15.00

ESSAYS ON THE

INTELLECTUAL POWERS OF MAN

THOMAS REID

Introduction by Baruch A. Brody

THE M.I.T. PRESS
Cambridge, Massachusetts, and London, England

First M.I.T. Press Edition, 1969

Reproduced from Volumes II and III of *The Works of Thomas Reid*
four volumes, printed and published by Samuel Etheridge, Jun'r
Charlestown, Massachusetts
1813 (Vol. I), 1814 (Vol. II), 1815 (Vols. III and IV)

Introduction by Baruch A. Brody copyright © 1969 by
The Massachusetts Institute of Technology

SBN 262 18040 5 (hardcover)
SBN 262 68012 2 (paperback)

Library of Congress Number: 71–84658
Printed in The United States of America

CONTENTS

ESSAY III.
CONCERNING MEMORY

ESSAY IV.
OF CONCEPTION

ESSAY V.
OF ABSTRACTION

ESSAY VI.
OF JUDGMENT

ESSAY VII.
OF REASONING

ESSAY VIII.
OF TASTE

INTRODUCTION

THOMAS REID, the founder of the Scottish school of common sense philosophy, was born on April 26, 1710, at Strachan in Kincardineshire, a parish situated about twenty miles from Aberdeen. Reid's paternal family had been very prominent in Scottish clerical and intellectual circles since the Reformation, while his maternal family was the Gregorys, another prominent Scottish intellectual family, the most important member of which was his mother's brother, David Gregory, Savilian professor of astronomy at Oxford and a close friend of Sir Isaac Newton. It is not surprising, therefore, that Reid was educated and trained for a career in the church or the university.

After spending two years at the parish school of Kincardine, Reid was sent to Aberdeen to pursue his classical studies, and at the age of twelve, he entered the Marischal College at Aberdeen. Like many another prominent scholar who did not show any signs of future eminence while he was a student, Reid was described by his teachers in later years as having shown through his industry that he would eventually do well. In any case, his work was good enough to earn for him an appointment as college librarian for a year or two, after which he was appointed, by King's College of Aberdeen, to the post of minister at New Machar.

Reid served as minister at New Machar from 1737 to 1752. Although his appointment to the post was originally opposed by many of the members of the parish, he left New Machar with the highest praise from all of his parishioners, so he must have been quite successful as a minister. Nevertheless, he seems to have spent most of his time engaged in his studies. The nature of his work during this period can be judged by the one paper that he published while at New Machar, an article in the *Philosophical Transactions of the Royal Society of London* for 1748 entitled "An Essay on Quantity." In this paper, Reid discussed the conditions under which a property can be treated quantitatively and, more specifically, the conditions for treating virtue and merit quantitatively. Although interesting enough, this paper gives no indication either of Reid's later interests or of the abilities that he would display in his more mature work.

In 1752 Reid was appointed professor of philosophy at King's College in Aberdeen. It is not entirely clear how Reid obtained this position. His biographer, Dugald Stewart, attributes this to the high opinion held of Reid despite the fact that he had published so little. One cannot help suspecting, however, that Reid's family connections were of great help to him at this point. In any case, the appointment was a great success. Although Reid was not a very organized and systematic lecturer, his students were very pleased with him as a teacher. They had ample opportunity to get to know him since Reid lectured at Aberdeen on mathematics and physics, as well as philosophy and logic, it being an old tradition in Scotland that a single professor should teach his students all the subjects that they studied at the university.

It was during his stay at Aberdeen that Reid began those activities that were to earn him his place in the history of philosophy. To begin with, he founded a weekly discussion group which was to last for many years and which was extremely influential in the development of Scottish thought in the latter half of the eighteenth century. The most prominent members of this group were Reid, James Beattie, James Gregory, George Campbell, and Alexander Gerard. Reid was clearly the dominant figure in this circle, and his ideas had a great influence on all of these thinkers. Secondly, in 1764 Reid published his first major work, the *Inquiry into the Human Mind*, where, for the first time, he offered his own theories as an alternative to Humean skepticism. Before sending the book to the publisher, Reid persuaded Hume to read the manuscript. Although Hume was originally somewhat cynical, believing that it was better for parsons to bother one another than to engage in philosophical controversies, he changed his mind as soon as he read the manuscript. Hume wrote to Reid, commending the book as a real challenge to his ideas. And there is no doubt that the appearance of Reid's *Inquiry* did pose a severe challenge to the many Scottish thinkers who had accepted Humean skepticism.

Later in 1764, Reid was invited by the University of Glasgow to accept its professorship in moral philosophy, a position from which Adam Smith had just resigned. One of the main attractions of this new position was that it only involved lecturing on philosophy. Reid was thus liberated from the task of teaching mathematics and physics, and he found himself freed, for the first time, of all professional responsibilities other than that of teaching and writing about ethics and epistemology. But even this freedom was not sufficient, and in 1780 he retired from all public activities so that he could systematize his thoughts on these topics and work them into full treatises. The results of this labor were his *Essays on the Intellectual Powers of Man* (1785) and his *Essays on the Active Powers of the Human Mind* (1788).

The publication of these works marked the end of Reid's literary career. But he was not the type of man who could retire intellectually, and he spent his remaining years renewing the scientific interests that he had abandoned years ago so that he could devote himself fully to the development of his philosophical ideas. He continued these studies until his death on October 7, 1796.

What type of man was Reid? His writings give us few hints about the man, but we do know that his contemporaries considered him a deeply moral man, one who was committed to the search for truth, and, above all, one who had complete control over his passions and emotions. It was also generally conceded that his philosophical achievements were due as much to his patience and perseverance as to his abilities. But one must not conclude from this description that Reid was a dull and cold man obsessed with virtue. His contemporaries also considered him a warm and concerned friend to many and a deeply devoted husband (to his cousin, Elizabeth, whom he married in 1740) and father of five.

Reid's life was clearly much less interesting than that of many of the eighteenth century philosophers, and he was certainly a far less interesting person than most of these other philosophers. But he compensated for all of this by the depth of his philosophical insight, which is, after all, our real concern. We turn, therefore, to a consideration of his ideas and insights.

PART II

The first of Reid's two major writings, his *Essays on the Intellectual Powers of Man*, is concerned with questions about understanding and knowledge, while the second of his major writings, his *Essays on the Active Powers of the Human Mind*, is concerned with the powers and freedom of the human will. We will not say anything else about this second work in this introduction; the reader is referred to our introduction to that book for further information about it.

Reid's work in the theory of knowledge must be studied from two different points of view. The first considers Reid's attempt to construct a theory of the human mind and its epistemic operations which would be analogous to the theory of material objects and their movements constructed by Galileo, Kepler, and Newton. Reid was not, of course, the first eighteenth century thinker who attempted to construct such a theory; but, as we shall see, the theory that he constructed was very different from most of the usual eighteenth century theories. The second point of view considers Reid's attack on Humean skepticism. Throughout his works Reid argued against this position, and no consideration of his work would be complete if it failed to deal with this aspect of it.

These two aspects of Reid's epistemology were intimately related to each other. Reid was convinced that Humean skepticism was the logical conclusion of the whole of philosophy since Descartes and Locke and not merely the product of an ingenious and sophistic mind, and he saw his own psychological theories as the basis for the only approach that could avoid this devastating skepticism.

Reid was convinced that earlier theories of the operations of the human mind were based upon mistaken approaches to this topic, and he therefore devoted the first essay in his book to a consideration of questions of methodology. Reid was strongly opposed to the use of hypotheses (theories not derived from data) and of analogies drawn from the physical world. He argued that these should be replaced by a careful reflection upon the operations of our own mind. But Reid was quite aware of the shortcomings of this introspective method, and he suggested that it should be supplemented by (a) a consideration of common distinctions drawn in all languages which usually reflect real distinctions in the world that mankind, in its ordinary activities, has had occasion to notice and (b) a consideration of the behavior that is the effect of the mental activity and that can shed light on it.

The Essays on the Intellectual Powers of Man contain, besides this first methodological essay, seven substantive essays, one each on the external senses, memory, conception, abstraction, judgment, reasoning, and taste. The introduction of a separate essay on taste is quite surprising; it undoubtedly reflects a desire on the part of Reid to emphasize his view that judgments of taste are true and false and are not mere expressions of likes and dislikes.

Reid begins his discussion of the external senses with a critique of a variety of theories about the mechanisms by which impressions affect our senses. His main objection to all of them is that they are unclear and unsubstantiated. But Reid's real concern was with our mental acts of perception and not with the impressions that precede them. Reid finds in any act of perception three elements: (1) the act of perceiving; (2) the object of the act; (3) a conviction that this object exists, this conviction not being derived from any reasoning process. There are several important points that must be noted about this analysis. First of all, Reid insists that there exists, at least in the case of perception, a real distinction between the mental act and its object. And he suggests at various points that a failure to draw this distinction has led thinkers like Locke astray. Secondly, Reid thinks that the objects of perception are real things like chairs, tables, and people, and not ideas or impressions in our mind. Indeed, as we shall see below, Reid was convinced that these "mental objects of perception" do not exist at all. And finally, Reid believes that this belief that we have which is not based upon any reasoning process is true and that our belief in it requires no justification.

Sensation, according to Reid, is very different. In acts of sensation, such as the feeling of a pain, there is no distinction to be drawn between the act and its object. On the contrary, there is no object, a pain, which can be distinguished from the act of sensing, the feeling of the pain. Reid feels that it is this difference that distinguishes sensations from perceptions.

Reid uses this distinction between perceptions and sensations to help explain the distinction between primary and secondary qualities. According to Reid, our perceptions and sensations often are mixed together. Now when we experience a primary quality, our attention is drawn to the quality in the object that we perceive and not to the accompanying sensation, and we therefore say that this quality, the primary quality, is in the object. But when we experience a secondary quality, our attention is drawn to the sensation and not to the quality in the object that we are perceiving which causes the sensation, and we therefore say either that the secondary quality (meaning the sensation) does not exist in the object or that it (meaning the cause of the sensation) does exist in the object but the only idea we have of it is as the cause of the sensation.

Reid discovers in acts of memory the same threefold distinction between an act, its object, and the belief in the existence of the object that he had discovered in the case of perception. And once more, Reid does not believe that there are any special mental objects of these acts of memory. The only difference between memory and perception is that the objects of the former existed in the past and our belief in their existence is a belief in their existence in the past while the objects of the latter exist at present and our belief in their existence is a belief in their present existence. In discussing memory, Reid also discusses the question of personal identity. While agreeing with the claim of the empiricist tradition that memory plays a central role in our concept of personal identity, Reid refused to define personal identity as the having of certain memories in common on the grounds that this definition would confuse the evidence for a claim with what is asserted in the claim.

The next type of mental act that Reid considers is the act of conception, of simple apprehension. Reid wants to make two important points about these acts of conception. The first is that since no judgments are involved in them, such acts are neither true nor false. The second is that although we have to distinguish the act of conception from its object, the act is not necessarily accompanied by a belief in the existence of the object and the object often does not exist. So conception, unlike perception and memory, can have a nonexistent object.

Philosophers have often, for one reason or another, found it difficult to understand the possibility of general conceptions; in Essay v, Reid uses his general theory of conception to offer a simple explanation of this possibility. A general conception involves two elements, the act of conception and its object. The former is a particular act of conceiving, involves no generality, and there is no difficulty in seeing how it can exist. The generality of a general conception lies in its object, which is a universal. Reid agrees with the empiricists that such a general object cannot exist. But we have seen that the object of an act of conception need not exist, and so there is no reason why a nonexistent universal cannot be the object of an act of conception. Reid therefore concludes that there is no difficulty in understanding the possibility of general conceptions.

It might be helpful, before turning to the different issues involved in Reid's analysis of judgment and reasoning, to summarize in the following chart the important distinctions that Reid has drawn between these four acts of perception, sensation, memory, and conception:

	Is there an act-object distinction?	Does the object exist now?	Is there an accompanying belief in the object?
Perception	yes	yes	yes
Sensation	no	—	—
Memory	yes	no	yes
Conception	yes	perhaps	no

These are important distinctions and, as we have seen
in our discussion of general conception and as we shall
see in the next section, Reid was convinced that a
failure to attend to these distinctions was an important
source of the failings of the empiricist tradition.

There are two major points that Reid makes in his
discussion of judgment. The first is that our judgments
are usually about ordinary objects and their properties
and they are usually not about mental objects. This
point is merely an extension of his earlier remarks about
the objects of other mental acts. The second, and far
more important, point concerns the distinction between
intuitive judgments and judgments that are grounded
upon arguments. This distinction, which is essentially
the distinction between propositions that we are justified in believing in even if there is no evidence for their
truth and propositions that we are justified in believing
in only when there is evidence for their truth, is a very
old one and Reid has no new arguments to offer for it.
His main argument is the old one that intuitive judgments must exist for they are the basis for all of our
other beliefs. But what is significantly different in Reid's
account of this distinction is the type of judgments that
he includes under the heading of intuitive judgments.
Besides necessary truths and judgments about our
present mental states, Reid also includes such judgments as the ones asserting the existence of the self,
of the objects that we perceive or that we remember.
of other minds, and of the uniformity of nature. Our
belief in all of these judgments is, according to Reid,
completely justified although we have no good arguments for their truth. They are therefore to be classified
as intuitive truths.

Reid was quite conscious of the very unusual nature
of his proposal. As he himself points out, the philosophical tradition since Descartes has tried to make do
with as few intuitive judgments as possible, usually
only some necessary truths and judgments about our

present mental states. But Reid was convinced that such a meager class of judgments could not serve as the basis for all of our knowledge, and he therefore widened the class of intuitive judgments. Reid often called these new intuitive judgments the judgments of common sense, and because he emphasized their importance and increased their number, his philosophy is often called the philosophy of common sense. This name has often misled people into supposing that Reid was arguing for the necessity of believing anything that is commonly believed by uneducated people; this is, of course, a travesty of Reid's position, and one that can easily be avoided if one simply keeps in mind what Reid means by a common sense, i.e., intuitive, judgment.

Reid's discussion of reasoning, which he defines as the process of passing from one judgment to another, is primarily concerned with a refutation of Hume's skeptical argument against the possibility of knowledge based upon reasoning. Hume's argument was that since it is always possible that any reasoning process be mistaken, the most that we are entitled to say is that a belief based upon some reasoning process is probably true. And as we try to check the original reasoning process, we use additional reasoning processes which might also be mistaken, and this additional possibility of error lowers the probability of having been originally right. Eventually, that probability will reach zero. Against this argument, Reid claims (1) that the mere possibility of error does not imply that the original reasoning was only probable, and (2) the additional checks, instead of necessarily lowering the original probability, actually may raise the probability of the original reasoning having been correct. In the course of making these claims, Reid offers many important observations about the relations between 'probable', 'fallible', and 'necessary'.

The last topic that Reid discusses in this book is the nature of judgments of taste. His whole point is that we must distinguish our sensations of pleasure and pain from the properties that we ascribe to the objects in our judgments of taste. And these judgments of taste then are true or false depending upon whether or not the objects in question have the properties ascribed to them.

PART III

Reid's own philosophical theories, as outlined in the previous section of this introduction, are clearly far-reaching and extremely important. But these theories represent only part of Reid's accomplishment; as we have already pointed out, the other part is his attack on Humean skepticism and the philosophical tradition that led to it, and it is to a consideration of this attack that we now turn.

Reid believed that Hume's skepticism was the logical consequence of two assumptions that had been prevalent in philosophy since the time of Descartes and Locke. They were

(a) The direct object of mental acts like perception, memory, and conception are ideas in the mind of the perceiver, rememberer, and conceiver.

(b) Philosophical arguments and proofs are needed in order to justify our belief in the existence of physical objects, the past, other minds, and the uniformity of nature.

Moreover, according to Reid the assumption of (a) often led these philosophers to at least part of (b). After all, since we do not directly see physical objects, but only ideas in our mind, and since the direct objects of our acts of memory are not previously existing physical objects, but only ideas in our mind, we seem to be in need of a proof that the existence of these ideas implies the existence of presently existing and previously existing physical objects.

It is easy to see why Reid thought that these assumptions were the foundation for Humean skepticism. After all, none of the philosophers from Descartes on had been able to advance any good proofs of the principles in question, and since it was assumed throughout the period in question that such a proof was needed, the skeptical conclusion seemed to follow.

This philosophical analysis led Reid to a view of the history of modern philosophy which, while quite common today, was very unusual in his time. Hume in his own day was viewed, at least as far as his purely philosophical works are concerned, primarily as an ingenuous sophist. Reid, as early as the 1750's, saw that this was a false view of Hume, that Hume was really the culmination of philosophical thought since Descartes and Locke, and that the arguments used by thinkers like Descartes and Locke to avoid the skeptical challenge do not hold up.

Reid argued that assumption (a), the thesis that the objects of all of our mental acts are objects in our mind, is an unwarranted assumption which is also contrary to the obvious fact that we often perceive, remember, or conceive of physical objects, events, and their properties. In a whole variety of passages, Reid returns to this theme and argues that there is absolutely no reason to even believe in the existence of these "mental objects." Reid agreed, of course, that there were mental acts and that these mental acts had objects; he was only concerned with challenging the claim that these objects were never ordinary physical objects.

In order to show how unwarranted assumption (a) was, Reid considered at great length the various arguments that philosophers had offered for it. One of the things that he quickly discovered was that philosophers usually assumed, rather than argued for, the truth of (a). In the central case of perception, he could find only three arguments that had been offered for (a):

(1) Locke's argument that since by 'idea' we mean the objects of mental acts, and since acts of perception obviously have objects, therefore there are ideas that

are the objects of acts of perception. This argument, as Reid points out, only proves that there are objects of the acts of perception (since that is all that 'idea' means here); it does not prove what Locke wants it to prove, viz., that these objects exist in the mind.

(2) Clarke's argument that since there can be no action at a distance, the mind cannot perceive (thereby either acting upon or being acted upon by) the physical object which is at a distance from it. Reid quickly points out that whatever the merit of the principle of no action at a distance in the case of a physical object exerting a force upon another physical object, it is totally unjustified to assume that the principle in question holds as well for the interaction between a percipient and what is perceived, a process whose nature is unknown and which may be very different in nature from physical interactions.

(3) Hume's version of the argument from illusion. This is the most important argument for the theory of ideas and Reid gives it the detailed scrutiny that it deserves. Hume's argument is that when we move away from a physical object, its size does not change but the size of what we see does change. Consequently, the object that we see cannot be identical with the physical object, and the most plausible assumption is that it is some idea in our mind. Reid claims, in reply, that this argument rests upon a confusion between real size and apparent size. It is obvious that when the physical object does not change, its real size does not change. But why cannot its apparent size change while it remains unchanged, i.e., why cannot an object, without changing, appear at one time to have one size and at another time to have a different size? Since there seems to be no reason why this cannot happen, we can say in Hume's case that the object that we see is a physical object whose real size has not changed and the change that we see is only in its apparent size. So Hume's argument collapses.

Although Reid was primarily concerned with the claim that the objects of our acts of perception are ideas in our mind, he also considered the arguments that philosophers had offered to show that the objects of other mental acts, like acts of memory and conception, are also ideas in the mind. In the case of conception, for example, philosophers had argued that since the object of the act of conception must exist, but the physical object which we think is the object of that act might not exist, therefore the true object of the act of conception cannot be the physical object; the most plausible assumption is that it is some idea in our mind. As Reid points out, however, this argument clearly rests upon the dubious assumption that the object of an act of conception must exist; after all, it seems to be the distinguishing feature of that type of mental act that its object need not exist. In other words, the argument derives all of its persuasiveness from a failure to attend to the difference between conception and other mental acts. And a similar fallacy is found in the argument that since the physical objects that we think are the objects of acts of memory may not exist at the time of the act of memory, but the object of that act must exist at the time of the act, therefore the physical objects cannot be the true objects of our acts of memory. This argument also derives all of its persuasiveness from a failure to attend to the distinguishing characteristic of memory, viz., that the objects of acts of memory need not exist at the time of the act.

In addition to arguing that the counterintuitive theory of ideas is totally unsupported by any arguments, Reid showed that the theory leads to many absurdities. For example, when I think of a centaur, the object of my thought is partially a horse and partially a man. But if some idea was the object of my thought, it would have to be partially a horse and partially a man (literally, and not merely in the sense of being about something which is partially a horse and partially a man), and this is clearly absurd. On the basis of all of these considerations, therefore, Reid claimed that the theory of ideas should be rejected.

Even if the theory of ideas is rejected, it does not, of course, follow that all of the skeptical arguments are refuted. To begin with, the skeptic can always argue that it is possible that the physical objects which are the objects of our acts of perception (or our acts of memory) do not exist. After all, Reid himself has pointed out that there are mental acts, viz., acts of conception, that can have nonexistent objects. Perhaps this is also so even in the case of perception and memory, despite the conviction that accompanies these acts that their objects exist. Moreover, there are other skeptical arguments, ones that challenge our knowledge of general truths or of the existence of other minds, that do not involve the theory of ideas at all and are not therefore challenged by the refutation of that theory. Reid was aware of all of these considerations, and he realized that he needed further arguments to refute these additional skeptical challenges.

Descartes, Locke, and others had attempted to refute the skeptic by offering arguments to meet some of these skeptical challenges. But Reid was well aware of the weaknesses in their arguments. Descartes, for example, in attempting to prove that the proper use of our faculties of reasoning would lead us from true premises to true conclusions, had to use an argument to prove this and had, therefore, to implicitly presuppose the legitimacy of the very faculty for whose legitimacy he was arguing. In the case of Locke's argument for the existence of the external world, Locke himself was very conscious of the weakness of the argument that he proposed. Moreover, it would appear that Reid felt that the enterprise of refuting the skeptic could never be carried out successfully, since we have no more basic principles to use as premises in defending the very basic principles that the skeptic challenges.

Reid therefore proposed a new way of meeting these skeptical challenges, one that claims that the skeptics are mistaken in their supposition that these basic beliefs and principles are not justified until they are proven. Reid claimed instead that they are intuitive principles that we are justified in believing in without having any proof for them. This is why Reid could say that the demand for proof of intuitive principles is the second major source of skepticism.

It is obvious that this type of move needs further substantiation. Even if we grant that there have to be some intuitive principles, what justification can Reid give for the claim that the principles in question are intuitive principles? To be sure, it would be most advantageous if they were, but (to paraphrase Russell) these advantages would just be the ordinary advantages of theft over honest toil.

Reid was well aware of the possibility of such an objection, and at several points in the text, most notably at the end of Chapter ii of the first essay and Chapter iv of the sixth essay, he offers various criteria for determining whether or not a given judgment is an intuitive judgment. These include

(1) The universality of the belief in it;

(2) The fact that the belief is held by all long before they reach the stage of philosophical reflection;

(3) The existence of a universally felt absurdity in the denial of the judgment;

(4) The fact that those who deny the judgment or are skeptical about it will nevertheless, in practice, act as though it were clearly true.

Reid was not the first philosopher who saw this new approach as a possible way out of skepticism. He himself pointed out that Père Buffier, a French Jesuit, had made a similar suggestion in his *Traité des Premiers Veritez*, first published in 1724, and had repeated it in his *Cours des Sciences* (1732). But Buffier's analysis of the nature of these truths was nowhere nearly as profound as Reid's, and Buffier's list of these truths was nowhere nearly as plausible. Moreover, there is good reason to suppose that Reid came to know about Buffier's work only after he had developed his own ideas independently. So the mere existence of Buffier's book should not detract from Reid's originality as a thinker.

In any case, on the basis of the above arguments, Reid rejected the two principles (a) and (b) that he felt were the basis for all of skepticism, thereby clearing the ground for his own nonskeptical account of the nature of our intellectual faculties.

PART IV

Reid's writings, unlike Hume's, were well received from the very beginning and they exercised considerable influence on the development of philosophical thought in many countries. As far as Scotland itself was concerned, Reid's ideas were the most important influence on philosophical writings for a hundred years. As early as 1770, only six years after the publication of Reid's *Inquiry into the Human Mind*, James Beattie (1735–1803), professor of philosophy at Marischal College, published his *Essay on the Nature and Immutability of Truth* which adopted Reid's position on most matters. Beattie was much more of a popularizer than a serious thinker, but he was extremely influential in spreading Reid's ideas. In fact, there is a picture by Reynolds showing Sophistry, Skepticism, and Infidelity fleeing before Truth. Beattie is standing at Truth's side, with a copy of the *Essay* underneath his arm. This gives one some idea of the impression that Beattie made on the public. Another important disciple of Reid was Dugald Stewart (1753–1828), who was professor at Edinburgh and who brought Reid's philosophy to Edinburgh. Besides writing a three volume exposition of Reid's position, his *Elements of the Philosophy of the Human Mind* (vol. 1, 1792; vol. 2, 1810; vol. 3, 1828), Stewart taught this philosophy to his many eminent students including James Mill, Lord Russell, Palmerston, and Scott.

Not all of the major Scottish thinkers were in total agreement with Reid. Thomas Brown (1778–1820), Stewart's coprofessor of philosophy at Edinburgh, was very critical of some aspects of Reid's philosophy. Nevertheless, Brown still followed Reid on many points, most notably on the theory of common sense. Sir William Hamilton (1788–1856) the last of the major figures in the Scottish school of common sense philosophy, was highly critical of Brown's attack on Reid. But Hamilton was not merely another follower of Reid. He attempted to combine Reid's ideas with a Kantian distinction between the noumenal and phenomenal world by arguing that the type of knowledge that Reid was talking about (and indeed all knowledge) only held for the phenomenal world.

Reid's influence was not confined to Great Britain. He was also highly regarded on the continent, particularly in France, where Pierre Paul Royeu-Collard made much use of Reid's ideas in his attack on Condillac. Royeu-Collard's student, Victor Cousin, adopted many of Reid's ideas as part of his so-called eclectic philosophy, which was quite influential in the schools throughout much of the nineteenth century, probably because Cousin served for some years as minister of education. Reid was much less influential in Germany, primarily because of Kant's condemnation of the appeal to common sense in philosophy, but we do know that Reid was much admired by Schopenhauer. Reid had some influence in Italy, primarily through a discussion of his ideas by Rosmini in his *Saggio sulli Origini delle Idee*, and in Belgium, where a school of ontologists at the Louvain built upon Reid's critique of representationalism a doctrine of the knowledge of God.

Reid's ideas were also extremely influential in America. Indeed, before the civil war Reid's common sense philosophy, which was first brought to America by

John Witherspoon and Samuel Stanhope of Princeton, was the only opposition faced by New England's transcendentalism. Moreover, Reid's ideas continued to remain influential in America long after they had lost their influence elsewhere. This was primarily due to the activities of James McCosh (1811–1894), a Scottish philosopher who was educated at Glasgow and Edinburgh and who was president of Princeton University from 1868 to 1888. McCosh was primarily known for his reconciliation of religion with Darwinism, but all of his works either expounded or presupposed the common sense philosophy. McCosh was a follower of Reid's original approach, and in his *An Examination of Mr. J. S. Mill's Philosophy* (1866), he criticized Hamilton's attempt to combine Reid and Kant.

The latter half of the nineteenth century witnessed a decline of Reid's reputation and influence. This was not due to the appearance of a series of devastating critiques of the Scottish philosophy. Indeed, the only serious critique was J. S. Mill's *An Examination of Sir William Hamilton's Philosophy*, and it was by no means devastating. The explanation of the decline lies, instead, in the fact that the latter half of the nineteenth century also witnessed the rise in Great Britain and America of very different philosophical movements, most notably absolute idealism and pragmatism, that ignored, rather than attacked, the Scottish tradition. And by the time that these movements declined, the Scottish philosophy had been forgotten.

Reid's common sense philosophy has had a strange fate in the twentieth century. Although Reid and his followers have been neglected so much that it has been almost impossible until now to obtain even a copy of Reid's major works, many of his ideas have been discovered independently and have played a prominent role in recent philosophical thought. The most obvious example is G. E. Moore's theory of common sense propositions, like the ones asserting the existence of physical objects and of other minds, whose truth we know independently of any philosophical arguments. But there are many other less obvious examples of this phenomenon. Reid's distinction between mental acts and their objects, and his claim that the objects of acts of conceiving need not exist and that this is the distinguishing feature of conception has played a prominent role both in British realism and in the phenomenological tradition. And Reid's remarks about ordinary language are paralleled to a remarkable degree in the writings of J. L. Austin.

It is not the purpose of this introduction to offer a final evaluation of Reid's significance for contemporary philosophy. But the many parallels between Reid and influential recent thinkers suggest that there is much in Reid that is still viable. There is no reason to suppose, moreover, that the only viable parts of Reid are those that have already been independently rediscovered; there may be many important insights in Reid that remain to be rediscovered. We will never know whether they exist unless Reid is given the serious study that he deserves, and it is hoped that this edition, which makes Reid's works conveniently available for the first time in over a hundred years, will help make this needed reexamination possible.

Cambridge, Massachusetts   BARUCH A. BRODY
March 1969

ESSAYS ON THE
INTELLECTUAL POWERS OF MAN

DEDICATION.

MR. DUGALD STEWART,

LATELY PROFESSOR OF MATHEMATICS, NOW PRO-
FESSOR OF MORAL PHILOSOPHY;

AND

DR. JAMES GREGORY,

PROFESSOR OF THE THEORY OF PHYSIC,

IN

THE UNIVERSITY OF EDINBURGH.

My dear Friends,

I KNOW not to whom I can address these Essays
with more propriety than to you; not only on account of a friendship begun in early life on your part,
though in old age on mine, and in one of you I may say
hereditary; nor yet on account of that correspondence
in our literary pursuits and amusements, which has always given me so great pleasure; but because, if these
Essays have any merit, you have a considerable share
in it, having not only encouraged me to hope that they
may be useful, but favoured me with your observations
on every part of them, both before they were sent to
press and while they were under it.

I have availed myself of your observations, so as to
correct many faults that might otherwise have escaped

me ; and I have a very grateful sense of your friendship, in giving this aid to one, who stood much in need of it ; having no shame, but much pleasure, in being instructed by those who formerly were my pupils, as one of you was.

It would be ingratitude to a man whose memory I most highly respect, not to mention my obligations to the late lord Kaimes for the concern he was pleased to take in this work. Having seen a small part of it, he urged me to carry it on ; took account of my progress from time to time ; revised it more than once, as far as it was carried, before his death ; and gave me his observations on it, both with respect to the matter and the expression. On some points we differed in opinion, and debated them keenly, both in conversation and by many letters, without any abatement of his affection, or of his zeal for the work's being carried on and published : for he had too much liberality of mind not to allow to others the same liberty in judging which he claimed to himself.

It is difficult to say whether that worthy man was more eminent in active life or in speculation. Very rare, surely, have been the instances where the talents for both were united in so eminent a degree.

His genius and industry, in many different branches of literature, will, by his works, be known to posterity. His private virtues, and public spirit, his assiduity, through a long and laborious life, in many honourable public offices with which he was intrusted, and his zeal to encourage and promote every thing that tended to the improvement of his country, in laws, literature, com-

merce, manufactures, and agriculture, are best known
to his friends and contemporaries.

The favourable opinion which he, and you my friends,
were pleased to express of this work, has been my
chief encouragement to lay it before the public ; and
perhaps, without that encouragement, it had never seen
the light : for I have always found, that, without social
intercourse, even a favourite speculation languishes ;
and that we cannot help thinking the better of our
own opinions when they are approved by those whom
we esteem good judges.

You know that the substance of these Essays was
delivered annually, for more than twenty years, in lectures to a large body of the more advanced students in
this university, and for several years before, in another university. Those who heard me with attention,
of whom I presume there are some hundreds alive, will
recognise the doctrine which they heard, some of them
thirty years ago, delivered to them more diffusely, and
with the repetitions and illustrations proper for such
audiences.

I am afraid, indeed, that the more intelligent reader,
who is conversant in such abstract subjects, may think
that there are repetitions still left, which might be
spared. Such, I hope, will consider, that what to one
reader is a superfluous repetition, to the greater part, less
conversant in such subjects, may be very useful. If
this apology be deemed insufficient, and be thought to be
the dictate of laziness, I claim some indulgence even for
that laziness, at my period of life.

You who are in the prime of life, with the vigour which it inspires, will, I hope, make more happy advances in this, or in any other branch of science to which your talents may be applied.

THOMAS REID.

GLASGOW COLLEGE,
June 1, 1785.

PREFACE.

Human knowledge may be reduced to two general heads, according as it relates to body or to mind; to things material, or to things intellectual.

The whole system of bodies in the universe, of which we know but a very small part, may be called the Material World; the whole system of minds, from the infinite Creator, to the meanest creature endowed with thought, may be called the Intellectual World. These are the two great kingdoms of nature that fall within our notice; and about the one, or the other, or things pertaining to them, every art, every science, and every human thought is employed; nor can the boldest flight of imagination carry us beyond their limits.

Many things there are, indeed, regarding the nature and the structure both of body and of mind, which our faculties cannot reach; many difficulties which the ablest philosopher cannot resolve; but of other natures, if any other there be, we have no knowledge, no conception at all.

That every thing that exists must be either corporeal or incorporeal, is evident. But it is not so evident, that every thing that exists must either be corporeal, or endowed with thought. Whether there be in the universe, beings which are neither extended, solid, and inert, like body, nor active and intelligent, like mind, seems to be beyond the reach of our knowledge. There appears to be a vast interval between body and mind, and whether there be any intermediate nature that connects them to-gether, we know not.

We have no reason to ascribe intelligence, or even sen-sation, to plants; yet there appears in them an active force and energy, which cannot be the result of any ar-rangement or combination of inert matter. The same thing may be said of those powers by which animals are nourished and grow, by which matter gravitates, by which magnetical and electrical bodies attract and repel each other, and by which the parts of solid bodies cohere.

Some have conjectured, that the phenomena of the ma-terial world which require active force, are produced by the continual operation of intelligent beings : others have conjectured, that there may be in the universe, beings that are active without intelligence, which, as a kind of incorporeal machinery, contrived by the Supreme Wis-dom, perform their destined task without any knowledge or intention. But, laying aside conjecture, and all pre-tences to determine in things beyond our reach, we must rest in this, that body and mind are the only kinds of be-ing of which we can have any knowledge, or can form any conception. If there be other kinds, they are not discov-erable by the faculties which God hath given us; and with regard to us, are as if they were not.

As, therefore, all our knowledge is confined to body and mind, or things belonging to them, there are two great branches of philosophy, one relating to body, the other to mind. The properties of body, and the laws that ob-tain in the material system, are the objects of natural phi-

●sophy, as that word is now used. The branch which treats of the nature and operations of minds has by some been called Pneumatology. And to the one or the other of these branches, the principles of all the sciences belong.

What variety there may be of minds or thinking beings throughout this vast universe, we cannot pretend to say. We dwell in a little corner of God's dominion, disjoined from the rest of it. The globe which we inhabit is but one of seven planets that encircle our sun. What various orders of beings may inhabit the other six, their secondaries, and the comets belonging to our system; and how many other suns may be encircled with like systems, are things altogether hid from us. Although human reason and industry have discovered with great accuracy the order and distances of the planets, and the laws of their motion, we have no means of corresponding with them. That they may be the habitation of animated beings is very probable; but of the nature, or powers of their inhabitants, we are perfectly ignorant. Every man is conscious of a thinking principle or mind in himself, and we have sufficient evidence of a like principle in other men. The actions of brute animals shew, that they have some thinking principle, though of a nature far inferior to the human mind. And every thing about us may convince us of the existence of a Supreme Mind, the Maker and Governor of the universe. These are all the minds of which reason can give us any certain knowledge.

The mind of man is the noblest work of God which reason discovers to us, and therefore, on account of its dignity, deserves our study. It must indeed be acknowledged, that although it is of all objects the nearest to us, and seems the most within our reach, it is very difficult to attend to its operations, so as to form a distinct notion of them ; and on that account there is no branch of knowledge in which the ingenious and speculative have fallen into so great errors, and even absurdities. These errors and absurdities have given rise to a general prejudice against all inquiries of this nature; and because ingenious men have, for many ages, given different and contradictory accounts of the powers of the mind, it is concluded, that all speculations concerning them are chimerical and visionary.

But whatever effect this prejudice may have with superficial thinkers, the judicious will not be apt to be carried away with it. About two hundred years ago, the opinions of men in natural philosophy were as various, and as contradictory, as they are now concerning the powers of the mind. GALILEO, TORRICELLI, KEPLER, BACON, and NEWTON, had the same discouragement in their attempts to throw light upon the material system, as we have with regard to the intellectual. If they had been deterred by such prejudices, we should never have reaped the benefit of their discoveries, which do honour to human nature, and will make their names immortal. The motto which Lord BACON prefixed to some of his writings was worthy of his genius, *Inveniam viam aut faciam.*

There is a natural order in the progress of the sciences, and good reasons may be assigned why the philosophy of body should be *elder sister* to that of mind, and of a quicker growth ; but the last hath the principle of life no less than the first, and will grow up, though slowly, to maturity. The remains of ancient philosophy upon this subject, are venerable ruins, carrying the marks of genius and industry, sufficient to inflame, but not to satisfy our curiosity. In later ages, Des Cartes was the first that pointed out the road we ought to take in those dark regions. Malebranche, Arnaud, Locke, Berkeley, Buffier, Hutcheson, Butler, Hume, Price, Lord Kaims, have laboured to make discoveries; nor have they laboured in vain. For, however different and contrary their conclusions are, however skeptical some of them, they have all given new light, and cleared the way to those who shall come after them.

We ought never to despair of human genius, but rather to hope, that in time it may produce a system of the powers and operations of the human mind, no less certain than those of optics or astronomy.

This is the more devoutly to be wished, that a distinct knowledge of the powers of the mind would undoubtedly give great light to many other branches of science. Mr. Hume hath justly observed, that " all the sciences have a relation to human nature; and, however wide any of them may seem to run from it, they still return back by one passage or another. This is the centre and capitol of the sciences, which being once masters of, we may easily extend our conquests every where."

The faculties of our minds are the tools and engines we must use in every disquisition; and the better we understand their nature and force, the more successfully we shall be able to apply them. Mr. Locke gives this account of the occasion of his entering upon his Essay concerning Human Understanding: " Five or six friends, says he, meeting at my chamber, and discoursing on a subject very remote from this, found themselves quickly at a stand by the difficulties that rose on every side. After we had for a while puzzled ourselves, without coming any nearer to a resolution of those doubts that perplexed us, it came into my thoughts that we took a wrong course; and that, before we set ourselves upon inquiries of that nature, it was necessary to examine our own abilities, and see what objects our understandings were fitted or not fitted to deal with. This I proposed to the company, who all readily assented; and thereupon it was agreed that this should be our first inquiry." If this be commonly the cause of perplexity in those disquisitions which have least relation to the mind, it must be so much more in those that have an immediate connection with it.

The sciences may be distinguished into two classes, according as they pertain to the material or to the intellectual world. The various parts of Natural Philosophy, the mechanical Arts, Chemistry, Medicine, and Agriculture belong to the first; but, to the last, belong Grammar, Logic, Rhetoric, Natural Theology; Morals, Jurisprudence, Law, Politics, and the fine Arts. The knowledge of the human mind is the root from which these grow, and draw their nourishment. Whether therefore we consider the dignity of this subject, or its subserviency to science in general, and to the noblest branches of science in particular, it highly deserves to be cultivated.

A very elegant writer, on the *Sublime and Beautiful*, concludes his account of the passions thus: " The variety of the passions is great, and worthy, in every branch of that variety, of the most diligent investigation. The more accurately we search into the human mind, the stronger traces we every where find of His wisdom who made it. If a discourse on the use of the parts of the body may be considered as a hymn to the Creator; the use of the passions, which are the organs of the mind, cannot be barren of praise to him, nor unproductive to ourselves of that noble and uncommon union of science and admiration, which a contemplation of the works of infinite Wisdom alone can afford to a rational mind; whilst referring to him whatever we find of right, or good, or fair, in ourselves, discovering his strength and wisdom even in our own weakness and imperfection, honouring them where we discover them clearly, and adoring their profundity where we are lost in our search, we may be inquisitive without impertinence, and elevated without pride; we may be admitted, if I may dare to say so, into the councils of the Almighty, by a consideration of his works. This elevation of the mind ought to be the principal end of all our studies, which, if they do not in some measure effect, they are of very little service to us."

ESSAYS

ON THE

INTELLECTUAL POWERS OF MAN.

ESSAY I.

PRELIMINARY.

CHAP. I.

EXPLICATION OF WORDS.

THERE is no greater impediment to the advancement of knowledge than the ambiguity of words. To this chiefly it is owing that we find sects and parties in most branches of science; and disputes, which are carried on from age to age, without being brought to an issue.

Sophistry has been more effectually excluded from mathematics and natural philosophy than from other sciences. In mathematics it had no place from the beginning; mathematicians having had the wisdom to define accurately the terms they use, and to lay down, as axioms, the first principles on which their reasoning is grounded. Accordingly we find no parties among mathematicians, and hardly any disputes.

In natural philosophy, there was no less **sophistry,** no less dispute and uncertainty, than in other sciences, until about a century and a half ago, this science began to be built upon the foundation of clear definitions and self-evident axioms. Since that time, the science, as if watered with the dew of heaven, hath grown apace; disputes have ceased, truth hath prevailed, and the science hath received greater increase in two centuries, than in two thousand years before.

It were to be wished, that this method, which hath been so successful in those branches of science, were attempted in others: for definitions and axioms are the foundations of all science. But that definitions may not be sought, where no definition can be given, nor logical definitions be attempted, where the subject does not admit of them, it may be proper to lay down some general principles concerning definition, for the sake of those who are less conversant in this branch of logic.

When one undertakes to explain any art or science, he will have occasion to use many words that are common to all who use the same language, and some that are peculiar to that art or science. Words of the last kind are called *terms of the art,* and ought to be distinctly explained, that their meaning may be understood.

A definition is nothing else but an explication of the meaning of a word, by words whose meaning is already known. Hence it is evident, that every word cannot be defined; for the definition must consist of words; and there could be no definition, if there were not words previously understood without definition. Common words, therefore, ought to be used in their common acceptation; and, when they have different acceptations in common language, these, when it is necessary, ought to be distinguished. But they require no

definition. It is sufficient to define words that are uncommon, or that are used in an uncommon meaning.

It may farther be observed, that there are many
words, which, though they may need explication, cannot be logically defined. A logical definition, that is,
a strict and proper definition, must express the kind of
the thing defined, and the specific difference, by which
the species defined, is distinguished from every other
species belonging to that kind. It is natural to the
mind of man to class things under various kinds, and
again to subdivide every kind into its various species.
A species may often be subdivided into subordinate
species, and then it is considered as a kind.

From what has been said of logical definition, it is
evident, that no word can be logically defined which
does not denote a species; because such things only
can have a specific difference; and a specific difference
is essential to a logical definition. On this account there
can be no logical definition of individual things, such as
London or Paris. Individuals are distinguished either by
proper names, or by accidental circumstances of time or
place, but they have no specific difference; and therefore
though they may be known by proper names, or may be
described by circumstances or relations, they cannot be
defined. It is no less evident, that the most general words
cannot be logically defined, because there is not a more
general term of which they are a species.

Nay, we cannot define every species of things, because it happens sometimes that we have not words to
express the specific difference. Thus a scarlet colour
is, no doubt, a species of colour; but how shall we express the specific difference by which scarlet is distinguished from green or blue? The difference of them
is immediately perceived by the eye, but we have not
words to express it. These things we are taught by
logic.

Without having recourse to the principles of logic, we may easily be satisfied that words cannot be defined, which signify things perfectly simple, and void of all composition. This observation, I think, was first made by Des Cartes, and afterward more fully illustrated by Locke. And however obvious it appears to be, many instances may be given of great philosophers who have perplexed and darkened the subjects they have treated, by not knowing, or not attending to it.

When men attempt to define things which cannot be defined, their definitions will always be either obscure or false. It was one of the capital defects of Aristotle's philosophy, that he pretended to define the simplest things, which neither can be, nor need to be defined; such as *time* and *motion*. Among modern philosophers, I know none that has abused definition so much as Wolfius, the famous German philosopher, who, in a work on the human mind, called Psychologia Empirica, consisting of many hundred propositions, fortified by demonstrations, with a proportional accompaniment of definitions, corollaries, and scholia, has given so many definitions of things which cannot be defined, and so many demonstrations of things self-evident, that the greatest part of the work consists of tautology, and ringing changes upon words.

There is no subject in which there is more frequent occasion to use words that cannot be logically defined, than in treating of the powers and operations of the mind. The simplest operations of our minds must all be expressed by words of this kind. No man can explain by a logical definition what it is to think, to apprehend, to believe, to will, to desire. Every man who understands the language has some notion of the meaning of these words : and every man, who is capable of reflection, may, by attending to the operations of his own mind, which are signified by them, form a clear and distinct notion of them, but they cannot be logically defined.

Since therefore it is often impossible to define words which we must use on this subject, we must as much as possible use common words in their common acceptation, pointing out their various senses where they are ambiguous ; and when we are obliged to use words less common, we must endeavour to explain them as well as we can, without affecting to give logical definitions, when the nature of the thing does not admit of them.

The following observations on the meaning of certain words are intended to supply, as far as we can, the want of definitions, by preventing ambiguity or obscurity in the use of them.

1. By the *mind* of a man, we understand that in him which thinks, remembers, reasons, wills. The essence both of body and of mind is unknown to us. We know certain properties of the first, and certain operations of the last, and by these only we can define or describe them. We define body to be that which is extended, solid, moveable, divisible. In like manner, we define mind to be that which thinks. We are conscious that we think, and that we have a variety of thoughts of different kinds ; such as seeing, hearing, remembering, deliberating, resolving, loving, hating, and many other kinds of thought, all which we are taught by nature to attribute to one internal principle ; and this principle of thought we call the *mind* or *soul* of a man.

2. By the *operations* of the mind, we understand every mode of thinking of which we are conscious.

It deserves our notice, that the various modes of thinking have always, and in all languages, as far as we know, been called by the name of *operations* of the mind, or by names of the same import. To body we

ascribe various properties, but not operations, properly
so called; it is extended, divisible, moveable, inert;
it continues in any state in which it is put; every
change of its state is the effect of some force impressed
upon it, and is exactly proportional to the force impressed, and in the precise direction of that force.
These are the general properties of matter, and these
are not operations : on the contrary, they all imply its
being a dead inactive thing, which moves only as it is
moved, and acts only by being acted upon.

But the mind is from its very nature a living and
active being. Every thing we know of it implies life
and active energy; and the reason why all its modes
of thinking are called its operations, is, that in all, or
in most of them, it is not merely passive, as body is,
but is really and properly active.

In all ages, and in all languages, ancient and modern,
the various modes of thinking have been expressed by
words of active signification, such as seeing, hearing,
reasoning, willing. and the like. It seems therefore to
be the natural judgment of mankind, that the mind is
active in its various ways of thinking; and for this reason they are called its operations, and are expressed
by active verbs.

It may be made a question, What regard is to be
paid to this natural judgment ; may it not be a vulgar
error? Philosophers who think so, have, no doubt, a
right to be heard. But until it is proved that the
mind is not active in thinking, but merely passive, the
common language with regard to its operations ought
to be used, and ought not to give place to a phraseology invented by philosophers, which implies its being merely passive.

3. The words *power* and *faculty*, which are often
used in speaking of the mind, need little explication.
Every operation supposes a power in the being that

operates; for, to suppose any thing to operate, which has no power to operate, is manifestly absurd. But, on the other hand, there is no absurdity in supposing a being to have power to operate, when it does not operate. Thus, I may have power to walk, when I sit; or to speak, when I am silent. Every operation therefore implies power; but the power does not imply the operation.

The *faculties* of the mind, and its *powers,* are often used as synonymous expressions. But as most synonymies have some minute distinction that deserves notice, I apprehend that the word *faculty* is most properly applied to those powers of the mind which are original and natural, and which make a part of the constitution of the mind. There are other powers which are acquired by use, exercise or study, which are not called faculties, but *habits.* There must be something in the constitution of the mind necessary to our being able to acquire habits, and this is commonly called *capacity.*

4. We frequently meet with a distinction, in writers upon this subject, between things *in the mind,* and things *external* to the mind. The powers, faculties, and operations of the mind, are things in the mind. Every thing is said to be in the mind, of which the mind is the *subject.* It is self-evident, that there are some things which cannot exist without a subject to which they belong, and of which they are attributes. Thus, colour must be in something coloured; figure in something figured; thought can only be in something that thinks; wisdom and virtue cannot exist but in some being that is wise and virtuous. When therefore we speak of things in the mind, we understand by this, things of which the mind is the subject. Excepting the mind itself, and things in the mind, all other things are said to be external. It ought there-

fore to be remembered, that this distinction between
things in the mind, and things external, is not meant
to signify the place of the things we speak of, but their
subject.

There is a figurative sense in which things are said
to be in the mind, which it is sufficient barely to mention. We say, such a thing was not in my mind,
meaning no more than that I had not the least thought
of it. By a figure, we put the thing for the thought
of it. In this sense, external things are in the mind
as often as they are the objects of our thought.

5. *Thinking* is a very general word, which includes
all the operations of our minds, and is so well understood as to need no definition.

To *perceive*, to *remember*, to be *conscious*, and to
conceive or *imagine*, are words common to philosophers,
and to the vulgar. They signify different operations
of the mind, which are distinguished in all languages,
and by all men that think. I shall endeavour to use
them in their most common and proper acceptation,
and I think they are hardly capable of strict definition. But as some philosophers, in treating of the
mind, have taken the liberty to use them very improperly, so as to corrupt the English language, and
to confound things, which the common understanding
of mankind hath always led them to distinguish, I
shall make some observations on the meaning of them,
that may prevent ambiguity or confusion in the use
of them.

6. First. We are never said to *perceive* things, of the
existence of which we have not a full conviction. I
may *conceive* or *imagine* a mountain of gold, or a winged
horse; but no man says that he perceives such a creature of imagination. Thus *perception* is distinguished
from *conception* or imagination. Secondly, Perception
is applied only to external objects, not to those that

are in the mind itself. When I am pained, I do not say that I perceive pain, but that I feel it, or that I am conscious of it. Thus *perception* is distinguished from *consciousness*. Thirdly, The immediate object of perception must be something present, and not what is past. We may remember what is past, but do not perceive it. I may say, I perceive such a person has had the small-pox; but this phrase is figurative, although the figure is so familiar that it is not observed. The meaning of it is, that I perceive the pits in his face, which are certain signs of his having had the small-pox. We say we perceive the thing signified, when we only perceive the sign. But when the word *perception* is used properly, and without any figure, it is never applied to things past. And thus it is distinguished from *remembrance*.

In a word, perception is most properly applied to the evidence which we have of external objects by our senses. But as this is a very clear and cogent kind of evidence, the word is often applied by analogy to the evidence of reason or of testimony, when it is clear and cogent. The perception of external objects by our senses, is an operation of the mind of a peculiar nature, and ought to have a name appropriated to it. It has so in all languages. And, in the English, I know no word more proper to express this act of the mind than perception. Seeing, hearing, smelling, tasting, and touching or feeling, are words that express the operations proper to each sense; perceiving expresses that which is common to them all.

The observations made on this word would have been unnecessary, if it had not been so much abused in philosophical writings upon the mind; for, in other writings, it has no obscurity. Although this abuse is not chargeable on Mr. Hume only, yet I think he has carried it to the highest pitch. The first sentence of his

Treatise of Human Nature runs thus; " All the perceptions of the human mind resolve themselves into
two distinct heads, which I shall call impressions and
ideas." He adds a little after, that, under the name
of impressions, he comprehends all our sensations, passions, and emotions. Here we learn, that our passions
and emotions are perceptions. I believe, no English
writer before him ever gave the name of a perception
to any passion or emotion. When a man is angry, we
must say that he has the perception of anger. When
he is in love, that he has the perception of love. He
speaks often of the perceptions of memory, and of the
perceptions of imagination; and he might as well
speak of the hearing of sight, or of the smelling of
touch: for, surely, hearing is not more different from
sight, or smelling from touch, than perceiving is from
remembering or imagining.

7. *Consciousness* is a word used by philosophers, to
signify that immediate knowledge which we have of
our present thoughts and purposes, and, in general, of
all the present operations of our minds. Whence we
may observe, that consciousness is only of things present. To apply consciousness to things past, which
sometimes is done in popular discourse, is to confound
consciousness with memory; and all such confusion of
words ought to be avoided in philosophical discourse.
It is likewise to be observed, that consciousness is only
of things in the mind, and not of external things. It
is improper to say, I am conscious of the table which
is before me. I perceive it, I see it, but I do not say
I am conscious of it. As that consciousness by which
we have a knowledge of the operations of our own
minds, is a different power from that by which we perceive external objects, and as these different powers
have different names in our language, and, I believe, in
all languages, a philosopher ought carefully to pre-

serve this distinction, and never to confound things so different in their nature.

8. *Conceiving, imagining.* and *apprehending,* are commonly used as synonymous in our language, and signify the same thing which the logicians call *simple apprehension.* This is an operation of the mind different from all those we have mentioned. Whatever we perceive, whatever we remember, whatever we are conscious of, we have a full persuasion or conviction of its existence. But we may conceive or imagine what has no existence, and what we firmly believe to have no existence. What never had an existence cannot be remembered; what has no existence *at present* cannot be the object of perception or of consciousness; but what never had, nor has any existence, may be conceived. Every man knows, that it is as easy to conceive a winged horse or a centaur, as it is to conceive a horse or a man. Let it be observed therefore, that to *conceive,* to *imagine,* to *apprehend,* when taken in the proper sense, signify an act of the mind which implies no belief or judgment at all. It is an act of the mind by which nothing is affirmed or denied, and which therefore can neither be true nor false.

But there is another and a very different meaning of those words, so common and so well authorized in language, that it cannot easily be avoided; and on that account we ought to be the more on our guard, that we be not misled by the ambiguity. Politeness and good breeding lead men, on most occasions, to express their opinions with modesty, especially when they differ from others whom they ought to respect. Therefore, when we would express our opinion modestly, instead of saying, " This is my opinion," or, " this is my judgment," which has the air of dogmaticalness, we say, " I conceive it to be thus, I imagine or apprehend it to be thus ;" which is understood as a modest declaration of our judgment. In like manner, when any thing is said which we take to be impossible, we say, "We cannot conceive it," meaning that we cannot believe it.

Thus we see, that the words *conceive, imagine, apprehend*, have two meanings, and are used to express two operations of the mind, which ought never to be confounded. Sometimes they express simple apprehension, which implies no judgment at all; sometimes they express judgment or opinion. This ambiguity ought to be attended to, that we may not impose upon ourselves or others in the use of them. The ambiguity is indeed remedied in a great measure by their construction. When they are used to express simple apprehension, they are followed by a noun in the *accusative case*, which signifies the object conceived. But when they are used to express opinion or judgment, they are commonly followed by a verb in the *infinitive mood*. "I conceive an Egyptian pyramid." This implies no judgment. "I conceive the Egyptian pyramids to be the most ancient monuments of human art." This implies judgment. When the words are used in the last sense, the thing conceived must be a proposition, because judgment cannot be expressed but by a proposition. When they are used in the first sense, the thing conceived may be no proposition, but a simple term only, as a pyramid, an obelisk. Yet it may be observed, that even a proposition may be simply apprehended without forming any judgment of its truth or falsehood: for it is one thing to conceive the meaning of a proposition; it is another thing to judge it to be true or false.

Although the distinction between simple apprehension, and every degree of assent or judgment, be perfectly evident to every man who reflects attentively on what passes in his own mind; although it is very necessary, in treating of the powers of the mind, to attend carefully to this distinction ; yet, in the affairs of common life, it is seldom necessary to observe it accurately.　On this account, we shall find, in all common languages, the words which express one of those operations frequently applied to the other.　To think, to suppose, to imagine, to conceive, to apprehend, are the words we use to express simple apprehension ; but they are all frequently used to express judgment.　Their ambiguity seldom occasions any inconvenience in the common affairs of life, for which language is framed. But it has perplexed philosophers, in treating of the operations of the mind. and will always perplex them, if they do not attend accurately to the different meanings which are put upon those words on different occasions.

9. Most of the operations of the mind, from their very nature, must have *objects* to which they are directed, and about which they are employed.　He that perceives, must perceive something ; and that which he perceives, is called the object of his perception.　To perceive, without having any object of perception, is impossible.　The mind that perceives, the object perceived, and the operation of perceiving that object, are distinct things, and are distinguished in the structure of all languages.　In this sentence, "I see, or perceive the moon ;" *I* is the person or *mind ;* the active verb *see* denotes the operation of the mind ; and the *moon* denotes the object.　What we have said of perceiving, is equally applicable to most operations of the mind. Such operations are, in all languages, expressed by active transitive verbs : and we know, that, in all languages, such verbs require a thing or person, which is the agent, and a noun following in an oblique case, which is the object.　Whence it is evident, that all mankind, both those who have contrived language, and

those who use it with understanding, have distinguished these three things as different ; to wit, the operations of the mind, which are expressed by active verbs, the mind itself, which is the nominative to those verbs, and the object, which is, in the oblique case, governed by them.

It would have been unnecessary to explain so obvious a distinction, if some systems of philosophy had not confounded it. Mr. Hume's system, in particular, confounds all distinction between the operations of the mind and their objects. When he speaks of the ideas of memory, the ideas of imagination, and the ideas of sense, it is often impossible, from the tenour of his discourse, to know whether, by those ideas, he means the operations of the mind, or the objects about which they are employed. And, indeed, according to his system, there is no distinction between the one and the other.

A philosopher is, no doubt, entitled to examine even those distinctions that are to be found in the structure of all languages ; and. if he is able to shew that there is no foundation for them in the nature of the things distinguished ; if he can point out some prejudice common to mankind which has led them to distinguish things that are not really different ; in that case, such a distinction may be imputed to a vulgar error, which ought to be corrected in philosophy. But when, in the first setting out, he takes it for granted, without proof, that distinctions found in the structure of all languages, have no foundation in nature; this surely is too fastidious a way of treating the common sense of mankind. When we come to be instructed by philosophers, we must bring the old light of common sense along with us, and by it judge of the new light which the philosopher communicates to us. But when we are required to put out the old light altogether, that we may follow the new, we have reason to be on our guard. There may be distinctions that have a real foundation, and which may be necessary in philosophy, which are not made in common language, because not necessary in the common business of life. But, I believe, no instance will be found of a distinction made in all languages, which has not a just foundation in nature.

10. The word *idea* occurs so frequently in modern philosophical writings upon the mind, and is so ambiguous in its meaning, that it is necessary to make some observations upon it. There are chiefly two meanings of this word in modern authors, a popular and a philosophical.

First, in popular language, *idea* signifies the same thing as conception, apprehension, notion. To have an idea of any thing, is to conceive it. To have a distinct idea, is to conceive it distinctly. To have no idea of it, is not to conceive it at all. It was before observed, that conceiving or apprehending has always been considered by all men as an act or operation of the mind, and on that account has been expressed in all languages by an active verb. When, therefore, we use the phrase of having ideas, in the popular sense, we ought to attend to this, that it signifies precisely the same thing which we commonly express by the active verbs conceiving or apprehending.

When the word *idea* is taken in this popular sense, no man can possibly doubt whether he has ideas. For he that doubts must think, and to think, is to have ideas.

Sometimes, in popular language, a man's ideas signify his opinions. The ideas of Aristotle, or of Epicurus, signify the opinions of these philosophers. What was formerly said of the words *imagine, conceive, apprehend,* that they are sometimes used to express judgment, is no less true of the word *idea.* This signification of the word seems, indeed, more common in

the French language than in English. But it is found
in this sense in good English authors, and even in Mr.
Locke. Thus we see, that having *ideas*, taken in the
popular sense, has precisely the same meaning with
conceiving, imagining, apprehending, and has likewise
the same ambiguity. It may, therefore, be doubted,
whether the introduc .on of this word into popular discourse, to signify the operation of conceiving or apprehending, was at all necessary. For, first, we have, as
has been shown, several words which are originally
English, or have been long naturalized, that express
the same thing; why therefore should we adopt a
Greek word in place of these, any more than a French
or a German word? Besides, the words of our own language are less ambiguous. For the word idea has, for
many ages, been used by philosophers as a term of art;
and in the different systems of philosophers means very
different things.

Secondly, according to the philosophical meaning of
the word idea, it does not signify that act of the mind
which we call thought or conception, but some object
of thought. Ideas, according to Mr. Locke, whose
very frequent use of this word has probably been the
occasion of its being adopted into common language,
"are nothing but the immediate objects of the mind
in thinking." But of those objects of thought called
ideas, the different sects of philosophers have given a
very different account. Bruckerus, a learned German, wrote a whole book giving the history of ideas.

The most ancient system we have concerning ideas,
is that which is explained in several dialogues of Plato, and which many ancient as well as modern writers have ascribed to Plato as the inventor. But it is
certain that Plato had his doctrine upon this subject,
as well as the name *idea*, from the school of Pythagoras. We have still extant a tract of Timæus the

Locrian, a Pythagorean philosopher, concerning the soul of the world, in which we find the substance of Plato's doctrine concerning ideas. They were held to be eternal, uncreated, and immutable forms or models, according to which the Deity, of an eternal matter, made every species of things that exists. Those philosophers held, that there are three first principles of all things. First, an eternal matter, of which all things were made : secondly, eternal and immaterial forms or ideas, according to which they were made : and, thirdly, an efficient cause, the Deity who made them. The mind of man, in order to its being fitted for the contemplation of these eternal ideas, must undergo a certain purification, and be weaned from sensible things. The eternal ideas are the only object of science ; but the objects of sense, being in a perpetual flux, there can be no real knowledge with regard to them.

The philosophers of the Alexandrian school, commonly called *the latter Platonists*, made some change upon the system of the ancient Platonists with respect to the eternal ideas. They held them not to be a principle distinct from the Deity, but to be the conceptions of things in the divine understanding, the natures and essenses of all things being perfectly known to him from eternity.

It ought to be observed, that the Pythagoreans, and the Platonists whether elder or latter, made the eternal ideas to be objects of science only, and of abstract contemplation, not the objects of sense. And in this the ancient system of eternal ideas differs from the modern one of father Malebranche. He held, in common with other modern philosophers, that no external thing is perceived by us immediately, but only by ideas : but he thought, that the ideas, by which we perceive an external world, are the ideas of the Deity himself, in whose mind the ideas of all things, past, present, and future, must have been from eternity ; for the Deity being intimately present to our minds at all times, may discover to us as much of his ideas as he sees proper, according to certain established laws of nature : and in his ideas, as in a mirror, we perceive whatever we do perceive of the external world.

Thus we have three systems, which maintain, that the ideas, which are the immediate objects of human knowledge, are eternal and immutable, and existed before the things which they represent. There are other systems, according to which, the ideas, which are the immediate objects of all our thoughts, are posterior to the things which they represent, and derived from them. We shall give some account of these : but as they have gradually sprung out of the ancient Peripatetic system, it is necessary to begin with some account of it.

Aristotle taught, that all the objects of our thought enter at first by the senses ; and, since the sense cannot receive external material objects themselves, it receives their species ; that is, their images or forms, without the matter ; as wax receives the form of the seal without any of the matter of it. These images or forms, impressed upon the senses, are called *sensible species*, and are the objects only of the sensitive part of the mind : but, by various internal powers, they are retained, refined, and spiritualized, so as to become objects of memory and imagination, and, at last, of pure intellection. When they are objects of memory and of imagination, they get the name of *phantasms*. When, by farther refinement, and being stripped of their particularities, they become objects of science ; they are called *intelligible species* : so that every immediate object, whether of sense, of memory, of imagination, or of reasoning, must be some phantasm or species in the mind itself.

The followers of Aristotle, especially the schoolmen, made great additions to this theory, which the
author himself mentions very briefly, and with an appearance of reserve. They entered into large disquisitions with regard to the sensible species, what kind
of things they are; how they are sent forth by the object, and enter by the organs of the senses; how they
are preserved and refined by various agents, called internal senses; concerning the number and offices of
which they had many controversies. But we shall not
enter into a detail of these matters.

The reason of giving this brief account of the theory of the Peripatetics, with regard to the immediate
objects of our thoughts, is, because the doctrine of
modern philosophers concerning ideas is built upon it.
Mr. Locke, who uses this word so very frequently, tells
us, that he means the same thing by it, as is commonly meant by *species* or *phantasm*. Gassendi, from whom
Locke borrowed more than from any other author,
says the same. The words *species* and *phantasm*, are
terms of art in the Peripatetic system, and the meaning of them is to be learned from it.

The theory of Democritus and Epicurus, on this
subject, was not very unlike to that of the Peripatetics. They held, that all bodies continually send
forth slender films or spectres from their surface, of
such extreme subtilty, that they easily penetrate our
gross bodies, or enter by the organs of sense, and
stamp their image upon the mind. The sensible species of Aristotle was mere forms without matter. The
spectres of Epicurus were composed of a very subtile
matter.

Modern philosophers, as well as the Peripatetics and
Epicureans of old, have conceived, that external objects cannot be the immediate objects of our thought;
that there must be some image of them in the mind

itself, in which, as in a mirror, they are seen. And
the name *idea*, in the philosophical sense of it, is given
to those internal and immediate objects of our thoughts.
The external thing is the remote or mediate object;
but the idea, or image of that object in the mind, is the
immediate object, without which we could have no perception, no remembrance, no conception of the mediate
object.

When, therefore, in common language, we speak of
having an idea of any thing, we mean no more by that
expression but thinking of it. The vulgar allow, that
this expression implies a mind that thinks; an act of
that mind which we call thinking, and an object about
which we think. But, besides these three, the philosopher conceives that there is a fourth, to wit, the *idea*,
which is the immediate object. The idea is in the
mind itself, and can have no existence but in a mind
that thinks; but the remote, or mediate ob ect may be
something external, as the sun or moon; it may be
something past or future; it may be something which
never existed. This is the philosophical meaning of
the word *idea;* and we may observe, that this meaning
of that word is built upon a philosophical opinion: for
if philosophers had not believed that there are such
immediate objects of all our thoughts in the mind, they
would never have used the word idea to express them.

I shall only add on this article, that although I may
have occasion to use the word idea in this philosophical
sense in explaining the opinions of others, I shall have
no occasion to use it in expressing my own, because I believe *ideas*, taken in this sense, to be a mere fiction of
philosophers. And in the popular meaning of the word,
there is the less occasion to use it, because the English
words, *thought, notion, apprehension,* answer the purpose as well as the Greek word *idea;* with this advantage, that they are less ambiguous. There is indeed a

meaning of the word idea, which I think most agreeable to its use in ancient philosophy, and which I would willingly adopt, if use, the arbiter of language, did permit. But this will come to be explained afterward.

11. The word *impression* is used by Mr. Hume, in speaking of the operations of the mind, almost as often as the word *idea* is by Mr. Locke. What the latter calls ideas, the former divides into two classes; one of which he calls impressions, the other ideas. I shall make some observations upon Mr. Hume's explication of *that* word, and then consider the proper meaning of it in the English language.

" We may divide, says Mr. Hume, Essays, vol. ii. page 18. all the perceptions of the human mind into two classes or species, which are distinguished by their different degrees of force and vivacity. " The less lively and forcible, are commonly denominated thoughts or ideas. The other species want a name in our language, and in most others ; let us therefore use a little freedom, and call them impressions. By this term *impressions*, then, I mean all our more lively perceptions, when we hear, or see, or feel, or love, or hate, or desire, or will. Ideas are the less lively perceptions, of which we are conscious, when we reflect on any of those sensations or movements above mentioned."

This is the explication Mr. Hume hath given in his Essays of the term *impressions,* when applied to the mind ; and his explication of it, in his Treatise of Human Nature, is to the same purpose.

Disputes about words belong rather to grammarians than to philosophers ; but philosophers ought not to escape censure when they corrupt a language, by using words in a way which the purity of the language will not admit. I find fault with Mr. Hume's phraseology in the words I have quoted,

First, Because he gives the name of perceptions to
every operation of the mind. Love is a perception,
hatred a perception. Desire is a perception, will is a
perception ; and, by the same rule, a doubt, a question,
a command, is a perception. This is an intolerable
abuse of language, which no philosopher has authority
to introduce.

Secondly, When Mr. Hume says, *that we may divide
all the perceptions of the human mind into two classes
or species, which are distinguished by their degrees of
force and vivacity*, the manner of expression is loose
and unphilosophical. To differ in species is one thing ;
to differ in degree is another. Things which differ in
degree only must be of the same species. It is a maxim of common sense, admitted by all men, that *greater*
and *less* do not make a change of species. The same
man may differ in the degree of his force and vivacity
in the morning and at night ; in health and in sickness :
but this is so far from making him a different species, that it does not so much as make him a different
individual. To say, therefore, that two different classes,
or species of perceptions, are distinguished by the degrees of their force and vivacity, is to confound a difference of *degree* with a difference of *species*, which
every man of understanding knows how to distinguish.

Thirdly, We may observe that this author, having
given the general name of perception to all the operations of the mind, and distinguished them into two
classes or species, which differ only in degree of force
and vivacity, tells us, that he gives the name of impressions to all our more lively perceptions ; to wit, when
we hear, or see, or feel, or love, or hate, or desire, or
will. There is great confusion in this account of the
meaning of the word *impression*. When I see, this is
an *impression*. But why has not the author told us,

whether he gives the name of *impression* to the object seen, or to that act of my mind by which I see it? When I see the full moon, the full moon is one thing, my perceiving it is another thing. Which of these two things does he call an impression? We are left to guess this; nor does all that this author writes about impressions clear this point. Every thing he says tends to darken it, and to lead us to think, that the full moon which I see, and my seeing it are not two things, but one and the same thing.

The same observation may be applied to every other instance the author gives to illustrate the meaning of the word *impression*. "When we hear, when we feel, when we love, when we hate, when we desire, when we will." In all these acts of the mind there must be an *object*, which is heard, or felt, or loved, or hated, or desired, or willed. Thus, for instance, I love my country. This, says Mr. Hume, is an *impression*. But what is the *impression?* Is it my country, or is it the affection I bear to it? I ask the philosopher this question; but I find no answer to it. And when I read all that he has *written* on this subject, I find this word *impression* sometimes used to signify an operation of the mind, sometimes the object of the operation; but, for the most part, it is a vague and indetermined word that signifies both.

I know not whether it may be considered as an apology for such abuse of words, in an author who understood the language so well, and used it with so great propriety in writing on other subjects, that Mr. Hume's system, with regard to the mind, required a language of a different structure from the common; or, if expressed in plain English, would have been too shocking to the common sense of mankind. To give an instance or two of this. If a man receives a present on which he puts a high value; if he see and handle it, and

put it in his pocket, this, says Mr. Hume, is an *impression*. If the man only dream that he received such a
present, this is an *idea*. Wherein lies the difference
between this impression and this idea; between the
dream and the reality? They are different classes or
species, says Mr. Hume: so far all men will agree with
him. But he adds, that they are distinguished only
by different degrees of force and vivacity. Here he insinuates a tenet of his own, in contradiction to the common sense of mankind. Common sense convinces every
man, that a lively dream is no nearer to a reality than
a faint one; and that if a man should dream that he
had all the wealth of Crœsus, it would not put one
farthing in his pocket. It is impossible to fabricate
arguments against such undeniable principles, without
confounding the meaning of words.

In like manner, if a man would persuade me, that
the moon which I see, and my seeing it, are not two
things, but one and the same thing, he will answer his
purpose less by arguing this point in plain English, than
by confounding the two under one name, such as that
of an *impression :* for such is the power of words, that
if we can be brought to the habit of calling two things
that are connected *by the same name,* we are the more
easily led to believe them one and the same thing.

Let us next consider the proper meaning of the word
impression in English, that we may see how far it is fit
to express either the operations of the mind, or their
objects.

When a figure is stamped upon a body by pressure,
that figure is called an *impression,* as the impression of
a seal on wax, of printing types, or of a copperplate, on
paper. This seems now to be the literal sense of the
word; the effect borrowing its name from the cause. But
by metaphor or analogy, like most other words, its meaning is extended, so as to signify any change produced

in a body by the operation of some external cause. A
blow of the hand makes no impression on a stone wall;
but a battery of cannon may. The moon raises a tide
in the ocean, but makes no impression on rivers and
lakes.

When we speak of making an impression on the
mind, the word is carried still farther from its literal
meaning; use, however, which is the arbiter of language, authorizes this application of it. As when we
say, that admonition and reproof make little impression
on those who are confirmed in bad habits. The same
discourse delivered in one way, makes a strong impression on the hearers; delivered in another way, it makes
no impression at all.

It may be observed, that in such examples, an impression made on the mind always implies some change
of purpose or will; some new habit produced, or some
former habit weakened; some passion raised or allay-
ed. When such changes are produced by persuasion,
example, or any external cause, we say that such causes
make an impression upon the mind. But when things
are seen, or heard, or apprehended, without producing
any passion or emotion, we say that they make no impression.

In the most extensive sense, an impression is a
change produced in some passive subject by the operation of an external cause. If we suppose an active being to produce any change in itself by its own active
power, this is never called an impression. It is the
act or operation of the being itself, not an impression
upon it. From this it appears, that to give the name
of an impression to any effect produced in the mind, is
to suppose that the mind does not act at all in the production of that effect. If seeing, hearing, desiring, willing, be operations of the mind, they cannot be impressions. If they be impressions, they cannot be opera-

tions of the mind. In the structure of all languages
they are considered as acts or operations of the mind
itself, and the names given them imply this. To call
them impressions, therefore, is to trespass against the
structure, not of a particular language only, but of all
languages.

If the word *impression* be an improper word to signify the operations of the mind, it is at least as improper to signify their objects; for would any man be
thought to speak with propriety, who should say that
the sun is an impression, that the earth and the sea
are impressions?

It is commonly believed, and taken for granted, that
every language, if it be sufficiently copious in words,
is equally fit to express all opinions, whether they be
true or false. I apprehend, however, that there is an
exception to this general rule, which deserves our notice. There are certain common opinions of mankind,
upon which the structure and grammar of all languages are founded. While these opinions are common to all men, there will be a great similarity in all
languages that are to be found on the face of the earth.
Such a similarity there really is; for we find in all languages the same parts of speech, the distinction of
nouns and verbs, the distinction of nouns into adjective and substantive, of verbs into active and passive.
In verbs we find like tenses, moods, persons, and numbers. There are general rules of grammar, the same
in all languages. This similarity of structure in all
languages shews an uniformity among men in those
opinions upon which the structure of language is founded.

If, for instance, we should suppose that there was a
nation who believed that the things which we call attributes might exist without a subject, there would be
in their language no distinction between adjectives and

substantives, nor would it be a rule with them that an adjective has no meaning, unless when joined to a substantive. If there was any nation who did not distinguish between acting and being acted upon, there would in their language be no distinction between active and passive verbs, nor would it be a rule that the active verb must have an agent in the nominative case: but that, in the passive verb, the agent must be in an oblique case.

The structure of all languages is grounded upon common notions, which Mr. Hume's philosophy opposes, and endeavours to overturn. This no doubt led him to warp the common language into a conformity with his principles; but we ought not to imitate him in this, until we are satisfied that his principles are built on a solid foundation.

12. Sensation is a name given by philosophers to an act of mind, which may be distinguished from all others by this, that it hath no object distinct from the act itself. Pain of every kind is an uneasy sensation. When I am pained, I cannot say that the pain I feel is one thing, and that my feeling it is another thing. They are one and the same thing, and cannot be disjoined, even in imagination. Pain, when it is not felt, has no existence. It can be neither greater nor less in degree or duration, nor any thing else in kind, than it is felt to be. It cannot exist by itself, nor in any subject, but in a sentient being. No quality of an inanimate insentient being can have the least resemblance to it.

What we have said of pain may be applied to every other sensation. Some of them are agreeable, others uneasy, in various degrees. These being objects of desire or aversion, have some attention given to them; but many are indifferent, and so little attended to, that they have no name in any language.

Most operations of the mind, that have names in common language, are complex in their nature, and made up of various ingredients, or more simple acts ; which, though conjoined in our constitution, must be disjoined by abstraction, in order to our having a distinct and scientific notion of the complex operation. In such operations, sensation for the most part makes an ingredient. Those who do not attend to the complex nature of such operations, are apt to resolve them into some one of the simple acts of which they are compounded, overlooking the others : and from this cause many disputes have been raised, and many errors have been occasioned with regard to the nature of such operations.

The perception of external objects is accompanied with some sensation corresponding to the object perceived, and such sensations have, in many cases, in all languages, the same name with the external object which they always accompany. The difficulty of disjoining by abstraction, things thus constantly conjoined in the course of nature, and things, which have one and the same name in all languages, has likewise been frequently an occasion of errors in the philosophy of the mind. To avoid such errors, nothing is of more importance than to have a distinct notion of that simple act of the mind, which we call *sensation*, and which we have endeavoured to describe. By this means we shall find it more easy to distinguish it from every external object that it accompanies, and from every other act of the mind that may be conjoined with it. For this purpose it is likewise of importance, that the name of *sensation* should, in philosophical writings, be appropriated to signify this simple act of the mind, without including any thing more in its signification, or being applied to other purposes.

I shall add an observation concerning the word *feel-ing*. This word has too meanings. First. it signifies the perceptions we have of external objects. by the sense of touch. When we speak of feeling a body to be hard or soft, rough or smooth, hot or cold, to feel these things, is to perceive them by touch. They are exter-nal things, and that act of the mind by which we feel them, is easily distinguished from the objects felt : sec-ondly, the word *feeling* is used to signify the same thing as *sensation*, which we have just now explained ; and, in this sense, it has no object ; the feeling and the thing felt are one and the same.

Perhaps betwixt feeling, taken in this last sense, and sensation. there may be this small difference, that sen-sation is most commonly used to signify those feelings which we have by our external senses and bodily appe-tites. and all our bodily pains and pleasures. But there are *feelings* of a nobler nature accompanying our affec-tions. our moral judgments, and our determinations in matters of taste. to which the word *sensation* is less properly applied.

I have premised these observations on the meaning of certain words that frequently occur in treating of this subject. for two reasons ; first, that I may be the better understood when I use them ; and, secondly, that those who would make any progress in this branch of science. may accustom themselves to attend very carefully to the meaning of words that are used in it. They may be assured of this, that the ambiguity of words, and the vague and improper application of them, have thrown more darkness upon this subject, than the subtilty and intricacy of things.

When we use common words, we ought to use them in the sense in which they are most commonly used by the best and purest writers in the language ; and, when we have occasion to enlarge or restrict the meaning of a common word, or to give it more precision than it has in common language, the reader ought to have warning of this, otherwise we shall impose upon ourselves and upon him.

A very respectable writer has given us a good example of this kind, by explaining, in an appendix to his Elements of Criticism, the terms he has occasion to use. In that Appendix, most of the words are explained on which I have been making observations. And the explication I have given, I think, agrees, for the most part, with his.

Other words that need explication shall be explained as they occur.

CHAP. II.

PRINCIPLES TAKEN FOR GRANTED.

As there are words common to philosophers and to the vulgar, which need no explication ; so there are principles common to both, which need no proof, and which do not admit of direct proof.

One who applies to any branch of science must be come to years of understanding, and consequently must have exercised his reason, and the other powers of his mind, in various ways. He must have formed various opinions and principles, by which he conducts himself in the affairs of life. Of those principles, some are common to all men, being evident in themselves, and so necessary in the conduct of life, that a man cannot live and act according to the rules of common prudence without them.

All men that have common understanding agree in such principles, and consider a man as lunatic, or destitute of common sense, who denies or calls them in question. Thus, if any man were found of so strange a turn as not to believe his own eyes; to put no trust in his senses, nor have the least regard to their testimony; would any man think it worth while to reason gravely with such a person, and, by argument, to convince him of his error? Surely no wise man would. For before men can reason together, they must agree in first principles; and it is impossible to reason with a man who has no principles in common with you.

There are, therefore, common principles, which are the foundation of all reasoning, and of all science. Such common principles seldom admit of direct proof; nor do they need it. Men need not to be taught them; for they are such as all men of common understanding know; or such, at least, as they give a ready assent to, as soon as they are proposed and understood.

Such principles, when we have occasion to use them in science, are called *axioms*. And, although it be not absolutely necessary, yet it may be of great use, to point out the principles or axioms on which a science is grounded.

Thus, mathematicians, before they prove any of the propositions of mathematics, lay down certain axioms, or common principles, upon which they build their reasonings. And although those axioms be truths which every man knew before; such as, that the whole is greater than a part, that equal quantities added to equal quantities make equal sums; yet when we see nothing assumed in the proof of mathematical propo-sitions, but such self-evident axioms, the propositions appear more certain, and leave no room for doubt or dispute.

In all other sciences, as well as in mathematics, it will be found, that there are a few common principles, upon which all the reasonings in that science are grounded, and into which they may be resolved. If these were pointed out and considered, we should be better able to judge what stress may be laid upon the conclusions in that science. If the principles be certain, the conclusions justly drawn from them must be certain. If the principles be only probable, the conclusions can only be probable. If the principles be false, dubious, or obscure, the superstructure that is built upon them must partake of the weakness of the foundation.

Sir Isaac Newton, the greatest of natural philosophers, has given an example well worthy of imitation, by laying down the common principles or axioms, on which the reasonings in natural philosophy are built. Before this was done, the reasonings of philosophers, in that science, were as vague and uncertain as they are in most others. Nothing was fixed; all was dispute and controversy: but, by this happy expedient, a solid foundation is laid in that science, and a noble superstructure is raised upon it, about which there is now no more dispute or controversy among men of knowledge, than there is about the conclusions of mathematics.

It may, however, be observed, that the first principles of natural philosophy are of a quite different nature from mathematical axioms. They have not the same kind of evidence, nor are they necessary truths, as mathematical axioms are. They are such as these: that similar effects proceed from the same or similar causes: that we ought to admit of no other causes of natural effects, but such as are true, and sufficient to account for the effects. These are principles, which, though they have not the same kind of evidence that mathematical axioms have, yet have such evidence, that every man of common understanding readily assents to them, and finds it absolutely necessary to conduct his actions and opinions by them, in the ordinary affairs of life.

Though it has not been usual, yet I conceive it may be useful, to point out some of those things which I shall take for granted, as first principles in treating of the mind and its faculties. There is the more occasion for this; because very ingenious men, such as Des Cartes, Malebranche, Arnaud, Locke, and many others, have lost much labour, by not distinguishing things which require proof, from things which, though they may admit of illustration, yet being self evident, do not admit of proof. When men attempt to deduce such self-evident principles from others more evident, they always fall into inconclusive reasoning: and the consequence of this has been, that others, such as Berkeley and Hume, finding the arguments brought to prove such first principles to be weak and inconclusive, have been tempted first to doubt of them, and afterward to deny them.

It is so irksome to reason with those who deny first principles, that wise men commonly decline it. Yet it is not impossible, that what is only a vulgar prejudice may be mistaken for a first principle. Nor is it impossible, that what is really a first principle, may, by the enchantment of words, have such a mist thrown about it, as to hide its evidence, and to make a man of candour doubt of it. Such cases happen more frequently perhaps in this science than in any other; but they are not altogether without remedy. There are ways by which the evidence of first principles may be made more apparent when they are brought into dispute; but they require to be handled in a way peculiar to themselves. Their evidence is not demonstrative, but intuitive. They require not proof, but to be placed in a proper point of view. This will be shown more fully in its proper place, and applied to those very principles which we now assume. In the mean time, when they are proposed as first principles, the reader is put on his guard, and warned to consider whether they have a just claim to that character.

1. First, then, I shall take it for granted, that I *think*, that I *remember*, that I *reason*, and, in general, that I really perform all those operations of mind of which I am conscious.

The operations of our minds are attended with *consciousness*; and this consciousness is the evidence, the only evidence, which we have or can have of their existence. If a man should take it into his head to think or to say that his consciousness may deceive him, and to require proof that it cannot, I know of no proof that can be given him; he must be left to himself, as a man that denies first principles, without which there can be no reasoning. Every man finds himself under a necessity of believing what consciousness testifies, and every thing that hath this testimony is to be taken as a first principle.

2. As by consciousness we know certainly the existence of our present thoughts and passions; so we know the past by *remembrance*. And when they are recent, and the remembrance of them fresh, the knowledge of them, from such distinct remembrance, is, in its certainty and evidence, next to that of consciousness.

3. But it is to be observed, that we are conscious of many things to which we give little or no attention. We can hardly attend to several things at the same time; and our attention is commonly employed about that which is the object of our thought, and rarely about the thought itself. Thus, when a man is angry, his attention is turned to the injury done him, or the injurious person; and he gives very little attention to the passion of anger, although he is conscious of it. It

is in our power, however, when we come to the years of understanding, to give attention to our own thoughts and passions, and the various operations of our minds. And when we make these the objects of our attention, either while they are present, or when they are recent and fresh in our memory, this act of the mind is called *reflection*.

We take it for granted, therefore, that, by attentive reflection, a man may have a clear and certain knowledge of the operations of his own mind; a knowledge no less clear and certain, than that which he has of an external object when it is set before his eyes.

This *reflection* is a kind of intuition; it gives a like conviction with regard to internal objects, or things in the mind, as the faculty of seeing gives with regard to objects of sight. A man must, therefore, be convinced beyond possibility of doubt of every thing with regard to the operations of his own mind, which he clearly and distinctly discerns by attentive reflection.

4. I take it for granted, that all the thoughts I am conscious of, or remember, are the thoughts of one and the same thinking principle, which I call *myself* or my *mind*. Every man has an immediate and irresistible conviction, not only of his present existence but of his continued existence and identity, as far back as he can remember. If any man should think fit to demand a proof that the thoughts he is successively conscious of, belong to one and the same thinking principle; if he should demand a proof that he is the same person to-day as he was yesterday, or a year ago, I know no proof that can be given him : he must be left to himself, either as a man that is lunatic, or as one who denies first principles, and is not to be reasoned with.

Every man of a sound mind finds himself under a necessity of believing his own identity, and continued existence. The conviction of this is immediate and irresistible; and if he should lose this conviction, it would be a certain proof of insanity, which is not to be remedied by reasoning.

5. I take it for granted, that there are some things which cannot exist by themselves, but must be in something else to which they belong, as qualities, or attributes.

Thus, motion cannot exist but in something that is moved. And to suppose that there can be motion while every thing is at rest, is a gross and palpable absurdity. In like manner, hardness and softness, sweetness and bitterness, are things which cannot exist by themselves; they are qualities of something which is hard or soft, sweet or bitter. That thing, whatever it be, of which they are qualities, is called their *subject*, and such qualities necessarily suppose a subject.

Things which may exist by themselves, and do not necessarily suppose the existence of any thing else, are called *substances*; and with relation to the qualities or attributes that belong to them, they are called the *subjects* of such qualities or attributes.

All the things which we immediately perceive by our senses, and all the things we are conscious of, are things which must be in something else as their subject. Thus by my senses, I perceive figure, colour, hardness, softness, motion, resistance, and such like things. But these are qualities, and must necessarily be in something that is figured, coloured, hard or soft, that moves, or resists. It is not to these qualities, but to that which is the subject of them, that we give the name of *body*. If any man should think fit to deny that these things are qualities, or that they require any subject, I leave him to enjoy his opinion, as a man who denies first principles, and is not fit to be reasoned with. If he has common understanding, he will find that he cannot converse half an hour without saying things which imply the contrary of what he professes to believe.

In like manner, the things I am conscious of, such as thought, reasoning, desire, necessarily suppose something that thinks, that reasons, that desires. We do not give the name of *mind* to thought, reason, or desire; but to that being which thinks, which reasons, and which desires.

That every act or operation, therefore, supposes an agent, that every quality supposes a subject, are things which I do not attempt to prove, but take for granted. Every man of common understanding discerns this immediately, and cannot entertain the least doubt of it. In all languages, we find certain words, which, by grammarians, are called adjectives. Such words denote attributes, and every adjective must have a substantive to which it belongs; that is, every attribute must have a subject. In all languages, we find active verbs, which denote some action or operation; and it is a fundamental rule in the grammar of all languages, that such a verb supposes a person; that is, in other words, that every action must have an agent. We take it, therefore, as a first principle, that goodness, wisdom, and virtue, can only be in some being that is good, wise, and virtuous; that thinking supposes a being that thinks; and that every operation we are conscious of supposes an agent that operates, which we call *mind*.

6. I take it for granted, that in most operations of the mind, there must be an *object* distinct from the operation itself. I cannot see, without seeing something. To see, without having any object of sight, is absurd. I cannot remember, without remembering something. The thing remembered is past, while the remembrance of it is present; and therefore the operation and the object of it must be distinct things. The operations of our minds are denoted, in all languages, by active transitive verbs, which, from their construction in grammar, re-

quire not only a person or agent, but likewise an object of the operation. Thus the verb *know* denotes an operation of mind. From the general structure of language, this verb requires a person; I know, you know, or he knows: but it requires no less a noun in the accusative case, denoting the thing known; for he that knows, must know something; and to know, without having any object of knowledge, is an absurdity too gross to admit of reasoning.

7. We ought likewise to take for granted, as first principles, things wherein we find an *universal agreement*, among the learned and unlearned, in the different nations and ages of the world. A consent of ages and nations, of the learned and vulgar, ought, at least, to have great authority, unless we can show some prejudice, as universal as that consent is, which might be the cause of it. Truth is one, but error is infinite. There are many truths so obvious to the human faculties, that it may be expected that men should universally agree in them. And this is actually found to be the case with regard to many truths, against which we find no dissent, unless perhaps that of a few skeptical philosophers, who may justly be suspected, in such cases, to differ from the rest of mankind, through pride, obstinacy, or some favourite passion. Where there is such universal consent in things not deep nor intricate, but which lie, as it were, on the surface, there is the greatest presumption that can be, that it is the natural result of the human faculties; and it must have great authority with every sober mind that loves truth. *Major enim pars eo fere deferri solet quo a natura deducitur.* Cic. de off. 1. 41.

Perhaps it may be thought that it is impossible to collect the opinions of all men upon any point whatsoever, and, therefore; that this maxim can be of no use. But there are many cases wherein it is otherwise. Who can doubt, for instance, whether mankind have, in all ages, believed the existence of a material world, and that those things which they see and handle are real, and not mere illusions and apparitions? Who can doubt, whether mankind have universally believed, that every thing that begins to exist, and every change that happens in nature, must have a cause? Who can doubt, whether mankind have been universally persuaded that there is a right and a wrong in human conduct? Some things which, in certain circumstances, they ought to do, and other things which they ought not to do? The universality of these opinions, and of many such that might be named, is sufficiently evident, from the whole tenor of men's conduct, as far as our acquaintance reaches, and from the records of history, in all ages and nations, that are transmitted to us.

There are other opinions that appear to be universal, from what is common in the structure of all languages, ancient and modern, polished and barbarous. Language is the express image and picture of human thoughts; and from the picture, we may draw very certain conclusions with regard to the original. We find, in all languages, the same parts of speech, nouns substantive and adjective, verbs active and passive, varied according to the tenses of past, present and future; we find adverbs, prepositions, and conjunctions. There are general rules of syntax, common to all languages. This uniformity in the structure of language, shows a certain degree of uniformity in those notions upon which the structure of language is grounded.

We find, in the structure of all languages, the distinction of acting, and being acted upon, the distinction of action and agent, of quality and subject, and many others of the like kind; which shews, that these distinctions are founded in the universal sense of mankind. We shall have frequent occasion to argue from the sense of mankind expresed in the structure of language; and therefore it was proper here to take notice of the force of argument drawn from this topic.

8. I need hardly say, that I shall also take for granted such facts as are attested to the conviction of all sober and reasonable men, either by our senses, by memory, or by human testimony. Although some writers on this subject have disputed the authority of the senses, of memory, and of every human faculty; yet we find, that such persons, in the conduct of life, in pursuing their ends, or in avoiding dangers, pay the same regard to the authority of their senses, and other faculties, as the rest of mankind. By this they give us just ground to doubt of their candour in their professions of skepticism.

This, indeed, has always been the fate of the few that have professed skepticism, that, when they have done what they can to discredit their senses, they find themselves, after all, under a necessity of trusting to them. Mr. Hume has been so candid as to acknowledge this; and it is no less true of those who have not shewn the same candour. For I never heard that any skeptic run his head against a post, or stepped into a kennel, because he did not believe his eyes.

Upon the whole, I acknowledge, that we ought to be cautious, that we do not adopt opinions as first principles, which are not entitled to that character. But there is surely the least danger of men's being imposed upon in this way, when such principles openly lay claim to the character, and are thereby fairly exposed to the examination of those who may dispute their authority. We do not pretend, that those things that are laid down as first principles may not be examined, and that we ought not to have our ears open to what may be pleaded against their being admitted as such. Let us deal with them, as an upright judge does with a witness who has a fair character. He pays a regard to the testi-

mony of such a witness, while his character is unim-
peached. But if it can be shewn that he was suborn-
ed, or that he is influenced by malice or partial favour,
his testimony loses all its credit, and is justly rejected.

CHAP. III.

OF HYPOTHESES.

EVERY branch of human knowledge hath its proper
principles, its proper foundation and method of reasoning; and, if we endeavour to build it upon any other
foundation, it will never stand firm and stable. Thus
the historian builds upon testimony, and rarely indulges
conjecture. The antiquarian mixes conjecture with
testimony: and the former often makes the larger ingredient. The mathematician pays not the least regard either to testimony or conjecture, but deduces
every thing, by demonstrative reasoning, from his definitions and axioms. Indeed, whatever is built upon
conjecture, is improperly called science; for conjecture
may beget opinion, but cannot produce knowledge.
Natural philosophy must be built upon the phenomena
of the material system, discovered by observation and
experiment.

When men first began to philosophize, that is, to
carry their thoughts beyond the objects of sense, and
to inquire into the causes of things, and the secret operations of nature, it was very natural for them to indulge conjecture; nor was it to be expected, that, in
many ages, they should discover the proper and scientific way of proceeding in philosophical disquisitions.
Accordingly we find, that the most ancient systems in
every branch of philosophy were nothing but the con-

jectures of men famous for their wisdom, whose fame
gave authority to their opinions. Thus, in early ages,
wise men conjectured, that this earth is a vast plain,
surrounded on all hands by a boundless ocean. That
from this ocean, the sun, moon, and stars, emerge at
their rising, and plunge into it again at their setting.

With regard to the mind, men in their rudest state
are apt to conjecture, that the principle of life in a man
is his breath; because the most obvious distinction between a living and a dead man is, that the one breathes,
and the other does not. To this it is owing, that, in
ancient languages, the word which denotes the soul, is
that which properly signifies breath or air.

As men advance in knowledge, their first conjectures appear silly and childish, and give place to others, which tally better with later observations and discoveries. Thus, one system of philosophy succeeds another, without any claim to superior merit, but this,
that it is a more ingenious system of conjectures, and
accounts better for common appearances.

To omit many ancient systems of this kind, Des
Cartes, about the middle of the last century, dissatisfied with the *materia prima,* the *substantial forms,* and
the *occult qualities* of the Peripatetics, conjectured
boldly, that the heavenly bodies of our system are carried round by a vortex or whirlpool of subtile matter,
just as straws and chaff are carried round in a tub of
water. He conjectured, that the soul is seated in a
small gland in the brain, called the *pineal gland :* that
there, as in her chamber of presence, she receives intelligence of every thing that affects the senses, by
means of a subtile fluid contained in the nerves, called
the animal spirits; and that she despatches these animal spirits, as her messengers, to put in motion the
several muscles of the body, as there is occasion. By
such conjectures as these, Des Cartes could account

for every phenomenon in nature, in such a plausible manner, as gave satisfaction to a great part of the learned world for more than half a century.

Such conjectures in philosophical matters have commonly got the name of *hypotheses* or *theories*. And the invention of a hypothesis, founded on some slight probabilities, which accounts for many appearances of nature, has been considered as the highest attainment of a philosopher. If the hypothesis hangs well together, is embellished by a lively imagination, and serves to account for common appearances; it is considered by many as having all the qualities that should recommend it to our belief; and all that ought to be required in a philosophical system.

There is such proneness in men of genius to invent hypotheses, and in others to acquiesce in them as the utmost which the human faculties can attain in philosophy, that it is of the last consequence to the progress of real knowledge, that men should have a clear and distinct understanding of the nature of hypotheses in philosophy, and of the regard that is due to them.

Although some conjectures may have a considerable degree of probability, yet it is evidently in the nature of conjecture to be uncertain. In every case, the assent ought to be proportioned to the evidence; for to believe firmly, what has but a small degree of probability, is a manifest abuse of our understanding. Now, though we may, in many cases, form very probable conjectures concerning the works of men, every conjecture we can form with regard to the works of God, has as little probability as the conjectures of a child with regard to the works of a man.

The wisdom of God exceeds that of the wisest man, more than that of the wisest man exceeds the wisdom of a child. If a child were to conjecture how an army is to be formed in the day of battle; how a city is to be fortified, or a state governed; what chance has he to guess right? As little chance has the wisest man when he pretends to conjecture how the planets move in their courses, how the sea ebbs and flows, and how our minds act upon our bodies.

If a thousand of the greatest wits that ever the world produced, were, without any previous knowledge in anatomy, to sit down and contrive how, and by what internal organs the various functions of the human body are carried on; how the blood is made to circulate, and the limbs to move, they would not in a thousand years hit upon any thing like the truth.

Of all the discoveries that have been made concerning the inward structure of the human body, never one was made by conjecture. Accurate observations of anatomists have brought to light innumerable artifices of nature in the contrivance of this machine of the human body, which we cannot but admire as excellently adapted to their several purposes. But the most sagacious physiologist never dreamed of them till they were discovered. On the other hand, innumerable conjectures, formed in different ages, with regard to the structure of the body, have been confuted by observation, and none ever confirmed.

What we have said of the internal structure of the human body, may be said, with justice, of every other part of the works of God, wherein any real discovery has been made. Such discoveries have always been made by patient observation, by accurate experiments, or by conclusions drawn by strict reasoning from observations and experiments, and such discoveries have always tended to refute, but not to confirm, the theories and hypotheses which ingenious men had invented.

As this is a fact confirmed by the history of philosophy in all past ages, it ought to have taught men, long ago, to treat with just contempt hypotheses in every branch of philosophy, and to despair of ever advancing real knowledge in that way. The Indian philosopher, being at a loss to know how the earth was supported, invented the hypothesis of a huge elephant; and this elephant he supposed to stand upon the back of a huge tortoise. This hypothesis, however ridiculous it appears to us, might seem very reasonable to other Indians, who knew no more than the inventor of it; and the same will be the fate of all hypotheses invented by men to account for the works of God: they may have a decent and plausible appearance to those who are not more knowing than the inventor; but, when men come to be more enlightened, they will always appear ridiculous and childish.

This has been the case with regard to hypotheses that have been revered by the most enlightened part of mankind for hundreds of years; and it will always be the case to the end of the world. For until the wisdom of men bear some proportion to the wisdom of God, their attempts to find out the structure of his works by the force of their wit and genius, will be vain.

The finest productions of human art are immensely short of the meanest works of nature. The nicest artist cannot make a feather, or the leaf of a tree. Human workmanship will never bear a comparison with divine. Conjectures and hypotheses are the invention and the workmanship of men, and must bear proportion to the capacity and skill of the inventor; and therefore will always be very unlike to the works of God, which it is the business of philosophy to discover.

The world has been so long befooled by hypotheses in all parts of philosophy, that it is of the utmost consequence to every man, who would make any progress in real knowledge, to treat them with just contempt as the reveries of vain and fanciful men, whose pride makes them conceive themselves able to unfold the mysteries of nature by the force of their genius. A learned man, in an epistle to Des Cartes, has the following observation, which very much deserved the attention of that philosopher, and of all that come after him. "When men, sitting in their closet, and consulting only their books, attempt disquisitions into nature, they may indeed tell how they would have made the world, if God had given them that in commission; that is, they may describe chimeras, which correspond with the imbecility of their own minds, no less than the admirable beauty of the universe corresponds with the infinite perfection of its Creator; but without an understanding truly divine, they can never form such an idea to themselves as the Deity had in creating things."

Let us, therefore, lay down this as a fundamental principle in our inquiries into the structure of the mind, and its operations, that no regard is due to the conjectures or hypotheses of philosophers, however ancient, however generally received. Let us accustom ourselves to try every opinion by the touchstone of fact and experience. What can fairly be deduced from facts duly observed, or sufficiently attested, is genuine and pure; it is the voice of God, and no fiction of human imagination.

The first rule of philosophizing laid down by the great Newton is this: *Causas rerum naturalium, non plures admitti debere, quam quæ et veræ sint, et earum phænomenis explicandis sufficiant.* "No more causes, nor any other causes of natural effects ought to be admitted, but such as are both true, and are sufficient for explaining their appearances." This is a golden rule; it is the true and proper test, by which what is sound and solid in philosophy may be distinguished from what is hollow and vaiu.

If a philosopher, therefore, pretend to shew us the cause of any natural effect, whether relating to matter or to mind; let us first consider whether there be sufficient evidence that the cause he assigns does really exist. If there be not, reject it with disdain as a fiction which ought to have no place in genuine philosoophy. If the cause assigned really exist, consider in the next place, whether the effect it is brought to explain necessarily follow from it. Unless it have these two conditions, it is good for nothing.

When Newton had shewn the admirable effects of gravitation in our planetary system, he must have felt a strong desire to know its cause. He could have invented a hypothesis for this purpose, as many had done before him. But his philosophy was of another complexion. Let us hear what he says. *Rationem harum gravitatis proprietatum ex phænomenis non potui deducere, et hypotheses non fingo. Quicquid enim ex phænomenis non deducitur, hypothesis vocanda est. Et hypotheses, seu metaphysicæ, seu physicæ, seu qualitatum occultarum, seu mechanicæ, in philosophia experimentali locum non habent.*

CHAP. IV.

OF ANALOGY.

IT is natural to men to judge of things less known
by some similitude they observe, or think they observe, between them and things more familiar or better known. In many cases, we have no better way of
judging. And where the things compared have really
a great similitude in their nature, when there is reason
to think that they are subject to the same laws, there
may be a considerable degree of probability in conclusions drawn from analogy.

Thus, we may observe a very great similitude between this earth which we inhabit, and the other
planets, Saturn, Jupiter, Mars, Venus, and Mercury.
They all revolve round the sun, as the earth does,
although at different distances, and in different periods.
They borrow all their light from the sun, as the earth
does. Several of them are known to revolve round
their axis like the earth, and, by that means, must
have a like succession of day and night. Some of
them have moons, that serve to give them light in the
absence of the sun, as our moon does to us. They are
all, in their motions, subject to the same law of gravitation, as the earth is. From all this similitude, it is
not unreasonable to think, that those planets may, like
our earth, be the habitation of various orders of living
creatures. There is some probability in this conclusion from analogy.

In medicine, physicians must, for the most part, be
directed in their prescriptions by analogy. The constitution of one human body is so like to that of another, that it is reasonable to think, that what is the

cause of health or sickness to one, may have the same effect upon another. And this generally is found true, though not without some exceptions.

In politics, we reason, for the most part, from analogy. The constitution of human nature is so similar in different societies or commonwealths, that the causes of peace and war, of tranquillity and sedition, of riches and poverty, of improvement and degeneracy, are much the same in all.

Analogical reasoning, therefore, is not, in all cases, to be rejected. It may afford a greater or a less degree of probability, according as the things compared are more or less similar in that nature. But it ought to be observed, that, as this kind of reasoning can afford only probable evidence at best, so, unless great caution be used, we are apt to be led into error by it. For men are naturally disposed to conceive a greater similitude in things than there really is.

To give an instance of this : anatomists, in ancient ages, seldom dissected human bodies ; but very often the bodies of those quadrupeds, whose internal structure was thought to approach nearest to that of the human body. Modern anatomists have discovered many mistakes the ancients were led into, by their conceiving a greater similitude between the structure of men and of some beasts than there is in reality. By this, and many other instances that might be given, it appears, that conclusions built on analogy stand on a slippery foundation ; and that we ought never to rest upon evidence of this kind, when we can have more direct evidence.

I know no author who has made a more just and a more happy use of this mode of reasoning, than bishop Butler, in his Analogy of Religion, Natural and Revealed, to the Constitution and Coúrse of Nature. In that excellent work, the author does not ground any of the truths of religion upon analogy, as their proper evidence. He only makes use of analogy to answer objections against them. When objections are made against the truths of religion, which may be made with equal strength against what we know to be true in the course of nature, such objections can have no weight.

Analogical reasoning, therefore, may be of excellent use in answering objections against truths which have other evidence. It may likewise give a greater or a less degree of probability in cases where we can find no other evidence. But all arguments, drawn from analogy, are still the weaker, the greater disparity there is between the things compared; and therefore must be weakest of all when we compare body with mind, because there are no two things in nature more unlike.

There is no subject in which men have always been so prone to form their notions by analogies of this kind, as in what relates to the mind. We form an early acquaintance with material things by means of our senses, and are bred up in a constant familiarity with them. Hence we are apt to measure all things by them; and to ascribe to things most remote from matter, the qualities that belong to material things. It is for this reason, that mankind have, in all ages, been so prone to conceive the mind itself to be some subtile kind of matter: that they have been disposed to ascribe human figure, and human organs, not only to angels, but even to the Deity. Though we are conscious of the operations of our own minds when they are exerted, and are capable of attending to them, so as to form a distinct notion of them; this is so difficult a work to men, whose attention is constantly solicited by external objects, that we give them names from things that are familiar, and which are conceived to have some similitude to them; and the notions we

form of them are no less analogical than the names we
give them. Almost all the words, by which we express the operations of the mind, are borrowed from
material objects. To *understand*, to *conceive*, to *imagine*, to *comprehend*, to *deliberate*, to *infer*, and many
others, are words of this kind; so that the very language of mankind, with regard to the operation of our
minds, is analogical. Because bodies are effected only
by contact and pressure, we are apt to conceive, that
what is an immediate object of thought, and affects
the mind, must be in contact with it, and make some
impression upon it. When we imagine any thing, the
very word leads us to think, that there must be some
image in the mind, of the thing conceived. It is evident, that these notions are drawn from some similitude conceived between body and mind, and between
the properties of body and the operations of mind.

To illustrate more fully that analogical reasoning
from a supposed similitude of mind to body, which I
conceive to be the most fruitful source of error with
regard to the operations of our minds, I shall give an
instance of it.

When a man is urged by contrary motives, those on
one hand inciting him to do some action, those on the
other to forbear it; he deliberates about it, and at last
resolves to do it, or not to do it. The contrary motives are here compared to the weights in the opposite
scales of a balance; and there is not perhaps any instance that can be named of a more striking analogy
between body and mind. Hence the phrases of weighing motives, of deliberating upon actions, are common
to all languages.

From this analogy, some philosophers draw very
important conclusions. They say, that, as the balance
cannot incline to one side more than the other, when
the opposite weights are equal; so a man cannot pos-

sibly determine himself, if the motives on both hands
are equal : and, as the balance must necessarily turn
to that side which has most weight; so the man must
necessarily be determined to that hand where the motive is strongest. And on this foundation, some of
the schoolmen maintained, that, if a hungry ass were
placed between two bundles of hay equally inviting, the
beast must stand still and starve to death, being unable to
turn to either, because there are equal motives to both.
This is an instance of that analogical reasoning, which
I conceive ought never to be trusted : for, the analogy
between a balance and a man deliberating, though one
of the strongest that can be found between matter and
mind, is too weak to support any argument. A piece
of dead inactive matter, and an active intelligent being, are things very unlike ; and because the one would
remain at rest in a certain case, it does not follow that
the other would be inactive in a case somewhat similar. The argument is no better than this, that, because
a dead animal moves only as it is pushed, and if pushed
with equal force in contrary directions, must remain
at rest; therefore the same thing must happen to a
living animal ; for surely the similitude between a dead
animal and a living, is as great as that between a balance and a man.

The conclusion I would draw from all that has been
said on analogy, is, that, in our inquiries concerning
the mind, and its operations, we ought never to trust
to reasonings, drawn from some supposed similitude of
body to mind ; and that we ought to be very much upon
our guard, that we be not imposed upon by those analogical terms and phrases, by which the operations of
the mind are expressed in all languages.

CHAP. V.

OF THE PROPER MEANS OF KNOWING THE OPERATIONS
OF THE MIND.

SINCE we ought to pay no regard to hypotheses, and to be very suspicious of analogical reasoning, it may be asked, from what source must the knowledge of the mind, and its faculties be drawn?

I answer, The chief and proper source of this branch of knowledge is accurate reflection upon the operations of our own minds. Of this source we shall speak more fully, after making some remarks upon two others that may be subservient to it. The first of them is, attention to the structure of language.

The language of mankind is expressive of their thoughts, and of the various operations of their minds.

The various operations of the understanding, will, and passions, which are common to mankind, have various forms of speech corresponding to them in all languages, which are the signs of them, and by which they are expressed: and a due attention to the signs may, in many cases, give considerable light to the things signified by them.

There are, in all languages, modes of speech, by which men signify their judgment, or give their testimony; by which they accept or refuse; by which they ask information or advice; by which they command, or threaten, or supplicate; by which they plight their faith in promises and contracts. If such operations were not common to mankind, we should not find in all languages forms of speech, by which they are expressed.

All languages, indeed, have their imperfections; they can never be adequate to all the varieties of human thought; and therefore things may be really distinct in their nature, and capable of being distinguished by the human mind, which are not distinguished in common language. We can only expect, in the structure of languages, those distinctions which all mankind in the common business of life have occasion to make.

There may be peculiarities in a particular language, of the causes of which we are ignorant, and from which, therefore, we can draw no conclusion. But whatever we find common to all languages, must have a common cause; must be owing to some common notion or sentiment of the human mind.

We gave some examples of this before, and shall here add another. All languages have a plural number in many of their nouns; from which we may infer, that all men have notions, not of individual things only, but of attributes, or things which are common to many individuals; for no individual can have a plural number.

Another source of information in this subject, is a due attention to the course of human actions and conduct. The actions of men are effects: their sentiments, their passions, and their affections, are the causes of those effects; and we may, in many cases, form a judgment of the cause from the effect.

The behaviour of parents toward their children, gives sufficient evidence, even to those who never had children, that the parental affection is common to mankind. It is easy to see, from the general conduct of men, what are the natural objects of their esteem, their admiration, their love, their approbation, their resentment, and of all their other original dispositions. It is obvious, from the conduct of men in all ages, that man is by his nature a social animal; that he delights to associate with his species; to converse, and to exchange good offices with them.

Not only the actions, but even the opinions of men may sometimes give light into the frame of the human

mind. The opinions of men may be considered as the
effects of their intellectual powers, as their actions are
the effects of their active principles. Even the prejudices and errors of mankind, when they are general,
must have some cause no less general ; the discovery
of which will throw some light upon the frame of the
human understanding.

I conceive this to be the principal use of the history
of philosophy. When we trace the history of the various philosophical opinions that have sprung up among
thinking men, we are led into a labyrinth of fanciful
opinions, contradictions, and absurdities, intermixed
with some truths ; yet we may sometimes find a clue
to lead us through the several windings of this labyrinth : we may find that point of view which presented things to the author of the system, in the light in
which they appeared to him. This will often give a
consistency to things seemingly contradictory, and
some degree of probability to those that appeared most
fanciful.

The history of philosophy, considered as a map of
the intellectual operations of men of genius, must always be entertaining, and may sometimes gives us
views of the human understanding, which could not
easily be had any other way.

I return to what I mentioned as the main source of
information on this subject; attentive reflection upon
the operations of our own mind.

All the notions we have of mind. and of its operations, are, by Mr. Locke, called *ideas of reflection*. A
man may have as distinct notions of remembrance, of
judgment, of will, of desire, as he has of any object
whatever. Such notions, as Mr. Locke justly observes,
are got by the power of reflection. But what is this
power of reflection? It is, says the same author, " that
power by which the mind turns its view inward, and
observes its own actions and operations." He observes

elsewhere, "That the understanding, like the eye, whilst it makes us see and perceive all other things, takes no notice of itself; and that it requires art and pains to set it at a distance, and make it its own object." Cicero has expressed this sentiment most beautifully, Tusc. i. 28.

This power of the understanding to make its own operations its object, to attend to them, and examine them on all sides, is the power of reflection, by which alone we can have any distinct notion of the powers of our own, or of other minds.

This reflection ought to be distinguished from consciousness, with which it is too often confounded, even by Mr. Locke. All men are conscious of the operations of their own minds, at all times, while they are awake; but there are few who reflect upon them, or make them objects of thought.

From infancy, till we come to the years of understanding, we are employed solely about external objects. And, although the mind is conscious of its operations, it does not attend to them; its attention is turned solely to the external objects, about which those operations are employed. Thus, when a man is angry, he is conscious of his passion; but his attention is turned to the person who offended him, and the circumstances of the offence, while the passion of anger is not in the least the object of his attention.

I conceive, this is sufficient to show the difference between consciousness of the operations of our minds, and reflection upon them; and to show that we may have the former without any degree of the latter. The difference between consciousness and reflection, is like to the difference between a superficial view of an object which presents itself to the eye, while we are engaged about something else, and that attentive examination which we give to an object when we are wholly employed in surveying it. Attention is a voluntary act; it requires an active exertion to begin and to continue it ; and it may be continued as long as we will; but consciousness is involuntary and of no continuance, changing with every thought.

The power of reflection upon the operations of their own minds does not appear at all in children. Men must be come to some ripeness of understanding before they are capable of it. Of all the powers of the human mind, it seems to be the last that unfolds itself. Most men seem incapable of acquiring it in any considerable degree. Like all our other powers, it is greatly improved by exercise ; and until a man has got the habit of attending to the operations of his own mind, he can never have clear and distinct notions of them, nor form any steady judgment concerning them. His opinions must be borrowed from others, his notions confused and indistinct, and he may easily be led to swallow very gross absurdities. To acquire this habit, is a work of time and labour, even in those who begin it early, and whose natural talents are tolerably fitted for it ; but the difficulty will be daily diminishing, and the advantage of it is great. They will thereby be enabled to think with precision and accuracy on every subject, especially on those subjects that are more abstract. They will be able to judge for themselves in many important points, wherein others must blindly follow a leader.

CHAP. VI.

OF THE DIFFICULTY OF ATTENDING TO THE OPERATIONS OF OUR OWN MINDS.

THE difficulty of attending to our mental operations ought to be well understood, and justly estimated, by those who would make any progress in this science; that they may neither on the one hand, expect success without pains and application of thought, nor, on the other, be discouraged, by conceiving that the obstacles that lie in the way are insuperable, and that there is no certainty to be attained in it. I shall, therefore, endeavour to point out the causes of this difficulty, and the effects that have arisen from it, that we may be able to form a true judgment of both.

1st, The number and quick succession of the operations of the mind make it difficult to give due attention to them. It is well known, that if a great number of objects be presented in quick succession, even to the eye, they are confounded in the memory and imagination. We retain a confused notion of the whole, and a more confused one of the several parts, especially if they are objects to which we have never before given particular attention. No succession can be more quick than that of thought. The mind is busy while we are awake, continually passing from one thought, and one operation, to another. The scene is constantly shifting. Every man will be sensible of this, who tries but for one minute to keep the same thought in his imagination, without addition or variation. He will find it impossible to keep the scene of his imagination fixed. Other objects will intrude without being called, and all he can do is to reject these intruders as quickly as possible, and return to his principal object.

2dly, In this exercise, we go contrary to habits which have been early acquired, and confirmed by long, unvaried practice. From infancy, we are accustomed to attend to objects of sense, and to them only; and, when sensible objects have got such strong hold of the attention by confirmed habit, it is not easy to dispossess them. When we grow up, a variety of external objects solicits our attention, excites our curiosity, engages our affections, or touches our passions; and the constant round of employment, about external objects, draws off the mind from attending to itself; so that nothing is more just than the observation of Mr. Locke before mentioned, " That the understanding, like the eye, while it surveys all the objects around it, commonly takes no notice of itself."

3dly, The operations of the mind, from their very nature, lead the mind to give its attention to some other object. Our sensations, as will be shown afterward, are natural signs, and turn our attention to the things signified by them; so much, that most of them, and those the most frequent and familiar, have no name in any language. In perception, memory, judgment, imagination, and reasoning, there is an object distinct from the operation itself; and, while we are led by a strong impulse to attend to the object, the operation escapes our notice. Our passions, affections, and all our active powers, have, in like manner, their objects which engross our attention, and divert it from the passion itself.

4thly, To this we may add a just observation made by Mr. Hume, That, " when the mind is agitated by any passion, as soon as we turn our attention from the object to the passion itself, the passion subsides or vanishes, and by that means escapes our inquiry. This, indeed, is common to almost every operation of the mind: when it is exerted, we are conscious of it; but then we do not attend to the operation, but to its object. When the mind is drawn off from the object to attend to its own operation, that operation ceases, and escapes our notice.

5thly, As it is not sufficient to the discovery of mathematical truths, that a man be able to attend to mathematical figures ; as it is necessary that he should have the ability to distinguish accurately things that differ, and to discern clearly the various relations of the quantities he compares ; an ability, which, though much greater in those who have the force of genius than in others, yet even in them requires exercise and habit to bring it to maturity ; so, in order to discover the truth in what relates to the operations of the mind, it is not enough that a man be able to give attention to them ; he must have the ability to distinguish accurately their minute differences ; to resolve and analyze complex operations into their simple ingredients ; to unfold the ambiguity of words, which in this science is greater than in any other, and to give them the same accuracy and precision that mathematical terms have. For, indeed, the same precision in the use of words ; the same cool attention to the minute differences of things ; the same talent for abstraction and analyzing, which fits a man for the study of mathematics, is no less necessary in this. But there is this great difference between the two sciences, that the objects of mathematics being things external to the mind, it is much more easy to attend to them, and fix them steadily in the imagination.

The difficulty attending our inquiries into the powers of the mind, serves to account for some events respecting this branch of philosophy, which deserve to be mentioned.

While most branches of science have, either in ancient or in modern times, been highly cultivated, and brought to a considerable degree of perfection, this remains, to this day, in a very low state, and as it were in its infancy.

Every science invented by men must have its beginning and its progress; and, from various causes, it may happen that one science shall be brought to a great degree of maturity, while another is yet in its infancy. The maturity of a science may be judged of by this : when it contains a system of principles, and conclusions drawn from them, which are so firmly established, that, among thinking and intelligent men, there remains no doubt or dispute about them; so that those who come after may raise the superstructure higher, but shall never be able to overturn what is already built, in order to begin on a new foundation.

Geometry seems to have been in its infancy about the time of Thales and Pythagoras; because many of the elementary propositions, on which the whole science is built, are ascribed to them as the inventors. Euclid's Elements, which were written some ages after Pythagoras, exhibit a system of geometry which deserves the name of a science; and though great additions have been made by Apollonius, Archimedes, Pappus, and others among the ancients, and still greater by the moderns; yet what was laid down in Euclid's Elements was never set aside. It remains as the firm foundation of all future superstructures in that science.

Natural philosophy remained in its infant state near two thousand years after geometry had attained to its manly form : for natural philosophy seems not to have been built on a stable foundation, nor carried to any degree of maturity, till the last century. The system of Des Cartes, which was all hypothesis, prevailed in the most enlightened part of Europe till toward the end of last century. Sir Isaac Newton has the merit of giving the form of a science to this branch of philosophy; and it need not appear surprising, if the philosophy of the human mind should be a century or two later in being brought to maturity.

It has received great accessions from the labours of
several modern authors; and perhaps wants little more
to entitle it to the name of a science, but to be purged
of certain hypotheses, which have imposed on some of
the most acute writers on this subject, and led them
into downright skepticism.

What the ancients have delivered to us concerning
the mind, and its operations, is almost entirely drawn,
not from accurate reflection, but from some conceived
amalogy between body and mind. And although the
modern authors I formerly named have given more attention to the operations of their own minds, and by that
means have made important discoveries; yet, by retaining some of the ancient analogical notions, their discoveries have been less useful than they might have
been, and have led to skepticism.

It may happen in science, as in building, that an
error in the foundation shall weaken the whole; and
the further the building is carried on, this weakness
shall become the more apparent and the more threatening.   Something of this kind seems to have happened in our systems concerning the mind.   The accession
they have received by modern discoveries, though very
important in itself, has thrown darkness and obscurity
upon the whole, and has led men rather to skepticism
than to knowledge.   This must be owing to some fundamental errors that have not been observed; and
when these are corrected, it is to be hoped, that the
improvements that have been made will have their due
effect.

The last effect I observe of the difficulty of inquiries
into the powers of the mind, is, that there is no other
part of human knowledge, in which ingenious authors
have been so apt to run into strange paradoxes, and
even into gross absurdities.

When we find philosophers maintaining, that there is no heat in the fire, nor colour in the rainbow: when we find the gravest philosophers, from Des Cartes down to bishop Berkeley, mustering up arguments to prove the existence of a material world, and unable to find any that will bear examination: when we find bishop Berkeley and Mr. Hume, the acutest metaphysicians of the age, maintaining that there is no such thing as matter in the universe; that sun, moon, and stars, the earth which we inhabit, our own bodies, and those of our friends, are only ideas in our minds, and have no existence but in thought: when we find the last maintaining, that there is neither body nor mind; nothing in nature but ideas and impressions, without any substance on which they are impressed: that there is no certainty nor indeed probability, even in mathematical axioms: I say, when we consider such extravagances of many of the most acute writers on this subject, we may be apt to think the whole to be only a dream of fanciful men, who have entangled themselves in cobwebs spun out of their own brain. But we ought to consider, that the more closely and ingeniously men reason from false principles, the more absurdities they will be led into; and when such absurdities help to bring to light the false principles from which they are drawn, they may be the more easily forgiven.

CHAP. VII.

DIVISION OF THE POWERS OF THE MIND.

THE powers of the mind are so many, so various, and so connected and complicated in most of their operations, that there never has been any division of them proposed which is not liable to considerable objections. We shall therefore take that general division which is the most common, into the powers of *understanding* and those of *will*. Under the will we comprehend our active powers, and all that lead to action, or influence the mind to act; such as appetites, passions, affections. The understanding comprehends our contemplative powers; by which we perceive objects; by which we conceive or remember them; by which we analyze or compound them; and by which we judge and reason concerning them.

Although this general division may be of use in order to our proceeding more methodically in our subject, we are not to understand it as if, in those operations which are ascribed to the understanding, there were no exertion of will or activity, or as if the understanding were not employed in the operations ascribed to the will; for I conceive there is no operation of the understanding wherein the mind is not active in some degree. We have some command over our thoughts, and can attend to this or to that, of many objects which present themselves to our senses, to our memory, or to our imagination. We can survey an object on this side or that, superficially or accurately, for a longer or a shorter time; so that our contemplative powers are under the guidance and direction of the active; and the former never pursue their object, without being led and directed, urged or restrained by the latter; and because the understanding is always more or less directed by the will, mankind have ascribed some degree of activity to the mind in its intellectual operations, as well as in those which belong to the will, and have expressed them by active verbs, such as seeing, hearing, judging, reasoning, and the like.

And as the mind exerts some degree of activity even in the operations of understanding, so it is certain, that there can be no act of will which is not accompanied with some act of understanding. The will must have an object, and that object must be apprehended or conceived in the understanding. It is therefore to be remembered, that in most, if not all operations of the mind, both faculties concur; and we range the operation under that faculty which has the largest share in it.

The intellectual powers are commonly divided into simple apprehension, judgment, and reasoning. As this division has in its favour the authority of antiquity, and of a very general reception, it would be improper to set it aside without giving any reason; I shall therefore explain it briefly, and give the reasons why I choose to follow another.

It may be observed, that, without apprehension of the objects concerning which we judge, there can be no judgment; as little can there be reasoning without both apprehension and judgment : these three operations, therefore, are not independent of each other. The second includes the first, and the third includes both the first and second; but the first may be exercised without either of the other two. It is on that account called *simple apprehension* ; that is, apprehension unaccompanied with any judgment about the object apprehended. This simple apprehension of an object is, in common language, called *having a notion*, or *having a conception* of the object, and by late authors is called *having an idea of it*. In speaking, it is expressed by a word, or by a part of a proposition, without that composition and structure which makes a complete sentence ; as *a man, a man of fortune*. Such words, taken by themselves, signify simple apprehensions. They neither affirm nor deny ; they imply no judgment or opinion of the thing signified by them, and therefore cannot be said to be either true or false.

The second operation in this division is *judgment* ; in which, say the philosophers, there must be two objects of thought compared, and some agreement or disagreement, or, in general, some relation discerned between them ; in consequence of which, there is an opinion or belief of that relation which we discern. This operation is expressed in speech by a proposition, in which some relation between the things compared is affirmed or denied ; as when we say, *All men are fallible*.

Truth and falsehood are qualities which belong to judgment only ; or to propositions by which judgment is expressed. Every judgment, every opinion, and every proposition, is either true or false. But words which neither affirm nor deny any thing, can have neither of those qualities ; and the same may be said of simple apprehensions, which are signified by such words.

The third operation is *reasoning* ; in which, from two or more judgments, we draw a conclusion.

This division of our intellectual powers corresponds perfectly with the account commonly given by philosophers, of the successive steps by which the mind proceeds in the acquisition of its knowledge ; which are these three : 1st, by the senses, or by other means, it is furnished with various simple apprehensions, notions

or ideas. These are the materials which nature gives
it to work upon ; and from the simple ideas it is furnished with by nature, it forms various others more complex. 2dly, By comparing its ideas, and by perceiving their agreements and disagreements, it forms its
judgments. And, lastly, from two or more judgments,
it deduces conclusions of reasoning.

Now, if all our knowledge is got by a procedure of
this kind, certainly the threefold division of the powers of understanding, into simple apprehension, judgment and reasoning, is the most natural, and the most
proper, that can be devised. This theory and that division are so closely connected, that it is difficult to
judge which of them has given rise to the other ; and
they must stand or fall together. But if all our knowledge is not got by a process of this kind ; if there are
other avenues of knowledge besides the comparing our
ideas, and perceiving their agreements and disagreements, it is probable that there may be operations of
the understanding which cannot be properly reduced
under any of the three that have been explained.

Let us consider some of the most familiar operations of our minds, and see to which of the three they
belong. I begin with consciousness. I know that I
think, and this of all knowledge is the most certain. Is
that operation of my mind, which gives me this certain
knowledge, to be called simple apprehension ? No, surely. Simple apprehension neither affirms nor denies.
It will not be said that it is by reasoning that I know
that I think. It remains, therefore, that it must be by
judgment, that is, according to the account given of
judgment, by comparing two ideas, and perceiving the
agreement between them. But what are the ideas compared ? They must be the idea of myself, and the idea
of thought, for they are the terms of the proposition *I*

think. According to this account then, first, I have the idea of myself, and the idea of thought ; then, by comparing these two ideas, I perceive that I think.

Let any man who is capable of reflection judge for himself, whether it is by an operation of this kind that he comes to be convinced that he thinks ? To me it appears evident, that the conviction I have that I think, is not got in this way ; and therefore I conclude, either that consciousness is not judgment, or that judgment is not rightly defined to be the perception of some agreement or disagreement between two ideas.

The perception of an object by my senses, is another operation of the understanding. I would know whether it be simple apprehension, or judgment, or reasoning. It is not simple apprehension, because I am persuaded of the existence of the object as much as I could be by demonstration. It is not judgment, if by judgment be meant the comparing ideas, and perceiving their agreements or disagreements. It is not reasoning, because those who cannot reason can perceive.

I find the same difficulty in classing memory under any of the operations mentioned.

There is not a more fruitful source of error in this branch of philosophy, than divisions of things which are taken to be complete when they are not really so. To make a perfect division of any class of things, a man ought to have the whole under his view at once. But the greatest capacity very often is not sufficient for this. Some thing is left out which did not come under the philosopher's view when he made his division : and to suit this to the division, it must be made what nature never made it. This has been so common a fault of philosophers, that one who would avoid error ought to be suspicious of divisions, though long received, and of great authority, especially when they are grounded on a theory that may be called in question. In a subject imperfectly known, we ought not to pretend to perfect divisions, but to leave room for such additions or alterations as a more perfect view of the subject may afterward suggest.

I shall not, therefore, attempt a complete enumeration of the powers of the human understanding. I shall only mention those which I propose to explain, and they are the following :

1st, The powers we have by means of our external senses. 2dly, Memory. 3dly, Conception. 4thly, The powers of resolving and analyzing complex objects, and compounding those that are more simple. 5thly, Judging. 6thly, Reasoning. 7thly, Taste. 8thly, Moral Perception. And, last of all, Consciousness.

CHAP. VIII.

OF SOCIAL OPERATIONS OF MIND.

THERE is another division of the powers of the mind, which, though it has been, ought not to be overlooked by writers on this subject, because it has a real foundation in nature. Some operations of our minds, from their very nature, are *social*, others are *solitary*.

By the first, I understand such operations as necessarily suppose an intercourse with some other intelligent being. A man may understand and will ; he may apprehend, and judge, and reason, though he should know of no intelligent being in the universe besides himself. But, when he asks information, or receives it ; when he bears testimony, or receives the testimony of another ; when he asks a favour, or accepts one ; when he gives a command to his servant, or receives one from a superior ; when he plights his faith in a promise or contract ; these are acts of social intercourse between intelligent beings, and can have no place in solitude. They suppose understanding and will ; but they suppose something more, which is neither understanding nor will ; that is, society with other intelligent beings. They may be called intellectual, because they can only be in intellectual beings : but they are neither simple apprehension, nor judgment, nor reasoning, nor are they any combination of these operations.

To ask a question is as simple an operation as to judge or to reason ; yet it is neither judgment, nor reasoning, nor simple apprehension, nor is it any composition of these. Testimony is neither simple apprehension, nor judgment, nor reasoning. The same may be said of a promise, or of a contract. These acts of mind

are perfectly understood by every man of common understanding ; but, when philosophers attempt to bring
them within the pale of their divisions, by analyzing
them, they find inexplicable mysteries, and even contradictions, in them. One may see an instance of this,
of many that might be mentioned, in Mr. Hume's Inquiry concerning the Principles of Morals, sect. 3.
part 2. note, near the end.

The attempts of philosophers to reduce the social operations under the common philosophical divisions, resemble very much the attempts of some philosophers to
reduce all our social affections to certain modifications
of self love. The Author of our being intended us to
be social beings, and has, for that end, given us social
intellectual powers, as well as social affections. Both
are original parts of our constitution, and the exertions
of both no less natural than the exertions of those powers that are solitary and selfish.

Our social intellectual operations, as well as our social affections, appear very early in life, before we are
capable of reasoning ; yet both suppose a conviction of
the existence of other intelligent beings. When a child
asks a question of his nurse, this act of his mind supposes,
not only a desire to know what he asks ; it supposes
likewise a conviction that the nurse is an intelligent
being, to whom he can communicate his thoughts,
and who can communicate her thoughts to him. How
he came by this conviction so early, is a question
of some importance in the knowledge of the human
mind, and therefore worthy of the consideration of
philosophers. But they seem to have given no attention either to this early conviction, or to those operations of mind which suppose it. Of this we shall
have occasion to treat afterward.

All languages are fitted to express the social as well as the solitary operations of the mind. It may indeed be affirmed, that, to express the former, is the primary and direct intention of language. A man, who had no intercourse with any other intelligent being, would never think of language. He would be as mute as the beasts of the field ; even more so, because they have some degree of social intercourse with one another and some of them with man. When language is once learned, it may be useful even in our solitary meditations ; and, by clothing our thoughts with words, we may have a firmer hold of them. But this was not its first intention ; and the structure of every language shows that it is not intended solely for this purpose.

In every language, a question, a command, a promise, which are social acts, can be expressed as easily and as properly as judgment, which is a solitary act. The expression of the last has been honoured with a particular name ; it is called a proposition ; it has been an object of great attention to philosophers ; it has been analyzed into its very elements, of subject, predicate, and copula. All the various modifications of these, and of propositions which are compounded of them, have been anxiously examined in many voluminous tracts. The expression of a question, of a command, or of a promise, is as capable of being analyzed as a proposition is ; but we do not find that this has been attempted ; we have not so much as given them a name different from the operations which they express.

Why have speculative men laboured so anxiously to analyze our solitary operations, and given so little attention to the social? I know no other reason but this, that, in the divisions that have been made of the mind's operations, the social have been omitted, and thereby thrown behind the curtain.

In all languages, the second person of verbs, the pronoun of the second person, and the vocative case in nouns, are appropriated to the expression of social operations of mind, and could never have had place in language but for this purpose: nor is it a good argument against this observation, that, by a rhetorical figure, we sometimes address persons that are absent, or even inanimated beings, in the second person. For it ought to be remembered, that all figurative ways of using words or phrases, suppose a natural and literal meaning of them.

ESSAY II.

OF THE POWERS WE HAVE BY MEANS OF OUR EXTER-
NAL SENSES.

CHAP. I.

OF THE ORGANS OF SENSE.

OF all the operations of our minds, the perception of external objects is the most familiar. The senses come to maturity even in infancy, when other powers have not yet sprung up. They are common to us with brute animals, and furnish us with the objects about which our other powers are the most frequently employed. We find it easy to attend to their operations; and because they are familiar, the names which properly belong to them are applied to other powers, which are thought to resemble them; for these reasons they claim to be first considered.

The perception of external objects is one main link of that mysterious chain, which connects the material world with the intellectual. We shall find many things in this operation unaccountable; sufficient to convince us, that we know but little of our own frame; and that a perfect comprehension of our mental powers, and of the manner of their operation, is beyond the reach of our understanding.

In perception there are impressions upon the organs of sense, the nerves, and brain, which, by the laws of

75

our nature, are followed by certain operations of mind. These two things are apt to be confounded; but ought most carefully to be distinguished. Some philosophers, without good reason, have concluded, that the impressions made on the body are the proper efficient cause of perception. Others, with as little reason, have concluded, that impressions are made on the mind similar to those made on the body. From these mistakes many others have arisen. The wrong notions men have rashly taken up with regard to the senses, have led to wrong notions with regard to other powers which are conceived to resemble them. Many important powers of mind have, especially of late, been called internal senses, from a supposed resemblance to the external; such as, the sense of beauty, the sense of harmony, the moral sense. And it is to be apprehended, that errors, with regard to the external, have, from analogy, led to similar errors with regard to the internal; it is therefore of some consequence, even with regard to other branches of our subject, to have just notions concerning the external senses.

In order to this, we shall begin with some observations on the organs of sense, and on the impressions which in perception are made upon them, and upon the nerves and brain.

We perceive no external object, but by means of certain bodily organs which God has given us for that purpose. The Supreme Being who made us, and placed us in this world, has given us such powers of mind as he saw to be suited to our state and rank in his creation. He has given us the power of perceiving many objects around us, the sun, moon, and stars, the earth and sea, and a variety of animals, vegetables, and inanimate bodies. But our power of perceiving these objects is limited in various ways, and particularly in this;

that without the organs of the several senses, we perceive no external object. We cannot see without eyes,
nor hear without ears : it is not only necessary that we
should have these organs, but that they should be in a
sound and natural state. There are many disorders of
the eye that cause total blindness; others that impair
the powers of vision, without destroying it altogether ;
and the same may be said of the organs of all the other
senses.

All this is so well known from experience, that it
needs no proof; but it ought to be observed, that we
know it from experience only. We can give no reason
for it, but that such is the will of our Maker. No man
can show it to be impossible to the Supreme Being to
have given us the power of perceiving external objects
without such organs. We have reason to believe, that
when we put off these bodies, and all the organs belonging to them, our perceptive powers shall rather be improved than destroyed or impaired. We have reason to
believe, that the Supreme Being perceives every thing in
a much more perfect manner than we do, without bodily
organs. We have reason to believe, that there are other
created beings endowed with powers of perception more
perfect and more extensive than ours, without any such
organs as we find necessary.

We ought not, therefore, to conclude, that such bodily organs are, in their own nature, necessary to perception ; but rather, that, by the will of God, our power of perceiving external objects is limited and circumscribed by our organs of sense ; so that we perceive
objects in a certain manner, and in certain circumstances, and in no other.

If a man was shut up in a dark room, so that he
could see nothing but through one small hole in the
shutter of a window, would he conclude, that the hole

was the cause of his seeing, and that it is impossible
to see any other way? Perhaps, if he had never in
his life seen but in this way, he might be apt to think
so; but the conclusion is rash and groundless. He
sees, because God has given him the power of seeing;
and he sees only through this small hole, because his
power of seeing is circumscribed by impediments on all
other hands.

Another necessary caution in this matter is, that we
ought not to confound the organs of perception with
the being that perceives. Perception must be the act
of some being that perceives. The eye is not that which
sees; it is only the organ by which we see. The ear is
not that which hears; but the organ by which we hear;
and so of the rest.

A man cannot see the satellites of Jupiter but by a
telescope. Does he conclude from this, that it is the
telescope that sees those stars? By no means; such a
conclusion would be absurd. It is no less absurd to
conclude, that it is the eye that sees, or the ear that
hears. The telescope is an artificial organ of sight,
but it sees not. The eye is a natural organ of sight,
by which we see; but the natural organ sees as little as
the artificial.

The eye is a machine most admirably contrived for
refracting the rays of light, and forming a distinct picture of objects upon the retina; but it sees neither the
object nor the picture. It can form the picture after it
is taken out of the head; but no vision ensues. Even
when it is in its proper place, and perfectly sound, it is
well known that an obstruction in the optic nerve takes
away vision, though the eye has performed all that belongs to it.

If any thing more were necessary to be said on a
point so evident, we might observe, that if the faculty of

seeing were in the eye, that of hearing in the ear, and so of the other senses, the necessary consequence of this would be, that the thinking principle, which I call myself, is not one, but many. But this is contrary to the irresistible conviction of every man.

When I say, I see, I hear, I feel, I remember, this implies that it is one and the same self that performs all these operations; and as it would be absurd to say, that my memory, another man's imagination, and a third man's reason, may make one individual intelligent being, it would be equally absurd to say, that one piece of matter seeing, another hearing, and a third feeling, may make one and the same percipient being.

These sentiments are not new; they have occurred to thinking men from early ages. Cicero, in his Tusculan Questions, lib. i. chap. 20. has expressed them very distinctly. Those who choose, may consult the passage.

CHAP. II.

OF THE IMPRESSIONS ON THE ORGANS, NERVES, AND BRAIN.

A SECOND law of our nature regarding perception is, that we perceive no object, unless some impression is made upon the organ of sense, either by the immediate application of the object, or by some medium which passes between the object and the organ.

In two of our senses, to wit, *touch* and *taste*, there must be an immediate application of the object to the organ. In the other three, the object is perceived at a distance, but still by means of a medium, by which some impression is made upon the organ.

The effluvia of bodies drawn into the nostrils with the breath, are the medium of smell; the undulations of the air, are the medium of hearing ; and the rays of light passing from visible objects to the eye, are the medium of sight. We see no object, unless rays of light come from it to the eye. We hear not the sound of any body, unless the vibrations of some elastic medium, occasioned by the tremulous motion of the sounding body, reach our ear. We perceive no smell, unless the effluvia of the smelling body enter into the nostrils. We perceive no taste, unless the sapid body be applied to the tongue, or some part of the organ of taste. Nor do we perceive any tangible quality of a body, unless it touch the hands, or some part of our body.

These are facts known from experience to hold universally and invariably, both in men and brutes. By this law of our nature, our powers of perceiving external objects are further limited and circumscribed. Nor can we give any other reason for this, than that it is the will of our Maker, who knows best what powers, and what degrees of them, are suited to our state. We were once in a state, I mean in the womb, wherein our powers of perception were more limited than in the present, and, in a future state, they may be more enlarged.

It is likewise a law of our nature, that, in order to our perceiving objects, the impressions made upon the organs of sense must be communicated to the nerves, and by them to the brain. This is perfectly known to those who know any thing of anatomy.

The nerves are fine cords, which pass from the brain, or from the spinal marrow, which is a production of the brain, to all parts of the body, dividing into smaller branches as they proceed, until at last they escape our eyesight : and it is found by experience, that all the voluntary and involuntary motions of the body are performed by their means. When the nerves that serve any limb, are cut, or tied hard, we have then no more power to move that limb, than if it was no part of the body.

As there are nerves that serve the muscular motions, so there are others that serve the several senses ; and, as without the former, we cannot move a limb, so without the latter, we can have no perception.

This train of machinery the wisdom of God has made necessary to our perceiving objects. Various parts of the body concur to it, and each has its own function. 1st, The object either immediately, or by some medium, must make an impression on the organ. The organ serves only as a medium, by which an impression is made on the nerve ; and the nerve serves as a medium to make an impression upon the brain. Here the material part ends ; at least we can trace it no further ; the rest is all intellectual.

The proof of these impressions upon the nerves and brain in perception is this, that, from many observations and experiments, it is found, that when the organ of any sense is perfectly sound, and has the impression made upon it by the object ever so strongly, yet, if the nerve which serves that organ be cut or tied hard, there is no perception : and it is well known, that disorders in the brain deprive us of the power of perception, when both the organ and its nerve are sound.

There is, therefore, sufficient reason to conclude, that, in perception, the object produces some change in the organ ; that the organ produces some change upon the nerve ; and that the nerve produces some change in the brain.   And we give the name of an *impression* to those changes, because we have not a name more proper to express, in a general manner, any change produced in a body, by an external cause, without specifying the nature of that change.   Whether it be pressure, or attraction, or repulsion, or vibration, or something unknown, for which we have no name, still it may be called an impression.   But with regard to the particular kind of this change or impression, philosophers have never been able to discover any thing at all.

But, whatever be the nature of those impressions upon the organs, nerves, and brain, we perceive nothing without them.   Experience informs that it is so ; but we cannot give a reason why it is so.   In the constitution of man, perception, by fixed laws of nature, is connected with those impressions ; but we can discover no necessary connection.   The Supreme Being has seen fit to limit our power of perception ; so that we perceive not without such impressions ; and this is all we know of the matter.

This, however, we have reason to conclude in general, that as the impressions on the organs, nerves, and brain, correspond exactly to the nature and conditions of the objects by which they are made ; so our perceptions and sensations correspond to those impressions, and vary in kind, and in degree, as they vary.   Without this exact correspondence, the information we receive by our senses would not only be imperfect, as it undoubtedly is, but would be fallacious, which we have no reason to think it is.

CHAP. III.

HYPOTHESES CONCERNING THE NERVES AND BRAIN.

WE are informed by anatomists, that although the
two coats which enclose a nerve, and which it derives
from the coats of the brain, are tough and elastic ; yet
the nerve itself has a very small degree of consistence,
being almost like marrow. It has, however, a fibrous
texture, and may be divided and subdivided, till its
fibres escape our senses : and as we know so very little
about the texture of the nerves, there is great room left
for those who choose to indulge themselves in conjecture.

The ancients conjectured, that the nervous fibres are
fine tubes, filled with a very subtile spirit, or vapour,
which they called *animal spirits;* that the brain is a
gland, by which the animal spirits are secreted from
the finer part of the blood, and their continual waste
repaired ; and that it is by these animal spirits that
the nerves perform their functions. Des Cartes has
shown how, by these animal spirits going and return-
ing in the nerves, muscular motion, perception, memory,
and imagination, are effected. All this he has described
as distinctly as if he had been an eye witness of all those
operations. But it happens, that the tubular structure
of the nerves was never perceived by the human eye,
nor shown by the nicest injections ; and all that has been
said about animal spirits through more than fifteen centuries, is mere conjecture.

Dr. Briggs, who was sir Isaac Newton's master in
anatomy, was the first, as far as I know, who advanced a
new system concerning the nerves. He conceived them
to be solid filaments of prodigious tenuity; and this
opinion, as it accords better with observation, seems

to have been more generally received since his time. As to the manner of performing their office, Dr. Briggs thought, that, like musical chords, they have vibrations differing according to their length and tension. They seem, however, very unfit for this purpose, on account of their want of tenacity, their moisture, and being through their whole length in contact with moist substances: So that, although Dr. Briggs wrote a book upon this system, called Nova Visionis Theoria, it seems not to have been much followed.

Sir Isaac Newton, in all his philosophical writings, took great care to distinguish his doctrines, which he pretended to prove by just induction, from his conjectures, which were to stand or fall, according as future experiments and observations should establish or refute them. His conjectures he has put in the form of queries, that they might not be received as truths, but be inquired into, and determined according to the evidence to be found for or against them. Those who mistake his queries for a part of his doctrine, do him great injustice, and degrade him to the rank of the common herd of philosophers, who have in all ages adulterated philosophy, by mixing conjecture with truth, and their own fancies with the oracles of nature. Among other queries, this truly great philosopher proposed this, Whether there may not be an elastic medium, or ether, immensely more rare than air, which pervades all bodies, and which is the cause of gravitation; of the refraction and reflection of the rays of light; of the transmission of heat, through spaces void of air; and of many other phenomena? In the 23d query subjoined to his Optics, he puts this question with regard to the impressions made on the nerves and brain in perception, Whether vision is effected chiefly by the vibrations of this medium, excited in the bottom of the eye by the rays of light, and propagated along the solid, pellucid, and uniform capillaments of the optic nerve? And whether hearing is effected by the vibrations of this or some other medium, excited by the tremor of the air in the auditory nerves, and propagated along the solid, pellucid, and uniform capillaments of those nerves? And so with regard to the other senses.

What Newton only proposed as a matter to be inquired into, Dr. Hartley conceived to have such evidence, that, in his Observations on Man, he has deduced, in a mathematical form, a very ample system concerning the faculties of the mind, from the doctrine of vibrations, joined with that of association.

His notion of the vibrations, excited in the nerves, is expressed in propositions 4 and 5. of the first part of his Observations on Man. "Proposition 4. External objects impressed on the senses, occasion first in the nerves, on which they are impressed, and then in the brain, vibrations of the small, and, as one may say, infinitesimal medullary particles. Prop. 5. The vibrations mentioned in the last proposition are excited, propagated, and kept up, partly by the ether, that is, by a very subtile elastic fluid ; partly by the uniformity, continuity, softness, and active powers of the medullary substance of the brain, spinal marrow, and nerves."

The modesty and diffidence with which Dr. Hartley offers his system to the world, by desiring his reader "to expect nothing but hints and conjectures in difficult and obscure matters, and a short detail of the principal reasons and evidences in those that are clear ; by acknowledging, that he shall not be able to execute, with any accuracy, the proper method of philosophizing, recommended and followed by sir Isaac Newton ; and that he will attempt a sketch only for the benefit of future inquirers," seem to forbid any criticism upon it. One cannot, without reluctance, criticise what is proposed in such a manner, and with so good intention ; yet, as

the tendency of this system of vibrations is to make all
the operations of the mind mere mechanism, dependent
on the laws of matter and motion ; and as it has been
held forth by its votaries, *as in a manner demonstrated,*
I shall make some remarks on that part of the system
which relates to the impressions made on the nerves
and brain in perception.

It may be observed in general, that Dr. Hartley's
work consists of a chain of propositions, with their
proofs and corollaries, digested in good order, and in a
scientific form.   A great part of them, however, are,
as he candidly acknowledges, conjectures and hints only ;
yet these are mixed with the propositions legitimately
proved, without any distinction. Corollaries are drawn
from them, and other propositions grounded upon them,
which, all taken together, make up a system. A system
of this kind resembles a chain, of which some links are
abundantly strong, others very weak.   The strength of
the chain is determined by that of the weakest links ;
for if they give way, the whole falls to pieces, and the
weight, supported by it, falls to the ground.

Philosophy has been in all ages adulterated by hypotheses ; that is, by systems built partly on facts, and
much upon conjecture.   It is pity that a man of Dr.
Hartley's knowledge and candour should have followed
the multitude in this fallacious tract, after expressing
his approbation of the proper method of philosophizing,
pointed out by Bacon and Newton.   The last considered it as a reproach, when his system was called his hypothesis ; and says, with disdain of such imputation,
hypotheses non fingo.   And it is very strange, that Dr.
Hartley should not only follow such a method of philosophizing himself, but that he should direct others in their
inquiries to follow it.   So he does in Proposition 87.
part 1. where he deduces rules for the ascertainment of

truth, from the rule of false, in arithmetic, and from the art of decyphering ; and in other places.

As to the vibrations and vibratiuncles, whether of an elastic ether, or of the infinitesimal particles of the brain and nerves, there may be such things for what we know ; and men may rationally inquire whether they can find any evidence of their existence ; but while we have no proof of their existence, to apply them to the solution of phenomena, and to build a system upon them, is what I conceive, we call, building a castle in the air.

When men pretend to account for any of the operations of nature, the causes assigned by them ought, as sir Isaac Newton has taught us, to have two conditions, otherwise they are good for nothing. 1st, They ought to be true, to have a real existence, and not to be barely conjectured to exist without proof. 2dly, They ought to be sufficient to produce the effect.

As to the existence of vibratory motions in the medullary substance of the nerves and brain, the evidence produced is this : 1st, It is observed, that the sensations of seeing and hearing, and some sensations of touch, have some short duration and continuance. 2dly, Though there be no direct evidence that the sensations of taste and smell, and the greater part of these of touch, have the like continuance ; yet, says the author, analogy would incline one to believe that they must resemble the sensations of sight and hearing in this particular. 3dly. The continuance of all our sensations being thus established, it follows, that external objects impress vibratory motions on the medullary substance of the nerves and brain ; because no motion, besides a vibratory one, can reside in any part for a moment of time.

This is the chain of proof ; in which the first link is strong, being confirmed by experience ; the second is very weak ; and the third still weaker. For other kinds of motion, besides that of vibration, may have some continuance, such as rotation, bending or unbending of a spring, and perhaps others which we are unacquainted with ; nor do we know whether it is motion that is produced in the nerves ; it may be pressure, attraction, repulsion, or something we do not know. This, indeed, is the common refuge of all hypotheses, that we know no other way in which the phenomena may be produced, and therefore they must be produced in this way. There is therefore no proof of vibrations in the infinitesimal particles of the brain and nerves.

It may be thought that the existence of an elastic vibrating ether stands on a firmer foundation, having the authority of sir Isaac Newton. But it ought to be observed, that although this great man had formed conjectures about this ether near fifty years before he died, and had it in his eye during that long space as a subject of inquiry ; yet it does not appear that he ever found any convincing proof of its existence, but considered it to the last as a question whether there be such an ether or not. In the premonition to the reader, prefixed to the second edition of his Optics, *anno* 1717, he expresses himself thus with regard to it : "Lest any one should think that I place gravity among the essential properties of bodies, I have subjoined one question concerning its cause ; a question, I say, for I do not hold it as a thing established." If, therefore, we regard the authority of sir Isaac Newton, we ought to hold the existence of such an ether as a matter not established by proof, but to be examined into by experiments ; and I have never heard that, since his time, any new evidence has been found of its existence.

But, says Dr. Hartley, "supposing the existence of the ether, and of its properties, to be destitute of all direct evidence, still, if it serves to account for a great variety of phenomena, it will have an indirect evidence in its favour by this means." There never was an hypothesis invented by an ingenious man which has not this evidence in its favour. The vortices of Des Cartes, the sylphs and gnomes of Mr. Pope, serve to account for a great variety of phenomena.

When a man has, with labour and ingenuity, wrought up an hypothesis into a system, he contracts a fondness for it, which is apt to warp the best judgment. This, I humbly think, appears remarkably in Dr. Hartley. In his preface, he declares his approbation of the method of philosophizing recommended and followed by sir Isaac Newton; but having first deviated from this method in his practice, he is brought at last to justify this deviation in theory, and to bring arguments in defence of a method diametrically opposite to it. "We admit, says he, the key of a cypher to be a true one, when it explains the cypher completely." I answer, To find the key requires an understanding equal or superior to that which made the cypher. This instance, therefore, will then be in point, when he who attempts to decypher the works of nature by an hypothesis, has an understanding equal or superior to that which made them. The votaries of hypotheses have often been challenged to show one useful discovery in the works of nature that was ever made in that way. If instances of this kind could be produced, we ought to conclude that lord Bacon and sir Isaac Newton have done great disservice to philosophy, by what they have said against hypotheses. But if no such instance can be produced, we must conclude, with those great men, that every system which pretends to account for the phenomena of nature by hypotheses or conjecture, is spurious and illegitimate, and serves only to flatter the pride of man with a vain conceit of knowledge which he has not attained.

The author tells us, " that any hypothesis that has so much plausibility as to explain a considerable number of facts, helps us to digest these facts in proper order, to bring new ones to light, and to make *experimenta crucis* for the sake of future inquirers."

Let hypotheses be put to any of these uses as far as they can serve: let them suggest experiments, or direct our inquiries; but let just induction alone govern our belief.

" The rule of false affords an obvious and strong instance of the possibility of being led, with precision and certainty, to a true conclusion from a false position. And it is of the very essence of algebra, to proceed in the way of supposition."

This is true; but, when brought to justify the accounting for natural phenomena by hypotheses, is foreign to the purpose. When an unknown number, or any unknown quantity is sought, which must have certain conditions, it may be found in a scientific manner by the rule of false, or by an algebraical analysis; and, when found, may be synthetically demonstrated to be the number or the quantity sought, by its answering all the conditions required. But it is one thing to find a quantity which shall have certain conditions; it is a very different thing to find out the laws by which it pleases God to govern the world and produce the phenomena which fall under our observation. And we can then only allow some weight to this argument in favour of hypotheses, when it can be shown that the cause of any one phenomenon in nature has been or can be found, as an unknown quantity is, by the rule of false, or by algebraical analysis. This, I apprehend, will never be, till the era arrives, which Dr. Hartley seems to foretell, "when future generations shall put all kinds of evidences and inquiries into mathematical forms, and, as it were, reduce Aristotle's ten Categories, and bishop Wilkin's forty Summa Genera, to the head of quantity alone, so as to make mathematics, and logic, natural history, and civil history, natural philosophy, and philosophy of all other kinds, coincide *omni ex parte.*"

Since sir Isaac Newton laid down the rules of philosophizing in our inquiries into the works of nature, many philosophers have deviated from them in practice; perhaps few have paid that regard to them which they deserve. But they have met with very general approbation, as being founded in reason, and pointing out the only path to the knowledge of nature's works. Dr. Hartley is the only author I have met with who reasons against them, and has taken pains to find out arguments in defence of the exploded method of hypotheses.

Another condition which sir Isaac Newton requires in the causes of natural things assigned by philosophers, is, that they be sufficient to account for the phenomena. Vibrations and vibratiuncles of the medullary substance of the nerves and brain, are assigned by Dr. Hartley to account for all our sensations and ideas, and, in a word, for all the operations of our minds. Let us consider very briefly how far they are sufficient for that purpose.

It would be injustice to this author to conceive him a materialist. He proposes his sentiments with great candour, and they ought not to be carried beyond what his words express. He thinks it a consequence of his theory, that matter, if it can be endued with the most simple kinds of sensation, might arrive at all that intelligence of which the human mind is possessed. He thinks that his theory overturns all the arguments that are usually brought for the immateriality of the soul, from the subtilty of the internal senses, and of the rational faculty ; but he does not take upon him to determine whether matter can be endued with sensation or not. He even acknowledges, that matter and motion, however subtilely divided and reasoned upon, yield nothing more than matter and motion still ; and therefore he would not be any way interpreted so as to oppose the immateriality of the soul.

It would, therefore, be unreasonable to require that his theory of vibrations should, in the proper sense, account for our sensations. It would, indeed, be ridiculous in any man to pretend that thought of any kind must necessarily result from motion, or that vibrations in the nerves must necessarily produce thought, any more than the vibrations of a pendulum. Dr. Hartley disclaims this way of thinking, and therefore it ought not to be imputed to him. All that he pretends is, that, in the human constitution, there is a certain connection between vibrations in the medullary substance of the nerves and brain, and the thoughts of the mind ; so that the last depend entirely upon the first, and every kind of thought in the mind arises in consequence of a corresponding vibration, or vibratiuncle in the nerves and brain. Our sensations arise from vibrations, and our ideas from vibratiuncles, or miniature vibrations; and he comprehends, under these two words of *sensations* and *ideas*, all the operations of the mind.

But how can we expect any proof of the connection between vibrations and thought, when the existence of such vibrations was never proved? The proof of their connection cannot be stronger than the proof of their existence: for as the author acknowledges that we cannot infer the existence of the thoughts from the existence of the vibrations, it is no less evident, that we cannot infer the existence of vibrations from the existence of our thoughts. The existence of both must be known before we can know their connection. As to the existence of our thoughts, we have the evidence of consciousness; a kind of evidence that never was called in question. But as to the existence of vibrations in the medullary substance of the nerves and brain, no proof has yet been brought.

All therefore we have to expect from this hypothesis, is, that in vibrations considered abstractly, there should be a variety in kind and degree, which tallies so exactly with the varieties of the thoughts they are to account for, as may lead us to suspect some connection between the one and the other. If the divisions and subdivisions of thought be found to run parallel with the divisions and subdivisions of vibrations, this would give that kind of plausibility to the hypothesis of their connection, which we commonly expect even in a mere hypothesis; but we do not find even this.

For, to omit all those thoughts and operations which the author comprehends under the name of *ideas*. and which he thinks are connected with vibratiuncles; to omit the perception of external objects, which he comprehends under the name of *sensations;* to omit the sensations, properly so called, which accompany our passions and affections, and to confine ourselves to the sensations which we have by means of our external senses, we can perceive no correspondence between the variety we find in their kinds and degrees, and that which may be supposed in vibrations.

We have five senses, whose sensations differ totally in kind. By each of these, excepting perhaps that of hearing, we have a variety of sensations, which differ specifically, and not in degree only. How many tastes and smells are there which are specifically different, each of them capable of all degrees of strength and weakness? Heat and cold, roughness and smoothness, hardness and softness, pain and pleasure, are sensations of touch that differ in kind, and each has an endless variety of degrees. Sounds have the qualities of acute and grave, loud and low, with all different degrees of each. The varieties of colour are many more than we have names to express. How shall we find varieties in vibrations corresponding to all this variety of sensations which we have by our five senses only?

I know two qualities of vibrations in an uniform elastic medium, and I know no more. They may be quick or slow in various degrees, and they may be strong or weak in various degrees; but I cannot find any division of our sensations that will make them tally with those divisions of vibrations. If we had no other sensations but those of hearing, the theory would answer well; for sounds are either acute or grave, which may answer to quick or slow vibrations; or they are loud or low, which answer to strong or weak vibrations. But then we have no variety of vibrations corresponding to the immense variety of sensations which we have by sight, smell, taste, and touch.

Dr. Hartley has endeavoured to find out other two qualities of vibrations; to wit, that they may primarily affect one part of the brain or another, and that they may vary in their direction, according as they enter by different external nerves; but these seem to be added to make a number: for, as far as we know, vibrations in an uniform elastic substance, spread over the whole, and in all directions. However, that we may be liberal, we shall grant him four different kinds of vibrations, each of them having as many degrees as he pleases. Can he or any man reduce all our sensations to four kinds? We have five senses, and by each of them a variety of sensations, more than sufficient to exhaust all the varieties we are able to conceive in vibrations.

Dr. Hartley, indeed, was sensible of the difficulty of finding vibrations to suit all the variety of our sensations. His extensive knowledge of physiology and pathology could yield him but a feeble aid; and therefore he is often reduced to the necessity of heaping supposition upon supposition, conjecture upon conjecture, to give some credibility to his hypothesis; and in seeking out vibrations which may correspond with the sensations of one sense, he seems to forget that those must be omitted which have been appropriated to another.

Philosophers have accounted in some degree for our various sensations of sound by the vibrations of elastic air. But it is to be observed, 1st, That we know that such vibrations do really exist; and, 2dly, that they tally exactly with the most remarkable phenomena of sound. We cannot, indeed, show how any vibration should produce the sensation of sound. This must be resolved into the will of God, or into some cause altogether unknown. But we know, that as the vibration is strong or weak, the sound is loud or low. We know, that as the vibration is quick or slow, the sound is acute or grave. We can point out that relation of synchronous vibrations which produces harmony or discord, and that relation of successive vibrations which produces melody : and all this is not conjectured, but proved by a sufficient induction. This account of sounds, therefore, is philosophical ; although, perhaps, there may be many things relating to sound that we cannot account for, and of which the causes remain latent. The connections described in this branch of philosophy are the work of God, and not the fancy of men.

If any thing similar to this could be shown in accounting for all our sensations by vibrations in the medullary substance of the nerves and brain, it would deserve a place in sound philosophy. But, when we are told of vibrations in a substance, which no man could ever prove to have vibrations, or to be capable of them ; when such imaginary vibrations are brought to account for all our sensations, though we can perceive no correspondence in their variety of kind and degree, to the variety of sensations ; the connections described in such a system, are the creatures of human imagination, not the work of God.

The rays of light make an impression upon the optic nerves ; but they make none upon the auditory or olfactory. The vibrations of the air make an impression upon the auditory nerves ; but none upon the optic or the olfactory. The effluvia of bodies make an impression upon the olfactory nerves ; but make none upon the optic or auditory. No man has been able to give a shadow of reason for this. While this is the case, is it not better to confess our ignorance of the nature of those impressions made upon the nerves and brain in perception, than to flatter our pride with the conceit of knowledge which we have not, and to adulterate philosophy with the spurious brood of hypotheses?

CHAP. IV.

FALSE CONCLUSIONS DRAWN FROM THE IMPRESSIONS BEFORE MENTIONED.

SOME philosophers among the ancients, as well as among the moderns, imagined that man is nothing but a piece of matter so curiously organized, that the impressions of external objects produce in it sensation, perception, remembrance, and all the other operations we are conscious of. This foolish opinion could only take its rise from observing the constant connection which the Author of nature has established between certain impressions made upon our senses, and our perception of the objects by which the impression is made; from which they weakly inferred, that those impressions were the proper efficient causes of the corresponding perception.

But no reasoning is more fallacious than this, that because two things are always conjoined, therefore one must be the cause of the other. Day and night have been joined in a constant succession since the beginning of the world; but who is so foolish as to conclude from this, that day is the cause of night, or night the cause of the following day? There is indeed nothing more ridiculous than to imagine that any motion or modification of matter should produce thought.

If one should tell of a telescope so exactly made as to have the power of seeing; of a whispering gallery that had the power of hearing; of a cabinet so nicely framed as to have the power of memory; or of a machine so delicate as to feel pain when it was touched; such absurdities are so shocking to common sense that they would not find belief even among savages ; yet it is the same absurdity to think, that the impressions of external objects upon the machine of our bodies, can be the real efficient cause of thought and perception.

Passing this therefore as a notion too absurd to admit of reasoning; another conclusion very generally made by philosophers, is, that in perception an impression is made upon the mind as well as upon the organ, nerves, and brain. Aristotle, as was before observed, thought that the form or image of the object perceived, enters by the organ of sense, and strikes upon the mind. Mr. Hume gives the name of *impressions* to all our perceptions, to all our sensations, and even to the objects which we perceive. Mr. Locke affirms very positively, that the ideas of external objects are produced in our minds by impulse, " that being the only way we can conceive bodies to operate in." It ought, however, to be observed, in justice to Mr. Locke, that he retracted this notion in his first letter to the bishop of Worcester, and promised, in the next edition of his essay to have that passage rectified ; but either from forgetfulness in the author, or negligence in the printer, the passage remains in all the subsequent editions I have seen.

There is no prejudice more natural to man, than to conceive of the mind as having some similitude to body in its operations. Hence, men have been prone to imagine, that as bodies are put in motion by some impulse or impression made upon them by contiguous bodies ; so the mind is made to think and to perceive by some impression made upon it, or some impulse given to it by contiguous objects. If we have such a notion of the mind as Homer had of his gods, who might be bruised or wounded with swords and spears, we may then understand what is meant by impressions made upon it by a body: but if we conceive the mind to be immaterial, of which I think we have very strong proofs, we shall find it difficult to affix a meaning to *impressions made upon it.*

There is a figurative meaning of impressions on the mind which is well authorized, and of which we took notice in the observations made on that word; but this meaning applies only to objects that are interesting. To say that an object which I see with perfect indifference makes an impression upon my mind, is not, as I apprehend, good English. If philosophers mean no more but that I see the object, why should they invent an improper phrase to express what every man knows how to express in plain English?

But it is evident, from the manner in which this phrase is used by modern philosophers, that they mean not barely to express by it my perceiving an object, but to explain the manner of perception. They think that the object perceived acts upon the mind, in some way similar to that in which one body acts upon another, by making an impression upon it. The impression upon the mind is conceived to be something wherein the mind is altogether passive, and has some effect produced in it by the object. But this is an hypothesis which contradicts the common sense of mankind, and which ought not to be admitted without proof.

When I look upon the wall of my room, the wall does not act at all, nor is capable of acting; the perceiving it is an act or operation in me. That this is the common apprehension of mankind with regard to perception, is evident from the manner of expressing it in all languages.

The vulgar give themselves no trouble how they perceive objects, they express what they are conscious of, and they express it with propriety; but philosophers have an avidity to know how we perceive objects; and conceiving some similitude between a body that is put in motion, and a mind that is made to perceive, they are led to think, that as the body must receive some impulse to make it move, so the mind must receive some impulse or impression to make it perceive. This analogy seems to be confirmed, by observing that we perceive objects only when they make some impression upon the organs of sense, and upon the nerves and brain; but it ought to be observed, that such is the nature of body that it cannot change its state, but by some force impressed upon it. This is not the nature of mind. All that we know about it shows it to be in its nature living and active, and to have the power of perception in its constitution, but still within those limits to which it is confined by the laws of nature.

It appears, therefore, that this phrase of the mind's having impressions made upon it by corporeal objects in perception, is either a phrase without any distinct meaning, and contrary to the propriety of the English language, or it is grounded upon an hypothesis which is destitute of proof. On that account, though we grant that in perception there is an impression made upon the organ of sense. and upon the nerves and brain, we do not admit that the object makes any impression upon the mind.

There is another conclusion drawn from the impressions made upon the brain in perception, which I conceive to have no solid foundation, though it has been adopted very generally by philosophers. It is, that by the impressions made on the brain, images are formed of the object perceived; and that the mind, being seated in the brain as its chamber of presence, immediately perceives those images only, and has no perception of the external object but by them. This notion of our perceiving external objects, not immediately, but in certain images or species of them conveyed by the senses, seems to be the most ancient philosophical hypothesis we have on the subject of perception, and to have, with small variations, retained its authority to this day.

Aristotle, as was before observed, maintained, that the species, images, or forms of external objects, coming from the object, are impressed on the mind. The followers of Democritus and Epicurus held the same thing, with regard to slender films of subtile matter coming from the object, that Aristotle did with regard to his immaterial species or forms.

Aristotle thought, that every object of human understanding enters at first by the senses; and that the notions got by them are by the powers of the mind refined and spiritualized, so as at last to become objects of the most sublime and abstracted sciences. Plato, on the other hand, had a very mean opinion of all the knowledge we get by the senses. He thought it did not deserve the name of knowledge, and could not be the foundation of science; because the objects of sense are individuals only, and are in a constant fluctuation. All science, according to him, must be employed about those eternal and immutable ideas, which existed before the objects of sense, and are not liable to any change. In this there was an essential difference between the systems of these two philosophers. The notion of eternal and immutable ideas, which Plato borrowed from the Pythagorean school, was totally rejected by Aristotle, who held it as a maxim, that there is nothing in the intellect, which was not at first in the senses.

But, notwithstanding this great difference in those
two ancient systems, they might both agree as to the
manner in which we perceive objects by our senses;
and that they did so, I think, is probable; because
Aristotle, as far as I know, neither takes notice of any
difference between himself and his master upon this
point, nor lays claim to his theory of the manner of our
perceiving objects as his own invention. It is still
more probable from the hints which Plato gives in the
seventh book of his Republic, concerning the manner
in which we perceive the objects of sense; which he
compares to persons in a deep and dark cave, who see
not external objects themselves, but only their shadows, by a light let into the cave through a small opening.

It seems, therefore, probable, that the Pythagoreans
and Platonists agreed with the Peripatetics in this general theory of perception; to wit, that the objects of
sense are perceived only by certain images, or shadows of them, let into the mind, as into a *camera ob-
scura*.

The notions of the ancients were very various with
regard to the seat of the soul. Since it has been discovered, by the improvements in anatomy, that the
nerves are the instruments of perception, and of the
sensations accompanying it, and that the nerves ulti-
mately terminate in the brain, it has been the general
opinion of philosophers that the brain is the seat of the
soul; and that she perceives the images that are
brought there, and external things only by means of
them.

Des Cartes, observing that the pineal gland is the
only part of the brain that is single, all the other parts
being double, and thinking that the soul must have one

seat, was determined by this to make that gland the soul's habitation, to which, by means of the animal spirits, intelligence is brought of all objects that affect the senses.

Others have not thought proper to confine the habitation of the soul to the pineal gland, but to the brain in general, or to some part of it, which they call the *sensorium*. Even the great Newton favoured this opinion, though he proposes it only as a query, with that modesty which distinguished him no less than his great genius. "Is not, says he, the sensorium of animals the place where the sentient substance is present, and to which the sensible species of things are brought through the nerves and brain, that there they may be perceived by the mind present in that place? And is there not an incorporeal, living, intelligent, and omnipresent Being, who, in infinite space, as if it were in his sensorium, intimately perceives things themselves, and comprehends them perfectly, as being present to them; of which things, that principle in us which perceives and thinks, discerns only, in its little sensorium, the images brought to it through the organs of the senses?"

His friend, Dr. Samuel Clarke, adopted the same sentiments with more confidence. In his papers to Leibnitz, we find the following passages: "Without being present to the images of the things perceived, it (the soul) could not possibly perceive them. A living substance can only there perceive where it is present, either to the things themselves, as the omnipresent God is to the whole universe, or to the images of things, as the soul of man is in its proper sensory. Nothing can any more act, or be acted upon, where it is not present, than it can be where it is not. We are sure the soul cannot perceive what it is not present to, because nothing can act, or be acted upon, where it is not."

Mr. Locke expresses himself so upon this point, that for the most part, one would imagine, that he thought that the ideas, or images of things, which he believed to be the immediate objects of perception, are impressions upon the mind itself; yet, in some passages, he rather places them in the brain, and makes them to be perceived by the mind there present. "There are some ideas, says he, which have admittance only through one sense; and if the organs or the nerves, which are the conduits to convey them from without to their audience in the brain, the mind's presence room, if I may so call it, are so disordered as not to perform their function, they have no postern to be admitted by.

"There seems to be a constant decay of all our ideas, even of those that are struck deepest. The pictures drawn in our minds are laid in fading colours. Whether the temper of the brain makes this difference, that in some it retains the characters drawn on it like marble, in others like freestone, and in others little better than sand, I shall not inquire."

From these passages of Mr. Locke, and others of a like nature, it is plain, that he thought that there are images of external objects conveyed to the brain. But whether he thought with Des Cartes and Newton, that the images in the brain are perceived by the mind there present, or that they are imprinted on the mind itself, is not so evident.

Now, with regard to this hypothesis, there are three things that deserve to be considered, because the hypothesis leans upon them; and, if any one of them fail, it must fall to the ground. The *first* is, that the soul has its seat, or, as Mr. Locke calls it, its presence room, in the brain. The *second*, that there are images formed in the brain of all the objects of sense. The *third,* that the mind or soul perceives these images in the brain; and that it perceives not external objects immediately, but only by means of their images.

As to the *first* point, that the soul has its seat in the brain, this, surely, is not so well established, as that we can safely build other principles upon it. There have been various opinions and much disputation about the place of spirits; whether they have a place? and if they have, how they occupy that place? After men had fought in the dark about those points for ages, the wiser part seem to have left off disputing about them, as matters beyond the reach of the human faculties.

As to the *second* point, that images of all the objects of sense are formed in the brain, we may venture to affirm, that there is no proof nor probability of this, with regard to any of the objects of sense; and that with regard to the greater part of them, it is words without any meaning.

We have not the least evidence, that the image of any external object is formed in the brain. The brain has been dissected times innumerable by the nicest anatomists; every part of it examined by the naked eye, and with the help of microscopes; but no vestige of an image of any external object was ever found. The brain seems to be the most improper substance that can be imagined for receiving or retaining images, being a soft moist medullary substance.

But how are these images formed? or whence do they come? Says Mr. Locke, the organs of sense and nerves convey them from without. This is just the Aristotelian hypothesis of sensible species, which modern philosophers have been at great pains to refute,

and which must be acknowledged to be one of the most
unintelligible parts of the Peripatetic system. Those
who consider species of colour, figure, sound, and smell,
coming from the object, and entering by the organs of
sense, as a part of the scholastic jargon, long ago discarded from sound philosophy, ought to have discarded
images in the brain along with them. There never
was a shadow of argument brought by any author, to
show that an image of any external object ever entered by any of the organs of sense.

That external objects make some impression on the
organs of sense, and by them on the nerves and brain,
is granted; but that those impressions resemble the
objects they are made by, so as that they may be called images of the objects, is most improbable. Every
hypothesis that has been contrived shows that there
can be no such resemblance; for neither the motions
of animal spirits, nor the vibrations of elastic chords,
or of elastic ether, or of the infinitesimal particles of
the nerves, can be supposed to resemble the objects by
which they are excited.

We know, that, in vision, an image of the visible
object is formed in the bottom of the eye by the rays of
light. But we know also, that this image cannot be
conveyed to the brain, because the optic nerve, and all
the parts that surround it, are opaque and impervious
to the rays of light; and there is no other organ of
sense in which any image of the object is formed.

It is further to be observed, that, with regard to
some objects of sense, we may understand what is
meant by an image of them imprinted on the brain;
but, with regard to most objects of sense, the phrase
is absolutely unintelligible, and conveys no meaning at all. As to objects of sight, I understand what

is meant by an image of their figure in the brain: but how shall we conceive an image of their colour where there is absolute darkness? And as to all other objects of sense, except figure and colour, I am unable to conceive what is meant by an image of them. Let any man say, what he means by an image of heat and cold, an image of hardness or softness, an image of sound, of smell, or taste. The word *image*, when applied to these objects of sense, has absolutely no meaning. Upon what a weak foundation, then, does this hypothesis stand, when it supposes, that images of all the objects of sense are imprinted on the brain, being conveyed thither by the conduits of the organs and nerves!

The *third* point in this hypothesis, is, that the mind perceives the images in the brain, and external objects only by means of them. This is as improbable, as that there are such images to be perceived. If our powers of perception be not altogether fallacious, the objects we perceive are not in our brain, but without us. We are so far from perceiving images in the brain, that we do not perceive our brain at all; nor would any man ever have known that he had a brain, if anatomy had not discovered, by dissection, that the brain is a constituent part of the human body.

To sum up what has been said with regard to the organs of perception, and the impressions made upon our nerves and brain. It is a law of our nature, established by the will of the Supreme Being, that we perceive no external object but by means of the organs given us for that purpose. But these organs do not perceive. The eye is the organ of sight, but it sees not. A telescope is an artificial organ of sight. The eye is a natural organ of sight, but it sees as little as the telescope. We know how the eye forms a picture

of the visible object upon the retina ; but how this picture makes us see the object we know not ; and if experience had not informed us that such a picture is
necessary to vision, we should never have known it.
We can give no reason why the picture on the retina
should be followed by vision, while a like picture on any
other part of the body produces nothing like vision.

It is likewise a law of our nature, that we perceive
not external objects, unless certain impressions be
made by the object upon the organ, and by means of
the organ upon the nerves and brain. But of the nature of those impressions we are perfectly ignorant ;
and though they are conjoined with perception by the
will of our Maker, yet it does not appear that they
have any necessary connection with it in their own
nature, far less that they can be the proper efficient
cause of it. We perceive, because God has given us
the power of perceiving, and not because we have impressions from objects.   We perceive nothing without
those impressions, because our Maker has limited and
circumscribed our powers of perception, by such laws
of nature as to his wisdom seemed meet, and such as
suited our rank in his creation.

CHAP. V.

OF PERCEPTION.

In speaking of the impressions made on our organs in perception, we build upon facts borrowed from anatomy and physiology, for which we have the testimony of our senses. But being now to speak of perception itself, which is solely an act of the mind, we must appeal to another authority. The operations of our minds are known not by sense, but by consciousness, the authority of which is as certain and as irresistible as that of sense.

In order, however, to our having a distinct notion of any of the operations of our own minds, it is not enough that we be conscious of them, for all men have this consciousness: it is further necessary that we attend to them while they are exerted, and reflect upon them with care, while they are recent and fresh in our memory. It is necessary that, by employing ourselves frequently in this way, we get the habit of this attention and reflection; and therefore, for the proof of facts which I shall have occasion to mention upon this subject, I can only appeal to the reader's own thoughts, whether such facts are not agreeable to what he is conscious of in his own mind.

If, therefore, we attend to that act of our mind which we call the perception of an external object of sense, we shall find in it these three things. *First*, Some conception or notion of the object perceived. *Secondly*, A strong and irresistible conviction and belief of its present existence. And, *thirdly*, That this conviction

and belief are immediate, and not the effect of reasoning.

1st, It is impossible to perceive an object without having some notion or conception of that which we perceive. We may indeed conceive an object which we
do not perceive ; but when we perceive the object, we
must have some conception of it at the same time ; and
we have commonly a more clear and steady notion of
the object while we perceive it, than we have from
memory or imagination when it is not perceived. Yet,
even in perception, the notion which our senses give of
the object may be more or less clear, more or less distinct, in all possible degrees.

Thus we see more distinctly an object at a small than
at a great distance. An object at a great distance is
seen more distinctly in a clear than in a foggy day. An
object seen indistinctly with the naked eye, on account
of its smallness, may be seen distinctly with a micro-
scope. The objects in this room will be seen by a person in the room less and less distinctly as the light of
the day fails ; they pass through all the various degrees
of distinctness according to the degrees of the light,
and at last. in total darkness, they are not seen at all.
What has been said of the objects of sight is so easily
applied to the objects of the other senses, that the application may be left to the reader.

In a matter so obvious to every person capable of reflection, it is necessary only further to observe, that the
notion which we get of an object, merely by our external sense, ought not to be confounded with that more scientific notion which a man, come to the years of understanding, may have of the same object, by attending to
its various attributes, or to its various parts, and their
relation to each other, and to the whole. Thus the

notion which a child has of a jack for roasting meat, will be acknowledged to be very different from that of a man who understands its construction, and perceives the relation of the parts to one another, and to the whole. The child sees the jack and every part of it as well as the man. The child, therefore, has all the notion of it which sight gives ; whatever there is more in the notion which the man forms of it, must be derived from other powers of the mind, which may afterward be explained. This observation is made here only, that we may not confound the operations of different powers of the mind, which, by being always conjoined after we grow up to understanding, are apt to pass for one and the same.

2dly, In perception we not only have a notion more or less distinct of the object perceived, but also an irresistible conviction and belief of its existence. This is always the case when we are certain that we perceive it. There may be a perception so faint and indistinct, as to leave us in doubt whether we perceive the object or not. Thus, when a star begins to twinkle as the light of the sun withdraws, one may, for a short time, think he sees it, without being certain, until the perception acquires some strength and steadiness. When a ship just begins to appear in the utmost verge of the horizon, we may at first be dubious whether we perceive it or not : but when the perception is in any degree clear and steady, there remains no doubt of its reality ; and when the reality of the perception is ascertained, the existence of the object perceived can no longer be doubted.

By the laws of all nations, in the most solemn judicial trials wherein men's fortunes and lives are at stake, the sentence passes according to the testimony of eye or ear witnesses of good credit. An upright judge will

give a fair hearing to every objection that can be made
to the integrity of a witness, and allow it to be possible
that he may be corrupted ; but no judge will ever
suppose, that witnesses may be imposed upon by trusting to their eyes and ears : and if a skeptical counsel
should plead against the testimony of the witnesses,
that they had no other evidence for what they declared, but the testimony of their eyes and ears, and that
we ought not to put so much faith in our senses, as to
deprive men of life or fortune upon their testimony ;
surely no upright judge would admit a plea of this
kind. I believe no counsel, however skeptical, ever
dared to offer such an argument ; and if it was offered,
it would be rejected with disdain.

Can any stronger proof be given, that it is the universal judgment of mankind that the evidence of sense
is a kind of evidence which we may securely rest
upon in the most momentous concerns of mankind ;
that it is a kind of evidence against which we ought not
to admit any reasoning ; and therefore, that to reason either for or against it, is an insult to common
sense ?

The whole conduct of mankind, in the daily occurrences of life, as well as the solemn procedure of judi-
catories in the trial of causes, civil and criminal, de-
monstrates this. I know only of two exceptions that
may be offered against this being the universal belief of
mankind.

The first exception is that of some lunatics, who
have been persuaded of things that seem to contradict
the clear testimony of their senses. It is said there
have been lunatics and hypochondriacal persons, who
seriously believed themselves to be made of glass ; and,
in consequence of this, lived in continual terror of having their brittle frame shivered into pieces.

All I have to say to this is, that our minds, in our present state, are, as well as our bodies, liable to strong disorders ; and as we do not judge of the natural constitution of the body, from the disorders or diseases to which it is subject from accidents, so neither ought we to judge of the natural powers of the mind from its disorders, but from its sound state. It is natural to man, and common to the species, to have two hands, and two feet ; yet I have seen a man, and a very ingenious one, who was born without either hands or feet. It is natural to man to have faculties superior to those of brutes ; yet we see some individuals, whose faculties are not equal to those of many brutes ; and the wisest man may, by various accidents, be reduced to this state. General rules that regard those whose intellects are sound, are not overthrown by instances of men whose intellects are hurt by any constitutional or accidental disorder.

The other exception that may be made to the principle we have laid down, is that of some philosophers who have maintained, that the testimony of sense is fallacious, and therefore ought never to be trusted. Perhaps it might be a sufficient answer to this to say, that there is nothing so absurd which some philosophers have not maintained. It is one thing to profess a doctrine of this kind, another seriously to believe it, and to be governed by it in the conduct of life. It is evident, that a man who did not believe his senses, could not keep out of harm's way an hour of his life ; yet, in all the history of philosophy, we never read of any skeptic that ever stepped into fire or water because he did not believe his senses, or that showed, in the conduct of life, less trust in his senses than other men have. This gives us just ground to apprehend, that philosophy was never able to conquer that natural belief which men have in their senses; and that all their subtile reasonings against this belief were never able to persuade themselves.

It appears, therefore, that the clear and distinct testimony of our senses carries irresistible conviction along with it, to every man in his right judgment.

I observed, 3dly, That this conviction is not only irresistible, but it is immediate; that is, it is not by a train of reasoning and argumentation that we come to be convinced of the existence of what we perceive; we ask no argument for the existence of the object, but that we perceive it; perception commands our belief upon its own authority, and disdains to rest its authority upon any reasoning whatsoever.

The conviction of a truth may be irresistible, and yet not immediate. Thus, my conviction that the three angles of every plain triangle, are equal to two right angles, is irresistible, but it is not immediate: I am convinced of it by demonstrative reasoning. There are other truths in mathematics of which we have not only an irresistible, but an immediate conviction. Such are the axioms. Our belief of the axioms in mathematics is not grounded upon argument. Arguments are grounded upon them, but their evidence is discerned immediately by the human understanding.

It is, no doubt, one thing to have an immediate conviction of a self evident axiom; it is another thing to have an immediate conviction of the existence of what we see: but the conviction is equally immediate and equally irresistible in both cases. No man thinks of seeking a reason to believe what he sees; and, before we are capable of reasoning, we put no less confidence in our senses than after. The rudest savage is as fully convinced of what he sees, and hears, and feels, as the most expert logician. The constitution of our understanding determines us to hold the truth of a mathematical axiom as a first principle, from which other truths may be deduced, but it is deduced from none ; and the constitution of our power of perception determines us to hold the existence of what we distinctly perceive as a first principle, from which other truths may be deduced, but it is deduced from none. What has been said of the irresistible and immediate belief of the existence of objects distinctly perceived, I mean only to affirm with regard to persons so far advanced in understanding, as to distinguish objects of mere imagination from things which have a real existence. Every man knows that he may have a notion of Don Quixote, or of Garagantua, without any belief that such persons ever existed ; and that of Julius Cesar and of Oliver Cromwell, he has not only a notion, but a belief that they did really exist. But whether children, from the time that they begin to use their senses, make a distinction between things which are only conceived or imagined, and things which really exist, may be doubted. Until we are able to make this distinction, we cannot properly be said to believe or to disbelieve the existence of any thing. The belief of the existence of any thing seems to suppose a notion of existence ; a notion too abstract, perhaps, to enter into the mind of an infant. I speak of the power of perception in those that are adult, and of a sound mind, who believe that there are some things which do really exist ; and that there are many things conceived by themselves, and by others, which have no existence. That such persons do invariably ascribe existence to every thing which they distinctly perceive, without seeking reasons or arguments for doing so, is perfectly evident from the whole tenor of human life.

The account I have given of our perception of external objects, is intended as a faithful delineation of

what every man, come to years of understanding, and
capable of giving attention to what passes in his own
mind, may feel in himself. In what manner the notion
of external objects, and the immediate belief of their
existence, is produced by means of our senses, I am not
able to show, and I do not pretend to show. If the
power of perceiving external objects in certain circumstances, be a part of the original constitution of the
human mind, all attempts to account for it will be vain.
No other account can be given of the constitution of
things, but the will of Him that made them. As we
can give no reason why matter is extended and inert,
why the mind thinks, and is conscious of its thoughts,
but the will of Him who made both; so I suspect we
can give no other reason why, in certain circumstances,
we perceive external objects, and in others do not.

The Supreme Being intended, that we should have
such knowledge of the material objects that surround
us, as is necessary in order to our supplying the wants
of nature, and avoiding the dangers to which we are
constantly exposed; and he has admirably fitted our
powers of perception to this purpose.   the intelligence we have of external objects were to be got by
reasoning only, the greatest part of men would be destitute of it; for the greatest part of men hardly ever
learn to reason; and in infancy and childhood no man
can reason. Therefore, as this intelligence of the objects that surround us, and from which we may receive
so much benefit or harm, is equally necessary to children and to men, to the ignorant and to the learned,
God in his wisdom conveys it to us in a way that puts
all upon a level. The information of the senses is as
perfect, and gives as full conviction to the most ignorant,
as to the most learned.

CHAP. VI.

WHAT IT IS TO ACCOUNT FOR A PHENOMENON IN NATURE.

An object placed at a proper distance, and in a good light, while the eyes are shut, is not perceived at all; but no sooner do we open our eyes upon it, than we have, as it were by inspiration, a certain knowledge of its existence, of its colour, figure, and distance. This is a fact which every one knows. The vulgar are satisfied with knowing the fact, and give themselves no trouble about the cause of it : but a philosopher is impatient to know how this event is produced, to account for it, or assign its cause.

This avidity to know the causes of things is the parent of all philosophy true and false. Men of speculation place a great part of their happiness in such knowledge. *Felix qui potuit rerum cognoscere causas,* has always been a sentiment of human nature. But as, in the pursuit of other kinds of happiness, men often mistake the road, so in none have they more frequently done it, than in the philosophical pursuit of the causes of things.

It is a dictate of common sense, that the causes we assign of appearances ought to be real, and not fictions of human imagination. It is likewise self evident, that such causes ought to be adequate to the effects that are conceived to be produced by them.

That those who are less accustomed to inquiries into the causes of natural appearances, may the better understand what it is to show the cause of such appearances, or to account for them; I shall borrow a plain instance of a phenomenon or appearance, of which a full and satisfactory account has been given. The phenomenon is this: that a stone, or any heavy body, falling from a height, continually increases its velocity as it descends; so that if it acquire a certain velocity in one second of time, it will have twice that velocity at the end of two seconds, thrice at the end of three seconds, and so on in proportion to the time. This accelerated velocity in a stone falling must have been observed from the beginning of the world; but the first person, as far as we know, who accounted for it in a proper and philosophical manner, was the famous Galileo; after innumerable false and fictitious accounts had been given of it.

He observed, that bodies once put in motion, continue that motion with the same velocity, and in the same direction, until they be stopped or retarded, or have the direction of their motion altered, by some force impressed upon them. This property of bodies is called their *inertia*, or inactivity; for it implies no more than that bodies cannot of themselves change their state from rest to motion, or from motion to rest. He observed also, that gravity acts constantly and equally upon a body, and therefore will give equal degrees of velocity to a body in equal times. From these principles, which are known from experience to be fixed laws of nature, Galileo showed, that heavy bodies must descend with a velocity uniformly accelerated, as by experience they are found to do.

For if the body by its gravitation acquire a certain velocity at the end of one second, it would, though its gravitation should cease that moment, continue to go on with that velocity; but its gravitation continues, and will in another second give it an additional velocity, equal to that which it gave in the first; so that the whole velocity at the end of two seconds will be twice

as great as at the end of one. In like manner, this velocity being continued through the third second, and
having the same addition by gravitation as in any of
the preceding, the whole velocity at the end of the
third second will be thrice as great as at the end of the
first, and so on continually.

We may here observe, that the causes assigned of
this phenomenon are two: 1st, That bodies once put
in motion, retain their velocity and their direction, until it is changed by some force impressed upon them.
2dly, That the weight or gravitation of a body is
always the same. These are laws of nature, confirmed by universal experience, and therefore are
not feigned, but true causes; then, they are precisely
adequate to the effect ascribed to them; they must
necessarily produce that very motion in descending
bodies which we find to take place ; and neither more
nor less. The account therefore given of this phenomenon is just and philosophical ; no other will ever be
required or admitted by those who understand this.

It ought likewise to be observed, that the causes assigned of this phenomenon are things of which we can
assign no cause. Why bodies once put in motion continue to move; why bodies constantly gravitate toward the earth with the same force, no man has been
able to show. These are facts confirmed by universal
experience, and they must no doubt have a cause;
but their cause is unknown, and we call them laws of
nature, because we know no cause of them but the
will of the Supreme Being.

But may we not attempt to find the cause of gravitation, and of other phenomena which we call laws of
nature? No doubt we may. We know not the limit
which has been set to human knowledge, and our knowledge of the works of God can never be carried too far :
but, supposing gravitation to be accounted for, by an

etherial elastic medium for instance, this can only be done, 1st, by proving the existence and the elasticity of this medium; and, 2dly, by showing, that this medium must necessarily produce that gravitation which bodies are known to have. Until this be done, gravitation is not accounted for, nor is its cause known; and when this is done, the elasticity of this medium will be considered as a law of nature, whose cause is unknown. The chain of natural causes has, not unfitly, been compared to a chain hanging down from heaven: a link that is discovered supports the links below it, but it must itself be supported; and that which supports it must be supported, until we come to the first link, which is supported by the throne of the Almighty. Every natural cause must have a cause, until we ascend to the first cause, which is uncaused, and operates not by necessity, but by will.

By what has been said in this chapter, those who are but little acquainted with philosophical inquiries may see what is meant by accounting for a phenomenon, or showing its cause, which ought to be well understood, in order to judge of the theories by which philosophers have attempted to account for our perception of external objects by the senses.

CHAP. VII.

SENTIMENTS OF PHILOSOPHERS ABOUT THE PERCEPTION
OF EXTERNAL OBJECTS ; AND, FIRST,

OF THE THEORY OF FATHER MALEBRANCHE.

How the correspondence is carried on between the thinking principle within us, and the material world without us, has always been found a very difficult problem to those philosophers who think themselves obliged to account for every phenomenon in nature. Many philosophers, ancient and modern, have employed their invention to discover how we are made to perceive external objects by our senses : and there appears to be a very great uniformity in their sentiments in the main, notwithstanding their variations in particular points.

Plato illustrates our manner of perceiving the objects of sense, in this manner : he supposes a dark subterraneous cave, in which men lie bound in such a manner, that they can direct their eyes only to one part of the cave. Far behind, there is a light, some rays of which come over a wall to that part of the cave which is before the eyes of our prisoners. A number of persons, variously employed, pass between them and the light, whose shadows are seen by the prisoners, but not the persons themselves.

In this manner, that philosopher conceived, that, by our senses, we perceive the shadows of things only, and not things themselves. He seems to have borrowed his notions on this subject from the Pythagoreans, and they very probably from Pythagoras himself. If we make allowance for Plato's allegorical genius, his sentiments on this subject correspond very well with

those of his scholar Aristotle, and of the Peripatetics.
The shadows of Plato may very well represent the species and phantasms of the Peripatetic school, and the
ideas and impressions of modern philosophers.

Two thousand years after Plato, Mr. Locke, who
studied the operations of the human mind so much,
and with se great success, represents our manner of
perceiving external objects, by a similitude very much
resembling that of the cave. "Methinks, says he, the
understanding is not much unlike a closet wholly shut
from light, with only some little opening left, to let in
external visible resemblances, or ideas of things without.
Would the pictures coming into such a dark room but
stay there, and lie so orderly as to be found upon occasion, it would very much resemble the understanding
of a man, in reference to all objects of sight, and the
ideas of them."

Plato's subterranean cave, and Mr. Locke's dark
closet, may be applied with ease to all the systems of
perception that have been invented ; for they all suppose that we perceive not external objects immediately,
and that the immediate objects of perception are only
certain shadows of the external objects. Those shadows or images, which we immediately perceive, were
by the ancients called *species, forms, phantasms*. Since
the time of Des Cartes, they have commonly been called
ideas, and by Mr. Hume *impressions*. But all philosophers, from Plato to Mr. Hume, agree in this, That
we do not perceive external objects immediately, and
that the immediate object of perception must be some
image present to the mind. So far there appears an
unanimity, rarely to be found among philosophers on
such abstruse points.

If it should be asked, Whether, according to the
opinion of philosophers, we perceive the images or ideas
only, and infer the existence and qualities of the ex-

ternal object from what we perceive in the image? or, whether we really perceive the external object as well as its image? The answer to this question is not quite obvious.

On the one hand, philosophers, if we except Berkeley and Hume, believe the existence of external objects of sense, and call them objects of perception, though not immediate objects. But what they mean by a mediate object of perception, I do not find clearly explained; whether they suit their language to popular opinion, and mean that we perceive external objects in that figurative sense, in which we say that we perceive an absent friend when we look on his picture; or whether they mean, that really, and without a figure, we perceive both the external object and its idea in the mind. If the last be their meaning, it would follow, that, in every instance of perception, there is a double object perceived: that I perceive, for instance, one sun in the heavens, and another in my own mind. But I do not find that they affirm this; and, as it contradicts the experience of all mankind, I will not impute it to them.

It seems, therefore, that their opinion is, that we do not really perceive the external object, but the internal only; and that when they speak of perceiving external objects, they mean it only in a popular or in a figurative sense, as above explained. Several reasons lead me to think this to be the opinion of philosophers, besides what is mentioned above. 1st, If we do really perceive the external object itself, there seems to be no necessity, no use, for an image of it. 2dly, Since the time of Des Cartes, philosophers have very generally thought that the existence of external objects of sense requires proof, and can only be proved from the existence of their ideas. 3dly, The way in which philosophers speak of ideas, seems to imply that they are the only objects of perception.

Having endeavoured to explain what is common to philosophers in accounting for our perception of external objects, we shall give some detail of their differences.

The ideas by which we perceive external objects, are said by some to be the ideas of the Deity; but it has been more generally thought, that every man's ideas are proper to himself, and are either in his mind, or in his *sensorium*, where the mind is immediately present. The *first* is the theory of Malebranche; the *second* we shall call the common theory.

With regard to that of Malebranche, it seems to have some affinity with the Platonic notion of ideas, but is not the same. Plato believed that there are three eternal first principles, from which all things have their origin; matter, ideas, and an efficient cause. Matter is that of which all things are made, which, by all the ancient philosophers, was conceived to be eternal. Ideas are forms without matter of every kind of things which can exist; which forms were also conceived by Plato to be eternal and immutable, and to be the models or patterns by which the efficient cause, that is the Deity, formed every part of this universe. These ideas were conceived to be the sole objects of science, and indeed of all true knowledge. While we are imprisoned in the body, we are prone to give attention to the objects of sense only; but these being individual things, and in a constant fluctuation, being indeed shadows rather than realities, cannot be the object of real knowledge. All science is employed, not about individual things, but about things universal and abstract from matter. Truth is eternal and immutable, and therefore must have for its object eternal and immutable ideas; these we are capable of contemplating in some degree even in our present state, but not without a certain purification of mind, and abstraction from the objects of sense. Such, as far as I am able to comprehend, were the sublime notions of Plato, and probably of Pythagoras.

The philosophers of the Alexandrian school, commonly called the latter Platonists, seem to have adopted the same system; but with this difference, that they made the eternal ideas not to be a principle distinct from the Deity, but to be in the Divine intellect, as the objects of those conceptions which the Divine mind must from all eternity have had, not only of every thing which he has made, but of every possible existence, and of all the relations of things. By a proper purification and abstraction from the objects of sense, we may be in some measure united to the Deity, and in the eternal light be enabled to discern the most sublime intellectual truths.

These Platonic notions, grafted upon Christianity, probably gave rise to the sect called Mystics, which, though in its spirit and principles extremely opposite to the Peripatetic, yet was never extinguished, but subsists to this day.

Many of the fathers of the Christian church have a tincture of the tenets of the Alexandrian school; among others St. Augustin. But it does not appear, as far as I know, that either Plato, or the latter Platonists, or St. Augustin, or the Mystics, thought that we perceive the objects of sense in the Divine ideas. They had too mean a notion of our perception of sensible objects to ascribe to it so high an origin. This theory, therefore, of our perceiving the objects of sense in the ideas of the Deity, I take to be the invention of father Malebranche himself. He indeed brings many passages of St. Augustin to countenance it, and seems very desirous to have that father of his party. But in those passages, though the father speaks in a very high strain of God's being the light of our minds, of our being illuminated immediately by the eternal

light, and uses other similar expressions; yet he seems
to apply those expressions only to our illumination in
moral and divine things, and not to the perception of
objects by the senses. Mr. Bayle imagines that some
traces of this opinion of Malebranche are to be found
in Amelius the Platonist, and even in Democritus;
but his authorities seem to be strained.

Malebranche, with a very penetrating genius, entered into a more minute examination of the powers of the
human mind than any one before him. He had the
advantage of the discoveries made by Des Cartes, whom
he followed without slavish attachment.

He lays it down as a principle admitted by all philosophers, and which could not be called in question,
that we do not perceive external objects immediately,
but by means of images or ideas of them present to
the mind. "I suppose, says he, that every one will
grant that we perceive not the objects that are without
us immediately, and of themselves. We see the sun,
the stars, and an infinity of objects without us; and
it is not at all likely that the soul sallies out of the
body, and, as it were, takes a walk through the heavens to contemplate all those objects. She sees them
not, therefore, by themselves; and the immediate
object of the mind, when it sees the sun, for example,
is not the sun, but something which is intimately
united to the soul; and it is that which I call an idea:
so that by the word *idea*, I understand nothing else
here but that which is the immediate object, or nearest to the mind, when we perceive any object. It ought
to be carefully observed, that, in order to the mind's
perceiving any object, it is absolutely necessary that
the idea of that object be actually present to it. Of
this it is not possible to doubt. The things which the
soul perceives are of two kinds. They are either in the
soul, or they are without the soul. Those that are in

the soul are its own thoughts, that is to say, all its different modifications. The soul has no need of ideas for perceiving these things. But with regard to things without the soul, we cannot perceive them but by means of ideas."

Having laid this foundation, as a principle which was common to all philosophers, and which admitted of no doubt, he proceeds to enumerate all the possible ways by which the ideas of sensible objects may be presented to the mind. Either, 1st, they come from the bodies which we perceive; or, 2dly, the soul has the power of producing them in itself; or, 3dly, they are produced by the Deity, either in our creation, or occasionally as there is use for them; or, 4thly, the soul has in itself virtually and eminently, as the schools speak, all the perfections which it perceives in bodies; or, 5thly, the soul is united with a Being possessed of all perfection, who has in himself the ideas of all created things.

This he takes to be a complete enumeration of all the possible ways in which the ideas of external objects may be presented to our minds. He employs a whole chapter upon each; refuting the four first, and confirming the last by various arguments. The Deity, being always present to our minds in a more intimate manner than any other being, may, upon occasion of the impressions made on our bodies, discover to us, as far as he thinks proper, and according to fixed laws, his own ideas of the object; and thus we see all things in God, or in the Divine ideas.

However visionary this system may appear on a superficial view, yet when we consider, that he agreed with the whole tribe of philosophers in conceiving ideas to be the immediate objects of perception, and that he found insuperable difficulties, and even absurdities in every other hypothesis concerning them, it will

not appear so wonderful that a man of very great genius should fall into this; and probably it pleased so
devout a man the more, that it sets in the most striking
light our dependence upon God, and his continual
presence with us.

He distinguished more accurately than any philosopher had done before, the objects which we perceive
from the sensations in our own minds, which by the
laws of nature always accompany the perception of
the object. As in many things, so particularly in
this he has great merit: for this, I apprehend, is
a key that opens the way to a right understanding
both of our external senses, and of other powers of
the mind. The vulgar confound sensation with other
powers of the mind, and with their objects, because
the purposes of life do not make a distinction necessary. The confounding of these in common language has led philosophers, in one period, to make
those things external which really are sensations
in our own minds; and in another period, running, as
is usual, into the contrary extreme, to make almost
every thing to be a sensation or feeling in our minds.

It is obvious that the system of Malebranche leaves
no evidence of the existence of a material world, from
what we perceive by our senses; for the Divine ideas,
which are the objects immediately perceived, were
the same before the world was created. Malebranche
was too acute not to discern this consequence of his
system, and too candid not to acknowledge it. He
fairly owns it, and endeavours to make advantage of it,
resting the complete evidence we have of the existence
of matter upon the authority of revelation. He shows
that the arguments brought by Des Cartes to prove
the existence of a material world, though as good as
any that reason could furnish, are not perfectly conclusive; and though he acknowledges with Des Cartes,

that we feel a strong propensity to believe the existence of a material world, yet he thinks this is not sufficient; and that to yield to such propensities without
evidence, is to expose ourselves to perpetual delusion.
He thinks, therefore, that the only convincing evidence
we have of the existence of a material world is, that
we are assured by revelation that God created the
heavens and the earth, and that the Word was made
flesh. He is sensible of the ridicule to which so strange
an opinion may expose him among those who are guided
by prejudice; but, for the sake of truth, he is willing
to bear it. But no author, not even bishop Berkeley,
has shown more clearly, that either upon his own
system, or upon the common principles of philosophers with regard to ideas, we have no evidence
left, either from reason or from our senses, of the
existence of a material world. It is no more than
justice to father Malebranche to acknowledge, that
bishop Berkeley's arguments are to be found in him
in their whole force.

Mr. Norris, an English divine, espoused the system
of Malebranche, in his Essay toward the Theory of
the Ideal or Intellectual World, published in two volumes 8vo. A.D. 1701. This author has made a feeble
effort to supply a defect which is to be found not in
Malebranche only, but in almost all the authors who
have treated of ideas; I mean, to prove their existence.
He has employed a whole chapter to prove, that material things cannot be an immediate object of perception.
His arguments are these : 1st, They are without the
mind, and therefore there can be no union between the
object and the percipient. 2dly, They are disproportioned to the mind, and removed from it by the whole
diameter of being. 3dly, Because, if material objects
were immediate objects of perception, there could be
no physical science; things necessary and immutable

being the only objects of science. 4thly, If material
things were perceived by themselves, they would be a
true light to our minds, as being the intelligible form
of our understandings, and consequently perfective of
them, and indeed superior to them.

Malebranche's system was adopted by many devout
people in France of both sexes; but it seems to have
had no great currency in other countries. Mr. Locke
wrote a small tract against it, which is found among
his posthumous works: but whether it was written
in haste, or after the vigour of his understanding
was impaired by age, there is less of strength and solidity in it, than in most of his writings. The most
formidable antagonist Malebranche met with was in
his own country; Antony Arnauld, doctor of the Sorbonne, and one of the acutest writers the Jansenists
have to boast of, though that sect has produced many.
Those who choose to see this system attacked on the
one hand, and defended on the other, with subtilty of
argument, and elegance of expression, and on the part
of Arnauld with much wit and humour, may find satisfaction by reading Malebranche's Inquiry after Truth;
Arnauld's book of True and False Ideas; Malebranche's
Defence; and some subsequent replies and defences.
In controversies of this kind, the assailant commonly
has the advantage, if they are not unequally matched;
for it is easier to overturn all the theories of philosophers upon this subject, than to defend any one of
them. Mr. Bayle makes a very just remark upon this
controversy, that the arguments of Mr. Arnauld against
the system of Malebranche were often unanswerable,
but they were capable of being retorted against his
own system: and his ingenious antagonist knew well
how to use this defence.

CHAP. VIII.

OF THE COMMON THEORY OF PERCEPTION, AND OF THE
SENTIMENTS OF THE PERIPATETICS, AND
OF DES CARTES.

THIS theory in general is, that we perceive external
objects only by certain images which are in our minds,
or in the sensorium to which the mind is immediately
present.   Philosophers, in different ages, have differed
both in the names they have given to those images, and
in their notions concerning them.   It would be a laborious task to enumerate all their variations, and perhaps would not requite the labour.   I shall only give
a sketch of the principal differences with regard to
their names and their nature.

By Aristotle and the Peripatetics, the images presented to our senses were called *sensible species or
forms ;* those presented to the memory or imagination
were called *phantasms;* and those presented to the
intellect were called *intelligible species ;* and they
thought, that there can be no perception, no imagination, no intellection, without species or phantasms.
What the ancient philosophers called species, sensible
and intelligible, and phantasms, in later times, and especially since the time of Des Cartes, came to be called by the common name of *ideas.*   The Cartesians divided our ideas into three classes, those of *sensation,* of
imagination, and of *pure intellection.*   Of the objects
of sensation and imagination, they thought the images
are in the brain, but of objects that are incorporeal,
the images are in the understanding, or pure intellect.

Mr. Locke, taking the word *idea* in the same sense
as Des Cartes had done before him, to signify whatever
is meant by phantasm, notion, or species, divides ideas

into those of *sensation*, and those of *reflection;* meaning by the first, the ideas of all corporeal objects, whether perceived, remembered, or imagined ; by the second, the ideas of the powers and operations of our minds. What Mr. Locke calls ideas, Mr. Hume divides into two distinct kinds, *impressions* and *ideas*. The difference between these, he says, consists in the degrees of force and liveliness with which they strike upon the mind. Under *impressions* he comprehends all our sensations, passions and emotions, as they make their first appearance in the soul. By *ideas* he means the faint images of these in thinking and reasoning.

Dr. Hartley gives the same meaning to ideas as Mr. Hume does, and what Mr. Hume calls impressions, he calls sensations ; conceiving our sensations to be occasioned by vibrations of the infinitesimal particles of the brain, and ideas by miniature vibrations, or vibratiuncles. Such differences we find among philosophers, with regard to the name of those internal images of objects of sense, which they hold to be the immediate objects of perception.

We shall next give a short detail of the sentiments of the Peripatetics and Cartesians, of Locke, Berkeley, and Hume, concerning them.

Aristotle seems to have thought that the soul consists of two parts, or, rather, that we have two souls, the animal and the rational ; or, as he calls them, the soul and the intellect. To the *first* belong the senses, memory, and imagination ; to the *last*, judgment opinion, belief, and reasoning. The first we have in common with brute animals ; the last is peculiar to man. The animal soul he held to be a certain form of the body, which is inseparable from it, and perishes at death. To this soul the senses belong : and he defines a sense to be that which is capable of receiving the sensible forms, or species of objects, without any of the matter of them; as wax receives the form of the seal without any of the matter of it. The forms of sound, of colour, of taste, and of other sensible qualities, are in like manner received by the senses.

It seems to be a necessary consequence of Aristotle's doctrine, that bodies are constantly sending forth, in all directions, as many different kinds of forms without matter as they have different sensible qualities; for the forms of colour must enter by the eye, the forms of sound by the ear, and so of the other senses. This accordingly was maintained by the followers of Aristotle, though not, as far as I know, expressly mentioned by himself. They disputed concerning the nature of those forms, or species, whether they were real beings or non-entities; and some held them to be of an intermediate nature between the two. The whole doctrine of the Peripatetics and schoolmen concerning forms, substantial and accidental, and concerning the transmission of sensible species from objects of sense to the mind, if it be at all intelligible, is so far above my comprehension, that I should perhaps do it injustice, by entering into it more minutely. Malebranche, in his Recherche de la Verité, has employed a chapter to show, that material objects do not send forth sensible species of their several sensible qualities.

The great revolution which Des Cartes produced in philosophy, was the effect of a superiority of genius, aided by the circumstances of the times. Men had, for more than a thousand years, looked up to Aristotle as an oracle in philosophy. His authority was the test of truth. The small remains of the Platonic system were confined to a few Mystics, whose principles and manner of life drew little attention. The feeble attempts of Ramus, and of some others, to make improvements in the system, had little effect. The Peripatetic doctrines were so interwoven with the whole system of

scholastic theology, that to dissent from Aristotle was
to alarm the church. The most useful and intelligible parts, even of Aristotle's writings, were neglected,
and philosophy was become an art of speaking learned-
ly, and disputing subtilely, without producing any invention of use in human life. It was fruitful of words,
but barren of works, and admirably contrived for drawing a veil over human ignorance, and putting a stop to
the progress of knowledge, by filling men with a conceit that they knew every thing. It was very fruitful
also in controversies ; but for the most part they were
controversies about words, or about things of no moment, or things above the reach of the human faculties :
and the issue of them was what might be expected, that
the contending parties fought, without gaining or losing
an inch of ground, till they were weary of the dispute,
or their attention was called off to some other subject.

Such was the philosophy of the schools of Europe,
during many ages of darkness and barbarism that succeeded the decline of the Roman empire ; so that
there was great need of a reformation in philosophy as
well as in religion. The light began to dawn at last ;
a spirit of inquiry sprang up, and men got the courage
to doubt of the dogmas of Aristotle, as well as of the
decrees of popes. The most important step in the
reformation of religion was to destroy the claim of infallibility, which hindered men from using their judgment in matters of religion : and the most important
step in the reformation of philosophy was to destroy
the authority, of which Aristotle had so long had
peaceable possession. The last had been attempted by
lord Bacon and others, with no less zeal than the first
by Luther and Calvin.

Des Cartes knew well the defects of the prevailing
system, which had begun to lose its authority. His
genius enabled him, and his spirit prompted him, to

attempt a new one. He had applied much to the mathematical sciences, and had made considerable improvement in them. He wished to introduce that perspicuity and evidence into other branches of philosophy which he found in them.

Being sensible how apt we are to be led astray by prejudices of education, he thought the only way to avoid error, was, to resolve to doubt of every thing, and hold every thing to be uncertain ; even those things which he had been taught to hold as most certain, until he had such clear and cogent evidence as compelled his assent.

In this state of universal doubt, that which first appeared to him to be clear and certain, was his own existence. Of this he was certain, because he was conscious that he thought, that he reasoned. and that he doubted. He used this argument, therefore, to prove his own existence, *Cogito, ergo sum.* This he conceived to be the first of all truths, the foundation stone upon which the whole fabric of human knowledge is built, and on which it must rest. And as Archimedes thought, that if he had one fixed point to rest his engines upon, he could move the earth ; so Des Cartes, charmed with the discovery of one certain principle, by which he emerged from the state of universal doubt, believed that this principle alone would be a sufficient foundation on which he might build the whole system of science. He seems therefore to have taken no great trouble to examine whether there might not be other first principles, which, on account of their own light and evidence, ought to be admitted by every man of sound judgment. The love of simplicity, so natural to the mind of man, led him to apply the whole force of his mind to raise the fabric of knowledge upon this one principle, rather than seek a broader foundation.

Accordingly, he does not admit the evidence of sense to be a first principle, as he does that of consciousness.

The arguments of the ancient skeptics here occurred to him ; that our senses often deceive us, and therefore ought never to be trusted on their own authority : that, in sleep, we often seem to see and hear things which we are convinced to have had no existence. But that which chiefly led Des Cartes to think that he ought not to trust to his senses without proof of their veracity, was, that he took it for granted, as all philosophers had done before him, that he did not perceive external objects themselves, but certain images of them in his own mind, called *ideas.* He was certain, by consciousness, that he had the ideas of sun and moon, earth and sea; but how could he be assured that there really existed external objects like to these ideas ?

Hitherto he was uncertain of every thing but of his own existence, and the existence of the operations and ideas of his own mind. Some of his disciples, it is said, remained at this stage of his system, and got the name of Egoists. They could not find evidence in the subsequent stages of his progress. But Des Cartes resolved not to stop here ; he endeavoured to prove, by a new argument, drawn from his idea of a Deity, the existence of an infinitely perfect Being, who made him, and all his faculties. From the perfection of this Being, he inferred that he could be no deceiver ; and therefore concluded, that his senses, and the other faculties he found in himself, are not fallacious, but may be trusted, when a proper use is made of them.

The system of Des Cartes is, with great perspicuity and acuteness, explained by himself in his writings, which ought to be consulted by those who would understand it.

The merit of Des Cartes cannot be easily conceived by those who have not some notion of the Peripatetic system, in which he was educated. To throw off the prejudices of education, and to create a system of na-

ture, totally different from that which had subdued
the understanding of mankind, and kept it in subjec-
tion for so many centuries, required an uncommon force
of mind.

The world which Des Cartes exhibits to our view,
is not only in its structure very different from that of
the Peripatetics, but is, as we may say, composed of different materials.

In the old system, every thing was, by a kind of
metaphysical sublimation, resolved into principles so
mysterious, that it may be a question, whether they
were words without meaning, or were notions too refined for human understanding.

All that we observe in nature, is, according to Aristotle, a constant succession of the operations of generation and corruption.   The principles of generation are
matter and form ; the principle of corruption is privation.   All natural things are produced or generated
by the union of matter and form; matter being, as it
were, the mother, and form the father.   As to matter,
or the first matter, as it is called, it is neither substance
nor accident; it has no quality nor property ; it is nothing actually, but every thing potentially.   It has so
strong an appetite for form, that it is no sooner divest-
ed of one form, than it is clothed with another, and is
equally susceptible of all forms successively.   It has
no nature, but only the capacity of having any one.

This is the account which the Peripatetics give of
the first matter.   The other principle of generation is
form, act, perfection ; for these three words signify the
same thing.   But we must not conceive form to consist
in the figure, size, arrangement, or motion, of the
parts of matter.   These, indeed, are accidental forms,
by which things artificial are formed : but every production of nature has a substantial form, which, joined
to matter, makes it to be what it is.   The substantial
form is a kind of informing soul, which gives the thing

its specific nature, and all its qualities, powers, and activity. Thus the substantial form of heavy bodies, is that which makes them descend ; of light bodies, that which makes them ascend. The substantial form of gold, is that which gives it its ductility, its fusibility, its weight, its colour, and all its qualities; and the same is to be understood of every natural production. A change in the accidental form of any body, is alteration only ; but a change in the substantial form, is generation and corruption : it is corruption, with respect to the substantial form of which the body is deprived : it is generation, with respect to the substantial form that succeeds. Thus, when a horse dies, and turns to dust, the philosophical account of the phenomenon is this : a certain portion of the *materia prima*, which was joined to the substantial form of a horse, is deprived of it by privation, and in the same instant, is invested with the substantial form of earth. As every substance must have a substantial form, there are some of those forms inanimate, some vegetative, some animal, and some rational. The three former kinds can only subsist in matter ; but the last, according to the schoolmen, is immediately created by God, and infused into the body, making one substance with it, while they are united ; yet capable of being disjoined from the body, and of subsisting by itself.

Such are the principles of natural things in the Peripatetic system. It retains so much of the ancient Pythagorean doctrine, that we cannot ascribe the invention of it solely to Aristotle ; although he, no doubt, made considerable alterations in it. The first matter was probably the same in both systems, and was in both held to be eternal. They differed more about form. The Pythagoreans and Platonists held forms, or ideas, as they called them, to be eternal, immutable, and self existent. Aristotle maintained, that they were not

eternal, nor self existent. On the other hand, he did
not allow them to be produced, but educed from matter; yet he held them not to be actually in the matter
from which they are educed, but potentially only.
But these two systems differed less from one another,
than that of Des Cartes did from both.

In the world of Des Cartes, we meet with two kinds
of beings only, to wit, body and mind ; the first, the
object of our senses, the other of consciousness ; both
of them things of which we have a distinct apprehension,
if the human mind be capable of distinct apprehension
at all.   To the first, no qualities are ascribed but
extension, figure, and motion ; to the last, nothing but
thought, and its various modifications, of which we
are conscious.   He could observe no common attribute,
no resembling feature in the attributes of body and
mind, and therefore concluded them to be distinct substances, and totally of a different nature ; and that
body, from its very nature, is inanimate and inert, incapable of any kind of thought or sensation, or of producing any change or alteration in itself.

Des Cartes must be allowed the honour of being the
first who drew a distinct line between the material and
intellectual world, which, in all the old systems, were
so blended together, that it was impossible to say
where the one ends, and the other begins.   How much
this distinction has contributed to the improvements
of modern times, in the philosophy both of body and
of mind, is not easy to say.

One obvious consequence of this distinction, was,
that accurate reflection on the operations of our own
mind, is the only way to make any progress in the
knowledge of it.   Malebranche, Locke, Berkeley, and
Hume, were taught this lesson by Des Cartes ; and to
it we owe their most valuable discoveries in this branch
of philosophy.   The analogical way of reasoning con-

cerning the powers of the mind from the properties of
body, which is the source of almost all the errors on
this subject, and which is so natural to the bulk of
mankind, was as contrary to the principles of Des
Cartes, as it was agreeable to the principles of the
old philosophy. We may, therefore, truly say, that in
that part of philosophy which relates to the mind, Des
Cartes laid the foundation, and put us into that track,
which all wise men now acknowledge to be the only
one in which we can expect success.

With regard to physics, or the philosophy of body,
if Des Cartes had not the merit of leading men into
the right track, we must allow him that of bringing
them out of a wrong one. The Peripatetics, by as-
signing to every species of body a particular substantial form, which produces, in an unknown manner, all
the effects we observe in it, put a stop to all improvement in this branch of philosophy. Gravity and levi-
ty, fluidity and hardness, heat and cold, were qualities
arising from the substantial form of the bodies to
which they belonged. Generation and corruption,
substantial forms, and occult qualities, were always
at hand, to resolve every phenomenon. This philosophy, therefore, instead of accounting for any of the
phenomena of nature, contrived only to give learned
names to their unknown causes, and fed men with the
husks of barbarous terms, instead of the fruit of real
knowledge.

By the spreading of the Cartesian system, *materia
prima*, substantial forms, and occult qualities, with all
the jargon of the Aristotelian physics, fell into utter
disgrace, and were never mentioned by the followers of
the new system, but as a subject of ridicule. Men became sensible that their understanding had been hood-
winked by those hard terms. They were now accustomed to explain the phenomena of nature, by the

figure, size, and motion of the particles of matter, things perfectly level to human understanding, and could relish nothing in philosophy that was dark and unintelligible. Aristotle, after a reign of more than a thousand years, was now exposed as an object of derision even to the vulgar, arrayed in the mock majesty of his substantial forms and occult qualities. The ladies became fond of a philosophy which was easily learned, and required no words too harsh for their delicate organs. Queens and princesses, the most distinguished personages of the age, courted the conversation of Des Cartes, and became adepts in his philosophy. Witness Christina, Queen of Sweden, and Elisabeth, daughter of Frederick, king of Bohemia, and sister to Sophia, the mother of our royal family. The last, though very young, when Des Cartes wrote his Principia, he declares to be the only person he knew, who perfectly understood, not only all his philosophical writings, but the most abstruse of his mathematical works.

That men should rush with violence from one extreme, without going more or less into the contrary extreme, is not to be expected from the weakness of human nature. Des Cartes and his followers were not exempted from this weakness ; they thought that extension, figure, and motion, were sufficient to resolve all the phenomena of the material system. To admit other qualities, whose cause is unknown, was to return to Egypt, from which they had been so happily delivered.

When sir Isaac Newton's doctrine of gravitation was published, the great objection to it, which hindered its general reception in Europe for half a century, was, that gravitation seemed to be an occult quality, as it could not be accounted for by extension, figure, and motion, the known attributes of body. They who defended him, found it difficult to answer this objection, to

the satisfaction of those who had been initiated in the
principles of the Cartesian system.   But, by degrees,
men came to be sensible, that, in revolting from Aristotle, the Cartesians had gone into the opposite extreme ; experience convinced them, that there are
qualities in the material world, whose existence is certain, though their cause be occult.   To acknowledge
this, is only a candid confession of human ignorance, than
which there is nothing more becoming a philosopher.

As all that we can know of the mind must be derived
from a careful observation of its operations in ourselves ;
so all that we can know of the material system must
be derived from what can be discovered by our senses.
Des Cartes was not ignorant of this ; nor was his system so unfriendly to observation and experiment as the
old system was.   He made many experiments, and
called earnestly upon all lovers of truth to aid him in
this way.   But, believing that all the phenomena of
the material world are the result of extension, figure,
and motion, and that the Deity always combines these,
so as to produce the phenomena in the simplest manner
possible, he thought, that, from a few experiments, he
might be able to discover the simplest way, in which
the obvious phenomena of nature can be produced, by
matter and motion only ; and that this must be the
way in which they are actually produced.   His conjectures were ingenious, upon the principles he had
adopted : but they are found to be so far from the
truth, that they ought for ever to discourage philosophers from trusting to conjecture in the operations of
nature.

The vortices or whirlpools of subtile matter, by
which Des Cartes endeavoured to account for the phenomena of the material world, are now found to be fictions, no less than the sensible species of Aristotle.

It was reserved for sir Isaac Newton to point out clearly the road to the knowledge of nature's works. Taught by lord Bacon to despise hypotheses as the fictions of human fancy, he laid it down as a rule of philosophizing, that no causes of natural things ought to be assigned but such as can be proved to have a real existence. He saw, that all the length men can go in accounting for phenomena, is to discover the laws of nature, according to which they are produced; and therefore, that the true method of philosophizing is this. from real facts ascertained by observation and experiment, to collect by just induction the laws of nature, and to apply the laws so discovered, to account for the phenomena of nature.

Thus the natural philosopher has the rules of his art fixed with no less precision than the mathematician, and may be no less certain when he keeps within them and when he deviates from them : and though the evidence of a law of nature from induction is not demonstrative, it is the only kind of evidence on which all the most important affairs of human life must rest.

Pursuing this road without deviation. Newton discovered the laws of our planetary system, and of the rays of light; and gave the first and the noblest examples of that chaste induction, which lord Bacon could only delineate in theory.

How strange is it, that the human mind should have wandered for so many ages, without falling into this track! How much more strange, that after it has been clearly discovered, and a happy progress made in it, many choose rather to wander in the fairy regions of hypothesis!

To return to Des Cartes's notions of the manner of our perceiving external objects, from which a concern to do justice to the merits of that great reformer in philosophy has led me to digress, he took it for granted, as the old philosophers had done, that what we immediately perceive must be either in the mind itself, or in the brain, to which the mind is immediately present. The impressions made upon our organs, nerves, and brain, could be nothing, according to his philosophy, but various modifications of extension, figure, and motion. There could be nothing in the brain like sound or colour, taste or smell, heat or cold; these are sensations in the mind, which, by the laws of the union of soul and body, are raised on occasion of certain traces in the brain; and although he gives the name of ideas to those traces in the brain, he does not think it necessary that they should be perfectly like to the things which they represent, any more than that words or signs should resemble the things they signify. But, says he, that we may follow the received opinion as far as is possible, we may allow a slight resemblance. Thus we know, that a print in a book may represent houses, temples, and groves; and so far is it from being necessary that the print should be perfectly like the thing it represents, that its perfection often requires the contrary: for a circle must often be represented by an ellipse, a square by a rhombus, and so of other things.

The perceptions of sense, he thought, are to be referred solely to the union of soul and body. They commonly exhibit to us only what may hurt or profit our bodies; and rarely, and by accident only, exhibit things as they are in themselves. It is by observing this, that we must learn to throw off the prejudices of sense, and to attend with our intellect to the ideas which are by nature implanted in it. By this means we shall understand, that the nature of matter does not consist in those things that affect our senses, such as colour, or smell, or taste; but only in this, that it is something extended in length, breadth, and depth.

The writings of Des Cartes have in general a remarkable degree of perspicuity; and he undoubtedly intended that, in this particular, his philosophy should be a
perfect contrast to that of Aristotle; yet, in what he
has said in different parts of his writings, of our perception of external objects, there seems to be some obscurity, and even inconsistency; whether owing to his
having had different opinions on the subject at different
times, or to the difficulty he found in it, I will not pretend to say.

There are two points in particular, wherein I cannot
reconcile him to himself: the *first*, regarding the
place of the ideas or images of external objects, which
are the immediate objects of perception; the *second*,
with regard to the veracity of our external senses.

As to the *first*, he sometimes places the ideas of material objects in the brain, not only when they are perceived, but when they are remembered or imagined;
and this has always been held to be the Cartesian doctrine; yet he sometimes says, that we are not to conceive the images or traces in the brain to be perceived
as if there were eyes in the brain; these traces are
only occasions on which, by the laws of the union of
soul and body, ideas are excited in the mind; and therefore it is not necessary that there should be an exact
resemblance between the traces and the things represented by them, any more than that words or signs
should be exactly like the things signified by them.

These two opinions, I think, cannot be reconciled.
For if the images or traces in the brain are perceived,
they must be the objects of perception, and not the
occasions of it only. On the other hand, if they are
only the occasions of our perceiving, they are not perceived at all. Des Cartes seems to have hesitated between the two opinions, or to have passed from the one
to the other. Mr. Locke seems, in like manner, to

have wavered between the two; sometimes representing the ideas of material things as being in the brain, but more frequently as in the mind itself. Neither Des Cartes nor Mr. Locke could, consistently with themselves, attribute any other qualities to images in the brain, but extension, figure, and motion; for as to those qualities which Mr. Locke distinguished by the name of secondary qualities, both philosophers believed them not to belong to body at all, and therefore could not ascribe them to images in the brain.

Sir Isaac Newton and Dr. Samuel Clarke, uniformly speak of the species or images of material things as being in that part of the brain called the *sensorium*, and perceived by the mind there present; but the former speaks of this point only incidentally, and with his usual modesty, in the form of a query. Malebranche is perfectly clear and unambiguous in this matter. According to his system, the images or traces in the brain are not perceived at all; they are only occasions upon which, by the laws of nature, certain sensations are felt by us, and certain of the Divine ideas discovered to our minds.

The *second* point on which Des Cartes seems to waver, is with regard to the credit that is due to the testimony of our senses.

Sometimes, from the perfection of the Deity, and his being no deceiver, he infers, that our senses and our other faculties cannot be fallacious : and since we seem clearly to perceive, that the idea of matter comes to us from things external, which it perfectly resembles, therefore, we must conclude, that there really exists something extended in length, breadth, and depth, having all the properties which we clearly perceive to belong to an extended thing.

At other times, we find Des Cartes and his followers making frequent complaints, as all the ancient philosophers did, of the fallacies of sense. He warns us to throw off its prejudices, and to attend only, with our intellect, to the ideas implanted there. By this means we may perceive, that the nature of matter does not consist in hardness, colour, weight, or any of those things that affect our senses, but in this only, that it is something extended in length, breadth, and depth. The senses, he says, are only relative to our present state; they exhibit things only, as they tend to profit or to hurt us, and rarely, and by accident only, as they are in themselves.

It was probably owing to an aversion to admit any thing into philosophy, of which we have not a clear and distinct conception, that Des Cartes was led to deny, that there is any substance of matter, distinct from those qualities of it which we perceive. We say, that matter is something extended, figured, moveable. Extension, figure, mobility, therefore, are not matter, but qualities, belonging to this something, which we call *matter*. Des Cartes could not relish this obscure *something*, which is supposed to be the subject or *substratum* of those qualities; and therefore maintained that extension is the very essence of matter. But, as we must ascribe extension to space as well as to matter, he found himself under a necessity of holding, that space and matter are the same thing, and differ only in our way of conceiving them; so that, wherever there is space there is matter, and no void left in the universe. The necessary consequence of this is, that the material world has no bounds nor limits. He did not, however, choose to call it infinite, but indefinite.

It was probably owing to the same cause that Des Cartes made the essence of the soul to consist in thought. He would not allow it to be an unknown something that has the power of thinking; it cannot therefore be without thought: and as he conceived there can be no

thought without ideas, the soul must have had ideas
in its first formation, which, of consequence, are innate.

The sentiments of those who come after Des Cartes,
with regard to the nature of body and mind, have been
various.   Many have maintained, that body is only a
collection of qualities to which we give one name; and
that the notion of a subject of inhesion, to which those
qualities belong, is only a fiction of the mind.   Some
have even maintained, that the soul is only a succession
of related ideas, without any subject of inhesion.   It
appears, by what has been said, how far these notions
are allied to the Cartesian system.

The triumph of the Cartesian system over that of
Aristotle, is one of the most remarkable revolutions in
the history of philosophy, and has led me to dwell longer upon it than the present subject perhaps required.
The authority of Aristotle was now no more.   That
reverence for hard words and dark notions, by which
men's understanding had been strangled in early years,
was turned into contempt, and every thing suspected
which was not clearly and distinctly understood.   This
is the spirit of the Cartesian philosophy, and is a more
important acquisition to mankind than any of its particular tenets ; and for exerting this spirit so zealously,
and spreading it so successfully, Des Cartes deserves
immortal honour.

It is to be observed, however, that Des Cartes rejected a part only of the ancient theory, concerning the perception of external objects by the senses, and that he
adopted the other part.   That theory may be divided
into two parts : the *first*, that images, species, or forms
of external objects, come from the object, and enter by
the avenues of the senses to the mind ; the *second* part
is, that the external object itself is not perceived, but
only the species or image of it in the mind.   The first

part Des Cartes and his followers rejected, and refuted
by solid arguments; but the second part neither he
nor his followers have thought of calling in question;
being persuaded that it is only a representative image,
in the mind, of the external object that we perceive,
and not the object itself. And this image, which the
Peripatetics called a species, he calls an idea, changing
the name only, while he admits the thing.

It seems strange, that the great pains which this
philosopher took to throw off the prejudices of education, to dismiss all his former opinions, and to assent
to nothing, till he found evidence that compelled his
assent, should not have led him to doubt of this opinion
of the ancient philosophy. It is evidently a philosophical
opinion; for the vulgar undoubtedly believe that it is
the external object which we immediately perceive, and
not a representative image of it only. It is for this
reason that they look upon it as a perfect lunacy to
call in question the existence of external objects.

It seems to be admitted as a first principle by the
learned and the unlearned, that what is really perceived must exist, and that to perceive what does not exist
is impossible. So far the unlearned man and the philosopher agree. The unlearned man says, I perceive the
external object, and I perceive it to exist. Nothing
can be more absurd than to doubt of it. The Peripatetic says, What I perceive is the very identical form
of the object, which came immediately from the object,
and makes an impression upon my mind, as a seal does
upon wax; and therefore I can have no doubt of the
existence of an object whose form I perceive. But
what says the Cartesian? I perceive not, says he, the
external object itself. So far he agrees with the Peripatetic, and differs from the unlearned man. But I perceive an image, or form, or idea, in my own mind, or
in my brain. I am certain of the existence of the idea,
because I immediately perceive it. But how this idea

is formed, or what it represents, is not self evident; and therefore I must find arguments, by which, from the existence of the idea which I perceive, I can infer the existence of an external object which it represents.

As I take this to be a just view of the principles of the unlearned man, of the Peripatetic, and of the Cartesian, so I think they all reason consequently from their several principles; that the Cartesian has strong grounds to doubt of the existence of external objects; the Peripatetic very little ground of doubt; and the unlearned man none at all: and that the difference of their situation arises from this, that the unlearned man has no hypothesis; the Peripatetic leans upon an hypothesis; and the Cartesian upon one half of that hypothesis.

Des Cartes, according to the spirit of his own philosophy, ought to have doubted of both parts of the Peripatetic hypothesis, or to have given his reasons why he adopted one part, as well as why he rejected the other part; especially since the unlearned, who have the faculty of perceiving objects by their senses in no less perfection than philosophers, and should therefore know as well as they what it is they perceive, have been unanimous in this, that the objects they perceive are not ideas in their own minds, but things external. It might have been expected, that a philosopher who was so cautious as not to take his own existence for granted without proof, would not have taken it for granted, without proof, that every thing he perceived was only ideas in his own mind.

But if Des Cartes made a rash step in this, as I apprehend he did, he ought not to bear the blame alone. His successors have still continued in the same track, and, after his example, have adopted one part of the ancient theory, to wit, that the objects we immediately perceive are ideas only. All their systems are built on this foundation.

CHAP. IX.

OF THE SENTIMENTS OF MR. LOCKE.

THE reputation which Locke's Essay on Human Understanding had at home from the beginning, and which it has gradually acquired abroad, is a sufficient testimony of its merit. There is perhaps no book of the metaphysical kind that has been so generally read by those who understand the language, or that is more adapted to teach men to think with precision, and to inspire them with that candour and love of truth, which is the genuine spirit of philosophy. He gave, I believe, the first example in the English language of writing on such abstract subjects, with a remarkable degree of simplicity and perspicuity; and in this he has been happily imitated by others that came after him. No author has more successfully pointed out the danger of ambiguous words, and the importance of having distinct and determinate notions in judging and reasoning. His observations on the various powers of the human understanding, on the use and abuse of words, and on the extent and limits of human knowledge, are drawn from attentive reflection on the operations of his own mind, the true source of all real knowledge on these subjects; and show an uncommon degree of penetration and judgment: but he needs no panegyric of mine; and I mention these things, only that when I have occasion to differ from him, I may not be thought insensible of the merit of an author whom I highly respect, and to whom I owe my first lights in those studies, as well as my attachment to them.

He sets out in his Essay with a full conviction, common to him with other philosophers, that ideas in the

mind are the objects of all our thoughts in every operation of the understanding. This leads him to use
the word *idea* so very frequently, beyond what was usual
in the English language, that he thought it necessary
in his introduction to make this apology : " It being
that term, says he, which, I think, serves best to stand
for whatsoever is the object of understanding, when a
man thinks ; I have used it to express whatever is
meant by phantasm, notion, species, or whatever it is
which the mind can be employed about in thinking ; and
I could not avoid frequently using it. I presume it
will be granted me, that there are such ideas in men's
minds ; every man is conscious of them in himself ; and
men's words and actions will satisfy him that they are
in others."

Speaking of the reality of our knowledge, he says,
" It is evident the mind knows not things immediately,
but only by the intervention of the ideas it has of them.
Our knowledge therefore is real, only so far as there
is a conformity between our ideas and the reality of
things. But what shall be here the criterion ? How
shall the mind, when it perceives nothing but its own
ideas, know that they agree with things themselves ?
This, though it seems not to want difficulty, yet I
think there are two sorts of ideas that we may be assured agree with things."

We see that Mr. Locke was aware no less than Des
Cartes, that the doctrine of ideas made it necessary,
and at the same time difficult, to prove the existence
of a material world without us ; because the mind, according to that doctrine, perceives nothing but a world
of ideas in itself. Not only Des Cartes, but Malebranche, Arnauld, and Norris, had perceived this difficulty, and attempted to remove it with little success.
Mr. Locke attempts the same thing ; but his arguments are feeble. He even seems to be conscious of

this : for he concludes his reasoning with this observation, " That we have evidence sufficient to direct us in
attaining the good and avoiding the evil, caused by external objects, and that this is the important concern
we have in being made acquainted with them." This
indeed is saying no more than will be granted by those
who deny the existence of a material world.

As there is no material difference between Locke and
Des Cartes with regard to the perception of objects by
the senses, there is the less occasion, in this place, to
take notice of all their differences in other points.
They differed about the origin of our ideas. Des Cartes thought some of them were innate : the other maintained, that there are no innate ideas, and that they are
all derived from two sources, to wit, *sensation* and *reflection ;* meaning by sensation, the operations of our
external senses ; and by reflection, that attention
which we are capable of giving to the operations of our
own minds.

They differed with regard to the essence both of
matter and of mind. The British philosopher holding
that the real essence of both is beyond the reach of human knowledge ; the other conceiving, that the very
essence of mind consists in thought ; and that of matter in extension ; by which he made matter and space
not to differ in reality, and no part of space to be void
of matter.

Mr. Locke explained more distinctly than had been
done before, the operations of the mind in classing the
various objects of thought, and reducing them to genera and species. He was the first, I think, who distinguished in substances what he calls the nominal essence,
which is only the notion we form of a genus or species,
and which we express by a definition, from the real essence or internal constitution of the thing, which makes
it to be what it is. Without this distinction, the sub-

tile disputes which tortured the schoolmen for so many ages, in the controversy between the nominalists and realists, could never be brought to an issue. He shows distinctly how we form abstract and general notions, and the use and necessity of them in reasoning. And as, according to the received principles of philosophers, every notion of our mind must have for its object an idea in the mind itself; he thinks that we form abstract ideas by leaving out of the idea of an individual every thing wherein it differs from other individuals of the same species or genus ; and that this power of forming abstract ideas is that which chiefly distinguishes us from brute animals, in whom he could see no evidence of any abstract ideas.

Since the time of Des Cartes, philosophers have differed much with regard to the share they ascribe to the mind itself, in the fabrication of those representative beings called *ideas,* and the manner in which this work is carried on.

Of the authors I have met with, Dr. Robert Hook is the most explicit. He was one of the most ingenious and active members of the Royal Society of London at its first institution ; and frequently read lectures to the Society, which were published among his posthumous works. In his lectures upon Light, sect. 7. he makes ideas to be material substances, and thinks that the brain is furnished with a proper kind of matter for fabricating the ideas of each sense. The ideas of sight, he thinks, are formed of a kind of matter resembling the Bononian stone, or some kind of phosphorus ; that the ideas of sound are formed of some matter resembling the chords or glasses which take a sound from the vibrations of the air ; and so of the rest.

The soul, he thinks, may fabricate some hundreds of those ideas in a day ; and that as they are formed they are pushed further off from the centre of the brain where the soul resides. By this means they make a continued chain of ideas, coiled up in the brain, the first end of which is furthest removed from the centre or seat of the soul; and the other end is always at the centre, being the last idea formed, which is always present the moment when considered; and therefore, according as there is a greater number of ideas between the present sensation or thought in the centre and any other, the soul is apprehensive of a larger portion of time interposed.

Mr. Locke has not entered into so minute a detail of this manufacture of ideas; but he ascribes to the mind a very considerable hand in forming its own ideas. With regard to our sensations, the mind is passive, "they being produced in us, only by different degrees and modes of motion in our animal spirits, variously agitated by external objects." These, however, cease to be, as soon as they cease to be perceived; "but, by the faculties of memory and imagination, the mind has an ability, when it wills, to revive them again, and, as it were, to paint them anew upon itself, though some with more, some with less difficulty."

As to the ideas of reflection, he ascribes them to no other cause but to that attention which the mind is capable of giving to its own operations. These, therefore, are formed by the mind itself. He ascribes likewise to the mind the power of compounding its simple ideas into complex ones of various forms; of repeating them, and adding the repetitions together; of dividing and classing them; of comparing them, and, from that comparison, of forming the ideas of their relation; nay, of forming a general idea of a species or genus, by taking from the idea of an individual every thing by which it is distinguished from other individuals of the kind, till at last it becomes an abstract general idea, common to all the individuals of the kind.

These, I think, are the powers which Mr. Locke ascribes to the mind itself in the fabrication of its ideas. Bishop Berkeley, as we shall see afterward, abridged them considerably, and Mr. Hume much more.

The ideas we have of the various qualities of bodies are not all, as Mr. Locke thinks, of the same kind. Some of them are images or resemblances of what is really in the body ; others are not. There are certain qualities inseparable from matter ; such as extension, solidity, figure, mobility. Our ideas of these are real resemblances of the qualities in the body ; and these he calls primary qualities ; but colour, sound, taste, smell, heat and cold, he calls secondary qualities, and thinks that they are only powers in bodies of producing certain sensations in us ; which sensations have nothing resembling them, though they are commonly thought to be exact resemblances of something in the body. "Thus, says he, the idea of heat or light, which we receive by our eye or touch from the sun, are commonly thought real qualities existing in the sun, and something more than mere powers in it."

The names of primary and secondary qualities, were, I believe, first used by Mr. Locke ; but the distinction, which they express, was well understood by Des Cartes, and is explained by him in his Principia, part 1. sect. 69, 70, 71.

Although no author has more merit than Mr. Locke in pointing out the ambiguity of words, and resolving by that means many knotty questions, which had tortured the wits of the schoolmen ; yet, I apprehend he has been sometimes misled by the ambiguity of the word *idea*, which he uses so often almost in every page of his Essay.

In the explication given of this word, we took notice of two meanings given to it ; a popular and a philosophical. In the popular meaning, to have an idea of any thing, signifies nothing more than to think of it.

Although the operations of the mind are most properly and naturally, and indeed most commonly in all vulgar languages, expressed by active verbs, there is another way of expressing them less common, but equally well understood. To think of a thing, and to have a thought of it; to believe a thing, and to have a belief of it; to see a thing, and have a sight of it; to conceive a thing, and to have a conception, notion, or idea of it, are phrases perfectly synonymous. In these phrases the thought means nothing but the act of thinking; the belief, the act of believing; and the conception, notion, or idea, the act of conceiving. To have a clear and distinct idea, is, in this sense, nothing else but to conceive the thing clearly and distinctly. When the word *idea* is taken in this popular sense, there can be no doubt of our having ideas in our minds. To think without ideas would be to think without thought, which is a manifest contradiction.

But there is another meaning of the word *idea* peculiar to philosophers, and grounded upon a philosophical theory, which the vulgar never think of. Philosophers, ancient and modern, have maintained, that the operations of the mind, like the tools of an artificer, can only be employed upon objects that are present in the mind, or in the brain, where the mind is supposed to reside. Therefore, objects that are distant, in time or place, must have a representative in the mind, or in the brain; some image or picture of them, which is the object that the mind contemplates. This representative image was, in the old philosophy, called a *species* or *phantasm*. Since the time of Des Cartes, it has more commonly been called an *idea;* and every thought is conceived to have an idea for its object. As this has been a common opinion among philosophers, as far back as we can trace philosophy, it is the less to be wondered at, that they should be apt to confound the operation of the mind in thinking, with the idea or object of thought, which is supposed to be its inseparable concomitant.

If we pay any regard to the common sense of mankind, thought and the object of thought are different things, and ought to be distinguished. It is true, thought cannot be without an object, for every man who thinks must think of something; but the object he thinks of is one thing, his thought of that object is another thing. They are distinguished in all languages even by the vulgar; and many things may be affirmed of thought, that is, of the operation of the mind in thinking, which cannot without error, and even absurdity, be affirmed of the object of that operation.

From this, I think it is evident, that if the word *idea* in a work where it occurs in every paragraph, be used without any intimation of the ambiguity of the word, sometimes to signify thought, or the operation of the mind in thinking, sometimes to signify those internal objects of thought which philosophers suppose, this must occasion confusion in the thoughts both of the author and of the readers. I take this to be the greatest blemish in the Essay on Human Understanding, I apprehend this is the true source of several paradoxical opinions in that excellent work, which I shall have occasion to take notice of.

Here it is very natural to ask, Whether it was Mr. Locke's opinion, that ideas are the only objects of thought? or, Whether it is not possible for men to think of things which are not ideas in the mind?

To this question it is not easy to give a direct answer. On the one hand, he says often, in distinct and studied expressions, that the term *idea* stands for whatever is the object of the understanding when a man thinks, or whatever it is which the mind can be employed about in thinking: that the mind perceives nothing but its own ideas: that all knowledge consists in the perception of the agreement or disagreement of our ideas : that we can have no knowledge further than we have ideas. These, and many other expressions of the like import, evidently imply, that every object of thought must be an idea, and can be nothing else.

On the other hand, I am persuaded that Mr. Locke would have acknowledged, that we may think of Alexander the Great, or of the planet Jupiter, and of numberless things, which he would have owned are not ideas in the mind, but objects which exist independent of the mind that thinks of them.

How shall we reconcile the two parts of this apparent contradiction ? All I am able to say upon Mr. Locke's principles to reconcile them, is this, That we cannot think of Alexander, or of the planet Jupiter, unless we have in our minds an idea, that is, an image or picture of those objects. The idea of Alexander is an image, or picture, or representation of that hero in my mind ; and this idea is the immediate object of my thought when I think of Alexander. That this was Locke's opinion, and that it has been generally the opinion of philosophers, there can be no doubt.

But, instead of giving light to the question proposed, it seems to involve it in greater darkness.

When I think of Alexander, I am told there is an image or idea of Alexander in my mind, which is the immediate object of this thought. The necessary consequence of this seems to be, that there are two objects of this thought ; the idea, which is in the mind, and the person represented by that idea ; the first, the immediate object of the thought, the last, the object of the same thought, but not the immediate object. This is a hard saying ; for it makes every thought of things external to have a double object. Every man is conscious of his thoughts, and yet, upon attentive

reflection, he perceives no such duplicity in the object he
thinks about. Sometimes men see objects double, but
they always know when they do so : and I know of no
philosopher who has expressly owned this duplicity in
the object of thought, though it follows necessarily
from maintaining, that, in the same thought, there is
one object that is immediate and in the mind itself ;
and another object, which is not immediate, and which
is not in the mind.

Besides this, it seems very hard, or rather impossible, to understand what is meant by an object of thought,
that is not an immediate object of thought. A body
in motion may move another that was at rest, by the
medium of a third body that is interposed. This is
easily understood ; but we are unable to conceive any
medium interposed between a mind and the thought of
that mind ; and, to think of any object by a medium,
seems to be words without any meaning. There is a
sense in which a thing may be said to be perceived by a
medium. Thus, any kind of sign may be said to be the
medium by which I perceive or understand the thing
signified. The sign by custom, or compact, or perhaps
by nature, introduces the thought of the thing signified. But here the thing signified, when it is introduced to the thought, is an object of thought no less
immediate than the sign was before : and there are
here two objects of thought, one succeeding another,
which we have shown is not the case with respect to an
idea, and the object it represents.

I apprehend, therefore, that if philosophers will
maintain, that ideas in the mind are the only immediate objects of thought, they will be forced to grant that
they are the sole objects of thought, and that it is impossible for men to think of any thing else. Yet, surely
Mr. Locke believed that we can think of many things
that are not ideas in the mind ; but he seems not to have

perceived, that the maintaining that ideas in the mind are the only immediate objects of thought, must necessarily draw this consequence along with it.

The consequence, however, was seen by bishop Berkeley and Mr. Hume, who rather chose to admit the consequence than to give up the principle from which it follows.

Perhaps it was unfortunate for Mr. Locke, that he used the word *idea* so very frequently, as to make it very difficult to give the attention necessary to put it always to the same meaning. And it appears evident, that, in many places, he means nothing more by it but the notion or conception we have of any object of thought ; that is, the act of the mind, in conceiving it, and not the object conceived.

In explaining this word, he says, that he uses it for whatever is meant by phantasm, notion, species. Here are three synonymes to the word *idea.* The first and last are very proper to express the philosophical meaning of the word, being terms of art in the Peripatetic philosophy, and signifying images of external things in the mind, which, according to that philosophy, are objects of thought. But the word *notion* is a word in common language, whose meaning agrees exactly with the popular meaning of the word *idea,* but not with the philosophical.

When these two different meanings of the word *idea* are confounded in a studied explication of it, there is little reason to expect that they should be carefully distinguished in the frequent use of it. There are many passages in the Essay, in which, to make them intelligible, the word *idea* must be taken in one of those senses, and many others, in which it must be taken in the other. It seems probable, that the author, not attending to this ambiguity of the word, used it in the one sense or the other, as the subject matter required ; and the far greater part of his readers have done the same.

There is a third sense, in which he uses the word not unfrequently, to signify objects of thought that are not in the mind, but external. Of this he seems to be sensible, and somewhere makes an apology for it. When he affirms, as he does in innumerable places, that all human knowledge consists in the perception of the agreement or disagreement of our ideas, it is impossible to put a meaning upon this, consistent with his principles, unless he means by *ideas* every object of human thought, whether mediate or immediate ; every thing, in a word, that can be signified by the subject, or by the predicate of a proposition.

Thus we see, that the word *idea* has three different meanings in the Essay ; and the author seems to have used it sometimes in one, sometimes in another, without being aware of any change in the meaning. The reader slides easily into the same fallacy, that meaning occurring most readily to his mind which gives the best sense to what he reads. I have met with persons professing no slight acquaintance with the Essay on Human Understanding, who maintained, that the word *idea*, wherever it occurs, means nothing more than thought ; and that where he speaks of ideas as images in the mind, and as objects of thought, he is not to be understood as speaking properly, but figuratively or analogically . and indeed I apprehend, that it would be no small advantage to many passages in the book, if they could admit of this interpretation.

It is not the fault of this philosopher alone to have given too little attention to the distinction between the operations of the mind and the objects of those operations. Although this distinction be familiar to the vulgar, and found in the structure of all languages, philosophers, when they speak of ideas, often confound the

two together ; and their theory concerning ideas has
led them to do so : for ideas being supposed to be a
shadowy kind of beings, intermediate between the
thought, and the object of thought, sometimes seem to
coalesce with the thought, sometimes with the object
of thought, and sometimes to have a distinct existence
of their own.

The same philosophical theory of ideas has led philosophers to confound the different operations of the understanding, and to call them all by the name of perception. Mr. Locke, though not free from this fault,
is not so often chargeable with it, as some who came
after him. The vulgar give the name of perception to
that immediate knowledge of external objects which
we have by our external senses. This is its proper
meaning in our language, though sometimes it may be
applied to other things metaphorically, or analogically. When I think of any thing that does not exist, as
of the republic of Oceana, I do not perceive it ; I only
conceive, or imagine it. When I think of what happened to me yesterday, I do not perceive, but remember it. When I am pained with the gout, it is not proper to say, I perceive the pain ; I feel it, or am conscious of it : it is not an object of perception, but of
sensation, and of consciousness. So far the vulgar distinguish very properly the different operations of the
mind, and never confound the names of things so different in their nature : but the theory of ideas leads philosophers to conceive all those operations to be of one
nature, and to give them one name. They are all, according to that theory, the perception of ideas in the
mind. Perceiving, remembering, imagining, being conscious, are all perceiving ideas in the mind, and are
called *perceptions.* Hence it is that philosophers speak
of the perceptions of memory, and the perceptions of
imagination. They make sensation to be a perception ;

and every thing we perceive by our senses to be an idea
of sensation. Sometimes they say, that they are conscious of the ideas in their own minds, sometimes
that they perceive them.

However improbable it may appear, that philosophers,
who have taken pains to study the operations of their
own minds, should express them less properly, and less
distinctly than the vulgar, it seems really to be the case ;
and the only account that can be given of this strange
phenomenon, I take to be this : that the vulgar seek
no theory to account for the operations of their minds ;
they know that they see, and hear, and remember, and
imagine ; and those who think distinctly, will express
these operations distinctly, as their consciousness represents them to the mind : but philosophers think they
ought to know, not only that there are such operations,
but how they are performed ; how they see, and hear,
and remember, and imagine ; and, having invented a
theory to explain these operations, by ideas or images
in the mind, they suit their expressions to their theory ;
and as a false comment throws a cloud upon the text,
so a false theory darkens the phenomena which it attempts to explain.

We shall examine this theory afterward. Here I
would only observe, that if it is not true, it may be expected that it should lead ingenious men who adopt it to
confound the operations of the mind with their objects,
and with one another, even where the common language of the unlearned clearly distinguishes them. One
that trusts to a false guide, is in greater danger of
being led astray than he who trusts his own eyes,
though he should be but indifferently acquainted with
the road.

CHAP. X.

OF THE SENTIMENTS OF BISHOP BERKELEY.

GEORGE BERKELEY, afterward bishop of Cloyne, published his new Theory of Vision in 1709 ; his treatise on the principles of human knowledge, in 1710 ; and his dialogues between Hylas and Phylonous, in 1713 ; being then a Fellow of Trinity College, Dublin. He is acknowledged universally to have great merit as an excellent writer, and a very acute and clear reasoner on the most abstract subjects, not to speak of his virtues as a man, which were very conspicuous. Yet the doctrine chiefly held forth in the treatises above mentioned, especially in the two last, has generally been thought so very absurd, that few can be brought to think that he either believed it himself, or that he seriously meant to persuade others of its truth.

He maintains, and thinks he has demonstrated, by a variety of arguments, grounded on principles of philosophy universally received, that there is no such thing as matter in the universe ; that sun and moon, earth and sea, our own bodies, and those of our friends, are nothing but ideas in the minds of those who think of them, and that they have no existence when they are not the objects of thought ; that all that is in the universe may be reduced to two categories, to wit, minds, and ideas in the mind.

But, however absurd this doctrine might appear to the unlearned, who consider the existence of the objects of sense as the most evident of all truths, and what no man in his senses can doubt ; the philosophers, who had been accustomed to consider ideas as the immediate objects of all thought, had no title to view this doctrine of Berkeley in so unfavourable a light.

They were taught by Des Cartes, and by all that came after him, that the existence of the objects of sense is not self evident, but requires to be proved by arguments ; and although Des Cartes, and many others, had laboured to find arguments for this purpose, there did not appear to be that force and clearness in them which might have been expected in a matter of such importance. Mr. Norris had declared, that after all the arguments that had been offered, the existence of an external world is only probable, but by no means certain. Malebranche thought it rested upon the authority of revelation, and that the arguments drawn from reason were not perfectly conclusive. Others thought, that the argument from revelation was a mere sophism, because revelation comes to us by our senses, and must rest upon their authority.

Thus we see, that the new philosophy had been making gradual approaches toward Berkeley's opinion ; and, whatever others might do, the philosophers had no title to look upon it as absurd, or unworthy of a fair examination. Several authors attempted to answer his arguments, but with little success, and others acknowledged that they could neither answer them nor assent to them. It is probable the bishop made but few converts to his doctrine ; but it is certain he made some; and that he himself continued, to the end of his life, firmly persuaded, not only of its truth, but of its great importance for the improvement of human knowledge, and especially for the defence of religion. Dial. Pref. " If the principles which I here endeavour to propagate are admitted for true, the consequences which I think evidently flow from thence are, that atheism and skepticism will be utterly destroyed, many intricate points made plain, great difficulties solved, several useless parts of science retrenched, speculation referred to practice, and men reduced from paradoxes to common sense."

In the Theory of Vision, he goes no further than to assert, that the objects of sight are nothing but ideas in the mind, granting, or at least not denying, that there is a tangible world, which is really external, and which exists whether we perceive it or not.   Whether the reason of this was, that his system had not, at that time, wholly opened to his own mind, or whether he thought it prudent to let it enter into the minds of his readers by degrees, I cannot say.   I think he insinuates the last as the reason in the Principles of Human Knowledge.

The Theory of Vision, however, taken by itself, and without relation to the main branch of his system, contains very important discoveries, and marks of great genius.   He distinguishes more accurately than any that went before him, between the immediate objects of sight, and those of the other senses which are early associated with them.   He shows, that distance, of itself, and immediately, is not seen; but that we learn to judge of it by certain sensations and perceptions which are connected with it.   This is a very important observation; and, I believe, was first made by this author. It gives much new light to the operations of our senses, and serves to account for many phenomena in optics, of which the greatest adepts in that science had always either given a false account, or acknowledged that they could give none at all.

We may observe, by the way, that the ingenious author seems not to have attended to a distinction, by which his general assertion ought to have been limited. It is true, that the distance of an object from the eye is not immediately seen; but there is a certain kind of distance of one object from another, which we see immediately.   The author acknowledges, that there is a visible extension, and visible figures, which are proper objects of sight; there must therefore be a visible distance. Astronomers call it angular distance ; and although they measure it by the angle, which is made by two lines drawn from the eye to the two distant objects, yet it is immediately perceived by sight, even by those who never thought of that angle.

He led the way in showing how we learn to perceive the distance of an object from the eye, though this speculation was carried further by others who came after him. He made the distinction between that extension and figure which we perceive by sight only, and that which we perceive by touch ; calling the first, visible, the last, tangible extension and figure. He showed likewise, that tangible extension, and not visible, is the object of geometry, although mathematicians commonly use visible diagrams in their demonstrations.

The notion of extension and figure which we get from sight only, and that which we get from touch, have been so constantly conjoined from our infancy in all the judgments we form of the objects of sense, that it required great abilities to distinguish them accurately, and to assign to each sense what truly belongs to it ; " so difficult a thing it is," as Berkeley justly observes, " to dissolve an union so early begun, and confirmed by so long a habit." This point he has laboured, through the whole of the Essay on Vision, with that uncommon penetration and judgment which he possessed, and with as great success as could be expected in a first attempt upon so abstruse a subject.

He concludes this Essay, by showing, in no less than seven sections, the notions which an intelligent being, endowed with sight, without the sense of touch, might form of the objects of sense. This speculation, to shallow thinkers, may appear to be egregious trifling. To bishop Berkeley it appeared in another light, and will do so to those who are capable of entering into it, and who know the importance of it, in solving many of the phenomena of vision. He seems, indeed, to have exerted more force of genius in this than in the main branch of his system.

In the new philosophy, the pillars by which the existence of a material world was supported were so feeble, that it did not require the force of a Samson to bring them down ; and in this we have not so much reason to admire the strength of Berkeley's genius, as his boldness in publishing to the world an opinion, which the unlearned would be apt to interpret as the sign of a crazy intellect. A man who was firmly persuaded of the doctrine universally received by philosophers concerning ideas, if he could but take courage to call in question the existence of a material world, would easily find unanswerable arguments in that doctrine. " Some truths there are, says Berkeley, so near and obvious to the mind, that a man need only open his eyes to see them. Such," he adds, "I take this important one to be, that all the choir of heaven, and furniture of the earth ; in a word, all those bodies which compose the mighty frame of the world, have not any subsistence without a mind." Princ. § 6.

The principle from which this important conclusion is obviously deduced, is laid down in the first sentence of his Principles of Knowledge as evident ; and indeed it had always been acknowledged by philosophers. "It is evident," says he, " to any one who takes a survey of the objects of human knowledge, that they are either ideas actually imprinted on the senses, or else such as are perceived, by attending to the passions and operations of the mind ; or, lastly, ideas formed by help of memory and imagination, either compounding, dividing, or barely representing those originally perceived in the foresaid ways."

This is the foundation on which the whole system rests. If this be true, then, indeed, the existence of a

material world must be a dream that has imposed upon
all mankind from the beginning of the world.

The foundation on which such a fabric rests ought to
be very solid, and well established ; yet Berkeley says
nothing more for it than that it is evident. If he means
that it is self evident, this indeed might be a good reason for not offering any direct argument in proof of it.
But I apprehend this cannot justly be said. Self evident propositions are those which appear evident to every man of sound understanding who apprehends the
meaning of them distinctly, and attends to them without prejudice. Can this be said of this proposition,
that all the objects of our knowledge are ideas in our
own minds? I believe, that, to any man uninstructed in
philosophy, this proposition will appear very improbable, if not absurd. However scanty his knowledge may
be, he considers the sun and moon, the earth and sea,
as objects of it : and it will be difficult to persuade
him, that those objects of his knowledge are ideas in his
own mind, and have no existence when he does not
think of them. If I may presume to speak my own
sentiments, I once believed this doctrine of ideas so
firmly, as to embrace the whole of Berkeley's system
in consequence of it ; till, finding other consequences
to follow from it, which gave me more uneasiness than
the want of a material world, it came into my mind
more than forty years ago, to put the question, What
evidence have I for this doctrine, that all the objects
of my knowledge are ideas in my own mind? From
that time to the present I have been candidly and im-
partially, as I think, seeking for the evidence of this
principle, but can find none, excepting the authority of
philosophers.

We shall have occasion to examine its evidence afterward. I would at present only observe, that all the
arguments brought by Berkeley against the exist-

ence of a material world are grounded upon it ; and
that he has not attempted to give any evidence for it,
but takes it for granted, as other philosophers had done
before him.

But supposing this principle to be true, Berkeley's
system is impregnable. No demonstration can be more
evident than his reasoning from it.   Whatever is perceived is an idea, and an idea can only exist in a mind.
It has no existence when it is not perceived ; nor can
there be any thing like an idea, but an idea.

So sensible he was, that it required no laborious reasoning to deduce his system from the principle laid down,
that he was afraid of being thought needlessly prolix
in handling the subject, and makes an apology for it.
Princ. § 22. " To what purpose is it," says he, " to di-
late upon that which may be demonstrated with the utmost evidence, in a line or two, to any one who is capable of the least reflection."   But though his demonstration might have been comprehended in a line or two,
he very prudently thought, that an opinion, which the
world would be apt to look upon as a monster of absurdity, would not be able to make its way at once, even by
the force of a naked demonstration. He observes justly,
Dial. 2. " That though a demonstration be never so
well grounded, and fairly proposed, yet, if there is,
withal, a strain of prejudice, or a wrong bias on the
understanding, can it be expected to perceive clearly,
and adhere firmly to the truth ? No ; there is need of
time and pains ; the attention must be awakened and
detained by a frequent repetition of the same thing,
placed often in the same, often in different lights." It
was therefore necessary to dwell upon it, and turn it
on all sides till it became familiar ; to consider all its
consequences, and to obviate every prejudice and prepossession that might hinder its admittance.   It was
even a matter of some difficulty to fit it to common lan-

guage, so far as to enable men to speak and reason
about it intelligibly. Those who have entered seriously into Berkeley's system have found, after all the
assistance which his writings give, that time and practice are necessary to acquire the habit of speaking and
thinking distinctly upon it.

Berkeley foresaw the opposition that would be made
to his system, from two different quarters ; *first*, from
the philosophers ; and, *secondly*, from the vulgar, who
are led by the plain dictates of nature. The first he had
the courage to oppose openly and avowedly ; the second he dreaded much more, and therefore takes a great
deal of pains, and, I think, uses some art to court into
his party. This is particularly observable in his Dialogues. He sets out with a declaration, Dial. 1. "That
of late he had quitted several of the sublime notions
he had got in the schools of the philosophers for vulgar
opinions," and assures Hylas, his fellow dialogist,
"That, since this revolt from metaphysical notions to the
plain dictates of nature, and common sense, he found his
understanding strangely enlightened ; so that he could
now easily comprehend a great many things, which before were all mystery and riddle." Pref. to Dial. " If
his principles are admitted for true, men will be reduced
from paradoxes to common sense." At the same time
he acknowledges, " That they carry with them a great
opposition to the prejudices of philosophers, which have
so far prevailed against the common sense and natural
notions of mankind."

When Hylas objects to him, Dial. 3. " You can never
persuade me Philonous, that the denying of matter or
corporeal substance is not repugnant to the universal
sense of mankind ;" he answers, " I wish both our opinions were fairly stated, and submitted to the judgment
of men who had plain common sense, without the prejudices of a learned education. Let me be represented

as one who trusts his senses, who thinks he knows the things he sees and feels, and entertains no doubt of their existence.   If by material substance is meant only sensible body, that which is seen and felt, and the unphilosophical part of the world, I dare say, mean no more, then I am more certain of matter's existence than you or any other philosopher pretend to be.   If there be any thing which makes the generality of mankind averse from the notions I espouse, it is a misapprehension that I deny the reality of sensible things : but as it is you who are guilty of that, and not I, it follows, that in truth their aversion is against your notions, and not mine.   I am content to appeal to the common sense of the world for the truth of my notion.   I am of a vulgar cast, simple enough to believe my senses, and to leave things as I find them.   I cannot, for my life, help thinking that snow is white, and fire hot."

When Hylas is at last entirely converted, he observes to Philonous, " After all, the controversy about matter, in the strict acceptation of it, lies altogether between you and the philosophers, whose principles, I acknowledge, are not near so natural, or so agreeable to the common sense of mankind, and Holy Scripture, as yours."   Philonous observes in the end, " That he does not pretend to be a setter up of new notions ; his endeavours tend only to unite, and to place in a clearer light, that truth which was before shared between the vulgar and the philosophers ; the former being of opinion, that those things they immediately perceive are the real things ; and the latter, that the things immediately perceived are ideas which exist only in the mind ; which two things put together do, in effect, constitute the substance of what he advances :" and he concludes by observing, " That those principles, which at first view lead to skepticism, pursued to a certain point, bring men back to common sense."

These passages show sufficiently the author's concern to reconcile his system to the plain dictates of nature and common sense, while he expresses no concern
to reconcile it to the received doctrines of philosophers.
He is fond to take part with the vulgar against the
philosophers, and to vindicate common sense against
their innovations.   What pity is it that he did not carry this suspicion of the doctrine of philosophers so far
as to doubt of that philosophical tenet on which his
whole system is built, to wit, that the things immediately perceived by the senses are ideas which exist only
in the mind !

After all, it seems no easy matter to make the vulgar opinion and that of Berkeley to meet. And to accomplish this, he seems to me to draw each out of its
line toward the other, not without some straining.

The vulgar opinion he reduces to this, that the very
things which we perceive by our senses do really exist.
This he grants : for these things, says he, are ideas in
our minds, or complexions of ideas, to which we give
one name, and consider as one thing; these are the
immediate objects of sense, and these do really exist.
As to the notion, that those things have an absolute external existence, independent of being perceived by any
mind, he thinks, that this is no notion of the vulgar, but
a refinement of philosophers ; and that the notion of material substance, as a *substratum*, or support of that
collection of sensible qualities to which we give the
name of an apple or a melon, is likewise an invention
of philosophers, and is not found with the vulgar till
they are instructed by philosophers. The substance
not being an object of sense, the vulgar never think of
it ; or, if they are taught the use of the word, they
mean no more by it but that collection of sensible qualities which they, from finding them conjoined in nature,
have been accustomed to call by one name, and to consider as one thing.

Thus he draws the vulgar opinion near to his own ; and, that he may meet it half way, he acknowledges, that material things have a real existence out of the mind of this or that person ; but the question, says he, between the materialist and me, is, Whether they have an absolute existence distinct from their being perceived by God, and exterior to all minds ? This, indeed, he says, some heathens and philosophers have affirmed ; but whoever entertains notions of the Deity, suitable to the Holy Scripture, will be of another opinion.

But here an objection occurs, which it required all his ingenuity to answer. It is this : the ideas in my mind cannot be the same with the ideas of any other mind ; therefore, if the objects I perceive be only ideas, it is impossible that the objects I perceive can exist any where, when I do not perceive them ; and it is impossible that two or more minds can perceive the same object.

To this Berkeley answers, that this objection presses no less the opinion of the materialist philosopher than his ; but the difficulty is, to make his opinion coincide with the notions of the vulgar, who are firmly persuaded, that the very identical objects which they perceive, continue to exist when they do not perceive them ; and who are no less firmly persuaded, that when ten men look at the sun or the moon, they all see the same individual object.

To reconcile this repugnancy, he observes, Dial. 3. " That if the term *same* be taken in the vulgar acceptation, it is certain, and not at all repugnant to the principles he maintains, that different persons may perceive the same thing ; or the same thing or idea exist in different minds. Words are of arbitrary imposition ; and since men are used to apply the word *same* where no distinction or variety is perceived, and he does not pretend to alter their perceptions, it follows, that as

men have said before, *several saw the same thing ;* so
they may, upon like occasions, still continue to use the
same phrase without any deviation, either from propriety of language or the truth of things ; but if the
term *same* be used in the acceptation of philosophers,
who pretend to an abstracted notion of identity, then,
according to their sundry definitions of this term, for
it is not yet agreed wherein that philosophic identity
consists, it may or may not be possible for divers persons to perceive the same thing; but whether philosophers shall think fit to call a thing the *same* or no, is,
I conceive, of small importance. Men may dispute
about identity and diversity, without any real difference in their thoughts and opinions, abstracted from
names.''

Upon the whole, I apprehend that Berkeley has carried this attempt to reconcile his system to the vulgar
opinion further than reason supports him ; and he was
no doubt tempted to do so, from a just apprehension
that, in a controversy of this kind, the common sense
of mankind is the most formidable antagonist.

Berkeley has employed much pains and ingenuity to
show that his system, if received and believed, would
not be attended with those bad consequences in the
conduct of life which superficial thinkers may be apt to
impute to it. His system does not take away or make
any alteration upon our pleasures or our pains. Our
sensations, whether agreeable or disagreeable, are the
same upon his system as upon any other. These are
real things, and the only things that interest us. They
are produced in us according to certain laws of nature,
by which our conduct will be directed in attaining the
one, and avoiding the other : and it is of no moment to
us, whether they are produced immediately by the
operation of some powerful intelligent being upon our

minds, or by the mediation of some inanimate being which we call *matter*.

The evidence of an all governing Mind, so far from being weakened, seems to appear even in a more striking light upon his hypothesis, than upon the common one. The powers which inanimate matter is supposed to possess, have always been the strong hold of atheists, to which they had recourse in defence of their system. This fortress of atheism must be most effectually overturned, if there is no such thing as matter in the universe. In all this the bishop reasons justly and acutely. But there is one uncomfortable consequence of his system, which he seems not to have attended to, and from which it will be found difficult, if at all possible, to guard it.

The consequence I mean, is this, that, although it leaves us sufficient evidence of a supreme intelligent Mind, it seems to take away all the evidence we have of other intelligent beings like ourselves. What I call a father, a brother, or a friend, is only a parcel of ideas in my own mind ; and being ideas in my mind, they cannot possibly have that relation to another mind which they have to mine, any more than the pain felt by me can be the individual pain felt by another. I can find no principle in Berkeley's system, which affords me even probable ground to conclude, that there are other intelligent beings like myself, in the relations of father, brother, friend, or fellow citizen. I am left alone, as the only creature of God in the universe, in that forlorn state of *Egoism*, into which, it is said, some of the disciples of Des Cartes were brought by his philosophy.

Of all the opinions that have ever been advanced by philosophers, this of bishop Berkeley, that there is no material world, seems the strangest, and the most apt to bring philosophy into ridicule with plain men, who are guided by the dictates of nature and common sense.

And it will not, I apprehend, be improper to trace this
progeny of the doctrine of ideas from its origin, and to
observe its gradual progress, till it acquired such
strength, that a pious and learned bishop had the boldness to usher it into the world, as demonstrable from
the principles of philosophy universally received, and
as an admirable expedient for the advancement of
knowledge, and for the defence of religion.

During the reign of the Peripatetic philosophy, men
were little disposed to doubt, and much to dogmatize.
The existence of the objects of sense was held as a first
principle ; and the received doctrine was, that the sensible species or idea is the very form of the external
object, just separated from the matter of it, and sent
into the mind that perceives it ; so that we find no appearance of skepticism about the existence of matter
under that philosophy.

Des Cartes taught men to doubt even of those things
that had been taken for first principles. He rejected
the doctrine of species or ideas coming from objects ;
but still maintained, that what we immediately perceive is not the external object, but an idea or image
of it in our mind. This led some of his disciples into
Egoism, and to disbelieve the existence of every
creature in the universe but themselves and their own
ideas.

But Des Cartes himself, either from dread of the
censure of the church, which he took great care not
to provoke, or to shun the ridicule of the world, which
might have crushed his system at once, as it did that
of the Egoists ; or, perhaps, from inward conviction,
was resolved to support the existence of matter. To
do this consistently with his principles, he found himself obliged to have recourse to arguments that are far-
fetched, and not very cogent. Sometimes he argues,
that our senses are given us by God, who is no deceiv-

er; and therefore we ought to believe their testimony. But this argument is weak; because, according to his principles, our senses testify no more but that we have certain ideas: and if we draw conclusions from this testimony, which the premises will not support, we deceive ourselves. To give more force to this weak argument, he sometimes adds, that we have by nature a strong propensity to believe that there is an external world corresponding to our ideas.

Malebranche thought, that this strong propensity is not a sufficient reason for believing the existence of matter; and that it is to be received as an article of faith, not certainly discoverable by reason. He is aware that faith comes by hearing; and that it may be said that prophets, apostles, and miracles, are only ideas in our minds. But to this he answers, That though these things are only ideas, yet faith turns them into realities; and this answer, he hopes, will satisfy those who are not too morose.

It may perhaps seem strange, that Locke, who wrote so much about ideas, should not see those consequences which Berkeley thought so obviously deducible from that doctrine. Mr. Locke surely was not willing that the doctrine of ideas should be thought to be loaded with such consequences. He acknowledges, that the existence of a material world is not to be received as a first principle; nor is it demonstrable; but he offers the best arguments for it he can; and supplies the weakness of his arguments by this observation, that we have such evidence as is sufficient to direct us in pursuing the good, and avoiding the ill we may receive from external things, beyond which we have no concern.

There is, indeed, a single passage in Locke's Essay, which may lead one to conjecture, that he had a glimpse of that system which Berkeley afterward advanced, but thought proper to suppress it within his own breast.

The passage is in book 4. chap. 10. where, having proved the existence of an eternal intelligent Mind, he comes to answer those who conceive that matter also must be eternal; because we cannot conceive how it could be made out of nothing; and having observed that the creation of minds requires no less power than the creation of matter, he adds what follows: "Nay, possibly, if we could emancipate ourselves from vulgar notions, and raise our thoughts, as far as they would reach, to a closer contemplation of things, we might be able to aim at some dim and seeming conception, how matter might at first be made, and begin to exist by the power of that eternal first Being; but to give beginning and being to a spirit, would be found a more inconceivable effect of Omnipotent power. But this being what would perhaps lead us too far from the notions on which the philosophy now in the world is built, it would not be pardonable to deviate so far from them, or to inquire, so far as grammar itself would authorize, if the common settled opinion opposes it; especially in this place, where the received doctrine serves well enough to our present purpose."

It appears from this passage, 1st, That Mr. Locke had some system in his mind, perhaps not fully digested, to which we might be led, by raising our thoughts to a closer contemplation of things, and emancipating them from vulgar notions. 2dly, That this system would lead so far from the notions on which the philosophy now in the world is built, that he thought proper to keep it within his own breast. 3dly, That it might be doubted whether this system differed so far from the common settled opinion in reality, as it seemed to do in words. 4thly, By this system, we might possibly be enabled to aim at some dim and seeming conception how matter might at first be made and begin to exist; but it would give no aid in conceiving how a spirit might be made. These are the characteristics of that system which Mr. Locke had in his mind, and thought it prudent to suppress. May they not lead to a probable conjecture, that it was the same, or something similar to that of bishop Berkeley? According to Berkeley's system, God's creating the material world at such a time, means no more but that he decreed from that time, to produce ideas in the minds of finite spirits, in that order, and according to those rules, which we call the laws of nature. This, indeed, removes all difficulty, in conceiving how matter was created; and Berkeley does not fail to take notice of the advantage of his system on that account. But his system gives no aid in conceiving how a spirit may be made. It appears, therefore, that every particular Mr. Locke has hinted, with regard to that system which he had in his mind, but thought it prudent to suppress, tallies exactly with the system of Berkeley. If we add to this, that Berkeley's system follows from Mr. Locke's, by very obvious consequence, it seems reasonable to conjecture, from the passage now quoted, that he was not unaware of that consequence, but left it to those who should come after him to carry his principles their full length, when they should by time be better established, and able to bear the shock of their opposition to vulgar notions. Mr. Norris, in his Essay toward the theory of the ideal or intelligible world, published in 1701, observes, that the material world is not an object of sense; because sensation is within us, and has no object. Its existence, therefore, he says, is a collection of reason, and not a very evident one.

From this detail we may learn, that the doctrine of ideas, as it was new modelled by Des Cartes, looked with an unfriendly aspect upon the material world; and although philosophers were very unwilling to give up either, they found it a very difficult task to recon-

cile them to each other.   In this state of things Berkeley, I think, is reputed the first who had the daring
resolution to give up the material world altogether, as
a sacrifice to the received philosophy of ideas.

But we ought not in this historical sketch to omit
an author of far inferior name, Arthur Collier, rector
of Langford Magna, near Sarum. He published a book
in 1713, which he calls Clavis Universalis ; or, a new
Inquiry after Truth ; being a demonstration of the
non-existence, or impossibility of an external world.
His arguments are the same in substance with Berkeley's; and he appears to understand the whole strength
of his cause.   Though he is not deficient in metaphysical acuteness, his style is disagreeable, being full of
conceits, of new coined words, scholastic terms, and
perplexed sentences.   He appears to be well acquainted with Des Cartes, Malebranche, and Norris, as well
as with Aristotle and the schoolmen : but, what is
very strange, it does not appear that he had ever heard
of Locke's Essay, which had been published twenty-four
years, or of Berkeley's Principles of Knowledge, which
had been published three years.

He says, he had been ten years firmly convinced of
the non-existence of an external world, before he ven-
tured to publish his book.   He is far from thinking as
Berkeley does, that the vulgar are of his opinion.   If
his book should make any converts to his system, of
which he expresses little hope, though he has supported it by nine demonstrations, he takes pains to
show that his disciples, notwithstanding their opinion,
may, with the unenlightened, speak of material things
in the common style.   He himself had scruples of conscience about this for some time ; and if he had not got
over them, he must have shut his lips for ever : but he
considered, that God himself has used this style in
speaking to men in the Holy Scripture, and has thereby

sanctified it to all the faithful: and that to the pure
all things are pure.   He thinks his opinion may be of
great use, especially in religion ; and applies it in particular, to put an end to the controversy about Christ's
presence in the sacrament.

I have taken the liberty to give this short account of
Collier's book, because I believe it is rare, and little
known. I have only seen one copy of it, which is in the
university library of Glasgow.

CHAP. XI.

BISHOP BERKELEY'S SENTIMENTS OF THE NATURE OF
IDEAS.

I PASS over the sentiments of bishop Berkeley, with respect to abstract ideas, and with respect to space and time, as things which may more properly be considered in another place. But I must take notice of one part of his system, wherein he seems to have deviated from the common opinion about ideas.

Though he sets out in his Principles of Knowledge by telling us, that it is evident the objects of human knowledge are ideas, and builds his whole system upon this principle; yet, in the progress of it, he finds that there are certain objects of human knowledge that are not ideas, but things which have a permanent existence. The objects of knowledge, of which we have no ideas, are our own minds, and their various operations, other finite minds, and the Supreme mind. The reason why there can be no ideas of spirits and their operations, the author informs us, is this, That ideas are passive, inert, unthinking beings; they cannot therefore be the image or likeness of things that have thought, and will, and active power; we have notions of minds and of their operations, but not ideas : we know what we mean by thinking, willing, and perceiving; we can reason about beings endowed with those powers, but we have no ideas of them. A spirit, or mind, is the only substance or support wherein the unthinking beings or ideas can exist ; but that this substance which supports or perceives ideas, should itself be an idea, or like an idea, is evidently absurd.

He observes further, Princip. sect. 142. that " of relations including an act of the mind, we cannot properly be said to have an idea, but rather a notion of the relations or habitudes between things. But if, in the modern way, the word *idea* is extended to spirits, and relations, and acts, this is, after all, an affair of verbal concern ; yet it conduces to clearness and propriety, that we distinguish things very different by different names."

This is an important part of Berkeley's system, and deserves attention. We are led by it to divide the objects of human knowledge into two kinds. The first is ideas, which we have by our five senses ; they have no existence when they are not perceived, and exist only in the minds of those who perceive them. The second kind of objects comprehends spirits, their acts, and the relations and habitudes of things. Of these we have notions, but no ideas. No idea can represent them, or have any similitude to them : yet we understand what they mean, and we can speak with understanding, and reason about them, without ideas.

This account of ideas is very different from that which Locke has given. In his system, we have no knowledge where we have no ideas. Every thought must have an idea for its immediate object. In Berkeley's, the most important objects are known without ideas. In Locke's system, there are two sources of our ideas, sensation and reflection. In Berkeley's, sensation is the only source, because of the objects of reflection there can be no ideas. We know them without ideas. Locke divides our ideas into those of substances, modes, and relations. In Berkeley's system, there are no ideas of substances, or of relations, but notions only. And even in the class of modes, the operations of our own minds are things of which we have distinct notions ; but no ideas.

We ought to do the justice to Malebranche to acknowledge, that in this point, as well as in many others,

his system comes nearer to Berkeley's than the latter
seems willing to own. That author tells us, that there
are four different ways in which we come to the knowledge of things. To know things by their ideas, is only
one of the four. He affirms, that we have no idea of
our own mind, or any of its modifications ; that we
know these things by consciousness, without ideas.
Whether these two acute philosophers foresaw the consequences that may be drawn from the system of ideas,
taken in its full extent, and which were afterward
drawn by Mr. Hume, I cannot pretend to say. If they
did, their regard to religion was too great to permit
them to admit those consequences, or the principles
with which they were necessarily connected.

However this may be, if there be so many things that
may be apprehended and known without ideas, this very
naturally suggests a scruple with regard to those that
are left : for it may be said, If we can apprehend and
reason about the world of spirits, without ideas, is it
not possible that we may apprehend and reason about a
material world, without ideas ? If consciousness and
reflection furnish us with notions of spirits, and of their
attributes, without ideas, may not our senses furnish
us with notions of bodies and their attributes, without
ideas ?

Berkeley foresaw this objection to his system, and
puts it in the mouth of Hylas, in the following words,
Dial. 3. Hylas. " If you can conceive the mind of God,
without having an idea of it, why may not I be allowed
to conceive the existence of matter, notwithstanding
that I have no idea of it ?" The answer of Philonous
is, " You neither perceive matter objectively, as you
do an inactive being or idea, nor know it, as you do
yourself, by a reflex act, neither do you immediately
apprehend it by similitude of the one or the other, nor
yet collect it by reasoning from that which you know

immediately. All which makes the case of matter widely different from that of the Deity."

Though Hylas declares himself satisfied with this answer, I confess I am not: because, if I may trust the faculties that God has given me, I do perceive matter objectively, that is, something which is extended and solid, which may be measured and weighed, is the immediate object of my touch and sight. And this object I take to be matter, and not an idea. And though I have been taught by philosophers, that what I immediately touch is an idea, and not matter; yet I have never been able to discover this by the most accurate attention to my own perceptions.

It were to be wished, that this ingenious author had explained what he means by ideas, as distinguished from notions. The word *notion*, being a word in common language, is well understood. All men mean by it, the conception, the apprehension, or thought which we have of any object of thought. A notion, therefore, is an act of the mind conceiving or thinking of some object. The object of thought may be either something that is in the mind, or something that is not in the mind. It may be something that has no existence, or something that did, or does, or shall exist. But the notion which I have of that object, is an act of my mind which really exists while I think of the object; but has no existence when I do not think of it. The word *idea*, in popular language, has precisely the same meaning as the word *notion*. But philosophers have another meaning to the word *idea*; and what that meaning is, I think, is very difficult to say.

The whole of bishop Berkeley's system depends upon the distinction between notions and ideas; and therefore it is worth while to find, if we are able, what those things are which he calls ideas, as distinguished from notions.

For this purpose, we may observe, that he takes notice of two kinds of ideas, the ideas of sense, and the
ideas of imagination. "The ideas imprinted on the
senses by the author of nature, he says, are called real
things; and those excited in the imagination, being
less regular, vivid, and constant, are more properly
termed ideas, or images of things, which they copy and
represent. But then our sensations, be they never so
vivid and distinct, are nevertheless ideas; that is, they
exist in the mind, or are perceived by it as truly as the
ideas of its own framing. The ideas of sense are allowed to have more reality in them; that is, to be more
strong, orderly, and coherent, than the creatures of the
mind. They are also less dependent on the spirit,
or thinking substance which perceives them, in that
they are excited by the will of another and more powerful spirit; yet still they are ideas; and certainly no
idea, whether faint or strong, can exist, otherwise than
in a mind perceiving it." Princip. sect. 33.

From this passage we see, that, by the ideas of sense,
the author means sensations: and this indeed is evident from many other passages, of which I shall mention a few, Princip. sect. 5. "Light and colours, heat
and cold, extension and figure, in a word, the things
we see and feel, what are they but so many sensations,
notions, ideas, or impressions on the sense; and is it
possible to separate, even in thought, any of these from
perception? For my part, I might as easily divide a
thing from itself." Sect. 18. "As for our senses, by
them we have the knowledge only of our sensations,
ideas, or those things that are immediately perceived
by sense; call them what you will. But they do not
inform us that things exist without the mind, or un-
perceived, like to those which are perceived." Sect.
25. "All our ideas, sensations, or the things which
we perceive, by whatever names they may be distin-

guished, are visibly inactive; there is nothing of power or agency included in them."

This therefore appears certain, that by the ideas of
sense, the author meant the sensations we have by
means of our senses. I have endeavoured to explain
the meaning of the word *sensation*, Essay 1. chap. 1.
and refer to the explication there given of it, which
appears to me to be perfectly agreeable to the sense in
which bishop Berkeley uses it.

As there can be no notion or thought but in a thinking being; so there can be no sensation but in a sentient being. It is the act, or feeling of a sentient being;
its very essence consists in its being felt. Nothing can
resemble a sensation, but a similar sensation in the same,
or in some other mind. To think that any quality in a
thing that is inanimate can resemble a sensation, is a
great absurdity. In all this, I cannot but agree perfectly with bishop Berkeley; and I think his notions of
sensation much more distinct and accurate than Locke's,
who thought that the primary qualities of body are resemblances of our sensations, but that the secondary
are not.

That we have many sensations by means of our external senses, there can be no doubt; and if he is pleased to call those ideas, there ought to be no dispute
about the meaning of a word. But, says bishop Berkeley, by our senses, we have the knowledge *only* of our
sensations or ideas, call them which you will. I allow
him to call them which he will; but I would have the
word *only* in this sentence to be well weighed, because
a great deal depends upon it.

For if it be true, that, by our senses, we have the
knowledge of our sensations only, then his system must
be admitted, and the existence of a material world must
be given up as a dream. No demonstration can be
more invincible than this. If we have any knowledge

of a material world, it must be by the senses ; but, by the senses, we have no knowledge but of our sensations only ; and our sensations have no resemblance of any thing that can be in a material world. The only proposition in this demonstration which admits of doubt is, that, by our senses, we have the knowledge of our sensations only, and of nothing else. If there are objects of the senses which are not sensations, his arguments do not touch them ; they may be things which do not exist in the mind, as all sensations do ; they may be things, of which, by our senses, we have notions, though no ideas ; just as, by consciousness and reflection, we have notions of spirits, and of their operations, without ideas or sensations.

Shall we say then, that, by our senses, we have the knowledge of our sensations only ; and that they give us no notion of any thing but of our sensations ? Perhaps this has been the doctrine of philosophers, and not of bishop Berkeley alone, otherwise he would have supported it by arguments. Mr. Locke calls all the notions we have by our senses, *ideas of sensation ;* and in this has been very generally followed. Hence it seems a very natural inference, that ideas of sensation are sensations. But philosophers may err. Let us hear the dictates of common sense upon this point.

Suppose I am pricked with a pin ; I ask, is the pain I feel, a sensation ? undoubtedly it is. There can be nothing that resembles pain in any inanimate being. But I ask again, is the pin a sensation? To this question I find myself under a necessity of answering, that the pin is not a sensation, nor can have the least resemblance to any sensation. The pin has length and thickness, and figure, and weight. A sensation can have none of those qualities. I am not more certain that the pain I feel is a sensation, than that the pin is not a sensation ; yet the pin is an object of sense ; and

I am as certain that I perceive its figure and hardness by my senses, as that I feel pain when pricked by it.

Having said so much of the ideas of sense in Berkeley's system, we are next to consider the account he gives of the ideas of imagination. Of these he says, Princip. sect. 28. "I find I can excite ideas in my mind at pleasure, and vary and shift the scene as often as I think fit. It is no more than willing ; and straightway this or that idea arises in my fancy ; and by the same power it is obliterated, and makes way for another. This making and unmaking of ideas, doth very properly denominate the mind active. This much is certain, and grounded on experience. Our sensations, he says, are called real things ; the ideas of imagination are more properly termed *ideas*, or *images of things;*" that is, as I apprehend, they are the images of our sensations. It might surely be expected, that we should be well acquainted with the ideas of imagination, as they are of our making ; yet, after all the bishop has said about them, I am at a loss to know what they are.

I would observe in the *first* place, with regard to these ideas of imagination, that they are not sensations ; for surely sensation is the work of the senses, and not of imagination ; and though pain be a sensation, the thought of pain, when I am not pained, is no sensation.

I observe, in the *second* place, that I can find no distinction between ideas of imagination, and notions, which the author says are not ideas. I can easily distinguish between a notion and a sensation. It is one thing to say, I have the sensation of pain. It is another thing to say, I have a notion of pain. The last expression signifies no more than that I understand what is meant by the word *pain*. The first signifies, that I really feel pain. But I can find no distinction between the notion of pain, and the imagination of it, or indeed between the notion of any thing else, and the imagination of it. I can therefore give no account of the distinction which Berkeley makes between ideas of imagination, and notions, which he says are not ideas. They seem to me perfectly to coincide.

He seems indeed to say, that the ideas of imagination differ not in kind from those of the senses, but only in the degree of their regularity, vivacity, and constancy. "They are," says he, "less regular, vivid, and constant." This doctrine was afterward greedily embraced by Mr. Hume, and makes a main pillar of his system; but it cannot be reconciled to common sense, to which bishop Berkeley professes a great regard. For, according to this doctrine, if we compare the state of a man racked with the gout, with his state, when being at perfect ease, he relates what he has suffered; the difference of these two states is only this, that, in the last, the pain is less regular, vivid, and constant, than in the first. We cannot possibly assent to this. Every man knows that he can relate the pain he suffered, not only without pain, but with pleasure; and that to suffer pain, and to think of it, are things which totally differ in kind, and not in degree only.

We see, therefore, upon the whole, that, according to this system, of the most important objects of knowledge, that is, of spirits, of their operations, and of the relations of things, we have no ideas at all: we have notions of them, but not ideas: the ideas we have are those of sense, and those of imagination. The first are the sensations we have by means of our senses, whose existence no man can deny, because he is conscious of them; and whose nature has been explained by this author with great accuracy. As to the ideas of imagination, he has left us much in the dark. He makes them images of our sensations, though, according to his own doctrine, nothing can resemble a sensation, but a sensation. He seems to think, that they differ from sensations only in the degree of their regularity, vivacity, and constancy: but this cannot be reconciled to the experience of mankind ; and besides this mark, which cannot be admitted, he has given us no other mark by which they may be distinguished from notions. Nay, it may be observed, that the very reason he gives why we can have no ideas of the acts of the mind about its ideas, nor of the relations of things, is applicable to what he calls ideas of imagination. Princip. sect. 142. " We may not, I think, strictly be said to have an idea of an active being, or of an action, although we may be said to have a notion of them. I have some knowledge or notion of my mind, and its acts about ideas, in as much as I know or understand what is meant by these words. It is also to be remarked, that all relations, including an act of the mind, we cannot so properly be said to have an idea, but rather a notion of the relations and habitudes between things." From this it follows, that our imaginations are not properly ideas, but notions, because they include an act of the mind. For he tells us, in a passage already quoted, that they are creatures of the mind, of its own framing, and that it makes and unmakes them as it thinks fit, and from this is properly denominated active. If it be a good reason why we have not ideas, but notions only of relations, because they include an act of the mind ; the same reason must lead us to conclude, that our imaginations are notions, and not ideas, since they are made and unmade by the mind as it thinks fit, and from this it is properly denominated active.

When so much has been written, and so many disputes raised, about ideas, it were desirable that we knew what they are, and to what category or class of beings they belong. In this we might expect satisfaction in the writings of bishop Berkeley, if any where, considering his known accuracy and precision in the use of words ; and it is for this reason that I have taken so much pains to find out what he took them to be.

After all, if I understand what he calls the ideas of sense, they are the sensations which we have by means of our five senses; but they are, he says, less properly termed ideas.

I understand likewise what he calls notions, but they, says he, are very different from ideas, though, in the modern way, often called by that name.

The ideas of imagination remain, which are most properly termed ideas, as he says; and, with regard to these, I am still very much in the dark. When I imagine a lion or an elephant, the lion or elephant is the object imagined. The act of the mind, in conceiving that object, is the notion, the conception, or imagination of the object. If, besides the object, and the act of the mind about it, there be something called the idea of the object, I know not what it is.

If we consult other authors who have treated of ideas, we shall find as little satisfaction with regard to the meaning of this philosophical term. The vulgar have adopted it; but they only mean by it the notion or conception we have of any object, especially our more abstract or general notions. When it is thus put to signify the operation of the mind about objects, whether in conceiving, remembering, or perceiving, it is well understood. But philosophers will have ideas to be the objects of the mind's operations, and not the operations themselves. There is, indeed, great variety of objects of thought. We can think of minds, and of their operations, of bodies, and of their qualities and relations. If ideas are not comprehended under any of these classes, I am at a loss to comprehend what they are.

In ancient philosophy, ideas were said to be immaterial forms, which, according to one system, existed from all eternity, and, according to another, are sent forth from the objects, whose form they are. In modern philosophy, they are things in the mind, which are the immediate objects of all our thoughts, and which have no existence when we do not think of them. They are called the images, the resemblances, the representatives of external objects of sense: yet they have neither colour, nor smell, nor figure, nor motion, nor any sensible quality. I revere the authority of philosophers, especially where they are so unanimous; but until I can comprehend what they mean by ideas, I must think and speak with the vulgar.

In sensation, properly so called, I can distinguish two things, the mind, or sentient being, and the sensation. Whether the last is to be called a feeling or an operation, I dispute not; but it has no object distinct from the sensation itself. If in sensation there be a third thing, called an idea, I know not what it is.

In perception, in remembrance, and in conception, or imagination, I distinguish three things, the mind that operates, the operation of the mind, and the object of that operation. That the object perceived is one thing, and the perception of that object another, I am as certain as I can be of any thing. The same may be said of conception, of remembrance, of love and hatred, of desire and aversion. In all these the act of the mind about its object is one thing, the object is another thing. There must be an object, real or imaginary, distinct from the operations of the mind about it. Now, if in these operations the idea be a fourth thing different from the three I have mentioned, I know not what it is, nor have been able to learn from all that has been written about ideas. And if the doctrine of philosophers about ideas confounds any two of these things which I have mentioned as distinct; if, for example, it confounds the object perceived with the perception of that object, and represents them as one and the same thing, such doctrine is altogether repugnant to all that I am able to discover of the operations of my own mind; and it is repugnant to the common sense of mankind, expressed in the structure of all languages.

CHAP. XII.

OF THE SENTIMENTS OF MR. HUME.

Two volumes of the Treatise of Human Nature were published in 1739, and the third in 1740. The doctrine contained in this Treatise was published anew in a more popular form in Mr. Hume's Philosophical Essays, of which there have been various editions. What other authors, from the time of Des Cartes, had called *ideas*, this author distinguished into two kinds, to wit, *impressions* and *ideas;* comprehending under the first, all our sensations, passions, and emotions ; and under the last, the faint images of these, when we remember or imagine them.

He sets out with this, as a principle that needed no proof, and of which therefore he offers none, That all the perceptions of the human mind resolve themselves into these two kinds, *impressions* and *ideas.*

As this proposition is the foundation upon which the whole of Mr. Hume's system rests, and from which it is raised with great acuteness indeed, and ingenuity, it were to be wished that he had told us upon what authority this fundamental proposition rests. But we are left to guess, whether it is held forth as a first principle, which has its evidence in itself; or whether it is to be received upon the authority of philosophers.

Mr. Locke had taught us, that all the immediate objects of human knowledge are ideas in the mind. Bishop Berkeley, proceeding upon this foundation, demonstrated very easily, that there is no material world. And he thought, that, for the purposes both of philosophy and religion, we should find no loss, but great benefit in the want of it. But the bishop, as became his order,

was unwilling to give up the world of spirits.   He saw
very well, that ideas are as unfit to represent spirits as
they are to represent bodies.   Perhaps he saw, that if
we perceive only the ideas of spirits, we shall find the
same difficulty in inferring their real existence from
the existence of their ideas, as we find in inferring the
existence of matter from the idea of it ; and therefore,
while he gives up the material world in favour of the
system of ideas, he gives up one half of that system in
favour of the world of spirits; and maintains, that we
can without ideas, think, and speak, and reason, intelligibly about spirits, and what belongs to them.

Mr. Hume shows no such partiality in favour of the
world of spirits.   He adopts the theory of ideas in its
full extent ; and, in consequence, shows that there is
neither matter nor mind in the universe ; nothing but
impressions and ideas.   What we call a *body*, is only a
bundle of sensations ; and what we call the *mind*, is
only a bundle of thoughts, passions, and emotions, without any subject.

Some ages hence it will perhaps be looked upon as a
curious anecdote, that two philosophers of the 18th
century, of very distinguished rank, were led by a philosophical hypothesis ; one to disbelieve the existence
of matter, and the other to disbelieve the existence
both of matter and of mind.   Such an anecdote may
not be uninstructive, if it prove a warning to philosophers to beware of hypotheses, especially when they
lead to conclusions which contradict the principles
upon which all men of common sense must act in common life.

The Egoists, whom we mentioned before, were left
far behind by Mr. Hume ; for they believed their own
existence, and perhaps also the existence of a Deity.
But Mr. Hume's system does not even leave him a *self*
to claim the property of his impressions and ideas.

A system of consequences, however absurd, acutely and justly drawn from a few principles, in very abstract matters, is of real utility in science, and may be made subservient to real knowledge. This merit Mr. Hume's metaphysical writings have in a great degree.

We had occasion before to observe, that, since the time of Des Cartes, philosophers, in treating of the powers of the mind, have in many instances confounded things, which the common sense of mankind has always led them to distinguish, and which have different names in all languages. Thus, in the perception of an external object, all languages distinguish three things, the *mind* that perceives, the operation of that mind, which is called *perception*, and the *object* perceived. Nothing appears more evident to a mind untutored by philosophy, than that these three are distinct things, which, though related, ought never to be confounded. The structure of all languages supposes this distinction, and is built upon it. Philosophers have introduced a fourth thing in this process, which they call the *idea* of the object, which is supposed to be an image, or representative of the object, and is said to be the immediate object. The vulgar know nothing about this idea; it is a creature of philosophy, introduced to account for, and explain, the manner of our perceiving external objects.

It is pleasant to observe, that while philosophers, for more than a century, have been labouring, by means of ideas, to explain perception, and the other operations of the mind, those ideas have by degrees usurped the place of perception, object, and even of the mind itself, and have supplanted those very things they were brought to explain. Des Cartes reduced all the operations of the understanding to perception; and what can be more natural to those who believe that they are only different modes of perceiving ideas in our own minds. Locke confounds ideas, sometimes with the perception of an external object, sometimes with the external object itself. In Berkeley's system, the idea is the only object, and yet is often confounded with the perception of it. But in Hume's, the idea or the impression, which is only a more lively idea, is mind, perception, and object, all in one : so that, by the term perception in Mr. Hume's system, we must understand the mind itself, all its operations, both of understanding and will, and all the objects of these operations. Perception, taken in this sense, he divides into our more lively perceptions, which he calls *impressions*, and the less lively, which he calls *ideas*. To prevent repetition, I must here refer the reader to some remarks made upon this division, Essay 1. chap. 1. in the explication there given of the words *perceive, object, impression.*

Philosophers have differed very much with regard to the origin of our ideas, or the sources whence they are derived. The Peripatetics held, that all knowledge is derived originally from the senses ; and this ancient doctrine seems to be revived by some late French philosophers, and by Dr. Hartley and Dr. Priestley among the British. Des Cartes maintained, that many of our ideas are innate. Locke opposed the doctrine of innate ideas with much zeal, and employs the whole first book of his Essay against it. But he admits two different sources of ideas ; the operations of our external senses, which he calls *sensation*, by which we get all our ideas of body, and its attributes ; and *reflection* upon the operations of our minds, by which we get the ideas of every thing belonging to the mind. The main design of the second book of Locke's Essay, is to show, that all our simple ideas, without exception, are derived from the one or the other, or both of these sources. In doing this, the author is led into some paradoxes, although, in general, he is not fond of paradoxes :

and had he foreseen all the consequences that may be
drawn from his account of the origin of our ideas, he
would probably have examined it more carefully.

Mr. Hume adopts Locke's account of the origin of
our ideas, and from that principle infers, that we have
no idea of substance, corporeal or spiritual, no idea of
power, no other idea of a cause, but that it is something antecedent, and constantly conjoined to that
which we call its effects; and, in a word, that we can
have no idea of any thing but our sensations, and the
operations of mind we are conscious of.

This author leaves no power to the mind in framing
its ideas and impressions; and no wonder, since he
holds that we have no idea of power; and the mind is
nothing but that succession of impressions and ideas of
which we are intimately conscious.

He thinks, therefore, that our impressions arise from
unknown causes, and that the impressions are the
causes of their corresponding ideas. By this he means
no more but that they always go before the ideas; for
this is all that is necessary to constitute the relation of
cause and effect.

As to the order and succession of our ideas, he holds
it to be determined by three laws of attraction or association, which he takes to be original properties of the
ideas, by which they attract, as it were, or associate
themselves with other ideas which either resemble
them, or which have been contiguous to them in time
and place, or to which they have the relations of cause
and effect.

We may here observe by the way, that the last of
these three laws seems to be included in the second,
since causation, according to him, implies no more than
contiguity in time and place.

It is not my design at present to show how Mr. Hume,
upon the principles he has borrowed from Locke and

Berkeley, has with great acuteness reared a system of
absolute skepticism, which leaves no rational ground to
believe any one proposition, rather than its contrary:
my intention in this place being only to give a detail of
the sentiments of philosophers concerning ideas since
they became an object of speculation, and concerning
the manner of our perceiving external objects by their
means.

CHAP. XIII.

OF THE SENTIMENTS OF ANTONY ARNAULD.

In this sketch of the opinions of philosophers concerning ideas, we must not omit Antony Arnauld, doctor of the Sorbonne, who, in the year 1683, published his book of True and False Ideas, in opposition to the system of Malebranche, before mentioned. It is only about ten years since I could find this book, and I believe it is rare.

Though Arnauld wrote before Locke, Berkeley, and Hume, I have reserved to the last place some account of his sentiments, because it seems difficult to determine whether he adopted the common theory of ideas, or whether he is singular in rejecting it altogether as a fiction of philosophers.

The controversy between Malebranche and Arnauld necessarily led them to consider what kind of things ideas are, a point upon which other philosophers had very generally been silent. Both of them professed the doctrine universally received, that we perceive not material things immediately, that it is their ideas that are the immediate objects of our thought, and that it is in the idea of every thing that we perceive its properties.

It is necessary to premise, that both these authors use the word *perception*, as Des Cartes had done before them, to signify every operation of the understanding. " To think, to know, to perceive, are the same thing," says Mr. Arnauld, chap. 5. def. 2. It is likewise to be observed, that the various operations of the mind are by both called modifications of the mind. Perhaps they were led into this phrase by the Cartesian doctrine, that the essence of the mind consists in thinking, as that of body consists in extension. I apprehend, therefore, that when they make sensation, perception, memory, and imagination, to be various modifications of the mind, they mean no more, but that these are things which can only exist in the mind as their subject. We express the same thing, by calling them various modes of thinking, or various operations of the mind.

The things which the mind perceives, says Malebranche, are of two kinds. They are either in the mind itself, or they are external to it. The things in the mind, are all its different modifications, its sensations, its imaginations, its pure intellections, its passions and affections. These are immediately perceived ; we are conscious of them, and have no need of ideas to represent them to us.

Things external to the mind, are either corporeal or spiritual. With regard to the last, he thinks it possible, that, in another state, spirits may be an immediate object of our understandings, and so be perceived without ideas ; that there may be such an union of spirits as that they may immediately perceive each other, and communicate their thoughts mutually, without signs, and without ideas.

But leaving this as a problematical point, he holds it to be undeniable, that material things cannot be perceived immediately, but only by the mediation of ideas. He thought it likewise undeniable. that the idea must be immediately present to the mind, that it must touch the soul, as it were, and modify its perception of the object.

From these principles we must necessarily conclude, either that the idea is some modification of the human mind, or that it must be an idea in the Divine Mind, which is always intimately present with our minds. The matter being brought to this alternative, Malebranche considers first, all the possible ways such a modification may be produced in our mind as that we call an idea of a material object, taking it for granted always, that it must be an object perceived, and something different from the act of the mind in perceiving it. He finds insuperable objections against every hypothesis of such ideas being produced in our minds, and therefore concludes, that the immediate objects of perception are the ideas of the Divine Mind.

Against this system Arnauld wrote his book of True and False Ideas. He does not object to the alternative mentioned by Malebranche; but he maintains, that ideas are modifications of our minds. And finding no other modification of the human mind which can be called the idea of an external object, he says it is only another word for perception. Chap. 5. def. 3. "I take the idea of an object, and the perception of an object, to be the same thing. I do not say whether there may be other things to which the name of idea may be given. But it is certain that there are ideas taken in this sense, and that these ideas are either attributes or modifications of our minds."

This, I think indeed, was to attack the system of Malebranche upon its weak side, and where, at the same time, an attack was least expected. Philosophers had been so unanimous in maintaining that we do not perceive external objects immediately, but by certain representative images of them called *ideas*, that Malebranche might well think his system secure upon that quarter, and that the only question to be determined was, in what subject those ideas are placed, whether in the human or in the Divine Mind?

But, says Mr. Arnauld, those ideas are mere chimeras, fictions of philosophers; there are no such beings in nature; and therefore it is to no purpose to inquire whether they are in the Divine or in the human mind.

The only true and real ideas are our perceptions, which are acknowledged by all philosophers, and by Malebranche himself, to be acts or modifications of our own minds. He does not say that the fictitious ideas were a fiction of Malebranche. He acknowledges, that they had been very generally maintained by the scholastic philosophers, and points out, very judiciously, the prejudices that had led them into the belief of such ideas.

Of all the powers of our mind, the external senses are thought to be the best understood, and their objects are the most familiar. Hence we measure other powers by them, and transfer to other powers the language which properly belongs to them. The objects of sense must be present to the sense, or within its sphere, in order to their being perceived. Hence, by analogy, we are led to say of every thing when we think of it, that it is present to the mind, or in the mind. But this presence is metaphorical, or analogical only; and Arnauld calls it objective presence, to distinguish it from that local presence which is required in objects that are perceived by sense. But both being called by the same name, they are confounded together, and those things that belong only to real or local presence, are attributed to the metaphorical.

We are likewise accustomed to see objects by their images in a mirror, or in water; and hence are led, by analogy, to think that objects may be presented to the memory or imagination, in some similar manner, by images, which philosophers have called *ideas*.

By such prejudices and analogies, Arnauld conceives, men have been led to believe, that the objects of memory and imagination must be presented to the mind by images or ideas; and the philosophers have been more carried away by these prejudices than even the vulgar, because the use made of this theory was to explain and account for the various operations of the mind, a matter in which the vulgar take no concern.

He thinks, however, that Des Cartes had got the
better of these prejudices, and that he uses the word
idea as signifying the same thing with perception, and
is therefore surprised that a disciple of Des Cartes, and
one who was so great an admirer of him as Malebranche
was, should be carried away by them. It is strange,
indeed, that the two most eminent disciples of Des
Cartes, and his contemporaries, should differ so essentially with regard to his doctrine concerning ideas.

I shall not attempt to give the reader an account of
the continuation of this controversy between those two
acute philosophers, in the subsequent defences and replies ; because I have not access to see them. After
much reasoning, and some animosity, each continued
in his own opinion, and left his antagonist where he
found him. Malebranche's opinion of our seeing all
things in God, soon died away of itself ; and Arnauld's
notion of ideas seems to have been less regarded than
it deserved, by the philosophers that came after him ;
perhaps for this reason, among others, that it seemed
to be in some sort given up by himself, in his attempting to reconcile it to the common doctrine concerning
ideas.

From the account I have given, one would be apt to
conclude, that Arnauld totally denied the existence of
ideas, in the philosophical sense of that word, and that
he adopted the notion of the vulgar, who acknowledge
no object of perception but the external object. But he
seems very unwilling to deviate so far from the common track, and what he had given up with one hand he
takes back with the other.

For, 1st, Having defined ideas to be the same thing
with perceptions, he adds this qualification to his definition : "I do not here consider whether there are
other things that may be called ideas ; but it is certain
there are ideas taken in this sense." I believe, indeed,

there is no philosopher who does not, on some occasions, use the word *idea* in this popular sense.

2dly, He supports this popular sense of the word by the authority of Des Cartes, who, in his demonstration of the existence of God from the idea of him in our minds, defines an idea thus: " By the word *idea*, I understand that form of any thought, by the immediate perception of which I am conscious of that thought; so that I can express nothing by words, with understanding, without being certain that there is in my mind the idea of that which is expressed by the words." This definition seems, indeed, to be of the same import with that which is given by Arnauld. But Des Cartes adds a qualification to it, which Arnauld, in quoting it, omits; and which shows, that Des Cartes meant to limit his definition to the idea then treated of, that is, to the idea of the Deity; and that there are other ideas to which this definition does not apply. For he adds: " And thus I give the name of idea, not solely to the images painted in the phantasy. Nay, in this place, I do not at all give the name of ideas to those images, in so far as they are painted in the corporeal phantasy, that is in some part of the brain, but only in so far as they inform the mind, turning its attention to that part of the brain."

3dly, Arnauld has employed the whole of his sixth chapter, to show that these ways of speaking, common among philosophers, to wit, *that we perceive not things immediately ; that it is their ideas that are the immediate objects of our thoughts ; that it is in the idea of every thing that we perceive its properties*, are not to be rejected, but are true when rightly understood. He labours to reconcile these expressions to his own definition of ideas, by observing, that every perception, and every thought is necessarily conscious of itself, and reflects upon itself; and that, by this consciousness and reflection, it is its own immediate object. Whence he infers, that the idea, that is, the perception, is the immediate object of perception.

This looks like a weak attempt to reconcile two inconsistent doctrines, by one who wishes to hold both. It is true, that consciousness always goes along with perception; but they are different operations of the mind, and they have their different objects. Consciousness is not perception, nor is the object of consciousness the object of perception. The same may be said of every operation of mind that has an object. Thus, injury is the object of resentment. When I resent an injury, I am conscious of my resentment; that is, my resentment is the immediate, and the only object of my consciousness; but it would be absurd to infer from this, that my resentment is the immediate object of my resentment.

Upon the whole, if Arnauld, in consequence of his doctrine, that ideas, taken for representative images of external objects, are a mere fiction of the philosophers, had rejected boldly the doctrine of Des Cartes, as well as of the other philosophers, concerning those fictitious beings, and all the ways of speaking that imply their existence, I should have thought him more consistent with himself, and his doctrine concerning ideas, more rational and more intelligible than that of any other author of my acquaintance who has treated of the subject.

CHAP. XIV.

REFLECTIONS ON THE COMMON THEORY OF IDEAS.

AFTER so long a detail of the sentiments of philosophers, ancient and modern, concerning ideas, it may
seem presumptuous to call in question their existence.
But no philosophical opinion, however ancient, however generally received, ought to rest upon authority.
There is no presumption in requiring evidence for it,
or in regulating our belief by the evidence we can find.

To prevent mistakes, the reader must again be re-
minded, that if by *ideas* are meant only the acts or operations of our minds in perceiving, remembering, or
imagining objects, I am far from calling in question
the existence of those acts ; we are conscious of them
every day, and every hour of life ; and I believe no man
of a sound mind ever doubted of the real existence of
the operations of mind, of which he is conscious.   Nor
is it to be doubted, that by the faculties which God has
given us, we can conceive things that are absent, as well
as perceive those that are within the reach of our senses ; and that such conceptions may be more or less distinct, and more or less lively and strong. We have reason to ascribe to the all knowing and all perfect Being,
distinct conceptions of all things existent and possible,
and of all their relations ; and if these conceptions are
called his *eternal ideas*, there ought to be no dispute
among philosophers about a word. The ideas, of whose
existence I require the proof, are not the operations of
any mind, but supposed objects of those operations.
They are not perception, remembrance, or conception,
but things that are said to be perceived, or remembered, or imagined.

Nor do I dispute the existence of what the vulgar call the objects of perception. These, by all who acknowledge their existence, are called *real things*, not *ideas*. But philosophers maintain, that, besides these, there are immediate objects of perception in the mind itself: that, for instance, we do not see the sun immediately, but an idea; or, as Mr. Hume calls it, an impression in our own minds. This idea is said to be the image, the resemblance, the representative of the sun, if there be a sun. It is from the existence of the idea that we must infer the existence of the sun. But the idea being immediately perceived, there can be no doubt, as philosophers think, of its existence.

In like manner, when I remember, or when I imagine any thing, all men acknowledge that there must be something that is remembered, or that is imagined; that is, some object of those operations. The object remembered must be something that did exist in time past. The object imagined, may be something that never existed. But, say the philosophers, besides these objects which all men acknowledge, there is a more immediate object which really exists in the mind at the same time we remember or imagine. This object is an idea, or image of the thing remembered or imagined.

The *first* reflection I would make on this philosophical opinion is, that it is directly contrary to the universal sense of men who have not been instructed in philosophy. When we see the sun or moon, we have no doubt that the very objects which we immediately see, are very far distant from us, and from one another. We have not the least doubt, that this is the sun and moon which God created some thousands of years ago, and which have continued to perform their revolutions in the heavens ever since. But how are we astonished when the philosopher informs us, that we are mistaken in all this; that the sun and moon which we see, are

not, as we imagine, many miles distant from us, and
from each other, but that they are in our own mind;
that they had no existence before we saw them, and
will have none when we cease to perceive and to think
of them; because the objects we perceive are only ideas
in our own minds, which can have no existence a moment longer than we think of them.

If a plain man, uninstructed in philosophy, has faith
to receive these mysteries, how great must be his as-
tonishment. He is brought into a new world, where
every thing he sees, tastes, or touches, is an idea; a
fleeting kind of being which he can conjure into existence, or can annihilate in the twinkling of an eye.

After his mind is somewhat composed, it will be natural for him to ask his philosophical instructor, pray,
sir, are there then no substantial and permanent beings
called the sun and moon, which continue to exist whether we think of them or not?

Here the philosophers differ. Mr. Locke, and those
that were before him, will answer to this question, that
it is very true, there are substantial and permanent beings called the sun and moon; but they never appear
to us in their own person, but by their representatives, the ideas in our own minds, and we know nothing
of them but what we can gather from those ideas.

Bishop Berkeley and Mr. Hume, would give a different answer to the question proposed. They would assure
the querist, that it is a vulgar error, a mere prejudice
of the ignorant and unlearned, to think that there are
any permanent and substantial beings called the sun and
moon; that the heavenly bodies, our own bodies, and
all bodies whatsoever, are nothing but ideas in our
minds; and that there can be nothing like the ideas of
one mind, but the ideas of another mind. There is nothing in nature but minds and ideas, says the bishop : nay,
says Mr. Hume, there is nothing in nature but ideas

only; for what we call a mind, is nothing but a train of ideas connected by certain relations between themselves.

In this representation of the theory of ideas, there is nothing exaggerated or misrepresented, as far as I am able to judge ; and surely nothing further is necessary to show, that, to the uninstructed in philosophy, it must appear extravagant and visionary, and most contrary to the dictates of common understanding.

There is the less need of any further proof of this, that it is very amply acknowledged by Mr. Hume in his Essay on the Academical or Skeptical Philosophy. "It seems evident, says he, that men are carried by a natural instinct, or prepossession, to repose faith in their senses ; and that without any reasoning, or even almost before the use of reason, we always suppose an external universe, which depends not on our perception, but would exist though we and every sensible creature were absent or annihilated. Even the animal creation are governed by a like opinion, and preserve this belief of external objects in all their thoughts, designs, and actions.

"It seems also evident, that when men follow this blind and powerful instinct of nature, they always suppose the very images presented by the senses to be the external objects, and never entertain any suspicion, that the one are nothing but representations of the other. This very table which we see white, and feel hard, is believed to exist independent of our perception, and to be something external to the mind which perceives it ; our presence bestows not being upon it ; our absence annihilates it not : it preserves its existence uniform and entire, independent of the situation of intelligent beings who perceive or contemplate it.

" But this universal and primary notion of all men is soon destroyed by the slightest philosophy, which teaches us, that nothing can ever be present to the mind, but in image or perception; and that the senses are only the inlets through which these images are received, without being ever able to produce any immediate intercourse between the mind and the object."

It is therefore acknowledged by this philosopher, to be a natural instinct or prepossession, an universal and primary opinion of all men, a primary instinct of nature, that the objects which we immediately perceive by our senses, are not images in our minds, but external objects, and that their existence is independent of us, and our perception.

In this acknowledgment, Mr. Hume, indeed, seems to me more generous, and even more ingenuous than bishop Berkeley, who would persuade us, that his opinion does not oppose the vulgar opinion, but only that of the philosophers; and that the external existence of a material world is a philosophical hypothesis, and not the natural dictate of our perceptive powers. The bishop shows a timidity of engaging such an adversary, as a primary and universal opinion of all men. He is rather fond to court its patronage. But the philosopher intrepidly gives a defiance to this antagonist, and seems to glory in a conflict that was worthy of his arm. *Optat aprum aut fulvum descendere monte leonem.* After all, I suspect that a philosopher, who wages war with this adversary, will find himself in the same condition as a mathematician who should undertake to demonstrate, that there is no truth in the axioms of mathematics.

A *second* reflection upon this subject is, that the authors who have treated of ideas, have generally taken their existence for granted, as a thing that could not be called in question; and such arguments as they have

mentioned incidentally, in order to prove it, seem too
weak to support the conclusion.

Mr. Locke, in the introduction to his Essay, tells us,
that he uses the word *idea* to signify whatever is the
immediate object of thought; and then adds, "I presume it will be easily granted me that there are such
ideas in men's minds; every one is conscious of them in
himself, and men's words and actions will satisfy him
that they are in others." I am indeed conscious of perceiving, remembering, imagining; but that the objects
of these operations are images in my mind I am not
conscious. I am satisfied by men's words and actions,
that they often perceive the same objects which I perceive, which could not be, if those objects were ideas in
their own minds.

Mr. Norris is the only author I have met with, who
professedly puts the question, Whether material things
can be perceived by us immediately? He has offered
four arguments to show that they cannot. 1st, "Material objects are without the mind, and therefore there
can be no union between the object and the percipient." *Answer*, This argument is lame, until it is shown
to be necessary that in perception there should be a union
between the object and the percipient. 2dly, "Material objects are disproportioned to the mind, and removed from it by the whole diameter of Being." This argument I cannot answer, because I do not understand
it. 3dly, "Because if material objects were immediate
objects of perception, there could be no physical science; things necessary and immutable being the only
object of science." *Answer*, Although things necessary and immutable be not the immediate objects of perception, they may be immediate objects of other powers
of the mind. 4thly, "If material things were perceived
by themselves, they would be a true light to our minds,
as being the intelligible form of our understandings,

and consequently perfective of them, and indeed superior to them." If I comprehend any thing of this mysterious argument, it follows from it, that the Deity perceives nothing at all, because nothing can be superior to his understanding, or perfective of it.

There is an argument which is hinted at by Malebranche, and by several other authors, which deserves to be more seriously considered. As I find it most clearly expressed, and most fully urged by Dr. Samuel Clarke, I shall give it in his words, in his second reply to Leibnitz, sect. 4. " The soul, without being present to the images of the things perceived, could not possibly perceive them. A living substance can only there perceive, where it is present, either to the things themselves, as the omnipresent God is to the whole universe, or to the images of things, as the soul is in its proper *sensorium*."

Sir Isaac Newton expresses the same sentiment, but with his usual reserve, in a query only.

The ingenious Dr. Porterfield, in his Essay concerning the motions of our eyes, adopts this opinion with more confidence. His words are: " How body acts upon mind, or mind upon body, I know not; but this I am very certain of, that nothing can act, or be acted upon, where it is not; and therefore, our mind can never perceive any thing but its own proper modifications, and the various states of the sensorium, to which it is present: so that it is not the external sun and moon which are in the heavens, which our mind perceives, but only their image or representation impressed upon the sensorium. How the soul of a seeing man sees these images, or how it receives those ideas, from such agitations in the sensorium, I know not; but I am sure it can never perceive the external bodies themselves, to which it is not present."

These, indeed, are great authorities; but, in matters of philosophy, we must not be guided by authority, but by reason. Dr. Clarke, in the place cited, mentions slightly, as the reason of his opinion, that "nothing can any more act, or be acted upon, when it is not present, than it can be where it is not." And again, in his third reply to Leibnitz, sect. 11. "We are sure the soul cannot perceive what it is not present to, because nothing can act, or be acted upon, where it is not." The same reason we see is urged by Dr. Porterfield.

That nothing can act immediately where it is not, I think, must be admitted; for I agree with sir Isaac Newton, that power without substance is inconceivable. It is a consequence of this, that nothing can be acted upon immediately where the agent is not present. Let this therefore be granted. To make the reasoning conclusive, it is further necessary that, when we perceive objects, either they act upon us, or we act upon them. This does not appear self evident, nor have I ever met with any proof of it. I shall briefly offer the reasons why I think it ought not to be admitted.

When we say that one being acts upon another, we mean that some power or force is exerted by the agent, which produces, or has a tendency to produce, a change in the thing acted upon. If this be the meaning of the phrase, as I conceive it is, there appears no reason for asserting, that, in perception, either the object acts upon the mind, or the mind upon the object.

An object, in being perceived, does not act at all. I perceive the walls of the room where I sit; but they are perfectly inactive, and therefore act not upon the mind. To be perceived, is what logicians call an external denomination, which implies neither action nor quality in the object perceived. Nor could men ever have gone into this notion, that perception is owing to

some action of the object upon the mind, were it not,
that we are so prone to form our notions of the mind
from some similitude we conceive between it and body.
Thought in the mind is conceived to have some analogy to motion in a body: and as a body is put in motion,
by being acted upon by some other body; so we are apt
to think the mind is made to perceive, by some impulse
it receives from the object. But reasonings, drawn
from such analogies, ought never to be trusted. They
are, indeed, the cause of most of our errors with regard to the mind. And we might as well conclude,
that minds may be measured by feet and inches, or
weighed by ounces and drachms, because bodies have
those properties.

I see as little reason, in the second place, to believe,
that in perception the mind acts upon the object. To
perceive an object is one thing, to act upon it is another; nor is the last at all included in the first. To
say, that I act upon the wall, by looking at it, is an
abuse of language, and has no meaning. Logicians
distinguish two kinds of operations of mind; the first
kind produces no effect without the mind; the last
does. The first they call *immanent acts*; the second
transitive. All intellectual operations belong to the
first class; they produce no effect upon any external
object. But without having recourse to logical distinctions, every man of common sense knows, that to
think of an object, and to act upon it, are very different things.

As we have therefore no evidence, that, in perception,
the mind acts upon the object, or the object upon the
mind, but strong reasons to the contrary; Dr. Clarke's
argument against our perceiving external objects immediately falls to the ground. This notion, that, in
perception, the object must be contiguous to the percipient, seems, with many other prejudices, to be bor-

rowed from analogy. In all the external senses, there must, as has been before observed, be some impression made upon the organ of sense by the object, or by something coming from the object. An impression supposes contiguity. Hence we are led by analogy to conceive something similar in the operations of the mind. Many philosophers resolve almost every operation of mind into impressions and feelings, words manifestly borrowed from the sense of touch. And it is very natural to conceive contiguity necessary between that which makes the impression, and that which receives it; between that which feels, and that which is felt. And though no philosopher will now pretend to justify such analogical reasoning as this, yet it has a powerful influence upon the judgment, while we contemplate the operations of our minds, only as they appear through the deceitful medium of such analogical notions and expressions.

When we lay aside those analogies, and reflect attentively upon our perception of the objects of sense, we must acknowledge, that, though we are conscious of perceiving objects, we are altogether ignorant how it is brought about : and know as little how we perceive objects as how we were made. And if we should admit an image in the mind, or contiguous to it, we know as little how perception may be produced by this image as by the most distant object. Why therefore should we be led, by a theory which is neither grounded on evidence, nor, if admitted, can explain any one phenomenon of perception, to reject the natural and immediate dictates of those perceptive powers, to which, in the conduct of life, we find a necessity of yielding implicit submission ?

There remains only one other argument that I have been able to find urged against our perceiving external objects immediately. It is proposed by Mr. Hume, who, in the Essay already quoted. after acknowledging that it is an universal and primary opinion of all men, that we perceive external objects immediately, subjoins what follows :

" But this universal and primary opinion of all men is soon destroyed by the slightest philosophy, which teaches us, that nothing can ever be present to the mind but an image or perception; and that the senses are only the inlets through which these images are received, without being ever able to produce any immediate intercourse between the mind and the object. The table, which we see, seems to diminish as we remove further from it ; but the real table, which exists independent of us, suffers no alteration. It was therefore nothing but its image which was present to the mind. These are the obvious dictates of reason ; and no man who reflects, ever doubted that the existences which we consider, when we say, *this house,* and *that tree,* are nothing but perceptions in the mind, and fleeting copies and representations of other existences, which remain uniform and independent. So far then, we are necessitated, by reasoning, to depart from the primary instincts of nature, and to embrace a new system, with regard to the evidence of our senses."

We have here a remarkable conflict between two contradictory opinions, wherein all mankind are engaged. On the one side, stand all the vulgar, who are unpractised in philosophical researches, and guided by the uncorrupted primary instincts of nature. On the other side, stand all the philosophers ancient and modern ; every man without exception who reflects. In this division, to my great humiliation, I find myself classed with the vulgar.

The passage now quoted is all I have found in Mr. Hume's writings upon this point ; and indeed there is more reasoning in it than I have found in any other author; I shall therefore examine it minutely.

First, He tells us, That " this universal and primary opinion of all men is soon destroyed by the slightest philosophy, which teaches us, that nothing can ever be present to the mind but an image or perception."

The phrase of being present to the mind has some obscurity; but I conceive he means being an immediate object of thought; an immediate object, for instance, of perception, of memory, or of imagination. If this be the meaning, and it is the only pertinent one I can think of, there is no more in this passage but an assertion of the proposition to be proved, and an assertion that philosophy teaches it. If this be so, I beg leave to dissent from philosophy till she gives me reason for what she teaches. For though common sense and my external senses demand my assent to their dictates upon their own authority, yet philosophy is not entitled to this privilege. But that I may not dissent from so grave a personage without giving a reason, I give this as the reason of my dissent. I see the sun when he shines; I remember the battle of Culloden; and neither of these objects is an image or perception.

He tells us in the *next* place, " That the senses are only the inlets through which these images are received."

I know that Aristotle and the schoolmen taught, that images or species flow from objects, and are let in by the senses, and strike upon the mind; but this has been so effectually refuted by Des Cartes, by Malebranche, and many others, that nobody now pretends to defend it. Reasonable men consider it as one of the most unintelligible and unmeaning parts of the ancient system. To what cause is it owing that modern philosophers are so prone to fall back into this hypothesis, as if they really believed it? For of this proneness I

could give many instances besides this of Mr. Hume;
and I take the cause to be, that images in the mind,
and images let in by the senses, are so nearly allied,
and so strictly connected, that they must stand or fall
together. The old system consistently maintained
both : but the new system has rejected the doctrine of
images let in by the senses, holding, nevertheless, that
there are images in the mind ; and, having made this
unnatural divorce of two doctrines which ought not to be
put asunder, that which they have retained often
leads them back involuntarily to that which they have
rejected.

Mr. Hume surely did not seriously believe that an
image of sound is let in by the ear, an image of smell
by the nose, an image of hardness and softness, of solidity and resistance, by the touch. For, besides the
absurdity of the thing, which has often been shown,
Mr. Hume, and all modern philosophers maintain, that
the images which are the immediate objects of perception, have no existence when they are not perceived :
whereas, if they were let in by the senses, they must be,
before they are perceived, and have a separate existence.

He tells us further, that philosophy teaches, that the
senses are unable to produce any immediate intercourse
between the mind and the object. Here I still require the
reasons that philosophy gives for this ; for, to my apprehension, I immediately perceive external objects, and this
I conceive is the immediate intercourse here meant.

Hitherto I see nothing that can be called an argument. Perhaps it was intended only for illustration.
The argument, the only argument follows :

The table, which we see, seems to diminish as we remove further from it ; but the real table, which exists
independent of us, suffers no alteration. It was therefore nothing but its image which was presented to the
mind. These are the obvious dictates of reason

To judge of the strength of this argument, it is necessary to attend to a distinction which is familiar to those who are conversant in the mathematical sciences, I mean the distinction between real and apparent magnitude. The real magnitude of a line is measured by some known measure of length, as inches, feet, or miles. The real magnitude of a surface or solid, by known measures of surface or of capacity. This magnitude is an object of touch only, and not of sight; nor could we even have had any conception of it, without the sense of touch; and bishop Berkeley, on that account, calls it *tangible magnitude*.

Apparent magnitude is measured by the angle which an object subtends at the eye. Supposing two right lines drawn from the eye to the extremities of the object, making an angle, of which the object is the subtense, the apparent magnitude is measured by this angle. This apparent magnitude is an object of sight, and not of touch. Bishop Berkeley calls it *visible magnitude*.

If it be asked, What is the apparent magnitude of the sun's diameter? the answer is, That it is about thirty-one minutes of a degree. But if it be asked, What is the real magnitude of the sun's diameter? The answer must be, So many thousand miles, or so many diameters of the earth. From which it is evident, that real magnitude, and apparent magnitude, are things of a different nature, though the name of magnitude is given to both. The first has three dimensions, the last only two. The first is measured by a line, the last by an angle.

From what has been said, it is evident that the real magnitude of a body must continue unchanged, while the body is unchanged. This we grant. But is it likewise evident, that the apparent magnitude must continue the same while the body is unchanged? So far otherwise, that every man who knows any thing of mathematics can easily demonstrate, that the same individual object, remaining in the same place, and unchanged, must necessarily vary in its apparent magnitude, according as the point from which it is seen is more or less distant; and that its apparent length or breadth will be nearly in a reciprocal proportion to the distance of the spectator. This is as certain as the principles of geometry.

We must likewise attend to this, that though the real magnitude of a body is not originally an object of sight, but of touch, yet we learn by experience to judge of the real magnitude in many cases by sight. We learn by experience to judge of the distance of a body from the eye within certain limits; and from its distance and apparent magnitude taken together, we learn to judge of its real magnitude.

And this kind of judgment, by being repeated every hour, and almost every minute of our lives, becomes, when we are grown up, so ready and so habitual, that it very much resembles the original perceptions of our senses, and may not improperly be called *acquired perception.*

Whether we call it judgment or acquired perception is a verbal difference. But it is evident, that, by means of it, we often discover by one sense things which are properly and naturally the objects of another. Thus I can say without impropriety, I hear a drum, I hear a great bell, or I hear a small bell; though it is certain that the figure or size of the sounding body is not originally an object of hearing. In like manner, we learn by experience how a body of such a real magnitude, and at such a distance, appears to the eye: but neither its real magnitude, nor its distance from the eye, are properly objects of sight, any more than the form of a drum, or the size of a bell, are properly objects of hearing.

If these things be considered, it will appear, that Mr. Hume's argument has no force to support his conclusion, nay, that it leads to a contrary conclusion. The argument is this. The table we see, seems to diminish as we remove further from it; that is, its apparent magnitude is diminished; but the real table suffers no alteration, to wit, in its real magnitude; therefore it is not the real table we see. I admit both the premises in this syllogism, but I deny the conclusion. The syllogism has what the logicians call two middle terms. Apparent magnitude is the middle term in the first premise; real magnitude in the second. Therefore, according to the rules of logic, the conclusion is not justly drawn from the premises; but, laying aside the rules of logic, let us examine it by the light of common sense.

Let us suppose, for a moment, that it is the real table we see. Must not this real table seem to diminish as we remove further from it? It is demonstrable that it must. How then can this apparent diminution be an argument that it is not the real table? When that which must happen to the real table, as we remove further from it, does actually happen to the table we see, it is absurd to conclude from this, that it is not the real table we see. It is evident, therefore, that this ingenious author has imposed upon himself, by confounding real magnitude with apparent magnitude, and that his argument is a mere sophism.

I observed that Mr. Hume's argument, not only has no strength to support his conclusion, but that it leads to the contrary conclusion; to wit, that it is the real table we see; for this plain reason, that the table we see has precisely that apparent magnitude which it is demonstrable the real table must have when placed at that distance.

The argument is made much stronger by considering, that the real table may be placed successively at a thousand different distances, and in every distance, in a thousand different positions; and it can be determined demonstratively, by the rules of geometry and perspective, what must be its apparent magnitude, and apparent figure, in each of those distances and positions. Let the table be placed successively in as many of these different distances, and different positions, as you will, or in them all; open your eyes, and you shall see a table precisely of that apparent magnitude, and that apparent figure, which the real table must have in that distance, and in that position. Is not this a strong argument that it is the real table you see?

In a word, the appearance of a visible object is infinitely diversified, according to its distance and position. The visible appearances are innumerable, when we confine ourselves to one object, and they are multiplied according to the variety of objects. Those appearances have been matter of speculation to ingenious men, at least since the time of Euclid. They have accounted for all this variety, on the supposition, that the objects we see are external, and not in the mind itself. The rules they have demonstrated about the various projections of the sphere, about the appearances of the planets in their progressions, stations, and retrogradations, and all the rules of perspective, are built on the supposition that the objects of sight are external. They can each of them be tried in thousands of instances. In many arts and professions, innumerable trials are daily made; nor were they ever found to fail in a single instance. Shall we say that a false supposition, invented by the rude vulgar, has been so lucky in solving an infinite number of phenomena of nature? This

surely would be a greater prodigy than philosophy
ever exhibited. Add to this, that upon the contrary
hypothesis, to wit, that the objects of sight are internal,
no account can be given of any one of those appearances,
nor any physical cause assigned why a visible object
should, in any one case, have one apparent figure and
magnitude rather than another.

Thus I have considered every argument I have found
advanced to prove the existence of ideas or images of
external things in the mind; and if no better arguments can be found, I cannot help thinking, that the
whole history of philosophy has never furnished an instance of an opinion so unanimously entertained by philosophers upon so slight grounds.

A *third* reflection I would make upon this subject is,
that philosophers, notwithstanding their unanimity as
to the existence of ideas, hardly agree in any one thing
else concerning them. If ideas be not a mere fiction,
they must be of all objects of human knowledge, the
things we have best access to know, and to be acquainted with; yet there is nothing about which men differ
so much.

Some have held them to be self existent, others to
be in the Divine mind, others in our own minds, and
others in the brain or *sensorium*. I considered the hypotheses of images in the brain, in the fourth chapter of
this Essay. As to images in the mind, if any thing
more is meant by the image of an object in the mind
than the thought of that object, I know not what it
means. The distinct conception of an object may, in a
metaphorical or analogical sense, be called an *image* of
it in the mind. But this image is only the conception
of the object, and not the object conceived. It is an act
of the mind, and not the object of that act.

Some philosophers will have our ideas, or a part of
them, to be innate; others will have them all to be adventitious. Some derive them from the senses alone;

others from sensation and reflection. Some think they are fabricated by the mind itself; others that they are produced by external objects; others that they are the immediate operation of the Deity; others say, that impressions are the causes of ideas, and that the causes of impressions are unknown. Some think that we have ideas only of material objects, but none of minds, of their operations, or of the relations of things; others will have the immediate object of every thought to be an idea. Some think we have abstract ideas, and that by this chiefly we are distinguished from the brutes; others maintain an abstract idea to be an absurdity, and that there can be no such thing. With some they are the immediate objects of thought, with others, the only objects.

A *fourth* reflection is, that ideas do not make any of the operations of the mind to be better understood, although it was probably with that view that they have been first invented, and afterward so generally received.

We are at a loss to know how we perceive distant objects; how we remember things past; how we imagine things that have no existence. Ideas in the mind seem to account for all these operations. They are all by the means of ideas reduced to one operation; to a kind of feeling, or immediate perception of things present, and in contact with the percipient; and feeling is an operation so familiar, that we think it needs no explication, but may serve to explain other operations.

But this feeling, or immediate perception, is as difficult to be comprehended, as the things which we pretend to explain by it. Two things may be in contact without any feeling or perception; there must therefore be in the percipient a power to feel or to perceive. How this power is produced, and how it operates, is quite beyond the reach of our knowledge. As little can we know whether this power must be limited to things present, and in contact with us. Nor can any man pretend to prove, that the Being who gave us the power to perceive things present, may not give us the power to perceive things that are distant, to remember things past, and to conceive things that never existed.

Some philosophers have endeavoured to make all our senses to be only different modifications of touch; a theory which serves only to confound things that are different, and to perplex and darken things that are clear. The theory of ideas resembles this, by reducing all the operations of the human understanding to the perception of ideas in our own minds. This power of perceiving ideas is as inexplicable as any of the powers explained by it: and the contiguity of the object contributes nothing at all to make it better understood; because there appears no connection between contiguity and perception, but what is grounded on prejudices, drawn from some imagined similitude between mind and body; and from the supposition, that, in perception, the object acts upon the mind, or the mind upon the object. We have seen how this theory has led philosophers to confound those operations of mind which experience teaches all men to be different, and teaches them to distinguish in common language; and that it has led them to invent a language inconsistent with the principles upon which all language is grounded.

The *last* reflection I shall make upon this theory is, that the natural and necessary consequences of it furnish a just prejudice against it to every man who pays a due regard to the common sense of mankind.

Not to mention, that it led the Pythagoreans and Plato to imagine that we see only the shadows of external things, and not the things themselves, and that it gave rise to the Peripatetic doctrine of sensible *species*, one of the greatest absurdities of that ancient system, let us only consider the fruits it has produced, since it was new modelled by Des Cartes. That great reformer in philosophy saw the absurdity of the doctrine of ideas coming from external objects, and refuted it effectually, after it had been received by philosophers for thousands of years; but he still retained ideas in the brain and in the mind. Upon this foundation, all our modern systems of the powers of the mind are built. And the tottering state of those fabrics, though built by skilful hands, may give a strong suspicion of the unsoundness of the foundation.

It was this theory of ideas that led Des Cartes, and those that followed him, to think it necessary to prove, by philosophical arguments, the existence of material objects. And who does not see that philosophy must make a very ridiculous figure in the eyes of sensible men, while it is employed in mustering up metaphysical arguments, to prove that there is a sun and a moon, an earth and a sea? Yet we find these truly great men, Des Cartes, Malebranche, Arnauld, and Locke, seriously employing themselves in this argument.

Surely their principles led them to think, that all men, from the beginning of the world, believed the existence of these things upon insufficient grounds, and to think that they would be able to place upon a more rational foundation this universal belief of mankind. But the misfortune is, that all the laboured arguments they have advanced, to prove the existence of those things we see and feel, are mere sophisms. Not one of them will bear examination.

I might mention several paradoxes, which Mr. Locke, though by no means fond of paradoxes, was led into by this theory of ideas. Such as, that the secondary qualities of body are no qualities of body at all, but sensations of the mind: That the primary qualities of body are resemblances of our sensations: That

we have no notion of duration, but from the succession
of ideas in our minds : That personal identity consists
in consciousness ; so that the same individual thinking
being may make two or three different persons, and
several different thinking beings make one person :
That judgment is nothing but a perception of the agreement or disagreement of our ideas. Most of these paradoxes I shall have occasion to examine.

However, all these consequences of the doctrine of
ideas were tolerable, compared with those which came
afterward to be discovered by Berkeley and Hume :
That there is no material world : No abstract ideas or
notions : That the mind is only a train of related impressions and ideas, without any subject on which they
may be impressed : That there is neither space nor
time, body nor mind, but impressions and ideas only :
And, to sum up all, That there is no probability, even
in demonstration itself, nor any one proposition more
probable than its contrary.

These are the noble fruits which have grown upon
this theory of ideas, since it began to be cultivated by
skilful hands. It is no wonder that sensible men
should be disgusted at philosophy, when such wild and
shocking paradoxes pass under its name. However, as
these paradoxes have, with great acuteness and ingenuity, been deduced by just reasoning from the theory
of ideas, they must at last bring this advantage, that
positions so shocking to the common sense of mankind,
and so contrary to the decisions of all our intellectual
powers, will open men's eyes, and break the force of the
prejudice which has held them entangled in that theory.

CHAP. XV.

ACCOUNT OF THE SYSTEM OF LEIBNITZ.

THERE is yet another system concerning perception, of which I shall give some account, because of the fame of its author. It is the invention of the famous German philosopher Leibnitz, who, while he lived, held the first rank among the Germans in all parts of philosophy, as well as in mathematics, in jurisprudence, in the knowledge of antiquities, and in every branch, both of science and of literature. He was highly respected by emperors, and by many kings and princes, who bestowed upon him singular marks of their esteem. He was a particular favourite of our queen Caroline, consort of George II. with whom he continued his correspondence by letters after she came to the crown of Britain, till his death.

The famous controversy between him and the British mathematicians, whether he or sir Isaac Newton was the inventor of that noble improvement in mathematics, called by Newton *the method of fluxions,* and by Leibnitz *the differential method,* engaged the attention of the mathematicians in Europe for several years. He had likewise a controversy with the learned and judicious Dr. Samuel Clarke, about several points of the Newtonian philosophy which he disapproved. The papers which gave occasion to this controversy, with all the replies and rejoinders, had the honour to be transmitted from the one party to the other through the hands of queen Caroline, and were afterward published.

His authority, in all matters of philosophy, is still so great in most parts of Germany, that they are considered as bold spirits, and a kind of heretics, who dissent

from him in any thing. Wolfius, the most voluminous writer in philosophy of this age, is considered as the
great interpreter and advocate of the Leibnitzian system, and reveres as an oracle whatever has dropped
from the pen of Leibnitz. This author proposed two
great works upon the mind. The first, which I have
seen, he published with the title of *Psychologia empirica, seu experimentalis.* The other was to have the
title of *Psychologia rationalis;* and to it he refers for
his explication of the theory of Leibnitz with regard
to the mind. But whether it was published I have not
learned.

I must therefore take the short account I am to give
of this system from the writings of Leibnitz himself,
without the light which his interpreter Wolfius may
have thrown upon it.

Leibnitz conceived the whole universe, bodies as
well as minds, to be made up of monads, that is, simple
substances, each of which is, by the Creator in the beginning of its existence, endowed with certain active and
perceptive powers. A monad, therefore, is an active
substance, simple, without parts or figure, which has
within itself the power to produce all the changes it
undergoes from the beginning of its existence to eternity. The changes which the monad undergoes, of what
kind soever, though they may seem to us the effect of
causes operating from without, yet they are only the
gradual and successive evolutions of its own internal
powers, which would have produced all the same
changes and motions, although there had been no other
being in the universe.

Every human soul is a monad joined to an organized body, which organized body consists of an infinite
number of monads, each having some degree of active
and of perceptive power in itself. But the whole machine of the body has a relation to that monad which

we call the soul, which is, as it were, the centre of the whole.

As the universe is completely filled with monads, without any chasm or void, and thereby every body acts upon every other body, according to its vicinity or distance, and is mutually re-acted upon by every other body, it follows, says Leibnitz, that every monad is a kind of living mirror, which reflects the whole universe, according to its point of view, and represents the whole more or less distinctly.

I cannot undertake to reconcile this part of the system with what was before mentioned. to wit, that every change in a monad is the evolution of its own original powers, and would have happened though no other substance had been created. But to proceed;

There are different orders of monads, some higher, and others lower. The higher orders he calls dominant; such is the human soul. The monads that compose the organized bodies of men, animals and plants, are of a lower order, and subservient to the dominant monads. But every monad of whatever order, is a complete substance in itself, indivisible, having no parts, indestructible, because, having no parts, it cannot perish by any kind of decomposition; it can only perish by annihilation, and we have no reason to believe that God will ever annihilate any of the beings which he has made.

The monads of a lower order may, by a regular evolution of their powers, rise to a higher order. They may successively be joined to organized bodies, of various forms and different degrees of perception; but they never die, nor cease to be in some degree active and percipient.

This philosopher makes a distinction between perception and what he calls *apperception*. The first is common to all monads, the last proper to the higher orders, among which are human souls.

By apperception he understands that degree of perception which reflects, as it were, upon itself; by which
we are conscious of our own existence, and conscious
of our perceptions; by which we can reflect upon the
operations of our own minds, and can comprehend
abstract truths. The mind, in many operations, he
thinks, particularly in sleep, and in many actions common to us with the brutes, has not this apperception,
although it is still filled with a multitude of obscure
and indistinct perceptions, of which we are not conscious.

He conceives that our bodies and minds are united
in such a manner, that neither has any physical influence upon the other. Each performs all its operations by its own internal springs and powers; yet the
operations of one correspond exactly with those of the
other, by a pre-established harmony; just as one clock
may be so adjusted as to keep time with another, although each has its own moving power, and neither receives any part of its motion from the other.

So that, according to this system, all our perceptions
of external objects would be the same, though external
things had never existed; our perception of them
would continue, although, by the power of God, they
should this moment be annihilated: we do not perceive external things because they exist, but because
the soul was originally so constituted as to produce in
itself all its successive changes, and all its successive
perceptions, independently of the external objects.

Every perception or apperception, every operation,
in a word, of the soul, is a necessary consequence of the
state of it immediately preceding that operation; and
this state is the necessary consequence of the state preceding it; and so backward, until you come to its first
formation, and constitution, which produces successively, and by necessary consequence, all its successive

states to the end of its existence ; so that in this respect the soul, and every monad, may be compared to
a watch wound up, which, having the spring of its
motion in itself, by the gradual evolution of its own
spring, produces all the successive motions we observe
in it.

In this account of Leibnitz's system concerning monads, and the pre-established harmony, I have kept as
nearly as I could to his own expressions, in his *new
system of the nature and communication of substances,
and of the union of soul and body;* and in the several illustrations of that new system which he afterward published ; and in his *principles of nature and grace founded in reason.* I shall now make a few remarks upon
this system.

1. To pass over the irresistible necessity of all human actions, which makes a part of this system, that
will be considered in another place, I observe first, that
the distinction made between perception and apperception is obscure and unphilosophical. As far as we
can discover, every operation of our mind is attended
with consciousness, and particularly that which we call
the perception of external objects ; and to speak of a
perception of which we are not conscious, is to speak
without any meaning.

As consciousness is the only power by which we discern the operations of our own minds, or can form any
notion of them, an operation of mind of which we are
not conscious, is, we know not what ; and to call such an
operation by the name of perception, is an abuse of
language. No man can perceive an object, without
being conscious that he perceives it. No man can
think, without being conscious that he thinks. What
men are not conscious of, cannot therefore, without impropriety, be called either perception or thought of any
kind. And if we will suppose operations of mind, of

which we are not conscious, and give a name to such creatures of our imagination, that name must signify what we know nothing about.

2. To suppose bodies organized or unorganized, to be made up of indivisible monads which have no parts, is contrary to all that we know of body. It is essential to a body to have parts; and every part of a body, is a body, and has parts also. No number of parts, without extension or figure, not even an infinite number, if we may use that expression, can, by being put together, make a whole that has extension and figure, which all bodies have.

3. It is contrary to all that we know of bodies, to ascribe to the monads, of which they are supposed to be compounded, perception and active force. If a philosopher thinks proper to say, that a clod of earth both perceives and has active force, let him bring his proofs. But he ought not to expect, that men who have understanding, will so far give it up as to receive without proof whatever his imagination may suggest.

4. This system overturns all authority of our senses, and leaves not the least ground to believe the existence of the objects of sense, or the existence of any thing which depends upon the authority of our senses; for our perception of objects, according to this system, has no dependence upon any thing external, and would be the same as it is, supposing external objects had never existed, or that they were from this moment annihilated.

It is remarkable that Leibnitz's system, that of Malebranche, and the common system of ideas, or images of external objects in the mind, do all agree in overturning all the authority of our senses; and this one thing, as long as men retain their senses, will always make all these systems truly ridiculous.

5. The last observation I shall make upon this system, which indeed is equally applicable to all the systems of perception I have mentioned, is, that it is all hypothesis, made up of conjectures and suppositions, without proof. The Peripatetics supposed sensible *species* to be sent forth by the objects of sense. The moderns suppose ideas in the brain, or in the mind. Malebranche supposed, that we perceive the ideas of the Divine mind. Leibnitz supposed monads and a pre-established harmony; and these monads being creatures of his own making, he is at liberty to give them what properties and powers his fancy may suggest. In like manner, the Indian philosopher supposed that the earth is supported by a huge elephant, and that the elephant stands on the back of a huge tortoise.

Such suppositions, while there is no proof of them offered, are nothing but the fictions of human fancy; and we ought no more to believe them, than we believe Homer's fictions of Apollo's silver bow, or Minerva's shield, or Venus's girdle. Such fictions in poetry are agreeable to the rules of the art. They are intended to please, not to convince. But the philosophers would have us to believe their fictions, though the account they give of the phenomena of nature has commonly no more probability than the account that Homer gives of the plague in the Grecian camp, from Apollo taking his station on a neighbouring mountain, and from his silver bow, letting fly his swift arrows into the camp.

Men then only begin to have a true taste in philosophy, when they have learned to hold hypotheses in just contempt; and to consider them as the reveries of speculative men, which will never have any similitude to the works of God.

The Supreme Being has given us some intelligence of his works, by what our senses inform us of external

things, and by what our consciousness and reflection inform us concerning the operations of our own minds.
Whatever can be inferred from these common informations, by just and sound reasoning, is true and legiti-
mate philosophy: but what we add to this from conjecture is all spurious and illegitimate.

After this long account of the theories advanced by
philosophers, to account for our perception of external
objects, I hope it will appear, that neither Aristotle's
theory of sensible species, nor Malebranche's, of our
seeing things in God, nor the common theory of our
perceiving ideas in our own minds, nor Leibnitz's theory of monads, and a pre-established harmony, give any
satisfying account of this power of the mind, or make
it more intelligible than it is without their aid. They
are conjectures, and if they were true, would solve no
difficulty, but raise many new ones. It is therefore
more agreeable to good sense, and to sound philosophy, to rest satisfied with what our consciousness and
attentive reflection discover to us of the nature of
perception, than by inventing hypotheses, to attempt
to explain things which are above the reach of human understanding. I believe no man is able to explain how we perceive external objects, any more
than how we are conscious of those that are internal.
Perception, consciousness, memory, and imagination,
are all original and simple powers of the mind, and
parts of its constitution. For this reason, though I
have endeavoured to show, that the theories of philosophers on this subject are ill-grounded and insufficient, I do not attempt to substitute any other theory in
their place.

Every man feels that perception gives him an invincible belief of the existence of that which he perceives ; and that this belief is not the effect of reasoning, but the immediate consequence of perception.

When philosophers have wearied themselves and their readers with their speculations upon this subject, they can neither strengthen this belief, nor weaken it; nor can they show how it is produced. It puts the philosopher and the peasant upon a level; and neither of them can give any other reason for believing his senses, than that he finds it impossible for him to do otherwise.

CHAPTER XVI.

OF SENSATION.

HAVING finished what I intend, with regard to that act of mind which we call the perception of an external object, I proceed to consider another, which, by our constitution, is conjoined with perception, and not with perception only, but with many other acts of our minds; and that is sensation. To prevent repetition, I must refer the reader to the explication of this word given in Essay I. chap. 1.

Almost all our perceptions have corresponding sensations which constantly accompany them, and, on that account, are very apt to be confounded with them. Neither ought we to expect, that the sensation, and its corresponding perception, should be distinguished in common language, because the purposes of common life do not require it. Language is made to serve the purposes of ordinary conversation; and we have no reason to expect that it should make distinctions that are not of common use. Hence it happens, that a quality perceived, and the sensation corresponding to that perception, often go under the same name.

This makes the names of most of our sensations ambiguous, and this ambiguity has very much perplexed philosophers. It will be necessary to give some instances, to illustrate the distinction between our sensations and the objects of perception.

When I smell a rose, there is in this operation both sensation and perception. The agreeable odour I feel, considered by itself, without relation to any external object, is merely a sensation. It affects the mind in a certain way; and this affection of the mind may be conceived, without a thought of the rose, or any other object. This sensation can be nothing else than it is felt to be. Its very essence consists in being felt; and when it is not felt, it is not. There is no difference between the sensation and the feeling of it; they are one and the same thing. It is for this reason, that we before observed, that, in sensation, there is no object distinct from that act of the mind by which it is felt; and this holds true with regard to all sensations.

Let us next attend to the perception which we have in smelling a rose. Perception has always an external object; and the object of my perception, in this case, is that quality in the rose which I discern by the sense of smell. Observing that the agreeable sensation is raised when the rose is near, and ceases when it is removed, I am led, by my nature, to conclude some quality to be in the rose, which is the cause of this sensation. This quality in the rose is the object perceived; and that act of my mind, by which I have the conviction and belief of this quality, is what in this case I call perception.

But it is here to be observed, that the sensation I feel, and the quality in the rose which I perceive, are both called by the same name. The smell of a rose is the name given to both: so that this name has two meanings; and the distinguishing its different meanings removes all perplexity, and enables us to give clear and distinct answers to questions, about which philosophers have held much dispute.

Thus, if it is asked, whether the smell be in the rose, or in the mind that feels it? The answer is obvious: that there are two different things signified by the smell of a rose; one of which is in the mind, and can be in nothing but in a sentient being; the other is truly and properly in the rose. The sensation which I feel is in my mind. The mind is the sentient being; and as the rose is insentient, there can be no sensation, nor any thing resembling sensation in it. But this sensation in my mind is occasioned by a certain quality in the rose, which is called by the same name with the sensation, not on account of any similitude, but because of their constant concomitancy.

All the names we have for smells, tastes, sounds, and for the various degrees of heat and cold, have a like ambiguity; and what has been said of the smell of a rose may be applied to them. They signify both a sensation, and a quality perceived by means of that sensation. The first is the sign, the last the thing signified. As both are conjoined by nature, and as the purposes of common life do not require them to be disjoined in our thoughts, they are both expressed by the same name: and this ambiguity is to be found in all languages, because the reason of it extends to all.

The same ambiguity is found in the names of such diseases as are indicated by a particular painful sensation; such as the toothache, the headache. The toothache signifies a painful sensation, which can only be in a sentient being; but it signifies also a disorder in the body, which has no similitude to a sensation, but is naturally connected with it.

Pressing my hand with force against the table, I feel pain, and I feel the table to be hard. The pain is a sensation of the mind, and there is nothing that resembles it in the table. The hardness is in the table, nor is there any thing resembling it in the mind. Feeling is applied to both; but in a different sense; being a word common to the act of sensation, and to that of perceiving by the sense of touch.

I touch the table gently with my hand, and I feel it to be smooth, hard, and cold. These are qualities of the table perceived by touch; but I perceive them by means of a sensation which indicates them. This sensation not being painful, I commonly give no attention to it. It carries my thought immediately to the thing signified by it, and is itself forgotten, as if it had never been. But by repeating it, and turning my attention to it, and abstracting my thought from the thing signified by it, 1 find it to be merely a sensation, and that it has no similitude to the hardness, smoothness, or coldness of the table which are signified by it.

It is indeed difficult, at first, to disjoin things in our attention which have always been conjoined, and to make that an object of reflection which never was so before; but some pains and practice will overcome this difficulty in those who have got the habit of reflecting on the operations of their own minds.

Although the present subject leads us only to consider the sensations which we have by means of our external senses, yet it will serve to illustrate what has been said, and I apprehend is of importance in itself to observe, that many operations of mind, to which we give one name, and which we always consider as one thing, are complex in their nature, and made up of several more simple ingredients; and of these ingredients sensation very often makes one. Of this we shall give some instances.

The appetite of hunger includes an uneasy sensation, and desire of food. Sensation and desire are different acts of mind. The last, from its nature, must have an object; the first has no object. These two ingredients may always be separated in thought; perhaps they sometimes are, in reality; but hunger includes both.

Benevolence toward our fellow creatures includes an agreeable feeling; but it includes also a desire of the happiness of others. The ancients commonly called it desire: many moderns choose rather to call it a feeling. Both are right; and they only err who exclude either of the ingredients. Whether these two ingredients are necessarily connected, is perhaps difficult for us to determine, there being many necessary connections which we do not perceive to be necessary; but we can disjoin them in thought. They are different acts of the mind.

An uneasy feeling, and a desire, are in like manner the ingredients of malevolent affections; such as malice, envy, revenge. The passion of fear includes an uneasy sensation or feeling, and an opinion of danger; and hope is made up of the contrary ingredients. When we hear of a heroic action, the sentiment which it raises in our mind is made up of various ingredients. There is in it an agreeable feeling, a benevolent affection to the person, and a judgment or opinion of his merit.

If we thus analyze the various operations of our minds, we shall find, that many of them which we consider as perfectly simple, because we have been accustomed to call them by one name, are compounded of more simple ingredients; and that sensation or feeling, which is only a more refined kind of sensation, makes one ingredient, not only in the perception of external objects, but in most operations of the mind.

A small degree of reflection may satisfy us, that the number and variety of our sensations and feelings is prodigious: for, to omit all those which accompany our appetites, passions, and affections, our moral sentiments, and sentiments of taste, even our external senses furnish a great variety of sensations differing in kind, and almost in every kind an endless variety of degrees. Every variety we discern, with regard to taste, smell, sound, colour, heat and cold, and in the tangible qualities of bodies, is indicated by a sensation corresponding to it.

The most general and the most important division of our sensations and feelings, is into the agreeable, the disagreeable, and the indifferent. Every thing we call pleasure, happiness, or enjoyment, on the one hand;

and on the other, every thing we call misery, pain, or
uneasiness, is sensation or feeling: for no man can for
the present be more happy, or more miserable than he
feels himself to be. He cannot be deceived with regard to the enjoyment or suffering of the present moment.

But I apprehend, that besides the sensations that are
either agreeable or disagreeable, there is still a greater
number that are indifferent. To these we give so little
attention that they have no name, and are immediately
forgotten, as if they had never been; and it requires attention to the operations of our minds to be convinced
of their existence.

For this end we may observe, that to a good ear
every human voice is distinguishable from all others.
Some voices are pleasant, some disagreeable; but the
far greater part can neither be said to be one or the
other. The same thing may be said of other sounds,
and no less of tastes, smells, and colours; and if we
consider that our senses are in continual exercise while
we are awake, that some sensation attends every object they present to us, and that familiar objects seldom raise any emotion pleasant or painful, we shall see
reason, besides the agreeable and disagreeable, to admit a third class of sensations, that may be called indifferent.

The sensations that are indifferent, are far from being useless. They serve as signs to distinguish things
that differ; and the information we have concerning
things external. comes by their means. Thus, if a man
had no ear to receive pleasure from the harmony or
melody of sounds, he would still find the sense of hearing of great utility. Though sounds gave him neither
pleasure nor pain of themselves, they would give him
much useful information; and the like may be said of
the sensations we have by all the other senses.

As to the sensations and feelings that are agreeable or disagreeable, they differ much, not only in degree, but in kind and in dignity. Some belong to the animal part of our nature, and are common to us with the brutes: others belong to the rational and moral part. The first are more properly called *sensations*, the last *feelings*. The French word *sentiment* is common to both.

The intention of nature in them is for the most part obvious, and well deserving our notice. It has been beautifully illustrated by a very elegant French writer, in his Theorie des sentimens agréables.

The Author of nature, in the distribution of agreeable and painful feelings, has wisely and benevolently consulted the good of the human species, and has even shown us, by the same means, what tenor of conduct we ought to hold. For, *first*, The painful sensations of the animal kind are admonitions to avoid what would hurt us; and the agreeable sensations of this kind, invite us to those actions that are necessary to the preservation of the individual, or of the kind. 2dly, By the same means nature invites us to moderate bodily exercise, and admonishes us to avoid idleness and inactivity on the one hand, and excessive labour and fatigue on the other. 3dly, The moderate exercise of all our rational powers gives pleasure. 4thly, Every species of beauty is beheld with pleasure, and every species of deformity with disgust; and we shall find all that we call beautiful, to be something estimable or useful in itself, or a sign of something that is estimable or useful. 5thly, The benevolent affections are all accompanied with an agreeable feeling, the malevolent with the contrary. And, 6thly, The highest, the noblest, and most durable pleasure, is that of doing well, and acting the part that becomes us; and the most bitter and painful sentiment, the anguish and remorse of a guilty conscience. These observations, with regard to the economy of nature in the distribution of our painful and agreeable sensations and feelings, are illustrated by the author last mentioned, so elegantly and judiciously, that I shall not attempt to say any thing upon them after him.

I shall conclude this chapter by observing, that as the confounding our sensations with that perception of external objects, which is constantly conjoined with them, has been the occasion of most of the errors and false theories of philosophers with regard to the senses; so the distinguishing these operations seems to me to be the key that leads to a right understanding of both.

Sensation, taken by itself, implies neither the conception nor belief of any external object. It supposes a sentient being, and a certain manner in which that being is affected; but it supposes no more. Perception implies an immediate conviction and belief of something external; something different both from the mind that perceives, and from the act of perception. Things so different in their nature ought to be distinguished; but by our constitution they are always united. Every different perception is conjoined with a sensation that is proper to it. The one is the sign, the other the thing signified. They coalesce in our imagination. They are signified by one name, and are considered as one simple operation. The purposes of life do not require them to be distinguished.

It is the philosopher alone who has occasion to distinguish them, when he would analyze the operation compounded of them. But he has no suspicion that there is any composition in it; and to discover this requires a degree of reflection which has been too little practised even by philosophers.

In the old philosophy, sensation and perception were perfectly confounded. The sensible species coming from the object, and impressed upon the mind, was the whole; and you might call it sensation or perception as you pleased.

Des Cartes and Locke, attending more to the operations of their own minds, say, that the sensations by which we have notice of secondary qualities, have no resemblance to any thing that pertains to body; but they did not see that this might with equal justice be applied to the primary qualities. Mr. Locke maintains, that the sensations we have from primary qualities are resemblances of those qualities. This shows how grossly the most ingenious men may err with regard to the operations of their minds. It must indeed be acknowledged, that it is much easier to have a distinct notion of the sensations that belong to secondary, than of those that belong to the primary qualities. The reason of this will appear in the next chapter.

But had Mr. Locke attended with sufficient accuracy to the sensations which he was every day and every hour receiving from primary qualities, he would have seen, that they can as little resemble any quality of an inanimated being, as pain can resemble a cube or a circle.

What had escaped this ingenious philosopher was clearly discerned by bishop Berkeley. He had a just notion of sensations, and saw that it was impossible that any thing in an insentient being could resemble them; a thing so evident in itself, that it seems wonderful that it should have been so long unknown.

But let us attend to the consequence of this discovery. Philosophers, as well as the vulgar, had been accustomed to comprehend both sensation and perception under one name, and to consider them as one uncompounded operation. Philosophers, even more than the vulgar, gave the name of sensation to the whole operation of the senses; and all the notions we have of material things were called ideas of sensation. This led bishop Berkeley to take one ingredient of a complex operation for the whole; and having clearly discovered the nature of sensation, taking it for granted, that all that the senses present to the mind is sensation, which can have no resemblance to any thing material, he concluded that there is no material world.

If the senses furnished us with no materials of thought but sensations, his conclusion must be just; for no sensation can give us the conception of material things, far less any argument to prove their existence. But if it is true that by our senses we have not only a variety of sensations, but likewise a conception, and an immediate natural conviction of external objects, he reasons from a false supposition, and his arguments fall to the ground.

CHAP. XVII.

THE objects of perception are the various qualities
of bodies. Intending to treat of these only in general,
and chiefly with a view to explain the notions which
our senses give us of them, I begin with the distinction
between primary and secondary qualities. These were
distinguished very early. The Peripatetic system confounded them, and left no difference. The distinction
was again revived by Des Cartes and Locke, and a second time abolished by Berkeley and Hume. If the
real foundation of this distinction can be pointed out, it
will enable us to account for the various revolutions in
the sentiments of philosophers concerning it.

Every one knows that extension, divisibility, figure,
motion, solidity, hardness, softness, and fluidity, were
by Mr. Locke called *primary qualities of body ;* and that
sound, colour, taste, smell, and heat or cold, were called *secondary qualities.* Is there a just foundation for
this distinction ? is there any thing common to the primary which belongs not to the secondary ? And what
is it ?

I answer, that there appears to me to be a real foundation for the distinction ; and it is this : that our
senses give us a direct and a distinct notion of the primary qualities, and inform us what they are in themselves :
but of the secondary qualities, our senses give us only
a relative and obscure notion. They inform us only,
that they are qualities that effect us in a certain manner, that is, produce in us a certain sensation ; but as

to what they are in themselves, our senses leave us in the dark.

Every man capable of reflection may easily satisfy himself, that he has a perfectly clear and distinct notion of extension, divisibility, figure, and motion. The solidity of a body means no more, but that it excludes other bodies from occupying the same place at the same time. Hardness, softness, and fluidity, are different degrees of cohesion in the parts of a body. It is fluid, when it has no sensible cohesion; soft when the cohesion is weak; and hard when it is strong. Of the cause of this cohesion we are ignorant, but the thing itself we understand perfectly, being immediately informed of it by the sense of touch. It is evident, therefore, that of the primary qualities we have a clear and distinct notion; we know what they are, though we may be ignorant of their causes.

I observed further, that the notion we have of primary qualities is direct, and not relative only. A relative notion of a thing, is, strictly speaking, no notion of the thing at all, but only of some relation which it bears to something else.

Thus gravity sometimes signifies the tendency of bodies toward the earth; sometimes it signifies the cause of that tendency. When it means the first, I have a direct and distinct notion of gravity: I see it, and feel it, and know perfectly what it is; but this tendency must have a cause: we give the same name to the cause; and that cause has been an object of thought and of speculation. Now what notion have we of this cause when we think and reason about it? It is evident, we think of it as an unknown cause, of a known effect. This is a relative notion, and it must be obscure, because it gives us no conception of what the thing is, but of what relation it bears to something else. Every relation which a thing unknown bears to something

that is known, may give a relative notion of it; and
there are many objects of thought, and of discourse, of
which our faculties can give no better than a relative
notion.

Having premised these things to explain what is
meant by a relative notion, it is evident, that our notion
of primary qualities is not of this kind; we know what
they are, and not barely what relation they bear to
something else.

It is otherwise with secondary qualities. If you ask
me, what is that quality or modification in a rose which
I call its smell, I am at a loss to answer directly. Upon reflection I find, that I have a distinct notion of the
sensation which it produces in my mind. But there
can be nothing like to this sensation in the rose, because it is insentient. The quality in the rose is something which occasions the sensation in me; but what
that something is, I know not. My senses give me no
information upon this point. The only notion therefore my senses give is this, that smell in the rose
is an unknown quality or modification, which is the
cause or occasion of a sensation which I know well.
The relation which this unknown quality bears to the
sensation with which nature has connected it, is all I
learn from the sense of smelling: but this is evidently
a relative notion. The same reasoning will apply to
every secondary quality.

Thus I think it appears, that there is a real foundation for the distinction of primary from secondary
qualities; and that they are distinguished by this, that
of the primary we have by our senses a direct and distinct notion; but of the secondary only a relative notion, which must, because it is only relative, be obscure;
they are conceived only as the unknown causes or occasions of certain sensations with which we are well acquainted.

The account I have given of this distinction is founded upon no hypothesis. Whether our notions of primary qualities are direct and distinct, those of the secondary relative and obscure, is a matter of fact, of which every man may have certain knowledge by attentive reflection upon them. To this reflection I appeal, as the proper test of what has been advanced, and proceed to make some reflections on this subject.

1st, The primary qualities are neither sensations, nor are they resemblances of sensations. This appears to me self-evident. I have a clear and distinct notion of each of the primary qualities. I have a clear and distinct notion of sensation. I can compare the one with the other; and when I do so, I am not able to discern a resembling feature. Sensation is the act, or the feeling, I dispute not which, of a sentient being. Figure, divisibility, solidity, are neither acts nor feelings. Sensation supposes a sentient being as its subject; for a sensation that is not felt by some sentient being, is an absurdity. Figure and divisibility suppose a subject that is figured and divisible, but not a subject that is sentient.

2dly, We have no reason to think, that the sensations by which we have notice of secondary qualities resemble any quality of body. The absurdity of this notion has been clearly shown by Des Cartes, Locke, and many modern philosophers. It was a tenet of the ancient philosophy, and is still by many imputed to the vulgar, but only as a vulgar error. It is too evident to need proof, that the vibrations of a sounding body do not resemble the sensation of sound, nor the effluvia of an odorous body the sensation of smell.

3dly, The distinctness of our notions of primary qualities prevents all questions and disputes about their nature. There are no different opinions about the nature of extension, figure, or motion, or the nature of any primary quality. Their nature is manifest to our senses, and cannot be unknown to any man, or mistaken by him, though their causes may admit of dispute.

The primary qualities are the object of the mathematical sciences; and the distinctness of our notions of them enables us to reason demonstratively about them to a great extent. Their various modifications are precisely defined in the imagination, and thereby capable of being compared, and their relations determined with precision and certainty.

It is not so with secondary qualities. Their nature not being manifest to the sense, may be a subject of dispute. Our feeling informs us that the fire is hot; but it does not inform us what that heat of the fire is. But does it not appear a contradiction, to say we know that the fire is hot, but we know not what that heat is? I answer, there is the same appearance of contradiction in many things, that must be granted. We know that wine has an inebriating quality; but we know not what that quality is. It is true, indeed, that if we had not some notion of what is meant by the heat of fire, and by an inebriating quality, we could affirm nothing of either with understanding. We have a notion of both; but it is only a relative notion. We know that they are the causes of certain known effects.

4thly, The nature of secondary qualities is a proper subject of philosophical disquisition; and in this, philosophy has made some progress. It has been discovered, that the sensation of smell is occasioned by the effluvia of bodies; that of sound by their vibration. The disposition of bodies to reflect a particular kind of light occasions the sensation of colour. Very curious discoveries have been made of the nature of heat, and an ample field of discovery in these subjects remains.

5thly, We may see why the sensations belonging to secondary qualities are an object of our attention, while those which belong to the primary are not.

The first are not only signs of the object perceived, but they bear a capital part in the notion we form of it. We conceive it only as that which occasions such a sensation, and therefore cannot reflect upon it without thinking of the sensation which it occasions. We have no other mark whereby to distinguish it. The thought of a secondary quality, therefore, always carries us back to the sensation which it produces. We give the same name to both, and are apt to confound them together.

But having a clear and distinct conception of primary qualities, we have no need when we think of them to recal their sensations. When a primary quality is perceived, the sensation immediately leads our thought to the quality signified by it, and is itself forgotten. We have no occasion afterward to reflect upon it; and so we come to be as little acquainted with it, as if we had never felt it. This is the case with the sensations of all primary qualities, when they are not so painful or pleasant as to draw our attention.

When a man moves his hand rudely against a pointed hard body, he feels pain, and may easily be persuaded that this pain is a sensation, and that there is nothing resembling it in the hard body; at the same time he perceives the body to be hard and pointed, and he knows that these qualities belong to the body only. In this case, it is easy to distinguish what he feels from what he perceives.

Let him again touch the pointed body gently, so as to give him no pain; and now you can hardly persuade him that he feels any thing but the figure and hardness of the body; so difficult it is to attend to the sensations belonging to primary qualities, when they are neither pleasant nor painful. They carry the thought to the external object, and immediately disappear and are forgotten. Nature intended them only as signs; and when they have served that purpose they vanish.

We are now to consider the opinions both of the vulgar, and of philosophers upon this subject. As to the former, it is not to be expected that they should make distinctions which have no connection with the common affairs of life ; they do not therefore distinguish the primary from the secondary qualities, but speak of both as being equally qualities of the external object. Of the primary qualities they have a distinct notion, as they are immediately and distinctly perceived by the senses ; of the secondary, their notions, as I apprehend, are confused and indistinct, rather than erroneous. A secondary quality is the unknown cause or occasion of a well known effect ; and the same name is common to the cause and the effect. Now, to distinguish clearly the different ingredients of a complex notion, and, at the same time, the different meanings of an ambiguous word, is the work of a philosopher; and is not to be expected of the vulgar, when their occasions do not require it.

I grant, therefore, that the notion which the vulgar have of secondary qualities, is indistinct and inaccurate. But there seems to be a contradiction between the vulgar and the philosopher upon this subject, and each charges the other with a gross absurdity. The vulgar say, that fire is hot, and snow cold, and sugar sweet; and that to deny this is a gross absurdity, and contradicts the testimony of our senses. The philosopher says, that heat, and cold, and sweetness, are nothing but sensations in our minds; and it is absurd to conceive, that these sensations are in the fire, or in the snow, or in the sugar.

I believe this contradiction between the vulgar and the philosopher is more apparent than real; and that it is owing to an abuse of language on the part of the philosopher, and to indistinct notions on the part of the

vulgar. The philosopher says, there is no heat in the
fire, meaning, that the fire has not the sensation of
heat. His meaning is just; and the vulgar will agree
with him, as soon as they understand his meaning; but
his language is improper; for there is really a quality
in the fire, of which the proper name is heat; and the
name of heat is given to this quality, both by philosophers and by the vulgar, much more frequently than to
the sensation of heat. This speech of the philosopher,
therefore, is meant by him in one sense; it is taken
by the vulgar in another sense. In the sense in which
they take it, it is indeed absurd, and so they hold it to
be. In the sense in which he means it, it is true; and
the vulgar, as soon as they are made to understand that
sense, will acknowledge it to be true. They know as
well as the philosopher, that the fire does not feel heat;
and this is all that he means by saying there is no heat
in the fire.

In the opinions of philosophers about primary and
secondary qualities, there have been, as was before observed, several revolutions. They were distinguished
long before the days of Aristotle, by the sect called
Atomists; among whom Democritus made a capital
figure. In those times, the name of *quality* was applied only to those we call secondary qualities; the primary being considered as essential to matter, were not
called qualities. That the atoms, which they held to
be the first principles of things, were extended, solid,
figured, and moveable, there was no doubt; but the
question was, whether they had smell, taste and colour? or, as it was commonly expressed, whether they
had qualities? The Atomists maintained, that they
had not; that the qualities were not in bodies, but were
something resulting from the operation of bodies upon
our senses.

It would seem, that when men began to speculate
upon this subject, the primary qualities appeared so

clear and manifest, that they could entertain no doubt
of their existence wherever matter existed; but the
secondary so obscure, that they were at a loss where to
place them. They used this comparison; as fire, which
is neither in the flint nor in the steel, is produced by
their collision, so those qualities, though not in bodies,
are produced by their impulse upon our senses.

This doctrine was opposed by Aristotle. He believed taste and colour to be substantial forms of bodies,
and that their species, as well as those of figure and
motion, are received by the senses.

In believing, that what we commonly call *taste* and
colour is something really inherent in body, and does
not depend upon its being tasted and seen, he followed
nature. But, in believing that our sensations of taste
and colour are the forms or species of those qualities
received by the senses, he followed his own theory,
which was an absurd fiction. Des Cartes not only
showed the absurdity of sensible species received by the
senses, but gave a more just and more intelligible account of secondary qualities than had been given before.
Mr. Locke followed him, and bestowed much pains upon this subject. He was the first, I think, that gave
them the name of secondary qualities, which has been
very generally adopted. He distinguished the sensation from the quality in the body, which is the cause or
occasion of that sensation, and showed that there neither is nor can be any similitude between them.

By this account, the senses are acquitted of putting
any fallacy upon us; the sensation is real, and no fallacy; the quality in the body, which is the cause or
occasion of this sensation, is likewise real, though the
nature of it is not manifest to our senses. If we impose upon ourselves, by confounding the sensation with
the quality that occasions it, this is owing to rash judgment, or weak understanding, but not to any false testimony of our senses.

This account of secondary qualities I take to be very just; and, if Mr. Locke had stopped here, he would have left the matter very clear. But he thought it necessary to introduce the theory of ideas, to explain the distinction between primary and secondary qualities, and by that means, as I think, perplexed and darkened it.

When philosophers speak about ideas, we are often at a loss to know what they mean by them, and may be apt to suspect that they are mere fictions, that have no existence. They have told us, that by the ideas which we have immediately from our senses, they mean our sensations. These, indeed, are real things, and not fictions. We may, by accurate attention to them, know perfectly their nature; and if philosophers would keep by this meaning of the word *idea*, when applied to the objects of sense, they would at least be more intelligible. Let us hear now how Mr. Locke explains the nature of those ideas, when applied to primary and secondary qualities, Book 2. chap. 8. sect. 7. 10th edition. " To discover the nature of our ideas the better, and to discourse of them intelligibly, it will be convenient to distinguish them, as they are ideas, or perceptions in our minds, and as they are modifications of matter in the bodies that cause such perceptions in us, that so we may not think, as perhaps usually is done, that they are exactly the images and resemblances of something inherent in the subject; most of those of sensation being, in the mind, no more the likeness of something existing without us, than the names that stand for them are the likeness of our ideas, which yet, upon hearing, they are apt to excite in us."

This way of distinguishing a thing, 1st, as what it is; and 2dly, as what it is not, is, I apprehend, a very extraordinary way of discovering its nature; and if ideas are ideas or perceptions in our minds, and at the same time the modifications of matter in the bodies that cause such perceptions in us, it will be no easy matter to discourse of them intelligibly.

The discovery of the nature of ideas is carried on in the next section, in a manner no less extraordinary.

" Whatsoever the mind perceives in itself, or is the immediate object of perception, thought, or understanding, that I call *idea;* and the power to produce any idea in our mind, I call *quality* of the subject wherein that power is. Thus, a snowball having the power to produce in us the ideas of white, cold, and round, the powers to produce those ideas in us, as they are in the snowball, I call *qualities;* and as they are sensations, or perceptions in our understandings, I call them *ideas;* which ideas, if I speak of them sometimes as in the things themselves, I would be understood to mean those qualities in the objects which produce them in us."

These are the distinctions which Mr. Locke thought convenient, in order to discover the nature of our ideas of the qualities of matter the better, and to discourse of them intelligibly. I believe it will be difficult to find two other paragraphs in the Essay so unintelligible. Whether this is to be imputed to the intractable nature of ideas, or to an oscitancy of the author, with which he is very rarely chargeable, I leave the reader to judge. There are, indeed, several other passages in the same chapter, in which a like obscurity appears; but I do not choose to dwell upon them. The conclusion drawn by him from the whole, is, that primary and secondary qualities are distinguished by this, that the ideas of the former are resemblances or copies of them; but the ideas of the other are not resemblances of them. Upon this doctrine, I beg leave to make two observations.

First, Taking it for granted, that, by the ideas of primary and secondary qualities, he means the sensations they excite in us; I observe, that it appears strange, that a sensation should be the idea of a quality in body, to which it is acknowledged to bear no resemblance. If the sensation of sound be the idea of that vibration of the sounding body which occasions it, a surfeit may, for the same reason, be the idea of a feast.

A second observation is, that when Mr. Locke affirms, that the ideas of primary qualities, that is, the sensations they raise in us, are resemblances of those qualities, he seems neither to have given due attention to those sensations, nor to the nature of sensation in general.

Let a man press his hand against a hard body, and let him attend to the sensation he feels, excluding from his thought every thing external, even the body that is the cause of his feeling. This abstraction indeed is difficult, and seems to have been little, if at all, practised : but it is not impossible, and it is evidently the only way to understand the nature of the sensation. A due attention to this sensation will satisfy him, that it is no more like hardness in a body, than the sensation of sound is like vibration in the sounding body.

I know of no ideas but my conceptions ; and my idea of hardness in a body, is the conception of such a cohesion of its parts as requires great force to displace them. I have both the conception and belief of this quality in the body, at the same time that I have the sensation of pain, by pressing my hand against it. The sensation and perception are closely conjoined by my constitution; but I am sure they have no similitude : I know no reason why the one should be called the idea of the other, which does not lead us to call every natural effect the idea of its cause.

Neither did Mr. Locke give due attention to the nature of sensation in general, when he affirmed, that the ideas of primary qualities, that is, the sensations excited by them, are resemblances of those qualities.

That there can be nothing like sensation in an insentient being, or like thought in an unthinking being, is self-evident, and has been shown, to the conviction of all men that think, by bishop Berkeley; yet this was unknown to Mr. Locke. It is an humbling consideration, that, in subjects of this kind, self-evident truths may be hid from the eyes of the most ingenious men. But we have, withal, this consolation, that when once discovered, they shine by their own light; and that light can no more be put out.

Upon the whole, Mr. Locke, in making secondary qualities to be powers in bodies to excite certain sensations in us, has given a just and distinct analysis of what our senses discover concerning them; but, in applying the theory of ideas to them, and to the primary qualities, he has been led to say things that darken the subject, and that will not bear examination.

Bishop Berkeley, having adopted the sentiments common to philosophers, concerning the ideas we have by our senses, to wit, that they are all sensations, saw more clearly the necessary consequence of this doctrine; which is, that there is no material world; no qualities primary or secondary; and, consequently, no foundation for any distinction between them. He exposed the absurdity of a resemblance between our sensations and any quality, primary or secondary, of a substance that is supposed to be insentient. Indeed, if it is granted that the senses have no other office but to furnish us with sensations, it will be found impossible to make any distinction between primary and secondary qualities, or even to maintain the existence of a material world.

From the account I have given of the various revolutions in the opinions of philosophers about primary and secondary qualities, I think it appears, that all the darkness and intricacy that thinking men have found in this subject, and the errors they have fallen into, have been owing to the difficulty of distinguishing clearly sensation from perception; what we feel from what we perceive.

The external senses have a double province; to make us feel, and to make us perceive. They furnish us with a variety of sensations, some pleasant, others painful, and others indifferent; at the same time they give us a conception, and an invincible belief of the existence of external objects. This conception of external objects is the work of nature. The belief of their existence, which our senses give, is the work of nature; so likewise is the sensation that accompanies it. This conception and belief which nature produces by means of the senses, we call *perception*. The feeling which goes along with the perception, we call *sensation*. The perception and its corresponding sensation are produced at the same time. In our experience we never find them disjoined. Hence we are led to consider them as one thing, to give them one name, and to confound their different attributes. It becomes very difficult to separate them in thought, to attend to each by itself, and to attribute nothing to it which belongs to the other.

To do this requires a degree of attention to what passes in our own minds, and a talent of distinguishing things that differ, which is not to be expected in the vulgar, and is even rarely found in philosophers; so that the progress made in a just analysis of the operations of our senses has been very slow. The hypothesis of ideas, so generally adopted. has, as I apprehend, greatly retarded this progress; and we might hope for a quicker advance, if philosophers could so far

humble themselves as to believe, that in every branch
of the philosophy of nature, the productions of human
fancy and conjecture will be found to be dross ; and
that the only pure metal that will endure the test, is
what is discovered by patient observation, and chaste
induction.

CHAP. XVIII.

OF OTHER OBJECTS OF PERCEPTION.

BESIDES primary and secondary qualities of bodies, there are many other immediate objects of perception. Without pretending to a complete enumeration, I think they mostly fall under one or other of the following classes. 1st, Certain states or conditions of our own bodies. 2dly, Mechanical powers or forces. 3dly, Chymical powers. 4thly, Medical powers or virtues. 5thly, Vegetable and animal powers.

That we perceive certain disorders in our own bodies by means of uneasy sensations, which nature has conjoined with them, will not be disputed. Of this kind are toothache, headache, gout, and every distemper and hurt which we feel. The notions which our sense gives of these, have a strong analogy to our notions of secondary qualities. Both are similarly compounded, and may be similarly resolved, and they give light to each other.

In the toothache, for instance, there is, first, a painful feeling; and, secondly, a conception and belief of some disorder in the tooth, which is believed to be the cause of the uneasy feeling. The first of these is a sensation, the second is perception; for it includes a conception and belief of an external object. But these two things, though of different natures, are so constantly conjoined in our experience, and in our imagination, that we consider them as one. We give the same name to both; for the toothache is the proper name of the pain we feel; and it is the proper name of the disorder in the tooth which causes that pain. If it should be made a question, whether the toothache be in the

mind that feels it, or in the tooth that is affected?
much might be said on both sides, while it is not observed that the word has two meanings. But a little
reflection satisfies us, that the pain is in the mind, and
the disorder in the tooth. If some philosopher should
pretend to have made a discovery, that the toothache,
the gout, the headache, are only sensations in the mind,
and that it is a vulgar error to conceive that they are
distempers of the body, he might defend his system in
the same manner as those, who affirm that there is no
sound nor colour nor taste in bodies, defend that paradox. But both these systems, like most paradoxes,
will be found to be only an abuse of words.

We say that we *feel* the toothache, not that we perceive it. On the other hand, we say that we *perceive*
the colour of a body, not that we feel it. Can any reason be given for this difference of phraseology? in answer to this question, I apprehend, that both when we
feel the toothache, and when we see a coloured body,
there is sensation and perception conjoined. But, in the
toothache, the sensation being very painful, engrosses
the attention; and therefore we speak of it, as if it
were felt only, and not perceived: whereas, in seeing a
coloured body, the sensation is indifferent, and draws
no attention. The quality in the body, which we call
its colour, is the only object of attention; and therefore we speak of it, as if it were perceived, and not felt.
Though all philosophers agree that in seeing colour
there is sensation, it is not easy to persuade the vulgar,
that, in seeing a coloured body, when the light is not
too strong, nor the eye inflamed, they have any sensation or feeling at all.

There are some sensations, which, though they are
very often felt, are never attended to, nor reflected upon.
We have no conception of them; and therefore, in language, there is neither any name for them, nor any

form of speech that supposes their existence. Such are the sensations of colour and of all primary qualities; and therefore those qualities are said to be perceived, but not to be felt. Taste and smell, and heat and cold, have sensations that are often agreeable or disagreeable, in such a degree as to draw our attention; and they are sometimes said to be felt, and sometimes to be perceived. When disorders of the body occasion very acute pain, the uneasy sensation engrosses the attention, and they are said to be felt, not to be perceived.

There is another question relating to phraseology, which this subject suggests. A man says, he feels pain in such a particular part of his body; in his toe, for instance. Now, reason assures us, that pain being a sensation, can only be in the sentient being, as its subject, that is, in the mind. And though philosophers have disputed much about the place of the mind, yet none of them ever placed it in the toe. What shall we say then in this case? do our senses really deceive us, and make us believe a thing which our reason determines to be impossible? I answer, 1st, that when a man says, he has pain in his toe, he is perfectly understood, both by himself, and those who hear him. This is all that he intends. He really feels what he and all men call a pain in the toe; and there is no deception in the matter. Whether therefore there be any impropriety in the phrase or not, is of no consequence in common life. It answers all the ends of speech, both to the speaker and the hearers.

In all languages, there are phrases which have a distinct meaning; while, at the same time, there may be something in the structure of them that disagrees with the analogy of grammar, or with the principles of philosophy. And the reason is, because language is not made either by grammarians or philosophers. Thus we speak of feeling pain, as if pain was something distinct from the feeling of it. We speak of a pain coming and going, and removing from one place to another. Such phrases are meant by those who use them in a sense that is neither obscure nor false. But the philosopher puts them into his alembic, reduces them to their first principles, draws out of them a sense that was never meant, and so imagines that he has discovered an error of the vulgar.

I observe, 2dly, that when we consider the sensation of pain by itself, without any respect to its cause, we cannot say with propriety, that the toe is either the place, or the subject of it. But it ought to be remembered, that when we speak of pain in the toe, the sensation is combined in our thought, with the cause of it, which really is in the toe. The cause and the effect are combined in one complex notion, and the same name serves for both. It is the business of the philosopher to analyze this complex notion, and to give different names to its different ingredients. He gives the name of *pain* to the sensation only, and the name of *disorder* to the unknown cause of it. Then it is evident that the disorder only is in the toe, and that it would be an error to think that the pain is in it. But we ought not to ascribe this error to the vulgar, who never made the distinction, and who under the name of pain comprehend both the sensation and its cause.

Cases sometimes happen, which give occasion even to the vulgar to distinguish the painful sensation from the disorder which is the cause of it. A man who has had his leg cut off, many years after feels pain in a toe of that leg. The toe has now no existence; and he perceives easily, that the toe can neither be the place, nor the subject of the pain which he feels; yet it is the same feeling he used to have from a hurt in the toe; and if he did not know that his leg was cut off, it would give

him the same immediate conviction of some hurt or disorder in the toe.

The same phenomenon may lead the philosopher in
all cases, to distinguish sensation from perception. We
say, that the man had a deceitful feeling, when he felt a
pain in his toe after the leg was cut off; and we have a
true meaning in saying so. But. if we will speak accurately, our sensations cannot be deceitful; they must be
what we feel them to be, and can be nothing else.
Where then lies the deceit? I answer, it lies not in the
sensation, which is real, but in the seeming perception
he had of a disorder in his toe. This perception, which
nature had conjoined with the sensation, was in this
instance fallacious.

The same reasoning may be applied to every phenomenon that can, with propriety, be called a deception of
sense. As when one, who has the jaundice, sees a body
yellow, which is really white; or when a man sees an
object double, because his eyes are not both directed to
it; in these, and other like cases, the sensations we
have are real, and the deception is only in the perception which nature has annexed to them.

Nature has connected our perception of external objects with certain sensations. If the sensation is produced, the corresponding perception follows even when
there is no object, and in that case is apt to deceive us.
In like manner, nature has connected our sensations
with certain impressions that are made upon the nerve
and brain: and, when the impression is made, from
whatever cause. the corresponding sensation and perception immediately follows. Thus, in the man who
feels pain in his toe after the leg is cut off, the nerve
that went to the toe, part of which was cut off with
the leg, had the same impression made upon the remaining part, which, in the natural state of his body,
was caused by a hurt in the toe: and immediately
this impression is followed by the sensation and perception which nature connected with it.

In like manner, if the same impressions, which are
made at present upon my optic nerves by the objects
before me, could be made in the dark, I apprehend that
I should have the same sensations, and see the same
objects which I now see. The impressions and sensations would in such a case be real, and the perception
only fallacious.

Let us next consider the notions which our senses
give us of those attributes of bodies called *powers*.
This is the more necessary, because power seems to
imply some activity; yet we consider body as a dead
inactive thing, which does not act, but may be acted
upon.

Of the mechanical powers ascribed to bodies, that
which is called their *vis insita* or *inertia*, may first be
considered. By this is meant no more, than that bodies never change their state of themselves, either
from rest to motion, or from motion to rest, or from
one degree of velocity, or one direction to another.
In order to produce any such change, there must be
some force impressed upon them; and the change
produced is precisely proportioned to the force impressed, and in the direction of that force.

That all bodies have this property, is a matter of
fact, which we learn from daily observation, as well as
from the most accurate experiments. Now it seems
plain, that this does not imply any activity in body,
but rather the contrary. A power in body to change
its state, would much rather imply activity than its
continuing in the same state: so that, although this
property of bodies is called their *vis insita*, or *vis iner-
tiæ*, it implies no proper activity.

If we consider, next, the power of gravity, it is a
fact, that all the bodies of our planetary system gravitate toward each other. This has been fully proved by
the great Newton. But this gravitation is not conceiv

ed by that philosopher to be a power inherent in bodies, which they exert of themselves, but a force impressed upon them, to which they must necessarily yield. Whether this force be impressed by some subtile ether, or whether it be impressed by the power of the Supreme Being, or of some subordinate spiritual being, we do not know; but all sound natural philosophy, particularly that of Newton, supposes it to be an impressed force, and not inherent in bodies.

So that, when bodies gravitate, they do not properly act, but are acted upon: they only yield to an impression that is made upon them. It is common in language to express, by active verbs, many changes in things, wherein they are merely passive; and this way of speaking is used chiefly when the cause of the change is not obvious to sense. Thus we say that a ship sails, when every man of common sense knows that she has no inherent power of motion, and is only driven by wind and tide. In like manner, when we say that the planets gravitate toward the sun, we mean no more, but that, by some unknown power, they are drawn or impelled in that direction.

What has been said of the power of gravitation may be applied to other mechanical powers, such as cohesion, magnetism, electricity; and no less to chymical and medical powers. By all these, certain effects are produced upon the application of one body to another. Our senses discover the effect; but the power is latent. We know there must be a cause of the effect, and we form a relative notion of it from its effect; and very often the same name is used to signify the unknown cause, and the known effect.

We ascribe to vegetables, the powers of drawing nourishment, growing, and multiplying their kind. Here likewise the effect is manifest, but the cause is latent to sense. These powers, therefore, as well as all the other powers we ascribe to bodies, are unknown causes of certain known effects. It is the business of philosophy to investigate the nature of those powers as far as we are able, but our senses leave us in the dark.

We may observe a great similarity in the notions which our senses give us of secondary qualities, of the disorders we feel in our own bodies, and of the various powers of bodies which we have enumerated. They are all obscure and relative notions, being a conception of some unknown cause of a known effect. Their names are, for the most part, common to the effect, and to its cause; and they are a proper subject of philosophical disquisition. They might therefore, I think, not improperly be called *occult* qualities.

This name, indeed, is fallen into disgrace since the time of Des Cartes. It is said to have been used by the Peripatetics to cloke their ignorance, and to stop all inquiry into the nature of those qualities called *occult*. Be it so. Let those answer for this abuse of the word who were guilty of it. To call a thing occult, if we attend to the meaning of the word, is rather modestly to confess ignorance, than to cloke it. It is to point it out as a proper subject for the investigation of philosophers, whose proper business it is to better the condition of humanity, by discovering what was before hid from human knowledge.

Were I therefore to make a division of the qualities of bodies as they appear to our senses, I would divide them first into those that are *manifest*, and those that are *occult*. The manifest qualities are those which Mr. Locke calls *primary;* such as extension, figure, divisibility, motion, hardness, softness, fluidity. The nature of these is manifest even to sense; and the business of the philosopher with regard to them, is not to find out their nature, which is well known, but to discover the effects produced by their various combinations; and with regard to those of them which are not essential to matter, to discover their causes as far as he is able.

The second class consists of occult qualities, which may be subdivided into various kinds; as 1st, the secondary qualities; 2dly, the disorders we feel in our own bodies; and, 3dly, all the qualities which we call powers of bodies, whether mechanical, chymical, medical, animal, or vegetable; or if there be any other powers not comprehended under these heads. Of all these the existence is manifest to sense, but the nature is occult; and here the philosopher has an ample field.

What is necessary for the conduct of our animal life, the bountiful Author of nature has made manifest to all men. But there are many other choice secrets of nature, the discovery of which enlarges the power, and exalts the state of man. These are left to be discovered by the proper use of our rational powers. They are hid, not that they may be always concealed from human knowledge, but that we may be excited to search for them. This is the proper business of a philosopher; and it is the glory of a man, and the best reward of his labour, to discover what nature has thus concealed.

CHAP. XIX.

OF MATTER AND OF SPACE.

THE objects of sense we have hitherto considered are qualities. But qualities must have a subject. We give the names of *matter, material substance,* and *body,* to the subject of sensible qualities; and it may be asked, what this *matter* is?

I perceive in a billiard ball, figure, colour, and motion; but the ball is not figure, nor is it colour, nor motion, nor all these taken together; it is something that has figure, and colour, and motion. This is a dictate of nature, and the belief of all mankind.

As to the nature of this something, I am afraid we can give little account of it, but that it has the qualities which our senses discover.

But how do we know that they are qualities, and cannot exist without a subject? I confess I cannot explain how we know that they cannot exist without a subject, any more than I can explain how we know that they exist. We have the information of nature for their existence; and I think we have the information of nature that they are qualities.

The belief that figure, motion, and colour, are qualities, and require a subject, must either be a judgment of nature, or it must be discovered by reason, or it must be a prejudice that has no just foundation. There are philosophers who maintain, that it is a mere prejudice; that a body is nothing but a collection of what we call sensible qualities; and that they neither have nor need any subject. This is the opinion of bishop Berkeley and Mr. Hume; and they were led to it by finding, that they had not in their minds any idea of substance. It could neither be an idea of sensation nor of reflection.

But to me nothing seems more absurd, than that there should be extension without any thing extended; or motion without any thing moved; yet I cannot give reasons for my opinion, because it seems to me self-evident, and an immediate dictate of my nature.

And that it is the belief of all mankind, appears in the structure of all languages; in which we find adjective nouns used to express sensible qualities. It is well known, that every adjective in language must belong to some substantive expressed or understood; that is, every quality must belong to some subject.

Sensible qualities make so great a part of the furniture of our minds, their kinds are so many, and their number so great, that if prejudice, and not nature, teach us to ascribe them all to a subject, it must have a great work to perform, which cannot be accomplished in a short time, nor carried on to the same pitch in every individual. We should find not individuals only, but nations and ages, differing from each other in the progress which this prejudice had made in their sentiments, but we find no such difference among men. What one man accounts a quality, all men do, and ever did.

It seems therefore to be a judgment of nature, that the things immediately perceived are qualities, which must belong to a subject; and all the information that our senses give us about this subject, is, that it is that to which such qualities belong. From this it is evident, that our notion of body or matter, as distinguished from its qualities, is a relative notion; and I am afraid it must always be obscure until men have other faculties.

The philosopher in this seems to have no advantage above the vulgar; for as they perceive colour, and figure, and motion by their senses as well as he does, and both are equally certain that there is a subject of those qualities, so the notions which both have of this subject are equally obscure. When the philosopher calls it a *substratum*, and a subject of inhesion, those learned words convey no meaning but what every man understands and expresses, by saying in common language, that it is a thing extended, and solid, and moveable.

The relation which sensible qualities bear to their subject, that is, to body, is not, however, so dark, but that it is easily distinguished from all other relations. Every man can distinguish it from the relation of an effect to its cause; of a mean to its end; or of a sign to the thing signified by it.

I think it requires some ripeness of understanding to distinguish the qualities of a body from the body. Perhaps this distinction is not made by brutes, nor by infants; and if any one thinks that this distinction is not made by our senses, but by some other power of the mind, I will not dispute this point, provided it be granted, that men, when their faculties are ripe, have a natural conviction, that sensible qualities cannot exist by themselves without some subject to which they belong.

I think, indeed, that some of the determinations we form concerning matter cannot be deduced solely from the testimony of sense, but must be referred to some other source.

There seems to be nothing more evident, than that all bodies must consist of parts; and that every part of a body is a body, and a distinct being which may exist without the other parts; and yet I apprehend this conclusion is not deduced solely from the testimony of sense: for, besides that it is a necessary truth, and therefore no object of sense there is a limit beyond which we cannot perceive any division of a body. The parts become too small to be perceived by our senses; but we cannot believe that it becomes then incapable of being

further divided, or that such division would make it
not to be a body.

We carry on the division and subdivision in our
thought far beyond the reach of our senses, and we
can find no end to it: nay, I think we plainly discern,
that there can be no limit beyond which the division
cannot be carried.

For if there be any limit to this division, one of two
things must necessarily happen. Either we have come
by division to a body which is extended, but has no
parts, and is absolutely indivisible ; or this body is divisible, but as soon as it is divided, it becomes no body.
Both these positions seem to me absurd, and one or
the other is the necessary consequence of supposing a
limit to the divisibility of matter.

On the other hand, if it is admitted that the divisibility of matter has no limit, it will follow, that no
body can be called one individual substance. You may
as well call it two, or twenty, or two hundred. For
when it is divided into parts, every part is a being or
substance distinct from all the other parts, and was so
even before the division : any one part may continue to
exist, though all the other parts were annihilated.

There is, indeed, a principle long received, as an axiom in metaphysics, which I cannot reconcile to the divisibility of matter. It is, That every being is one,
omne ens est unum. By which, I suppose, is meant, that
every thing that exists must either be one indivisible
being, or composed of a determinate number of indivisible beings. Thus an army may be divided into regi-
ments, a regiment into companies, and a company into
men. But here the division has its limit; for you cannot divide a man without destroying him, because
he is an individual; and every thing, according to
this axiom, must be an individual, or made up of individuals.

That this axiom will hold with regard to an army, and with regard to many other things, must be granted; but I require the evidence of its being applicable to all beings whatsoever.

Leibnitz, conceiving that all beings must have this metaphysical unity, was by this led to maintain, that matter, and indeed the whole universe, is made up of monads, that is, simple and indivisible substances.

Perhaps the same apprehension might lead Boscovich into his hypothesis, which seems much more ingenious; to wit, that matter is composed of a definite number of mathematical points, endowed with certain powers of attraction and repulsion.

The divisibility of matter without any limit, seems to me more tenable than either of these hypotheses; nor do I lay much stress upon the metaphysical axiom, considering its origin. Metaphysicians thought proper to make the attributes common to all beings the subject of a science. It must be a matter of some difficulty to find out such attributes: and, after racking their invention, they have specified three, to wit, unity, verity, and goodness; and these I suppose have been invented to make a number, rather than from any clear evidence of their being universal.

There are other determinations concerning matter, which, I think, are not solely founded upon the testimony of sense; such as, that it is impossible that two bodies should occupy the same place at the same time; or that the same body should be in different places at the same time; or that a body can be moved from one place to another, without passing through the intermediate places, either in a straight course, or by some circuit. These appear to be necessary truths, and therefore cannot be conclusions of our senses; for our senses testify only what is, and not what must necessarily be.

We are next to consider our notion of space. It may be observed, that although space be not perceived by any of our senses when all matter is removed; yet, when we perceive any of the primary qualities, space presents itself as a necessary concomitant: for there can neither be extension, nor motion, nor figure, nor division, nor cohesion of parts without space.

There are only two of our senses by which the notion of space enters into the mind; to wit, touch and sight. If we suppose a man to have neither of these senses, I do not see how he could ever have any conception of space. Supposing him to have both, until he sees or feels other objects, he can have no notion of space. It has neither colour nor figure to make it an object of sight. It has no tangible quality to make it an object of touch. But other objects of sight and touch carry the notion of space along with them; and not the notion only, but the belief of it: for a body could not exist if there was no space to contain it: it could not move if there was no space. Its situation, its distance, and every relation it has to other bodies, suppose space.

But though the notion of space seems not to enter at first into the mind, until it is introduced by the proper objects of sense; yet, being once introduced, it remains in our conception and belief, though the objects which introduced it be removed. We see no absurdity in supposing a body to be annihilated; but the space that contained it remains; and to suppose that annihilated, seems to be absurd. It is so much allied to nothing or emptiness, that it seems incapable of annihilation or of creation.

Space not only retains a firm hold of our belief, even when we suppose all the objects that introduced it to be annihilated, but it swells to immensity. We can set no limits to it, either of extent or of duration.

Hence we call it immense, eternal, immoveable, and indestructible. But it is only an immense, eternal, immoveable, and indestructible void or emptiness. Perhaps we may apply to it, what the Peripatetics said of their first matter, that whatever it is, it is potentially only, not actually.

When we consider parts of space that have measure and figure, there is nothing we understand better, nothing about which we can reason so clearly, and to so great extent. Extension and figure are circumscribed parts of space, and are the object of geometry, a science in which human reason has the most ample field, and can go deeper, and with more certainty than in any other. But when we attempt to comprehend the whole of space, and to trace it to its origin, we lose ourselves in the search. The profound speculations of ingenious men upon this subject differ so widely, as may lead us to suspect, that the line of human understanding is too short to reach the bottom of it.

Bishop Berkeley, I think, was the first who observed, that the extension, figure, and space, of which we speak in common language, and of which geometry treats, are originally perceived by the sense of touch only; but that there is a notion of extension, figure, and space, which may be got by sight, without any aid from touch. To distinguish these, he calls the first tangible extension, tangible figure, and tangible space; the last he calls visible.

As I think this distinction very important in the philosophy of our senses, I shall adopt the names used by the inventor to express it; remembering what has been already observed, that space, whether tangible or visible, is not so properly an object of sense, as a necessary concomitant of the objects both of sight and touch.

The reader may likewise be pleased to attend to this, that when I use the names of tangible and visible space,

I do not mean to adopt bishop Berkeley's opinion, so far as to think that they are really different things, and altogether unlike. I take them to be different conceptions of the same thing; the one very partial, and the other more complete; but both distinct and just, as far as they reach.

Thus when I see a spire at a very great distance, it seems like the point of a bodkin; there appears no vane at the top, no angles. But when I view the same object at a small distance, I see a huge pyramid of several angles with a vane on the top. Neither of these appearances is fallacious. Each of them is what it ought to be, and what it must be, from such an object seen at such different distances. These different appearances of the same object may serve to illustrate the different conceptions of space, according as they are drawn from the information of sight alone, or as they are drawn from the additional information of touch.

Our sight alone, unaided by touch, gives a very partial notion of space, but yet a distinct one. When it is considered according to this partial notion, I call it visible space. The sense of touch gives a much more complete notion of space; and when it is considered according to this notion, I call it tangible space. Perhaps there may be intelligent beings of a higher order, whose conceptions of space, are much more complete than those we have from both senses. Another sense added to those of sight and touch, might, for what I know, give us conceptions of space, as different from those we can now attain, as tangible space is from visible; and might resolve many knotty points concerning it, which, from the imperfection of our faculties, we cannot by any labour untie.

Berkeley acknowledges that there is an exact correspondence between the visible figure and magnitude of objects, and the tangible; and that every modification

of the one has a modification of the other corresponding. He acknowledges likewise, that nature has established such a connection between the visible figure
and magnitude of an object, and the tangible, that we
learn by experience to know the tangible figure and
magnitude from the visible. And having been accustomed to do so from infancy, we get the habit of doing it with such facility and quickness, that we think
we see tangible figure, magnitude, and distance of
bodies, when, in reality, we only collect those tangible
qualities from the corresponding visible qualities, which
are natural signs of them.

The correspondence and connection which Berkeley shows to be between the visible figure and magnitude of objects, and their tangible figure and magnitude,
is in some respects very similar to that which we have
observed between our sensations, and the primary qualities with which they are connected. No sooner is the
sensation felt, than immediately we have the conception
and belief of the corresponding quality. We give no
attention to the sensation; it has not a name; and it is
difficult to persuade us that there was any such thing.

In like manner, no sooner is the visible figure and
magnitude of an object seen, than immediately we have
the conception and belief of the corresponding tangible
figure and magnitude. We give no attention to the visible figure and magnitude. It is immediately forgotten,
as if it had never been perceived; and it has no name
in common language; and indeed, until Berkeley pointed
it out as a subject of speculation, and gave it a name, it
had none among philosophers, excepting in one instance,
relating to the heavenly bodies, which are beyond the
reach of touch. With regard to them, what Berkeley
calls visible magnitude, was, by astronomers, called
apparent magnitude.

There is surely an apparent magnitude, and an apparent figure of terrestrial objects, as well as of celes-

tial; and this is what Berkeley calls their visible figure and magnitude. But this was never made an object of thought among philosophers, until that author gave it a name, and observed the correspondence and connection between it and tangible magnitude and figure, and how the mind gets the habit of passing so instantaneously from the visible figure, as a sign to the tangible figure, as the thing signified by it, that the first is perfectly forgotten, as if it had never been perceived.

Visible figure, extension, and space, may be made a subject of mathematical speculation, as well as the tangible. In the visible, we find two dimensions only; in the tangible three. In the one, magnitude is measured by angles; in the other by lines. Every part of visible space bears some proportion to the whole; but tangible space being immense, any part of it bears no proportion to the whole.

Such differences in their properties led bishop Berkeley to think, that visible and tangible magnitude and figure, are things totally different and dissimilar, and cannot both belong to the same object.

And upon this dissimilitude is grounded one of the strongest arguments by which his system is supported. For it may be said, if there be external objects which have a real extension and figure, it must be either tangible extension and figure, or visible, or both. The last appears absurd; nor was it ever maintained by any man, that the same object has two kinds of extension and figure, totally dissimilar. There is then only one of the two really in the object; and the other must be ideal. But no reason can be assigned why the perceptions of one sense should be real, whilst those of another are only ideal: and he who is persuaded that the objects of sight are ideas only, has equal reason to believe so of the objects of touch.

This argument, however, loses all its force, if it be true, as was formerly hinted, that visible figure and ex-

tension are only a partial conception, and the tangible
figure and extension a more complete conception of
that figure and extension which is really in the object.

It has been proved very fully by bishop Berkeley,
that sight alone, without any aid from the informations
of touch, gives us no perception, nor even conception
of the distance of any object from the eye. But he
was not aware that this very principle overturns the
argument for his system, taken from the difference between visible and tangible extension and figure: for,
supposing external objects to exist, and to have that
tangible extension and figure which we perceive, it
follows demonstrably, from the principle now mentioned, that their visible extension and figure must be just
what we see it to be.

The rules of perspective, and of the projection of
the sphere, which is a branch of perspective, are demonstrable. They suppose the existence of external
objects, which have a tangible extension and figure;
and, upon that supposition, they demonstrate what
must be the visible extension and figure of such objects,
when placed in such a position, and at such a distance.

Hence it is evident, that the visible figure and extension of objects is so far from being incompatible with
the tangible, that the first is a necessary consequence
from the last, in beings that see as we do. The correspondence between them is not arbitrary, like that
between words and the thing they signify, as Berkeley thought; but it results necessarily from the nature
of the two senses; and this correspondence being always found in experience to be exactly what the rules
of perspective show that it ought to be, if the senses
give true information, is an argument of the truth of
both.

CHAP. XX.

OF THE EVIDENCE OF SENSE, AND OF BELIEF IN GENERAL.

THE intention of nature in the powers which we call the external senses, is evident. They are intended to give us that information of external objects which the Supreme Being saw to be proper for us in our present state; and they give to all mankind the information necessary for life, without reasoning, without any art or investigation on our part.

The most uninstructed peasant has as distinct a conception, and as firm a belief of the immediate objects of his senses, as the greatest philosopher; and with this he rests satisfied, giving himself no concern how he came by this conception and belief. But the philosopher is impatient to know how his conception of external objects, and his belief of their existence, is produced. This, I am afraid, is hid in impenetrable darkness. But where there is no knowledge, there is the more room for conjecture : and of this philosophers have always been very liberal.

The dark cave and shadows of Plato, the species of Aristotle, the films of Epicurus, and the ideas and impressions of modern philosophers, are the productions of human fancy, successively invented to satisfy the eager desire of knowing how we perceive external objects; but they are all deficient in the two essential characters of a true and philosophical account of the phenomenon : for we neither have any evidence of their existence; nor, if they did exist, can it be shown how they would produce perception.

It was before observed, that there are two ingredients in this operation of perception : 1st, the concep-

tion or notion of the object; and, 2dly, the belief of
its present existence.   Both are unaccountable.

That we can assign no adequate cause of our first
conceptions of things, I think, is now acknowledged by
the most enlightened philosophers.   We know that
such is our constitution, that in certain circumstances we
have certain conceptions; but how they are produced, we
know no more than how we ourselves were produced.

When we have got the conception of external objects
by our senses, we can analyze them in our thought into
their simple ingredients; and we can compound those
ingredients into various new forms, which the senses
never presented.   But it is beyond the power of human imagination to form any conception, whose simple
ingredients have not been furnished by nature in a
manner unaccountable to our understanding.

We have an immediate conception of the operations
of our own minds, joined with a belief of their existence; and this we call consciousness.   But this is only
giving a name to this source of our knowledge.   It is
not a discovery of its cause.   In like manner, we have,
by our external senses, a conception of external objects,
joined with a belief of their existence; and this we call
perception.   But this is only giving a name to another
source of our knowledge, without discovering its cause.

We know, that when certain impressions are made
upon our organs, nerves, and brain, certain corresponding sensations are felt, and certain objects are both
conceived and believed to exist.   But in this train of
operations nature works in the dark.   We can neither
discover the cause of any one of them, nor any necessary
connection of one with another; and whether they are
connected by any necessary tie, or only conjoined in
our constitution by the will of Heaven, we know not.

That any kind of impression upon a body should be
the efficient cause of sensation, appears very absurd.

Nor can we perceive any necessary connection between sensation and the conception and belief of an external object.   For any thing we can discover, we might have been so framed as to have all the sensations we now have by our senses, without any impressions upon our organs, and without any conception of any external object.   For any thing we know, we might have been so made as to perceive external objects, without any impressions on bodily organs, and without any of those sensations which invariably accompany perception in our present frame.

If our conception of external objects be unaccountable, the conviction and belief of their existence, which we get by our senses, is no less so.

Belief, assent, conviction, are words which I think do not admit of logical definition, because the operation of mind signified by them is perfectly simple, and of its own kind.   Nor do they need to be defined, because they are common words, and well understood.

Belief must have an object.   For he that believes, must believe something; and that which he believes is called the object of his belief.   Of this object of his belief, he must have some conception, clear or obscure; for although there may be the most clear and distinct conception of an object, without any belief of its existence, there can be no belief without conception.

Belief is always expressed in language by a proposition, wherein something is affirmed or denied.   This is the form of speech which in all languages is appropriated to that purpose, and without belief there could be neither affirmation nor denial, nor should we have any form of words to express either.   Belief admits of all degrees from the slightest suspicion to the fullest assurance.   These things are so evident to every man that reflects, that it would be abusing the reader's patience to dwell upon them.

I proceed to observe, that there are many operations of mind in which, when we analyze them as far as we are able, we find belief to be an essential ingredient. A man cannot be conscious of his own thoughts, without believing that he thinks. He cannot perceive an object of sense, without believing that it exists. He cannot distinctly remember a past event, without believing that it did exist. Belief therefore is an ingredient in consciousness, in perception, and in remembrance.

Not only in most of our intellectual operations, but in many of the active principles of the human mind, belief enters as an ingredient. Joy and sorrow, hope and fear, imply a belief of good or ill, either present or in expectation. Esteem, gratitude, pity, and resentment, imply a belief of certain qualities in their objects. In every action that is done for an end, there must be a belief of its tendency to that end. So large a share has belief in our intellectual operations, in our active principles, and in our actions themselves, that as faith in things divine is represented as the main spring in the life of a Christian, so belief in general is the main spring in the life of a man.

That men often believe what there is no just ground to believe, and thereby are led into hurtful errors, is too evident to be denied : and, on the other hand, that there are just grounds of belief, can as little be doubted by any man who is not a perfect skeptic.

We give the name of evidence to whatever is a ground of belief. To believe without evidence is a weakness which every man is concerned to avoid, and which every man wishes to avoid. Nor is it in a man's power to believe any thing longer than he thinks he has evidence.

What this evidence is, is more easily felt than described. Those who never reflected upon its nature, feel its influence in governing their belief. It is the business of the logician to explain its nature, and to distinguish its various kinds and degrees; but every man of understanding can judge of it, and commonly judges right, when the evidence is fairly laid before him, and his mind is free from prejudice. A man who knows nothing of the theory of vision, may have a good eye; and a man who never speculated about evidence in the abstract, may have a good judgment.

The common occasions of life lead us to distinguish evidence into different kinds, to which we give names that are well understood; such as the evidence of sense, the evidence of memory, the evidence of consciousness, the evidence of testimony, the evidence of axioms, the evidence of reasoning. All men of common understanding agree, that each of these kinds of evidence may afford just ground of belief, and they agree very generally in the circumstances that strengthen or weaken them.

Philosophers have endeavoured, by analyzing the different sorts of evidence, to find out some common nature wherein they all agree, and thereby to reduce them all to one. This was the aim of the schoolmen in their intricate disputes about the criterion of truth. Des Cartes placed this criterion of truth in clear and distinct perception; and laid it down as a maxim, that whatever we clearly and distinctly perceive to be true, is true; but it is difficult to know what he understands by clear and distinct perception in this maxim. Mr. Locke placed it in a perception of the agreement or disagreement of our ideas, which perception is immediate in intuitive knowledge, and by the intervention of other ideas in reasoning.

I confess that, although I have, as I think, a distinct notion of the different kinds of evidence above mentioned, and perhaps of some others, which it is unnecessary here to enumerate, yet I am not able to find any common nature to which they may all be reduced.

They seem to me to agree only in this, that they are all fitted by nature to produce belief in the human mind ; some of them in the highest degree, which we call certainty, others in various degrees according to circumstances.

I shall take it for granted, that the evidence of sense, when the proper circumstances concur, is good evidence, and a just ground of belief. My intention in this place is only to compare it with the other kinds that have been mentioned, that we may judge whether it be reducible to any of them, or of a nature peculiar to itself.

1st, It seems to be quite different from the evidence of reasoning. All good evidence is commonly called reasonable evidence, and very justly, because it ought to govern our belief as reasonable creatures. And, according to this meaning, I think the evidence of sense no less reasonable than that of demonstration. If nature give us information of things that concern us, by other means than by reasoning, reason itself will direct us to receive that information with thankfulness, and to make the best use of it.

But when we speak of the evidence of reasoning as a particular kind of evidence, it means the evidence of propositions that are inferred by reasoning, from propositions already known and believed. Thus the evidence of the fifth proposition of the first book of Euclid's elements consists in this, that it is shown to be the necessary consequence of the axioms, and of the preceding propositions. In all reasoning, there must be one or more premises, and a conclusion drawn from them. And the premises are called the reason why we must believe the conclusion which we see to follow from them.

That the evidence of sense is of a different kind, needs little proof. No man seeks a reason for believing

what he sees or feels; and if he did, it would be difficult to find one. But though he can give no reason for
believing his senses, his belief remains as firm as if it
were grounded on demonstration.

Many eminent philosophers, thinking it unreasonable
to believe, when they could not show a reason, have laboured to furnish us with reasons for believing our
senses; but their reasons are very insufficient, and will
not bear examination. Other philosophers have shown
very clearly the fallacy of these reasons, and have, as
they imagine, discovered invincible reasons against this
belief; but they have never been able either to shake it
in themselves, or to convince others. The statesman
continues to plod, the soldier to fight, and the merchant
to export and import, without being in the least moved
by the demonstrations that have been offered of the non-
existence of those things about which they are so seriously employed. And a man may as soon, by reasoning,
pull the moon out of her orbit, as destroy the belief of
the objects of sense.

Shall we say then that the evidence of sense is the
same with that of axioms, or self-evident truths? I
answer, 1st, that all modern philosophers seem to
agree, that the existence of the objects of sense is not
self-evident, because some of them have endeavoured
to prove it by subtile reasoning, others to refute it.
Neither of these can consider it as self-evident.

2dly, I would observe, that the word *axiom* is taken
by philosophers in such a sense, as that the existence of
the objects of sense cannot, with propriety, be called
an axiom. They give the name of axiom only to self-
evident truths that are necessary, and are not limited
to time and place, but must be true at all times, and in
all places. The truths attested by our senses are not
of this kind; they are contingent, and limited to time
and place.

Thus, that one is the half of two, is an axiom.   It is
equally true at all times, and in all places.   We perceive, by attending to the proposition itself, that it cannot but be true; and therefore it is called an eternal,
necessary and immutable truth.   That there is at present a chair on my right hand, and another on my left,
is a truth attested by my senses; but it is not necessary,
nor eternal, nor immutable.   It may not be true next
minute; and therefore, to call it an axiom, would, I apprehend, be to deviate from the common use of the
word.

3dly, If the word *axiom* be put to signify every truth
which is known immediately, without being deduced
from any antecedent truth, then the existence of the
objects of sense may be called an axiom.   For my senses
give me as immediate conviction of what they testify,
as my understanding gives me of what is commonly
called an axiom.

There is no doubt an analogy between the evidence
of sense and the evidence of testimony.   Hence we find in
all languages the analogical expressions of the *testimony
of sense,* of giving *credit* to our senses, and the like.
But there is a real difference between the two, as well
as a similitude.   In believing upon testimony, we rely
upon the authority of a person who testifies : but we
have no such authority for believing our senses.

Shall we say then that this belief is the inspiration of
the Almighty?   I think this may be said in a good sense;
for I take it to be the immediate effect of our constitution, which is the work of the Almighty.   But if inspiration be understood to imply a persuasion of its coming
from God, our belief of the objects of sense is not inspiration; for a man would believe his senses though he
had no notion of a Deity.   He who is persuaded that
he is the workmanship of God, and that it is a part of
his constitution to believe his senses, may think that a

good reason to confirm his belief: but he had the belief
before he could give this or any other reason for it.

If we compare the evidence of sense with that of
memory, we find a great resemblance, but still some
difference. I remember distinctly to have dined yesterday with such a company. What is the meaning of
this? It is, that I have a distinct conception and firm
belief of this past event; not by reasoning, not by testimony, but immediately from my constitution : and I
give the name of memory to that part of my constitution, by which I have this kind of conviction of past
events.

I see a chair on my right hand. What is the
meaning of this? It is, that I have, by my constitution, a distinct conception and firm belief of the present existence of the chair in such a place, and in
such a position ; and I give the name of seeing to
that part of my constitution, by which I have this immediate conviction. The two operations agree in the
immediate conviction which they give. They agree in
this also, that the things believed are not necessary,
but contingent, and limited to time and place. But
they differ in two respects ; 1st, that memory has something for its object that did exist in time past ; but the
object of sight, and of all the senses, must be something
which exists at present. And, 2dly, that I see by my
eyes, and only when they are directed to the object,
and when it is illuminated. But my memory is not
limited by any bodily organ that I know, nor by light
and darkness, though it has its limitations of another
kind.

These differences are obvious to all men, and very
reasonably lead them to consider seeing and remembering as operations specifically different. But the nature of the evidence they give has a great resemblance.
A like difference and a like resemblance there is be-

tween the evidence of sense and that of consciousness, which I leave the reader to trace.

As to the opinion, that evidence consists in a perception of the agreement or disagreement of ideas, we may have occasion to consider it more particularly in another place. Here I only observe, that, when taken in the most favourable sense, it may be applied with propriety to the evidence of reasoning, and to the evidence of some axioms. But I cannot see how, in any sense, it can be applied to the evidence of consciousness, to the evidence of memory, or to that of the senses.

When I compare the different kinds of evidence above mentioned, I confess, after all, that the evidence of reasoning, and that of some necessary and self-evident truths, seems to be the least mysterious, and the most perfectly comprehended ; and therefore I do not think it strange that philosophers should have endeavoured to reduce all kinds of evidence to these.

When I see a proposition to be self-evident and necessary, and that the subject is plainly included in the predicate, there seems to be nothing more that I can desire, in order to understand why I believe it. And when I see a consequence that necessarily follows from one or more self-evident propositions, I want nothing more with regard to my belief of that consequence. The light of truth so fills my mind in these cases, that I can neither conceive, nor desire any thing more satisfying.

On the other hand, when I remember distinctly a past event, or see an object before my eyes, this commands my belief no less than an axiom. But when, as a philosopher, I reflect upon this belief, and want to trace it to its origin, I am not able to resolve it into necessary and self-evident axioms, or conclusions that are necessarily consequent upon them. I seem to want that evidence which I can best comprehend, and which gives perfect satisfaction to an inquisitive mind; yet it is ridiculous to doubt, and I find it is not in my power. An attempt to throw off this belief, is like an attempt to fly, equally ridiculous and impracticable.

To a philosopher, who has been accustomed to think that the treasure of his knowledge is the acquisition of that reasoning power of which he boasts, it is no doubt humiliating to find, that his reason can lay no claim to the greater part of it.

By his reason, he can discover certain abstract and necessary relations of things; but his knowledge of what really exists, or did exist, comes by another channel, which is open to those who cannot reason. He is led to it in the dark, and knows not how he came by it.

It is no wonder that the pride of philosophy should lead some to invent vain theories, in order to account for this knowledge; and others who see this to be impracticable, to spurn at a knowledge they cannot account for, and vainly attempt to throw it off, as a reproach to their understanding. But the wise and the humble will receive it as the gift of Heaven, and endeavour to make the best use of it.

CHAP. XXI.

OF THE IMPROVEMENT OF THE SENSES.

OUR senses may be considered in two views; 1st, as they afford us agreeable sensations, or subject us to such as are disagreeable; and, 2dly, as they give us information of things that concern us.

In the 1st view, they neither require nor admit of improvement. Both the painful and the agreeable sensations of our external senses are given by nature for certain ends; and they are given in that degree which is the most proper for their end. By diminishing or increasing them, we should not mend, but mar the work of nature.

Bodily pains are indications of some disorder or hurt of the body, and admonitions to use the best means in our power to prevent or remove their causes. As far as this can be done by temperance, exercise, regimen, or the skill of the physician, every man has sufficient inducement to do it.

When pain cannot be prevented or removed, it is greatly alleviated by patience and fortitude of mind. While the mind is superior to pain, the man is not unhappy, though he may be exercised. It leaves no sting behind it, but rather matter of triumph and agreeable reflection, when borne properly, and in a good cause. The Canadians have taught us, that even savages may acquire a superiority to the most excruciating pains; and, in every region of the earth, instances will be found, where a sense of duty, of honour, or even of worldly interest, have triumphed over it.

It is evident, that nature intended for man in his present state, a life of labour and toil, wherein he may be occasionally exposed to pain and danger: and the happiest man is not he who has felt least of those evils, but he whose mind is fitted to bear them by real magnanimity.

Our active and perceptive powers are improved and perfected by use and exercise. This is the constitution of nature. But, with regard to the agreeable and disagreeable sensations we have by our senses, the very contrary is an established constitution of nature: the frequent repetition of them weakens their force. Sensations at first very disagreeable, by use become tolerable, and at last perfectly indifferent. And those that are at first very agreeable, by frequent repetition become insipid, and at last perhaps give disgust. Nature has set limits to the pleasures of sense, which we cannot pass; and all studied gratification of them, as it is mean and unworthy of a man, so it is foolish and fruitless.

The man who, in eating and drinking, and in other gratifications of sense, obeys the calls of nature, without affecting delicacies and refinements, has all the enjoyment that the senses can afford. If one could, by a soft and luxurious life, acquire a more delicate sensibility to pleasure, it must be at the expense of a like sensibility to pain, from which he can never promise exemption; and at the expense of cherishing many diseases which produce pain.

The improvement of our external senses, as they are the means of giving us information, is a subject more worthy of our attention: for although they are not the noblest and most exalted powers of our nature, yet they are not the least useful. All that we know or can know of the material world, must be grounded upon their information; and the philosopher, as well as the day labourer, must be indebted to them for the largest part of his knowledge.

Some of our perceptions by the senses may be called original, because they require no previous experience or learning; but the far greatest part is acquired, and the fruit of experience.

Three of our senses, to wit, smell, taste, and hearing, originally give us only certain sensations, and a conviction that these sensations are occasioned by some external object. We give a name to that quality of the object by which it is fitted to produce such a sensation, and connect that quality with the object, and with its other qualities.

Thus we learn, that a certain sensation of smell is produced by a rose; and that quality in the rose, by which it is fitted to produce this sensation, we call the smell of the rose. Here it is evident that the sensation is original. The perception, that the rose has that quality, which we call its smell, is acquired. In like manner, we learn all those qualities in bodies, which we call their smell, their taste, their sound. These are all secondary qualities, and we give the same name to them which we give to the sensations they produce; not from any similitude between the sensation and the quality of the same name, but because the quality is signified to us by the sensation as its sign, and because our senses give us no other knowledge of the quality, but that it is fit to produce such a sensation.

By the other two senses, we have much more ample information. By sight, we learn to distinguish objects by their colour, in the same manner as by their sound, taste, and smell. By this sense, we perceive visible objects to have extension in two dimensions, to have visible figure and magnitude, and a certain angular distance from one another. These I conceive are the original perceptions of sight.

By touch, we not only perceive the temperature of bodies as to heat and cold, which are secondary qualities, but we perceive originally their three dimensions, their tangible figure and magnitude, their linear distance from one another, their hardness, softness, or fluidity. These qualities we originally perceive by touch only; but, by experience, we learn to perceive all or most of them by sight.

We learn to perceive, by one sense, what originally could have been perceived only by another, by finding a connection between the objects of the different senses. Hence the original perceptions, or the sensations of one sense become signs of whatever has always been found connected with them; and from the sign the mind passes immediately to the conception and belief of the thing signified: and although the connection in the mind between the sign and the thing signified by it, be the effect of custom, this custom becomes a second nature, and it is difficult to distinguish it from the original power of perception.

Thus, if a sphere of one uniform colour be set before me, I perceive evidently by my eye its spherical figure, and its three dimensions. All the world will acknowledge, that by sight only, without touching it, I may be certain that it is a sphere; yet it is no less certain, that, by the original power of sight, I could not perceive it to be a sphere, and to have three dimensions. The eye originally could only perceive two dimensions, and a gradual variation of colour on the different sides of the object.

It is experience that teaches me that the variation of colour is an effect of spherical convexity, and of the distribution of light and shade. But so rapid is the progress of the thought from the effect to the cause, that we attend only to the last, and can hardly be persuaded that we do not immediately see the three dimensions of the sphere.

Nay, it may be observed, that, in this case, the acquired perception in a manner effaces the original one;

for the sphere is seen to be of one uniform colour, though originally there would have appeared a gradual variation of colour : but that apparent variation, we learn to interpret as the effect of light and shade falling upon a sphere of one uniform colour.

A sphere may be painted upon a plane, so exactly, as to be taken for a real sphere, when the eye is at a proper distance, and in the proper point of view. We say in this case, that the eye is deceived, that the appearance is fallacious. But there is no fallacy in the original perception, but only in that which is acquired by custom. The variation of colour, exhibited to the eye by the painter's art, is the same which nature exhibits by the different degrees of light falling upon the convex surface of a sphere.

In perception, whether original or acquired, there is something which may be called the sign, and something which is signified to us, or brought to our knowledge by that sign.

In original perception, the signs are the various sensations which are produced by the impressions made upon our organs. The things signified, are the objects perceived in consequence of those sensations, by the original constitution of our nature.

Thus, when I grasp an ivory ball in my hand, I have a certain sensation of touch. Although this sensation be in the mind, and have no similitude to any thing material, yet, by the laws of my constitution, it is immediately followed by the conception and belief. that there is in my hand a hard smooth body of a spherical figure, and about an inch and a half in diameter. This belief is grounded neither upon reasoning, nor upon experience ; it is the immediate effect of my constitution, and this I call original perception.

In acquired perception, the sign may be either a sensation, or something originally perceived. The thing signified is something, which, by experience, has been found connected with that sign.

Thus, when the ivory ball is placed before my eye, I perceive by sight what I before perceived by touch, that the ball is smooth, spherical, of such a diameter, and at such a distance from the eye ; and to this is added the perception of its colour.   All these things I perceive by sight distinctly, and with certainty : yet it is certain from principles of philosophy, that if I had not been accustomed to compare the informations of sight with those of touch, I should not have perceived these things by sight.   I should have perceived a circular object, having its colour gradually more faint toward the shaded side.   But I should not have perceived it to have three dimensions, to be spherical, to be of such a linear magnitude, and at such a distance from the eye.   That these last mentioned are not original perceptions of sight, but acquired by experience, is sufficiently evident from the principles of optics, and from the art of painters, in painting objects of three dimensions, upon a plane which has only two.   And it has been put beyond all doubt, by observations recorded of several persons, who having, by cataracts in their eyes, been deprived of sight from their infancy, have been couched and made to see, after they came to years of understanding.

Those who have had their eyesight from infancy, acquire such perceptions so early, that they cannot recollect the time when they had them not, and therefore make no distinction between them and their original perceptions ; nor can they be easily persuaded, that there is any just foundation for such a distinction. In all languages men speak with equal assurance of their seeing objects to be spherical or cubical, as of their feeling them to be so ; nor do they ever dream, that these perceptions of sight were not as early and original, as the perceptions they have of the same objects by touch.

This power which we acquire of perceiving things by our senses, which originally we should not have perceived, is not the effect of any reasoning on our part: it is the result of our constitution, and of the situations in which we happen to be placed.

We are so made, that when two things are found to be conjoined in certain circumstances, we are prone to believe that they are connected by nature, and will always be found together in like circumstances. The belief which we are led into in such cases is not the effect of reasoning, nor does it arise from intuitive evidence in the thing believed; it is, as I apprehend, the immediate effect of our constitution. Accordingly it is strongest in infancy, before our reasoning power appears, before we are capable of drawing a conclusion from premises. A child who has once burnt his finger in a candle, from that single instance connects the pain of burning with putting his finger in the candle, and believes that these two things must go together. It is obvious, that this part of our constitution is of very great use before we come to the use of reason, and guards us from a thousand mischiefs, which, without it, we would rush into; it may sometimes lead us into error, but the good effects of it far overbalance the ill.

It is no doubt the perfection of a rational being to have no belief but what is grounded on intuitive evidence, or on just reasoning : but man, I apprehend, is not such a being; nor is it the intention of nature that he should be such a being, in every period of his existence. We come into the world without the exercise of reason; we are merely animal before we are rational creatures;

and it is necessary for our preservation, that we should believe many things before we can reason. How then is our belief to be regulated before we have reason to regulate it ? has nature left it to be regulated by chance ? By no means. It is regulated by certain principles, which are parts of our constitution. Whether they ought to be called animal principles, or instinctive principles, or what name we give to them, is of small moment; but they are certainly different from the faculty of reason. They do the office of reason while it is in its infancy, and must, as it were, be carried in a nurse's arms, and they are leading strings to it in its gradual progress.

From what has been said, I think it appears, that our original powers of perceiving objects by our senses receive great improvement by use and habit; and without this improvement, would be altogether insufficient for the purposes of life. The daily occurrences of life not only add to our stock of knowledge, but give additional perceptive powers to our senses; and time gives us the use of our eyes and ears, as well as of our hands and legs.

This is the greatest and most important improvement of our external senses. It is to be found in all men come to years of understanding, but is various in different persons according to their different occupations, and the different circumstances in which they are placed. Every artist acquires an eye as well as a hand in his own profession. His eye becomes skilled in perceiving, no less than his hand in executing, what belongs to his employment.

Besides this improvement of our senses, which nature produces without our intent on, there are various ways in which they may be improved, or their defects remedied by art. As, 1st, by a due care of the organs of sense, that they be in a sound and natural state. This belongs to the department of the Medical Faculty.

2dly, By accurate attention to the objects of sense. The effects of such attention in improving our senses appear in every art. The artist, by giving more attention to certain objects than others do, by that means perceives many things in those objects which others do not. Those who happen to be deprived of one sense, frequently supply that defect in a great degree, by giving more accurate attention to the objects of the senses they have. The blind have often been known to acquire uncommon acuteness in distinguishing things by feeling and hearing; and the deaf are uncommonly quick in reading men's thoughts in their countenance.

A *third* way in which our senses admit of improvement, is, by additional organs or instruments contrived by art. By the invention of optical glasses, and the gradual improvement of them, the natural power of vision is wonderfully improved, and a vast addition made to the stock of knowledge which we acquire by the eye. By speaking trumpets, and ear trumpets, some improvement has been made in the sense of hearing. Whether by similar inventions the other senses may be improved, seems uncertain.

A *fourth* method by which the information got by our senses may be improved, is, by discovering the connection which nature has established between the sensible qualities of objects and their more latent qualities.

By the sensible qualities of bodies, I understand those that are perceived immediately by the senses, such as their colour, figure, feeling, sound, taste, smell. The various modifications, and various combinations of these, are innumerable; so that there are hardly two individual bodies in nature that may not be distinguished by their sensible qualities.

The latent qualities are such as are not immediately discovered by our senses; but discovered, sometimes by accident, sometimes by experiment or observation. The most important part of our knowledge of bodies, is the knowledge of the latent qualities of the several species, by which they are adapted to certain purposes, either for food, or medicine, or agriculture, or for the materials or utensils of some art or manufacture.

I am taught, that certain species of bodies have certain latent qualities ; but how shall I know that this individual is of such a species? This must be known by the sensible qualities which characterize the species. I must know that this is bread, and that wine, before I eat the one or drink the other. I must know that this is rhubarb, and that opium, before I use the one or the other for medicine.

It is one branch of human knowledge to know the names of the various species of natural and artificial bodies, and to know the sensible qualities by which they are ascertained to be of such a species, and by which they are distinguished from one another. It is another branch of knowledge to know the latent qualities of the several species, and the uses to which they are subservient.

The man who possesses both these branches, is informed by his senses of innumerable things of real moment, which are hid from those who possess only one, or neither.   This is an improvement in the information got by our senses, which must keep pace with the improvements made in natural history, in natural philosophy, and in the arts.

It would be an improvement still higher, if we were able to discover any connection between the sensible qualities of bodies and their latent qualities, without knowing the species, or what may have been discovered with regard to it.

Some philosophers of the first rate have made attempts toward this noble improvement, not without promising hopes of success.   Thus the celebrated Linnæus has attempted to point out certain sensible qualities by which a plant may very probably be concluded to be poisonous, without knowing its name or species. He has given several other instances, wherein certain medical and economical virtues of plants are indicated by their external appearances.   Sir Isaac Newton has attempted to show, that from the colours of bodies we may form a probable conjecture of the size of their constituent parts, by which the rays of light are reflected.

No man can pretend to set limits to the discoveries that may be made by human genius and industry, of such connections between the latent and the sensible qualities of bodies.   A wide field here opens to our view, whose boundaries no man can ascertain, of improvements that may hereafter be made in the information conveyed to us by our senses.

CHAP. XXII.

OF THE FALLACY OF THE SENSES.

COMPLAINTS of the fallacy of the senses have been very common in ancient and in modern times, especially among the philosophers : and if we should take for granted all that they have said on this subject, the natural conclusion from it might seem to be, that the senses are given to us by some malignant demon on purpose to delude us, rather than that they are formed by the wise and beneficent Author of nature, to give us true information of things necessary to our preservation and happiness.

The whole sect of Atomists among the ancients, led by Democritus, and afterward by Epicurus, maintained, that all the qualities of bodies which the moderns call secondary qualities, to wit, smell, taste, sound, colour, heat, and cold, are mere illusions of sense, and have no real existence. Plato maintained that we can attain no real knowledge of material things ; and that eternal and immutable ideas are the only objects of real knowledge. The Academics and Skeptics anxiously sought for arguments to prove the fallaciousness of our senses, in order to support their favourite doctrine, that even in things that seem most evident, we ought to withhold assent.

Among the Peripatetics we find frequent complaints that the senses often deceive us, and that their testimony is to be suspected, when it is not confirmed by reason, by which the errors of sense may be corrected. This complaint they supported by many common place instances ; such as, the crooked appearance of an oar in water; objects being magnified, and their distance mistaken in a fog; the sun and moon appearing about a foot or two in diameter, while they are really thousands of miles; a square tower being taken at a distance to be round. These, and many similar appearances, they thought to be sufficiently accounted for from the fallacy of the senses: and thus the fallacy of the senses was used as a decent cover to conceal their ignorance of the real causes of such phenomena, and served the same purpose as their occult qualities and substantial forms.

Des Cartes and his followers joined in the same complaint. Antony le Grand, a philosopher of that sect, in the first chapter of his Logic, expresses the sentiments of the sect as follows: "Since all our senses are fallacious, and we are frequently deceived by them, common reason advises, that we should not put too much trust in them, nay, that we should suspect falsehood in every thing they represent; for it is imprudence and temerity to trust to those who have but once deceived us; and if they err at any time, they may be believed always to err. They are given by nature for this purpose only, to warn us of what is useful and what is hurtful to us. The order of nature is perverted when we put them to any other use, and apply them for the knowledge of truth."

When we consider that the active part of mankind, in all ages from the beginning of the world, have rested their most important concerns upon the testimony of sense, it will be very difficult to reconcile their conduct with the speculative opinion so generally entertained of the fallaciousness of the senses. And it seems to be a very unfavourable account of the workmanship of the Supreme Being, to think that he has given us one faculty to deceive us, to wit, our senses, and another faculty, to wit, our reason, to detect the fallacy.

It deserves, therefore, to be considered, whether the fallaciousness of our senses be not a common error, which men have been led into, from a desire to conceal their ignorance, or to apologize for their mistakes.

There are two powers which we owe to our external senses, sensation, and the perception of external objects.

It is impossible that there can be any fallacy in sensation : for we are conscious of all our sensations, and they can neither be any other in their nature, nor greater or less in their degree than we feel them. It is impossible that a man should be in pain, when he does not feel pain ; and when he feels pain, it is impossible that his pain should not be real, and in its degree what it is felt to be : and the same thing may be said of every sensation whatsoever. An agreeable or an uneasy sensation may be forgotten when it is past, but when it is present, it can be nothing but what we feel.

If, therefore, there be any fallacy in our senses, it must be in the perception of external objects, which we shall next consider.

And here I grant that we can conceive powers of perceiving external objects more perfect than ours, which, possibly, beings of a higher order may enjoy. We can perceive external objects only by means of bodily organs ; and these are liable to various disorders, which sometimes affect our powers of perception. The nerves and brain, which are interior organs of perception, are likewise liable to disorders, as every part of the human frame is.

The imagination, the memory, the judging and reasoning powers, are all liable to be hurt, or even destroyed, by disorders of the body, as well as our powers of perception ; but we do not on this account call them fallacious.

Our senses, our memory, and our reason, are all limited and imperfect : this is the lot of humanity :

but they are such as the Author of our being saw to be
best fitted for us in our present state. Superior natures may have intellectual powers which we have not,
or such as we have, in a more perfect degree, and less
liable to accidental disorders : but we have no reason
to think that God has given fallacious powers to any
of his creatures. This would be to think dishonoura-
bly of our Maker, and would lay a foundation for universal skepticism.

The appearances commonly imputed to the fallacy
of the senses are many, and of different kinds ; but I
think they may be reduced to the four following classes.

1st, Many things called deceptions of the senses are
only conclusions rashly drawn from the testimony of
the senses. In these cases the testimony of the senses
is true, but we rashly draw a conclusion from it, which
does not necessarily follow. We are disposed to impute our errors rather to false information than to inconclusive reasoning, and to blame our senses for the
wrong conclusions we draw from their testimony.

Thus, when a man has taken a counterfeit guinea for
a true one, he says his senses deceived him ; but he
lays the blame where it ought not to be laid : for we
may ask him, did your senses give a false testimony of
the colour, or of the figure, or of the impression ? No.
But this is all that they testified, and this they testified
truly.   From these premises you concluded that it was
a true guinea, but this conclusion does not follow ; you
erred therefore, not by relying upon the testimony of
sense, but by judging rashly from its testimony. Not
only are your senses innocent of this error, but it is
only by their information that it can be discovered.   If
you consult them properly, they will inform you that
what you took for a guinea is base metal, or is deficient
in weight, and this can only be known by the testimony of sense.

I remember to have met with a man who thought the argument used by Protestants against the Popish doctrine of transubstantiation, from the testimony of our senses, inconclusive; because, said he, instances may be given where several of our senses may deceive us: how do we know then that there may not be cases wherein they all deceive us, and no sense is left to detect the fallacy? I begged of him to know an instance wherein several of our senses deceive us. I take, said he, a piece of soft turf, I cut it into the shape of an apple; with the essence of apples, I give it the smell of an apple; and with paint, I can give it the skin and colour of an apple. Here then is a body, which, if you judge by your eye, by your touch, or by your smell, is an apple.

To this I would answer, that no one of our senses deceives us in this case. My sight and touch testify that it has the shape and colour of an apple: this is true. The sense of smelling testifies that it has the smell of an apple: this is likewise true, and is no deception. Where then lies the deception? It is evident it lies in this, that because this body has some qualities belonging to an apple, I conclude that it is an apple. This is a fallacy, not of the senses, but of inconclusive reasoning.

Many false judgments that are accounted deceptions of sense, arise from our mistaking relative motion for real or absolute motion. These can be no deceptions of sense, because by our senses we perceive only the relative motions of bodies; and it is by reasoning that we infer the real from the relative which we perceive. A little reflection may satisfy us of this.

It was before observed, that we perceive extension to be one sensible quality of bodies, and thence are necessarily led to conceive space, though space be of itself no object of sense. When a body is removed out of its place, the space which it filled remains empty till it is filled by some other body, and would remain if it should never be filled. Before any body existed, the space which bodies now occupy was empty space, capable of receiving bodies; for no body can exist where there is no space to contain it. There is space therefore wherever bodies exist, or can exist.

Hence it is evident that space can have no limits. It is no less evident that it is immoveable. Bodies placed in it are moveable, but the place where they were cannot be moved; and we can as easily conceive a thing to be moved from itself, as one part of space brought nearer to, or removed further from another.

This space, therefore, which is unlimited and immoveable, is called by philosophers *absolute space*. Absolute, or real motion, is a change of place in absolute space.

Our senses do not testify the absolute motion or absolute rest of any body. When one body removes from another, this may be discerned by the senses; but whether any body keeps the same part of absolute space, we do not perceive by our senses. When one body seems to remove from another, we can infer with certainty that there is absolute motion, but whether in the one or the other, or partly in both, is not discerned by sense.

Of all the prejudices which philosophy contradicts, I believe there is none so general as that the earth keeps its place unmoved. This opinion seems to be universal, till it is corrected by instruction, or by philosophical speculation. Those who have any tincture of education are not now in danger of being held by it, but they find at first a reluctance to believe that there are antipodes; that the earth is spherical, and turns round its axis every day, and round the sun every year.

They can recollect the time when reason struggled with prejudice upon these points, and prevailed at length, but not without some effort.

The cause of a prejudice so very general is not unworthy of investigation. But that is not our present business. It is sufficient to observe, that it cannot justly be called a fallacy of sense ; because our senses testify only the change of situation of one body in relation to other bodies, and not its change of situation in absolute space. It is only the relative motion of bodies that we perceive, and that we perceive truly. It is the province of reason and philosophy, from the relative motions which we perceive, to collect the real and absolute motions which produce them.

All motion must be estimated from some point or place which is supposed to be at rest. We perceive not the points of absolute space, from which real and absolute motion must be reckoned : and there are obvious reasons that lead mankind in the state of ignorance, to make the earth the fixed place from which they may estimate the various motions they perceive. The custom of doing this from infancy, and of using constantly a language which supposes the earth to be at rest, may perhaps be the cause of the general prejudice in favour of this opinion.

Thus it appears, that if we distinguish accurately between what our senses really and naturally testify, and the conclusions which we draw from their testimony, by reasoning, we shall find many of the errors, called fallacies of the senses, to be no fallacy of the senses, but rash judgments, which are not to be imputed to our senses.

2dly, Another class of errors imputed to the fallacy of the senses, are those which we are liable to in our acquired perceptions. Acquired perception is not properly the testimony of those senses which God has given us, but a conclusion drawn from what the senses testify. In our past experience, we have found certain things conjoined with what our senses testify. We are led by our constitution to expect this conjunction in time to come; and when we have often found it in our experience to happen, we acquire a firm belief, that the things which we have found thus conjoined are connected in nature, and that one is a sign of the other. The appearance of the sign immediately produces the belief of its usual attendant, and we think we perceive the one as well as the other.

That such conclusions are formed even in infancy, no man can doubt; nor is it less certain that they are confounded with the natural and immediate perceptions of sense, and in all languages are called by the same name. We are therefore authorized by language to call them perception, and must often do so, or speak unintelligibly. But philosophy teaches us in this, as in many other instances, to distinguish things which the vulgar confound. I have therefore given the name of acquired perception to such conclusions, to distinguish them from what is naturally, originally, and immediately testified by our senses. Whether this acquired perception is to be resolved into some process of reasoning, of which we have lost the remembrance, as some philosophers think, or whether it results from some part of our constitution distinct from reason, as I rather believe, does not concern the present subject. If the first of these opinions be true, the errors of acquired perception will fall under the first class before mentioned. If not, it makes a distinct class by itself. But whether the one or the other be true, it must be observed, that the errors of acquired perception are not properly fallacies of our senses.

Thus when a globe is set before me, I perceive by my eyes that it has three dimensions and a spherical

figure. To say that this is not perception, would be
to reject the authority of custom in the use of words,
which no wise man will do: but that it is not the testimony of my sense of seeing, every philosopher knows.
I see only a circular form, having the light and colour
distributed in a certain way over it. But being accustomed to observe this distribution of light and colour
only in a spherical body, I immediately, from what I
see, believe the object to be spherical, and say that I
see or perceive it to be spherical. When a painter,
by an exact imitation of that distribution of light and
colour, which I have been accustomed to see only in a
real sphere, deceives me, so as to make me take that
to be a real sphere, which is only a painted one, the
testimony of my eye is true; the colour and visible figure of the object is truly what I see it to be: the error
lies in the conclusion drawn from what I see, to wit,
that the object has three dimensions and a spherical
figure. The conclusion is false in this case; but whatever be the origin of this conclusion, it is not properly
the testimony of sense.

To this class we must refer the judgments we are
apt to form of the distance and magnitude of the heavenly bodies, and of terrestrial objects seen on high. The
mistakes we make of the magnitude and distance of objects seen through optical glasses, or through an atmo-
sphere uncommonly clear, or uncommonly foggy, belong
likewise to this class.

The errors we are led into in acquired perception are
very rarely hurtful to us in the conduct of life; they
are gradually corrected by a more enlarged experience,
and a more perfect knowledge of the laws of nature;
and the general laws of our constitution, by which we
are sometimes led into them, are of the greatest utility.

We come into the world ignorant of every thing, and
by our ignorance exposed to many dangers and to many

mistakes. The regular train of causes and effects, which Divine Wisdom has established, and which directs every step of our conduct in advanced life, is unknown, until it is gradually discovered by experience.

We must learn much from experience before we can reason, and therefore must be liable to many errors. Indeed, I apprehend, that, in the first part of life, reason would do us much more hurt than good. Were we sensible of our condition in that period, and capable of reflecting upon it, we should be like a man in the dark, surrounded with dangers, where every step he takes may be into a pit. Reason would direct him to sit down, and wait till he could see about him.

In like manner, if we suppose an infant endowed with reason, it would direct him to do nothing, till he knew what could be done with safety. This he can only know by experiment, and experiments are dangerous. Reason directs, that experiments that are full of danger should not be made without a very urgent cause. It would therefore make the infant unhappy, and hinder his improvement by experience.

Nature has followed another plan. The child, unapprehensive of danger, is led by instinct to exert all his active powers, to try every thing without the cautious admonitions of reason, and to believe every thing that is told him. Sometimes he suffers by his rashness what reason would have prevented: but his suffering proves a salutary discipline, and makes him for the future avoid the cause of it. Sometimes he is imposed upon by his credulity; but it is of infinite benefit to him upon the whole. His activity and credulity are more useful qualities, and better instructors than reason would be; they teach him more in a day than reason would do in a year; they furnish a stock of materials for reason to work upon; they make him easy and happy in a period of his existence, when reason could only serve to suggest a thousand tormenting anxieties and fears : and he acts agreeably to the constitution and intention of nature, even when he does and believes what reason would not justify. So that the wisdom and goodness of the Author of nature is no less conspicuous in withholding the exercise of our reason in this period, than in bestowing it when we are ripe for it.

A third class of errors, ascribed to the fallacy of the senses, proceeds from ignorance of the laws of nature.

The laws of nature, I mean not moral but physical laws, are learned, either from our own experience, or the experience of others, who have had occasion to observe the course of nature.

Ignorance of those laws, or inattention to them, is apt to occasion false judgments with regard to the objects of sense, especially those of hearing and of sight ; which false judgments are often, without good reason, called fallacies of sense.

Sounds affect the ear differently, according as the sounding body is before or behind us, on the right hand or on the left, near or at a great distance. We learn, by the manner in which the sound affects the ear, on what hand we are to look for the sounding body ; and in most cases we judge right. But we are sometimes deceived by echoes, or by whispering galleries, or speaking trumpets, which return the sound, or alter its direction, or convey it to a distance without diminution.

The deception is still greater, because more uncommon, which is said to be produced by gastriloquists, that is, persons who have acquired the art of modifying their voice, so that it shall affect the ear of the hearers, as if it came from another person, or from the clouds, or from under the earth.

I never had the fortune to be acquainted with any of these artists, and therefore cannot say to what degree of perfection the art may have been carried.

I apprehend it to be only such an imperfect imitation as may deceive those who are inattentive, or under a panic. For if it could be carried to perfection, a gastriloquist would be as dangerous a man in society as was the shepherd Giges, who, by turning a ring upon his finger, could make himself invisible, and by that means, from being the king's shepherd, became king of Lydia.

If the gastriloquists have all been too good men to use their talents to the detriment of others, it might at least be expected that some of them should apply it to their own advantage. If it could be brought to any considerable degree of perfection, it seems to be as proper an engine for drawing money by the exhibition of it, as legerdemain or rope dancing. But I have never heard of any exhibition of this kind, and therefore am apt to think, that it is too coarse an imitation to bear exhibition even to the vulgar.

Some are said to have the art of imitating the voice of another so exactly, that in the dark they might be taken for the person whose voice they imitate. I am apt to think, that this art also, in the relations made of it, is magnified beyond the truth, as wonderful relations are apt to be, and that an attentive ear would be able to distinguish the copy from the original.

It is indeed a wonderful instance of the accuracy, as well as of the truth of our senses, in things that are of real use in life, that we are able to distinguish all our acquaintance by their countenance, by their voice, and by their hand writing, when at the same time we are often unable to say by what minute difference the distinction is made; and that we are so very rarely deceived in matters of this kind, when we give proper attention to the informations of sense.

However, if any case should happen, in which sounds produced by different causes are not distinguishable by the ear, this may prove that our senses are imperfect, but not that they are fallacious. The ear may not be able to draw the just conclusion, but it is only our ignorance of the laws of sound that leads us to a wrong conclusion.

Deceptions of sight, arising from ignorance of the laws of nature, are more numerous, and more remarkable than those of hearing.

The rays of light, which are the means of seeing, pass in right lines from the object to the eye, when they meet with no obstruction; and we are by nature led to conceive the visible object to be in the direction of the rays that come to the eye. But the rays may be reflected, refracted, or inflected in their passage from the object to the eye, according to certain fixed laws of nature; by which means their direction may be changed, and consequently the apparent place, figure, or magnitude of the object.

Thus a child seeing himself in a mirror, thinks he sees another child behind the mirror, that imitates all his motions. But even a child soon gets the better of this deception, and knows that he sees himself only.

All the deceptions made by telescopes, microscopes, camera obscuras, magic lanterns, are of the same kind, though not so familiar to the vulgar. The ignorant may be deceived by them; but to those who are acquainted with the principles of optics, they give just and true information; and the laws of nature by which they are produced, are of infinite benefit to mankind.

There remains another class of errors, commonly called deceptions of sense, and the only one, as I apprehend, to which that name can be given with propriety; I mean such as proceed from some disorder or preternatural state, either of the external organ, or of the nerves and brain, which are internal organs of perception.

In a delirium, or in madness, perception, memory, imagination, and our reasoning powers, are strangely disordered and confounded. There are likewise disorders which affect some of our senses, while others are sound. Thus, a man may feel pain in his toes after the leg is cut off. He may feel a little ball double, by crossing his fingers. He may see an object double, by not directing both eyes properly to it. By pressing the ball of his eye, he may see colours that are not real. By the jaundice in his eyes, he may mistake colours. These are more properly deceptions of sense than any of the classes before mentioned.

We must acknowledge it to be the lot of human nature, that all the human faculties are liable, by accidental causes, to be hurt, and unfitted for their natural functions, either wholly or in part : but as this imperfection is common to them all. it gives no just ground for accounting any one of them fallacious more than another.

Upon the whole, it seems to have been a common error of philosophers, to account the senses fallacious. And to this error they have added another, that one use of reason is to detect the fallacies of sense.

It appears, I think, from what has been said, that there is no more reason to account our senses fallacious, than our reason, our memory, or any other faculty of judging which nature has given us. They are all limited and imperfect ; but wisely suited to the present condition of man. We are liable to error and wrong judgment in the use of them all ; but as little in the informations of sense as in the deductions of reasoning. And the errors we fall into with regard to objects of sense are not corrected by reason, but by more accurate attention to the informations we may receive by our senses themselves.

Perhaps the pride of philosophers may have given occasion to this error. Reason is the faculty wherein they assume a superiority to the unlearned. The informations of sense are common to the philosopher and to the most illiterate: they put all men upon a level, and therefore are apt to be undervalued. We must, however, be beholden to the informations of sense for the greatest and most interesting part of our knowledge. The wisdom of nature has made the most useful things most common, and they ought not to be despised on that account. Nature likewise forces our belief in those informations, and all the attempts of philosophy to weaken it are fruitless and vain.

I add only one observation to what has been said upon this subject. It is, that there seems to be a contradiction between what philosophers teach concerning ideas, and their doctrine of the fallaciousness of the senses. We are taught that the office of the senses is only to give us the ideas of external objects. If this be so, there can be no fallacy in the senses. Ideas can neither be true nor false. If the senses testify nothing, they cannot give false testimony. If they are not judging faculties, no judgment can be imputed to them, whether false or true. There is, therefore, a contradiction between the common doctrine concerning ideas, and that of the fallaciousness of the senses. Both may be false, as I believe they are, but both cannot be true.

ESSAY III.

CONCERNING MEMORY.

CHAP. I.

THINGS OBVIOUS AND CERTAIN WITH REGARD TO MEMORY.

In the gradual progress of man, from infancy to maturity, there is a certain order in which his faculties are unfolded, and this seems to be the best order we can follow in treating of them.

The external senses appear first; memory soon follows, which we are now to consider.

It is by memory that we have an immediate knowledge of things past. The senses give us information of things only as they exist in the present moment; and this information, if it were not preserved by memory, would vanish instantly, and leave us as ignorant as if it had never been.

Memory must have an object. Every man who remembers must remember something, and that which he remembers is called the object of his remembrance. In this, memory agrees with perception, but differs from sensation, which has no object but the feeling itself.

Every man can distinguish the thing remembered from the remembrance of it. We may remember any thing which we have seen, or heard, or known, or done, or suffered; but the remembrance of it is a particular act of the mind which now exists, and of which we are conscious. To confound these two is an absurdity, which a thinking man could not be led into, but by some false hypothesis which hinders him from reflecting upon the thing which he would explain by it.

In memory we do not find such a train of operations connected by our constitution as in perception. When we perceive an object by our senses, there is, first, some impression made by the object upon the organ of sense, either immediately or by means of some medium. By this an impression is made upon the nerves and brain, in consequence of which we feel some sensation; and that sensation is attended by that conception and belief of the external object which we call perception. These operations are so connected in our constitution, that it is difficult to disjoin them in our conceptions, and to attend to each without confounding it with the others. But in the operations of memory we are free from this embarrassment; they are easily distinguished from all other acts of the mind, and the names which denote them are free from all ambiguity.

The object of memory, or thing remembered, must be something that is past; as the object of perception and of consciousness must be something which is present. What now is, cannot be an object of memory; neither can that which is past and gone be an object of perception or of consciousness.

Memory is always accompanied with the belief of that which we remember, as perception is accompanied with the belief of that which we perceive, and consciousness with the belief of that whereof we are conscious. Perhaps in infancy, or in a disorder of mind, things remembered may be confounded with those which are merely imagined; but in mature years, and in a sound state of mind, every man feels that he must believe what he distinctly remembers, though he can give no other reason of his belief, but that he remembers the thing distinctly; whereas, when he merely imagines a thing ever so distinctly, he has no belief of it upon that account.

This belief, which we have from distinct memory, we account real knowledge, no less certain than if it was grounded on demonstration; no man in his wits calls it in question, or will hear any argument against it. The testimony of witnesses in causes of life and death depends upon it, and all the knowledge of mankind of past events is built on this foundation.

There are cases in which a man's memory is less distinct and determinate, and where he is ready to allow that it may have failed him; but this does not in the least weaken its credit, when it is perfectly distinct.

Memory implies a conception and belief of past duration; for it is impossible that a man should remember a thing distinctly, without believing some interval of duration, more or less, to have passed between the time it happened, and the present moment; and I think it is impossible to show how we could acquire a notion of duration if we had no memory.

Things remembered must be things formerly perceived or known. I remember the transit of Venus over the sun in the year 1769. I must therefore have perceived it at the time it happened, otherwise I could not now remember it. Our first acquaintance with any object of thought cannot be by remembrance. Memory can only produce a continuance or renewal of a former acquaintance with the thing remembered.

The remembrance of a past event is necessarily accompanied with the conviction of our own existence at the time the event happened. I cannot remember a thing that happened a year ago, without a conviction as strong as memory can give, that I, the same identical person who now remember that event, did then exist.

What I have hitherto said concerning memory, I consider as principles, which appear obvious and certain to every man who will take the pains to reflect upon the operations of his own mind. They are facts of which every man must judge by what he feels; and they admit of no other proof but an appeal to every man's own reflection. I shall therefore take them for granted in what follows, and shall first draw some conclusions from them, and then examine the theories of philosophers concerning memory, and concerning duration, and our personal identity, of which we acquire the knowledge by memory.

CHAP. II.

MEMORY AN ORIGINAL FACULTY.

FIRST, I think it appears that memory is an original faculty given us by the Author of our being, of which we can give no account, but that we are so made.

The knowledge which I have of things past, by my memory, seems to me as unaccountable as an immediate knowledge would be of things to come : and I can give no reason why I should have the one and not the other, but that such is the will of my Maker. I find in my mind a distinct conception, and a firm belief of a series of past events; but how this is produced I know not. I call it memory, but this is only giving a name to it; it is not an account of its cause.   I believe most firmly what I distinctly remember ; but I can give no reason of this belief.   It is the inspiration of the Almighty that gives me this understanding.

When I believe the truth of a mathematical axiom, or of a mathematical proposition, I see that it must be so.   Every man who has the same conception of it sees the same.   There is a necessary and an evident connection between the subject and the predicate of the proposition ; and I have all the evidence to support my belief which I can possibly conceive.

When I believe that I washed my hands and face this morning, there appears no necessity in the truth of this proposition.   It might be, or it might not be.   A man may distinctly conceive it without believing it at all. How then do I come to believe it ? I remember it distinctly.   This is all I can say.   This remembrance is an act of my mind.   It is impossible that this act should be, if the event had not happened.   I confess I do not see any necessary connection between the one and the other. If any man can show such a necessary connection, then I think that belief which we have of what we remember will be fairly accounted for; but if this cannot be done, that belief is unaccountable, and we can say no more but that it is the result of our constitution.

Perhaps it may be said, that the experience we have had of the fidelity of memory is a good reason for relying upon its testimony. I deny not that this may be a reason to those who have had this experience, and who reflect upon it. But I believe there are few who ever thought of this reason, or who found any need of it. It must be some very rare occasion that leads a man to have recourse to it; and in those who have done so, the testimony of memory was believed before the experience of its fidelity; and that belief could not be caused by the experience which came after it.

We know some abstract truths, by comparing the terms of the proposition which expresses them, and perceiving some necessary relation or agreement between them. It is thus I know that two and three make five; that the diameters of a circle are all equal. Mr. Locke having discovered this source of knowledge, too rashly concluded that all human knowledge might be derived from it; and in this he has been followed very generally; by Mr. Hume in particular.

But I apprehend, that our knowledge of the existence of things contingent can never be traced to this source. I know that such a thing exists, or did exist. This knowledge cannot be derived from the perception of a necessary agreement between existence and the thing that exists, because there is no such necessary agreement; and therefore no such agreement can be perceived either immediately, or by a chain of reasoning.

The thing does not exist necessarily, but by the will and power of him that made it ; and there is no contradiction follows from supposing it not to exist.

Whence I think it follows, that our knowledge of the existence of our own thoughts, of the existence of all the material objects about us, and of all past contingencies, must be derived, not from a perception of necessary relations or agreements, but from some other source.

Our Maker has provided other means for giving us the knowledge of these things; means which perfectly answer their end, and produce the effect intended by them. But in what manner they do this, is, I fear, beyond our skill to explain. We know our own thoughts, and the operations of our minds, by a power which we call consciousness : but this is only giving a name to this part of our frame. It does not explain its fabric, nor how it produces in us an irresistible conviction of its informations. We perceive material objects and their sensible qualities by our senses; but how they give us this information, and how they produce our belief in it, we know not. We know many past events by memory ; but how it gives this information, I believe, is inexplicable.

It is well known what subtile disputes were held through all the scholastic ages, and are still carried on about the prescience of the Deity. Aristotle had taught, that there can be no certain foreknowledge of things contingent ; and in this he has been very generally followed, upon no other grounds, as I apprehend, but that we cannot conceive how such things should be foreknown, and therefore conclude it to be impossible. Hence has arisen an opposition and supposed inconsistency between Divine prescience and human liberty. Some have given up the first in favour of the last, and others have given up the last in order to support the first.

It is remarkable, that these disputants have never apprehended that there is any difficulty in reconciling with liberty the knowledge of what is past, but only of what is future. It is prescience only, and not memory, that is supposed to be hostile to liberty, and hardly reconcileable to it.

Yet I believe the difficulty is perfectly equal in the one case and in the other. I admit, that we cannot account for prescience of the actions of a free agent. But I maintain, that we can as little account for memory of the past actions of a free agent. If any man thinks he can prove that the actions of a free agent cannot be foreknown, he will find the same arguments of equal force to prove that the past actions of a free agent cannot be remembered. It is true, that what is past did certainly exist. It is no less true, that what is future will certainly exist. I know no reasoning from the constitution of the agent, or from his circumstances, that has not equal strength, whether it be applied to his past or to his future actions. The past was, but now is not. The future will be, but now is not. The present is equally connected, or unconnected with both.

The only reason why men have apprehended so great disparity in cases so perfectly like, I take to be this, that the faculty of memory in ourselves convinces us from fact, that it is not impossible that an intelligent being, even a finite being, should have certain knowledge of past actions of free agents, without tracing them from any thing necessarily connected with them. But having no prescience in ourselves corresponding to our memory of what is past, we find great difficulty in admitting it to be possible even in the Supreme Being.

A faculty which we possess in some degree, we easily admit that the Supreme Being may possess in a more perfect degree; but a faculty, which has nothing corresponding to it in our constitution, we will hardly allow to be possible. We are so constituted as to have an intuitive knowledge of many things past; but we have no intuitive knowledge of the future. We might perhaps have been so constituted as to have an intuitive knowledge of the future, but not of the past; nor would this constitution have been more unaccountable than the present, though it might be much more inconvenient. Had this been our constitution, we should have found no difficulty in admitting that the Deity may know all things future, but very much in admitting his knowledge of things that are past.

Our original faculties are all unaccountable. Of these memory is one. He only who made them, comprehends fully how they are made, and how they produce in us, not only a conception, but a firm belief and assurance of things which it concerns us to know.

CHAP. III.

OF DURATION.

FROM the principles laid down in the first chapter of this Essay, I think it appears, that our notion of duration, as well as our belief of it, is got by the faculty of memory. It is essential to every thing remembered that it be something which is past; and we cannot conceive a thing to be past, without conceiving some duration, more or less, between it and the present. As soon, therefore, as we remember any thing, we must have both a notion and a belief of duration. It is necessarily suggested by every operation of our memory; and to that faculty it ought to be ascribed. This is therefore a proper place to consider what is known concerning it.

Duration, extension, and number, are the measures of all things subject to mensuration. When we apply them to finite things which are measured by them, they seem of all things to be the most distinctly conceived, and most within the reach of human understanding.

Extension having three dimensions, has an endless variety of modifications, capable of being accurately defined; and their various relations furnish the human mind with its most ample field of demonstrative reasoning. Duration having only one dimension, has fewer modifications; but these are clearly understood; and their relations admit of measure, proportion, and demonstrative reasoning.

Number is called discrete quantity, because it is compounded of units, which are all equal and similar, and it can only be divided into units. This is true, in some sense, even of fractions of unity, to which we now commonly give the name of number. For in every fractional number the unit is supposed to be subdivided into a certain number of equal parts, which are the units of that denomination, and the fractions of that denomination are only divisible into units of the same denomination. Duration and extension are not discrete, but continued quantity. They consist of parts perfectly similar, but divisible without end.

In order to aid our conception of the magnitude and proportions of the various intervals of duration, we find it necessary to give a name to some known portion of it, such as an hour, a day, a year. These we consider as units, and by the number of them contained in a larger interval, we form a distinct conception of its magnitude. A similar expedient we find necessary to give us a distinct conception of the magnitudes and proportions of things extended. Thus, number is found necessary, as a common measure of extension and duration. But this perhaps is owing to the weakness of our understanding. It has even been discovered by the sagacity of mathematicians, that this expedient does not in all cases answer its intention. For there are proportions of continued quantity, which cannot be perfectly expressed by numbers; such as that between the diagonal and side of a square, and many others.

The parts of duration have to other parts of it the relations of prior and posterior, and to the present they have the relations of past and future. The notion of past is immediately suggested by memory, as has been before observed. And when we have got the notions of present and past, and of prior and posterior, we can from these frame a notion of the future; for the future is that which is posterior to the present. Nearness and distance are relations equally applicable to time and to place. Distance in time, and distance in place, are things so different in their nature, and so like in their relation, that it is difficult to determine whether the name of distance is applied to both in the same or an analogical sense.

The extension of bodies which we perceive by our senses, leads us necessarily to the conception and belief of a space, which remains immoveable when the body is removed; and the duration of events which we remember leads us necessarily to the conception and belief of a duration, which would have gone on uniformly, though the event had never happened.

Without space there can be nothing that is extended. And without time there can be nothing that has duration. This I think undeniable. And yet we find, that extension and duration are not more clear and intelligible than space and time are dark and difficult objects of contemplation.

As there must be space wherever any thing extended does or can exist, and time when there is or can be any thing that has duration, we can set no bounds to either even in our imagination. They defy all limitation. The one swells in our conception to immensity, the other to eternity.

An eternity past is an object which we cannot comprehend; but a beginning of time, unless we take it in a figurative sense, is a contradiction. By a common figure of speech, we give the name of time to those motions and revolutions by which we measure it, such as days and years. We can conceive a beginning of these sensible measures of time, and say that there was a time when they were not, a time undistinguished by any motion or change; but to say that there was a time before all time, is a contradiction.

All limited duration is comprehended in time, and all limited extension in space. These, in their capacious womb, contain all finite existences, but are con-

tained by none. Created things have their particular
place in space, and their particular place in time; but
time is every where, and space at all times. They
embrace each the other, and have that mysterious
union which the schoolmen conceived between soul and
body. The whole of each is in every part of the other.

We are at a loss to what category or class of things
we ought to refer them. They are not beings, but rather the receptacles of every created being, without
which it could not have had the possibility of existence.
Philosophers have endeavoured to reduce all the objects of human thought to these three classes, of substances, modes, and relations. To which of them
shall we refer time, space, and number, the most common objects of thought?

Sir Isaac Newton thought, that the Deity, by existing every where, and at all times, constitutes time and
space, immensity and eternity. This probably suggested to his great friend Dr. Clarke what he calls the
argument *a priori* for the existence of an immense
and eternal Being. Space and time, he thought, are
only abstract or partial conceptions of an immensity
and eternity, which forces itself upon our belief. And
as immensity and eternity are not substances, they
must be the attributes of a Being, who is necessarily
immense and eternal. These are the speculations of
men of superior genius. But whether they be as solid
as they are sublime, or whether they be the wander-
ings of imagination in a region beyond the limits of
human understanding, I am unable to determine.

The schoolmen made eternity to be a *nunc stans*,
that is, a moment of time that stands still. This was
to put a spoke into the wheel of time, and might give
satisfaction to those who are to be satisfied by words
without meaning. But I can as easily believe a circle
to be a square as time to stand still.

Such paradoxes and riddles, if I may so call them, men are involuntarily led into when they reason about time and space, and attempt to comprehend their nature. They are probably things of which the human faculties give an imperfect and an inadequate conception. Hence difficulties arise which we in vain attempt to overcome, and doubts which we are unable to resolve. Perhaps some faculty which we possess not, is necessary to remove the darkness which hangs over them, and makes us so apt to bewilder ourselves when we reason about them.

CHAP. IV.

OF IDENTITY.

THE conviction which every man has of his identity, as far back as his memory reaches, needs no aid of philosophy to strengthen it, and no philosophy can weaken it, without first producing some degree of insanity.

The philosopher, however, may very properly consider this conviction as a phenomenon of human nature worthy of his attention. If he can discover its cause, an addition is made to his stock of knowledge; if not, it must be held as a part of our original constitution, or an effect of that constitution produced in a manner unknown to us.

We may observe, first of all, that this conviction is indispensably necessary to all exercise of reason. The operations of reason, whether in action or in speculation, are made up of successive parts. The antecedent are the foundation of the consequent, and without the conviction that the antecedent have been seen or done by me, I could have no reason to proceed to the consequent, in any speculation, or in any active project whatever.

There can be no memory of what is past without the conviction that we existed at the time remembered. There may be good arguments to convince me that I existed before the earliest thing I can remember; but to suppose that my memory reaches a moment further back than my belief and conviction of my existence, is a contradiction.

The moment a man loses this conviction, as if he had drunk the water of Lethe, past things are done away;

and, in his own belief, he then begins to exist. Whatever was thought, or said, or done, or suffered, before that period, may belong to some other person; but he can never impute it to himself, or take any subsequent step that supposes it to be his doing.

From this it is evident, that we must have the conviction of our own continued existence and identity, as soon as we are capable of thinking or doing any thing, on account of what we have thought, or done, or suffered before; that is, as soon as we are reasonable creatures.

That we may form as distinct a notion as we are able of this phenomenon of the human mind, it is proper to consider what is meant by identity in general, what by our own personal identity, and how we are led into that invincible belief and conviction which every man has of his own personal identity, as far as his memory reaches.

Identity in general, I take to be a relation between a thing which is known to exist at one time, and a thing which is known to have existed at another time. If you ask whether they are one and the same, or two different things, every man of common sense understands the meaning of your question perfectly. Whence we may infer with certainty, that every man of common sense has a clear and distinct notion of identity.

If you ask a definition of identity, I confess I can give none; it is too simple a notion to admit of logical definition: I can say it is a relation, but I cannot find words to express the specific difference between this and other relations, though I am in no danger of confounding it with any other. I can say that diversity is a contrary relation, and that similitude and dissimilitude are another couple of contrary relations which every man easily distinguishes in his conception from identity and diversity.

I see evidently that identity supposes an uninterrupted continuance of existence. That which has ceased
to exist, cannot be the same with that which afterward
begins to exist; for this would be to suppose a being to
exist after it ceased to exist, and to have had existence
before it was produced, which are manifest contradictions. Continued uninterrupted existence is therefore
necessarily implied in identity.

Hence we may infer, that identity cannot, in its proper sense, be applied to our pains, our pleasures, our
thoughts, or any operation of our minds. The pain
felt this day is not the same individual pain which I
felt yesterday, though they may be similar in kind and
degree, and have the same cause. The same may be
said of every feeling, and of every operation of
mind. They are all successive in their nature, like
time itself, no two moments of which can be the same
moment.

It is otherwise with the parts of absolute space.
They always are, and were, and will be the same. So
far, I think, we proceed upon clear ground in fixing
the notion of identity in general.

It is perhaps more difficult to ascertain with precision the meaning of personality; but it is not necessary
in the present subject: it is sufficient for our purpose
to observe, that all mankind place their personality in
something that cannot be divided, or consist of parts.
A part of a person is a manifest absurdity.

When a man loses his estate, his health, his strength,
he is still the same person, and has lost nothing of his
personality. If he has a leg or an arm cut off, he is
the same person he was before. The amputated member is no part of his person, otherwise it would have a
right to a part of his estate, and be liable for a part of
his engagements. It would be entitled to a share of his
merit and demerit, which is manifestly absurd. A per-

son is something indivisible, and is what Leibnitz calls a *monad*.

My personal identity, therefore, implies the continued existence of that indivisible thing which I call *myself*. Whatever this self may be, it is something which thinks, and deliberates, and resolves, and acts, and suffers. I am not thought, I am not action, I am not feeling; I am something that thinks, and acts, and suffers. My thoughts, and actions, and feelings, change every moment; they have no continued, but a successive existence; but that *self* or *I*, to which they belong, is permanent, and has the same relation to all the succeeding thoughts, actions and feelings, which I call mine.

Such are the notions that I have of my personal identity. But perhaps it may be said, this may all be fancy without reality. How do you know; what evidence have you, that there is such a permanent self which has a claim to all the thoughts, actions, and feelings, which you call yours?

To this I answer, that the proper evidence I have of all this is remembrance. I remember that twenty years ago I conversed with such a person; I remember several things that passed in that conversation; my memory testifies not only that this was done, but that it was done by me who now remember it. If it was done by me, I must have existed at that time, and continued to exist from that time to the present. If the identical person whom I call myself, had not a part in that conversation, my memory is fallacious; it gives a distinct and positive testimony of what is not true. Every man in his senses believes what he distinctly remembers, and every thing he remembers convinces him that he existed at the time remembered.

Although memory gives the most irresistible evidence of my being the identical person that did such a thing, at such a time, I may have other good evidence of things which befell me, and which I do not remember: I know who bare me, and suckled me, but I do not remember these events.

It may here be observed, though the observation would have been unnecessary, if some great philosophers had not contradicted it, that it is not my remembering any action of mine that makes me to be the person who did it. This remembrance makes me to know assuredly that I did it; but I might have done it, though I did not remember it. That relation to me, which is expressed by saying that I did it, would be the same, though I had not the least remembrance of it. To say that my remembering that I did such a thing, or, as some choose to express it, my being conscious that I did it, makes me to have done it, appears to me as great an absurdity as it would be to say, that my belief that the world was created, made it to be created.

When we pass judgment on the identity of other persons besides ourselves, we proceed upon other grounds, and determine from a variety of circumstances, which sometimes produce the firmest assurance, and sometimes leave room for doubt. The identity of persons has often furnished matter of serious litigation before tribunals of justice. But no man of a sound mind ever doubted of his own identity, as far as he distinctly remembered.

The identity of person is a perfect identity; wherever it is real, it admits of no degrees; and it is impossible that a person should be in part the same, and in part different; because a person is a *monad*, and is not divisible into parts. The evidence of identity in other persons besides ourselves, does indeed admit of all degrees, from what we account certainty, to the least degree of probability. But still it is true, that the same person is perfectly the same, and cannot be so in part, or in some degree only.

For this cause, I have first considered personal identity, as that which is perfect in its kind, and the natural measure of that which is imperfect.

We probably at first derive our notion of identity from that natural conviction which every man has from the dawn of reason of his own identity and continued existence. The operations of our minds are all successive, and have no continued existence. But the thinking being has a continued existence, and we have an invincible belief, that it remains the same when all its thoughts and operations change.

Our judgments of the identity of objects of sense, seem to be formed much upon the same grounds as our judgments of the identity of other persons besides ourselves.

Wherever we observe great similarity, we are apt to presume identity, if no reason appears to the contrary. Two objects ever so like, when they are perceived at the same time, cannot be the same: but if they are presented to our senses at different times, we are apt to think them the same, merely from their similarity.

Whether this be a natural prejudice, or from whatever cause it proceeds, it certainly appears in children from infancy; and, when we grow up, it is confirmed in most instances by experience: for we rarely find two individuals of the same species that are not distinguishable by obvious differences.

A man challenges a thief whom he finds in possession of his horse or his watch, only on similarity. When the watchmaker swears that he sold this watch to such a person, his testimony is grounded on similarity. The testimony of witnesses to the identity of a person is commonly grounded on no other evidence.

Thus it appears, that the evidence we have of our own identity, as far back as we remember, is totally of a different kind from the evidence we have of the identity of other persons, or of objects of sense. The first

is grounded on memory, and gives undoubted certainty.
The last is grounded on similarity, and on other circumstances, which in many cases are not so decisive as to
leave no room for doubt.

It may likewise be observed that the identity of objects of sense is never perfect. All bodies, as they consist of innumerable parts that may be disjoined from
them by a great variety of causes, are subject to continual changes of their substance, increasing, diminishing, changing insensibly. When such alterations are
gradual, because language could not afford a different
name for every different state of such a changeable
being, it retains the same name, and is considered as the
same thing. Thus we say of an old regiment, that it
did such a thing a century ago, though there now is not
a man alive who then belonged to it. We say a tree is
the same in the seed bed and in the forest. A ship of
war, which has successively changed her anchors, her
tackle, her sails, her masts, her planks, and her tim-
bers, while she keeps the same name, is the same.

The identity therefore which we ascribe to bodies,
whether natural or artificial, is not perfect identity; it
is rather something which, for the conveniency of
speech, we call identity. It admits of a great change
of the subject, providing the change be gradual, sometimes even of a total change. And the changes which
in common language are made consistent with identity,
differ from those that are thought to destroy it, not in
kind, but in number and degree. It has no fixed nature when applied to bodies; and questions about the
identity of a body are very often questions about words.
But identity, when applied to persons, has no ambiguity, and admits not of degrees, or of more and less:
it is the foundation of all rights and obligations, and of
all accountableness; and the notion of it is fixed and
precise.

CHAP. V.

MR. LOCKE'S ACCOUNT OF THE ORIGIN OF OUR IDEAS, AND
PARTICULARLY OF THE IDEA OF DURATION.

It was a very laudable attempt of Mr. Locke " to inquire into the original of those ideas, notions, or whatever you please to call them, which a man observes,
and is conscious to himself he has in his mind; and
the ways whereby the understanding comes to be furnished with them." No man was better qualified for
this investigation; and I believe no man ever engaged
in it with a more sincere love of truth.

His success, though great, would, I apprehend, have
been greater, if he had not too early formed a system,
or hypothesis, upon this subject, without all the caution
and patient induction, which is necessary in drawing
general conclusions from facts.

The sum of his doctrine I take to be this, " That all
our ideas or notions may be reduced to two classes, the
simple and the complex: that the simple are purely
the work of nature, the understanding being merely
passive in receiving them : that they are all suggested
by two powers of the mind, to wit, sensation and reflection; and that they are the materials of all our
knowledge: that the other class of complex ideas are
formed by the understanding itself, which being once
stored with simple ideas of sensation and reflection, has
the power to repeat, to compare, and to combine them
even to an almost infinite variety, and so can make at
pleasure new complex ideas; but that it is not
in the power of the most exalted wit, or enlarged
understanding, by any quickness or variety of thought,
to invent or frame one new simple idea in the
mind, not taken in by the two ways before mentioned.

That as our power over the material world reaches only to the compounding, dividing, and putting together, in various forms, the matter which God has made, but reaches not to the production or annihilation of a single atom; so we may compound, compare, and abstract the original and simple ideas which nature has given us; but are unable to fashion in our understanding any simple idea, not received in by our senses from external objects, or by reflection from the operations of our own mind about them."

This account of the origin of all our ideas is adopted by bishop Berkeley and Mr. Hume; but some very ingenious philosophers, who have a high esteem of Locke's Essay, are dissatisfied with it.

Dr. Hutcheson of Glasgow, in his Inquiry into the ideas of beauty and virtue, has endeavoured to show, that these are original and simple ideas, furnished by original powers, which he calls the sense of beauty and the moral sense.

Dr. Price, in his Review of the principal questions and difficulties in Morals, has observed very justly, that if we take the words *sensation* and *reflection.* as Mr. Locke has defined them in the beginning of his excellent Essay. it will be impossible to derive some of the most important of our ideas from them; and that, by the understanding, that is, by our judging and reasoning power, we are furnished with many simple and original notions.

Mr. Locke says, that by reflection he would be understood to mean, "the notice which the mind takes of its own operations, and the manner of them." This, I think, we commonly call consciousness; from which, indeed, we derive all the notions we have of the operations of our own minds; and he often speaks of the operations of our own minds, as the only objects of reflection.

When reflection is taken in this confined sense, to say, that all our ideas are ideas either of sensation or reflection, is to say, that every thing we can conceive is either some object of sense or some operation of our own minds, which is far from being true.

But the word reflection is commonly used in a much more extensive sense; it is applied to many operations of the mind, with more propriety than to that of consciousness. We reflect, when we remember, or call to mind what is past, and survey it with attention. We reflect, when we define, when we distinguish, when we judge, when we reason, whether about things material or intellectual.

When reflection is taken in this sense, which is more common, and therefore more proper than the sense which Mr. Locke has put upon it, it may be justly said to be the only source of all our distinct and accurate notions of things. For, although our first notions of material things are got by the external senses, and our first notions of the operations of our own minds by consciousness, these first notions are neither simple nor clear. Our senses and our consciousness are continually shifting from one object to another: their operations are transient and momentary, and leave no distinct notion of their objects, until they are recalled by memory, examined with attention, and compared with other things.

This reflection is not one power of the mind; it comprehends many; such as recollection, attention, distinguishing, comparing, judging. By these powers our minds are furnished, not only with many simple and original notions, but with all our notions which are accurate and well defined, and which alone are the proper materials of reasoning. Many of these, are neither notions of the objects of sense, nor of the operations of our own minds, and therefore neither ideas of sensation,

nor of reflection, in the sense that Mr. Locke gives to
reflection. But if any one chooses to call them ideas
of reflection, taking the word in the more common and
proper sense, I have no objection.

Mr. Locke seems to me to have used the word reflection sometimes in that limited sense which he has
given to it in the definition before mentioned, and
sometimes to have fallen unawares into the common
sense of the word; and by this ambiguity his account
of the origin of our ideas is darkened and perplexed.

Having premised these things in general of Mr.
Locke's theory of the origin of our ideas or notions, I
proceed to some observations on his account of the idea
of duration.

" Reflection, he says, upon the train of ideas, which
appear one after another in our minds, is that which
furnishes us with the idea of succession; and the
distance between any two parts of that succession, is
that we call duration."

If it be meant that the idea of succession is prior to
that of duration, either in time, or in the order of nature, this, I think, is impossible, because succession, as
Dr. Price justly observes, presupposes duration, and
can in no sense be prior to it; and therefore it would
be more proper to derive the idea of succession from
that of duration.

But how do we get the idea of succession? It is, says
he, by reflecting upon the train of ideas, which appear
one after another in our minds.

Reflecting upon the train of ideas can be nothing
but remembering it, and giving attention to what our
memory testifies concerning it: for if we did not remember it, we could not have a thought about it. So
that it is evident, that this reflection includes remembrance, without which there could be no reflection on
what is past, and consequently no idea of succession.

It may here be observed, that if we speak strictly and philosophically, no kind of succession can be an object, either of the senses, or of consciousness ; because the operations of both are confined to the present point of time, and there can be no succession in a point of time ; and on that account the motion of a body, which is a successive change of place, could not be observed by the senses alone without the aid of memory.

As this observation seems to contradict the common sense and common language of mankind, when they affirm that they see a body move, and hold motion to be an object of the senses, it is proper to take notice, that this contradiction between the philosopher and the vulgar is apparent only, and not real. It arises from this, that philosophers and the vulgar differ in the meaning they put upon what is called the *present* time, and are thereby led to make a different limit between sense and memory.

Philosophers give the name of the *present* to that indivisible point of time, which divides the future from the past : but the vulgar find it more convenient in the affairs of life, to give the name of *present* to a portion of time, which extends more or less, according to circumstances, into the past or the future. Hence we say, the present hour, the present year, the present century, though one point only of these periods can be present in the philosophical sense.

It has been observed by grammarians, that the present tense in verbs is not confined to an indivisible point of time, but it is so far extended as to have a beginning, a middle, and an end ; and that in the most copious and accurate languages, these different parts of the present are distinguished by different forms of the verb.

As the purposes of conversation make it convenient to extend what is called the present, the same reason leads men to extend the province of sense, and to carry its limit as far back as they carry the present. Thus a man may say, I saw such a person just now; it would be ridiculous to find fault with this way of speaking, because it is authorized by custom, and has a distinct meaning: but if we speak philosophically, the senses do not testify what we saw, but only what we see; what I saw last moment I consider as the testimony of sense, though it is now only the testimony of memory.

There is no necessity in common life of dividing accurately the provinces of sense and of memory; and therefore we assign to sense, not an indivisible point of time, but that small portion of time which we call the present, which has a beginning, a middle, and an end.

Hence it is easy to see, that though in common language we speak with perfect propriety and truth, when we say, that we see a body move, and that motion is an object of sense, yet when as philosophers we distinguish accurately the province of sense from that of memory, we can no more see what is past, though but a moment ago, than we can remember what is present: so that speaking philosophically, it is only by the aid of memory that we discern motion, or any succession whatsoever. We see the present place of the body; we remember the successive advance it made to that place. The first can then only give us a conception of motion, when joined to the last.

Having considered the account given by Mr. Locke, of the idea of succession, we shall next consider how, from the idea of succession, he derives the idea of duration.

"The distance, he says, between any parts of that succession, or between the appearance of any two ideas in our minds, is that we call duration."

To conceive this the more distinctly, let us call the distance between an idea and that which immediately succeeds it, one element of duration; the distance between an idea and the second that succeeds it, two elements, and so on. If ten such elements make duration, then one must make duration, otherwise duration must be made up of parts that have no duration, which is impossible.

For, suppose a succession of as many ideas as you please, if none of these ideas have duration, nor any interval of duration be between one and another, then it is perfectly evident there can be no interval of duration between the first and the last, how great soever their number be. I conclude therefore, that there must be duration in every single interval or element of which the whole duration is made up. Nothing indeed is more certain, than that every elementary part of duration must have duration, as every elementary part of extension must have extension.

Now it must be observed, that in these elements of duration, or single intervals of successive ideas, there is no succession of ideas, yet we must conceive them to have duration; whence we may conclude with certainty, that there is a conception of duration, where there is no succession of ideas in the mind.

We may measure duration by the succession of thoughts in the mind, as we measure length by inches or feet; but the notion or idea of duration must be antecedent to the mensuration of it, as the notion of length is antecedent to its being measured.

Mr. Locke draws some conclusions from his account of the idea of duration, which may serve as a touchstone to discover how far it is genuine. One is, that if it were possible for a man awake, to keep only one idea in his mind without variation, or the succession of others, he would have no perception of duration at all; and the moment he began to have this idea, would seem to have no distance from the moment he ceased to have it.

Now that one idea should seem to have no duration, and that a multiplication of that *no duration* should seem to have duration, appears to me as impossible, as that the multiplication of nothing should produce something.

Another conclusion which the author draws from this theory is, that the same period of duration appears long to us, when the succession of ideas in our mind is quick, and short when the succession is slow.

There can be no doubt but the same length of duration appears in some circumstances much longer than in others; the time appears long when a man is impatient under any pain or distress, or when he is eager in the expectation of some happiness. On the other hand, when he is pleased and happy in agreeable conversation, or delighted with a variety of agreeable objects that strike his senses, or his imagination, time flies away and appears short.

According to Mr. Locke's theory, in the first of these cases, the succession of ideas is very quick, and in the last very slow. I am rather inclined to think that the very contrary is the truth. When a man is racked with pain, or with expectation, he can hardly think of any thing but his distress; and the more his mind is occupied by that sole object, the longer the time appears. On the other hand, when he is entertained with cheerful music, with lively conversation, and brisk sallies of wit, there seems to be the quickest succession of ideas, but the time appears shortest.

I have heard a military officer, a man of candour and observation, say, that the time he was engaged in hot action always appeared to him much shorter than it really was. Yet I think it cannot be supposed that the succession of ideas was then slower than usual.

If the idea of duration were got merely by the succession of ideas in our minds, that succession must to
ourselves appear equally quick at all times, because
the only measure of duration is the number of succeeding ideas ; but I believe every man capable of reflection will be sensible, that at one time his thoughts come
slowly and heavily, and at another time have a much
quicker and livelier motion.

I know of no ideas or notions that have a better
claim to be accounted simple and original than those
of space and time. It is essential both to space and
time to be made up of parts, but every part is similar
to the whole, and of the same nature.   Different parts
of space, as it has three dimensions, may differ both in
figure and in magnitude ; but time having only one
dimension, its parts can differ only in magnitude ; and,
as it is one of the simplest objects of thought, the conception of it must be purely the effect of our constitution, and given us by some original power of the
mind.

The sense of seeing, by itself, gives us the conception and belief of only two dimensions of extension,
but the sense of touch discovers three ; and reason,
from the contemplation of finite extended things, leads
us necessarily to the belief of an immensity that contains them. In like manner, memory gives us the
conception and belief of finite intervals of duration.
From the contemplation of these, reason leads us necessarily to the belief of an eternity, which comprehends all things that have a beginning and end. Our
conceptions, both of space and time, are probably partial and inadequate, and therefore we are apt to lose
ourselves, and to be embarrassed in our reasonings
about them.

Our understanding is no less puzzled when we consider the minutest parts of time and space, than when

we consider the whole. We are forced to acknowledge, that in their nature they are divisible without end or limit; but there are limits beyond which our faculties can divide neither the one nor the other.

It may be determined by experiment, what is the least angle under which an object may be discerned by the eye, and what is the least interval of duration that may be discerned by the ear. I believe these may be different in different persons: but surely there is a limit which no man can exceed: and what our faculties can no longer divide is still divisible in itself, and, by beings of superior perfection, may be divided into thousands of parts.

I have reason to believe, that a good eye in the prime of life may see an object under an angle not exceeding half a minute of a degree; and I believe there are some human eyes still more perfect. But even this degree of perfection will appear great, if we consider how small a part of the retina of the eye it must be which subtends an angle of half a minute.

Supposing the distance between the centre of the eye and the retina to be six or seven tenths of an inch, the subtense of an angle of half a minute to that radius, or the breadth of the image of an object seen under that angle, will not be above the ten thousandth part of an inch. This shows such a wonderful degree of accuracy in the refracting power of a good eye, that a pencil of rays coming from one point of the object shall meet in one point of the retina, so as not to deviate from that point the ten thousandth part of an inch. It shows, likewise, that such a motion of an object as makes its image on the retina to move the ten thousandth part of an inch, is discernible by the mind.

In order to judge to what degree of accuracy we can measure short intervals of time, it may be observed, that one who has given attention to the motion of a

second pendulum, will be able to beat seconds for a
minute with a very small error. When he continues
this exercise long, as for five or ten minutes, he is apt
to err, more even than in proportion to the time, for
this reason, as I apprehend, that it is difficult to attend
long to the moments at they pass, without wandering
after some other object of thought.

I have found, by some experiments, that a man may
beat seconds for one minute, without erring above one
second in the whole sixty; and I doubt not but by long
practice he might do it still more accurately. From
this, I think, it follows, that the sixtieth part of a second of time is discernible by the human mind.

CHAP. VI.

OF MR. LOCKE'S ACCOUNT OF PERSONAL IDENTITY.

IN a long chapter upon identity and diversity, Mr. Locke has made many ingenious and just observations, and some which, I think, cannot be defended. I shall only take notice of the account he gives of our own personal identity. His doctrine upon this subject has been censured by bishop Butler, in a short essay subjoined to his Analogy, with whose sentiments I perfectly agree.

Identity, as was observed chap. 4, of this Essay, supposes the continued existence of the being of which it is affirmed, and therefore can be applied only to things which have a continued existence. While any being continues to exist, it is the same being; but two beings which have a different beginning or a different ending of their existence, cannot possibly be the same. To this I think Mr. Locke agrees.

He observes very justly, that to know what is meant by the same person, we must consider what the word *person* stands for; and he defines a person to be an intelligent being, endowed with reason and with consciousness, which last he thinks inseparable from thought.

From this definition of a person, it must necessarily follow, that while the intelligent being continues to exist and to be intelligent, it must be the same person. To say that the intelligent being is the person, and yet that the person ceases to exist, while the intelligent being continues, or that the person continues while the intelligent being ceases to exist, is, to my apprehension, a manifest contradiction.

One would think that the definition of a person should perfectly ascertain the nature of personal identity, or wherein it consists, though it might still be a question how we come to know and be assured of our personal identity.

Mr. Locke tells us, however, " that personal identity, that is, the sameness of a rational being, consists in consciousness alone; and, as far as this consciousness can be extended backward to any past action or thought, so far reaches the identity of that person. So that whatever has the consciousness of present and past actions, is the same person to whom they belong."

This doctrine has some strange consequences, which the author was aware of. Such as, that if the same consciousness can be transferred from one intelligent being to another, which he thinks we cannot show to be impossible, then two or twenty intelligent beings may be the same person. And if the intelligent being may lose the consciousness of the actions done by him, which surely is possible, then he is not the person that did those actions; so that one intelligent being may be two or twenty different persons, if he shall so often lose the consciousness of his former actions.

There is another consequence of this doctrine, which follows no less necessarily, though Mr. Locke probably did not see it. It is, that a man may be, and at the same time not be, the person that did a particular action.

Suppose a brave officer to have been flogged when a boy at school, for robbing an orchard, to have taken a standard from the enemy in his first campaign, and to have been made a general in advanced life. Suppose also, which must be admitted to be possible, that when he took the standard, he was conscious of his having been flogged at school; and that when made a general, he was conscious of his taking the standard, but had absolutely lost the consciousness of his flogging.

These things being supposed, it follows, from Mr.
Locke's doctrine, that he who was flogged at school is
the same person who took the standard ; and that he who
took the standard is the same person who was made a
general. Whence it follows, if there be any truth in logic,
that the general is the same person with him who was
flogged at school. But the general's consciousness does
not reach so far back as his flogging, therefore, according to Mr. Locke's doctrine, he is not the person
who was flogged. Therefore the general is, and at the
same time is not, the same person with him who was
flogged at school.

Leaving the consequences of this doctrine to those
who have leisure to trace them, we may observe, with
regard to the doctrine itself;

1st, That Mr. Locke attributes to consciousness
the conviction we have of our past actions, as if a man
may now be conscious of what he did twenty years ago.
It is impossible to understand the meaning of this, unless by consciousness be meant memory, the only faculty by which we have an immediate knowledge of our
past actions.

Sometimes, in popular discourse, a man says he is
conscious that he did such a thing, meaning that he
distinctly remembers that he did it. It is unnecessary,
in common discourse, to fix accurately the limits between consciousness and memory. This was formerly shown to be the case with regard to sense and memory : and therefore distinct remembrance is sometimes called sense, sometimes consciousness, without
any inconvenience.

But this ought to be avoided in philosophy, otherwise we confound the different powers of the mind, and
ascribe to one what really belongs to another. If a man
can be conscious of what he did twenty years, or twenty minutes ago, there is no use for memory, nor ought

we to allow that there is any such faculty. The faculties of consciousness and memory are chiefly distinguished by this, that the first is an immediate knowledge of the present, the second an immediate knowledge of the past.

When, therefore, Mr. Locke's notion of personal
identity is properly expressed, it is, that personal identity consists in distinct remembrance: for, even in the
popular sense, to say that I am conscious of a past action, means nothing else than that I distinctly remember that I did it.

2dly, It may be observed, that in this doctrine, not
only is consciousness confounded with memory, but,
which is still more strange, personal identity is confounded with the evidence which we have of our personal identity.

It is very true, that my remembrance that I did
such a thing is the evidence I have that I am the identical person who did it. And this, I am apt to think,
Mr. Locke meant: but to say that my remembrance
that I did such a thing, or my consciousness, makes
me the person who did it, is, in my apprehension, an
absurdity too gross to be entertained by any man who
attends to the meaning of it: for it is to attribute to
memory or consciousness, a strange magical power of
producing its object, though that object must have
existed before the memory or consciousness which produced it.

Consciousness is the testimony of one faculty; memory is the testimony of another faculty: and to say
that the testimony is the cause of the thing testified,
this surely is absurd, if any thing be, and could
not have been said by Mr. Locke, if he had not
confounded the testimony with the thing testified.

When a horse that was stolen is found and claimed
by the owner, the only evidence he can have, or that

a judge or witnesses can have, that this is the very
identical horse which was his property, is similitude.

But would it not be ridiculous from this to infer
that the identity of a horse consists in similitude only?
The only evidence I have that I am the identical person who did such actions, is, that I remember distinctly
I did them; or, as Mr. Locke expresses it, I am conscious I did them. To infer from this, that personal
identity consists in consciousness, is an argument,
which, if it had any force, would prove the identity of a
stolen horse to consist solely in similitude.

3dly, Is it not strange that the sameness or identity
of a person should consist in a thing which is continually changing, and is not any two minutes the same?

Our consciousness, our memory, and every operation
of the mind, are still flowing like the water of a river,
or like time itself. The consciousness I have this
moment can no more be the same consciousness I had
last moment, than this moment can be the last moment.
Identity can only be affirmed of things which have a
continued existence. Consciousness, and every kind
of thought, is transient and momentary, and has no
continued existence; and therefore, if personal identity
consisted in consciousness, it would certainly follow,
that no man is the same person any two moments of his
life; and as the right and justice of reward and punishment is founded on personal identity, no man could be
responsible for his actions.

But though I take this to be the unavoidable consequence of Mr. Locke's doctrine concerning personal
identity, and though some persons may have liked
the doctrine the better on this account, I am far from
imputing any thing of this kind to Mr. Locke. He was
too good a man not to have rejected with abhorrence
a doctrine which he believed to draw this consequence
after it.

4thly, There are many expressions used by Mr. Locke in speaking of personal identity, which to me are altogether unintelligible, unless we suppose that he confounded that sameness, or identity, which we ascribe to an individual, with the identity which in common discourse is often ascribed to many individuals of the same species.

When we say that pain and pleasure, consciousness and memory, are the same in all men, this sameness can only mean similarity, or sameness of kind; but that the pain of one man can be the same individual pain with that of another man, is no less impossible, than that one man should be another man; the pain felt by me yesterday, can no more be the pain I feel today, than yesterday can be this day; and the same thing may be said of every passion and of every operation of the mind. The same kind or species of operation may be in different men, or in the same man at different times; but it is impossible that the same individual operation should be in different men, or in the same man at different times.

When Mr. Locke therefore speaks of "the same consciousness being continued through a succession of different substances;" when he speaks of "repeating the idea of a past action, with the same consciousness we had of it at the first," and of "the same consciousness extending to actions past and to come;" these expressions are to me unintelligible, unless he means, not the same individual consciousness, but a consciousness that is similar, or of the same kind.

If our personal identity consists in consciousness, as this consciousness cannot be the same individually any two moments, but only of the same kind, it would follow. that we are not for any two moments the same individual persons, but the same kind of persons.

As our consciousness sometimes ceases to exist, as in sound sleep, our personal identity must cease with it. Mr. Locke allows, that the same thing cannot have two beginnings of existence, so that our identity would be irrecoverably gone every time we cease to think, if it was but for a moment.

CHAP. VII.

THEORIES CONCERNING MEMORY.

THE common theory of ideas, that is, of images in the brain, or in the mind, of all the objects of thought, has been very generally applied to account for the faculties of memory and imagination, as well as that of perception by the senses.

The sentiments of the Peripatetics are expressed by Alexander Aphrodisiensis, one of the earliest Greek commentators on Aristotle, in these words, as they are translated by Mr. Harris in his Hermes: "Now what fancy or imagination is, we may explain as follows: we may conceive to be formed within us, from the operations of our senses about sensible objects, some impression, as it were, or picture in our original sensorium, being a relict of that motion caused within us by the external object; a relict, which, when the external object is no longer present, remains, and is still preserved, being, as it were, its image; and which, by being thus preserved, becomes the cause of our having memory. Now such a sort of relict, and as it were impression, they call fancy or imagination."

Another passage from Alcinous, of the doctrines of Plato, chap. 4. shows the agreement of the ancient Platonists and Peripatetics in this theory. "When the form or type of things is imprinted on the mind by the organs of the senses, and so imprinted as not to be deleted by time, but preserved firm and lasting, its preservation is called *memory*."

Upon this principle Aristotle imputes the shortness of memory in children to this cause, that their brain is too moist and soft to retain impressions made upon it: and the defect of memory in old men he imputes, on the contrary, to the hardness and rigidity of the brain, which hinders its receiving any durable impression.

This ancient theory of the cause of memory is defective in two respects: 1st, if the cause assigned did really exist, it by no means accounts for the phenomenon : and, 2dly, there is no evidence, nor even probability, that that cause exists.

It is probable, that in perception some impression is made upon the brain as well as upon the organ and nerves, because all the nerves terminate in the brain, and because disorders and hurts of the brain are found to affect our powers of perception when the external organ and nerve are sound ; but we are totally ignorant of the nature of this impression upon the brain. It can have no resemblance to the object perceived, nor does it in any degree account for that sensation and perception which are consequent upon it. These things have been argued in the second Essay, and shall now be taken for granted, to prevent repetition.

If the impression upon the brain be insufficient to account for the perception of objects that are present, it can as little account for the memory of those that are past.

So that if it were certain, that the impressions made on the brain in perception remain as long as there is any memory of the object; all that could be inferred from this, is, that, by the laws of nature, there is a connection established between that impression, and the remembrance of that object. But how the impression contributes to this remembrance, we should be quite ignorant; it being impossible to discover how thought of any kind should be produced, by an impression on the brain, or upon any part of the body.

To say that this impression is memory, is absurd, if understood literally. If it is only meant that it is the cause of memory, it ought to be shown how it produces this effect, otherwise memory remains as unaccountable as before.

If a philosopher should undertake to account for the force of gunpowder, in the discharge of a musket, and then tell us gravely, that the cause of this phenomenon is the drawing of the trigger, we should not be much wiser by this account. As little are we instructed in the cause of memory, by being told that it is caused by a certain impression on the brain. For, supposing that impression on the brain were as necessary to memory as the drawing of the trigger is to the discharge of the musket, we are still as ignorant as we were how memory is produced; so that, if the cause of memory, assigned by this theory, did really exist, it does not in any degree account for memory.

Another defect in this theory is, that there is no evidence, nor probability, that the cause assigned does exist; that is, that the impression made upon the brain in perception remains after the object is removed.

That impression, whatever be its nature, is caused by the impression made by the object upon the organ of sense, and upon the nerve. Philosophers suppose, without any evidence, that when the object is removed, and the impression upon the organ and nerve ceases, the impression upon the brain continues, and is permanent; that is, that when the cause is removed the effect continues. The brain surely does not appear more fitted to retain an impression than the organ and nerve.

But granting that the impression upon the brain continues after its cause is removed, its effects ought to continue while it continues; that is, the sensation and perception should be as permanent as the impression upon the brain, which is supposed to be their cause. But here again the philosopher makes a second supposition, with as little evidence, but of a contrary nature, to wit, that, while the cause remains, the effect ceases.

If this should be granted also, a third must be made, that the same cause, which at first produced sensation and perception, does afterward produce memory; an operation essentially different, both from sensation and perception.

A fourth supposition must be made, that this cause, though it be permanent, does not produce its effect at all times; it must be like an inscription which is sometimes covered with rubbish, and on other occasions made legible: for the memory of things is often interrupted for a long time, and circumstances bring to our recollection what had been long forgotten. After all, many things are remembered which were never perceived by the senses, being no objects of sense, and therefore, which could make no impression upon the brain by means of the senses.

Thus, when philosophers have piled one supposition upon another, as the giants piled the mountains, in order to scale the heavens, all is to no purpose; memory remains unaccountable; and we know as little how we remember things past, as how we are conscious of the present.

But here it is proper to observe, that although impressions upon the brain give no aid in accounting for memory, yet it is very probable, that, in the human frame, memory is dependent on some proper state or temperament of the brain.

Although the furniture of our memory bears no resemblance to any temperament of brain whatsoever, as indeed it is impossible it should; yet nature may have subjected us to this law, that a certain constitution or state of the brain is necessary to memory. That this

is really the case, many well known facts lead us to
conclude.

It is possible, that, by accurate observation, the proper
means may be discovered of preserving that temperament of the brain which is favourable to memory,
and of remedying, the disorders of that temperament.
This would be a very noble improvement of the medical art. But if it should ever be attained. it would
give no aid to understand how one state of the brain
assists memory, and another hurts it.

I know certainly, that the impression made upon
my hand by the prick of a pin occasions acute pain.
But can any philosopher show how this cause produces
the effect ? The nature of the impression is here perfectly known; but it gives no help to understand how
that impression affects the mind; and if we knew as
distinctly that state of the brain which causes memory,
we should still be as ignorant as before how that state
contributes to memory. We might have been so constituted, for any thing that I know, that the prick of a
pin in the hand, instead of causing pain, should cause
remembrance; nor would that constitution be more unaccountable than the present.

The body and mind operate on each other, according
to fixed laws of nature ; and it is the business of a philosopher to discover those laws by observation and experiment : but, when he has discovered them, he must rest
in them as facts, whose cause is inscrutable to the human understanding.

Mr. Locke, and those who have followed him, speak
with more reserve than the ancients, and only incidentally, of impressions on the brain as the cause of
memory, and impute it rather to our retaining in our
minds the ideas, got either by sensation or reflection.

This, Mr. Locke says, may be done two ways; "1st,
by keeping the idea for some time actually in view,

which is called *contemplation*. 2dly, By the power to revive again in our minds those ideas, which, after imprinting, have disappeared, or have been, as it were, laid out of sight; and this is memory, which is, as it were, the storehouse of our ideas."

To explain this more distinctly, he immediately adds the following observation : " But our ideas being nothing but actual perceptions in the mind, which cease to be any thing, when there is no perception of them, this laying up of our ideas in the repository of the memory, signifies no more but this, that the mind has a power, in many cases, to revive perceptions which it once had, with this additional perception annexed to them, that it has had them before ; and in this sense it is, that our ideas are said to be in our memories, when indeed they are actually no where ; but only there is an ability in the mind, when it will, to revive them again, and, as it were, paint them anew upon itself, though some with more, some with less difficulty, some more lively, and others more obscurely."

In this account of memory, the repeated use of the phrase, *as it were*, leads one to judge that it is partly figurative ; we must therefore endeavour to distinguish the figurative part from the philosophical. The first being addressed to the imagination, exhibits a picture of memory, which, to have its effect, must he viewed at a proper distance, and from a particular point of view. The second being addressed to the understanding, ought to bear a near inspection, and a critical examination.

The analogy between memory and a repository, and between remembering and retaining, is obvious, and is to be found in all languages ; it being very natural to express the operations of the mind by images taken from things material. But in philosophy we ought to draw aside the veil of imagery, and to view them naked.

When therefore memory is said to be a repository or storehouse of ideas, where they are laid up when not perceived, and again brought forth as there is occasion, I take this to be popular and rhetorical. For the author tells us, that when they are not perceived, they are nothing, and no where, and therefore can neither be laid up in a repository, nor drawn out of it.

But we are told, "That this laying up of our ideas in the repository of the memory signifies no more than this, that the mind has a power to revive perceptions, which it once had, with this additional perception annexed to them, that it has had them before." This, I think, must be understood literally and philosophically.

But it seems to me as difficult to revive things that have ceased to be any thing, as to lay them up in a repository, or to bring them out of it. When a thing is once annihilated, the same thing cannot be again produced, though another thing similar to it may. Mr. Locke, in another place, acknowledges, that the same thing cannot have two beginnings of existence; and that things that have different beginnings are not the same, but diverse. From this it follows, that an ability to revive our ideas or perceptions, after they have ceased to be, can signify no more but an ability to create new ideas or perceptions similar to those we had before.

They are said "to be revived, with this additional perception, that we have had them before." This, surely, would be a fallacious perception, since they could not have two beginnings of existence; nor could we believe them to have two beginnings of existence. We can only believe, that we had formerly ideas or perceptions very like to them, though not identically the same. But whether we perceive them to be the same, or only like to those we had before, this perception, one would think, supposes a remembrance of those we had before, otherwise the similitude or identity could not be perceived.

Another phrase is used to explain this reviving of our perceptions. "The mind, as it were, paints them anew upon itself." There may be something figurative in this; but making due allowance for that, it must imply, that the mind, which paints the things that have ceased to exist, must have the memory of what they were, since every painter must have a copy either before his eye, or in his imagination and memory.

These remarks upon Mr. Locke's account of memory are intended to show, that his system of ideas gives no light to this faculty, but rather tends to darken it; as little does it make us understand how we remember, and by that means have the certain knowledge of things past.

Every man knows what memory is, and has a distinct notion of it: but when Mr. Locke speaks of a power to revive in the mind those ideas, which, after imprinting, have disappeared, or have been, as it were, laid out of sight, one would hardly know this to be memory, if he had not told us. There are other things which it seems to resemble at least as much. I see before me the picture of a friend. I shut my eyes, or turn them another way; and the picture disappears, or is, as it were, laid out of sight. I have a power to turn my eyes again toward the picture, and immediately the perception is revived. But is this memory? no, surely; yet it answers the definition as well as memory itself can do.

We may observe, that the word *perception* is used by Mr. Locke in too indefinite a way, as well as the word *idea*.

Perception, in the chapter upon that subject, is said to be the first faculty of the mind exercised about our ideas. Here we are told, that ideas are nothing but perceptions: yet I apprehend it would sound oddly to say, that perception is the first faculty of the mind exercised about perception; and still more strangely to say, that ideas are the first faculty of the mind exercised about our ideas. But why should not ideas be a faculty as well as perception, if both are the same?

Memory is said to be a power to revive our perceptions. Will it not follow from this, that every thing that can be remembered is a perception? If this be so, it will be difficult to find any thing in nature but perceptions.

Our ideas, we are told, are nothing but actual perceptions; but in many places of the Essay, ideas are said to be the objects of perception, and that the mind, in all its thoughts and reasonings, has no other immediate object which it does or can contemplate but its own ideas. Does it not appear from this, either that Mr. Locke held the operations of the mind to be the same thing with the objects of those operations, or that he used the word *idea* sometimes in one sense and sometimes in another, without any intimation, and probably without any apprehension of its ambiguity? It is an article of Mr. Hume's philosophy, that there is no distinction between the operations of the mind and their objects. But I see no reason to impute this opinion to Mr. Locke. I rather think, that, notwithstanding his great judgment and candour, his understanding was entangled by the ambiguity of the word *idea,* and that most of the imperfections of his Essay are owing to that cause.

Mr. Hume saw further into the consequences of the common system concerning ideas than any author had done before him. He saw the absurdity of making every object of thought double, and splitting it into a remote object, which has a separate and permanent existence, and an immediate object, called an idea or impression, which is an image of the former, and has no existence, but when we are conscious of it. According to this system, we have no intercourse with the external world, but by means of the internal world of ideas, which represents the other to the mind.

He saw it was necessary to reject one of these worlds as a fiction, and the question was, which should be rejected? Whether all mankind, learned and unlearned, had feigned the existence of the external world without good reason? or whether philosophers had feigned the internal world of ideas, in order to account for the intercourse of the mind with the external? Mr. Hume adopted the first of these opinions, and employed his reason and eloquence in support of it.

Bishop Berkeley had gone so far in the same track as to reject the material world as fictitious; but it was left to Mr. Hume to complete the system.

According to his system, therefore, impressions and ideas in his own mind are the only things a man can know, or can conceive : nor are these ideas representatives, as they were in the old system. There is nothing else in nature, or at least within the reach of our faculties, to be represented. What the vulgar call the perception of an external object, is nothing but a strong impression upon the mind. What we call the remembrance of a past event, is nothing but a present impression or idea, weaker than the former. And what we call imagination, is still a present idea, but weaker than that of memory.

That I may not do him injustice, these are his words in his Treatise of Human Nature, p. 193.

" We find by experience, that when any impression has been present with the mind, it again makes its appearance there as an idea; and this it may do after two different ways, either when in its new appearance it re-

tains a considerable degree of its first vivacity, and is
somewhat intermediate betwixt an impression and an
idea, or when it entirely loses that vivacity, and is a
perfect idea.   The faculty by which we repeat our impressions in the first manner, is called the memory, and
the other the imagination."

Upon this account of memory and imagination I
shall make some remarks.

1st, I wish to know, what we are here to understand
by experience? It is said, we find all this by experience; and I conceive nothing can be meant by this experience but memory.   Not that memory which our
author defines, but memory in the common acceptation
of the word.   According to vulgar apprehension, memory is an immediate knowledge of something past.
Our author does not admit that there is any such
knowledge in the human mind.   He maintains that
memory is nothing but a present idea or impression.
But, in defining what he takes memory to be, he takes
for granted that kind of memory which he rejects.
For can we find by experience, that an impression, after its first appearance to the mind, makes a second,
and a third, with different degrees of strength and vivacity, if we have not so distinct a remembrance of its
first appearance, as enables us to know it, upon its second and third, notwithstanding that, in the interval, it
has undergone a very considerable change ?

All experience supposes memory; and there can be
no such thing as experience, without trusting to our
own memory, or that of others: so that it appears
from Mr. Hume's account of this matter, that he
found himself to have that kind of memory, which he
acknowledges and defines, by exercising that kind
which he rejects.

2dly, What is it we find by experience or memory ?
It is, " That when an impression has been present with

the mind, it again makes its appearance there as an idea, and that after two different ways."

If experience informs us of this, it certainly deceives us; for the thing is impossible, and the author shows it to be so. Impressions and ideas are fleeting, perishable things, which have no existence, but when we are conscious of them. If an impression could make a second and a third appearance to the mind, it must have a continued existence during the interval of these appearances, which Mr. Hume acknowledges to be a gross absurdity. It seems then, that we find by experience, a thing which is impossible. We are imposed upon by our experience, and made to believe contradictions.

Perhaps it may be said, that these different appearances of the impression are not to be understood literally, but figuratively; that the impression is personified, and made to appear at different times, and in different habits, when no more is meant, but that an impression appears at one time; afterward a thing of a middle nature, between an impression and an idea, which we call memory; and last of all a perfect idea, which we call imagination : that this figurative meaning agrees best with the last sentence of the period, where we are told, that memory and imagination are faculties, whereby we repeat our impressions in a more or less lively manner. To repeat an impression is a figurative way of speaking, which signifies making a new impression similar to the former.

If, to avoid the absurdity implied in the literal meaning, we understand the philosopher in this figurative one, then his definitions of memory and imagination. when stripped of the figurative dress, will amount to this, that memory is the faculty of making a weak impression, and imagination the faculty of making an impression still weaker, after a corresponding strong one. These definitions of memory and imagination labour under two defects; 1st, that they convey no notion of the thing defined; and, 2dly, that they may be applied to things of a quite different nature from those that are defined.

When we are said to have a faculty of making a weak impression after a corresponding strong one, it would not be easy to conjecture that this faculty is memory. Suppose a man strikes his head smartly against the wall, this is an impression; now he has a faculty by which he can repeat this impression with less force, so as not to hurt him; this, by Mr. Hume's account, must be memory. He has a faculty by which he can just touch the wall with his head, so that the impression entirely loses its vivacity. This surely must be imagination; at least it comes as near to the definition given of it by Mr. Hume as any thing I can conceive.

3dly, We may observe, that when we are told that we have a faculty of repeating our impressions in a more or less lively manner, this implies that we are the efficient causes of our ideas of memory and imagination; but this contradicts what the author says a little before, where he proves, by what he calls a convincing argument, that impressions are the cause of their corresponding ideas. The argument that proves this, had need indeed to be very convincing; whether we make the idea to be a second appearance of the impression, or a new impression similar to the former.

If the first be true, then the impression is the cause of itself. If the second, then the impression, after it is gone, and has no existence, produces the idea. Such are the mysteries of Mr. Hume's philosophy.

It may be observed, that the common system, that ideas are the only immediate objects of thought, leads to skepticism with regard to memory, as well as with regard to the objects of sense, whether those ideas are placed in the mind or in the brain.

Ideas are said to be things internal and present, which have no existence but during the moment they are in the mind. The objects of sense are things external, which have a continued existence. When it is maintained, that all that we immediately perceive is only ideas or phantasms, how can we, from the existence of those phantasms, conclude the existence of an external world corresponding to them?

This difficult question seems not to have occurred to the Peripatetics. Des Cartes saw the difficulty, and endeavoured to find out arguments by which, from the existence of our phantasms or ideas, we might infer the existence of external objects. The same course was followed by Malebranche, Arnauld, and Locke; but Berkeley and Hume easily refuted all their arguments, and demonstrated that there is no strength in them.

The same difficulty with regard to memory naturally arises from the system of ideas; and the only reason why it was not observed by philosophers, is, because they give less attention to the memory than to the senses; for since ideas are things present, how can we, from our having a certain idea presently in our mind, conclude that an event really happened ten or twenty years ago corresponding to it?

There is the same need of arguments to prove, that the ideas of memory are pictures of things that really did happen, as that the ideas of sense are pictures of external objects which now exist. In both cases, it will be impossible to find any argument that has real weight. So that this hypothesis leads us to absolute skepticism, with regard to those things which we most distinctly remember, no less than with regard to the external objects of sense.

It does not appear to have occurred either to Locke or to Berkeley, that their system has the same tendency to overturn the testimony of memory as the testimony of the senses.

Mr. Hume saw further than both, and found this consequence of the system of ideas perfectly corresponding to his aim of establishing universal skepticism. His system is therefore more consistent than theirs, and the conclusions agree better with the premises.

But if we should grant to Mr. Hume, that our ideas of memory afford no just ground to believe the past existence of things which we remember, it may still be asked, How it comes to pass that perception and memory are accompanied with belief, while bare imagination is not? Though this belief cannot be justified upon his system, it ought to be accounted for as a phenomenon of human nature.

This he has done, by giving us a new theory of belief in general; a theory which suits very well with that of ideas, and seems to be a natural consequence of it, and which at the same time reconciles all the belief that we find in human nature to perfect skepticism.

What then is this belief? It must either be an idea, or some modification of an idea; we conceive many things which we do not believe. The idea of an object is the same whether we believe it to exist, or barely conceive it. The belief adds no new idea to the conception; it is therefore nothing but a modification of the idea of the thing believed, or a different manner of conceiving it. Hear himself:

" All the perceptions of the mind are of two kinds, impressions and ideas, which differ from each other only in their different degrees of force and vivacity. Our ideas are copied from our impressions, and represent them in all their parts. When you would vary

the idea of a particular object, you can only increase
or diminish its force and vivacity: If you make any
other change upon it, it represents a different object or
impression.   The case is the same as in colours   A
particular shade of any colour may acquire a new degree of liveliness or brightness, without any other
variation; but when you produce any other variation,
it is no longer the same shade or colour. So that as
belief does nothing but vary the manner in which we
conceive any object, it can only bestow on our ideas
an additional force and vivacity. An opinion, therefore, or belief, may be most accurately defined a lively idea, related to, or associated with a present impression."

   This theory of belief is very fruitful of consequences, which Mr. Hume traces with his usual acuteness, and brings into the service of his system. A
great part of his system indeed is built upon it; and
it is of itself sufficient to prove what he calls his hypothesis, " that belief is more properly an act of
the sensitive than of the cogitative part of our natures."

   It is very difficult to examine this account of belief
with the same gravity with which it is proposed. It
puts one in mind of the ingenious account given by
Martinus Scriblerus of the power of syllogism, by
making the *major* the male, and the *minor* the female,
which being coupled by the middle *term*, generate the
conclusion. There is surely no science in which men
of great parts and ingenuity have fallen into such
gross absurdities as in treating of the powers of the
mind. I cannot help thinking, that never any thing
more absurd was gravely maintained by any philosopher, than this account of the nature of belief, and
of the distinction of perception, memory, and imagination.

The belief of a proposition is an operation of mind of which every man is conscious, and what it is, he understands perfectly, though, on account of its simplicity, he cannot give a logical definition of it. If he compares it with the strength or vivacity of his ideas, or with any modification of ideas, they are so far from appearing to be one and the same, that they have not the least similitude.

That a strong belief and a weak belief differ only in degree, I can easily comprehend; but that belief and no belief should differ only in degree, no man can believe who understands what he speaks : for this is in reality to say that something and nothing differ only in degree, or that nothing is a degree of something.

Every proposition that may be the object of belief, has a contrary proposition that may be the object of a contrary belief. The ideas of both, according to Mr. Hume, are the same, and differ only in degrees of vivacity. That is, contraries differ only in degree; and so pleasure may be a degree of pain, and hatred a degree of love. But it is to no purpose to trace the absurdities that follow from this doctrine, for none of them can be more absurd than the doctrine itself.

Every man knows perfectly what it is to see an object with his eyes, what it is to remember a past event, and what it is to conceive a thing which has no existence. That these are quite different operations of his mind, he is as certain as that sound differs from colour, and both from taste; and I can as easily believe that sound, and colour, and taste, differ only in degree, as that seeing, and remembering, and imagining, differ only in degree.

Mr. Hume, in the third volume of his treatise of Human Nature, is sensible that his theory of belief is liable to strong objections, and seems, in some measure, to retract it; but in what measure it is not easy to say. He seems still to think, that belief is only a modification of the idea, but that vivacity is not a proper term to express that modification. Instead of it he uses some analogical phrases to explain that modification, such as "apprehending the idea more strongly, or taking faster hold of it."

There is nothing more meritorious in a philosopher than to retract an error upon conviction; but in this instance I humbly apprehend Mr. Hume claims that merit upon too slight a ground : for I cannot perceive that the apprehending an idea more strongly, or taking faster hold of it, expresses any other modification of the idea than what was before expressed by its strength and vivacity, or even that it expresses the same modification more properly. Whatever modification of the idea he makes belief to be, whether its vivacity, or some other without a name, to make perception, memory, and imagination, to be the different degrees of that modification, is chargeable with the absurdities we have mentioned.

Before we leave this subject of memory, it is proper to take notice of a distinction which Aristotle makes between memory and reminiscence, because the distinction has a real foundation in nature, though in our language, I think, we do not distinguish them by different names.

Memory is a kind of habit which is not always in exercise with regard to things we remember, but is ready to suggest them when there is occasion. The most perfect degree of this habit is, when the thing presents itself to our remembrance spontaneously, and without labour, as often as there is occasion. A second degree is, when the thing is forgotten for a longer or a shorter time, even when there is occasion to remember it, yet at last some incident brings it to mind without any search. A third degree is, when we cast about and search for what we would remember, and so at last find it out. It is this last, I think, which Aristotle calls reminiscence, as distinguished from memory.

Reminiscence, therefore, includes a will to recollect something past, and a search for it. But here a difficulty occurs. It may be said, that what we will to remember we must conceive, as there can be no will without a conception of the thing willed. A will to remember a thing, therefore, seems to imply that we remember it already, and have no occasion to search for it. But this difficulty is easily removed. When we will to remember a thing, we must remember something relating to it, which gives us a relative conception of it; but we may, at the same time, have no conception what the thing is, but only what relation it bears to something else. Thus, I remember that a friend charged me with a commission to be executed at such a place; but I have forgotten what the commission was. By applying my thought to what I remember concerning it, that it was given by such a person, upon such an occasion, in consequence of such a conversation, I am led, in a train of thought, to the very thing I had forgotten, and recollect distinctly what the commission was.

Aristotle says, that brutes have not reminiscence, and this I think is probable; but, says he, they have memory. It cannot, indeed, be doubted but they have something very like to it, and in some instances in a very great degree. A dog knows his master after long absence. A horse will trace back a road he has once gone as accurately as a man; and this is the more strange, that the train of thought which he had in going, must be reversed in his return. It is very

like to some prodigious memories we read of, where a
person, upon hearing an hundred names, or unconnected words pronounced, can begin at the last, and go
backward to the first, without losing or misplacing one.
Brutes certainly may learn much from experience,
which seems to imply memory.

Yet I see no reason to think that brutes measure
time as men do, by days, months, or years, or that
they have any distinct knowledge of the interval between things which they remember, or of their distance from the present moment. If we could not re-
cord transactions according to their dates, human memory would be something very different from what it is,
and perhaps resemble more the memory of brutes.

ESSAY IV.

OF CONCEPTION.

CHAP. I.

OF CONCEPTION, OR SIMPLE APPREHENSION IN GEN-ERAL.

CONCEIVING, imagining, apprehending, understanding, having a notion of a thing, are common words, used to express that operation of the understanding, which the logicians call *simple apprehension*. The having an idea of a thing, is in common language used in the same sense, chiefly I think since Mr. Locke's time.

Logicians define simple apprehension to be the bare conception of a thing, without any judgment or belief about it. If this were intended for a strictly logical definition, it might be a just objection to it, that conception and apprehension are only synonymous words; and that we may as well define conception by apprehension, as apprehension by conception; but it ought to be remembered, that the most simple operations of the mind cannot be logically defined. To have a distinct notion of them, we must attend to them as we feel them in our own minds. He that would have a distinct notion of a scarlet colour, will never attain it by a definition; he must set it before his eye, attend to it, compare it with the colours that come nearest to it, and observe the specific difference, which he will in vain attempt to define.

Every man is conscious that he can conceive a thousand things, of which he believes nothing at all; as a horse with wings, a mountain of gold: but although conception may be without any degree of belief, even the weakest belief cannot be without conception. He that believes, must have some conception of what he believes.

Without attempting a definition of this operation of the mind, I shall endeavour to explain some of its properties; consider the theories about it; and take notice of some mistakes of philosophers concerning it.

1st, It may be observed, that conception enters as an ingredient in every operation of the mind. Our senses cannot give us the belief of any object, without giving some conception of it at the same time. No man can either remember or reason about things of which he has no conception. When we will to exert any of our active powers, there must be some conception of what we will to do. There can be no desire nor aversion, love nor hatred, without some conception of the object. We cannot feel pain without conceiving it, though we can conceive it without feeling it. These things are self evident.

In every operation of the mind, therefore, in every thing we call thought, there must be conception. When we analyze the various operations either of the understanding or of the will, we shall always find this at the bottom, like the *caput mortuum* of the chymists, or the *materia prima* of the Peripatetics; but though there is no operation of mind without conception, yet it may be found naked, detached from all others, and then it is called simple apprehension, or the bare conception of a thing.

As all the operations of our mind are expressed by language, every one knows, that it is one thing to understand what is said, to conceive or apprehend its meaning, whether it be a word, a sentence, or a discourse; it is another thing to judge of it, to assent or dissent, to be persuaded or moved. The first is simple apprehension, and may be without the last, but the last cannot be without the first.

2dly, In bare conception, there can neither be truth nor falsehood, because it neither affirms nor denies. Every judgment, and every proposition by which judgment is expressed, must be true or false; and the qualities of true and false, in their proper sense, can belong to nothing but to judgments, or to propositions which express judgment. In the bare conception of a thing there is no judgment, opinion, or belief included, and therefore it cannot be either true or false.

But it may be said, Is there any thing more certain than that men may have true or false conceptions, true or false apprehensions, of things? I answer, that such ways of speaking are indeed so common, and so well authorized by custom, the arbiter of language, that it would be presumption to censure them. It is hardly possible to avoid using them. But we ought to be upon our guard, that we be not misled by them, to confound things, which, though often expressed by the same words, are really different. We must therefore remember what was before observed, Essay I. chap. 1. that all the words, by which we signify the bare conception of a thing, are likewise used to signify our opinions, when we wish to express them with modesty and diffidence. And we shall always find, that, when we speak of true or false conceptions, we mean true or false opinions. An opinion, though ever so wavering, or ever so modestly expressed, must be either true or false; but a bare conception, which expresses no opinion or judgment, can be neither.

If we analyze those speeches, in which men attribute truth or falsehood to our conceptions of things, we shall

find in every case, that there is some opinion or
judgment implied in what they call conception. A
child conceives the moon to be flat, and a foot or two
broad ; that is, this is his opinion : and when we say it
is a false notion, or a false conception, we mean that it
is a false opinion. He conceives the city of London to
be like his country village ; that is, he believes it to be
so till he is better instructed. He conceives a lion to
have horns ; that is, he believes that the animal which
men call a lion, has horns. Such opinions language
authorizes us to call conceptions; and they may be true
or false. But bare conception, or what the logicians call simple apprehension, implies no opinion,
however slight, and therefore can neither be true nor
false.

What Mr. Locke says of ideas, by which word he
very often means nothing but conceptions, is very just,
when the word *idea* is so understood, book 2. chap. 32.
§ 1. " Though truth and falsehood belong in propriety of speech only to propositions, yet ideas are often
termed true or false, as what words are there that are
not used with great latitude, and with some deviation
from their strict and proper signification; though I
think, that when ideas themselves are termed true or
false, there is still some secret, or tacit proposition,
which is the foundation of that denomination; as we
shall see, if we examine the particular occasions wherein they come to be called true or false ; in all which we
shall find some kind of affirmation or negation, which is
the reason of that denomination : for our ideas being
nothing but bare appearances, or perceptions in our
minds, cannot properly and simply in themselves be said
to be true or false, no more than a simple name of any
thing can be said to be true or false."

It may be here observed, by the way, that in this
passage, as in many others, Mr. Locke uses the word

perception, as well as the word *idea,* to signify what I
call *conception,* or *simple apprehension.* And in his
chapter upon perception, book 2. chap. 9. he uses it
in the same sense. "Perception, he says, as it is the
first faculty of the mind, exercised about our ideas; so
it is the first and simplest idea we have from reflection,
and is by some called thinking in general. It seems to
be that which puts the distinction betwixt the animal
kingdom and the inferior parts of nature. It is the
first operation of all our faculties, and the inlet of all
knowledge into our minds."

Mr. Locke has followed the example given by Des
Cartes, Gassendi, and other Cartesians, in giving the
name of *perception* to the bare conception of things;
and he has been followed in this by bishop Berkeley,
Mr. Hume, and many late philosophers, when they
treat of ideas. They have probably been led into this
impropriety, by the common doctrine concerning ideas,
which teaches us, that conception, perception by the
senses, and memory, are only different ways of perceiving ideas in our own minds. If that theory be well
founded, it will indeed be very difficult to find any specific distinction between conception and perception.
But there is reason to distrust any philosophical theory,
when it leads men to corrupt language, and to confound,
under one name, operations of the mind, which common sense and common language teach them to distinguish.

I grant that there are some states of the mind,
wherein a man may confound his conceptions with what
he perceives or remembers, and mistake the one for
the other; as, in the delirium of a fever, in some cases
of lunacy and of madness, in dreaming, and perhaps in
some momentary transports of devotion, or of other
strong emotions, which cloud his intellectual faculties,
and for a time carry a man out of himself, as we usually express it.

Even in a sober and sound state of mind, the memory of a thing may be so very weak, that we may be in doubt whether we only dreamed or imagined it.

It may be doubted, whether children, when their imagination first begins to work, can distinguish what they barely conceive from what they remember. I have been told by a man of knowledge and observation, that one of his sons, when he began to speak, very often told lies with great assurance, without any intention, as far as appeared, or any consciousness of guilt. From which the father concluded, that it is natural to some children to lie. I am rather inclined to think, that the child had no intention to deceive, but mistook the rovings of his own fancy, for things which he remembered. This, however, I take to be very uncommon, after children can communicate their sentiments by language, though perhaps not so in a more early period.

Granting all this, if any man will affirm, that they whose intellectual faculties are sound, and sober, and ripe, cannot with certainty distinguish what they perceive or remember, from what they barely conceive, when those operations have any degree of strength and distinctness, he may enjoy his opinion; I know not how to reason with him. Why should philosophers confound those operations in treating of ideas, when they would be ashamed to do it on other occasions? To distinguish the various powers of our minds, a certain degree of understanding is necessary: and if some, through a defect of understanding, natural or accidental, or from unripeness of understanding, may be apt to confound different powers, will it follow that others cannot clearly distinguish them?

To return from this digression, into which the abuse of the word *perception*, by philosophers, has led me, it appears evident, that the bare conception of an object, which includes no opinion or judgment, can neither be true nor false. Those qualities, in their proper sense, are altogether inapplicable to this operation of the mind.

3dly, Of all the analogies between the operations of body and those of the mind, there is none so strong and so obvious to all mankind as that which there is between painting, or other plastic arts, and the power of conceiving objects in the mind. Hence in all languages, the words, by which this power of the mind and its various modifications are expressed, are analogical, and borrowed from those arts. We consider this power of the mind as a plastic power, by which we form to ourselves images of the objects of thought.

In vain should we attempt to avoid this analogical language, for we have no other language upon the subject ; yet it is dangerous, and apt to mislead. All analogical and figurative words have a double meaning; and, if we are not very much upon our guard, we slide insensibly from the borrowed and figurative meaning into the primitive. We are prone to carry the parallel between the things compared further than it will hold, and thus very naturally to fall into error.

To avoid this as far as possible in the present subject, it is proper to attend to the dissimilitude between conceiving a thing in the mind, and painting it to the eye, as well as to their similitude. The similitude strikes and gives pleasure. The dissimilitude we are less disposed to observe. But the philosopher ought to attend to it, and to carry it always in mind, in his reasonings on this subject, as a monitor, to warn him against the errors into which the analogical language is apt to draw him.

When a man paints, there is some work done which remains when his hand is taken off, and continues to exist, though he should think no more of it. Every stroke of his pencil produces an effect, and this effect is different from his action in making it; for it remains and continues to exist when the action ceases. The action of painting is one thing, the picture produced is another thing. The first is the cause, the second is the effect.

Let us next consider what is done when he only conceives this picture. He must have conceived it before he painted it; for this is a maxim universally admitted, that every work of art must first be conceived in the mind of the operator. What is this conception? It is an act of the mind, a kind of thought. This cannot be denied. But does it produce any effect besides the act itself? Surely common sense answers this question in the negative: for every one knows, that it is one thing to conceive, another thing to bring forth into effect. It is one thing to project, another to execute. A man may think for a long time what he is to do, and after all do nothing. Conceiving as well as projecting or resolving, are what the schoolmen called *immanent* acts of the mind, which produce nothing beyond themselves. But painting is a transitive act, which produces an effect distinct from the operation, and this effect is the picture. Let this therefore be always remembered, that what is commonly called the image of a thing in the mind, is no more than the act or operation of the mind in conceiving it.

That this is the common sense of men who are untutored by philosophy, appears from their language. If one ignorant of the language should ask, what is meant by conceiving a thing? we should very naturally answer, that it is having an image of it in the

mind; and perhaps we could not explain the word
better. This shows, that conception, and the image
of a thing in the mind, are synonymous expressions.
The image in the mind, therefore, is not the object of
conception, nor is it any effect produced by conception
as a cause. It is conception itself. That very mode
of thinking, which we call conception, is by another
name called an image in the mind.

Nothing more readily gives the conception of a
thing than the seeing an image of it. Hence, by a
figure common in language, conception is called an
image of the thing conceived. But to show that it
is not a real, but a metaphorical image, it is called an
image in the mind. We know nothing that is properly in the mind but thought; and when any thing
else is said to be in the mind, the expression must be
figurative, and signify some kind of thought.

I know that philosophers very unanimously maintain,
that in conception there is a real image in the mind,
which is the immediate object of conception, and distinct from the act of conceiving it. I beg the reader's
indulgence to defer what may be said for or against
this philosophical opinion to the next chapter; intending in this only to explain what appears to me to belong to this operation of mind, without considering the
theories about it. I think it appears from what has
been said, that the common language of those who
have not imbibed any philosophical opinion upon this
subject, authorizes us to understand *the conception of
a thing*, and *an image of it in the mind*, not as two
different things, but as two different expressions, to
signify one and the same thing; and I wish to use common words in their common acceptation.

4thly, Taking along with us what is said in the last
article, to guard us against the seduction of the analogical language used on this subject, we may observe

a very strong analogy, not only between conceiving and painting in general, but between the different kinds of our conceptions, and the different works of the painter. He either makes fancy pictures, or he copies from the painting of others, or he paints from the life; that is, from real objects of art or nature which he has seen. I think our conceptions admit of a division very similar.

1st, There are conceptions which may be called fancy pictures. They are commonly called creatures of fancy, or of imagination. They are not the copies of any original that exists, but are originals themselves. Such was the conception which Swift formed of the island of Laputa and of the country of the Lilliputians; Cervantes of Don Quixote and his Squire; Harrington of the government of Oceana; and sir Thomas More of that of Utopia. We can give names to such creatures of imagination, conceive them distinctly, and reason consequentially concerning them, though they never had an existence. They were conceived by their creators, and may be conceived by others, but they never existed. We do not ascribe the qualities of true or false to them, because they are not accompanied with any belief, nor do they imply any affirmation or negation.

Setting aside those creatures of imagination, there are other conceptions, which may be called copies, because they have an original or archetype to which they refer, and with which they are believed to agree: and we call them true or false conceptions, according as they agree or disagree with the standard to which they are referred. These are of two kinds, which have different standards or originals.

The *first* kind is analogous to pictures taken from the life. We have conceptions of individual things that really exist, such as the city of London, or the

government of Venice. Here the things conceived
are the originals ; and our conceptions are called
true when they agree with the thing conceived. Thus,
my conception of the city of London is true when I
conceive it to be what it really is.

Individual things which really exist, being the
creatures of God, though some of them may receive
their outward form from man, he only who made
them knows their whole nature ; we know them but
in part, and therefore our conceptions of them must
in all cases be imperfect and inadequate ; yet they
may be true and just, as far as they reach.

The *second* kind is analogous to the copies which
the painter makes from pictures done before. Such
I think are the conceptions we have of what the ancients called universals ; that is, of things which belong,
or may belong to many individuals. These are kinds
and species of things ; such as, man, or elephant,
which are species of substances ; wisdom, or courage,
which are species of qualities ; equality, or similitude,
which are species of relations. It may be asked,
from what original are these conceptions formed ? And
when are they said to be true or false ?

It appears to me, that the original from which they
are copied, that is, the thing conceived, is the conception or meaning which other men who understand the
language affix to the same words.

Things are parcelled into kinds and sorts, not by
nature, but by men. The individual things we are
connected with, are so many, that to give a proper
name to every individual would be impossible. We
could never attain the knowledge of them that is necessary, nor converse nor reason about them, without
sorting them according to their different attributes.
Those that agree in certain attributes are thrown into
ne parcel, and have a general name given them, which

belongs equally to every individual in that parcel. This common name must therefore signify those attributes which have been observed to be common to every individual in that parcel, and nothing else.

That such general words may answer their intention, all that is necessary is, that those who use them should affix the same meaning or notion, that is, the same conception to them. The common meaning is the standard by which such conceptions are formed, and they are said to be true or false, according as they agree or disagree with it. Thus, my conception of felony is true and just, when it agrees with the meaning of that word in the laws relating to it, and in authors who understand the law. The meaning of the word is the thing conceived; and that meaning is the conception affixed to it by those who best understand the language.

An individual is expressed in language either by a proper name, or by a general word joined to such circumstances as distinguish that individual from all others: if it is unknown, it may, when an object of sense and within reach, be pointed out to the senses; when beyond the reach of the senses, it may be ascertained by a description, which, though very imperfect, may be true and sufficient to distinguish it from every other individual. Hence it is, that, in speaking of individuals, we are very little in danger of mistaking the object, or taking one individual for another.

Yet, as was before observed, our conception of them is always inadequate and lame. They are the creatures of God, and there are many things belonging to them which we know not, and which cannot be deduced by reasoning from what we know: they have a real essence, or constitution of nature, from which all their qualities flow: but this essence our faculties do not comprehend: they are therefore incapable of definition; for a definition ought to comprehend the whole nature or essence of the thing defined.

Thus, Westminster bridge is an individual object; though I had never seen or heard of it before, if I am only made to conceive that it is a bridge from Westminster over the Thames, this conception, however imperfect, is true, and is sufficient to make me distinguish it, when it is mentioned, from every other object that exists. The architect may have an adequate conception of its structure, which is the work of man; but of the materials, which are the work of God, no man has an adequate conception; and therefore, though the object may be described, it cannot be defined.

Universals are always expressed by general words; and all the words of language, excepting proper names, are general words; they are the signs of general conceptions, or of some circumstance relating to them. These general conceptions are formed for the purpose of language and reasoning; and the object from which they are taken, and to which they are intended to agree, is the conception which other men join to the same words; they may therefore be adequate, and perfectly agree with the thing conceived. This implies no more than that men who speak the same language may perfectly agree in the meaning of many general words.

Thus mathematicians have conceived what they call a plane triangle. They have defined it accurately; and when I conceive it to be a plane surface, bounded by three right lines, I have both a true and an adequate conception of it. There is nothing belonging to a plane triangle which is not comprehended in this conception of it, or deducible from it by just reasoning. This definition expresses the whole essence of the thing de-

fined, as every just definition ought to do; but this essence is only what Mr. Locke very properly calls a
nominal essence ; it is a general conception formed by
the mind, and joined to a general word as its sign.

If all the general words of a language had a precise
meaning, and were perfectly understood, as mathematical terms are, all verbal disputes would be at an end,
and men would never seem to differ in opinion, but
when they differ in reality; but this is far from being
the case. The meaning of most general words is not
learned like that of mathematical terms, by an accurate definition, but by the experience we happen to
have, by hearing them used in conversation. From
such experience we collect their meaning by a kind of
induction; and as this induction is for the most part
lame and imperfect, it happens that different persons
join different conceptions to the same general word;
and though we intend to give them the meaning which
use, the arbiter of language, has put upon them, this
is difficult to find, and apt to be mistaken, even by the
candid and attentive. Hence, in innumerable disputes,
men do not really differ in their judgments, but in the
way of expressing them.

Our conceptions, therefore, appear to be of three
kinds. They are either the conceptions of individual
things, the creatures of God; or they are conceptions
of the meaning of general words; or they are the
creatures of our own imagination; and these different
kinds have different properties which we have endeavoured to describe.

5thly. Our conception of things may be strong and
lively, or it may be faint and languid in all degrees.
These are qualities which properly belong to our conceptions, though we have no names for them but such
as are analogical. Every man is conscious of such a
difference in his conceptions, and finds his lively con-

ceptions most agreeable, when the object is not of such a nature as to give pain.

Those who have lively conceptions, commonly express them in a lively manner, that is, in such a manner as to raise lively conceptions and emotions in others. Such persons are the most agreeable companions in conversation, and the most acceptable in their writings.

The liveliness of our conceptions proceeds from different causes. Some objects, from their own nature, or from accidental associations, are apt to raise strong emotions in the mind. Joy and hope, ambition, zeal, and resentment, tend to enliven our conceptions. Disappointment, disgrace, grief, and envy, tend rather to flatten them. Men of keen passions are commonly lively and agreeable in conversation ; and dispassionate men often make dull companions. There is in some men a natural strength and vigour of mind, which gives strength to their conceptions on all subjects, and in all the occasional variations of temper.

It seems easier to form a lively conception of objects that are familiar, than of those that are not ; our conceptions of visible objects are commonly the most lively, when other circumstances are equal. Hence poets not only delight in the description of visible objects, but find means by metaphor, analogy, and allusion, to clothe every object they describe with visible qualities. The lively conception of these makes the object appear, as it were, before our eyes. Lord Kaimes, in his Elements of Criticism, has shown of what importance it is in works of taste, to give to objects described, what he calls *ideal presence.* To produce this in the mind, is indeed the capital aim of poetical and rhetorical description. It carries the man, as it were, out of himself, and makes him a spectator of the scene described. This ideal presence seems to me to be nothing else but a lively conception of the appearance which the object would make if really present to the eye.

Abstract and general conceptions are never lively, though they may be distinct; and therefore, however necessary in philosophy, seldom enter into poetical description, without being particularized or clothed in some visible dress.

It may be observed, however, that our conceptions of visible objects become more lively by giving them motion, and more still by giving them life, and intellectual qualities. Hence in poetry, the whole creation is animated, and endowed with sense and reflection.

Imagination, when it is distinguished from conception, seems to me to signify one species of conception; to wit, the conception of visible objects. Thus, in a mathematical proposition, I imagine the figure, and I conceive the demonstration; it would not I think be improper to say, I conceive both; but it would not be so proper to say, I imagine the demonstration.

6thly, Our conceptions of things may be clear, distinct, and steady; or they may be obscure, indistinct, and wavering. The liveliness of our conceptions gives pleasure, but it is their distinctness and steadiness that enables us to judge right, and to express our sentiments with perspicuity.

If we inquire into the cause, why among persons speaking or writing on the same subject, we find in one so much darkness, in another so much perspicuity, I believe the chief cause will be found to be, that one had a distinct and steady conception of what he said or wrote, and the other had not. Men generally find means to express distinctly what they have conceived distinctly. Horace observes, that proper words spontaneously follow distinct conceptions, " *Verbaque provisam rem non invita sequuntur.*" But it is impossible that a man should distinctly express what he has not distinctly conceived.

We are commonly taught, that perspicuity depends upon a proper choice of words, a proper structure of sentences, and a proper order in the whole composition. All this is very true, but it supposes distinctness in our conceptions, without which there can be neither propriety in our words, nor in the structure of our sentences, nor in our method.

Nay, I apprehend, that indistinct conceptions of things are, for the most part, the cause, not only of obscurity in writing and speaking, but of error in judging.

Must not they who conceive things in the same manner form the same judgment of their agreements and disagreements? Is it possible for two persons to differ with regard to the conclusion of a syllogism who have the same conception of the premises?

Some persons find it difficult to enter into a mathematical demonstration. I believe we shall always find the reason to be, that they do not distinctly apprehend it. A man cannot be convinced by what he does not understand. On the other hand, I think a man cannot understand a demonstration without seeing the force of it. I speak of such demonstrations as those of Euclid, where every step is set down, and nothing left to be supplied by the reader.

Sometimes one who has got through the first four books of Euclid's Elements, and sees the force of the demonstrations, finds difficulty in the fifth. What is the reason of this? You may find, by a little conversation with him, that he has not a clear and steady conception of ratios, and of the terms relating to them. When the terms used in the fifth book have become familiar, and readily excite in his mind a clear and steady conception of their meaning, you may venture to affirm that he will be able to understand the demonstrations of that book, and to see the force of them.

If this be really the case, as it seems to be, it leads us to think, that men are very much upon a level with regard to mere judgment, when we take that faculty apart from the apprehension or conception of the things about which we judge; so that a sound judgment seems to be the inseparable companion of a clear and steady apprehension: and we ought not to consider these two as talents, of which the one may fall to the lot of one man, and the other to the lot of another, but as talents which always go together.

It may, however, be observed, that some of our conceptions may be more subservient to reasoning than others which are equally clear and distinct. It was before observed, that some of our conceptions are of individual things, others of things general and abstract. It may happen, that a man who has very clear conceptions of things individual, is not so happy in those of things general and abstract. And this I take to be the reason why we find men who have good judgment in matters of common life, and perhaps good talents for poetical or rhetorical composition, who find it very difficult to enter into abstract reasoning.

That I may not appear singular in putting men so much upon a level in point of mere judgment, I beg leave to support this opinion by the authority of two very thinking men, Des Cartes and Cicero. The former, in his Dissertation on Method, expresses himself to this purpose: "Nothing is so equally distributed among men as judgment. Wherefore it seems reasonable to believe, that the power of distinguishing

What is true from what is false, which we properly
call judgment or right reason, is by nature equal
in all men; and therefore that the diversity of our
opinions does not arise from one person being endowed with a greater power of reason than another,
but only from this, that we do not lead our thoughts
in the same track, nor attend to the same things."

Cicero, in his third book De Oratore, makes this
observation "It is wonderful, when the learned and
unlearned differ so much in art, how little they differ in judgment. For art being derived from nature, is good for nothing, unless it move and delight
nature."

From what has been said in this article, it follows,
that it is so far in our power to write and speak per-
spicuously, and to reason justly, as it is in our power
to form clear and distinct conceptions of the subject
on which we speak or reason. And though nature
has put a wide difference between one man and another in this respect, yet that it is in a very considerable degree in our power to have clear and distinct
apprehensions of things about which we think and
reason, cannot be doubted.

7thly, It has been observed by many authors, that,
when we barely conceive any object, the ingredients
of that conception must either be things with which
we were before acquainted by some other original
power of the mind, or they must be parts or attributes
of such things. Thus a man cannot conceive colours,
if he never saw, nor sounds, if he never heard. If a
man had not a conscience, he could not conceive what
is meant by moral obligation, or by right and wrong
in conduct.

Fancy may combine things that never were combined in reality. It may enlarge or diminish, multiply or divide, compound and fashion the objects which

nature presents; but it cannot, by the utmost effort of
that creative power which we ascribe to it, bring any
one simple ingredient into its productions, which nature has not framed, and brought to our knowledge by
some other faculty.

This Mr. Locke has expressed as beautifully as
justly. "The dominion of man, in this little world of
his own understanding, is much the same as in the
great world of visible things; wherein his power, however managed by art and skill, reaches no further than
to compound and divide the materials that are made to
his hand, but can do nothing toward making the least
particle of matter, or destroying one atom that is already in being. The same inability will every one find
in himself, to fashion in his understanding any simple
idea not received by the powers which God has given
him."

I think all philosophers agree in this sentiment. Mr.
Hume, indeed, after acknowledging the truth of the
principle in general, mentions what he thinks a single
exception to it. That a man, who had seen all the
shades of a particular colour except one, might frame
in his mind a conception of that shade which he
never saw. I think this is not an exception; because
a particular shade of a colour differs not specifically,
but only in degree, from other shades of the same
colour.

It is proper to observe, that our most simple conceptions are not those which nature immediately presents
to us. When we come to years of understanding, we
have the power of analyzing the objects of nature, of
distinguishing their several attributes and relations, of
conceiving them one by one, and of giving a name to
each, whose meaning extends only to that single attribute or relation: and thus our most simple conceptions

are not those of any object in nature, but of some single attribute or relation of such objects.

Thus nature presents to our senses, bodies that are extended in three dimensions, and solid. By analyzing the notion we have of body from our senses, we form to ourselves the conceptions of extension, solidity, space, a point, a line, a surface; all which are more simple conceptions than that of a body. But they are the elements, as it were, of which our conception of a body is made up, and into which it may be analyzed. This power of analyzing objects we propose to consider particularly in another place. It is only mentioned here, that what is said in this article may not be understood, so as to be inconsistent with it.

8thly, Though our conceptions must be confined to the ingredients mentioned in the last article, we are unconfined with regard to the arrangement of those ingredients. Here we may pick and choose, and form an endless variety of combinations and compositions, which we call creatures of the imagination. These may be clearly conceived, though they never existed: and indeed every thing that is made, must have been conceived before it was made. Every work of human art, and every plan of conduct, whether in public or in private life, must have been conceived before it is brought to execution. And we cannot avoid thinking, that the Almighty, before he created the universe by his power, had a distinct conception of the whole and of every part, and saw it to be good, and agreeable to his intention.

It is the business of man, as a rational creature, to employ this unlimited power of conception, for planning his conduct and enlarging his knowledge. It seems to be peculiar to beings endowed with reason to act by a preconceived plan. Brute animals seem either to want this power, or to have it in a very low degree. They

are moved by instinct, habit, appetite, or natural affection, according as these principles are stirred by the
present occasion. But I see no reason to think that
they can propose to themselves a connected plan of life,
or form general rules of conduct. Indeed, we see
that many of the human species, to whom God has
given this power, make little use of it. They act without a plan, as the passion or appetite which is strongest
at the time leads them.

9thly, The last property I shall mention of this faculty, is that which essentially distinguishes it from every
other power of the mind; and it is, that it is not employed solely about things which have existence. I
can conceive a winged horse or a centaur, as easily
and as distinctly as I can conceive a man whom I
have seen. Nor does this distinct conception incline
my judgment in the least to the belief, that a winged
horse or a centaur ever existed.

It is not so with the other operations of our minds.
They are employed about real existences, and carry
with them the belief of their objects. When I feel
pain, I am compelled to believe that the pain that I
feel has a real existence. When I perceive any external object, my belief of the real existence of the object
is irresistible. When I distinctly remember any
event, though that event may not now exist, I can
have no doubt but it did exist. That consciousness
which we have of the operations of our own minds, implies a belief of the real existence of those operations.

Thus we see, that the powers of sensation, of perception, of memory, and of consciousness, are all employed solely about objects that do exist, or have existed. But conception is often employed about objects
that neither do, nor did, nor will exist. This is the
very nature of this faculty, that its object, though distinctly conceived, may have no existence. Such an ob-

ject we call a creature of imagination; but this creature never was created.

That we may not impose upon ourselves in this matter, we must distinguish between that act or operation of the mind, which we call conceiving an object, and the object which we conceive. When we conceive any thing, there is a real act or operation of the mind; of this we are conscious, and can have no doubt of its existence; but every such act must have an object; for he that conceives, must conceive something. Suppose he conceives a centaur, he may have a distinct conception of this object, though no centaur ever existed.

I am afraid, that, to those who are unacquainted with the doctrine of philosophers upon this subject, I shall appear in a very ridiculous light, for insisting upon a point so very evident, as that men may barely conceive things that never existed. They will hardly believe, that any man in his wits ever doubted of it. Indeed, I know no truth more evident to the common sense and to the experience of mankind. But if the authority of philosophy, ancient and modern, opposes it, as I think it does, I wish not to treat that authority so fastidiously, as not to attend patiently to what may be said in support of it.

CHAP. II.

THEORIES CONCERNING CONCEPTION.

THE theory of ideas has been applied to the conception of objects as well as to perception and memory. Perhaps it will be irksome to the reader, as it is to the writer, to return to that subject, after so much has been said upon it; but its application to the conception of objects, which could not properly have been introduced before, gives a more comprehensive view of it, and of the prejudices which have led philosophers so unanimously into it.

There are two prejudices which seem to me to have given rise to the theory of ideas in all the various forms in which it has appeared in the course of above two thousand years; and though they have no support from the natural dictates of our faculties, or from attentive reflection upon their operations, they are prejudices which those who speculate upon this subject, are very apt to be led into by analogy.

The *first* is, that in all the operations of the understanding there must be some immediate intercourse between the mind and its object, so that the one may act upon the other. The *second*, that in all the operations of understanding there must be an object of thought, which really exists while we think of it; or, as some philosophers have expressed it, that which is not, cannot be intelligible.

Had philosophers perceived, that these are prejudices grounded only upon analogical reasoning, we had never heard of ideas in the philosophical sense of that word.

The first of these principles has led philosophers to think, that as the external objects of sense are too remote to act upon the mind immediately, there must be some image or shadow of them that is present to the mind, and is the immediate object of perception. That there is such an immediate object of perception, distinct from the external object, has been very unanimously held by philosophers, though they have differed much about the name, the nature, and the origin of those immediate objects.

We have considered what has been said in the support of this principle, Essay II. chap. 14. to which the reader is referred, to prevent repetition.

I shall only add to what is there said, that there appears no shadow of reason why the mind must have an object immediately present to it in its intellectual operations, any more than in its affections and passions. Philosophers have not said, that ideas are the immediate objects of love or resentment, of esteem or disapprobation. It is, I think, acknowledged, that persons and not ideas are the immediate objects of those affections; persons, who are as far from being immediately present to the mind as other external objects, and sometimes persons who have now no existence in this world at least, and who can neither act upon the mind, nor be acted upon by it.

The second principle, which I conceive to be likewise a prejudice of philosophers grounded upon analogy, is now to be considered.

It contradicts directly what was laid down in the last article of the preceding chapter, to wit, that we may have a distinct conception of things which never existed. This is undoubtedly the common belief of those who have not been instructed in philosophy; and they will think it as ridiculous to defend it by reasoning, as to oppose it.

The philosopher says, though there may be a remote object which does not exist, there must be an immediate object which really exists; for that which is not, cannot be an object of thought. The idea must be perceived by the mind, and if it does not exist there, there can be no perception of it, no operation of the mind about it.

This principle deserves the more to be examined, because the other before mentioned depends upon it; for although the last may be true, even if the first was false, yet if the last be not true, neither can the first. If we can conceive objects which have no existence, it follows, that there may be objects of thought which neither act upon the mind, nor are acted upon by it; because that which has no existence can neither act nor be acted upon.

It is by these principles that philosophers have been led to think, that in every act of memory and of conception, as well as of perception, there are two objects. The one, the immediate object, the idea, the species, the form; the other, the mediate or external object. The vulgar know only of one object, which in perception is something external that exists; in memory, something that did exist; and in conception, may be something that never existed: but the immediate object of the philosophers, the idea, is said to exist, and to be perceived in all these operations.

These principles have not only led philosophers to split objects into two, where others can find but one, but likewise have led them to reduce the three operations now mentioned to one, making memory and conception, as well as perception, to be the perception of ideas. But nothing appears more evident to the vulgar, than that, what is only remembered, or only conceived, is not perceived: and to speak of the perceptions of memory, appears to them as absurd, as to speak of the hearing of sight.

In a word, these two principles carry us into the whole philosophical theory of ideas, and furnish every argument that ever was used for their existence. If they are true, that system must be admitted with all its consequences: if they are only prejudices, grounded upon analogical reasoning, the whole system must fall to the ground with them.

It is, therefore, of importance to trace those principles, as far as we are able, to their origin, and to see, if possible, whether they have any just foundation in reason, or whether they are rash conclusions, drawn from a supposed analogy between matter and mind.

The unlearned, who are guided by the dictates of nature, and express what they are conscious of concerning the operations of their own mind, believe, that the object which they distinctly perceive certainly exists; that the object which they distinctly remember certainly did exist, but now may not; but as to things that are barely conceived, they know that they can conceive a thousand things that never existed, and that the bare conception of a thing does not so much as afford a presumption of its existence. They give themselves no trouble to know how these operations are performed, or to account for them from general principles.

But philosophers, who wish to discover the causes of things, and to account for these operations of mind, observing, that in other operations there must be not only an agent, but something to act upon, have been led by analogy to conclude, that it must be so in the operations of the mind.

The relation between the mind and its conceptions bears a very strong and obvious analogy to the relation between a man and his work. Every scheme he forms, every discovery he makes by his reasoning powers, is very properly called the work of his mind. These works of the mind are sometimes great and important works, and draw the attention and admiration of men.

It is the province of the philosopher to consider how such works of the mind are produced, and of what materials they are composed. He calls the materials ideas. There must, therefore, be ideas, which the mind can arrange and form into a regular structure. Every thing that is produced must be produced of something ; and from nothing, nothing can be produced.

Some such reasoning as this seems to me to have given the first rise to the philosophical notions of ideas. These notions were formed into a system by the Pythagoreans two thousand years ago; and this system was adopted by Plato, and embellished with all the powers of a fine and lofty imagination. I shall, in compliance with custom, call it the Platonic system of ideas, though, in reality, it was the invention of the Pythagorean school.

The most arduous question which employed the wits of men in the infancy of the Grecian philosophy, was, What was the origin of the world? From what principles and causes did it proceed? To this question very different answers were given in the different schools. Most of them appear to us very ridiculous. The Pythagoreans, however, judged very rationally, from the order and beauty of the universe, that it must be the workmanship of an eternal, intelligent and good Being: and therefore they concluded the Deity to be one first principle or cause of the universe.

But they conceived there must be more. The universe must be made of something. Every workman must have materials to work upon. That the world

should be made out of nothing seemed to them absurd, because every thing that is made must be made
of something.

Nullam rem e nihilo gigni divinitus unquam.   LUCR.

De nihilo nihil, in nihilum nil posse reverti.   PERS.

This maxim never was brought into doubt. Even in
Cicero's time it continued to be held by all philosophers. What natural philosopher, says that author
in his second book of Divination, ever asserted that
any thing could take its rise from nothing, or be reduced to nothing? Because men must have materials
to work upon, they concluded it must be so with the
Deity. This was reasoning from analogy.

From this it followed, that an eternal uncreated
matter was another first principle of the universe.
But this matter, they believed, had no form nor quality. It was the same with the *materia prima*, or first
matter of Aristotle, who borrowed this part of his
philosophy from his predecessors.

To us it seems more rational to think that the Deity
created matter with its qualities, than that the matter
of the universe should be eternal and self-existent.
But so strong was the prejudice of the ancient philosophers against what we call creation, that they rather
chose to have recourse to this eternal and unintelligible matter, that the Deity might have materials to
work upon.

The same analogy which led them to think that
there must be an eternal matter of which the world
was made, led them also to conclude that there must
be an eternal pattern or model according to which it
was made. Works of design and art must be distinctly conceived before they are made. The Deity, as
an intelligent Being, about to execute a work of perfect

beauty and regularity, must have had a distinct conception of his work before it was made. This appears
very rational.

But this conception, being the work of the Divine
intellect, something must have existed as its object.
This could only be ideas, which are the proper and immediate object of intellect.

From this investigation of the principles or causes
of the universe, those philosophers concluded them to
be three in number, to wit, an eternal matter as the
material cause, eternal ideas as the model or exempla-
ry cause, and an eternal intelligent mind as the efficient
cause.

As to the nature of those eternal ideas, the philosophers of that sect ascribed to them the most magnificent attributes. They were immutable and uncreated ;
the object of the Divine intellect before the world was
made ; and the only object of intellect and of science
to all intelligent beings. As far as intellect is superior to sense, so far are ideas superior to all the objects of sense. The objects of sense being in a
constant flux, cannot properly be said to exist. Ideas
are the things which have a real and permanent existence. They are as various as the species of things,
there being one idea of every species, but none of individuals. The idea is the essence of the species, and
existed before any of the species was made. It is
entire in every individual of the species, without being
either divided or multiplied.

In our present state, we have but an imperfect conception of the eternal ideas ; but it is the highest fe-
licity and perfection of men to be able to contemplate
them. While we are in this prison of the body, sense,
as a dead weight, bears us down from the contemplation of the intellectual objects, and it is only by a due
purification of the soul, and abstraction from sense,

that the intellectual eye is opened, and that we are enabled to mount upon the wings of intellect to the celestial world of ideas.

Such was the most ancient system concerning ideas, of which we have any account.   And, however different from the modern, it appears to be built upon the prejudices we have mentioned ; to wit, that in every operation, there must be something to work upon ; and that even in conception there must be an object which really exists.

For if those ancient philosophers had thought it possible that the Deity could operate without materials in the formation of the world, and that he could conceive the plan of it without a model, they could have seen no reason to make matter and ideas eternal and necessarily existent principles, as well as the Deity himself.

Whether they believed that the ideas were not only eternal, but eternally, and without a cause, arranged in that beautiful and perfect order, which they ascribe to this intelligible world of ideas, I cannot say ; but this seems to be a necessary consequence of the system ; for if the Deity could not conceive the plan of the world which he made, without a model which really existed, that model could not be his work, nor contrived by his wisdom ; for if he made it, he must have conceived it before it was made ; it must therefore have existed in all its beauty and order independent of the Deity ; and this I think they acknowledged, by making the model, and the matter of this world, first principles, no less than the Deity.

If the Platonic system be thus understood, and I do not see how it can hang together otherwise, it leads to two consequences that are unfavourable to it.

1st, Nothing is left to the Maker of this world but the skill to work after a model. The model had all the perfection and beauty that appears in the copy, and the Deity had only to copy after a pattern that existed independent of him. Indeed the copy, if we believe those philosophers, falls very far short of the original; but this they seem to have ascribed to the refractoriness of matter, of which it was made.

2dly, If the world of ideas, without being the work of a perfectly wise and good intelligent Being, could have so much beauty and perfection, how can we infer from the beauty and order of this world, which is but an imperfect copy of the other, that it must have been made by a perfectly wise and good Being? The force of this reasoning, from the beauty and order of the universe, to its being the work of a wise Being, which appears invincible to every candid mind, and appeared so to those ancient philosophers, is entirely destroyed by the supposition of the existence of a world of ideas, of greater perfection and beauty, which never was made. Or, if the reasoning be good, it will apply to the world of ideas, which must of consequence have been made by a wise and good intelligent Being, and must have been conceived before it was made.

It may further be observed, that all that is mysterious and unintelligible in the Platonic ideas arises from attributing existence to them. Take away this one attribute, all the rest, however pompously expressed, are easily admitted and understood.

What is a Platonic idea? It is the essence of a species. It is the exemplar, the model, according to which all the individuals of that species are made. It is entire in every individual of the species, without being multiplied or divided. It was an object of the Divine intellect from eternity, and is an object of contemplation and of science to every intelligent being. It is eternal, immutable, and uncreated; and, to crown all, it not only exists, but has a more real and permanent existence than any thing that ever God made.

Take this description altogether, and it would require an Oedipus to unriddle it. But take away the last part of it, and nothing is more easy. It is easy to find five hundred things which answer to every article in the description except the last.

Take for an instance the nature of a circle, as it is defined by Euclid, an object which every intelligent being may conceive distinctly, though no circle had ever existed; it is the exemplar, the model, according to which all the individual figures of that species that ever existed were made, for they are all made according to the nature of a circle. It is entire in every individual of the species, without being multiplied or divided: for every circle is an entire circle; and all circles, in as far as they are circles, have one and the same nature. It was an object of the Divine intellect from all eternity, and may be an object of contemplation and of science to every intelligent being. It is the essence of a species, and, like all other essences, it is eternal, immutable, and uncreated. This means no more, but that a circle always was a circle, and can never be any thing but a circle. It is the necessity of the thing, and not any act of creating power, that makes a circle to be a circle.

The nature of every species, whether of substance, of quality, or of relation, and in general every thing which the ancients called an universal, answers to the description of a Platonic idea, if in that description you leave out the attribute of existence.

If we believe that no species of things could be conceived by the Almighty without a model that really existed, we must go back to the Platonic system, however mysterious. But if it be true, that the

Deity could have a distinct conception of things which did not exist, and that other intelligent beings may conceive objects which do not exist, the system has no better foundation than this prejudice, that the operations of mind must be like those of the body.

Aristotle rejected the ideas of his master Plato as visionary; but he retained the prejudices that gave rise to them, and therefore substituted something in their place, but under a different name, and of a different origin.

He called the objects of intellect, intelligible species; those of the memory and imagination, phantasms, and those of the senses, sensible species. This change of the name was indeed very small; for the Greek word of Aristotle, which we translate *species* or *form*, is so near to the Greek word *idea*, both in its sound and signification, that, from their etymology, it would not be easy to give them different meanings. Both are derived from the Greek word which signifies *to see*, and both may signify a vision, or appearance to the eye. Cicero, who understood Greek well, often translates the Greek word *idea* by the Latin word *visio*. But both words being used as terms of art, one in the Platonic system, the other in the Peripatetic, the Latin writers generally borrowed the Greek word *idea* to express the Platonic notion, and translated Aristotle's word, by the word *species* or *forma;* and in this they have been followed in the modern languages.

Those forms or species were called intelligible, to distinguish them from sensible species, which Aristotle held to be the immediate objects of sense.

He thought that the sensible species come from the external object, and defined a *sense* to be that which has the capacity to receive the form of sensible things without the matter; as wax receives the form of a seal without any of the matter of it. In like manner, he thought that the intellect receives the forms of things intelligible, and he calls it the place of forms.

I take it to have been the opinion of Aristotle, that the intelligible forms in the human intellect are derived from the sensible by abstraction, and other operations of the mind itself. As to the intelligible forms in the Divine intellect, they must have had another origin; but I do not remember that he gives any opinion about them. He certainly maintained, however, that there is no intellection without intelligible species; no memory or imagination without phantasms; no perception without sensible species. Treating of memory he proposes a difficulty, and endeavours to resolve it, how a phantasm, that is a present object in the mind, should represent a thing that is past.

Thus, I think, it appears, that the Peripatetic system of species and phantasms, as well as the Platonic system of ideas, is grounded upon this principle, that in every kind of thought there must be some object that really exists; in every operation of the mind, something to work upon. Whether this immediate object be called an idea with Plato, or a phantasm or species with Aristotle; whether it be eternal and uncreated, or produced by the impressions of external objects, is of no consequence in the present argument. In both systems it was thought impossible, that the Deity could make the world without matter to work upon. In both it was thought impossible, that an intelligent being could conceive any thing that did not exist, but by means of a model that really existed.

The philosophers of the Alexandrian school, commonly called the latter Platonists, conceived the

eternal ideas of things to be in the Divine intellect,
and thereby avoided the absurdity of making them a
principle distinct from, and independent of the Deity ; but still they held them to exist really in
the Divine mind as the objects of conception, and
as the patterns and archetypes of things that are
made.

Modern philosophers, still persuaded that of every
thought there must be an immediate object that really exists, have not thought it necessary to distinguish
by different names the immediate objects of intellect,
of imagination, and of the senses, but have given the
common name of *idea* to them all.

Whether these ideas be in the sensorium, or in the
mind, or partly in the one, and partly in the other;
whether they exist when they are not perceived, or
only when they are perceived; whether they are the
workmanship of the Deity or of the mind itself, or
of external natural causes; with regard to these
points, different authors seem to have different opinions, and the same author sometimes to waver or be
diffident ; but as to their existence, there seems to be
great unanimity.

So much is this opinion fixed in the minds of philosophers, that I doubt not but it will appear to most
a very strange paradox, or rather a contradiction, that
men should think without ideas.

That it has the appearance of a contradiction, I
confess. But this appearance arises from the ambiguity of the word *idea*. If the idea of a thing means
only the thought of it, or the operation of the
mind in thinking about it, which is the most common meaning of the word, to think without ideas, is
to think without thought, which is undoubtedly a contradiction.

But an idea, according to the definition given of it by philosophers, is not thought, but an object of thought, which really exists, and is perceived. Now, whether is it a contradiction to say, that a man may think of an object that does not exist?

I acknowledge that a man cannot perceive an object that does not exist; nor can he remember an object that did not exist; but there appears to me no contradiction in his conceiving an object that neither does, nor ever did exist.

Let us take an example. I conceive a centaur. This conception is an operation of the mind, of which I am conscious, and to which I can attend. The sole object of it is a centaur, an animal which I believe never existed. I can see no contradiction in this.

The philosopher says, I cannot conceive a centaur without having an idea of it in my mind. I am at a loss to understand what he means. He surely does not mean that I cannot conceive it without conceiving it. This would make me no wiser. What then is this idea? Is it an animal, half horse and half man? No. Then I am certain it is not the thing I conceive. Perhaps he will say, that the idea is an image of the animal, and is the immediate object of my conception, and that the animal is the mediate or remote object.

To this I answer: 1st, I am certain there are not two objects of this conception, but one only; which is as immediate an object of my conception as any can be.

2dly, This one object which I conceive, is not the image of an animal, it is an animal. I know what it is to conceive an image of an animal, and what it is to conceive an animal; and I can distinguish the one of these from the other without any danger of mistake. The thing I conceive is a body of a certain

figure and colour, having life and spontaneous motion. The philosopher says that the idea is an image
of the animal, but that it has neither body, nor colour,
nor life, nor spontaneous motion. This I am not able
to comprehend.

3dly, I wish to know how this idea comes to be
an object of my thought, when I cannot even conceive what it means; and if I did conceive it, this
would be no evidence of its existence, any more than
my conception of a centaur is of its existence. Philosophers sometimes say that we perceive ideas, sometimes that we are conscious of them. I can have no
doubt of the existence of any thing which I either perceive, or of which I am conscious; but I cannot
find that I either perceive ideas or am conscious of
them.

Perception and consciousness are very different
operations, and it is strange that philosophers have
never determined by which of them ideas are discerned. This is as if a man should positively affirm that
he perceived an object, but whether by his eyes, or
his ears, or his touch, he could not say.

But may not a man who conceives a centaur say,
that he has a distinct image of it in his mind? I think
he may. And if he means by this way of speaking
what the vulgar mean, who never heard of the philosophical theory of ideas, I find no fault with it. By
a distinct image in the mind, the vulgar mean a distinct conception; and it is natural to call it so, on
account of the analogy between an image of a thing
and the conception of it. On account of this analogy,
obvious to all mankind, this operation is called imagination, and an image in the mind is only a periphrasis for imagination. But to infer from this that
there is really an image in the mind, distinct from the
operation of conceiving the object, is to be misled by

an analogical expression; as if, from the phrases of deliberating and balancing things in the mind, we should infer that there is really a balance existing in the mind for weighing motives and arguments.

The analogical words and phrases, used in all languages to express conception, do no doubt facilitate their being taken in a literal sense. But if we only attend carefully to what we are conscious of in this operation, we shall find no more reason to think that images do really exist in our minds, than that balances and other mechanical engines do.

We know of nothing that is in the mind but by consciousness, and we are conscious of nothing but various modes of thinking; such as understanding, willing, affection, passion, doing, suffering. If philosophers choose to give the name of an idea to any mode of thinking of which we are conscious, I have no objection to the name; but that it introduces a foreign word into our language without necessity, and a word that is very ambiguous, and apt to mislead. But if they give that name to images in the mind, which are not thought, but only objects of thought, I can see no reason to think that there are such things in nature. If they be, their existence and their nature must be more evident than any thing else, because we know nothing but by their means. I may add, that if they be, we can know nothing besides them. For, from the existence of images, we can never, by any just reasoning, infer the existence of any thing else, unless perhaps the existence of an intelligent Author of them. In this bishop Berkeley reasoned right.

In every work of design, the work must be conceived before it is executed, that is, before it exists. If a model, consisting of ideas, must exist in the mind, as the object of this conception, that model is a work of design no less than the other, of which it is the model; and therefore, as a work of design, it must have been conceived before it existed. In every work of design, therefore, the conception must go before the existence. This argument we applied before to the Platonic system of eternal and immutable ideas, and it may be applied with equal force to all the systems of ideas.

If now it should be asked, what is the idea of a circle? I answer, It is the conception of a circle. What is the immediate object of this conception? The immediate and the only object of it is a circle. But where is this circle? It is no where. If it was an individual, and had a real existence, it must have a place; but being an universal, it has no existence, and therefore no place. Is it not in the mind of him that conceives it? The conception of it is in the mind, being an act of the mind; and in common language, a thing being in the mind, is a figurative expression, signifying that the thing is conceived or remembered.

It may be asked, Whether this conception is an image or resemblance of a circle? I answer, I have already accounted for its being, in a figurative sense, called the image of a circle in the mind. If the question is meant in the literal sense, we must observe, that the word *conception* has two meanings. Properly it signifies that operation of the mind which we have been endeavouring to explain; but sometimes it is put for the object of conception, or thing conceived.

Now, if the question be understood in the last of these senses, the object of this conception is not an image or resemblance of a circle; for it is a circle, and nothing can be an image of itself.

If the question be, Whether the operation of mind in conceiving a circle be an image or resemblance of a circle? I think it is not; and that no two things can be more perfectly unlike, than a species of thought and a species of figure. Nor is it more strange that conception should have no resemblance to the object conceived, than that desire should have no resemblance to the object desired, or resentment to the object of resentment.

I can likewise conceive an individual object that really exists, such as St. Paul's church in London. I have an idea of it; that is, I conceive it. The immediate object of this conception is four hundred miles distant; and I have no reason to think that it acts upon me, or that I act upon it; but I can think of it notwithstanding. I can think of the first year, or the last year of the Julian period.

If, after all, it should be thought, that images in the mind serve to account for this faculty of conceiving things most distant in time and place, and even things which do not exist, which otherwise would be altogether inconceivable; to this I answer, that accounts of things, grounded upon conjecture, have been the bane of true philosophy in all ages. Experience may satisfy us, that it is an hundred times more probable that they are false than that they are true.

This account of the faculty of conception, by images in the mind, or in the brain, will deserve the regard of those who have a true taste in philosophy, when it is proved by solid arguments, 1st, that there are images in the mind, or in the brain, of the things we conceive. 2dly, That there is a faculty in the mind, of perceiving such images. 3dly, That the perception of such images produces the conception of things most distant, and even of things that have no

existence. And, 4thly, that the perception of individual images in the mind, or in the brain, gives us
the conception of universals, which are the attributes
of many individuals. Until this is done, the theory of
images existing in the mind, or in the brain, ought to
be placed in the same category with the sensible species, and *materia prima* of Aristotle, and the vortices
of Des Cartes.

CHAP. III.

MISTAKES CONCERNING CONCEPTION.

1st, WRITERS on logic, after the example of Aristotle, divide the operations of the understanding into three; simple apprehension, which is another word for conception, judgment, and reasoning. They teach us, that reasoning is expressed by a syllogism, judgment by a proposition, and simple apprehension by a term only, that is, by one or more words which do not make a full proposition, but only the subject or predicate of a proposition. If by this they mean, as I think they do, that a proposition, or even a syllogism, may not be simply apprehended, I believe this is a mistake.

In all judgment, and in all reasoning, conception is included. We can neither judge of a proposition, nor reason about it, unless we conceive or apprehend it. We may distinctly conceive a proposition, without judging of it at all. We may have no evidence on one side or the other; we may have no concern whether it be true or false. In these cases we commonly form no judgment about it, though we perfectly understand its meaning.

A man may discourse, or plead, or write, for other ends than to find the truth. His learning, and wit, and invention, may be employed, while his judgment is not at all, or very little. When it is not truth, but some other end he pursues, judgment would be an impediment, unless for discovering the means of attaining his end; and therefore it is laid aside, or employed solely for that purpose.

The business of an orator is said to be to find out what is fit to persuade. This a man may do with much ingenuity, who never took the trouble to examine whether it ought to persuade or not. Let it not be thought, therefore, that a man judges of the truth of every proposition he utters, or hears uttered. In our commerce with the world, judgment is not the talent that bears the greatest price; and therefore those who are not sincere lovers of truth, lay up this talent, where it rusts and corrupts, while they carry others to market, for which there is greater demand.

2dly, The division commonly made by logicians, of simple apprehension, into sensation, imagination, and pure intellection, seems to me very improper in several respects.

1st, Under the word *sensation*, they include not only what is properly so called, but the perception of external objects by the senses. These are very different operations of the mind; and, although they are commonly conjoined by nature, ought to be carefully distinguished by philosophers.

2dly, Neither sensation, nor the perception of external objects, is simple apprehension. Both include judgment and belief, which are excluded from simple apprehension.

3dly, They distinguish imagination from pure intellection by this, that in imagination the image is in the brain, in pure intellection it is in the intellect. This is to ground a distinction upon an hypothesis. We have no evidence that there are images either in the brain or in the intellect.

I take imagination, in its most proper sense, to signify a lively conception of objects of sight. This is a talent of importance to poets and orators, and deserves a proper name, on account of its connection with those arts. According to this strict meaning of the word, imagination is distinguished from conception as a part from the whole. We conceive the objects of the other senses, but it is not so proper to say that we imagine them. We conceive judgment, reasoning, propositions, and arguments; but it is rather improper to say that we imagine these things.

This distinction between imagination and conception, may be illustrated by an example, which Des Cartes uses to illustrate the distinction between imagination and pure intellection. We can imagine a triangle or a square so clearly as to distinguish them from every other figure. But we cannot imagine a figure of a thousand equal sides and angles so clearly. The best eye, by looking at it, could not distinguish it from every figure of more or fewer sides. And that conception of its appearance to the eye, which we properly call imagination, cannot be more distinct than the appearance itself, yet we can conceive a figure of a thousand sides, and even can demonstrate the properties which distinguish it from all figures of more or fewer sides. It is not by the eye, but by a superior faculty, that we form the notion of a great number, such as a thousand: and a distinct notion of this number of sides not being to be got by the eye, it is not imagined, but it is distinctly conceived, and easily distinguished from every other number.

3dly, Simple apprehension is commonly represented as the first operation of the understanding; and judgment, as being a composition or combination of simple apprehensions.

This mistake has probably arisen from the taking sensation and the perception of objects by the senses, to be nothing but simple apprehension. They are very probably the first operations of the mind, but they are not simple apprehension.

It is generally allowed, that we cannot conceive sounds if we have never heard, nor colours if we have never seen: and the same thing may be said of the objects of the other senses. In like manner, we must have judged or reasoned before we have the conception or simple apprehension of judgment, and of reasoning.

Simple apprehension, therefore, though it be the simplest, is not the first operation of the understanding; and instead of saying, that the more complex operations of the mind are formed by compounding simple apprehensions, we ought rather to say, that simple apprehensions are got by analyzing more complex operations.

A similar mistake, which is carried through the whole of Mr. Locke's Essay, may be here mentioned. It is, that our simplest ideas or conceptions are got immediately by the senses, or by consciousness, and the complex afterward formed by compounding them. I apprehend, it is far otherwise.

Nature presents no object to the senses, or to consciousness, that is not complex. Thus, by our senses we perceive bodies of various kinds; but every body is a complex object; it has length, breadth, and thickness; it has figure, and colour, and various other sensible qualities, which are blended together in the same subject; and I apprehend, that brute animals, who have the same senses that we have, cannot separate the different qualities belonging to the same subject, and have only a complex and confused notion of the whole: such also would be our notions of the objects of sense, if we had not superior powers of understanding, by which we can analyze the complex object, abstract every particular attribute from the rest, and form a distinct conception of it.

So that it is not by the senses immediately, but rather by the powers of analyzing and abstraction, that we get the most simple, and the most distinct no-

tions even of the objects of sense. This will be more
fully explained in another place.

4thly, There remains another mistake concerning
conception, which deserves to be noticed. It is, that
our conception of things is a test of their possibility, so
that, what we can distinctly conceive, we may conclude to be possible; and of what is impossible, we
can have no conception.

This opinion has been held by philosophers for
more than an hundred years, without contradiction or
dissent, as far as I know ; and if it be an error. it may
be of some use to inquire into its origin, and the
causes that it has been so generally received as a maxim, whose truth could not be brought into doubt.

One of the fruitless questions agitated among the
scholastic philosophers in the dark ages was, What is
the criterion of truth? as if men could have any other
way to distinguish truth from error, but by the right
use of that power of judging which God has given
them.

Des Cartes endeavoured to put an end to this controversy, by making it a fundamental principle in
his system, that whatever we clearly and distinctly
perceive, is true.

To understand this principle of Des Cartes, it must
be observed, that he gave the name of perception
to every power of the human understanding ; and
in explaining this very maxim, he tells us, that sense,
imagination, and pure intellection, are only different
modes of perceiving, and so the maxim was understood by all his followers.

The learned Dr. Cudworth seems also to have adopted this principle. "The criterion of true knowledge,
says he, is only to be looked for in our knowledge
and conceptions themselves : for the entity of all
theoretical truth is nothing else but clear intelligi-

bility, and whatever is clearly conceived is an entity
and a truth; but that which is false, Divine power
itself cannot make it to be clearly and distinctly
understood. A falsehood can never be clearly conceived or apprehended to be true." Etern. and Immut.
Morality, p. 172, &c.

This Cartesian maxim seems to me to have led the
way to that now under consideration, which seems to
have been adopted as the proper correction of the former. When the authority of Des Cartes declined,
men began to see that we may clearly and distinctly
conceive what is not true, but thought, that our conception, though not in all cases a test of truth, might
be a test of possibility.

This indeed seems to be a necessary consequence of
the received doctrine of ideas; it being evident, that
there can be no distinct image, either in the mind or
any where else, of that which is impossible. The ambiguity of the word *conceive*, which we observed, Essay
I. chap. 1. and the common phraseology of saying *we
cannot conceive such a thing*, when we would signify
that we think it impossible, might likewise contribute
to the reception of this doctrine.

But whatever was the origin of this opinion, it
seems to prevail universally, and to be received as a
maxim.

"The bare having an idea of the proposition proves
the thing not to be impossible; for of an impossible
proposition there can be no idea." Dr. Sam. Clarke.

" Of that which neither does nor can exist we can
have no idea." Lord Bolingbroke.

"The measure of impossibility to us is inconceiv-
ableness, that of which we can have no idea, but
that reflecting upon it, it appears to be nothing, we
pronounce to be impossible." Abernethy.

"In every idea is implied the possibility of the existence of its object, nothing being clearer than that

there can be no idea of an impossibility, or conception of what cannot exist." Dr. Price.

"Impossibile est cujus nullam notionem formare possumus ; possibile e contra, cui aliqua respondet notio." Wolfii Ontolog.

"It is an established maxim in metaphysics, that whatever the mind conceives, includes the idea of possible existence, or, in other words, that nothing we imagine is absolutely impossible." D. Hume.

It were easy to muster up many other respectable authorities for this maxim, and I have never found one that called it in question.

If the maxim be true in the extent which the famous Wolfius has given it, in the passage above quoted, we shall have a short road to the determination of every question about the possibility or impossibility of things. We need only look into our own breast, and that, like the Urim and Thummim, will give an infallible answer. If we can conceive the thing, it is possible : if not, it is impossible. And surely every man may know whether he can conceive what is affirmed or not.

Other philosophers have been satisfied with one half of the maxim of Wolfius. They say, that whatever we can conceive is possible ; but they do not say, that whatever we cannot conceive is impossible.

I cannot help thinking even this to be a mistake, which philosophers have been unwarily led into, from the causes before mentioned. My reasons are these.

1st, Whatever is said to be possible or impossible is expressed by a proposition. Now, what is it to conceive a proposition? I think it is no more than to understand distinctly its meaning. I know no more that can be meant by simple apprehension or conception, when applied to a proposition. The axiom, therefore, amounts to this : every proposition, of which you understand the meaning distinctly, is possible. I am persuaded, that I understand as distinctly the meaning of this proposition, *Any two sides of a triangle are together equal to the third*, as of this, *Any two sides of a triangle are together greater than the third ;* yet the first of these is impossible.

Perhaps it will be said, that though you understand the meaning of the impossible proposition, you cannot suppose or conceive it to be true.

Here we are to examine the meaning of the phrases of *supposing* and *conceiving* a proposition to be true. I can certainly suppose it to be true, because I can draw consequences from it which I find to be impossible, as well as the proposition itself.

If by conceiving it to be true be meant giving some degree of assent to it, however small, this, I confess, I cannot do. But will it be said, that every proposition to which I can give any degree of assent is possible? This contradicts experience, and therefore the maxim cannot be true in this sense.

Sometimes, when we say that *we cannot conceive a thing to be true,* we mean by that expression that *we judge it to be impossible.* In this sense, I cannot, indeed, conceive it to be true, that two sides of a triangle are equal to the third. I judge it to be impossible. If, then, we understand in this sense that maxim, that nothing we can conceive is impossible, the meaning will be, that nothing is impossible which we judge to be possible. But does it not often happen, that what one man judges to be possible, another man judges to be impossible? The maxim, therefore, is not true in this sense.

I am not able to find any other meaning of *conceiving a proposition,* or of *conceiving it to be true,* besides these I have mentioned. I know nothing that can be meant by having the idea of a proposition, but either the understanding its meaning, or the judging of its truth. I can understand a proposition that is false or impossible, as well as one that is true or possible ; and I find that men have contradictory judgments about what is possible or impossible, as well as about other things. In what sense then can it be said, that the having an idea of a proposition gives certain evidence that it is possible?

If it be said, that the idea of a proposition is an image of it in the mind ; I think indeed there cannot be a distinct image either in the mind, or elsewhere, of that which is impossible : but what is meant by the image of a proposition I am not able to comprehend, and I shall be glad to be informed.

2dly, Every proposition, that is necessarily true, stands opposed to a contradictory proposition that is impossible; and he that conceives one, conceives both. Thus a man who believes that two and three necessarily make five, must believe it to be impossible that two and three should not make five. He conceives both propositions when he believes one. Every proposition carries its contradictory in its bosom, and both are conceived at the same time. "It is confessed, says Mr. Hume, that in all cases where we dissent from any person, we conceive both sides of the question, but we can believe only one." From this it certainly follows, that when we dissent from any person about a necessary proposition, we conceive one that is impossible ; yet I know no philosopher who has made so much use of the maxim, that whatever we conceive is possible, as Mr. Hume. A great part of his peculiar tenets is built upon it ; and if it is true, they must be true. But he did not perceive, that in the passage now quoted, the truth of which is evident, he contradicts it himself.

3dly, Mathematicians have, in many cases, proved some things to be possible and others to be im-

possible, which, without demonstration, would not have
been believed; yet I have never found that any mathematician has attempted to prove a thing to be possible,
because it can be conceived; or impossible, because it
cannot be conceived. Why is not this maxim applied
to determine whether it is possible to square the circle?
a point about which very eminent mathematicians have
differed. It is easy to conceive, that in the infinite series of numbers, and intermediate fractions, some one
number, integral, or fractional, may bear the same ratio to another, as the side of a square bears to its diagonal; yet, however conceivable this may be, it may
be demonstrated to be impossible.

4thly, Mathematicians often require us to conceive
things that are impossible, in order to prove them to be
so. This is the case in all their demonstrations, *ad absurdum*. Conceive, says Euclid, a right line drawn
from one point of the circumference of a circle to
another, to fall without the circle; I conceive this, I
reason from it, until I come to a consequence that is
manifestly absurd; and from thence conclude, that the
thing which I conceived is impossible.

Having said so much to show, that our power of conceiving a proposition is no criterion of its possibility
or impossibility, I shall add a few observations on the
extent of our knowledge of this kind.

1st, There are many propositions which, by the faculties God has given us, we judge to be necessary, as
well as true. All mathematical propositions are of this
kind, and many others. The contradictories of such
propositions must be impossible. Our knowledge,
therefore, of what is impossible, must at least be as extensive as our knowledge of necessary truth.

2dly, By our senses, by memory, by testimony, and
by other means, we know many things to be true, which
do not appear to be necessary. But whatever is true, is

possible. Our knowledge, therefore, of what is possible, must at least extend as far as our knowledge of truth.

3dly, If a man pretends to determine the possibility or impossibility of things beyond these limits, let him bring proof. I do not say that no such proof can be brought. It has been brought in many cases, particularly in mathematics. But I say, that his being able to conceive a thing, is no proof that it is possible. Mathematics afford many instances of impossibilities in the nature of things, which no man would have believed, if they had not been strictly demonstrated. Perhaps, if we were able to reason demonstratively in other subjects, to as great extent as in mathematics, we might find many things to be impossible, which we conclude, without hesitation, to be possible.

It is possible, you say, that God might have made an universe of sensible and rational creatures, into which neither natural nor moral evil should ever enter. It may be so, for what I know : but how do you know that it is possible? That you can conceive it, I grant ; but this is no proof. I cannot admit, as an argument, or even as a pressing difficulty, what is grounded on the supposition that such a thing is possible, when there is no good evidence that it is possible, and, for any thing we know, it may in the nature of things be impossible.

CHAP. IV.

OF THE TRAIN OF THOUGHT IN THE MIND.

EVERY man is conscious of a succession of thoughts which pass in his mind while he is awake, even when they are not excited by external objects.

The mind on this account may be compared to liquor in a state of fermentation. When it is not in this state, being once at rest, it remains at rest, until it is moved by some external impulse. But, in the state of fermentation, it has some cause of motion in itself, which, even when there is no impulse from without, suffers it not to be at rest a moment, but produces a constant motion, an ebullition, while it continues to ferment.

There is surely no similitude between motion and thought; but there is an analogy, so obvious to all men, that the same words are often applied to both; and many modifications of thought have no name but such as is borrowed from the modifications of motion. Many thoughts are excited by the senses. The causes or occasions of these may be considered as external: but when such external causes do not operate upon us, we continue to think from some internal cause. From the constitution of the mind itself there is a constant ebullition of thought, a constant intestine motion; not only of thoughts barely speculative, but of sentiments, passions and affections, which attend them.

This continued succession of thought has, by modern philosophers, been called the *imagination*. I think it was formerly called the *fancy*, or the *phantasy*. If the old name be laid aside, it were to be wished that it had got a name less ambiguous than that of imagination, a name which had two or three meanings besides.

It is often called the *train of ideas.* This may lead one to think, that it is a train of bare conceptions; but this would surely be a mistake. It is made up of many other operations of mind, as well as of conceptions, or ideas.

Memory, judgment, reasoning, passions, affections and purposes, in a word, every operation of the mind excepting those of sense, is exerted occasionally in this train of thought, and has its share as an ingredient: so that we must take the word *idea* in a very extensive sense, if we make the train of our thoughts to be only a train of ideas.

To pass from the name, and consider the thing, we may observe, that the trains of thought in the mind are of two kinds; they are either such as flow spontaneously, like water from a fountain, without any exertion of a governing principle to arrange them; or they are regulated and directed by an active effort of the mind, with some view and intention.

Before we consider these in their order, it is proper to emise, that these two kinds, however distinct in their nature, are for the most part mixed, in persons awake and come to years of understanding.

On the one hand, we are rarely so vacant of all project and design, as to let our thoughts take their own course, without the least check or direction: or if at any time we should be in this state, some object will present itself, which is too interesting not to engage the attention, and rouse the active or contemplative powers that were at rest.

On the other hand, when a man is giving the most intense application to any speculation, or to any scheme of conduct, when he wills to exclude every thought that is foreign to his present purpose, such thoughts will often impertinently intrude upon him, in spite of his endeavours to the contrary, and occupy, by a kind of violence, some part of the time destined to another purpose. One man may have the command of his thoughts more than another man, and the same man more at one time than at another. But I apprehend, in the best trained mind, the thoughts will sometimes be restive, sometimes capricious and self-willed, when we wish to have them most under command.

It has been observed very justly, that we must not ascribe to the mind the power of calling up any thought at pleasure, because such a call or volition supposes that thought to be already in the mind; for otherwise, how should it be the object of volition? As this must be granted on the one hand, so it is no less certain on the other, that a man has a considerable power in regulating and disposing his own thoughts. Of this every man is conscious, and I can no more doubt of it, than I can doubt whether I think at all.

We seem to treat the thoughts that present themselves to the fancy in crowds, as a great man treats those that attend his levee. They are all ambitious of his attention; he goes round the circle, bestowing a bow upon one, a smile upon another; asks a short question of a third; while a fourth is honoured with a particular conference; and the greater part have no particular mark of attention, but go as they came. It is true, he can give no mark of his attention to those who were not there, but he has a sufficient number for making a choice and distinction.

In like manner, a number of thoughts present themselves to the fancy spontaneously; but if we pay no attention to them, nor hold any conference with them, they pass with the crowd, and are immediately forgotten, as if they had never appeared. But those to which we think proper to pay attention, may be stopped, examined, and arranged, for any particular purpose we have in view.

It may likewise be observed, that a train of thought, which was at first composed by application and judgment, when it has been often repeated, and becomes familiar. will present itself spontaneously. Thus when a man has composed an air in music, so as to please his own ear; after he has played, or sung it often, the notes will arrange themselves in just order; and it requires no effort to regulate their succession.

Thus we see, that the fancy is made up of trains of thinking ; some of which are spontaneous, others studied and regulated, and the greater part are mixed of both kinds, and take their denomination from that which is most prevalent: and that a train of thought, which at first was studied and composed, may by habit present itself spontaneously. Having premised these things, let us return to those trains of thought which are spontaneous, which must be first in the order of nature.

When the work of the day is over, and a man lies down to relax his body and mind, he cannot cease from thinking, though he desires it. Something occurs to his fancy; that is followed by another thing, and so his thoughts are carried on from one object to another, until sleep closes the scene.

In this operation of the mind, it is not one faculty only that is employed; there are many that join together in its production. Sometimes the transactions of the day are brought upon the stage, and acted over again, as it were, upon this theatre of the imagination. In this case, memory surely acts the most considerable part, since the scenes exhibited are not fictions, but realities, which we remember; yet in this case the memory does not act alone, other powers are employed, and attend upon their proper objects. The transactions remembered will be more or less interesting ; and we cannot then review our own conduct, nor that of others, without passing some judgment upon it. This we approve, that we disapprove. This elevates, that humbles and depresses us. Persons that are not absolutely indifferent to us, can hardly appear even to the imagination, without some friendly or unfriendly emotion. We judge and reason about things, as well as persons in such reveries. We remember what a man said and did; from this we pass to his designs, and to his general character, and frame some hypothesis to make the whole consistent. Such trains of thought we may call historical.

There are others which we may call romantic, in which the plot is formed by the creative power of fancy, without any regard to what did or will happen. In these also, the powers of judgment, taste, moral sentiment, as well as the passions and affections, come in and take a share in the execution.

In these scenes, the man himself commonly acts a very distinguished part, and seldom does any thing which he cannot approve. Here the miser will be generous, the coward brave, and the knave honest. Mr. Addison, in the Spectator, calls this play of the fancy, *castle building*.

The young politician, who has turned his thoughts to the affairs of government, becomes in his imagination a minister of state. He examines every spring and wheel of the machine of government with the nicest eye, and the most exact judgment. He finds a proper remedy for every disorder of the commonwealth, quickens trade and manufactures by salutary laws, encourages arts and sciences, and makes the nation happy at home, and respected abroad. He feels

the reward of his good administration, in that self approbation which attends it, and is happy in acquiring, by his wise and patriotic conduct, the blessings
of the present age, and the praises of those that are to
come.

It is probable, that, upon the stage of imagination,
more great exploits have been performed in every age,
than have been upon the stage of life from the beginning of the world. An innate desire of self approbation is undoubtedly a part of the human constitution. It is a powerful spur to wo thy conduct, and
is intended as such by the Author of our being. A
man cannot be easy or happy, unless this desire be in
some measure gratified. While he conceives himself
worthless and base, he can relish no enjoyment. The
humiliating, mortifying sentiment must be removed,
and this natural desire of self approbation will either
produce a noble effort to acquire real worth, which is
its proper direction, or it will lead into some of those
arts of self deceit, which create a false opinion of
worth.

A castle builder, in the fictitious scenes of his fancy,
will figure, not according to his real character, but
according to the highest opinion he has been able to
form of himself, and perhaps far beyond that opinion.
For in those imaginary conflicts, the passions easily
yield to reason, and a man exerts the noblest efforts
of virtue and magnanimity, with the same ease, as, in
his dreams, he flies through the air, or plunges to the
bottom of the ocean.

The romantic scenes of fancy are most commonly
the occupation of young minds, not yet so deeply engaged in life as to have their thoughts taken up by its
real cares and business.

Those active powers of the mind, which are most
luxuriant by constitution, or have been most cherished

by education, impatient to exert themselves, hurry the thought into scenes that give them play; and the boy commences in imagination, according to the bent of his mind, a general or a statesman, a poet or an orator.

When the fair ones become castle builders, they use different materials; and while the young soldier is carried into the field of Mars, where he pierces the thickest squadrons of the enemy, despising death in all its forms, the gay and lovely nymph, whose heart has never felt the tender passion, is transported into a brilliant assembly, where she draws the attention of every eye, and makes an impression on the noblest heart.

But no sooner has Cupid's arrow found its way into her own heart, than the whole scenery of her imagination is changed. Balls and assemblies have now no charms. Woods and groves, the flowery bank, and the crystal fountain, are the scenes she frequents in imagination. She becomes an Arcadian shepherdess, feeding her flock beside that of her Strephon, and wants no more to complete her happiness.

In a few years the love-sick maid is transformed into the solicitous mother. Her smiling offspring play around her. She views them with a parent's eye. Her imagination immediately raises them to manhood, and brings them forth upon the stage of life. One son makes a figure in the army, another shines at the bar; her daughters are happily disposed of in marriage, and bring new alliances to the family. Her children's children rise up before her, and venerate her gray hairs.

Thus, the spontaneous sallies of fancy are as various as the cares and fears, the desires and hopes, of man.

Quicquid agunt homines, votum, timor, ira, voluptas,
Gaudia, discursus :

These fill up the scenes of fancy, as well as the page of the satyrist.   Whatever possesses the heart makes occasional excursions into the imagination, and acts such scenes upon that theatre as are agreeable to the prevailing passion.   The man of traffic, who has committed a rich cargo to the inconstant ocean, follows it in his thought; and, according as his hopes or his fears prevail, he is haunted with storms, and rocks, and shipwreck; or he makes a happy and a lucrative voyage; and before his vessel has lost sight of land, he has disposed of the profit which she is to bring at her return.

The poet is carried into the Elysian fields, where he converses with the ghosts of Homer and Orpheus. The philosopher makes a tour through the planetary system, or goes down to the centre of the earth, and examines its various strata.   In the devout man, likewise, the great objects that possess his heart often play in his imagination; sometimes he is transported to the regions of the blessed, whence he looks down with pity upon the folly and the pageantry of human life; or he prostrates himself before the throne of the Most High, with devout veneration; or he converses with celestial spirits about the natural and moral kingdom of God, which he now sees only by a faint light, but hopes hereafter to view with a steadier and brighter ray.

In persons come to maturity, there is even in these spontaneous sallies of fancy, some arrangement of thought; and I conceive that it will be readily allowed, that in those who have the greatest stock of knowledge, and the best natural parts, even the spontaneous movements of fancy will be the most regular and connected.   They have an order, connection, and unity,

by which they are no less distinguished from the dreams
of one asleep, or the ravings of one delirious on the one
hand, than from the finished productions of art on the
other.

How is this regular arrangement brought about ? It
has all the marks of judgment and reason, yet it seems
to go before judgment, and to spring forth spontaneously.

Shall we believe with Leibnitz, that the mind was
originally formed like a watch wound up ; and that all
its thoughts, purposes, passions and actions, are effected by the gradual evolution of the original spring
of the machine, and succeed each other in order, as
necessarily as the motions and pulsations of a watch?

If a child of three or four years, were put to account for the phenomena of a watch, he would conceive that there is a little man within the watch, or
some other little animal that beats continually, and
produces the motion.   Whether the hypothesis of this
young philosopher in turning the watch spring into a
man, or that of the German philosopher in turning a
man into a watch spring, be the most rational, seems
hard to determine.

To account for the regularity of our first thoughts,
from motions of animal spirits, vibrations of nerves, attractions of ideas, or from any other unthinking cause,
whether mechanical or contingent, seems equally irra-
tional.

If we be not able to distinguish the strongest marks
of thought and design from the effects of mechanism
or contingency, the consequence will be very melancholy : for it must necessarily follow, that we
have no evidence of thought in any of our fellow men,
nay, that we have no evidence of thought or design
in the structure and government of the universe.   If a
good period or sentence was ever produced without

having had any judgment previously employed about it,
why not an Iliad or Eneid? They differ only in less
and more; and we should do injustice to the philosopher of Laputa, in laughing at his project of making
poems by the turning of a wheel, if a concurrence of
unthinking causes may produce a rational train of
thought.

It is, therefore, in itself highly probable, to say no
more, that whatsoever is regular and rational in a train
of thought, which presents itself spontaneously to a
man's fancy, without any study, is a copy of what had
been before composed by his own rational powers, or
those of some other person.

We certainly judge so in similar cases.   Thus, in a
book I find a train of thinking, which has the marks
of knowledge and judgment.   I ask how it was produced?   It is printed in a book.   This does not satisfy
me, because the book has no knowledge nor reason.   I
am told that a printer printed it, and a compositor set
the types.   Neither does this satisfy me.   These causes
perhaps knew very little of the subject.   There must
be a prior cause of the composition.   It was printed
from a manuscript.   True.   But the manuscript is as
ignorant as the printed book.   The manuscript was
written or dictated by a man of knowledge and judgment.   This, and this only, will satisfy a man of common understanding; and it appears to him extremely
ridiculous to believe, that such a train of thinking could
originally be produced by any cause that neither reasons nor thinks.

Whether such a train of thinking be printed in a
book, or printed, so to speak, in his mind, and issue
spontaneously from his fancy, it must have been composed with judgment by himself, or by some other rational being.

This, I think, will be confirmed by tracing the progress of the human fancy as far back as we are able.

We have not the means of knowing how the fancy is employed in infants. Their time is divided between the employment of their senses and sound sleep: so that there is little time left for imagination, and the materials it has to work upon are probably very scanty. A few days after they are born, sometimes a few hours, we see them smile in their sleep. But what they smile at, is not easy to guess; for they do not smile at any thing they see, when awake, for some months after they are born. It is likewise common to see them move their lips in sleep, as if they were sucking.

These things seem to discover some working of the imagination; but there is no reason to think that there is any regular train of thought in the mind of infants.

By a regular train of thought, I mean that which has a beginning, a middle, and an end, an arrangement of its parts, according to some rule, or with some intention. Thus, the conception of a design, and of the means of executing it; the conception of a whole, and the number and order of the parts. These are instances of the most simple trains of thought that can be called regular.

Man has undoubtedly a power, whether we call it taste or judgment, is not of any consequence in the present argument, whereby he distinguishes between a composition, and a heap of materials ; between a house, for instance, and a heap of stones ; between a sentence, and a heap of words ; between a picture, and a heap of colours. It does not appear to me that children have any regular trains of thought until this power begins to operate. Those who are born such idiots as never to show any signs of this power, show as little any signs of regularity of thought.   It seems, therefore, that this power is connected with all regular trains of thought, and may be the cause of them.

Such trains of thought discover themselves in children about two years of age.   They can then give attention to the operations of older children in making their little houses, and ships, and other such things, in imitation of the works of men.   They are then capable of understanding a little of language, which shows both a regular train of thinking, and some degree of abstraction.   I think we may perceive a distinction between the faculties of children of two or three years of age, and those of the most sagacious brutes.   They can then perceive design and regularity in the works of others, especially of older children; their little minds are fired with the discovery; they are eager to imitate it, and never at rest till they can exhibit something of the same kind.

When a child first learns by imitation to do something that requires design, how does he exult! Pythagoras was not more happy in the discovery of his famous theorem.   He seems then first to reflect upon himself, and to swell with self esteem.   His eyes sparkle.   He is impatient to show his performance to all about him, and thinks himself entitled to their applause.   He is applauded by all, and feels the same emotion from this applause, as a Roman consul did from a triumph.   He has now a consciousness of some worth in himself.   He assumes a superiority over those who are not so wise; and pays respect to those who are wiser than himself.   He attempts something else, and is every day reaping new laurels.

As children grow up, they are delighted with tales, with childish games, with designs and stratagems: every thing of this kind stores the fancy with a new regular train of thought, which becomes familiar by repetition, so that one part draws the whole after it in the imagination.

The imagination of a child, like the hand of a painter, is long employed in copying the works of others, before it attempts any invention of its own.

The power of invention is not yet brought forth, but is coming forward, and, like the bud of a tree, is ready to burst its integuments, when some accident aids its eruption.

There is no power of the understanding that gives so much pleasure to the owner as that of invention : whether it be employed in mechanics, in science, in the conduct of life, in poetry, in wit, or in the fine arts. One who is conscious of it, acquires thereby a worth and importance in his own eye which he had not before. He looks upon himself as one who formerly lived upon the bounty and gratuity of others, but who has now acquired some property of his own. When this power begins to be felt in the young mind, it has the grace of novelty added to its other charms, and, like the youngest child of the family, is caressed beyond all the rest.

We may be sure, therefore, that as soon as children are conscious of this power, they will exercise it in such ways as are suited to their age, and to the objects they are employed about. This gives rise to innumerable new associations, and regular trains of thought, which make the deeper impression upon the mind, as they are its exclusive property.

I am aware that the power of invention is distributed among men more unequally than almost any other. When it is able to produce any thing that is interesting to mankind, we call it genius; a talent which is the lot of very few. But there is perhaps a lower kind, or lower degree of invention that is more common. However this may be, it must be allowed, that the power of invention in those who have it, will produce many new regular trains of thought; and these being expressed in works of art, in writing, or in discourse, will be copied by others.

Thus I conceive the minds of children, as soon as they have judgment to distinguish what is regular, orderly, and connected, from a mere medley of thought, are furnished with regular trains of thinking by these means.

1st, And chiefly, by copying what they see in the works and in the discourse of others.   Man is the most imitative of all animals; he not only imitates with intention, and purposely, what he thinks has any grace or beauty, but even without intention, he is led by a kind of instinct, which it is difficult to resist, into the modes of speaking, thinking, and acting, which he has been accustomed to see in his early years. The more children see of what is regular and beautiful in what is presented to them, the more they are led to observe and to imitate it.

This is the chief part of their stock, and descends to them by a kind of tradition from those who came before them; and we shall find, that the fancy of most men is furnished from those they have conversed with, as well as their religion, language, and manners.

2dly, By the additions or innovations that are properly their own, these will be greater or less, in proportion to their study and invention; but in the bulk of mankind are not very considerable.

Every profession, and every rank in life, has a manner of thinking, and turn of fancy that is proper to it; by which it is characterized in comedies and works of humour.   The bulk of men of the same nation, of the same rank, and of the same occupation, are cast as it were in the same mould.   This mould itself changes gradually, but slowly, by new inventions, by intercourse with strangers, or by other accidents.

The condition of man requires a longer infancy and youth than that of other animals ; for this reason, among others, that almost every station in civil society requires a multitude of regular trains of thought, to be not only acquired, but to be made so familiar by frequent repetition, as to present themselves spontaneously, when there is occasion for them.

The imagination even of men of good parts never serves them readily but in things wherein it has been much exercised. A minister of state holds a conference with a foreign ambassador, with no greater emotion than a professor in a college prelects to his audience. The imagination of each presents to him what the occasion requires to be said, and how. Let them change places, and both would find themselves at a loss.

The habits which the human mind is capable of acquiring by exercise are wonderful in many instances ; in none more wonderful, than in that versatility of imagination which a well bred man acquires, by being much exercised in the various scenes of life. In the morning he visits a friend in affliction. Here his imagination brings forth from its store every topic of consolation ; every thing that is agreeable to the laws of friendship and sympathy, and nothing that is not so. From thence he drives to the minister's levee, where imagination readily suggests what is proper to be said or replied to every man, and in what manner, according to the degree of acquaintance or familiarity, of rank or dependence, of opposition or concurrence of interests, of confidence or distrust, that is between them. Nor does all this employment hinder him from carrying on some design with much artifice, and en-

deavouring to penetrate into the views of others
through the closest disguises. From the levee he
goes to the House of Commons, and speaks upon the
affairs of the nation; from thence to a ball or assembly, and entertains the ladies. His imagination puts
on the friend, the courtier, the patriot, the fine gentleman, with more ease than we put off one suit and
put on another.

This is the effect of training and exercise. For a
man of equal parts and knowledge, but unaccustomed
to those scenes of public life, is quite disconcerted when
first brought into them. His thoughts are put to flight,
and he cannot rally them.

There are feats of imagination to be learned by application and practice, as wonderful as the feats of bal-
ancers and rope dancers, and often as useless.

When a man can make a hundred verses standing
on one foot, or play three or four games at chess at
the same time without seeing the board, it is probable
he has spent his life in acquiring such a feat. However, such unusual phenomena show what habits of
imagination may be acquired.

When such habits are acquired and perfected, they
are exercised without any laborious effort; like the
habit of playing upon an instrument of music. There
are innumerable motions of the fingers upon the stops
or keys, which must be directed in one particular train
or succession. There is only one arrangement of those
motions that is right, while there are ten thousand that
are wrong, and would spoil the music. The musician
thinks not in the least of the arrangement of those motions; he has a distinct idea of the tune, and wills to
play it. The motions of the fingers arrange themselves so as to answer his intention.

In like manner, when a man speaks upon a subject
with which he is acquainted, there is a certain arrange-

ment of his thoughts and words necessary to make his discourse sensible, pertinent, and grammatical. In every sentence, there are more rules of grammar, logic, and rhetoric, that may be transgressed, than there are words and letters. He speaks without thinking of any of those rules, and yet observes them all, as if they were all in his eye.

This is a habit so similar to that of a player on an instrument, that I think both must be got in the same way, that is, by much practice, and the power of habit.

When a man speaks well and methodically upon a subject without study, and with perfect ease, I believe we may take it for granted that his thoughts run in a beaten track. There is a mould in his mind, which has been formed by much practice, or by study, for this very subject, or for some other so similar and analogous, that his discourse falls into this mould with ease, and takes its form from it.

Hitherto we have considered the operations of fancy that are either spontaneous, or at least require no laborious effort to guide and direct them, and have endeavoured to account for that degree of regularity and arrangement which is found even in them. The natural powers of judgment and invention, the pleasure that always attends the exercise of those powers, the means we have of improving them by imitation of others, and the effect of practice and habits, seems to me sufficiently to account for this phenomenon, without supposing any unaccountable attractions of ideas by which they arrange themselves.

But we are able to direct our thoughts in a certain course, so as to perform a destined task.

Every work of art has its model framed in the imagination. Here the Iliad of Homer, the Republic of Plato, the Principia of Newton, were fabricated.

Shall we believe, that those works took the form in which they now appear of themselves? That the sentiments, the manners, and the passions, arranged themselves at once in the mind of Homer, so as to form the Iliad? Was there no more effort in the composition, than there is in telling a well known tale, or singing a favourite song? This cannot be believed.

Granting that some happy thought first suggested the design of singing the wrath of Achilles; yet, surely, it was a matter of judgment and choice where the narration should begin, and where it should end.

Granting that the fertility of the poet's imagination suggested a variety of rich materials; was not judgment necessary to select what was proper, to reject what was improper, to arrange the materials into a just composition, and to adapt them to each other, and to the design of the whole?

No man can believe that Homer's ideas, merely by certain sympathies and antipathies, by certain attractions and repulsions inherent in their natures, arranged themselves according to the most perfect rules of epic poetry; and Newton's, according to the rules of mathematical composition.

I should sooner believe that the poet, after he invoked his muse, did nothing at all but listen to the song of the goddess. Poets indeed, and other artists, must make their works appear natural; but nature is the perfection of art, and there can be no just imitation of nature without art. When the building is finished, the rubbish, the scaffolds, the tools and engines, are carried out of sight; but we know it could not have been reared without them.

The train of thinking, therefore, is capable of being guided and directed, much in the same manner as the horse we ride. The horse has his strength, his agility, and his mettle in himself; he has been taught certain movements, and many useful habits that make him more subservient to our purposes, and obedient to our will; but to accomplish a journey, he must be directed by the rider.

In like manner, fancy has its original powers, which are very different in different persons; it has likewise more regular motions, to which it has been trained by a long course of discipline and exercise; and by which it may *extempore,* and without much effort, produce things that have a considerable degree of beauty, regularity, and design.

But the most perfect works of design are never extemporary. Our first thoughts are reviewed; we place them at a proper distance; examine every part, and take a complex view of the whole. By our critical faculties, we perceive this part to be redundant, that deficient; here is a want of nerves, there a want of delicacy; this is obscure, that too diffuse; things are marshalled anew, according to a second and more deliberate judgment; what was deficient, is supplied; what was dislocated, is put in joint; redundancies are lopped off, and the whole polished.

Though poets of all artists make the highest claim to inspiration, yet if we believe Horace a competent judge, no production in that art can have merit, which has not cost such labour as this in the birth.

> Vos O!
> Pompilius sanguis; carmen reprehendite quod non
> Multa dies, et multa litura coercuit, atque
> Perfectum decies non castigavit ad unguem.

The conclusion I would draw from all that has been said upon this subject is, that every thing that is regular in that train of thought, which we call fancy, or imagination, from the little designs and reveries of children, to the grandest productions of human genius, was originally the offspring of judgment or taste, applied with some effort greater or less. What one person composed with art and judgment, is imitated by another with great ease. What a man himself at first composed with pains, becomes by habit so familiar, as to offer itself spontaneously to his fancy afterward : but nothing that is regular, was ever at first conceived, without design, attention and care.

I shall now make a few reflections upon a theory which has been applied to account for this successive train of thought in the mind. It was hinted by Mr. Hobbes, but has drawn more attention since it was distinctly explained by Mr. Hume.

That author thinks that the train of thought in the mind is owing to a kind of attraction which ideas have for other ideas that bear certain relations to them. He thinks the complex ideas, which are the common subjects of our thoughts and reasoning, are owing to the same cause. The relations which produce this attraction of ideas, he thinks, are these three only, to wit, causation, contiguity in time or place, and similitude. He asserts, that these are the only general principles that unite ideas. And having, in another place, occasion to take notice of contrariety as a principle of connection among ideas, in order to reconcile this to his system, he tells us gravely, that contrariety may perhaps be considered as a mixture of causation and resemblance. That ideas which have any of these three relations do mutually attract each other, so that one of them being presented to the fancy, the other is drawn along with it, this he seems to think an original property of the mind, or rather of the ideas, and therefore inexplicable.

1st, I observe with regard to this theory, that although it is true that the thought of any object is apt to lead us to the thought of its cause or effect, of things contiguous to it in time or place, or of things resembling it, yet this enumeration of the relations of things which are apt to lead us from one object to another, is very inaccurate.

The enumeration is too large upon his own principles; but it is by far too scanty in reality. Causation, according to his philosophy, implies nothing more than a constant conjunction observed between the cause and the effect, and therefore contiguity must include causation, and his three principles of attraction are reduced to two.

But when we take all the three, the enumeration is in reality very incomplete. Every relation of things has a tendency, more or less, to lead the thought, in a thinking mind, from one to the other; and not only every relation, but every kind of contrariety and opposition. What Mr. Hume says, that contrariety may perhaps be considered as a mixture " of causation and resemblance," I can as little comprehend as if he had said that figure may perhaps be considered as a mixture of colour and sound.

Our thoughts pass easily from the end to the means; from any truth to the evidence on which it is founded, the consequences that may be drawn from it, or the use that may be made of it. From a part we are easily led to think of the whole, from a subject to its qualities, or from things related to the relation. Such transitions in thinking must have been made thousands of times by every man who thinks and reasons, and thereby become, as it were, beaten tracks for the imagination.

Not only the relations of objects to each other influence our train of thinking, but the relation they bear to the present temper and disposition of the mind; their relation to the habits we have acquired, whether moral or intellectual; to the company we have kept, and to the business in which we have been chiefly employed. The same event will suggest very different reflections to different persons, and to the same person at different times, according as he is in good or bad humour, as he is lively or dull, angry or pleased, melancholy or cheerful.

Lord Kaimes in his Elements of Criticism, and Dr. Gerard in his Essay on Genius, have given a much fuller and juster enumeration of the causes that influence our train of thinking, and I have nothing to add to what they have said on this subject.

2dly, Let us consider how far this attraction of ideas must be resolved into original qualities of human nature.

I believe the original principles of the mind, of which we can give no account, but that such is our constitution, are more in number than is commonly thought. But we ought not to multiply them without necessity.

That trains of thinking, which by frequent repetition have become familiar, should spontaneously offer themselves to our fancy, seems to require no other original quality but the power of habit.

In all rational thinking, and in all rational discourse, whether serious or facetious, the thought must have some relation to what went before. Every man, therefore, from the dawn of reason, must have been accustomed to a train of related objects. These please the understanding, and by custom become like beaten tracks which invite the traveller.

As far as it is in our power to give a direction to our thoughts, which it is, undoubtedly, in a great degree, they will be directed by the active principles common to men, by our appetites, our passions, our affections, our reason, and conscience. And that the trains of thinking in our minds are chiefly governed by these, according as one or another prevails at the time, every man will find in his experience.

If the mind is at any time vacant from every passion and desire, there are still some objects that are more acceptable to us than others. The facetious man is pleased with surprising similitudes or contrasts; the philosopher with the relations of things that are subservient to reasoning; the merchant with what tends to profit; and the politician with what may mend the state.

A good writer of comedy or romance can feign a train of thinking for any of the persons of his fable, which appears very natural, and is approved by the best judges. Now, what is it that entitles such a fiction to approbation? Is it that the author has given a nice attention to the relations of causation, contiguity, and similitude in the ideas? This, surely, is the least part of its merit. But the chief part consists in this, that it corresponds perfectly with the general character, the rank, the habits, the present situation and passions of the person. If this be a just way of judging in criticism, it follows necessarily, that the circumstances last mentioned have the chief influence in suggesting our trains of thought.

It cannot be denied, that the state of the body has an influence upon our imagination, according as a man is sober or drunk, as he is fatigued or refreshed. Crudities and indigestion are said to give uneasy dreams, and have probably a like effect upon the waking thoughts. Opium gives to some persons pleasing dreams, and pleasing imaginations when awake, and to others such as are horrible and distressing.

These influences of the body upon the mind can only be known by experience, and I believe we can give no account of them.

Nor can we, perhaps, give any reason why we must think without ceasing while we are awake. I believe we are likewise originally disposed, in imagination, to pass from any one object of thought to others that are contiguous to it in time or place. This, I think, may be observed in brutes and in idiots, as well as in children, before any habit can be acquired that might account for it. The sight of an object is apt to suggest to the imagination what has been seen or felt in conjunction with it, even when the memory of that conjunction is gone.

Such conjunctions of things influence not only the imagination, but the belief and the passions, especially in children and in brutes; and perhaps all that we call memory in brutes, is something of this kind.

They expect events in the same order and succession in which they happened before; and by this expectation, their actions and passions, as well as their thoughts, are regulated. A horse takes fright at the place where some object frightened him before. We are apt to conclude from this, that he remembers the former accident. But perhaps there is only an association formed in his mind between the place and the passion of fear, without any distinct remembrance.

Mr. Locke has given us a very good chapter upon the association of ideas; and by the examples he has given to illustrate this doctrine, I think it appears that very strong associations may be formed at once; not of ideas to ideas only, but of ideas to passions and emotions; and that strong associations are never formed at once, but when accompanied by some strong passion or emotion. I believe this must be resolved into the constitution of our nature.

Mr. Hume's opinion, that the complex ideas, which are the common objects of discourse and reasoning, are formed by those original attractions of ideas, to which he ascribes the train of thoughts in the mind, will come under consideration in another place.

To put an end to our remarks upon this theory of Mr. Hume, I think he has real merit in bringing this curious subject under the view of philosophers, and carrying it a certain length. But I see nothing in this theory that should hinder us from concluding that every thing in the trains of our thought, which bears the marks of judgment and reason, has been the product of judgment and reason previously exercised, either by the person himself at that or some former time, or by some other person. The attraction of ideas will be the same in a man's second thoughts upon any subject as in his first. Or if some change in his circumstances, or in the objects about him, should make any change in the attractions of his ideas, it is an equal chance whether the second be better than the first, or whether they be worse. But it is certain, that every man of judgment and taste will, upon a review, correct that train of thought which first presented itself. If the attractions of ideas are the sole causes of the regular arrangement of thought in the fancy, there is no use for judgment or taste in any composition, nor indeed any room for their operation.

There are other reflections of a more practical nature, and of higher importance, to which this subject leads.

I believe it will be allowed by every man, that our happiness or misery in life, that our improvement in any art or science which we profess, and that our improvement in real virtue and goodness, depend in a very great degree on the train of thinking, that occupies the mind both in our vacant and in our more serious hours. As far, therefore, as the direction of our thoughts is in our power, and that it is so in a great measure, cannot be doubted, it is of the last importance to give them that direction which is most subservient to those valuable purposes.

What enjoyment can he have worthy a man, whose imagination is occupied only about things low and base, and grovels in a narrow field of mean, unanimating and uninteresting objects, insensible to those finer and more delicate sentiments, and blind to those more enlarged and nobler views which elevate the soul, and make it conscious of its dignity.

How different from him, whose imagination, like an eagle in her flight, takes a wide prospect, and observes whatever it presents, that is new or beautiful, grand or important; whose rapid wing varies the scene every moment, carrying him sometimes through the fairy regions of wit and fancy, sometimes through the more regular and sober walks of science and philosophy.

The various objects which he surveys, according to their different degrees of beauty and dignity, raise in him the lively and agreeable emotions of taste. Illustrious human characters, as they pass in review, clothed with their moral qualities, touch his heart still more deeply. They not only awaken the sense of beauty, but excite the sentiment of approbation, and kindle the glow of virtue.

While he views what is truly great and glorious in human conduct, his soul catches divine flame, and burns with desire to emulate what it admires.

The human imagination is an ample theatre, upon which every thing in human life, good or bad, great or mean, laudable or base, is acted.

In children, and in some frivolous minds, it is a mere toy shop. And in some, who exercise their memory without their judgment, its furniture is made up of old scraps of knowledge, that are threadbare and worn out.

In some, this theatre is often occupied by ghastly superstition, with all her train of *gorgons, and hydras,*

and chimeras dire. Sometimes it is haunted with all
the infernal demons, and made the forge of plots, and
rapine, and murder. Here every thing that is black
and detestable is first contrived, and a thousand wicked
designs conceived that are never executed. Here too
the furies act their part, taking a severe, though secret
vengeance upon the self condemned criminal.

How happy is that mind, in which the light of real
knowledge dispels the phantoms of superstition; in
which the belief and reverence of a perfect, all governing Mind casts out all fear but the fear of acting wrong;
in which serenity and cheerfulness, innocence, humanity, and candour, guard the imagination against the en-
trance of every unhallowed intruder, and invite more
amiable and worthier guests to dwell!

There shall the muses, the graces, and the virtues,
fix their abode: for every thing that is great and worthy in human conduct must have been conceived in the
imagination before it was brought into act. And many
great and good designs have been formed there, which,
for want of power and opportunity, have proved abortive.

The man, whose imagination is occupied by these
guests, must be wise, he must be good, and he must be
happy.

ESSAY V.

OF ABSTRACTION.

───

CHAP. I.

OF GENERAL WORDS.

THE words we use in language are either general words, or proper names. Proper names are intended to signify one individual only. Such are the names of men, kingdoms, provinces, cities, rivers, and of every other creature of God, or work of man, which we choose to distinguish from all others of the kind, by a name appropriated to it. All the other words of language are general words, not appropriated to signify any one individual thing, but equally related to many.

Under general words, therefore, I comprehend, not only those which logicians call general terms; that is, such general words as may make the subject or the predicate of a proposition; but likewise their auxiliaries or accessories, as the learned Mr. Harris calls them ; such as prepositions, conjunctions, articles, which are all general words, though they cannot properly be called general terms.

In every language, rude or polished, general words make the greatest part, and proper names the least. Grammarians have reduced all words to eight or nine classes, which are called parts of speech. Of these there is only one, to wit, that of *nouns*, wherein proper names are found. All *pronouns, verbs, participles, adverbs, articles, prepositions, conjunctions,* and *interjections,* are general words. Of *nouns,* all *adjectives* are general words, and the greater part of *substantives.* Every substantive that has a plural number, is a general word ; for no proper name can have a plural number, because it signifies only one individual. In all the fifteen books of Euclid's Elements, there is not one word that is not general ; and the same may be said of many large volumes.

At the same time it must be acknowledged, that all the objects we perceive are individuals. Every object of sense, of memory, or of consciousness, is an individual object. All the good things we enjoy or desire, and all the evils we feel or fear, must come from individuals ; and I think we may venture to say, that every creature which God has made, in the heavens above, or in the earth beneath, or in the waters under the earth, is an individual.

How comes it to pass then, that in all languages, general words make the greatest part of the language, and proper names but a very small and inconsiderable part of it.

This seemingly strange phenomenon may, I think, be easily accounted for by the following observations.

First, Though there be a few individuals that are obvious to the notice of all men, and therefore have proper names in all languages ; such as the sun and moon. the earth and sea ; yet the greatest part of the things to which we think fit to give proper names are local; known perhaps to a village or to a neighbourhood, but unknown to the greater part of those who speak the same language, and to all the rest of mankind. The names of such things being confined to a corner, and having no names answering to them in other languages, are not accounted a part of the language, any more than the customs of a particular hamlet are accounted part of the law of the nation.

For this reason, there are but few proper names that belong to a language. It is next to be considered why there must be many general words in every language.

Secondly, It may be observed, that every individual object that falls within our view has various attributes; and it is by them that it becomes useful or hurtful to us. We know not the essence of any individual object; all the knowledge we can attain of it, is the knowledge of its attributes; its quantity, its various qualities, its various relations to other things, its place, its situation, and motions. It is by such attributes of things only that we can communicate our knowledge of them to others. By their attributes, our hopes or fears from them are regulated; and it is only by attention to their attributes that we can make them subservient to our ends; and therefore we give names to such attributes.

Now all attributes must from their nature be expressed by general words, and are so expressed in all languages. In the ancient philosophy, attributes in general were called by two names which express their nature. They were called *universals,* because they might' belong equally to many individuals, and are not confined to one; they were also called *predicables,* because whatever is predicated, that is, affirmed or denied of one subject, may be of more, and therefore is an universal, and expressed by a general word. A predicable therefore signifies the same thing as an attribute, with this difference only, that the first is Latin, the last English. The attributes we find either in the creatures of God, or in the works of men, are common to many individuals. We either find it to be so, or presume it may be so, and give them the same name in every subject to which they belong.

There are not only attributes belonging to individual subjects, but there are likewise attributes of attributes, which may be called secondary attributes. Most attributes are capable of different degrees, and different modifications, which must be expressed by general words.

Thus it is an attribute of many bodies to be moved; but motion may be in an endless variety of directions. It may be quick or slow, rectilineal or curvilineal; it may be equable, or accellerated, or retarded.

As all attributes, therefore, whether primary or secondary, are expressed by general words, it follows, that in every proposition we express in language, what is affirmed or denied of the subject of the proposition must be expressed by general words: and that the subject of the proposition may often be a general word, will appear from the next observation.

Thirdly, The same faculties by which we distinguish the different attributes belonging to the same subject, and give names to them, enables us likewise to observe, that many subjects agree in certain attributes, while they differ in others. By this means we are enabled to reduce individuals which are infinite, to a limited number of classes, which are called kinds and sorts; and in the scholastic language, *genera* and *species*.

Observing many individuals to agree in certain attributes, we refer them all to one class, and give a name

to the class. This name comprehends in its signification not one attribute only, but all the attributes which
distinguish that class; and by affirming this name of
any individual, we affirm it to have all the attributes
which characterize the class. Thus men, dogs, horses
elephants, are so many different classes of animals.
In like manner we marshal other substances, vegetable
and inanimate, into classes.

Nor is it only substances that we thus form into
classes. We do the same, with regard to qualities, relations, actions, affections, passions, and all other things.

When a class is very large, it is divided into subordinate classes in the same manner. The higher class
is called a *genus* or kind; the lower a *species* or sort of
the higher. Sometimes a species is still subdivided
into subordinate species; and this subdivision is carried on as far as is found convenient for the purpose of
language, or for the improvement of knowledge.

In this distribution of things into *genera* and *species*,
it is evident that the name of the species comprehends
more attributes than the name of the genus. The
species comprehends all that is in the genus, and those
attributes likewise which distinguish that species from
others belonging to the same genus; and the more
subdivisions we make, the names of the lower become
still the more comprehensive in their signification, but
the less extensive in their application to individuals.

Hence it is an axiom in logic, that the more extensive any general term is, it is the less comprehensive;
and on the contrary, the more comprehensive, the less
extensive. Thus, in the following series of subordinate general terms, animal, man, Frenchman, Parisian,
every subsequent term comprehends in its signification
all that is in the preceding, and sometimes more; and
every antecedent term extends to more individuals than
the subsequent.

Such divisions and subdivisions of things into *genera* and *species* with general names, are not confined to the learned and polished languages; they are found in those of the rudest tribes of mankind: from which we learn, that the invention and the use of general words, both to signify the attributes of things, and to signify the *genera* and *species* of things, is not a subtile invention of philosophers, but an operation which all men perform by the light of common sense. Philosophers may speculate about this operation, and reduce it to canons and aphorisms; but men of common undertsanding, without knowing any thing of the philosophy of it, can put it in practice; in like manner as they can see objects, and make use of their eyes, although they know nothing of the structure of the eye, or of the theory of vision.

Every genus, and every species of things, may be either the subject or the predicate of a proposition, nay, of innumerable propositions; for every attribute common to the genus or species may be affirmed of it; and the genus may be affirmed of every species, and both genus and species of every individual to which it extends.

Thus of man it may be affirmed, that he is an animal made up of body and mind; that he is of few days, and full of trouble; that he is capable of various improvements in arts, in knowledge, and in virtue. In a word, every thing common to the species may be affirmed of man; and of all such propositions, which are innumerable, man is the subject.

Again, of every nation and tribe, and of every individual of the human race that is, or was, or shall be, it may be affirmed that they are men. In all such propositions, which are innumerable, man is the predicate of the proposition.

We observed above an extension and a comprehension in general terms; and that in any subdivision of

things the name of the lowest species is most comprehensive, and that of the highest genus most extensive.
I would now observe, that, by means of such general
terms, there is also an extension and comprehension
of propositions, which is one of the noblest powers
of language, and fits it for expressing, with great
ease and expedition, the highest attainments in knowledge, of which the human understanding is capable.

When the predicate is a *genus* or a *species*, the proposition is more or less comprehensive, according as
the predicate is. Thus, when I say that this seal is
gold, by this single proposition, I affirm of it all the
properties which that metal is known to have. When
I say of any man that he is a mathematician, this ap-
pellation comprehends all the attributes that belong to
him as an animal, as a man, and as one who has studied
mathematics. When I say that the orbit of the planet
Mercury is an ellipsis, I thereby affirm of that orbit
all the properties which Apollonius and other Geo-
metricians have discovered, or may discover, of that
species of figure.

Again, when the subject of a proposition is a *genus*
or a *species*, the proposition is more or less extensive,
according as the subject is. Thus when I am taught,
that the three angles of a plane triangle are equal to
two right angles, this property extends to every species of plane triangle, and to every individual plane
triangle that did, or does, or can exist.

It is by means of such extensive and comprehensive propositions that human knowledge is condensed,
as it were, into a size adapted to the capacity of the
human mind, with great addition to its beauty, and
without any diminution of its distinctness and perspicuity.

General propositions in science may be compared
to the seed of a plant, which, according to some phi-

losophers, has not only the whole future plant enclosed within it, but the seeds of that plant, and the plants that shall spring from them through all future generations.

But the similitude falls short in this respect, that time and accidents, not in our power, must concur to disclose the contents of the seed, and bring them into our view; whereas the contents of a general proposition may be brought forth, ripened, and exposed to view at our pleasure, and in an instant.

Thus the wisdom of ages, and the most sublime theorems of science, may be laid up, like an Iliad in a nut shell, and transmitted to future generations. And this noble purpose of language can only be accomplished, by means of general words annexed to the divisions and subdivisions of things.

What has been said in this chapter, I think, is sufficient to show, that there can be no language, not so much as a single proposition, without general words; that they must make the greatest part of every language, and that it is by them only that language is fitted to express, with wonderful ease and expedition, all the treasures of human wisdom and knowledge.

CHAP. II.

OF GENERAL CONCEPTIONS.

As general words are so necessary in language, it is natural to conclude that there must be general conceptions, of which they are the signs.

Words are empty sounds, when they do not signify the thoughts of the speaker; and it is only from their signification that they are denominated general. Every word that is spoken, considered merely as a sound, is an individual sound. And it can only be called a general word, because that which it signifies, is general. Now, that which it signifies, is conceived by the mind both of the speaker and hearer, if the word have a distinct meaning, and be distinctly understood. It is therefore impossible that words can have a general signification, unless there be conceptions in the mind of the speaker, and of the hearer, of things that are general. It is to such that I give the name of general conceptions: and it ought to be observed, that they take this denomination, not from the act of the mind in conceiving, which is an individual act, but from the object, or thing conceived, which is general.

We are therefore here to consider whether we have such general conceptions, and how they are formed.

To begin with the conceptions expressed by general terms, that is, by such general words as may be the subject or the predicate of a proposition. They are either attributes of things, or they are *genera* or *species* of things.

It is evident, with respect to all the individuals we are acquainted with, that we have a more clear and

distinct conception of their attributes, than of the subject to which those attributes belong.

Take, for instance, any individual body we have
access to know, what conception do we form of
it? Every man may know this from his consciousness. He will find that he conceives it as a thing that
has length, breadth, and thickness, such a figure, and
such a colour; that it is hard, or soft, or fluid; that
it has such qualities, and is fit for such purposes. If
it is a vegetable, he may know where it grew, what is
the form of its leaves, and flower, and seed. If an
animal, what are its natural instincts, its manner of
life, and of rearing its young. Of these attributes belonging to this individual, and numberless others, he
may surely have a distinct conception; and he will
find words in language by which he can clearly and
distinctly express each of them.

If we consider, in like manner, the conception we
form of any individual person of our acquaintance, we
shall find it to be made up of various attributes, which
we ascribe to him; such as, that he is the son of such a
man, the brother of such another, that he has such an
employment or office, has such a fortune, that he is
tall or short, well or ill made, comely or ill favoured,
young or old, married or unmarried; to this we may
add, his temper, his character, his abilities, and perhaps some anecdotes of his history.

Such is the conception we form of individual persons
of our acquaintance. By such attributes we describe
them to those who know them not; and by such attributes historians give us a conception of the personages of former times. Nor is it possible to do it in
any other way.

All the distinct knowledge we have or can attain
of any individual, is the knowledge of its attributes: for we know not the essence of any indi

vidual. This seems to be beyond the reach of the human faculties.

Now, every attribute is what the ancients called an universal. It is, or may be, common to various individuals. There is no attribute belonging to any creature of God which may not belong to others; and, on this account, attributes, in all languages, are expressed by general words.

It appears likewise, from every man's experience, that he may have as clear and distinct a conception of such attributes as we have named, and of innumerable others, as he can have of any individual to which they belong.

Indeed the attributes of individuals is all that we distinctly conceive about them. It is true, we conceive a subject, to which the attributes belong; but of this subject, when its attributes are set aside, we have but an obscure and relative conception, whether it be body or mind.

This was before observed with regard to bodies, Essay 2. chap. 19. to which we refer, and it is no less evident with regard to minds. What is it we call a mind? It is a thinking, intelligent, active being. Granting, that thinking, intelligence, and activity, are attributes of mind, I want to know what the thing or being is, to which these attributes belong? To this question I can find no satisfying answer. The attributes of mind, and particularly its operations, we know clearly; but of the thing itself we have only an obscure notion.

Nature teaches us, that thinking and reasoning are attributes, which cannot exist without a subject; but of that subject I believe the best notion we can form implies little more than that it is the subject of such attributes.

Whether other created beings may have the knowledge of the real essence of created things, so as to be able to deduce their attributes from their essence and constitution, or whether this be the prerogative of Him who made them, we cannot tell; but it is a knowledge which seems to be quite beyond the reach of the human faculties.

We know the essence of a triangle, and from that essence can deduce its properties. It is an universal, and might have been conceived by the human mind, though no individual triangle had ever existed. It has only what Mr. Locke calls a nominal essence, which is expressed in its definition. But every thing that exists has a real essence, which is above our comprehension; and therefore we cannot deduce its properties or attributes from its nature, as we do in the triangle. We must take a contrary road in the knowledge of God's works, and satisfy ourselves with their attributes as facts, and with the general conviction that there is a subject to which those attributes belong.

Enough, I think, has been said, to show, not only that we may have clear and distinct conceptions of attributes, but that they are the only things, with regard to individuals, of which we have a clear and distinct conception.

The other class of general terms are those that signify the *genera* and *species* into which we divide and subdivide things. And if we be able to form distinct conceptions of attributes, it cannot surely be denied that we may have distinct conceptions of *genera* and *species;* because they are only collections of attributes which we conceive to exist in a subject, and to which we give a general name. If the attributes comprehended under that general name be distinctly conceived, the thing meant by the name must be distinctly conceived. And the name may justly be attributed to every individual which has those attributes.

Thus, I conceive distinctly what it is to have wings, to be covered with feathers, to lay eggs. Suppose then that we give the name of *bird* to every animal that has these three attributes. Here undoubtedly my conception of a bird is as distinct as my notion of the attributes which are common to this species : and if this be admitted to be the definition of a bird, there is nothing I conceive more distinctly. If I had never seen a bird, and can but be made to understand the definition, I can easily apply it to every individual of the species, without danger of mistake.

When things are divided and subdivided by men of science, and names given to the *genera* and *species,* those names are defined. Thus, the genera and species of plants, and of other natural bodies, are accurately defined by the writers in the various branches of natural history ; so that, to all future generations, the definition will convey a distinct notion of the genus or species defined.

There are, without doubt, many words signifying genera and species of things, which have a meaning somewhat vague and indistinct ; so that those who speak the same language do not always use them in the same sense. But if we attend to the cause of this indistinctness, we shall find, that it is not owing to their being general terms, but to this, that there is no definition of them that has authority. Their meaning therefore, has not been learned by a definition, but by a kind of induction, by observing to what individuals they are applied by those who understand the language. We learn by habit to use them as we see others do, even when we have not a precise meaning annexed to them. A man may know, that to certain individuals they may be applied with propriety ; but whether they can be applied to certain other individuals, he may be uncertain, either from want of good authorities, or from having contrary authorities, which leave him in doubt.

Thus, a man may know, that when he applies the name of beast to a lion or a tyger, and the name of bird to an eagle or a turkey, he speaks properly. But whether a bat be a bird or a beast, he may be uncertain. If there was any accurate definition of a beast and of a bird, that was of sufficient authority, he could be at no loss.

It is said to have been sometimes a matter of dispute, with regard to a monstrous birth of a woman, whether it was a man or not. Although this be in reality a question about the meaning of a word, it may be of importance, on account of the privileges which laws have annexed to the human character. To make such laws perfectly precise, the definition of a man would be necessary. which I believe legislators have seldom or never thought fit to give. It is, indeed, very difficult to fix a definition of so common a word, and the cases wherein it would be of any use so rarely occur, that perhaps it may be better, when they do occur, to leave them to the determination of a judge or of a jury, than to give a definition, which might be attended with unforeseen consequences.

A genus or species, being a collection of attributes, conceived to exist in one subject, a definition is the only way to prevent any addition or diminution, of its ingredients in the conception of different persons; and when there is no definition that can be appealed to as a standard, the name will hardly retain the most perfect precision in its signification.

From what has been said, I conceive it is evident, that the words which signify genera and species of things have often as precise and definite a signification as any words whatsoever; and that when it is otherwise, their want of precision is not owing to their being general words, but to other causes.

Having shown that we may have a perfectly clear and distinct conception of the meaning of general terms, we may, I think, take it for granted, that the same may be said of other general words, such as prepositions, conjunctions, articles. My design at present being only to show, that we have general conceptions no less clear and distinct than those of individuals, it is sufficient for this purpose, if this appears with regard to the conceptions expressed by general terms. To conceive the meaning of a general word, and to conceive that which it signifies, is the same thing. We conceive distinctly the meaning of general terms, therefore we conceive distinctly that which they signify. But such terms do not signify any individual, but what is common to many individuals; therefore we have a distinct conception of things common to many individuals, that is, we have distinct general conceptions.

We must here beware of the ambiguity of the word *conception,* which sometimes signifies the act of the mind in conceiving, sometimes the thing conceived, which is the object of that act. If the word be taken in the first sense, I acknowledge that every act of the mind is an individual act; the universality, therefore, is not in the act of the mind, but in the object, or thing conceived. The thing conceived is an attribute common to many subjects, or it is a genus or species common to many individuals.

Suppose I conceive a triangle, that is, a plain figure terminated by three right lines. He that understands this definition distinctly has a distinct conception of a triangle. But a triangle is not an individual; it is a species. The act of my understanding in conceiving it is an individual act, and has a real existence; but the thing conceived is general, and cannot exist without other attributes, which are not included in the definition.

Every triangle that really exists must have a certain length of sides and measure of angles; it must have place and time. But the definition of a triangle includes neither existence, nor any of those attributes; and therefore they are not included in the conception of a triangle, which cannot be accurate if it comprehend more than the definition.

Thus I think it appears to be evident, that we have general conceptions that are clear and distinct, both of attributes of things, and of genera and species of things.

CHAP. III.

OF GENERAL CONCEPTIONS FORMED BY ANALYZING OBJECTS.

WE are next to consider the operations of the understanding, by which we are enabled to form general conceptions.

These appear to me to be three; *first*, the resolving or analyzing a subject into its known attributes, and giving a name to each attribute, which name shall signify that attribute, and nothing more.

Secondly, The observing one or more such attributes to be common to many subjects. The first is by philosophers called *abstraction*; the second may be called *generalizing*; but both are commonly included under the name of *abstraction*.

It is difficult to say which of them goes first, or whether they are not so closely connected that neither can claim the precedence. For on the one hand, to perceive an agreement between two or more objects in the same attribute, seems to require nothing more than to compare them together. A savage, upon seeing snow and chalk, would find no difficulty in perceiving that they have the same colour. Yet, on the other hand, it seems impossible that he should observe this agreement without abstraction, that is, distinguishing in his conception the colour, wherein those two objects agree, from the other qualities wherein they disagree.

It seems, therefore, that we cannot generalize without some degree of abstraction; but I apprehend we may abstract without generalizing: for what hinders me from attending to the whiteness of the paper before me, without applying that colour to any

other object ? The whiteness of this individual object
is an abstract conception, but not a general one, while
applied to one individual only. These two operations, however, are subservient to each other ; for the
more attributes we observe and distinguish in any one
individual, the more agreements we shall discover between it and other individuals.

A *third* operation of the understanding, by which we
form abstract conceptions, is the combining into one
whole a certain number of those attributes of which we
have formed abstract notions, and giving a name to
that combination. It is thus we form abstract notions
of the genera and species of things. These three operations we shall consider in order.

With regard to abstraction, strictly so called, I can
perceive nothing in it that is difficult either to be understood or practised. What can be more easy than
to distinguish the different attributes which we know
to belong to a subject ? In a man, for instance, to distinguish his size, his complexion, his age, his fortune, his
birth, his profession, and twenty other things that belong to him. To think and speak of these things with
understanding, is surely within the reach of every man
endowed with the human faculties.

There may be distinctions that require nice discernment, or an acquaintance with the subject that is
not common. Thus, a critic in painting, may discern
the style of Raphael or Titian, when another man could
not. A lawyer may be acquainted with many distinctions in crimes, and contracts, and actions, which never
occurred to a man who has not studied law. One man
may excel another in the talent of distinguishing, as
he may in memory or in reasoning : but there is a certain degree of this talent, without which a man would
have no title to be considered as a reasonable creature.

It ought likewise to be observed, that attributes may with perfect ease be distinguished and disjoined in our conception, which cannot be actually separated in the subject. Thus, in a body, I can distinguish its solidity from its extension, and its weight from both. In extension I can distinguish length, breadth, and thickness, yet none of these can be separated from the body, or from one another. There may be attributes belonging to a subject, and inseparable from it, of which we have no knowledge, and consequently no conception; but this does not hinder our conceiving distinctly those of its attributes which we know.

Thus, all the properties of a circle are inseparable from the nature of a circle, and may be demonstrated from its definition; yet a man may have a perfectly distinct notion of a circle, who knows very few of those properties of it which mathematicians have demonstrated; and a circle probably has many properties which no mathematician ever dreamed of.

It is therefore certain, that attributes, which in their nature are absolutely inseparable from their subject, and from one another, may be disjoined in our conception; one cannot exist without the other, but one can be conceived without the other.

Having considered abstraction, strictly so called, let us next consider the operation of generalizing, which is nothing but the observing one or more attributes to be common to many subjects.

If any man can doubt whether there be attributes that are really common to many individuals, let him consider whether there be not many men that are above six feet high, and many below it; whether there be not many men that are rich, and many more that are poor; whether there be not many that were born in Britain, and many that were born in France. To multiply instances of this kind, would be to affront the reader's

understanding. It is certain therefore, that there are
innumerable attributes that are really common to many
individuals ; and if this be what the schoolmen called
universale a parte rei, we may affirm with certainty,
that there are such universals.

There are some attributes expressed by general
words, of which this may seem more doubtful. Such
are the qualities which are inherent in their several
subjects. It may be said that every subject has its
own qualities, and that which is the quality of one
subject, cannot be the quality of another subject. Thus
the whiteness of the sheet of paper upon which I write,
cannot be the whiteness of another sheet, though both
are called white. The weight of one guinea is not the
weight of another guinea, though both are said to have
the same weight.

To this I answer, that the whiteness of this sheet is
one thing, whiteness is another; the conceptions signified by these two forms of speech are as different as
the expressions : the first signifies an individual quality really existing, and is not a general conception,
though it be an abstract one; the second signifies a
general conception, which implies no existence, but
may be predicated of every thing that is white, and in
the same sense. On this account, if one should say,
that the whiteness of this sheet is the whiteness of
another sheet, every man perceives this to be absurd ;
but when he says both sheets are white, this is true
and perfectly understood. The conception of whiteness implies no existence ; it would remain the same,
though every thing in the universe that is white were
annihilated.

It appears, therefore, that the general names of
qualities, as well as of other attributes, are applicable
to many individuals in the same sense, which cannot
be if there be not general conceptions signified by such
names.

If it should be asked, how early, or at what period of life, men begin to form general conceptions? I answer, as soon as a child can say, with understanding, that he has two brothers or two sisters; as soon as he can use the plural number, he must have general conceptions; for no individual can have a plural number.

As there are not two individuals in nature that agree in every thing, so there are very few that do not agree in some things. We take pleasure from very early years in observing such agreements. One great branch of what we call *wit*, which, when innocent gives pleasure to every good natured man, consists in discovering unexpected agreements in things. The author of Hudibras could discern a property common to the morning and a boiled lobster, that both turn from black to red. Swift could see something common to wit and an old cheese. Such unexpected agreements may show wit; but there are innumerable agreements of things which cannot escape the notice of the lowest understanding; such as agreements in colour, magnitude, figure, features, time, place, age, and so forth. These agreements are the foundation of so many common attributes, which are found in the rudest languages.

The ancient philosophers called these universals, or predicables, and endeavoured to reduce them to five classes; to wit, genus, species, specific difference, properties, and accidents. Perhaps there may be more classes of universals or attributes; for enumerations, so very general, are seldom complete; but every attribute, common to several individuals, may be expressed by a general term, which is the sign of a general conception.

How prone men are to form general conceptions we may see from the use of metaphor, and of the other figures of speech grounded on similitude. Similitude is nothing else than an agreement of the objects compared in one or more attributes; and if there be no attribute comnon to both, there can be no similitude.

The similtudes and analogies between the various objects that nature presents to us, are infinite and inexhaustible. They not only please, when displayed by the poet or vit in works of taste, but they are highly useful in the ordinary communication of our thoughts and sentimeits by language. In the rude languages of barbarousnations, similitudes and analogies supply the want of proper words to express men's sentiments, so much, that in such languages, there is hardly a sentence without a metaphor; and if we examine the most copious and polished languages, we shall find that a great proportion of the words and phrases which are accounted the most proper, may be said to be the progeny of metaphor.

As foreigners, who settle in a nation as their home, come at last to be incorporated, and lose the denomination of foreigners, so words and phrases, at first borrowed and figurative, by long use become denizens in the language, and lose the denomination of figures of speech. When we speak of the extent of knowledge, the steadiness of virtue, the tenderness of affection, the perspicuity of expression, no man conceives these to be metaphorical expressions; they are as proper as any in the language: yet it appears upon the very face of them, that they must have been metaphorical in those who used them first; and that it is by use and prescription that they have lost the denomination of figurative, and acquired a right to be considered proper words. This observation will be found to extend to a great part, perhaps the greatest part, of the words of the most perfect languages. Sometimes the name of an individual is given to a general conception, and thereby the individual in a manner generalized. As when the Jew Shylock, in Shakespeare, says, A Daniel come to judgment ; yea, a Daniel! In this speech, a Daniel, is an attribute, or an universal. The character of Daniel, as a man of singular wisdom, is abstracted from his person, and considered as capable of being attributed to other persons.

Upon the whole, these two operations of abstracting and generalizing appear common to all men that have understanding. The practice of them is, and must be, familiar to every man that uses language; but it is one thing to practise them, and another to explain how they are performed; as it is one thing to see, another to explain how we see. The first is the province of all men, and is the natural and easy operation of the faculties which God has given us. The second is the province of philosophers, and though a matter of no great difficulty in itself, has been much perplexed by the ambiguity of words, and still more by the hypotheses of philosophers.

Thus when I consider a billiard ball, its colour is one attribute, which I signify by calling it white; its figure is another, which is signified by calling it spherical; the firm cohesion of its parts is signified by calling it hard; its recoiling, when it strikes a hard body, is signified by its being called elastic; its origin, as being part of the tooth of an elephant, is signified by calling it ivory: and its use by calling it a billiard ball.

The words, by which each of those attributes is signified, have one distinct meaning, and in this meaning are applicable to many individuals. They signify not any individual thing, but attributes common to many individuals; nor is it beyond the capacity of a child to understand them perfectly, and to apply them properly to every individual in which they are found.

As it is by analyzing a complex object into its several attributes that we acquire our simplest abstract conceptions, it may be proper to compare this analysis with that which a chymist makes of a compounded body into the ingredients which enter into its composition; for although there be such an analogy between these two operations, that we give to both the name of analysis or resolution, there is at the same time so great a dissimilitude in some respects, that we may be led into error, by applying to one what belongs to the other.

It is obvious, that the chymical analysis is an operation of the hand upon matter, by various material instruments. The analysis we are now explaining is purely an operation of the understanding, which requires no material instrument, nor produces any change upon any external thing; we shall therefore call it the intellectual or mental analysis.

In the chymical analysis, the compound body itself is the subject analyzed. A subject so imperfectly known, that it may be compounded of various ingredients, when to our senses it appears perfectly simple; and even when we are able to analyze it into the different ingredients of which it is composed, we know not how or why the combination of those ingredients produces such a body.

Thus pure sea salt is a body to appearance, as simple as any in nature. Every the least particle of it, discernible by our senses, is perfectly similar to every other particle in all its qualities. The nicest taste, the quickest eye, can discern no mark of its being made up of different ingredients; yet, by the chymical art, it can be analyzed into an acid and an alkali, and can be again produced by the combination of those two ingredients. But how this combination produces sea salt, no man has been able to discover. The ingredients are both as unlike the compound as any bodies we know. No man could have guessed, before the thing was known, that sea salt is compounded of those two in-

gredients; no man could have guessed, that the union
of those two ingredients should produce such a compound as sea salt. Such in many cases are the phenomena of the chymical analysis of a compound body.

If we consider the intellectual analysis of an object,
it is evident that nothing of this kind can happen;
because the thing analyzed is not an external object
imperfectly known; it is a conception of the mind itself. And to suppose that there can be any thing in
a conception that is not conceived, is a contradiction.

The reason of observing this difference between
those two kinds of analysis is, that some philosophers,
in order to support their systems, have maintained,
that a complex idea may have the appearance of the
most perfect simplicity, and retain no similitude of any
of the simple ideas of which it is compounded; just as
a white colour may appear perfectly simple, and retain
no similitude to any of the seven primary colours of
which it is compounded; or as a chymical composition
may appear perfectly simple, and retain no similitude
to any of the ingredients.

From which those philosophers have drawn this important conclusion, that a cluster of the ideas of sense,
properly combined, may make the idea of a mind; and
that all the ideas, which Mr. Locke calls ideas of reflection, are only compositions of the ideas which we
have by our five senses. From this the transition is
easy, that if a proper composition of the ideas of matter may make the idea of a mind, then a proper composition of matter itself may make a mind, and that
man is only a piece of matter curiously formed.

In this curious system, the whole fabric rests upon
this foundation, that a complex idea, which is made
up of various simple ideas, may appear to be perfectly
simple, and to have no marks of composition, because

a compound body may appear to our senses to be perfectly simple.

Upon this fundamental proposition of this system I beg leave to make two remarks.

1st. Supposing it to be true, it affirms only what *may be*. We are indeed in most cases very imperfect judges of what may be. But this we know, that were we ever so certain that a thing may be, this is no good reason for believing that it really is. A *may be* is a mere hypothesis, which may furnish matter of investigation, but is not entitled to the least degree of belief. The transition from what may be to what really is, is familiar and easy to those who have a predilection for a hypothesis; but to a man who seeks truth without prejudice or prepossession, it is a very wide and difficult step, and he will never pass from the one to the other, without evidence, not only that the thing may be, but that it really is.

2dly. As far as I am able to judge, this, which it is said may be, cannot be. That a complex idea should be made up of simple ideas, so that to a ripe understanding reflecting upon that idea, there should be no appearance of composition, nothing similar to the simple ideas of which it is compounded, seems to me to involve a contradiction. The idea is a conception of the mind. If any thing more than this is meant by the idea, I know not what it is; and I wish both to know what it is, and to have proof of its existence. Now that there should be any thing in the conception of an object which is not conceived, appears to me as manifest a contradiction, as that there should be an existence which does not exist, or that a thing should be conceived, and not conceived at the same time.

But, say these philosophers, a white colour is produced by the composition of the primary colours, and yet has no resemblance to any of them. I grant it.

But what can be inferred from this with regard to the composition of ideas? To bring this argument home to the point, they must say, that because a white colour is compounded of the primary colours, therefore the idea of a white colour is compounded of the ideas of the primary colours. This reasoning, if it was admitted, would lead to innumerable absurdities. An opaque fluid may be compounded of two or more pellucid fluids. Hence we might infer with equal force, that the idea of an opaque fluid may be compounded of the idea of two or more pellucid fluids.

Nature's way of compounding bodies, and our way of compounding ideas, are so different in many respects, that we cannot reason from the one to the other, unless it can be found, that ideas are combined by fermentations and elective attractions, and may be analyzed in a furnace by the force of fire and of menstruums. Until this discovery be made, we must hold those to be simple ideas, which, upon the most attentive reflection, have no appearance of composition; and those only to be the ingredients of complex ideas, which, by attentive reflection, can be perceived to be contained in them.

If the idea of mind, and its operations, may be compounded of the ideas of matter and its qualities, why may not the idea of matter be compounded of the ideas of mind? There is the same evidence for the last *may be* as for the first. And why may not the idea of sound be compounded of the ideas of colour; or the idea colour of those of sound? Why may not the idea of wisdom be compounded of ideas of folly; or the idea of truth of ideas of absurdity? But we leave those mysterious *may bes* to them that have faith to receive them.

CHAP. IV.

OF GENERAL CONCEPTIONS FORMED BY COMBINATION.

As, by an intellectual analysis of objects, we form general conceptions of single attributes, which, of all conceptions that enter into the human mind, are the most simple, so by combining several of these into one parcel, and giving a name to that combination, we form general conceptions that may be very complex, and at the same time very distinct.

Thus one, who, by analyzing extended objects, has got the simple notions of a point, a line, straight or curve, an angle, a surface, a solid, can easily conceive a plain surface, terminated by four equal straight lines meeting in four points at right angles. To this species of figure he gives the name of a square. In like manner, he can conceive a solid terminated by six equal squares, and give it the name of a cube. A square, a cube, and every name of mathematical figure, is a general term, expressing a complex general conception, made by a certain combination of the simple elements into which we analyze extended bodies.

Every mathematical figure is accurately defined, by enumerating the simple elements of which it is formed, and the manner of their combination. The definition contains the whole essence of it: and every property that belongs to it may be deduced by demonstrative reasoning from its definition. It is not a thing that exists, for then it would be an individual; but it is a thing that is conceived without regard to existence.

A farm, a manor, a parish, a county, a kingdom, are complex general conceptions, formed by various combinations and modifications of inhabited territory, under certain forms of government.

Different combinations of military men form the notions of a company, a regiment, an army.

The several crimes which are the objects of criminal law, such as theft, murder, robbery, piracy, what are they but certain combinations of human actions and intentions, which are accurately defined in criminal law, and which it is found convenient to comprehend under one name, and consider as one thing?

When we observe, that nature, in her animal, vegetable, and inanimate productions, has formed many individuals that agree in many of their qualities and attributes, we are led by natural instinct to expect their agreement in other qualities, which we have not had occasion to perceive. Thus, a child who has once burnt his finger, by putting it in the flame of one candle, expects the same event if he puts it in the flame of another candle, or in any flame, and is thereby led to think that the quality of burning belongs to all flame. This instinctive induction is not justified by the rules of logic, and it sometimes leads men into harmless mistakes, which experience may afterward correct; but it preserves us from destruction in innumerable dangers to which we are exposed.

The reason of taking notice of this principle in human nature in this place is, that the distribution of the productions of nature into *genera* and *species* becomes, on account of this principle, more generally useful.

The physician expects, that the rhubarb which has never yet been tried will have like medical virtues with that which he has prescribed on former occasions. Two parcels of rhubarb agree in certain sensible qualities, from which agreement they are both called by the same general name *rhubarb*. Therefore it is expected that they will agree in their medical virtues. And as experience, has discovered certain virtues in one parcel, or in many parcels, we presume, without

experience, that the same virtues belong to all parcels
of rhubarb that shall be used.

If a traveller meets a horse, an ox, or a sheep, which
he never saw before, he is under no apprehension, believing these animals to be of a species that is tame
and inoffensive. But he dreads a lion or a tiger, because they are of a fierce and ravenous species.

We are capable of receiving innumerable advantages,
and are exposed to innumerable dangers, from the
various productions of nature, animal, vegetable, and
inanimate. The life of man, if an hundred times longer
than it is, would be insufficient to learn from experience
the useful and hurtful qualities of every individual production of nature taken singly.

The Author of nature has made provision for our
attaining that knowledge of his works which is necessary for our subsistence and preservation, partly by
the constitution of the productions of nature, and
partly by the constitution of the human mind.

For, *first*, In the productions of nature, great numbers of individuals are made so like to one another,
both in their obvious and in their more occult qualities, that we are not only enabled, but invited, as it
were, to reduce them into classes, and to give a general
name to a class; a name which is common to every individual of the class, because it comprehends in its signification those qualities or attributes only that are
common to all the individuals of that class.

Secondly, The human mind is so framed, that, from
the agreement of individuals in the more obvious qualities by which we reduce them into one class, we are
naturally led to expect that they will be found to agree
in their more latent qualities, and in this we are seldom
disappointed.

We have, therefore, a strong and rational inducement,
both to distribute natural substances into classes,

genera and *species,* under general names; and to do this with all the accuracy and distinctness we are able. For the more accurate our divisions are made, and the more distinctly the several species are defined, the more securely we may rely, that the qualities we find in one or in a few individuals will be found in all of the same species.

Every species of natural substances which has a name in language, is an attribute of many individuals, and is itself a combination of more simple attributes, which we observe to be common to those individuals.

We shall find a great part of the words of every language, nay, I apprehend, the far greater part, to signify combinations of more simple general conceptions, which men have found proper to be bound up, as it were, in one parcel, by being designed by one name.

Some general conceptions there are, which may more properly be called *compositions* or *works* than mere combinations. Thus, one may conceive a machine which never existed. He may conceive an air in music, a poem, a plan of architecture, a plan of government, a plan of conduct in public or in private life, a sentence, a discourse, a treatise. Such compositions are things conceived in the mind of the author, not individuals that really exist; and the same general conception which the author had may be communicated to others by language.

Thus, the Oceana of Harrington was conceived in the mind of its author. The materials of which it is composed are things conceived, not things that existed. His senate, his popular assembly, his magistrates, his elections, are all conceptions of his mind, and the whole is one complex conception. And the same may be said of every work of the human understanding.

Very different from these are the works of God, which we behold. They are works of creative power, not of understanding only. They have a real existence. Our best conceptions of them are partial and imperfect. But of the works of the human understanding our conception may be perfect and complete. They are nothing but what the author conceived, and what he can express by language, so as to convey his conception perfectly to men like himself.

Although such works are indeed complex general conceptions, they do not so properly belong to our present subject. They are more the objects of judgment and of taste, than of bare conception or simple apprehension.

To return therefore to those complex conceptions which are formed merely by combining those that are more simple. Nature has given us the power of combining such simple attributes, and such a number of them as we find proper; and of giving one name to that combination, and considering it as one object of thought.

The simple attributes of things, which fall under our observation, are not so numerous but that they may all have names in a copious language. But to give names to all the combinations that can be made of two, three, or more of them, would be impossible. The most copious languages have names but for a very small part.

It may likewise be observed, that the combinations that have names are nearly, though not perfectly, the same in the different languages of civilized nations, that have intercourse with another. Hence it is, that the Lexicographer, for the most part, can give words in one language answering perfectly, or very nearly, to those of another; and what is wrote in a simple style in one language, can be translated almost word for word into another.

From these observations we may conclude, that there are either certain common principles of human nature, or certain common occurrences of human life, which dispose men, out of an infinite number that might be formed, to form certain combinations rather than others.

Mr. Hume, in order to account for this phenomenon, has recourse to what he calls the associating qualities of ideas; to wit, causation, contiguity in time, and place, and similitude. He conceives, "that one of the most remarkable effects of those associating qualities, is the complex ideas which are the common subjects of our thoughts. That this also is the cause why languages so nearly correspond to one another. Nature in a manner pointing out to every one those ideas which are most proper to be united into a complex one."

I agree with this ingenious author, that nature in a manner points out those simple ideas which are most proper to be united into a complex one; but nature does this, not solely or chiefly by the relations between the simple ideas, of contiguity, causation, and resemblance; but rather by the fitness of the combinations we make, to aid our own conceptions, and to convey them to others by language easily and agreeably.

The end and use of language, without regard to the associating qualities of ideas, will lead men that have common understanding to form such complex notions as are proper for expressing their wants, their thoughts, and their desires; and in every language we shall find these to be the complex notions that have names.

In the rudest state of society, men must have occasion to form the general notions of man, woman, father, mother, son, daughter, sister, brother, neighbour, friend, enemy, and many others, to express the common relations of one person to another.

If they are employed in hunting, they must have general terms to express the various implements and operations of the chase. Their houses and clothing, however simple, will furnish another set of general terms, to express the materials, the workmanship, and excellencies and defects of those fabrics. If they sail upon rivers, or upon the sea, this will give occasion to a great number of general terms, which otherwise would never have occurred to their thoughts.

The same thing may be said of agriculture, of pasturage, of every art they practise, and of every branch of knowledge they attain. The necessity of general terms for communicating our sentiment is obvious; and the invention of them, as far as we find them necessary, requires no other talent but that degree of understanding which is common to men.

The notions of debtor and creditor, of profit and loss, of account, balance, stock on hand, and many others, are owing to commerce. The notions of latitude, longitude, course, distance run; and those of ships, and of their various parts, furniture and operations, are owing to navigation. The anatomist must have names, for the various similar and dissimilar parts of the human body, and words, to express their figure, position, structure, and use. The physician must have names for the various diseases of the body, their causes, symptoms, and means of cure.

The like may be said of the grammarian, the logician, the critic, the rhetorician, the moralist, the naturalist, the mechanic, and every man that professes any art or science.

When any discovery is made in art or in nature, which requires new combinations and new words to express it properly, the invention of these is easy to those who have a distinct notion of the thing to be expressed; and such words will readily be adopted, and receive the public sanction.

If, on the other hand, any man of eminence, through vanity or want of judgment, should invent new words, to express combinations that have neither beauty nor utility, or which may as well be expressed in the current language, his authority may give them currency for a time with servile imitators, or blind admirers: but the judicious will laugh at them, and they will soon lose their credit. So true was the observation made by Pomponius Marcellus, an ancient grammarian, to Tiberius Cesar. "You Cesar, have power to make a man a denizen of Rome, but not to make a word a denizen of the Roman language."

Among nations that are civilized, and have intercourse with one another, the most necessary and useful arts will be common; the important parts of human knowledge will be common; their several languages will be fitted to it, and consequently to one another.

New inventions of general use give an easy birth to new complex notions and new names, which spread as far as the invention does. How many new complex notions have been formed, and names for them invented in the languages of Europe, by the modern inventions of printing, of gunpowder, of the mariner's compass, of optical glasses! The simple ideas combined in those complex notions, and the associating qualities of those ideas, are very ancient; but they never produced those complex notions until there was use for them.

What is peculiar to a nation in its customs, manners, or laws, will give occasion to complex notions and words peculiar to the language of that nation. Hence it is easy to see, why an *impeachment*, and an *attainder*, in the English language, and *ostracism* in the Greek language, have not names answering to them in other languages.

I apprehend, therefore, that it is utility, and not the associating qualities of the ideas, that has led men to form only certain combinations, and to give names to them in language, while they neglect an infinite number that might be formed.

The common occurrences of life, in the intercourse of men, and in their occupations, give occasion to many complex notions. We see an individual occurrence, which draws our attention more or less, and may be a subject of conversation. Other occurrences, similar to this in many respects, have been observed, or may be expected. It is convenient that we should be able to speak of what is common to them all, leaving out the unimportant circumstances of time, place, and persons. This we can do with great ease, by giving a name to what is common to all those individual occurrences. Such a name is a great aid to language, because it comprehends, in one word, a great number of simple notions, which it would be very tedious to express in detail.

Thus men have formed the complex notions of eating, drinking sleeping, walking, riding, running, buying, selling, ploughing, sowing, a dance, a feast, war, a battle, victory, triumph ; and others without number.

Such things must frequently be the subject of conversation ; and if we had not a more compendious way of expressing them than by a detail of all the simple notions they comprehend, we should lose the benefit of speech.

The different talents, dispositions, and habits of men in society, being interesting to those who have to do with them, will in every language have general names ; such as wise, foolish, knowing, ignorant, plain, cunning. In every operative art, the tools, instruments, materials, the work produced, and the various excellencies and defects of these, must have general names.

The various relations of persons, and of things which cannot escape the observation of men in society, lead us to many complex general notions ; such as father, brother, friend, enemy, master, servant, property, theft, rebellion.

The terms of art in the sciences make another class of general names of complex notions ; as in mathematics, axiom, definition, problem, theorem, demonstration.

I do not attempt a complete enumeration even of the classes of complex general conceptions. Those I have named as a specimen, I think, are mostly comprehended under what Mr. Locke calls mixed modes and relations ; which, he justly observes, have names given them in language, in preference to innumerable others that might be formed ; for this reason only, that they are useful for the purpose of communicating our thoughts by language.

In all the languages of mankind, not only the writings and discourses of the learned, but the conversation of the vulgar, is almost entirely made up of general words, which are the signs of general conceptions, either simple or complex. And in every language, we find the terms signifying complex notions to be such, and only such, as the use of language requires.

There remains a very large class of complex general terms, on which I shall make some observations ; I mean those by which we name the species, genera, and tribes of natural substances.

It is utility, indeed, that leads us to give general names to the various species of natural substances ; but, in combining the attributes which are included under the specific name, we are more aided and directed by nature, than in forming other combinations of mixed modes and relations. In the last, the ingredients are brought together in the occurrences of life, or in the actions or thoughts of men. But, in the first, the ingredients are united by nature in many individual substances which God has made. We form a general notion of those attributes, wherein many individuals agree. We give a specific name to this combination; which name is common to all substances having those attributes, which either do or may exist. The specific name comprehends neither more nor fewer attributes than we find proper to put into its definition. It comprehends not time, nor place, nor even existence, although there can be no individual without these.

This work of the understanding is absolutely necessary for speaking intelligibly of the productions of nature, and for reaping the benefits we receive, and avoiding the dangers we are exposed to from them. The individuals are so many, that to give a proper name to each would be beyond the power of language. If a good or bad quality was observed in an individual, of how small use would this be, if there was not a species in which the same quality might be expected.

Without some general knowledge of the qualities of natural substances, human life could not be preserved. And there can be no general knowledge of this kind, without reducing them to species under specific names. For this reason, among the rudest nations, we find names for fire, water, earth, air, mountains, fountains, rivers; for the kinds of vegetables they use; of animals they hunt or tame, or that are found useful or hurtful.

Each of those names signifies in general a substance having a certain combination of attributes. The name therefore must be common to all substances in which those attributes are found.

Such general names of substances being found in all vulgar languages, before philosophers began to make accurate divisions, and less obvious distinctions, it is not to be expected that their meaning should be more precise than is necessary for the common purposes of life.

As the knowledge of nature advances, more species of natural substances are observed, and their useful qualities discovered. In order that this important part of human knowledge may be communicated, and handed down to future generations, it is not sufficient that the species have names. Such is the fluctuating state of language, that a general name will not always retain the same precise signification, unless it have a definition in which men are disposed to acquiesce.

There was undoubtedly a great fund of natural knowledge among the Greeks and Romans in the time of Pliny. There is a great fund in his Natural History; but much of it is lost to us, for this reason among others, that we know not what species of substance he means by such a name.

Nothing could have prevented this loss but an accurate definition of the name, by which the species might have been distinguished from all others, as long as that name and its definition remained.

To prevent such loss in future times, modern philosophers have very laudably attempted to give names and accurate definitions of all the known species of substances, wherewith the bountiful Creator has enriched our globe.

This is necessary, in order to form a copious and distinct language concerning them, and consequently to facilitate our knowledge of them, and to convey it to future generations.

Every species that is known to exist ought to have a name; and that name ought to be defined by such attributes as serve best to distinguish the species from all others.

Nature invites to this work, by having formed things so as to make it both easy and important.

For, *first*, We perceive numbers of individual substances so like in their obvious qualities, that the most

unimproved tribes of men consider them as of one
species, and give them one common name.

Secondly, The more latent qualities of substances
are generally the same in all the individuals of a species: so that what, by observation or experiment, is
found in a few individuals of a species, is presumed,
and commonly found to belong to the whole. By this
we are enabled, from particular facts, to draw general
conclusions. This kind of induction is indeed the master key to the knowledge of nature, without which we
could form no general conclusions in that branch of
philosophy.

And, *thirdly,* By the very constitution of our nature,
we are led, without reasoning, to ascribe to the whole
species what we have found to belong to the individuals. It is thus we come to know that fire burns,
and water drowns; that bodies gravitate, and bread
nourishes.

The species of two of the kingdoms of nature, to
wit, the animal and the vegetable, seem to be fixed
by nature, by the power they have of producing their
like. And in these, men in all ages and nations have
accounted the parent and the progeny of the same
species. The differences among naturalists, with regard to the species of these two kingdoms, are very inconsiderable, and may be occasioned by the changes
produced by soil, climate, and culture, and sometimes by monstrous productions, which are compara-
tively rare.

In the inanimate kingdom we have not the same
means of dividing things into species, and therefore
the limits of species seem to be more arbitrary. But
from the progress already made, there is ground to
hope, that even in this kingdom, as the knowledge of
it advances, the various species may be so well distinguished and defined as to answer every valuable
purpose.

When the species are so numerous as to burden the memory, it is greatly assisted by distributing them into *genera;* the *genera* into tribes, the tribes into orders, and the orders into classes.

Such a regular distribution of natural substances, by divisions and subdivisions, has got the name of a system.

It is not a system of truths, but a system of general terms, with their definitions; and it is not only a great help to memory, but facilitates very much the definition of the terms. For the definition of the genus is common to all the species of that genus, and so is understood in the definition of each species, without the trouble of repetition. In like manner, the definition of a tribe is understood in the definition of every genus, and every species of that tribe; and the same may be said of every superior division.

The effect of such a systematical distribution of the productions of nature, is seen in our systems of zoology, botany, and mineralogy; in which a species is commonly defined accurately in a line or two, which, without the systematical arrangement, could hardly be defined in a page.

With regard to the utility of systems of this kind, men have gone into contrary extremes; some have treated them with contempt, as a mere dictionary of words; others, perhaps, rest in such systems, as all that is worth knowing in the works of nature.

On the one hand, it is not the intention of such systems to communicate all that is known of the natural productions which they describe. The properties most fit for defining and distinguishing the several species, are not always those that are most useful to be known. To discover and to communicate the uses of natural substances in life and in the arts, is

no doubt that part of the business of a naturalist
which is the most important; and the systematical
arrangement of them is chiefly to be valued for its subserviency to this end. This every judicious naturalist
will grant.

But, on the other hand, the labour is not to be despised, by which the road to an useful and important
branch of knowledge is made easy in all time to come;
especially when this labour requires both extensive
knowledge and great abilities.

The talent of arranging properly, and defining accurately, is so rare, and at the same time so useful,
that it may very justly be considered as a proof of
real genius, and as entitled to a high degree of praise.
There is an intrinsic beauty in arrangement, which
captivates the mind, and gives pleasure, even abstracting from its utility; as in most other things, so in
this particularly, nature has joined beauty with utility.
The arrangement of an army in the day of battle is a
grand spectacle. The same men crowded in a fair,
have no such effect. It is not more strange therefore
that some men spend their days in studying systems of
nature, than that other men employ their lives in the
study of languages. The most important end of those
tystems, surely, is to form a copious and an unambiguous language concerning the productions of
nature, by which every useful discovery concerning
them may be communicated to the present, and transmitted to all future generations, without danger of
mistake.

General terms, especially such as are complex in
their signification, will never keep one precise meaning without accurate definition; and accurate definitions of such terms can in no way be formed so easily
and advantageously, as by reducing the things they
signify into a regular system.

Very eminent men in the medical profession, in order to remove all ambiguity in the names of diseases, and to advance the healing art, have of late attempted to reduce into a systematical order, the diseases of the human body, and to give distinct names, and accurate definitions, of the several species, *genera*, orders, and classes, into which they distribute them; and I apprehend, that in every art and science, where the terms of the art have any ambiguity that obstructs its progress, this method will be found the easiest and most successful for the remedy of that evil.

It were even to be wished, that the general terms which we find in common language, as well as those of the arts and sciences, could be reduced to a systematical arrangement, and defined so as that they might be free from ambiguity; but perhaps the obstacles to this are insurmountable. I know no man who has attempted it but Bishop Wilkins in his Essay toward a real character and a philosophical language. The attempt was grand, and worthy of a man of genius.

The formation of such systems, therefore, of the various productions of nature, instead of being despised, ought to be ranked among the valuable improvements of modern ages; and to be the more esteemed that its utility reaches to the most distant future times, and, like the invention of writing, serves to embalm a most important branch of human knowledge, and to preserve it from being corrupted or lost.

CHAP. V.

OBSERVATIONS CONCERNING THE NAMES GIVEN TO
OUR GENERAL NOTIONS.

HAVING now explained, as well as I am able, those operations of the mind by which we analyze the objects which nature presents to our observation, into their simple attributes, giving a general name to each, and by which we combine any number of such attributes into one whole, and give a general name to that combination, I shall offer some observations relating to our general notions, whether simple or complex.

I apprehend that the names given to them by modern philosophers have contributed to darken our speculations about them, and to render them difficult and abstruse.

We call them general notions, conceptions, ideas. The words *notion* and *conception*, in their proper and most common sense, signify the act or operation of the mind in conceiving an object. In a figurative sense, they are sometimes put for the object conceived. And I think they are rarely, if ever, used in this figurative sense, except when we speak of what we call general notions or general conceptions. The word idea, as it is used in modern times, has the same ambiguity.

Now, it is only in the last of these senses, and not in the first, that we can be said to have general notions or conceptions. The generality is in the object conceived, and not in the act of the mind by which it is conceived. Every act of the mind is an individual act, which does or did exist. But we have power to conceive things which neither do nor ever did exist. We have power to conceive attributes without regard

to their existence. The conception of such an attribute is a real and individual act of the mind ; but the
attribute conceived is common to many individuals
that do or may exist. We are too apt to confound an
object of conception with the conception of that object.
But the danger of doing this must be much greater
when the object of conception is called a conception.

The Peripatetics gave to such objects of conception
the names of universals, and of predicables. Those
names had no ambiguity, and I think were much more
fit to express what was meant by them than the names
we use.

It is for this reason that I have so often used the
word attribute, which has the same meaning with
predicable. And for the same reason, I have thought
it necessary repeatedly to warn the reader, that when,
in compliance with custom, I speak of general notions or general conceptions, I always mean things
conceived, and not the act of the mind in conceiving
them.

The Pythagoreans and Platonists gave the name of
ideas to such general objects of conception, and to
nothing else. As we borrowed the word idea from
them, so that it is now familiar in all the languages of
Europe, I think it would have been happy if we had
also borrowed their meaning, and had used it only to
signify what they meant by it. I apprehend we want
an unambiguous word to distinguish things barely
conceived from things that exist. If the word *idea*
was used for this purpose only, it would be restored
to its original meaning, and supply that want.

We may surely agree with the Platonists in the
meaning of the word *idea*, without adopting their
theory concerning ideas. We need not believe, with
them, that ideas are eternal and self-existent, and that
they have a more real existence than the things we see
and feel.

They were led to give existence to ideas, from the common prejudice, that every thing which is an object of conception must really exist ; and having once given existence to ideas, the rest of their mysterious system about ideas followed of course ; for things merely conceived, have neither beginning nor end, time nor place ; they are subject to no change ; they are the patterns and exemplars according to which the Deity made every thing that he made ; for the work must be conceived by the artificer before it is made.

These are undeniable attributes of the ideas of Plato, and if we add to them that of real existence, we have the whole mysterious system of Platonic ideas. Take away the attribute of existence, and suppose them not to be things that exist, but things that are barely conceived, and all the mystery is removed ; all that remains is level to the human understanding.

The word *essence* came to be much used among the schoolmen, and what the Platonists called the idea of a species, they called its essence. The word *essentia* is said to have been made by Cicero ; but even his authority could not give it currency, until long after his time. It came at last to be used, and the schoolmen fell into much the same opinions concerning essences, as the Platonists held concerning ideas. The essences of things were held to be uncreated, eternal, and immutable.

Mr. Locke distinguishes two kinds of essence, the real and the nominal. By the real essence he means the constitution of an individual, which makes it to be what it is. This essence must begin and end with the individual to which it belongs. It is not therefore a Platonic idea. But what Mr. Locke calls the nominal essence, is the constitution of a species, or that which makes an individual to be of such a species ; and this is nothing but that combination of attributes which is signified by the name of the species, and which we conceive without regard to existence.

The essence of a species therefore is what the Platonists called the idea of the species.

If the word *idea* be restricted to the meaning which it bore among the Platonists and Pythagoreans, many things which Mr. Locke has said with regard to ideas will be just and true, and others will not.

It will be true, that most words, indeed all general words, are the signs of ideas; but proper names are not; they signify individual things, and not ideas. It will be true, not only that there are general and abstract ideas, but that all ideas are general and abstract. It will be so far from the truth, that all our simple ideas are got immediately, either from sensation, or from consciousness; that no simple idea is got by either, without the co-operation of other powers. The objects of sense, of memory, and of consciousness, are not ideas but individuals; they must be analyzed by the understanding into their simple ingredients, before we can have simple ideas; and those simple ideas must be again combined by the understanding, in distinct parcels with names annexed, in order to give us complex ideas. It will be probable, not only that brutes have no abstract ideas, but they have no ideas at all.

I shall only add, that the learned author of the Origin and Progress of Language. and perhaps his learned friend Mr. Harris, are the only modern authors I have met with, who restrict the word *idea* to this meaning. Their acquaintance with ancient philosophy led them to this. What pity is it that a word, which in ancient philosophy had a distinct meaning, and which if kept to that meaning, would have been a real acquisition to our language, should be used by the moderns in so vague and ambiguous a manner, that it is more apt to perplex and darken our speculations, than to convey useful knowledge.

From all that has been said about abstract and general conceptions, I think we may draw the following conclusions concerning them.

1st, That it is by abstraction that the mind is furnished with all its most simple, and most distinct notions. The simplest objects of sense appear both complex and indistinct, until by abstraction they are analyzed into their more simple elements; and the same may be said of the objects of memory and of consciousness.

2dly, Our most distinct complex notions are those that are formed by compounding the simple notions got by abstraction.

3dly, Without the powers of abstracting and generalizing, it would be impossible to reduce things into any order and method, by dividing them into genera and species.

4thly, Without those powers there could be no definition; for definition can only be applied to universals, and no individual can be defined.

5thly, Without abstract and general notions there can neither be reasoning nor language.

6thly, As brute animals show no signs of being able to distinguish the various attributes of the same subject; of being able to class things into genera and species; to define, to reason, or to communicate their thoughts by artificial signs, as men do; I must think with Mr. Locke, that they have not the powers of abstracting and generalizing; and that in this particular, nature has made a specific difference between them and the human species.

CHAP. VI.

OPINIONS OF PHILOSOPHERS ABOUT UNIVERSALS.

IN the ancient philosophy, the doctrine of universals, that is, of things which we express by general terms, makes a great figure. The ideas of the Pythagoreans and Platonists, of which so much has been already said, were universals. All science is employed about universals as its object. It was thought that there can be no science, unless its object be something real and immutable; and therefore those who paid homage to truth and science, maintained that ideas, or universals, have a real and immutable existence.

The skeptics, on the contrary, for there were skeptical philosophers in those early days, maintained, that all things are mutable, and in a perpetual fluctuation; and from this principle inferred, that there is no science, no truth; that all is uncertain opinion.

Plato, and his masters of the Pythagorean school, yielded this with regard to objects of sense, and acknowledged that there could be no science or certain knowledge concerning them: but they held, that there are objects of intellect of a superior order and nature, which are permanent and immutable. These are ideas, or universal natures, of which the objects of sense are only the images and shadows.

To these ideas they ascribed, as I have already observed, the most magnificent attributes. Of man, of a rose, of a circle, and of every species of things, they believed that there is one idea or form, which existed from eternity, before any individual of the species was formed: that this idea is the exemplar or pattern, according to which the Deity formed the individuals of the species: that every individual of the species par-

ticipates of this idea, which constitutes its essence;
and that this idea is likewise an object of the human
intellect, when, by due abstraction, we discern it to be
one in all the individuals of the species.

Thus the idea of every species, though one and immutable, might be considered in three different views
or respects; 1st, as having an eternal existence before
there was any individual of the species; 2dly, as existing in every individual of that species, without division or multiplication, and making the essence of the
species; and, 3dly, as an object of intellect and of science in man.

Such I take to be the doctrine of Plato, as far as I
am able to comprehend it. His disciple Aristotle rejected the first of these views of ideas as visionary, but
differed little from his master with regard to the two
last. He did not admit the existence of universal natures antecedent to the existence of individuals; but he
held, that every individual consists of matter and form:
that the form, which I take to be what Plato calls the
idea, is common to all the individuals of the species,
and that the human intellect is fitted to receive the
forms of things as objects of contemplation. Such profound speculations about the nature of universals, we
find even in the first ages of philosophy. I wish I
could make them more intelligible to myself and to
the reader.

The division of universals into five classes; to wit,
genus, species, specific difference, properties, and accidents, is likewise very ancient, and I conceive was borrowed by the Peripatetics from the Pythagorean school

Porphyry has given us a very distinct treatise upon
these, as an introduction to Aristotle's categories.
But he has omitted the intricate metaphysical questions
that were agitated about their nature; such as, Whether genera and species do really exist in nature? Or.

Whether they are only conceptions of the human mind?
If they exist in nature, Whether they are corporeal
or incorporeal? And whether they are inherent in the
objects of sense, or disjoined from them? These questions he tells us, for brevity's sake, he omits, because
they are very profound, and require accurate discussion.
It is probable, that these questions exercised the wits
of the philosophers till about the twelfth century.

About that time, Roscelinus or Ruscelinus, the
master of the famous Abelard, introduced a new doctrine, that there is nothing universal but words or names.
For this, and other heresies, he was much persecuted.
However, by his eloquence and abilities, and those of
his disciple Abelard, the doctrine spread, and those
who followed it were called Nominalists. His antagonists, who held that there are things that are really
universal, were called Realists. The scholastic philosophers, from the beginning of the twelfth century,
were divided into these two sects. Some few took a
middle road between the contending parties. That
universality, which the Realists held to be in things
themselves, Nominalists in names only, they held to be
neither in things nor in names only, but in our conceptions. On this account they were called Concep-
tualists : but being exposed to the batteries of both
the opposite parties, they made no great figure.

When the sect of Nominalists was like to expire,
it received new life and spirit from Occam, the disciple of Scotus, in the fourteenth century. Then the
dispute about universals, *a parte rei*, was revived with
the greatest animosity in the schools of Britain, France,
and Germany, and carried on, not by arguments only,
but by bitter reproaches, blows, and bloody affrays, until the doctrines of Luther and the other reformers,
turned the attention of the learned world to more important subjects.

After the revival of learning, Mr. Hobbes adopted the opinion of the Nominalists. Human Nature, chap. 5. sect. 6. "It is plain, therefore," says he, "that there is nothing universal but names." And in his Leviathan, part 1. chap. 4. "There being nothing universal but names, proper names bring to mind one thing only ; universals recal any one of many."

Mr. Locke, according to the division before mentioned, I think, may be accounted a Conceptualist. He does not maintain that there are things that are universal ; but that we have general, or universal ideas which we form by abstraction ; and this power of forming abstract and general ideas, he conceives to be that which makes the chief distinction in point of understanding between men and brutes.

Mr. Locke's doctrine about abstraction has been combated by two very powerful antagonists, bishop Berkeley and Mr. Hume, who have taken up the opinion of the Nominalists. The former thinks, "That the opinion, that the mind has a power of forming abstract ideas, or notions of things, has had a chief part in rendering speculation intricate and perplexed, and has occasioned innumerable errors and difficulties in almost all parts of knowledge." That "abstract ideas are like a fine and subtile net, which has miserably perplexed and entangled the minds of men, with this peculiar circumstance, that by how much the finer and more curious was the wit of any man, by so much the deeper was he like to be ensnared, and faster held therein." That "among all the false principles that have obtained in the world, there is none has a more wide influence over the thoughts of speculative men than this of abstract general ideas."

The good bishop therefore, in twenty-four pages of the introduction to his Principles of Human Knowledge, encounters this principle with a zeal proportioned to his apprehension of its malignant and extensive influence.

That the zeal of the skeptical philosopher against abstract ideas was almost equal to that of the bishop, appears from his words, Treatise of Human Nature, book 1. part 1. sect. 7. " A very material question has been started concerning abstract or general ideas, whether they be general or particular in the mind's conception of them? A great philosopher (he means Dr. Berkeley) has disputed the received opinion in this particular, and has asserted, that all general ideas are nothing but particular ones annexed to a certain term, which gives them a more extensive signification, and makes them recal upon occasion other individuals which are similar to them.   As I look upon this to be one of the greatest and most valuable discoveries that have been made of late years in the republic of letters, I shall here endeavour to confirm it by some arguments, which, I hope, will put it beyond all doubt and controversy."

I shall make an end of this subject, with some reflections on what has been said upon it by these two eminent philosophers.

1. *First,* I apprehend that we cannot, with propriety, be said to have abstract and general ideas, either in the popular or in the philosophical sense of that word. In the popular sense an idea is a thought : it is the act of the mind in thinking, or in conceiving any object.   This act of the mind is always an individual act, and therefore there can be no general idea in this sense.   In the philosophical sense, an idea is an image in the mind, or in the brain, which, in Mr. Locke's system is the immediate object of thought ; in the system of Berkeley and Hume the only object of thought.   I believe there are no ideas of this kind, and therefore no abstract general ideas.   Indeed, if there were really such images in the mind, or in the brain, they could

not be general, because every thing that really exists is an individual. Universals are neither acts of the mind, nor images in the mind.

As therefore there are no general ideas in either of the senses in which the word *idea* is used by the moderns, Berkeley and Hume have in this question an advantage over Mr. Locke; and their arguments against him are good *ad hominem.* They saw farther than he did into the just consequences of the hypothesis concerning ideas, which was common to them and to him; and they reasoned justly from this hypothesis, when they concluded from it, that there is neither a material world, nor any such power in the human mind as that of abstraction.

A triangle, in general, or any other universal, might be called an idea by a Platonist; but, in the style of modern philosophy, it is not an idea, nor do we ever ascribe to ideas the properties of triangles. It is never said of any idea, that it has three sides and three angles. We do not speak of equilateral, isosceles, or scalene ideas, nor of right angled, acute angled, or obtuse angled ideas. And if these attributes do not belong to ideas, it follows necessarily, that a triangle is not an idea. The same reasoning may be applied to every other universal.

Ideas are said to have a real existence in the mind, at least, while we think of them; but universals have no real existence. When we ascribe existence to them, it is not an existence in time or place, but existence in some individual subject; and this existence means no more but that they are truly attributes of such a subject. Their existence is nothing but predicability, or the capacity of being attributed to a subject. The name of predicables, which was given them in ancient philosophy, is that which most properly expresses their nature.

2. I think it must be granted, in the *second* place, that universals cannot be the objects of imagination, when we take that word in its strict and proper sense. " I find," says Berkeley, " I have a faculty of imagining or representing to myself the ideas of those particular things I have perceived, and of variously compounding and dividing them. I can imagine a man with two heads, or the upper parts of a man joined to the body of a horse. I can imagine the hand, the eye, the nose, each by itself, abstracted or separated from the rest of the body. But then, whatever hand or eye I imagine, it must have some particular shape or colour. Likewise, the idea of a man that I frame to myself must be either of a white, or a black, or a tawny, a straight, or a crooked, a tall, or a low, or a middle sized man."

I believe every man will find in himself what this ingenious author found, that he cannot imagine a man without colour, or stature, or shape.

Imagination, as we before observed, properly signifies a conception of the appearance an object would make to the eye, if actually seen. An universal is not an object of any external sense, and therefore cannot be imagined; but it may be distinctly conceived. When Mr. Pope says, " The proper study of mankind is man," I conceive his meaning distinctly, though I neither imagine a black, or a white, a crooked, or a straight man. The distinction between conception and imagination is real, though it be too often overlooked, and the words taken to be synonimous. I can conceive a thing that is impossible, but I cannot distinctly imagine a thing that is impossible. I can conceive a proposition or a demonstration, but I cannot imagine either. I can conceive understanding and will, virtue and vice, and other attributes of mind, but I cannot imagine them. In like manner, I can distinctly conceive universals, but I cannot imagine them.

As to the manner how we conceive universals, I confess my ignorance. I know not how I hear, or see, or remember, and as little do I know how I conceive things that have no existence. In all our original faculties, the fabric and manner of operation is, I apprehend, beyond our comprehension, and perhaps is perfectly understood by him only who made them.

But we ought not to deny a fact of which we are conscious, though we know not how it is brought about. And I think we may be certain that universals are not conceived by means of images of them in our minds, because there can be no image of an universal.

3dly, It seems to me, that on this question Mr. Locke and his two antagonists have divided the truth between them. He saw very clearly, that the power of forming abstract and general conceptions is one of the most distinguishing powers of the human mind, and puts a specific difference between man and the brute creation. But he did not see that this power is perfectly irreconcileable to his doctrine concerning ideas.

His opponents saw this inconsistency; but, instead of rejecting the hypothesis of ideas, they explain away the power of abstraction, and leave no specific distinction between the human understanding, and that of brutes.

4thly, Berkeley, in his reasoning against abstract general ideas, seems unwilling or unwarily to grant all that is necessary to support abstract and general conceptions.

" A man," he says, " may consider a figure merely as triangular, without attending to the particular qualities of the angles, or relations of the sides. So far he may abstract. But this will never prove that he can frame an abstract general inconsistent idea of a triangle."

If a man may consider a figure merely as triangular, he must have some conception of this object of his consideration: for no man can consider a thing which he does not conceive. He has a conception, therefore, of a triangular figure, merely as such. I know no more that is meant by an abstract general conception of a triangle.

He that considers a figure merely as triangular, must understand what is meant by the word *triangular*. If to the conception he joins to this word, he adds any particular quality of angles or relation of sides, he misunderstands it, and does not consider the figure merely as triangular. Whence I think it is evident, that he who considers a figure merely as triangular must have the conception of a triangle, abstracting from any quality of angles or relation of sides.

The bishop, in like manner, grants, "That we may consider Peter so far forth as man, or so far forth as animal, without framing the forementioned abstract idea, in as much as all that is perceived is not considered." It may here be observed, that he who considers Peter so far forth as man, or so far forth as animal, must conceive the meaning of those abstract general words *man* and *animal*, and he who conceives the meaning of them, has an abstract general conception.

From these concessions, one would be apt to conclude that the bishop thinks that we can abstract, but that we cannot frame abstract ideas; and in this I should agree with him. But I cannot reconcile his concessions with the general principle he lays down before. "To be plain," says he, "I deny that I can abstract one from another, or conceive separately those qualities which it is impossible should exist so separated." This appears to me inconsistent with the concessions above mentioned, and inconsistent with experience.

If we can consider a figure merely as triangular, without attending to the particular quality of the angles or relation of the sides, this, I think, is conceiving separately things which cannot exist so separated : for surely a triangle cannot exist without a particular quality of angles and relation of sides. And it is well known from experience, that a man may have a distinct conception of a triangle, without having any conception or knowledge of many of the properties without which a triangle cannot exist.

Let us next consider the bishop's notion of generalizing. He does not absolutely deny that there are general ideas, but only that there are abstract general ideas. "An idea," he says, "which, considered in itself, is particular, becomes general, by being made to represent or stand for all other particular ideas of the same sort. To make this plain by an example, suppose a geometrician is demonstrating the method of cutting a line in two equal parts. He draws, for instance, a black line of an inch in length. This, which is in itself a particular line, is nevertheless, with regard to its signification, general ; since, as it is there used, it represents all particular lines whatsoever ; so that what is demonstrated of it, is demonstrated of all lines, or, in other words, of a line in general. And as that particular line becomes general by being made a sign, so the name *line*, which, taken absolutely, is particular, by being a sign, is made general."

Here I observe, that when a particular idea is made a sign to represent and stand for all of a sort, this supposes a distinction of things into sorts or species. To be of a sort implies having those attributes which characterize the sort, and are common to all the individuals that belong to it. There cannot, therefore, be a sort without general attributes, nor can there be any conception of a sort without a conception of those general attributes which distinguish it. The conception of a sort, therefore, is an abstract general conception.

The particular idea cannot surely be made a sign of a thing of which we have no conception. I do not say that you must have an idea of the sort, but surely you ought to understand or conceive what it means, when you make a particular idea a representative of it, otherwise your particular idea represents, you know not what.

When I demonstrate any general property of a triangle, such as, that the three angles are equal to two right angles, I must understand or conceive distinctly what is common to all triangles. I must distinguish the common attributes of all triangles from those wherein particular triangles may differ. And if I conceive distinctly what is common to all triangles, without confounding it with what is not so, this is to form a general conception of a triangle. And without this, it is impossible to know that the demonstration extends to all triangles.

The bishop takes particular notice of this argument, and makes this answer to it. " Though the idea I have in view, whilst I make the demonstration be, for instance, that of an isosceles rectangular triangle, whose sides are of a determinate length, I may nevertheless be certain that it extends to all other rectilinear triangles, of what sort or bigness soever; and that because neither the right angle, nor the equality or determinate length of the sides, are at all concerned in the demonstration."

But if he do not, in the idea he has in view, clearly distinguish what is common to all triangles from what is not, it would be impossible to discern whether something that is not common be concerned in the demonstration or not. In order, therefore, to perceive that the demonstration extends to all triangles, it is necessary to have a distinct conception of what is common

to all triangles, excluding from that conception all that
is not common.   And this is all I understand by an abstract general conception of a triangle.

Berkeley catches an advantage to his side of the
question, from what Mr. Locke expresses, too strongly indeed, of the difficulty of framing abstract general
ideas, and the pains and skill necessary for that purpose.   From which the bishop infers, that a thing so
difficult cannot be necessary for communication by language, which is so easy and familiar to all sorts of men.

There may be some abstract and general conceptions
that are difficult, or even beyond the reach of persons
of weak understanding ; but there are innumerable,
which are not beyond the reach of children.   It is impossible to learn language without acquiring general
conceptions ; for there cannot be a single sentence
without them.   I believe the forming these, and being
able to articulate the sounds of language, make up the
whole difficulty that children find in learning language
at first.

But this difficulty, we see, they are able to overcome so early as not to remember the pains it cost
them.   They have the strongest inducement to exert
all their labour and skill, in order to understand, and
to be understood ; and they no doubt do so.

The labour of forming abstract notions, is the labour
of learning to speak, and to understand what is spoken.
As the words of every language, excepting a few proper
names, are general words, the minds of children are
furnished with general conceptions, in proportion as
they learn the meaning of general words.   I believe
most men have hardly any general notions but those
which are expressed by the general words they hear
and use in conversation.   The meaning of some of
these is learned by a definition, which at once conveys
a distinct and accurate general conception.   The

meaning of other general words we collect, by a kind of induction, from the way in which we see them used on various occasions, by those who understand the language. Of these our conception is often less distinct, and in different persons is perhaps not perfectly the same.

" Is it not a hard thing," says the bishop, " that a couple of children cannot prate together of their sugarplums and rattles, and the rest of their little trinkets, till they have first tacked together numberless inconsistencies, and so formed in their minds abstract general ideas, and annexed them to every common name they make use of."

However hard a thing it may be, it is an evident truth, that a couple of children, even about their sugar-plums and their rattles, cannot prate so as to understand, and be understood, until they have learned to conceive the meaning of many general words, and this, I think, is to have general conceptions.

5thly, Having considered the sentiments of Bishop Berkeley on this subject, let us next attend to those of Mr. Hume, as they are expressed, part 1. sect. 7. Treatise of Human Nature. He agrees perfectly with the bishop, " That all general ideas are nothing but particular ones annexed to a certain term, which gives them a more extensive signification, and makes them recal upon occasion other individuals which are similar to them. A particular idea becomes general, by being annexed to a general term; that is, to a term, which, from a customary conjunction, has a relation to many other particular ideas, and readily recals them in the imagination. Abstract ideas are therefore in themselves individual, however they may become general in their representation. The image in the mind is only that of a particular object, though the application of it in our reasoning be the same as if it was universal."

Although Mr. Hume looks upon this to be one of the greatest and most valuable discoveries that has been made of late years in the republic of letters, it appears to be no other than the opinion of the Nominalists, about which so much dispute was held from the beginning of the twelfth century down to the reformation, and which was afterward supported by Mr. Hobbes. I shall briefly consider the arguments, by which Mr. Hume hopes to have put it beyond all doubt and controversy.

1st, He endeavours to prove, by three arguments, that it is utterly impossible to conceive any quantity or quality, without forming a precise notion of its degrees.

This is indeed a great undertaking; but if he could prove it, it is not sufficient for his purpose; for two reasons.

1st, Because there are many attributes of things, besides quantity and quality; and it is incumbent upon him to prove, that it is impossible to conceive any attribute, without forming a precise notion of its degree. Each of the ten categories of Aristotle is a genus, and may be an attribute: and if he should prove of two of them, to wit, quantity and quality, that there can be no general conception of them, there remain eight behind, of which this must be proved.

The other reason is, because though it were impossible to conceive any quantity or quality, without forming a precise notion of its degree, it does not follow that it is impossible to have a general conception even of quantity and quality. The conception of a pound troy is the conception of a quantity, and of the precise degree of that quantity; but it is an abstract general conception notwithstanding, because it may be the attribute of many individual bodies, and of many kinds of bodies. He ought therefore to have proved, that we cannot conceive quantity or quality, or any other attribute, without joining it inseparably to some individual subject.

This remains to be proved, which will be found no easy matter. For instance, I conceive what is meant by a Japanese as distinctly as what is meant by an Englishman or a Frenchman. It is true, a Japanese is neither quantity nor quality, but it is an attribute common to every individual of a populous nation. I never saw an individual of that nation, and, if I can trust my consciousness, the general term does not lead me to imagine one individual of the sort as a representative of all others.

Though Mr. Hume, therefore, undertakes much, yet, if he could prove all he undertakes to prove, it would by no means be sufficient to show that we have no abstract general conceptions.

Passing this, let us attend to his arguments for proving this extraordinary position, that it is impossible to conceive any quantity or quality, without forming a precise notion of its degree.

The first argument is, that it is impossible to distinguish things that are not actually separable. " The precise length of a line is not different or distinguishable from the line."

I have before endeavoured to show, that things inseparable in their nature may be distinguished in our conception. And we need go no farther to be convinced of this, than the instance here brought to prove the contrary. The precise length of a line, he says, is not distinguishable from the line. When I say, *this is a line*, I say and mean one thing. When I say *it is a line of three inches*, I say and mean another thing. If this be not to distinguish the precise length of the line from the line, I know not what it is to distinguish.

Second argument. " Every object of sense, that is, every impression, is an individual, having its de-

terminate degrees of quantity and quality : but whatever is true of the impression is true of the idea,
as they differ in nothing but their strength and vivacity."

The conclusion in this argument is indeed justly
drawn from the premises. If it be true that ideas differ in nothing from objects of sense but in strength
and vivacity, as it must be granted that all the objects
of sense are individuals, it will certainly follow that
all ideas are individuals. Granting therefore the just-
ness of this conclusion, I beg leave to draw two other
conclusions from the same premises, which will follow no less necessarily.

1st, If ideas differ from the object of sense only in
strength and vivacity, it will follow, that the idea
of a lion is a lion of less strength and vivacity. And
hence may arise a very important question, Whether
the idea of a lion may not tear in pieces and devour
the ideas of sheep, oxen, and horses, and even of men,
women, and children ?

2dly, If ideas differ only in strength and vivacity
from the objects of sense, it will follow, that objects,
merely conceived, are not ideas; for such objects
differ from the objects of sense in respects of a very
different nature from strength and vivacity. Every
object of sense must have a real existence, and time
and place : but things merely conceived may neither
have existence, nor time nor place ; and therefore,
though there should be no abstract ideas, it does not
follow, that things abstract and general may not be
conceived.

The third argument is this : " It is a principle generally received in philosophy, that every thing in
nature is individual ; and that it is utterly absurd to
suppose a triangle really existent, which has no precise proportion of sides and angles. If this, there-

fore, be absurd in fact and reality, it must be absurd in idea, since nothing of which we can form a clear and distinct idea is absurd or impossible."

I acknowledge it to be impossible, that a triangle should really exist which has no precise proportion of sides and angles ; and impossible that any being should exist which is not an individual being ; for I think, a being and an individual being mean the same thing : but that there can be no attributes common to many individuals, I do not acknowledge. Thus, to many figures that really exist, it may be common that they are triangles ; and to many bodies that exist, it may be common that they are fluid. Triangle and fluid are not beings, they are attributes of beings.

As to the principle here assumed, that nothing of which we can form a clear and distinct idea is absurd or impossible, I refer to what was said upon it, chap. 3. Essay 4. It is evident, that in every mathematical demonstration, *ad absurdum*, of which kind almost one half of mathematics consists, we are required to suppose, and consequently to conceive a thing that is impossible. From that supposition we reason, until we come to a conclusion that is not only impossible but absurd. From this we infer, that the proposition supposed at first is impossible, and therefore that its contradictory is true.

As this is the nature of all demonstrations *ad absurdum*, it is evident, I do not say that we can have a clear and distinct idea, but that we can clearly and distinctly conceive things impossible.

The rest of Mr. Hume's discourse upon this subject is employed in explaining how an individual idea, annexed to a general term, may serve all the purposes in reasoning, which have been ascribed to abstract general ideas.

" When we have found a resemblance among several objects that often occur to us, we apply the same name to all of them, whatever differences we may observe in the degrees of their quantity and quality, and whatever other differences may appear among them. After we have acquired a custom of this kind, the hearing of that name revives the idea of one of these objects, and makes the imagination conceive it, with all its circumstances and proportions." But along with this idea, there is a readiness to survey any other of the individuals to which the name belongs, and to observe, that no conclusion be formed contrary to any of them. If any such conclusion is formed, those individual ideas which contradict it, immediately crowd in upon us, and make us perceive the falsehood of the proposition. If the mind suggest not always these ideas upon occasion, it proceeds from some imperfection in its faculties; and such a one as is often the source of false reasoning and sophistry.

This is in substance the way in which he accounts for what he calls " the foregoing paradox, that some ideas are particular in their nature, but general in their representation." Upon this account I shall make some remarks.

1st, He allows that we find a resemblance among several objects, and such a resemblance as leads us to apply the same name to all of them. This concession is sufficient to show that we have general conceptions. There can be no resemblance in objects that have no common attribute; and if there be attributes belonging in common to several objects, and in man a faculty to observe and conceive these, and to give names to them, this is to have general conceptions.

I believe indeed we may have an indistinct perception of resemblance, without knowing wherein it lies. Thus, I may see a resemblance between one face and

another, when I cannot distinctly say in what feature
they resemble: but by analyzing the two faces, and
comparing feature with feature, I may form a distinct
notion of that which is common to both. A painter,
being accustomed to an analysis of this kind, would
have formed a distinct notion of this resemblance at
first sight; to another man it may require some attention.

There is therefore an indistinct notion of resemblance when we compare the objects only in gross;
and this I believe brute animals may have. There is
also a distinct notion of resemblance, when we analyze the objects into their different attributes, and
perceive them to agree in some, while they differ in
others. It is in this case only that we give a name to
the attributes wherein they agree, which must be a
common name, because the thing signified by it is
common. Thus, when I compare cubes of different
matter, I perceive them to have this attribute in common, that they are comprehended under six equal
squares; and this attribute only, is signified by applying the name of *cube* to them all. When I compare clean linen with snow, I perceive them to agree
in colour; and when I apply the name of white to
both, this name signifies neither snow nor clean linen,
but the attribute which is common to both.

2dly, The author says, that when we have found a
resemblance among several objects, we apply the same
name to all of them.

It must here be observed, that there are two kinds
of names which the author seems to confound, though
they are very different in nature, and in the power
they have in language. There are proper names, and
there are common names, or appellatives. The first
are the names of individuals. The same proper name
is never applied to several individuals on account of

their similitude, because the very intention of a proper name is to distinguish one individual from all others ; and hence it is a maxim in grammar, that proper names have no plural number. A proper name signifies nothing but the individual, whose name it is ; and when we apply it to the individual, we neither affirm nor deny any thing concerning him.

A common name or appellative is not the name of any individual, but a general term, signifying something that is, or may be common to several individuals. Common names therefore signify common attributes. Thus, when I apply the name of son or brother to several persons, this signifies and affirms that this attribute is common to all of them.

From this it is evident, that the applying the same name to several individuals, on account of their resemblance, can, in consistence with grammar and common sense, mean nothing else than the expressing by a general term something that is common to those individuals, and which therefore may be truly affirmed of them all.

3dly, The author says, " It is certain that we form the idea of individuals, whenever we use any general term. The word raises up an individual idea, and makes the imagination conceive it, with all its particular circumstances and proportions."

This fact he takes a great deal of pains to account for, from the effect of custom.

But the fact should be ascertained before we take pains to account for it. I can see no reason to believe the fact ; and I think a farmer can talk of his sheep, and his black cattle, without conceiving in his imagination one individual, with all its circumstances and proportions. If this be true, the whole of his theory of general ideas falls to the ground. To me it appears, that when a general term is well understood, it is only

by accident if it suggest some individual of the kind ;
but this effect is by no means constant.

I understand perfectly what mathematicians call a
line of the fifth order ; yet I never conceived in my imagination any one of the kind in all its circumstances
and proportions. Sir Isaac Newton first formed a distinct general conception of lines of the third order ; and
afterward, by great labour and deep penetration, found
out and described the particular species comprehended
under that general term. According to Mr. Hume's
theory, he must first have been acquainted with the
particulars, and then have learned by custom, to apply
one general name to all of them.

The author observes, " that the idea of an equilateral triangle of an inch perpendicular, may serve us in
talking of a figure, a rectilinear figure, a regular figure, a triangle, and an equilateral triangle."

I answer, the man that uses these general terms,
either understands their meaning, or he does not. If he
does not understand their meaning, all his talk about
them will be sound only without sense, and the particular idea mentioned cannot enable him to speak of
them with understanding. If he understands the meaning of the general terms, he will find no use for the
particular idea.

4thly, He tells us gravely, " That in a globe of white
marble the figure and the colour are undistinguishable,
and are in effect the same." How foolish have mankind been to give different names, in all ages and in all
languages, to things undistinguishable, and in effect
the same? Henceforth, in all books of science and of
entertainment, we may substitute figure for colour, and
colour for figure. By this we shall make numberless
curious discoveries, without danger of error.

ESSAY VI.

OF JUDGMENT.

CHAP. I.

OF JUDGMENT IN GENERAL.

JUDGING is an operation of the mind so familiar to every man who has understanding, and its name is so common and so well understood, that it needs no definition.

As it is impossible by a definition to give a notion of colour to a man who never saw colours; so it is impossible by any definition to give a distinct notion of judgment to a man who has not often judged. and who is not capable of reflecting attentively upon this act of his mind. The best use of a definition is to prompt him to that reflection; and without it the best definition will be apt to mislead him.

The definition commonly given of judgment, by the more ancient writers in logic. was, that it is an act of the mind, whereby one thing is affirmed or denied of another. I believe this is as good a definition of it as can be given. Why I prefer it to some later definitions, will afterward appear. Without pretending to give any other, I shall make two remarks upon it, and then offer some general observations on this subject.

1st, It is true, that it is by affirmation or denial that we express our judgments; but there may be judgment which is not expressed. It is a solitary act of the mind, and the expression of it by affirmation or denial is not at all essential to it. It may be tacit, and not expressed. Nay, it is well known that men may judge contrary to what they affirm or deny; the definition therefore must be understood of mental affirmation or denial, which indeed is only another name for judgment.

2dly. Affirmation and denial is very often the expression of testimony, which is a different act of the mind, and ought to be distinguished from judgment.

A judge asks of a witness what he knows of such a matter to which he was an eye or ear witness. He answers, by affirming or denying something. But his answer does not express his judgment; it is his testimony. Again, I ask a man his opinion in a matter of science or of criticism. His answer is not testimony; it is the expression of his judgment.

Testimony is a social act, and it is essential to it to be expressed by words or signs. A tacit testimony is a contradiction: but there is no contradiction in a tacit judgment; it is complete without being expressed.

In testimony, a man pledges his veracity for what he affirms; so that a false testimony is a lie: but a wrong judgment is not a lie; it is only an error.

I believe, in all languages, testimony and judgment are expressed by the same form of speech. A proposition affirmative or negative, with a verb in what is called the indicative mood, expresses both. To distinguish them by the form of speech, it would be necessary that verbs should have two indicative moods, one for testimony, and another to express judgment. I know not that this is found in any language. And the reason is, not surely that the vulgar cannot distinguish the two, for every man knows the difference between a lie and an error of judgment, but that, from the matter and circumstances, we can easily see whether a man intends to give his testimony, or barely to express his judgment.

Although men must have judged in many cases before tribunals of justice were erected, yet it is very probable that there were tribunals before men began to speculate about judgment, and that the word may be borrowed from the practice of tribunals. As a judge, after taking the proper evidence, passes sentence in a cause, and that sentence is called his judgment; so the mind, with regard to whatever is true or false, passes sentence, or determines according to the evidence that appears. Some kinds of evidence leave no room for doubt. Sentence is passed immediately, without seeking or hearing any contrary evidence, because the thing is certain and notorious. In other cases, there is room for weighing evidence on both sides before sentence is passed. The analogy between a tribunal of justice and this inward tribunal of the mind, is too obvious to escape the notice of any man who ever appeared before a judge. And it is probable, that the word *judgment*, as well as many other words we use in speaking of this operation of mind, are grounded on this analogy.

Having premised these things, that it may be clearly understood what I mean by judgment, I proceed to make some general observations concerning it.

1st, Judgment is an act of the mind specifically different from simple apprehension, or the bare conception of a thing. It would be unnecessary to observe this, if some philosophers had not been led by their theories to a contrary opinion.

Although there can be no judgment without a conception of the things about which we judge; yet conception may be without any judgment. Judgment can be expressed by a proposition only, and a proposition is a complete sentence; but simple apprehension may be expressed by a word or words, which make no complete sentence. When simple apprehension is employed about a proposition, every man knows that it is one thing to apprehend a proposition, that is, to conceive what it means; but it is quite another thing to judge it to be true or false.

It is self-evident, that every judgment must be either true or false ; but simple apprehension or conception can neither be true nor false, as was shown before.

One judgment may be contradictory to another; and it is impossible for a man to have two judgments at the same time, which he perceives to be contradictory. But contradictory propositions may be conceived at the same time without any difficulty. That the sun is greater than the earth, and that the sun is not greater than the earth, are contradictory propositions. He that apprehends the meaning of one, apprehends the meaning of both. But it is impossible for him to judge both to be true at the same time. He knows that if the one is true, the other must be false. For these reasons, I hold it to be certain, that judgment and simple apprehension are acts of the mind specifically different.

2dly, There are notions or ideas that ought to be referred to the faculty of judgment as their source ; because, if we had not that faculty, they could not enter into our minds; and to those that have that faculty, and are capable of reflecting upon its operations, they are obvious and familiar.

Among these we may reckon the notion of judgment itself; the notions of a proposition, of its subject, predicate, and copula; of affirmation and negation, of true and false, of knowledge, belief, disbelief, opinion, assent, evidence. From no source could we acquire these notions, but from reflecting upon our judgments. Relations of things make one great class of our notions or ideas; and we cannot have the idea of any relation without some exercise of judgment, as will appear afterward.

3dly, In persons come to years of understanding, judgment necessarily accompanies all sensation, perception by the senses, consciousness, and memory, but not conception.

I restrict this to persons come to the years of understanding, because it may be a question, whether infants, in the first period of life, have any judgment or belief at all. The same question may be put with regard to brutes and some idiots. This question is foreign to the present subject; and I say nothing here about it, but speak only of persons who have the exercise of judgment.

In them it is evident, that a man who feels pain, judges and believes that he is really pained. The man who perceives an object, believes that it exists, and is what he distinctly perceives it to be; nor is it in his power to avoid such judgment. And the like may be said of memory, and of consciousness. Whether judgment ought to be called a necessary concomitant of these operations, or rather a part or ingredient of them, I do not dispute; but it is certain, that all of them are accompanied with a determination that something is true or false, and a consequent belief. If this determination be not judgment, it is an operation that has got no name; for it is not simple apprehension, neither is it reasoning; it is a mental affirmation or negation; it may be expressed by a proposition affirmative or negative, and it is accompanied with the firmest belief. These are the characteristics of judgment; and I must call it judgment, till I can find another name to it.

The judgments we form, are either of things necessary, or of things contingent. That three times three are nine; that the whole is greater than a part; are judgments about things necessary. Our assent to such necessary propositions is not grounded upon any operation of sense, of memory, or of consciousness, nor does it require their concurrence; it is unaccompanied by any other operation but that of conception, which must accompany all judgment; we may therefore call this judgment of things necessary, pure judgment. Our judgment of things contingent must always rest upon some other operation of the mind, such as sense, or memory, or consciousness, or credit in testimony, which is itself grounded upon sense.

That I now write upon a table covered with green cloth, is a contingent event, which I judge to be most undoubtedly true. My judgment is grounded upon my perception, and is a necessary concomitant or ingredient of my perception. That I dined with such a company yesterday, I judge to be true, because I remember it; and my judgment necessarily goes along with this remembrance, or makes a part of it.

There are many forms of speech in common language which show that the senses, memory and consciousness, are considered as judging faculties. We say that a man judges of colours by his eye, of sounds by his ear. We speak of the evidence of sense, the evidence of memory, the evidence of consciousness. Evidence is the ground of judgment, and when we see evidence, it is impossible not to judge.

When we speak of seeing or remembering any thing, we indeed hardly ever add that we judge it to be true. But the reason of this appears to be, that such an addition would be mere superfluity of speech, because every one knows, that what I see or remember, I must judge to be true, and cannot do otherwise.

And for the same reason, in speaking of any thing that is self-evident or strictly demonstrated, we do not say that we judge it to be true. This would be superfluity of speech, because every man knows that we must judge that to be true which we hold self-evident or demonstrated.

When you say you saw such a thing, or that you distinctly remember it, or when you say of any proposition that it is self-evident, or strictly demonstrated, it would be ridiculous after this to ask whether you judge it to be true; nor would it be less ridiculous in you to inform us that you do. It would be a superfluity of speech of the same kind as if, not content with saying that you saw such an object, you should add that you saw it with your eyes.

There is therefore good reason why, in speaking or writing, judgment should not be expressly mentioned, when all men know it to be necessarily implied; that is, when there can be no doubt. In such cases, we barely mention the evidence. But when the evidence mentioned leaves room for doubt, then, without any superfluity or tautology, we say we judge the thing to be so, because this is not implied in what was said before. A woman with child never says, that, going such a journey, she carried her child along with her. We know that, while it is in her womb, she must carry it along with her. There are some operations of mind that may be said to carry judgment in their womb, and can no more leave it behind them than the pregnant woman can leave her child. Therefore, in speaking of such operations, it is not expressed.

Perhaps this manner of speaking may have led philosophers into the opinion, that in perception by the senses, in memory, and in consciousness. there is no judgment at all. Because it is not mentioned in speaking of these faculties, they conclude that it does not accompany them; that they are only different modes of simple apprehension, or of acquiring ideas; and that it is no part of their office to judge.

I apprehend the same cause has led Mr. Locke into a notion of judgment which I take to be peculiar to him. He thinks that the mind has two faculties conversant about truth and falsehood: 1st, knowledge; and, 2dly, judgment. In the first, the perception of the agreement or disagreement of the ideas is certain. In the second, it is not certain, but probable only.

According to this notion of judgment, it is not by judgment that I perceive that two and three make five; it is by the faculty of knowledge. I apprehend there can be no knowledge without judgment, though there may be judgment without that certainty which we commonly call knowledge.

Mr. Locke, in another place of his Essay, tells us, "that the notice we have by our senses of the existence of things without us, though not altogether so certain as our intuitive knowledge, or the deductions of our reason about abstract ideas, yet is an assurance that deserves the name of knowledge." I think, by this account of it, and by his definitions before given of knowledge and judgment, it deserves as well the name of *judgment*.

That I may avoid disputes about the meaning of words, I wish the reader to understand, that I give the name of judgment to every determination of the mind concerning what is true or what is false. This, I think, is what logicians, from the days of Aristotle, have called judgment. Whether it be called one faculty, as I think it has always been, or whether a philosopher chooses to split it into two, seems not very material. And if it be granted, that by our senses, our memory and consciousness, we not only have ideas, or simple apprehensions, but form determinations concerning what is true, and what is false; whether these determinations ought to be called *knowledge* or *judgment*, is of small moment.

The judgments grounded upon the evidence of sense, of memory, and of consciousness, put all men upon a level. The philosopher, with regard to these, has no prerogative above the illiterate, or even above the savage.

Their reliance upon the testimony of these faculties is as firm and as well grounded as his. His superiority is in judgments of another kind; in judgments about things abstract and necessary. And he is unwilling to give the name of judgment to that wherein the most ignorant and unimproved of the species are his equals.

But philosophers have never been able to give any definition of judgment which does not apply to the determinations of our senses, our memory, and consciousness, nor any definition of simple apprehension which can comprehend those determinations.

Our judgments of this kind are purely the gift of nature, nor do they admit of improvement by culture. The memory of one man may be more tenacious than that of another; but both rely with equal assurance upon what they distinctly remember. One man's sight may be more acute, or his feeling more delicate than that of another; but both give equal credit to the distinct testimony of their sight and touch.

And as we have this belief by the constitution of our nature, without any effort of our own, so no effort of ours can overturn it.

The skeptic may perhaps persuade himself in general, that he has no ground to believe his senses or his memory: but, in particular cases that are interesting, his disbelief vanishes, and he finds himself under a necessity of believing both.

These judgments, may, in the strictest sense, be called *judgments of nature.* Nature has subjected us to them whether we will or not. They are neither got, nor can they be lost by any use or abuse of our faculties ; and it is evidently necessary for our preservation that it shóuld be so. For if belief in our senses and in our memory were to be learned by culture, the race of men would perish before they learned this lesson. It is necessary to all men for their being and preservation, and therefore is unconditionally given to all men by the Author of nature.

I acknowledge, that if we were to rest in those judgments of nature of which we now speak, without building others upon them, they would not entitle us to the denomination of reasonable beings. But yet they ought not to be despised, for they are the foundation upon which the grand superstructure of human knowledge must be raised. And as in other superstructures the foundation is commonly overlooked, so it has been in this. The more sublime attainments of the human mind have attracted the attention of philosophers, while they have bestowed but a careless glance upon the humble foundation on which the whole fabric rests.

A fourth observation is, that some exercise of judgment is necessary in the formation of all abstract and general conceptions whether more simple or more complex ; in dividing, in defining, and in general, in forming all clear and distinct conceptions of things, which are the only fit materials of reasoning.

These operations are allied to each other, and therefore I bring them under one observation. They are more allied to our rational nature than those mentioned in the last observation, and therefore are considered by themselves.

That I may not be mistaken, it may be observed, that I do not say that abstract notions, or other accurate notions of things, after they have been formed, cannot be barely conceived without any exercise of judgment about them. I doubt not that they may : but what I say, is, that, in their formation in the mind at first, there must be some exercise of judgment.

It is impossible to distinguish the different attributes belonging to the same subject, without judging that they are really different and distinguishable, and that they have that relation to the subject which logicians express, by saying that they may be *predicated* of it. We cannot generalize, without judging that the same attribute does or may belong to many individuals. It has been shown, that our simplest general notions are formed by these two operations of distinguishing and generalizing : judgment therefore is exercised in forming the simplest general notions.

In those that are more complex, and which have been shown to be formed by combining the more simple, there is another act of the judgment required ; for such combinations are not made at random, but for an end ; and judgment is employed in fitting them to that end. We form complex general notions for conveniency of arranging our thoughts in discourse and reasoning ; and therefore, of an infinite number of combinations that might be formed, we choose only those that are useful and necessary.

That judgment must be employed in dividing, as well as in distinguishing, appears evident. It is one thing to divide a subject properly, another to cut it in pieces. *Hoc non est dividere, sed frangere rem*, said Cicero, when he censured an improper division of Epicurus. Reason has discovered rules of division, which have been known to logicians more than two thousand years.

There are rules likewise of definition of no less antiquity and authority. A man may no doubt divide or define properly without attending to the rules, or even without knowing them. But this can only be, when he has judgment to perceive that to be right in a particular case, which the rule determines to be right in all cases.

I add in general, that, without some degree of judgment, we can form no accurate and distinct notions of things ; so that, one province of judgment is to aid us in forming clear and distinct conceptions of things, which are the only fit materials for reasoning.

This will probably appear to be a paradox to philosophers who have always considered the formation of ideas of every kind as belonging to simple apprehension ; and that the sole province of judgment is to put them together in affirmative or negative propositions ; and therefore it requires some confirmation.

1st, I think it necessarily follows from what has been already said in this observation. For if, without some degree of judgment, a man can neither distinguish, nor divide, nor define, nor form any general notion, simple or complex, he surely, without some degree of judgment, cannot have in his mind the materials necessary to reasoning.

There cannot be any proposition in language which does not involve some general conception. The proposition, *that I exist*, which Des Cartes thought the first of all truths, and the foundation of all knowledge, cannot be conceived without the conception of existence, one of the most abstract general conceptions. A man cannot believe his own existence, or the existence of any thing he sees or remembers, until he has so much judgment as to distinguish things that really exist from things which are only conceived. He sees a man six feet high ; he conceives a man sixty feet high ; he judges the first object to exist, because he sees it ; the second he does not judge to exist, because he only conceives it. Now, I would ask, Whether he can attribute existence to the first object, and not to the second, without knowing what existence means? It is impossible.

How early the notion of existence enters into the mind, I cannot determine; but it must certainly be in the mind, as soon as we can affirm of any thing, with understanding, that it exists.

In every other proposition, the predicate at least must be a general notion; a *predicable* and an *universal* being one and the same. Besides this, every proposition either affirms or denies. And no man can have a distinct conception of a proposition, who does not understand distinctly the meaning of affirming or denying; but these are very general conceptions, and, as was before observed, are derived from judgment as their source and origin.

I am sensible that a strong objection may be made to this reasoning, and that it may seem to lead to an absurdity, or a contradiction. It may be said, that every judgment is a mental affirmation or negation. If therefore some previous exercise of judgment be necessary to understand what is meant by affirmation or negation, the exercise of judgment must go before any judgment, which is absurd.

In like manner, every judgment may be expressed by a proposition, and a proposition must be conceived before we can judge of it. If therefore we cannot conceive the meaning of a proposition without a previous exercise of judgment, it follows that judgment must be previous to the conception of any proposition, and at the same time that the conception of a proposition must be previous to all judgment, which is a contradiction.

The reader may please to observe, that I have limited what I have said to distinct conception, and some degree of judgment; and it is by this means I hope to avoid this labyrinth of absurdity and contradiction.

The faculties of conception and judgment have an infancy and a maturity as man has. What I have said is limited to their mature state. I believe in their infant state they are very weak and indistinct; and that, by imperceptible degrees, they grow to maturity, each giving aid to the other, and receiving aid from it. But which of them first began this friendly intercourse, is beyond my ability to determine. It is like the question concerning the bird and the egg.

In the present state of things, it is true, that every bird comes from an egg, and every egg from a bird; and each may be said to be previous to the other. But if we go back to the origin of things, there must have been some bird that did not come from any egg, or some egg that did not come from any bird.

In like manner, in the mature state of man, distinct conception of a proposition supposes some previous exercise of judgment, and distinct judgment supposes distinct conception. Each may truly be said to come from the other, as the bird from the egg, and the egg from the bird. But if we trace back this succession to its origin, that is, to the first proposition that was ever conceived by the man, and the first judgment he ever formed, I determine nothing about them, nor do I know in what order, or how they were produced, any more than how the bones grow in the womb of her that is with child.

The first exercise of these faculties of conception and judgment is hid, like the sources of the Nile, in an unknown region.

The necessity of some degree of judgment to clear and distinct conceptions of things, may, I think, be illustrated by this similitude.

An artist, suppose a carpenter, cannot work in his art without tools, and these tools must be made by art. The exercise of the art therefore is necessary to make the tools, and the tools are necessary to the exercise of the art. There is the same appearance of contradiction, as in what I have advanced concerning the necessity of some degree of judgment, in order to form clear and distinct conceptions of things. These are the tools we must use in judging and in reasoning, and without them must make very bungling work; yet these tools cannot be made without some exercise of judgment.

The necessity of some degree of judgment in forming accurate and distinct notions of things will further appear, if we consider attentively what notions we can form, without any aid of judgment, of the objects of sense, of the operations of our own minds, or of the relations of things.

To begin with the objects of sense. It is acknowledged on all hands, that the first notions we have of sensible objects are got by the external senses only, and probably before judgment is brought forth; but these first notions are neither simple, nor are they accurate and distinct: they are gross and indistinct, and like the *chaos*, a *rudis indigestaque moles*. Before we can have any distinct notion of this mass, it must be analyzed; the heterogeneous parts must be separated in our conception, and the simple elements, which before lay hid in the common mass, must first be distinguished, and then put together into one whole.

In this way it is that we form distinct notions even of the objects of sense; but this analysis and composition, by habit, becomes so easy, and is performed so readily, that we are apt to overlook it, and to impute the distinct notion we have formed of the object to the senses alone; and this we are the more prone to do, because, when once we have distinguished the sensible qualities of the object from one another, the sense gives testimony to each of them.

You perceive, for instance, an object white, round, and a foot in diameter: I grant that you perceive all these attributes of the object by sense; but if you had not been able to distinguish the colour from the figure, and both from the magnitude, your senses would only have given you one complex and confused notion of all these mingled together.

A man who is able to say with understanding, or to determine in his own mind, that this object is white, must have distinguished whiteness from other attributes. If he has not made this distinction, he does not understand what he says.

Suppose a cube of brass to be presented at the same time to a child of a year old and to a man. The regularity of the figure will attract the attention of both. Both have the senses of sight and of touch in equal perfection; and therefore, if any thing be discovered in this object by the man, which cannot be discovered by the child, it must be owing, not to the senses, but to some other faculty which the child has not yet attained.

1st, Then, the man can easily distinguish the body from the surface which terminates it; this the child cannot do. 2dly, The man can perceive, that this surface is made up of six planes of the same figure and magnitude; the child cannot discover this. 3dly, The man perceives that each of these planes has four equal sides, and four equal angles; and that the opposite sides of each plane, and the opposite planes are parallel.

It will surely be allowed, that a man of ordinary judgment may observe all this in a cube which he makes an object of contemplation, and takes time to consider; that he may give the name of a square, to a plane terminated by four equal sides, and four equal angles: and the name of a cube, to a solid terminated by six equal squares; all this is nothing else but analyzing the figure of the object presented to his senses into its simplest elements, and again compounding it of those elements.

By this analysis and composition, two effects are produced. 1st, From the one complex object which his senses presented, though one of the most simple the senses can present, he educes many simple and distinct notions of right lines, angles, plain surface, solid, equality, parallelism; notions which the child has not yet faculties to attain. 2dly, When he considers the cube as compounded of these elements, put together in a certain order, he has then, and not before, a distinct and scientific notion of a cube. The child neither conceives those elements, nor in what order they must be put together in order to make a cube; and therefore has no accurate notion of a cube, which can make it a subject of reasoning.

Whence I think we may conclude, that the notion which we have from the senses alone, even of the simplest objects of sense, is indistinct and incapable of being either described or reasoned upon, until it is analyzed into its simple elements, and considered as compounded of those elements.

If we should apply this reasoning to more complex objects of sense, the conclusion would be still more evident. A dog may be taught to turn a jack, but he can never be taught to have a distinct notion of a ack. He sees every part as well as a man : but the relation of the parts to one another, and to the whole, he has not judgment to comprehend.

A distinct notion of an object, even of sense, is never got in an instant ; but the sense performs its office in an instant. Time is not required to see it better, but to analyze it, to distinguish the different parts, and their relation to one another, and to the whole.

Hence it is, that when any vehement passion or emotion hinders the cool application of judgment, we get no distinct notion of an object, even though the sense be long directed to it. A man who is put into a panic, by thinking he sees a ghost, may stare at it long, without having any distinct notion of it ; it is his understanding, and not his sense that is disturbed by his horror. If he can lay that aside, judgment immediately enters upon its office, and examines the length and breadth, the colour, and figure, and distance of the ob ect. Of these, while his panic lasted, he had no distinct notion, though his eyes were open all the time.

When the eye of sense is open, but that of judgment shut by a panic, or any violent emotion that engrosses the mind, we see things confusedly, and probably much in the same manner that brutes and perfect idiots do, and infants before the use of judgment.

There are therefore notions of the objects of sense which are gross and indistinct; and there are others that are distinct and scientific. The former may be got from the senses alone ; but the latter cannot be obtained without some degree of judgment.

The clear and accurate notions which geometry presents to us of a point, a right line, an angle, a square, a circle, of ratios direct and inverse, and others of that kind, can find no admittance into a mind that has not some degree of judgment. They are not properly ideas of the senses, nor are they got by compounding ideas of the senses: but, by analyzing the ideas or notions we get by the senses into their simplest elements, and again combining these elements into various, accurate, and elegant forms, which the senses never did nor can exhibit.

Had Mr. Hume attended duly to this, it ought to have prevented a very bold attempt, which he has prosecuted through fourteen pages of his Treatise of Human Nature, to prove that geometry is founded upon ideas that are not exact, and axioms that are not precisely true.

A mathematician might be tempted to think, that the man who seriously undertakes this has no great acquaintance with geometry; but I apprehend it is to be imputed to another cause, to a zeal for his own system. We see that even men of genius may be drawn into strange paradoxes, by an attachment to a favourite idol of the understanding, when it demands so costly a sacrifice.

We Protestants think, that the devotees of the Roman church pay no small tribute to her authority, when they renounce their five senses in obedience to her decrees. Mr. Hume's devotion to his system carries him even to trample upon mathematical demonstration.

The fundamental articles of his system are, that all the perceptions of the human mind are either impressions or ideas; and that ideas are only faint copies of impressions. The idea of a right line, therefore, is only a faint copy of some line that has been seen, or felt by touch; and the faint copy cannot be more perfect than the original. Now of such right lines, it is evident that the axioms of geometry are not precisely true; for two lines that are straight to our sight or touch may include a space, or they may meet in more points than one. If therefore we cannot form any notion of a straight line more accurate than that which we have from the senses of sight and touch, geometry has no solid foundation. If, on the other hand, the geometrical axioms are precisely true, the idea of a right line is not copied from any impression of sight or touch, but must have a different origin, and a more perfect standard.

As the geometrician, by reflecting only upon the extension and figure of matter, forms a set of notions more accurate and scientific than any which the senses exhibit; so the natural philosopher, reflecting upon other attributes of matter, forms another set, such as those of density, quantity of matter, velocity, momentum, fluidity, elasticity, centres of gravity, and of oscillation. These notions are accurate and scientific; but they cannot enter into a mind that has not some degree of judgment, nor can we make them intelligible to children, until they have some ripeness of understanding.

In navigation, the notions of latitude, longitude, course, leeway, cannot be made intelligible to children; and so it is with regard to the terms of every science, and of every art about which we can reason. They have had their five senses as perfect as men, for years before they are capable of distinguishing, comparing, and perceiving the relations of things, so as to be able to form such notions. They acquire the intellectual powers by a slow progress, and by imperceptible degrees, and by means of them learn to form distinct and accurate notions of things, which the senses could never have imparted.

Having said so much of the notions we get from the senses alone of the objects of sense, let us next consider what notions we can have from consciousness alone of the operations of our minds.

Mr. Locke very properly calls consciousness an internal sense. It gives the like immediate knowledge of things in the mind, that is, of our own thoughts and feelings, as the senses give us of things external. There is this difference, however, that an external object may be at rest, and the sense may be employed about it for some time. But the objects of consciousness are never at rest; the stream of thought flows like a river, without stopping a moment; the whole train of thought passes in succession under the eye of consciousness, which is always employed about the present. But is it consciousness that analyzes complex operations, distinguishes their different ingredients, and combines them in distinct parcels under general names? This surely is not the work of consciousness, nor can it be performed without reflection, recollecting, and judging of what we were conscious of, and distinctly remember. This reflection does not appear in children. Of all the powers of the mind, it seems to be of the latest growth, whereas consciousness is coeval with the earliest.

Consciousness, being a kind of internal sense, can no more give us distinct and accurate notions of the operations of our minds. than the external senses can give of external objects. Reflection upon the operations of our minds is the same kind of operation with that by which we form distinct notions of external objects. They differ not in their nature, but in this only, that one is employed about external, and the other about internal objects; and both may, with equal propriety, be called reflection.

Mr. Locke has restricted the word reflection to that which is employed about the operations of our minds, without any authority, as I think, from custom, the arbiter of language: for surely I may reflect upon what I have seen or heard, as well as upon what I have thought. The word, in its proper and common meaning, is equally applicable to objects of sense, and to objects of consciousness. He has likewise confounded reflection with consciousness, and seems not to have been aware that they are different powers, and appear at very different periods of life.

If that eminent philosopher had been aware of these mistakes about the meaning of the word *reflection*, he would, I think, have seen, that as it is by reflection upon the operations of our own minds that we can form any distinct and accurate notions of them, and not by consciousness without reflection; so it is by reflection upon the objects of sense, and not by the senses without reflection, that we can form distinct notions of them. Reflection upon any thing, whether external or internal, makes it an object of our intellectual powers, by which we survey it on all sides, and form such judgments about it as appear to be just and true.

I proposed, in the *third* place, to consider our notions of the relations of things: and here I think, that, without judgment, we cannot have any notion of relations.

There are two ways in which we get the notion of relations. The first is, by comparing the related objects, when we have before had the conception of both. By this comparison, we perceive the relation, either immediately, or by a process of reasoning. That my foot is longer than my finger, I perceive immediately; and that three is the half of six. This immediate perception is immediate and intuitive judgment. That the angles at the base of an isosceles triangle are equal, I perceive by a process of reasoning, in which it will be acknowledged there is judgment.

Another way in which we get the notion of relations, which seems not to have occurred to Mr. Locke, is, when, by attention to one of the related objects, we perceive, or judge, that it must, from its nature, have a certain relation to something else, which before, perhaps, we never thought of; and thus our attention to one of the related objects produces the notion of a correlate, and of a certain relation between them.

Thus when I attend to colour, figure, weight, I cannot help judging these to be qualities which cannot exist without a subject; that is, something which is coloured, figured, heavy. If I had not perceived such things to be qualities, I should never have had any notion of their subject, or of their relation to it.

By attending to the operations of thinking, memory, reasoning, we perceive or judge, that there must be something which thinks, remembers, and reasons, which we call the mind. When we attend to any change that happens in nature, judgment informs us, that there must be a cause of this change, which had power to produce it; and thus we get the notions of cause and effect, and of the relation between them. When we attend to body, we perceive that it cannot exist without space; hence we get the notion of space, which is neither an object of sense nor of consciousness, and of the relation which bodies have to a certain portion of unlimited space, as their place.

I apprehend, therefore, that all our notions of relations may more properly be ascribed to judgment as their source and origin, than to any other power of the mind. We must first perceive relations by our judgment, before we can conceive them without judging of them; as we must first perceive colours by sight, before we can conceive them without seeing them. I think Mr. Locke, when he comes to speak of the ideas of relations, does not say that they are ideas of sensation or reflection, but only that they terminate in, and are concerned about ideas of sensation or reflection.

The notions of unity and number are so abstract, that it is impossible they should enter into the mind until it has some degree of judgment. We see with what difficulty, and how slowly, children learn to use, with understanding, the names even of small numbers, and how they exult in this acquisition when they have attained it. Every number is conceived by the relation which it bears to unity, or to known combinations of units; and upon that account, as well as on account of its abstract nature, all distinct notions of it require some degree of judgment.

In its proper place, I shall have occasion to show, that judgment is an ingredient in all determinations of taste; in all moral determinations; and in many of our passions and affections. So that this operation, after we come to have any exercise of judgment, mixes with most of the operations of our minds, and, in analyzing them, cannot be overlooked without confusion and error.

CHAP. II.

OF COMMON SENSE.

THE word *sense*, in common language, seems to have a different meaning from that which it has in the writings of philosophers; and those different meanings are apt to be confounded, and to occasion embarrassment and error.

Not to go back to ancient philosophy upon this point, modern philosophers consider sense as a power that has nothing to do with judgment. Sense they consider as the power by which we receive certain ideas or impressions from objects; and judgment as the power by which we compare those ideas, and perceive their necessary agreements and disagreements.

The external senses give us the idea of colour, figure, sound, and other qualities of body, primary or secondary. Mr. Locke gave the name of an internal sense to consciousness, because by it we have the ideas of thought, memory, reasoning, and other operations of our own minds. Dr. Hutcheson of Glasgow, conceiving that we have simple and original ideas which cannot be imputed either to the external senses, or to consciousness, introduced other internal senses; such as the sense of harmony, the sense of beauty, and the moral sense. Ancient philosophers also spake of internal senses, of which memory was accounted one.

But all these senses, whether external or internal, have been represented by philosophers, as the means of furnishing our minds with ideas, without including any kind of judgment. Dr. Hutcheson defines a sense to be a determination of the mind to receive any idea from the presence of an object independent on our will.

" By this term, sense, philosophers in general have denominated those faculties, in consequence of which we are liable to feelings relative to ourselves only, and from which they have not pretended to draw any conclusions concerning the nature of things ; whereas truth is not relative, but absolute, and real." Dr. Priestly's Exam. of Dr. Reid, &c. page 123.

On the contrary, in common language, sense always implies judgment. A man of sense is a man of judgment. Good sense is good judgment. Nonsense is what is evidently contrary to right judgment. Common sense is that degree of judgment which is common to men with whom we can converse and transact business.

Seeing and hearing by philosophers are called senses, because we have ideas by them ; by the vulgar they are called senses, because we judge by them. We judge of colours by the eye ; of sounds by the ear ; of beauty and deformity by taste ; of right and wrong in conduct, by our moral sense, or conscience.

Sometimes philosophers, who represent it as the sole province of sense to furnish us with ideas, fall unawares into the popular opinion, that they are judging faculties. Thus Locke, book 4. chap. 11. " And of this, that the quality or accident of colour does really exist, and has a being without me, the greatest assurance I can possibly have, and to which my faculties can attain, is the testimony of my eyes, which are the proper and sole judges of this thing."

This popular meaning of the word *sense* is not peculiar to the English language. The corresponding words in Greek, Latin, and I believe in all the European languages, have the same latitude. The Latin words *sentire, sententia, sensa, sensus,* from the last of which the English word *sense* is borrowed, express judgment or opinion, and are applied indifferently to objects of external sense, of taste, of morals, and of the understanding.

I cannot pretend to assign the reason why a word, which is no term of art, which is familiar in common conversation, should have so different a meaning in philosophical writings. I shall only observe, that the philosophical meaning corresponds perfectly with the account which Mr. Locke and other modern philosophers give of judgment. For if the sole province of the senses, external and internal, be to furnish the mind with the ideas about which we judge and reason, it seems to be a natural consequence, that the sole province of judgment should be to compare those ideas, and to perceive their necessary relations.

These two opinions seem to be so connected, that one may have been the cause of the other. I apprehend, however, that if both be true, there is no room left for any knowledge or judgment, either of the real existence of contingent things, or of their contingent relations.

To return to the popular meaning of the word sense, I believe it would be much more difficult to find good authors who never use it in that meaning, than to find such as do.

We may take Mr. Pope as good authority for the meaning of an English word. He uses it often, and in his epistle to the Earl of Burlington, has made a little descant upon it.

> "Oft have you hinted to your brother Peer,
> A certain truth, which many buy too dear;
> Something there is more needful than expense,
> And something previous ev'n to taste, ——'tis sense.
> Good sense, which only is the gift of Heaven;
> And though no science, fairly worth the seven;
> A light, which in yourself you must perceive,
> Jones and Le Notre have it not to give."

This inward light or sense is given by Heaven to different persons in different degrees. There is a certain degree of it which is necessary to our being subjects of law and government, capable of managing our own affairs, and answerable for our conduct toward others. This is called common sense, because it is common to all men with whom we can transact business, or call to account for their conduct.

The laws of all civilized nations distinguish those who have this gift of Heaven, from those who have it not. The last may have rights which ought not to be violated, but having no understanding in themselves to direct their actions, the laws appoint them to be guided by the understanding of others. It is easily discerned by its effects in men's actions, in their speeches, and even in their looks; and when it is made a question, whether a man has this natural gift or not, a judge or a jury, upon a short conversation with him, can, for the most part, determine the question with great assurance.

The same degree of understanding which makes a man capable of acting with common prudence in the conduct of life, makes him capable of discovering what is true and what is false in matters that are self-evident, and which he distinctly apprehends.

All knowledge, and all science, must be built upon principles that are self-evident; and of such principles, every man who has common sense is a competent judge, when he conceives them distinctly. Hence it is, that disputes very often terminate in an appeal to common sense.

While the parties agree in the first principles on which their arguments are grounded, there is room for reasoning; but when one denies what to the other appears too evident to need, or to admit of proof, reasoning seems to be at an end; an appeal is made to common sense, and each party is left to enjoy his own opinion.

There seems to be no remedy for this, nor any way left to discuss such appeals, unless the decisions of common sense can be brought into a code, in which all reasonable men shall acquiesce. This indeed, if it be possible, would be very desirable, and would supply a desideratum in logic; and why should it be thought impossible that reasonable men should agree in things that are self-evident?

All that is intended in this chapter, is to explain the meaning of common sense, that it may not be treated, as it has been by some, as a new principle, or as a word without any meaning. I have endeavoured to show, that sense, in its most common, and therefore its most proper meaning, signifies *judgment*, though philosophers often use it in another meaning. From this it is natural to think, that common sense should mean common judgment; and so it really does.

What the precise limits are which divide common judgment from what is beyond it on the one hand, and from what falls short of it on the other, may be difficult to determine; and men may agree in the meaning of the word who have different opinions about those limits, or who even never thought of fixing them. This is as intelligible as, that all Englishmen should mean the same thing by the county of York, though perhaps not a hundredth part of them can point out its precise limits.

Indeed, it seems to me, that *common sense*, is as unambiguous a word, and as well understood as the *county of York*. We find it in innumerable places in good writers; we hear it on innumerable occasions in conversation; and, as far as I am able to judge, always in the same meaning. And this is probably the reason why it is so seldom defined or explained.

Dr. Johnson, in the authorities he gives, to show that the word *sense* signifies understanding, soundness of faculties, strength of natural reason, quotes Dr. Bentley for what may be called a definition of common sense, though probably not intended for that purpose, but mentioned accidentally : "God has endowed mankind with power and abilities, which we call natural light and reason, and common sense."

It is true, that common sense is a popular, and not a scholastic word ; and by most of those who have treated systematically of the powers of the understanding, it is only occasionally mentioned, as it is by other writers. But I recollect two philosophical writers, who are exceptions to this remark. One is Buffier, who treated largely of common sense, as a principle of knowledge, above fifty years ago. The other is bishop Berkeley, who, I think, has laid as much stress upon common sense, in opposition to the doctrines of philosophers, as any philosopher that has come after him. If the reader chooses to look back to Essay 2. chap. 10. he will be satisfied of this, from the quotations there made for another purpose, which it is unnecessary here to repeat.

Men rarely ask what common sense is ; because every man believes himself possessed of it, and would take it for an imputation upon his understanding to be thought unacquainted with it. Yet I remember two very eminent authors who have put this question ; and it is not improper to hear their sentiments upon a subject so frequently mentioned, and so rarely canvassed.

It is well known, that lord Shaftesbury gave to one of his Treatises the title of Sensus Communis ; an Essay on the Freedom of Wit and Humour, in a letter to a friend ; in which he puts his friend in mind of a free conversation with some of their friends on the subjects of morality and religion. Amidst the different opinions started and maintained with great life and ingenuity, one or other would every now and then take the liberty to appeal to common sense. Every one allowed the appeal; no one would offer to call the authority of the court in question, till a gentleman, whose good understanding was never yet brought in doubt, desired the company very gravely that they would tell him what common sense was.

"If," said he, "by the word *sense*, we were to understand opinion and judgment; and by the word *common*, the generality, or any considerable part of mankind, it would be hard to discover where the subject of common sense could lie; for that which was according to the sense of one part of mankind, was against the sense of another: and if the majority were to determine common sense, it would change as often as men changed. That in religion, common sense was as hard to determine as *catholic* or *orthodox*. What to one was absurdity, to another was demonstration.

"In policy, if plain British or Dutch sense were right, Turkish and French must certainly be wrong, and as mere nonsense as passive obedience seemed, we found it to be the common sense of a great party amongst ourselves, a greater party in Europe, and perhaps the greatest part of all the world besides. As for morals, the difference was still wider; for even the philosophers could never agree in one and the same system. And some even of our most admired modern philosophers had fairly told us, that virtue and vice had no other law or measure than mere fashion and vogue."

This is the substance of the gentleman's speech, which, I apprehend, explains the meaning of the word perfectly, and contains all that has been said, or can be said against the authority of common sense, and the propriety of appeals to it.

As there is no mention of any answer immediately made to this speech, we might be apt to conclude, that the noble author adopted the sentiments of the intelligent gentleman, whose speech he recites. But the contrary is manifest, from the title of Sensus Communis given to his Essay, from his frequent use of the word, and from the whole tenor of the Essay.

The author appears to have a double intention in that Essay, corresponding to the double title prefixed to it. One intention is, to justify the use of wit, humour, and ridicule, in discussing among friends the gravest subjects. " I can very well suppose," says he, " men may be frighted out of their wits ; but I have no apprehension they should be laughed out of them. I can hardly imagine, that, in a pleasant way, they should ever be talked out of their love for society, or reasoned out of humanity and common sense."

The other intention, signified by the title Sensus Communis, is carried on hand in hand with the first, and is to show, that common sense is not so vague and uncertain a thing as it is represented to be in the skeptical speech before recited. " I will try," says he, " what certain knowledge or assurance of things may be recovered in that very way, to wit, of humour, by which all certainty, you thought, was lost, and an endless skepticism introduced."

He gives some criticisms upon the word *sensus communis* in Juvenal, Horace, and Seneca ; and after showing, in a facetious way throughout the Treatise, that the fundamental principles of morals, of politics, of criticism, and of every branch of knowledge, are the dictates of common sense, he sums up the whole in these words : " That some moral and philosophical truths there are so evident in themselves, that it would be easier to imagine half mankind run mad, and joined precisely in the same species of folly, than to admit any thing as truth, which should be advanced against such natural knowledge, fundamental reason, and common sense." And, on taking leave, he adds : " And now, my friend, should you find I had moralized in any tolerable manner, according to common sense, and without canting, I should be satisfied with my performance."

Another eminent writer who has put the question what common sense is, is Fenelon, the famous Archbishop of Cambray.

That ingenious and pious author, having had an early prepossession in favour of the Cartesian philosophy, made an attempt to establish, on a sure foundation, the metaphysical arguments which Des Cartes had invented to prove the being of the Deity. For this purpose, he begins with the Cartesian doubt. He proceeds to find out the truth of his own existence, and then to examine wherein the evidence and certainty of this, and other such primary truths consisted. This, according to Cartesian principles, he places in the clearness and distinctness of the ideas. On the contrary, he places the absurdity of the contrary propositions, in their being repugnant to his clear and distinct ideas.

To illustrate this, he gives various examples of questions manifestly absurd and ridiculous, which every man of common understanding would at first sight perceive to be so, and then goes on to this purpose.

" What is it that makes these questions ridiculous ? Wherein does this ridicule precisely consist ? It will perhaps be replied, that it consists in this, that they shock common sense. But what is this same common sense ? It is not the first notions that all men have equally of the same things. This common sense, which is always and in all places the same ; which prevents inquiry ; which makes inquiry in some cases ridiculous ; which, instead of inquiring, makes a man laugh whether he will or not ; which puts it out of a man's power to doubt ; this sense, which only waits to be consulted ; which shows itself at the first glance, and immediately discovers the evidence or the absurdity of a question ; is not this the same that I call my ideas ?

" Behold then those ideas or general notions, which it is not in my power either to contradict or examine, and by which I examine and decide in every case, insomuch that I laugh instead of answering, as often as any thing is proposed to me, which is evidently contrary to what these immutable ideas represent."

I shall only observe upon this passage, that the interpretation it gives of Des Cartes's criterion of truth, whether just or not, is the most intelligible and the most favourable I have met with.

I beg leave to mention one passage from Cicero, and to add two or three from late writers, which show that this word is not become obsolete, nor has changed its meaning.

De Oratore, lib. 3. " Omnes enim tacito quodam sensu, sine ulla arte aut ratione, in artibus ac rationibus, recta ac prava dijudicant. Idque cum faciant in picturis, et in signis, et in aliis operibus, ad quorum intelligentiam a natura minus habent instrumenti, tum multo ostendunt magis in verborum, numerorum, vocumque judicio; quod ea sint in communibus infixa sensibus ; neque earum rerum quemquam funditus natura voluit expertem."

Hume's Essays and Treatises, vol. i. p. 5. " But a philosopher who proposes only to represent the common sense of mankind in more beautiful and more engaging colours, if by accident he commits a mistake, goes no further, but renewing his appeal to common sense, and the natural sentiments of the mind, returns into the right path, and secures himself from any dangerous illusion."

Hume's Inquiry concerning the principles of Morals, p. 2. " Those who have refused the reality of moral distinctions may be ranked among the disingenuous disputants. The only way of converting an antagonist of this kind is to leave him to himself : for, finding that nobody keeps up the controversy with him, it is prob-able he will at last, of himself, from mere weariness, come over to the side of common sense and reason."

Priestly's Institutes, Prelim. Essay, vol. i. p. 27. "Because common sense is a sufficient guard against many errors in religion, it seems to have been taken for granted, that common sense is a sufficient instruct-er also, whereas in fact, without positive instruction, men would naturally have been mere savages with re-spect to religion; as, without similar instruction, they would be savages with respect to the arts of life and the sciences. Common sense can only be compared to a judge; but what can a judge do without evidence and proper materials from which to form a judgment?"

Priestly's Examination of Dr. Reid, &c. page 127. "But should we, out of complaisance, admit that what has hitherto been called judgment may be called sense, it is making too free with the established signification of words to call it common sense, which, in common ac-ceptation, has long been appropriated to a very different thing, *viz.* to that capacity for judging of common things that persons of middling capacities are capable of." Page 129. "I should therefore expect, that if a man was so totally deprived of common sense as not to be able to distinguish truth from falsehood in one case, he would be equally incapable of distinguishing it in another."

From this cloud of testimonies, to which hundreds might be added, I apprehend, that whatever censure is thrown upon those who have spoke of common sense as a principle of knowledge, or who have ap-pealed to it in matters that are self-evident, will fall light, when there are so many to share in it. Indeed, the authority of this tribunal is too sacred and venera-ble, and has prescription too long in its favour to be now wisely called in question. Those who are disposed to do so, may remember the shrewd saying of Mr. Hobbes, "When reason is against a man, a man will be against reason." This is equally applicable to common sense.

From the account 1 have given of the meaning of this term, it is easy to judge both of the proper use and of the abuse of it.

It is absurd to conceive that there can be any opposition between reason and common sense. It is indeed the first born of reason, and as they are commonly joined together in speech and in writing, they are inseparable in their nature.

We ascribe to reason two offices, or two degrees. The first is to judge of things self-evident; the second to draw conclusions that are not self-evident from those that are. The first of these is the province, and the sole province of common sense; and therefore it coincides with reason in its whole extent, and is only another name for one branch or one degree of reason. Perhaps it may be said, Why then should you give it a particular name, since it is acknowledged to be only a degree of reason? It would be a sufficient answer to this, Why do you abolish a name which is to be found in the language of all civilized nations, and has acquired a right by prescription? Such an attempt is equally foolish and ineffectual. Every wise man will be apt to think, that a name which is found in all languages as far back as we can trace them, is not without some use.

But there is an obvious reason why this degree of reason should have a name appropriated to it; and that is, that in the greatest part of mankind no other degree of reason is to be found. It is this degree that entitles them to the denomination of reasonable creatures. It is this degree of reason, and this only, that makes a man capable of managing his own affairs, and answerable for his conduct toward others. There is therefore the best reason why it should have a name appropriated to it.

These two degrees of reason differ in other respects, which would be sufficient to entitle them to distinct names.

The first is purely the gift of Heaven. And where Heaven has not given it, no education can supply the want. The second is learned by practice and rules, when the first is not wanting. A man who has common sense may be taught to reason. But if he has not that gift, no teaching will make him able either to judge of first principles or to reason from them.

I have only this further to observe, that the province of common sense is more extensive in refutation than in confirmation. A conclusion drawn by a train of just reasoning from true principles cannot possibly contradict any decision of common sense, because truth will always be consistent with itself. Neither can such a conclusion receive any confirmation from common sense, because it is not within its jurisdiction.

But it is possible, that, by setting out from false principles, or by an error in reasoning, a man may be led to a conclusion that contradicts the decisions of common sense. In this case, the conclusion is within the jurisdiction of common sense, though the reasoning on which it was grounded be not; and a man of common sense may fairly reject the conclusion, without being able to show the error of the reasoning that led to it.

Thus, if a mathematician, by a process of intricate demonstration, in which some false step was made, should be brought to this conclusion, that two quantities, which are both equal to a third, are not equal to each other, a man of common sense, without pretending to be a judge of the demonstration, is well entitled to reject the conclusion, and to pronounce it absurd.

CHAP. III.

SENTIMENTS OF PHILOSOPHERS CONCERNING JUDG-
MENT.

A DIFFERENCE about the meaning of a word ought not
to occasion disputes among philosophers : but it is often
very proper to take notice of such differences, in order
to prevent verbal disputes. There are, indeed, no
words in language more liable to ambiguity than those
by which we express the operations of the mind; and
the most candid and judicious may sometimes be led
into different opinions about their precise meaning.

I hinted before what I take to be a peculiarity in
Mr. Locke with regard to the meaning of the word
judgment, and mentioned what I apprehend may have
led him into it. But let us hear himself; Essay, book 4.
chap. 14. " The faculty which God has given to man to
supply the want of clear and certain knowledge, where
that cannot be had, is judgment; whereby the mind
takes its ideas to agree or disagree ; or, which is the
same, any proposition to be true or false, without perceiving a demonstrative evidence in the proofs. Thus
the mind has two faculties, conversant about truth and
falsehood. 1st, Knowledge ; whereby it certainly perceives, and is undoubtedly satisfied of the agreement or
disagreement of any ideas. 2dly, Judgment ; which is
the putting ideas together, or separating them from
one another in the mind, when their certain agreement,
or disagreement is not perceived, but presumed to be
so."

Knowledge, I think, sometimes signifies things
known ; sometimes that act of the mind by which we
know them. And in like manner opinion sometimes
signifies things believed ; sometimes the act of the

mind by which we believe them. But judgment is the faculty which is exercised in both these acts of the mind. In knowledge, we judge without doubting ; in opinion, with some mixture of doubt. But I know no authority, besides that of Mr. Locke, for calling knowledge a faculty, any more than for calling opinion a faculty.

Neither do I think that knowledge is confined within the narrow limits which Mr. Locke assigns to it ; because the far greatest part of what all men call human knowledge, is in things which neither admit of intuitive nor of demonstrative proof.

I have all along used the word *judgment* in a more extended sense than Mr. Locke does in the passage above mentioned. I understand by it that operation of the mind, by which we determine, concerning any thing that may be expressed by a proposition, whether it be true or false. Every proposition is either true or false : so is every judgment. A proposition may be simply conceived without judging of it. But when there is not only a conception of the proposition, but a mental affirmation or negation, an assent or dissent of the understanding, whether weak or strong, that is judgment.

I think, that since the days of Aristotle, logicians have taken the word in this sense, and other writers, for the most part, though there are other meanings, which there is no danger of confounding with this.

We may take the authority of Dr. Isaac Watts, as a logician, as a man who understood English, and who had a just esteem of Mr. Locke's Essay. Logic, Introd. p. 5. " Judgment is that operation of the mind, wherein we join two or more ideas together by one affirmation or negation ; that is, we either affirm or deny *this* to be *that. So this tree is high ; that horse is not swift ; the mind of man is a thinking being ; mere matter has no thought belonging to it; God is just; good men are often miserable in this world; a righteous governor will make a difference betwixt the evil and the good;* which sentences are the effect of judgment, and are called propositions." And part 2. chap. 2. sect. 9. "The evidence of sense is, when we frame a proposition according to the dictates of any of our senses. So we judge, *that grass is green; that a trumpet gives a pleasant sound; that fire burns wood; water is soft; and iron hard.*"

In this meaning, judgment extends to every kind of evidence, probable or certain, and to every degree of assent or dissent. It extends to all knowledge, as well as to all opinion; with this difference only, that in knowledge it is more firm and steady, like a house founded upon a rock. In opinion it stands upon a weaker foundation, and is more liable to be shaken and overturned.

These differences about the meaning of words are not mentioned as if truth was on one side, and error on the other, but as an apology for deviating in this instance from the phraseology of Mr. Locke, which is for the most part accurate and distinct; and because attention to the different meanings that are put upon words by different authors is the best way to prevent our mistaking verbal differences for real differences of opinion.

The common theory concerning ideas, naturally leads to a theory concerning judgment, which may be a proper test of its truth; for as they are necessarily connected, they must stand or fall together. Their connection is thus expressed by Mr. Locke, book 4. chap. 1. "Since the mind, in all its thoughts and reasonings, has no other immediate object but its own ideas, which it alone does, or can contemplate, it is evident that our knowledge is only conversant about them. Knowledge then seems to me to be nothing but

the *perception of the connection and agreement, or disagreement and repugnancy of any of our ideas. In
this alone it consists.*"

There can only be one objection to the justice of
this inference ; and that is, that the antecedent proposition from which it is inferred, seems to have some
ambiguity : for, in the first clause of that proposition,
the mind is said to have no other *immediate* object but
its own ideas ; in the second, that it has no other object at all ; that it does, or can contemplate ideas
alone.

If the word *immediate* in the first clause be a mere
expletive, and be not intended to limit the generality
of the proposition, then the two clauses will be perfectly consistent, the second being only a repetition or
explication of the first ; and the inference that our
knowledge is only conversant about ideas, will be perfectly just and logical.

But if the word *immediate* in the first clause be intended to limit the general proposition, and to imply,
that the mind has other objects besides its own ideas,
though no other immediate objects ; then it will not
be true that it does or can contemplate ideas alone ;
nor will the inference be justly drawn, that our knowledge is only conversant about ideas.

Mr. Locke must either have meant his antecedent
proposition, without any limitation by the word *immediate*, or he must have meant to limit it by that word,
and to signify that there are objects of the mind which
are not ideas.

The first of these suppositions appears to me most
probable, for several reasons.

1st, Because, when he purposely defines the word
idea, in the introduction to the Essay, he says it is
whatsoever is the object of the understanding when a
man thinks ; or whatever the mind can be employed
about in thinking. Here there is no room left for ob-

jects of the mind that are not ideas. The same definition is often repeated throughout the Essay. Sometimes, indeed, the word *immediate* is added, as in the
passage now under consideration; but there is no intimation made that it ought to be understood when it
is not expressed. Now if it had really been his opinion, that there are objects of thought which are not
ideas, this definition, which is the ground work of the
whole Essay, would have been very improper, and apt
to mislead his reader.

2dly, He has never attempted to show how there
can be objects of thought, which are not immediate
objects; and indeed this seems impossible. For whatever the object be, the man either thinks of it, or he
does not. There is no medium between these. If he
thinks of it, it is an immediate object of thought while
he thinks of it. If he does not think of it, it is no object of thought at all. Every object of thought, therefore, is an immediate object of thought, and the word
immediate, joined to objects of thought, seems to be a
mere expletive.

3dly, Though Malebranche and Bishop Berkeley believed, that we have no ideas of minds, or of the operations of minds, and that we may think and reason
about them without ideas, this was not the opinion of
Mr. Locke. He thought that there are ideas of minds,
and of their operations, as well as of the objects of
sense; that the mind perceives nothing but its own
ideas, and that all words are the signs of ideas.

A fourth reason is, that to suppose that he intended to
limit the antecedent proposition by the word *immediate,*
is to impute to him a blunder in reasoning, which I do
not think Mr. Locke could have committed; for what
can be a more glaring paralogism than to infer, that
since ideas are partly, though not solely, the objects
of thought, it is evident that all our knowledge is only

conversant about them. If, on the contrary, he meant that ideas are the only objects of thought, then the conclusion drawn is perfectly just and obvious; and he might very well say, *that since it is ideas only that the mind does or can contemplate, it is evident that our knowledge is only conversant about them.*

As to the conclusion itself, I have only to observe, that though he extends it only to what he calls knowledge, and not to what he calls judgment, there is the same reason for extending it to both.

It is true of judgment, as well as of knowledge, that it can only be conversant about objects of the mind, or about things which the mind can contemplate. Judgment, as well as knowledge supposes the conception of the object about which we judge; and to judge of objects that never were nor can be objects of the mind, is evidently impossible.

This therefore we may take for granted, that if knowledge be conversant about ideas only, because there is no other object of the mind, it must be no less certain, that judgment is conversant about ideas only, for the same reason.

Mr. Locke adds, as the result of his reasoning, knowledge then seems to me to be nothing but the perception of the connection and agreement, or disagreement and repugnancy, of any of our ideas. In this alone it consists.

This is a very important point, not only on its own account, but on account of its necessary connection with his system concerning ideas, which is such, as that both must stand or fall together; for if there is any part of human knowledge which does not consist in the perception of the agreement or disagreement of ideas, it must follow, that there are objects of thought and of contemplation which are not ideas.

This point, therefore, deserves to be carefully examined. With this view, let us first attend to its meaning, which I think can hardly be mistaken, though it may need some explication.

Every point of knowledge, and every judgment is expressed by a proposition, wherein something is affirmed or denied of the subject of the proposition.

By perceiving the connection or agreement of two ideas, I conceive is meant perceiving the truth of an affirmative proposition, of which the subject and predicate are ideas. In like manner, by perceiving the disagreement and repugnancy of any two ideas, I conceive is meant perceiving the truth of a negative proposition, of which both subject and predicate are ideas. This I take to be the only meaning the words can bear, and it is confirmed by what Mr. Locke says in a passage already quoted in this chapter, that " the mind, taking its ideas to agree or disagree, is the same as taking any proposition to be true or false." Therefore, if the definition of knowledge given by Mr. Locke be a just one, the subject, as well as the predicate of every proposition, by which any point of knowledge is expressed, must be an idea, and can be nothing else ; and the same must hold of every proposition by which judgment is expressed, as has been shown above.

Having ascertained the meaning of this definition of human knowledge, we are next to consider how far it is just.

1st, I would observe, that if the word *idea* be taken in the meaning which it had at first among the Pythagoreans and Platonists, and if by knowledge be meant only abstract and general knowledge, which I believe Mr. Locke had chiefly in his view, I think the proposition is true, that such knowledge consists solely in perceiving the truth of propositions whose subject and predicate are ideas.

By ideas here I mean things conceived abstractly, without regard to their existence. We commonly call them abstract notions, abstract conceptions, abstract ideas; the Peripatetics called them universals; and the Platonists, who knew no other ideas, called them ideas without addition.

Such ideas are both subject and predicate in every proposition which expresses abstract knowledge.

The whole body of pure mathematics is an abstract science; and in every mathematical proposition, both subject and predicate are ideas, in the sense above explained. Thus, when I say the side of a square is not commensurable to its diagonal; in this proposition *the side and the diagonal of a square* are the subjects, for being a relative proposition it must have two subjects. A square, its side, and its diagonal, are ideas, or universals; they are not individuals, but things predicable of many individuals. Existence is not included in their definition, nor in the conception we form of them. The predicate of the proposition is *commensurable*, which must be an universal, as the predicate of every proposition is so. In other branches of knowledge many abstract truths may be found, but, for the most part, mixed with others that are not abstract.

I add, that I apprehend that what is strictly called demonstrative evidence, is to be found in abstract knowledge only. This was the opinion of Aristotle, of Plato, and I think of all the ancient philosophers; and I believe in this they judged right. It is true, we often meet with demonstration in astronomy, in mechanics, and in other branches of natural philosophy; but I believe we shall always find that such demonstrations, are grounded upon principles or suppositions, which have neither intuitive nor demonstrative evidence.

Thus when we demonstrate, that the path of a projectile *in vacuo* is a parabola, we suppose that it is acted upon with the same force, and in the same direction through its whole path by gravity. This is not intuitively known, nor is it demonstrable: and in the demonstration, we reason from the laws of motion, which are principles not capable of demonstration, but grounded on a different kind of evidence.

Ideas, in the sense above explained, are creatures of the mind; they are fabricated by its rational powers; we know their nature and their essence; for they are nothing more than they are conceived to be: and because they are perfectly known, we can reason about them with the highest degree of evidence.

And as they are not things that exist, but things conceived, they neither have place nor time, nor are they liable to change.

When we say that they are in the mind, this can mean no more but that they are conceived by the mind, or that they are objects of thought. The act of conceiving them is no doubt in the mind; the things conceived have no place, because they have no existence. Thus a circle, considered abstractly, is said figuratively to be in the mind of him that conceives it; but in no other sense than the city of London or the kingdom of France is said to be in his mind when he thinks of those objects.

Place and time belong to finite things that exist, but not to things that are barely conceived. They may be objects of conception to intelligent beings in every place, and at all times. Hence the Pythagoreans and Platonists were led to think that they are eternal and omnipresent. If they had existence, they must be so; for they have no relation to any one place or time, which they have not to every place and to every time.

The natural prejudice of mankind, that what we conceive must have existence, led those ancient philosophers to attribute existence to ideas; and by this they were led into all the extravagant and mysterious parts of their system. When it is purged of these, I apprehend it to be the only intelligible and rational system concerning ideas.

I agree with them therefore, that ideas are immutably the same in all times and places: for this means no more but that a circle is always a circle, and a square always a square.

I agree with them, that ideas are the patterns or exemplars, by which every thing was made that had a beginning: for an intelligent artificer must conceive his work before it is made; he makes it according to that conception; and the thing conceived, before it exists, can only be an idea.

I agree with them, that every species of things considered abstractly, is an idea; and that the idea of the species is in every individual of the species, without division or multiplication. This indeed is expressed somewhat mysteriously, according to the manner of the sect; but it may easily be explained.

Every idea is an attribute; and it is a common way of speaking, to say, that the attribute is in every subject of which it may truly be affirmed. Thus, *to be above fifty years of age*, is an attribute or idea. This attribute may be in, or affirmed of, fifty different individuals, and be the same in all, without division or multiplication.

I think, that not only every species, but every genus, higher or lower, and every attribute considered abstractly, is an idea. These are things conceived without regard to existence; they are universals, and therefore ideas, according to the ancient meaning of that word.

It is true, that, after the Platonists entered into disputes with the Peripatetics, in order to defend the existence of eternal ideas, they found it prudent to contract the line of defence, and maintained only that there is an idea of every species of natural things, but not of the genera, nor of things artificial. They were unwilling to multiply beings beyond what was necessary; but in this I think they departed from the genuine principles of their system.

The definition of a species, is nothing but the definition of the genus, with the addition of a specific difference; and the division of things into species is the work of the mind, as well as their division into genera and classes. A species, a genus, an order, a class, is only a combination of attributes made by the mind, and called by one name. There is therefore the same reason for giving the name of *idea* to every attribute, and to every species and genus, whether higher or lower. These are only more complex attributes, or combinations of the more simple. And though it might be improper. without necessity, to multiply beings, which they believed to have a real existence; yet, had they seen that ideas are not things that exist, but things that are conceived, they would have apprehended no danger nor expense from their number.

Simple attributes, species and genera, lower or higher, are all things conceived, without regard to existence; they are universals, they are expressed by general words, and have an equal title to be called by the name of *ideas*.

I likewise agree with those ancient philosophers, that ideas are the object, and the sole object of science, strictly so called; that is, of demonstrative reasoning.

And as ideas are immutable, so their agreements and disagreements, and all their relations and attributes are immutable. All mathematical truths are immutably true. Like the ideas about which they are conversant, they have no relation to time or place, no dependence upon existence or change. That the angles of a plane triangle are equal to two right angles, always was and always will be true, though no triangle had ever existed.

The same may be said of all abstract truths. On that account they have often been called eternal truths : and for the same reason, the Pythagoreans ascribed eternity to the ideas about which they are conversant. They may very properly be called necessary truths; because it is impossible they should not be true at all times and in all places.

Such is the nature of all truth that can be discovered, by perceiving the agreements and disagreements of *ideas*, when we take that word in its primitive sense. And that Mr. Locke, in his definition of knowledge, had chiefly in his view abstract truths, we may be led to think from the examples he gives to illustrate it.

But there is another great class of truths, which are not abstract and necessary, and therefore cannot be perceived in the agreements and disagreements of ideas. These are all the truths we know concerning the real existence of things; the truth of our own existence; of the existence of other things, inanimate, animal, and rational, and of their various attributes and relations.

These truths may be called contingent truths. I except only the existence and attributes of the Supreme Being, which is the only necessary truth I know regarding existence.

All other beings that exist, depend for their existence, and all that belongs to it, upon the will and power of the first cause; therefore neither their existence, nor their nature, nor any thing that befals them, is necessary, but contingent.

But although the existence of the Deity be necessary, I apprehend we can only deduce it from contingent truths. The only arguments for the existence of a Deity which I am able to comprehend, are grounded upon the knowledge of my own existence, and the existence of other finite beings. But these are contingent truths.

I believe, therefore, that by perceiving agreements and disagreements of ideas, no contingent truth whatsoever can be known, nor the real existence of any thing, not even our own existence, nor the existence of a Deity, which is a necessary truth. Thus I have endeavoured to show what knowledge may, and what cannot be attained, by perceiving the agreements and disagreements of ideas, when we take that word in its primitive sense.

We are, in the *next* place, to consider, whether knowledge consists in perceiving the agreement or disagreement of ideas, taking *ideas* in any of the senses in which the word is used by Mr. Locke and other modern philosophers.

1st, Very often the word *idea* is used so, that to have the idea of any thing is a *periphrasis* for conceiving it. In this sense, an idea is not an object of thought, it is thought itself. It is the act of the mind by which we conceive any object. And it is evident that this could not be the meaning which Mr. Locke had in view in his definition of knowledge.

2dly, A second meaning of the word *idea* is that which Mr. Locke gives in the Introduction to his Essay, when he is making an apology for the frequent use of it. "It being that term, I think, which serves best to stand for whatsoever is the object of the understanding when a man thinks, or whatever it is which a man can be employed about in thinking."

By this definition, indeed, every thing that can be
the object of thought is an idea. The objects of our
thoughts may, I think, be reduced to two classes.

The first class comprehends all those objects which
we not only can think of, but which we believe to have
a real existence. Such as the Creator of all things,
and all his creatures that fall within our notice. I can
think of the sun and moon, the earth and sea, and of
the various animal, vegetable, and inanimate productions with which it has pleased the bountiful Creator
to enrich our globe. I can think of myself, of my
friends and acquaintance. I think of the author of
the Essay with high esteem. These, and such as these,
are objects of the understanding which we believe to
have real existence.

A second class of objects of the understanding which
a man may be employed about in thinking, are things
which we either believe never to have existed, or which
we think of without regard to their existence.

Thus, I can think of Don Quixote, of the island of
Laputa, of Oceana, and of Utopia, which I believe
never to have existed. Every attribute, every species,
and every genus of things, considered abstractly, without any regard to their existence or non-existence, may
be an object of the understanding.

To this second class of objects of the understanding,
the name of idea does very properly belong, according
to the primitive sense of the word, and I have already
considered what knowledge does, and what does not consist in perceiving the agreements and disagreements of
such ideas.

But if we take the word *idea* in so extensive a sense
as to comprehend, not only the second, but also the
first class of objects of the understanding, it will undoubtedly be true, that all knowledge consists in perceiving the agreements and disagreements of ideas: for

it is impossible that there can be any knowledge, any judgment, any opinion, true or false, which is not employed about the objects of the understanding. But whatsoever is an object of the understanding is an idea, according to this second meaning of the word.

Yet I am persuaded that Mr. Locke, in his definition of knowledge, did not mean that the word *idea* should extend to all those things which we commonly consider as objects of the understanding.

Though bishop Berkeley believed that sun, moon, and stars, and all material things, are ideas, and nothing but ideas, Mr. Locke no where professes this opinion. He believed that we have ideas of bodies, but not that bodies are ideas. In like manner, he believed that we have ideas of minds, but not that minds are ideas. When he inquired so carefully into the origin of all our ideas, he did not surely mean to find the origin of whatsoever may be the object of the understanding, nor to resolve the origin of every thing that may be an object of understanding into sensation and reflection.

3dly, Setting aside, therefore, the two meanings of the word *idea* before mentioned, as meanings which Mr. Locke could not have in his view in the definition he gives of knowledge, the only meaning that could be intended in this place is that which I before called the philosophical meaning of the word *idea*, which has a reference to the theory commonly received about the manner in which the mind perceives external objects, and in which it remembers and conceives objects that are not present to it. It is a very ancient opinion, and has been very generally received among philosophers, that we cannot perceive or think of such objects immediately, but by the medium of certain images or representatives of them really existing in the mind at the time.

To those images the ancients gave the name of species and phantasms.   Modern philosophers have given
them the name of ideas.   " It is evident," says Mr.
Locke, book 4. chapter 4. " the mind knows not things
immediately, but only by the intervention of the ideas
it has of them."   And in the same paragraph he puts
this question : " How shall the mind when it perceives
nothing but its own ideas, know that they agree with
things themselves ?"

This theory I have already considered, in treating
of perception, of memory, and of conception.   The
reader will there find the reasons that lead me to think,
that it has no solid foundation in reason, or in attentive reflection upon those operations of our minds ;
that it contradicts the immediate dictates of our natural faculties, which are of higher authority than any
theory ; that it has taken its rise from the same prejudices which led all the ancient philosophers to think,
that the Deity could not make this world without some
eternal matter to work upon, and which led the Pythagoreans and Platonists to think, that he could not
conceive the plan of the world he was to make without
eternal ideas really existing as patterns to work by :
and that this theory, when its necessary consequences
are fairly pursued, leads to absolute skepticism, though
those consequences were not seen by most of the philosophers who have adopted it.

I have no intention to repeat what has before been
said upon those points ; but only, taking ideas in this
sense, to make some observations upon the definition
which Mr. Locke gives of knowledge.

1st, If all knowledge consists in perceiving the agreements and disagreements of ideas, that is, of representative images of things existing in the mind, it obviously follows, that if there be no such ideas, there can
be no knowledge : so that, if there should be found
good reason for giving up this philosophical hypothesis,
all knowledge must go along with it.

I hope, however, it is not so; and that though this hypothesis, like many others, should totter and fall to the ground, knowledge will continue to stand firm, upon a more permanent basis.

The cycles and epicycles of the ancient astronomers were for a thousand years thought absolutely necessary to explain the motions of the heavenly bodies. Yet now, when all men believe them to have been mere fictions, astronomy has not fallen with them, but stands upon a more rational foundation than before. Ideas, or images of things existing in the mind, have for a longer time been thought necessary for explaining the operations of the understanding. If they should likewise at last be found to be fictions, human knowledge and judgment would suffer nothing by being disengaged from an unwieldy hypothesis. Mr. Locke surely did not look upon the existence of ideas as a philosophical hypothesis. He thought that we are conscious of their existence, otherwise he would not have made the existence of all our knowledge to depend upon the existence of ideas.

2dly, Supposing this hypothesis to be true, I agree with Mr. Locke, that it is an evident and necessary consequence that our knowledge can be conversant about ideas only, and must consist in perceiving their attributes and relations. For nothing can be more evident than this, that all knowledge, and all judgment and opinion, must be about things which are, or may be immediate objects of our thought. What cannot be the object of thought, or the object of the mind in thinking, cannot be the object of knowledge or of opinion.

Every thing we can know of any object must be either some attribute of the object, or some relation it bears to some other object or objects. By the agreements and disagreements of objects, I apprehend Mr. Locke intended to express both their attributes and

their relations. If ideas then be the only objects of
thought, the consequence is necessary, that they must
be the only objects of knowledge, and all knowledge
must consist in perceiving their agreements and disagreements, that is, their attributes and relations.

The use I would make of this consequence, is to
show, that the hypothesis must be false, from which it
necessarily follows : for if we have any knowledge of
things that are not ideas, it will follow no less evidently, that ideas are not the only objects of our thoughts.

Mr. Locke has pointed out the extent and limits of
human knowledge in his fourth book, with more accuracy and judgment than any philosopher had done before ; but he has not confined it to the agreements and
disagreements of ideas. And I cannot help thinking,
that a great part of that book is an evident refutation
of the principles laid down in the beginning of it.

Mr. Locke did not believe that he himself was an
idea; that his friends and acquaintance were ideas ;
that the Supreme Being, to speak with reverence, is
an idea ; or that the sun and moon, the earth and the
sea, and other external objects of sense, are ideas. He
believed that he had some certain knowledge of all
those objects. His knowledge, therefore, did not consist solely in perceiving the agreements and disagreements of his ideas : for, surely, to perceive the existence, the attributes, and relations of things, which are
not ideas, is not to perceive the agreements and disagreements of ideas. And if things which are not ideas
be objects of knowledge, they must be objects of
thought. On the contrary, if ideas be the only objects
of thought, there can be no knowledge either of our own
existence, or of the existence of external objects, or of
the existence of a Deity.

This consequence, as far as concerns the existence
of external objects of sense, was afterward deduced

from the theory of ideas by bishop Berkeley with the clearest evidence; and that author chose rather to adopt the consequence than to reject the theory on which it was grounded. But, with regard to the existence of our own minds, of other minds, and of a Supreme mind, the bishop, that he might avoid the consequence, rejected a part of the theory, and maintained, that we can think of minds, of their attributes and relations, without ideas.

Mr. Hume saw very clearly the consequences of this theory, and adopted them in his speculative moments; but candidly acknowledges, that, in the common business of life, he found himself under a necessity of believing with the vulgar. His Treatise of Human Nature is the only system to which the theory of ideas leads; and, in my apprehension, is, in all its parts, the necessary consequence of that theory.

Mr. Locke, however, did not see all the consequences of that theory; he adopted it without doubt or examination, carried along by the stream of philosophers that went before him; and his judgment and good sense have led him to say many things, and to believe many things that cannot be reconciled to it.

He not only believed his own existence, the existence of external things, and the existence of a Deity; but he has shown very justly how we come by the knowledge of these existences.

It might here be expected, that he should have pointed out the agreements and disagreements of ideas from which these existences are deduced; but this is impossible, and he has not even attempted it.

Our own existence, he observes, *we know intuitively;* but this intuition is not a perception of the agreement or disagreement of ideas; for the subject of the proposition, *I exist,* is not an idea, but a person.

The knowledge of external objects of sense, he observes, *we can have only by sensation. This sensation* he afterward expresses more clearly by *the testimony of our senses, which are the proper and sole judges of this thing ;* whose testimony *is the greatest assurance we can possibly have, and to which our faculties can attain.* This is perfectly agreeable to the common sense of mankind, and is perfectly understood by those who never heard of the theory of ideas.   Our senses testify immediately the existence, and many of the attributes and relations of external material beings ; and, by our constitution, we rely with assurance upon their testimony, without seeking a reason for doing so.   This assurance, Mr. Locke acknowledges, deserves the name of knowledge.   But those external things are not ideas, nor are their attributes and relations the agreements and disagreements of ideas, but the agreements and disagreements of things which are not ideas.

To reconcile this to the theory of ideas, Mr. Locke says, *that it is the actual receiving of ideas from without, that gives us notice of the existence of those external things.*

This, if understood literally, would lead us back to the doctrine of Aristotle, that our ideas, or species, come from without from the external objects, and are the image or form of those objects.   But Mr. Locke, I believe, meant no more by it, but that our ideas of sense must have a cause, and that we are not the cause of them ourselves.

Bishop Berkeley acknowledges all this, and shows very clearly, that it does not afford the least shadow of reason for the belief of any material object.   Nay, that there can be nothing external that has any resemblance to our ideas but the ideas of other minds.

It is evident, therefore, that the agreements and disagreements of ideas can give us no knowledge of the existence of any material thing. If any knowledge can be attained of things which are not ideas, that knowledge is a perception of agreements and disagreements, not of ideas, but of things that are not ideas.

As to the existence of a Deity, though Mr. Locke was aware that Des Cartes, and many after him, had attempted to prove it merely from the agreements and disagreements of ideas; yet " he thought it an ill way of establishing that truth, and silencing Atheists, to lay the whole stress of so important a point upon that sole foundation." And therefore he proves this point with great strength and solidity, from our own existence, and the existence of the sensible parts of the universe. By memory, Mr. Locke says, we have the knowledge of the past existence of several things : but all conception of past existence, as well as of external existence, is irreconcileable to the theory of ideas : because it supposes that there may be immediate objects of thought, which are not ideas presently existing in the mind.

I conclude, therefore, that if we have any knowledge of our own existence, or of the existence of what we see about us, or of the existence of a Supreme Being ; or if we have any knowledge of things past by memory, that knowledge cannot consist in perceiving the agreements and disagreements of ideas.

This conclusion, indeed, is evident of itself : for if knowledge consists solely in the perception of the agreement or disagreement of ideas, there can be no knowledge of any proposition which does not express some agreement or disagreement of ideas ; consequently there can be no knowledge of any proposition ; which expresses either the existence, or the attributes or relations of things, which are not ideas. If therefore the theory of ideas be true, there can be no knowledge of any thing but of ideas. And, on the other hand, if we have any knowledge of any thing besides ideas, that theory must be false.

There can be no knowledge, no judgment, or opinion about things which are not immediate objects of thought. This I take to be self-evident. If, therefore, ideas be the only immediate objects of thought, they must be the only things in nature of which we can have any knowledge, and about which we can have any judgment or opinion.

This necessary consequence of the common doctrine of ideas Mr. Hume saw, and has made evident in his Treatise of Human Nature; but the use he made of it was not to overturn the theory with which it is necessarily connected, but to overturn all knowledge, and to leave no ground to believe any thing whatsoever. If Mr. Locke had seen this consequence, there is reason to think that he would have made another use of it.

That a man of Mr. Locke's judgment and penetration did not perceive a consequence so evident, seems indeed very strange; and I know no other account that can be given of it but this, that the ambiguity of the word *idea* has misled him in this, as in several other instances. Having at first defined ideas to be whatsoever is the object of the understanding when we think, he takes it very often in that unlimited sense; and so every thing that can be an object of thought is an idea. At other times, he uses the word to signify certain representative images of things in the mind, which philosophers have supposed to be immediate objects of thought. At other times, things conceived abstractly, without regard to their existence, are called ideas. Philosophy is much indebted to Mr. Locke for his observations on the abuse of words. It is pity he did not apply these observations to the word *idea*, the ambiguity and abuse of which has very much hurt his excellent Essay.

There are some other opinions of philosophers concerning judgment, of which I think it unnecessary to say much.

Mr. Hume sometimes adopts Mr. Locke's opinion, that it is the perception of the agreement or disagreement of our ideas; sometimes he maintains, that judgment and reasoning resolve themselves into conception, and are nothing but particular ways of conceiving objects; and he says, that an opinion or belief may most accurately be defined, *a lively idea related to, or associated with a present impression.* Treatise of Human Nature, vol. i. page 172.

I have endeavoured before, in the first chapter of this Essay, to show that judgment is an operation of mind specifically distinct from the bare conception of an object. I have also considered his notion of belief, in treating of the theories concerning memory.

Dr. Hartly says, "That assent and dissent must come under the notion of ideas, being only those very complex internal feelings which adhere by association to such clusters of words as are called propositions in general, or affirmations and negations in particular."

This, if I understand its meaning, agrees with the opinion of Mr. Hume above mentioned, and has therefore been before considered.

Dr. Priestly has given another definition of judgment. " It is nothing more than the perception of the universal concurrence, or the perfect coincidence of two ideas; or the want of that concurrence or coincidence." This I think coincides with Mr. Locke's definition, and therefore has been already considered.

There are many particulars which deserve to be known, and which might very properly be considered in this Essay on judgment; concerning the various kinds of propositions by which our judgments are expressed; their subjects and predicates; their conver-

sions and oppositions : but as these are to be found in
every system of logic from Aristotle down to the present age, I think it unnecessary to swell this Essay with
the repetition of what has been said so often. The remarks which have occurred to me upon what is commonly said on these points, as well as upon the art of
syllogism; the utility of the school logic, and the improvements that may be made in it, will be found in a
short account of Aristotle's Logic, with remarks, vol. i.
Lord Kames has honoured it with a place in his Sketches
of the History of Man.

CHAP. IV.

OF FIRST PRINCIPLES IN GENERAL.

ONE of the most important distinctions of our judgments is, that some of them are intuitive, others grounded on argument.

It is not in our power to judge as we will. The judgment is carried along necessarily by the evidence, real or seeming, which appears to us at the time. But in propositions that are submitted to our judgment, there is this great difference; some are of such a nature that a man of ripe understanding may apprehend them distinctly, and perfectly understand their meaning without finding himself under any necessity of believing them to be true or false, probable or improbable. The judgment remains in suspense, until it is inclined to one side or another by reasons or arguments.

But there are other propositions which are no sooner understood than they are believed. The judgment follows the apprehension of them necessarily, and both are equally the work of nature, and the result of our original powers. There is no searching for evidence; no weighing of arguments; the proposition is not deduced or inferred from another; it has the light of truth in itself, and has no occasion to borrow it from another.

Propositions of the last kind, when they are used in matters of science, have commonly been called *axioms;* and on whatever occasion they are used, are called *first principles, principles of common sense, common notions, self-evident truths.* Cicero calls them *naturæ judicia, judicia communibus hominum sensibus infixa.* Lord Shaftesbury expresses them by the words, *natural knowledge, fundamental reason,* and *common sense.*

What has been said, I think, is sufficient to distinguish first principles, or intuitive judgments, from those which may be ascribed to the power of reasoning ; nor is it a just objection against this distinction, that there may be some judgments concerning which we may be dubious to which class they ought to be referred. There is a real distinction between persons within the house, and those that are without ; yet it may be dubious to which the man belongs that stands upon the threshold.

The power of reasoning, that is of drawing a conclusion from a chain of premises, may with some propriety be called an art. " All reasoning," says Mr. Locke, " is search and casting about, and requires pains and application." It resembles the power of walking, which is acquired by use and exercise. Nature prompts to it, and has given the power of acquiring it ; but must be aided by frequent exercise before we are able to walk. After repeated efforts, much stumbling, and many falls, we learn to walk ; and it is in a similar manner that we learn to reason.

But the power of judging in self-evident propositions, which are clearly understood, may be compared to the power of swallowing our food. It is purely natural, and therefore common to the learned, and the unlearned ; to the trained, and the untrained : it requires ripeness of understanding, and freedom from prejudice, but nothing else.

I take it for granted, that there are self-evident principles. Nobody, I think, denies it. ' And if any man were so skeptical as to deny that there is any proposition that is self-evident, I see not how it would be possible to convince him by reasoning.

But yet there seems to be great difference of opinions among philosophers about first principles. What one takes to be self-evident, another labours to prove by arguments, and a third denies altogether.

Thus, before the time of Des Cartes, it was taken for a first principle, that there is a sun and a moon, an earth and sea, which really exist, whether we think of them or not. Des Cartes thought that the existence of those things ought to be proved by argument; and in this he has been followed by Malebranche, Arnauld, and Locke. They have all laboured to prove, by very weak reasoning, the existence of external objects of sense; and Berkeley, and Hume, sensible of the weakness of their arguments, have been led to deny their existence altogether.

The ancient philosophers granted, that all knowledge must be grounded on first principles, and that there is no reasoning without them. The Peripatetic philosophy was redundant rather than deficient in first principles. Perhaps the abuse of them in that ancient system may have brought them into discredit in modern times; for as the best things may be abused, so that abuse is apt to give a disgust to the thing itself; and as one extreme often leads into the opposite, this seems to have been the case in the respect paid to first principles in ancient and in modern times.

Des Cartes thought one principle, expressed in one word *cogito*, a sufficient foundation for his whole system, and asked no more.

Mr. Locke seems to think first principles of very small use. Knowledge consisting, according to him, in the perception of the agreement or disagreement of our ideas; when we have clear ideas, and are able to compare them together, we may always fabricate first principles as often as we have occasion for them. Such differences we find among philosophers about first principles.

It is likewise a question of some moment, whether the differences among men about first principles can be brought to any issue? When, in disputes, one man

maintains that to be a first principle, which another denies, commonly both parties appeal to common sense,
and so the matter rests. Now, is there no way of discussing this appeal? Is there no mark or criterion,
whereby first principles that are truly such, may be
distinguished from those that assume the character
without a just title? I shall humbly offer in the following propositions what appears to me to be agreeable
to truth in these matters, always ready to change my
opinion upon conviction.

1st, *First*, I hold it to be certain, and even demonstrable, that all knowledge got by reasoning must be built
upon first principles.

This is as certain as that every house must have a
foundation. The power of reasoning, in this respect,
resembles the mechanical powers or engines; it must
have a fixed point to rest upon, otherwise it spends its
force in the air, and produces no effect.

When we examine, in the way of analysis, the evidence of any proposition, either we find it self-evident,
or it rests upon one or more propositions that support
it. The same thing may be said of the propositions
that support it; and of those that support them, as far
back as we can go. But we cannot go back in this
track to infinity. Where then must this analysis stop?
It is evident that it must stop only when we come to
propositions, which support all that are built upon
them, but are themselves supported by none, that is,
to self-evident propositions.

Let us again consider a synthetical proof of any
kind, where we begin with the premises, and pursue
a train of consequences, until we come to the last conclusion, or thing to be proved. Here we must begin, either with self-evident propositions, or with such
as have been already proved. When the last is the
case, the proof of the propositions, thus assumed, is a

part of our proof; and the proof is deficient without it.
Suppose then the deficiency supplied, and the proof
completed, is it not evident that it must set out with
self-evident propositions, and that the whole evidence
must rest upon them? So that it appears to be demonstrable that, without first principles, analytical reasoning could have no end, and synthetical reasoning could
have no beginning; and that every conclusion got by
reasoning must rest with its whole weight upon first
principles, as the building does upon its foundation.

2dly, A *second* proposition is, that some first principles yield conclusions that are certain, others such as
are probable, in various degrees, from the highest probability to the lowest.

In just reasoning, the strength or weakness of the
conclusion will always correspond to that of the principles on which it is grounded.

In a matter of testimony, it is self-evident, that the
testimony of two is better than that of one, supposing
them equal in character, and in their means of knowledge; yet the single testimony may be true, and that
which is preferred to it may be false.

When an experiment has succeeded in several trials,
and the circumstances have been marked with care,
there is a self-evident probability of its succeeding in a
new trial; but there is no certainty. The probability,
in some cases, is much greater than in others; because,
in some cases, it is much easier to observe all the circumstances that may have influence upon the event than
in others. And it is possible, that, after many experiments made with care, our expectation may be frustrated in a succeeding one, by the variation of some
circumstance that has not, or perhaps could not be
observed.

Sir Isaac Newton has laid it down as a first principle
in natural philosophy, that a property which has been

found in all bodies upon which we have had access to make experiments, and which has always been found in its quantity to be in exact proportion to the quantity of matter in every body, is to be held as an universal property of matter.

This principle, as far as I know, has never been called in question. The evidence we have, that all matter is divisible, moveable, solid, and inert, is resolvable into this principle; and if it be not true, we cannot have any rational conviction that all matter has those properties. From the same principle that great man has shown, that we have reason to conclude, that all bodies gravitate toward each other.

This principle, however, has not that kind of evidence which mathematical axioms have. It is not a necessary truth whose contrary is impossible; nor did sir Isaac ever conceive it to be such. And if it should ever be found, by just experiments, that there is any part in the composition of some bodies which has not gravity, the fact, if duly ascertained, must be admitted as an exception to the general law of gravitation.

In games of chance, it is a first principle, that every side of a die has an equal chance to be turned up; and that, in a lottery every ticket has an equal chance of being drawn out. From such first principles as these, which are the best we can have in such matters, we may deduce, by demonstrative reasoning, the precise degree of probability of every event in such games.

But the principles of all this accurate and profound reasoning can never yield a certain conclusion, it being impossible to supply a defect in the first principles by any accuracy in the reasoning that is grounded upon them. As water, by its gravity, can rise no higher in its course than the fountain, however artfully it be conducted; so no conclusion of reasoning can have a greater degree of evidence than the first principles from which it is drawn.

From these instances, it is evident, that as there are some first principles that yield conclusions of absolute certainty; so there are others that can only yield probable conclusions; and that the lowest degree of probability must be grounded on first principles as well as absolute certainty.

3dly, A *third* proposition is, that it would contribute greatly to the stability of human knowledge, and consequently to the improvement of it, if the first principles upon which the various parts of it are grounded were pointed out and ascertained.

We have ground to think so, both from facts, and from the nature of the thing.

There are two branches of human knowledge, in which this method has been followed, to wit, mathematics and natural philosophy; in mathematics, as far back as we have books. It is in this science only, that, for more than two thousand years since it began to be cultivated, we find no sects, no contrary systems, and hardly any disputes; or, if there have been disputes, they have ended as soon as the animosity of parties subsided, and have never been again revived. The science, once firmly established upon the foundation of a few axioms and definitions, as upon a rock, has grown from age to age, so as to become the loftiest and the most solid fabric that human reason can boast.

Natural philosophy, till less than two hundred years ago, remained in the same fluctuating state with the other sciences. Every new system pulled up the old by the roots. The system builders, indeed, were always willing to accept of the aid of first principles, when they were of their side; but finding them insufficient to support the fabric which their imagination had raised, they were only brought in as auxiliaries, and so intermixed with conjectures, and with lame inductions, that their systems were like Nebuchadnez-

zar's image, whose feet were partly of iron and partly of clay.

Lord Bacon first delineated the only solid foundation on which natural philosophy can be built; and sir
Isaac Newton reduced the principles laid down by Bacon into three or four axioms, which he calls *regulæ
philosophandi*. From these, together with the phenomena observed by the senses, which he likewise lays
down as first principles, he deduces, by strict reasoning, the propositions contained in the third book of his
Principia, and in his Optics; and by this means has
raised a fabric in those two branches of natural philosophy, which is not liable to be shaken by doubtful disputation, but stands immoveable upon the basis of self-
evident principles.

This fabric has been carried on by the accession
of new discoveries; but is no more subject to revolutions.

The disputes about *materia prima*, substantial forms,
nature's abhorring a vacuum, and bodies having no
gravitation in their proper place, are now no more.
The builders in this work are not put to the necessity of holding a weapon in one hand while they build
with the other; their whole employment is to carry
on the work.

Yet it seems to be very probable, that if natural
philosophy had not been reared upon this solid foundation of self-evident principles, it would have been
to this day a field of battle, wherein every inch of
ground would have been disputed, and nothing fixed
and determined.

I acknowledge, that mathematics and natural philosophy, especially the former, have this advantage of
most other sciences, that it is less difficult to form distinct and determinate conceptions of the objects about
which they are employed; but as this difficulty is not

insuperable, it affords a good reason, indeed, why other sciences should have a longer infancy ; but no reason at all why they may not at last arrive at maturity, by the same steps as those of quicker growth.

The facts I have mentioned may therefore lead us to conclude, that if in other branches of philosophy the first principles were laid down, as has been done in mathematics and natural philosophy, and the subsequent conclusions grounded upon them, this would make it much more easy to distinguish what is solid and well supported from the vain fictions of human fancy.

But laying aside facts, the nature of the thing leads to the same conclusion.

For when any system is grounded upon first principles, and deduced regularly from them, we have a thread to lead us through the labyrinth. The judgment has a distinct and determinate object. The heterogeneous parts being separated, can be examined each by itself.

The whole system is reduced to axioms, definitions, and deductions. These are materials of very different nature, and to be measured by a very different standard; and it is much more easy to judge of each, taken by itself, than to judge of a mass wherein they are kneaded together without distinction. Let us consider how we judge of each of them.

1st, As to definitions, the matter is very easy. They relate only to words, and differences about them may produce different ways of speaking, but can never produce different ways of thinking, while every man keeps to his own definitions.

But as there is not a more plentiful source of fallacies in reasoning than men's using the same word sometimes in one sense and at other times in another, the best means of preventing such fallacies, or of detecting

them when they are committed, is definitions of words
as accurate as can be given.

2dly. As to deductions drawn from principles granted on both sides, I do not see how they can long be a
matter of dispute among men who are not blinded by
prejudice or partiality : for the rules of reasoning by
which inferences may be drawn from premises have
been for two thousand years fixed with great unanimity.
No man pretends to dispute the rules of reasoning laid
down by Aristotle, and repeated by every writer in di-
alectics.

And we may observe by the way, that the reason
why logicians have been so unanimous in determining
the rules of reasoning, from Aristotle down to this day,
seems to be, that they were by that great genius raised, in a scientific manner, from a few definitions and
axioms. It may further be observed, that when men
differ about a deduction, whether it follows from certain premises, this I think is always owing to their differing about some first principle. I shall explain this
by an example.

Suppose that, from a thing having begun to exist,
one man infers that it must have had a cause ; another
man does not admit the inference. Here it is evident,
that the first takes it for a self-evident principle, that
every thing which begins to exist must have a cause ;
the other does not allow this to be self-evident. Let
them settle this point, and the dispute will be at an
end.

Thus I think it appears, that in matters of science,
if the terms be properly explained, the first principles
upon which the reasoning is grounded be laid down and
exposed to examination, and the conclusions regularly
deduced from them, it might be expected, that men of
candour and capacity, who love truth, and have patience
to examine things coolly, might come to unanimity with

regard to the force of the deductions, and that their differences might be reduced to those they may have about first principles.

4thly, A fourth proposition is, that nature has not left us destitute of means whereby the candid and honest part of mankind may be brought to unanimity when they happen to differ about first principles.

When men differ about things that are taken to be first principles or self-evident truths, reasoning seems to be at an end.   Each party appeals to common sense. When one man's common sense gives one determination, another man's a contrary determination, there seems to be no remedy but to leave every man to enjoy his own opinion.   This is a common observation, and I believe a just one, if it be rightly understood.

It is in vain to reason with a man who denies the first principles on which the reasoning is grounded. Thus, it would be in vain to attempt the proof of a proposition in Euclid to a man who denies the axioms. Indeed, we ought never to reason with men who deny first principles from obstinacy and unwillingness to yield to reason.

But is it not possible, that men who really love truth, and are open to conviction, may differ about first principles?

I think it is possible, and that it cannot, without great want of charity, be denied to be possible.

When this happens, every man who believes that there is a real distinction between truth and error, and that the faculties which God has given us are not in their nature fallacious, must be convinced that there is a defect, or a perversion of judgment on the one side or the other.

A man of candour and humility will, in such a case, very naturally suspect his own judgment, so far as to be desirous to enter into a serious examination, even of what he has long held as a first principle. He will think it not impossible, that although his heart be upright, his judgment may have been perverted, by education, by authority, by party zeal, or by some other of the common causes of error, from the influence of which neither parts nor integrity exempt the human understanding.

In such a state of mind, so amiable, and so becoming every good man, has nature left him destitute of any rational means by which he may be enabled, either to correct his judgment if it be wrong, or to confirm it if it be right ?

I hope it is not so. I hope that, by the means which nature has furnished, controversies about first principles may be brought to an issue, and that the real lovers of truth may come to unanimity with regard to them.

It is true, that, in other controversies, the process by which the truth of a proposition is discovered, or its falsehood detected, is, by showing its necessary connection with first principles, or its repugnancy to them. It is true, likewise, that when the controversy is, whether a proposition be itself a first principle, this process cannot be applied. The truth, therefore, in controversies of this kind, labours under a peculiar disadvantage. But it has advantages of another kind to compensate this.

1st, For, in the *first* place, in such controversies, every man is a competent judge; and therefore it is difficult to impose upon mankind.

To judge of first principles, requires no more than a sound mind free from prejudice, and a distinct conception of the question. The learned and the unlearned, the philosopher and the day labourer, are upon a level, and will pass the same judgment, when they are not misled by some bias, or taught to renounce their understanding from some mistaken religious principle.

In matters beyond the reach of common understanding, the many are led by the few, and willingly yield to their authority. But, in matters of common sense, the few must yield to the many, when local and temporary prejudices are removed. No man is now moved by the subtile arguments of Zeno against motion, though perhaps he knows not how to answer them.

The ancient skeptical system furnishes a remarkable instance of this truth. That system, of which Pyrrho was reputed the father, was carried down, through a succession of ages, by very able and acute philosophers, who taught men to believe nothing at all, and esteemed it the highest pitch of human wisdom to withhold assent from every proposition whatsoever. It was supported with very great subtilty and learning, as we see from the writings of Sextus Empiricus, the only author of that sect whose writings have come down to our age. The assault of the skeptics against all science seems to have been managed with more art and address than the defence of the dogmatists.

Yet, as this system was an insult upon the common sense of mankind, it died away of itself; and it would be in vain to attempt to revive it. The modern skepticism is very different from the ancient, otherwise it would not have been allowed a hearing; and, when it has lost the grace of novelty, it will die away also, though it should never be refuted.

The modern skepticism, I mean that of Mr. Hume, is built upon principles which were very generally maintained by philosophers, though they did not see that they led to skepticism. Mr. Hume, by tracing, with great acuteness and ingenuity, the consequences of principles commonly received, has shown that they overturn all knowledge, and at last overturn themselves, and leave the mind in perfect suspense.

2dly, *Secondly*, We may observe, that opinions which contradict first principles are distinguished from other errors by this; that they are not only false, but absurd: and, to discountenance absurdity, nature has given us a particular emotion, to wit, that of ridicule, which seems intended for this very purpose of putting out of countenance what is absurd, either in opinion or practice.

This weapon, when properly applied, cuts with as keen an edge as argument. Nature has furnished us with the first to expose absurdity; as with the last to refute error. Both are well fitted for their several offices, and are equally friendly to truth when properly used.

Both may be abused to serve the cause of error: but the same degree of judgment, which serves to detect the abuse of argument, in false reasoning, serves to detect the abuse of ridicule when it is wrongly directed.

Some have from nature a happier talent for ridicule than others; and the same thing holds with regard to the talent of reasoning. Indeed, I conceive there is hardly any absurdity, which, when touched with the pencil of a Lucian, a Swift, or a Voltaire, would not be put out of countenance, when there is not some religious panic, or very powerful prejudice, to blind the understanding.

But it must be acknowledged, that the emotion of ridicule, even when most natural, may be stifled by an emotion of a contrary nature, and cannot operate till that is removed.

Thus, if the notion of sanctity is annexed to an object, it is no longer a laughable matter, and this visor must be pulled off before it appears ridiculous. Hence we see, that notions which appear most ridiculous to all who consider them coolly and indifferently, have no such appearance to those who never thought of them, but under the impression of religious awe and dread.

Even where religion is not concerned, the novelty of an opinion to those who are too fond of novelties; the gravity and solemnity with which it is introduced; the opinion we have entertained of the author: its apparent connection with principles already embraced, or subserviency to interests which we have at heart; and, above all, its being fixed in our minds at that time of life when we receive implicitly what we are taught; may cover its absurdity, and fascinate the understanding for a time.

But if ever we are able to view it naked and stripped of those adventitious circumstances from which it borrowed its importance and authority, the natural emotion of ridicule will exert its force. An absurdity can be entertained by men of sense no longer than it wears a mask. When any man is found, who has the skill or the boldness to pull off the mask, it can no longer bear the light; it slinks into dark corners for a while, and then is no more heard of, but as an object of ridicule.

Thus I conceive, that first principles, which are really the dictates of common sense, and directly opposed to absurdities in opinion, will always, from the constitution of human nature, support themselves, and gain, rather than lose ground among mankind.

3dly, *Thirdly*, It may be observed, that although it is contrary to the nature of first principles to admit of direct, or *apodictical* proof; yet there are certain ways of reasoning even about them, by which those that are just and solid may be confirmed, and those that are false may be detected. It may here be proper to mention some of the topics from which we may reason in matters of this kind.

1st, It is a good argument *ad hominem*, if it can be shown, that a first principle which a man rejects, stands upon the same footing with others which he admits: for, when this is the case, he must be guilty of an inconsistency who holds the one and rejects the other.

Thus the faculties of consciousness, of memory, of external sense, and of reason, are all equally the gifts of nature. No good reason can be assigned for receiving the testimony of one of them, which is not of equal force with regard to the others. The greatest skeptics admit the testimony of consciousness, and allow, that what it testifies is to be held as a first principle. If therefore they reject the immediate testimony of sense, or of memory, they are guilty of an inconsistency.

2dly, A first principle may admit of a proof *ad absurdum*.

In this kind of proof, which is very common in mathematics, we suppose the contradictory proposition to be true. We trace the consequences of that supposition in a train of reasoning; and if we find any of its necessary consequences to be manifestly absurd, we conclude the supposition from which it followed to be false; and therefore its contradictory to be true.

There is hardly any proposition, especially of those that may claim the character of first principles, that stands alone and unconnected. It draws many others along with it in a chain that cannot be broken. He that takes it up must bear the burden of all its consequences; and if that is too heavy for him to bear, he must not pretend to take it up.

3dly, I conceive, that the consent of ages and nations, of the learned and unlearned, ought to have great authority with regard to first principles, where every man is a competent judge.

Our ordinary conduct in life is built upon first principles, as well as our speculations in philosophy; and every motive to action supposes some belief. When we find a general agreement among men, in principles that concern human life, this must have great authority with every sober mind that loves truth.

It is pleasant to observe the fruitless pains which bishop Berkeley takes to show, that his system of the non-existence of a material world did not contradict the sentiments of the vulgar, but those only of the philosophers.

With good reason he dreaded more to oppose the authority of vulgar opinion in a matter of this kind, than all the schools of philosophers.

Here perhaps it will be said, What has authority to do in matters of opinion? Is truth to be determined by most votes? Or is authority to be again raised out of its grave to tyrannise over mankind?

I am aware that, in this age, an advocate for authority has a very unfavourable plea; but I wish to give no more to authority than is its due.

Most justly do we honour the names of those benefactors to mankind who have contributed more or less to break the yoke of that authority which deprives men of the natural, the unalienable right of judging for themselves; but while we indulge a just animosity against this authority, and against all who would subject us to its tyranny, let us remember how common the folly is, of going from one faulty extreme into the opposite.

Authority, though a very tyrannical mistress to private judgment, may yet, on some occasions, be a useful handmaid; this is all she is entitled to, and this is all I plead in her behalf.

The justice of this plea will appear by putting a case in a science, in which, of all sciences, authority is acknowledged to have least weight.

Suppose a mathematician has made a discovery in that science, which he thinks important; that he has put his demonstration in just order; and, after examining it with an attentive eye, has found no flaw in it; I would ask, Will there not be still in his breast some diffidence, some jealousy lest the ardour of invention may have made him overlook some false step? This must be granted.

He commits his demonstration to the examination of a mathematical friend, whom he esteems a competent judge, and waits with impatience the issue of his judgment. Here I would ask again, Whether the verdict of his friend, according as it has been favourable or unfavourable, will not greatly increase or diminish his confidence in his own judgment? Most certain it will, and it ought.

If the judgment of his friend agrees with his own, especially if it be confirmed by two or three able judges, he rests secure of his discovery without further examination; but if it be unfavourable, he is brought back into a kind of suspense, until the part that is suspected undergoes a new and a more rigorous examination.

I hope what is supposed in this case is agreeable to nature, and to the experience of candid and modest men on such occasions: yet here we see a man's judgment, even in a mathematical demonstration, conscious of some feebleness in itself, seeking the aid of authority to support it, greatly strengthened by that authority, and hardly able to stand erect against it, without some new aid.

Society in judgment, of those who are esteemed fair and competent judges has effects very similar to those of civil society; it gives strength and courage to every individual; it removes that timidity which is as naturally the companion of solitary judgment, as of a solitary man in the state of nature.

Let us judge for ourselves therefore, but let us not disdain to take that aid from the authority of other competent judges, which a mathematician thinks it necessary to take in that science, which of all sciences has least to do with authority.

In a matter of common sense, every man is no less a competent judge, than a mathematician is in a mathematical demonstration; and there must be a great presumption that the judgment of mankind, in such a matter, is the natural issue of those faculties which God has given them. Such a judgment can be erroneous only when there is some cause of the error, as general as the error is: when this can be shown to be the case, I acknowledge it ought to have its due weight. But to suppose a general deviation from truth among mankind in things self evident, of which no cause can be assigned, is highly unreasonable.

Perhaps it may be thought impossible to collect the general opinion of men upon any point whatsoever; and therefore, that this authority can serve us in no stead in examining first principles. But I apprehend, that, in many cases, this is neither impossible nor difficult.

Who can doubt whether men have universally believed the existence of a material world? who can doubt whether men have universally believed, that every change that happens in nature must have a cause? who can doubt whether men have universally believed, that there is a right and a wrong in human conduct; some things that merit blame, and others that are entitled to approbation?

The universality of these opinions, and of many such that might be named, is sufficiently evident, from the whole tenor of human conduct, as far as our acquaintance reaches, and from the history of all ages and nations of which we have any records.

There are other opinions that appear to be universal, from what is common in the structure of all languages.

Language is the express image and picture of human thoughts; and from the picture we may draw some certain conclusions concerning the original.

We find in all languages the same parts of speech; we find nouns, substantive and adjective; verbs active and passive, in their various tenses, numbers, and moods. Some rules of syntax are the same in all languages.

Now what is common in the structure of languages, indicates an uniformity of opinion in those things upon which that structure is grounded.

The distinction between substances, and the qualities belonging to them; between thought and the being that thinks; between thought, and the objects of thought; is to be found in the structure of all languages: and therefore, systems of philosophy, which abolish those distinctions, wage war with the common sense of mankind.

We are apt to imagine, that those who formed languages were no metaphysicians; but the first principles of all sciences are the dictates of common sense, and lie open to all men; and every man who has considered the structure of language in a philosophical light, will find infallible proofs that those who have framed it, and those who use it with understanding, have the power of making accurate distinctions, and of forming general conceptions, as well as philosophers. Nature has given those powers to all men, and they can use them when their occasions require it; but they leave it to the philosophers to give names to them, and to descant upon their nature. In like manner, Nature has given eyes to all men, and they can make good use of them; but the structure of the eye, and the theory of vision, is the business of philosophers.

4thly, Opinions that appear so early in the minds of men, that they cannot be the effect of education, or of false reasoning, have a good claim to be considered as first principles. Thus the belief we have, that the persons about us are living and intelligent beings, is a belief for which perhaps we can give some reason, when we are able to reason; but we had this belief before we could reason, and before we could learn it by instruction. It seems therefore to be an immediate effect of our constitution.

The *last* topic I shall mention is, when an opinion is so necessary in the conduct of life, that without the belief of it, a man must be led into a thousand absurdities in practice, such an opinion, when we can give no other reason for it, may safely be taken for a first principle.

Thus I have endeavoured to show, that although first principles are not capable of direct proof, yet differences, that may happen with regard to them among men of candour, are not without remedy; that nature has left us destitute of means by which we may discover errors of this kind; and that there are ways of reasoning, with regard to first principles by which those that are truly such may be distinguished from vulgar errors or prejudices.

CHAP. V.

THE FIRST PRINCIPLES OF CONTINGENT TRUTHS.

"Surely, says bishop Berkeley, it is a work well deserving our pains, to make a strict inquiry concerning the first principles of knowledge ; to sift and examine them on all sides." What was said in the last chapter, is intended both to show the importance of this inquiry, and to make it more easy.

But, in order that such an inquiry may be actually made, it is necessary that the first principles of knowledge be distinguished from other truths, and presented to view, that they may be sifted and examined on all sides. In order to this end, I shall attempt a detail of those I take to be such, and of the reasons why I think them entitled to that character.

If the enumeration should appear to some redundant, to others deficient, and to others both ; if things, which I conceive to be first principles, should to others appear to be vulgar errors, or to be truths which derive their evidence from other truths, and therefore not first principles ; in these things every man must judge for himself. I shall rejoice to see an enumeration more perfect in any or in all of those respects ; being persuaded, that the agreement of men of judgment and candour in first principles, would be of no less consequence to the advancement of knowledge in general, than the agreement of mathematicians in the axioms of geometry has been to the advancement of that science.

The truths that fall within the compass of human knowledge, whether they be self-evident, or deduced from those that are self-evident, may be reduced to two classes. They are either necessary and immutable truths, whose contrary is impossible; or they are contingent and mutable, depending upon some effect of will and power, which had a beginning, and may have an end.

That a cone is the third part of a cylinder of the same base and the same altitude, is a necessary truth. It depends not upon the will and power of any being. It is immutably true, and the contrary impossible. That the sun is the centre, about which the earth, and the other planets of our system, perform their revolutions, is a truth; but it is not a necessary truth. It depends upon the power and will of that Being who made the sun and all the planets, and who gave them those motions that seemed best to him.

If all truths were necessary truths, there would be no occasion for different tenses in the verbs by which they are expressed. What is true in the present time, would be true in the past and future; and there would be no change or variation of any thing in nature.

We use the present tense in expressing necessary truths; but it is only because there is no flexion of the verb which includes all times. When I say that three is the half of six, I use the present tense only; but I mean to express not only what now is, but what always was, and always will be; and so every proposition is to be understood by which we mean to express a necessary truth. Contingent truths are of another nature. As they are mutable, they may be true at one time, and not at another; and therefore the expression of them must include some point or period of time.

If language had been a contrivance of philosophers, they would probably have given some flexion to the indicative mood of verbs, which extended to all times past, present, and future; for such a flexion only would be fit to express necessary propositions, which have no relation to time. But there is no language, as far as I know, in which such a flexion of verbs is to be found. Because the thoughts and discourse of men are seldom employed about necessary truths, but commonly about such as are contingent; languages are fitted to express the last rather than the first.

The distinction commonly made between abstract truths, and those that express matters of fact, or real existences, coincides in a great measure, but not altogether, with that between necessary and contingent truths. The necessary truths that fall within our knowledge are for the most part abstract truths. We must except the existence and nature of the Supreme Being, which is necessary. Other existences are the effects of will and power. They had a beginning, and are mutable. Their nature is such as the Supreme Being was pleased to give them. Their attributes and relations must depend upon the nature God has given them; the powers with which he has endowed them; and the situation in which he has placed them.

The conclusions deduced by reasoning from first principles, will commonly be necessary or contingent, according as the principles are from which they are drawn. On the one hand, I take it to be certain, that whatever can, by just reasoning, be inferred from a principle that is necessary, must be a necessary truth; and that no contingent truth can be inferred from principles that are necessary.

Thus, as the axioms in mathematics are all necessary truths; so are all the conclusions drawn from them; that is, the whole body of that science. But from no mathematical truth can we deduce the existence of any thing; not even of the objects of the science.

On the other hand, I apprehend there are very few cases in which we can, from principles that are contingent, deduce truths that are necessary. I can only recollect one instance of this kind, namely, that, from the existence of things contingent and mutable, we can infer the existence of an immutable and eternal cause of them.

As the minds of men are occupied much more about truths that are contingent than about those that are necessary, I shall first endeavour to point out the principles of the former kind.

1st. *First,* Then, I hold, as a first principle, the existence of every thing of which I am conscious.

Consciousness is an operation of the understanding of its own kind, and cannot be logically defined. The objects of it are our present pains, our pleasures, our hopes, our fears, our desires, our doubts, our thoughts of every kind; in a word, all the passions, and all the actions and operations of our own minds, while they are present. We may remember them when they are past; but we are conscious of them only while they are present.

When a man is conscious of pain, he is certain of its existence; when he is conscious that he doubts, or believes, he is certain of the existence of those operations.

But the irresistible conviction he has of the reality of those operations is not the effect of reasoning; it is immediate and intuitive. The existence therefore of those passions and operations of our minds, of which we are conscious, is a first principle, which nature requires us to believe upon her authority.

If I am asked to prove that I cannot be deceived by consciousness, to prove that it is not a fallacious sense; I can find no proof. I cannot find any antecedent truth from which it is deduced, or upon which its evidence depends. It seems to disdain any such derived authority, and to claim my assent in its own right.

If any man could be found so frantic as to deny that he thinks, while he is conscious of it; I may wonder,

I may laugh, or I may pity him, but I cannot reason the matter with him. We have no common principles from which we may reason, and therefore can never join issue in an argument.

This, I think, is the only principle of common sense that has never directly been called in question. It seems to be so firmly rooted in the minds of men, as to retain its authority with the greatest skeptics. Mr. Hume, after annihilating body and mind, time and space, action and causation, and even his own mind, acknowledges the reality of the thoughts, sensations, and passions of which he is conscious.

No philosopher has attempted by any hypothesis to account for this consciousness of our own thoughts, and the certain knowledge of their real existence which accompanies it. By this they seem to acknowledge, that this at least is an original power of the mind; a power by which we not only have ideas, but original judgments, and the knowledge of real existence.

I cannot reconcile this immediate knowledge of the operations of our own minds with Mr. Locke's theory, that all knowledge consists in perceiving the agreement and disagreement of ideas. What are the ideas, from whose comparison the knowledge of our own thoughts results? Or what are the agreements or disagreements which convince a man that he is in pain when he feels it?

Neither can I reconcile it with Mr. Hume's theory, that to believe the existence of any thing, is nothing else than to have a strong and lively conception of it; or, at most, that belief is only some modification of the idea which is the object of belief. For not to mention, that propositions, not ideas, are the object of belief; in all that variety of thoughts and passions, of which we are conscious, we believe the existence of the weak as well as of the strong, the faint as well as the lively. No modification of the operations of our minds disposes us to the least doubt of their real existence.

As therefore the real existence of our thoughts, and of all the operations and feelings of our own minds, is believed by all men ; as we find ourselves incapable of doubting it, and as incapable of offering any proof of it, it may justly be considered as a first principle, or dictate of common sense.

But although this principle rests upon no other, a very considerable and important branch of human knowledge rests upon it.

For from this source of consciousness is derived all that we know, and indeed all that we can know, of the structure, and of the powers of our own minds ; from which we may conclude, that there is no branch of knowledge that stands upon a firmer foundation ; for surely no kind of evidence can go beyond that of consciousness.

How does it come to pass then, that in this branch of knowledge there are so many and so contrary systems ? so many subtile controversies that are never brought to an issue, and so little fixed and determined ? Is it possible that philosophers should differ most where they have the surest means of agreement ; where every thing is built upon a species of evidence which all men acquiesce in, and hold to be the most certain ?

This strange phenomenon may, I think, be accounted for, if we distinguish between consciousness and reflection, which are often improperly confounded.

The first is common to all men at all times, but is insufficient of itself to give us clear and distinct notions of the operations of which we are conscious, and of their mutual relations, and minute distinctions. The second, to wit, attentive reflection upon those operations, making them objects of thought, surveying them attentively, and examining them on all sides, is so far from being common to all men, that it is the lot of very few. The greatest part of men, either through want of capacity, or from other causes, never reflect attentively upon the operations of their own minds. The habit of this reflection, even in those whom nature has fitted for it, is not to be attained without much pains and practice. We can know nothing of the immediate objects of sight, but by the testimony of our eyes; and I apprehend, that if mankind had found as great difficulty in giving attention to the objects of sight, as they find in attentive reflection upon the operations of their own minds, our knowledge of the first might have been in as backward a state as our knowledge of the last.

But this darkness will not last for ever. Light will arise upon this benighted part of the intellectual globe. When any man is so happy as to delineate the powers of the human mind as they really are in nature, men that are free from prejudice, and capable of reflection, will recognise their own features in the picture; and then the wonder will be, how things so obvious could be so long wrapped up in mystery and darkness; how men could be carried away by false theories and conjectures, when the truth was to be found in their own breasts if they had but attended to it.

2dly, Another first principle, I think, is, That the thoughts of which I am conscious, are the thoughts of a being which I call *myself*, my *mind*, my *person*.

The thoughts and feelings of which we are conscious are continually changing, and the thought of this moment is not the thought of the last; but something which I call myself, remains under this change of thought. This self has the same relation to all the successive thoughts I am conscious of, they are all my thoughts; and every thought which is not my thought, must be the thought of some other person.

If any man asks a proof of this, I confess I can give none; there is an evidence in the proposition itself which I am unable to resist. Shall I think, that thought can stand by itself without a thinking being? Or that ideas can feel pleasure or pain? My nature dictates to me that it is impossible.

And that nature has dictated the same to all men, appears from the structure of all languages: for in all languages men have expressed thinking, reasoning, willing, loving, hating, by personal verbs, which from their nature require a person who thinks, reasons, wills, loves, or hates. From which it appears, that men have been taught by nature to believe that thought requires a thinker, reason a reasoner, and love a lover.

Here we must leave Mr. Hume, who conceives it to be a vulgar error, that besides the thoughts we are conscious of, there is a mind which is the subject of those thoughts. If the mind be any thing else than impressions and ideas, it must be a word without a meaning. The mind therefore, according to this philosopher, is a word which signifies a bundle of perceptions; or, when he defines it more accurately, "It is that succession of related ideas and impressions, of which we have an intimate memory and consciousness."

I am, therefore, that succession of related ideas and impressions of which I have the intimate memory and consciousness.

But who is the *I* that has this memory and consciousness of a succession of ideas and impressions? Why, it is nothing but that succession itself.

Hence I learn, that this succession of ideas and impressions intimately remembers, and is conscious of itself. I would wish to be further instructed, whether the impressions remember and are conscious of the ideas, or the ideas remember and are conscious of the impressions, or if both remember and are conscious of both? And whether the ideas remember those that come after them, as well as those that were before them? These are questions naturally arising from this system, that have not yet been explained.

This, however, is clear, that this succession of ideas and impressions, not only remembers and is conscious, but that it judges, reasons, affirms, denies; nay, that it eats and drinks, and is sometimes merry, and sometimes sad.

If these things can be ascribed to a succession of ideas and impressions, in a consistency with common sense, I should be very glad to know what is nonsense.

The scholastic philosophers have been wittily ridiculed, by representing them as disputing upon this question, *Num chimæra bombinans in vacuo possit comedere secundas intentiones?* And I believe the wit of man cannot invent a more ridiculous question. But, if Mr. Hume's philosophy be admitted, this question deserves to be treated more gravely: for if, as we learn from this philosophy, a succession of ideas and impressions may eat, and drink, and be merry, I see no good reason why a chimera, which if not the same, is of kin to an idea, may not chew the cud upon that kind of food, which the schoolmen call second intentions.

3dly, Another first principle I take to be, That those things did really happen which I distinctly remember.

This has one of the surest marks of a first principle; for no man ever pretended to prove it, and yet no man in his wits calls it in question; the testimony of memory, like that of consciousness, is immediate; it claims our assent upon its own authority.

Suppose that a learned counsel, in defence of a client against the concurring testimony of witnesses of credit, should insist upon a new topic to invalidate the testimony. "Admitting," says he, "the integrity of the witnesses, and that they distinctly remember what they have given in evidence; it does not follow that the prisoner is guilty. It has never been proved that the most distinct memory may not be fallacious. Show me any necessary connection between that act of the mind which we call memory, and the past existence of the event remembered. No man has ever offered a shadow of argument to prove such a connection; yet this is one link of the chain of proof against the prisoner; and if it have no strength, the whole proof falls to the ground. Until this, therefore, be made evident, until it can be proved, that we may safely rest upon the testimony of memory for the truth of past events, no judge or jury can justly take away the life of a citizen upon so doubtful a point."

I believe we may take it for granted, that this argument from a learned counsel would have no other effect upon the judge or jury, than to convince them that he was disordered in his judgment. Counsel is allowed to plead every thing for a client that is fit to persuade or to move; yet I believe no counsel ever had the boldness to plead this topic. And for what reason? For no other reason, surely, but because it is absurd. Now, what is absurd at the bar, is so in the philosopher's chair. What would be ridiculous, if delivered to a jury of honest, sensible citizens, is no less so when delivered gravely in a philosophical dissertation.

Mr. Hume has not, as far as I remember, directly called in question the testimony of memory; but he has laid down the premises by which its authority is overturned, leaving it to his reader to draw the conclusion.

He labours to show, that the belief or assent which always attends the memory and senses is nothing but the vivacity of those perceptions which they present.

He shows very clearly, that this vivacity gives no ground to believe the existence of external objects. And it is obvious, that it can give as little ground to believe the past existence of the objects of memory.

Indeed the theory concerning ideas, so generally received by philosophers, destroys all the authority of memory, as well as the authority of the senses. Des Cartes, Malebranche, and Locke, were aware that this theory made it necessary for them to find out arguments to prove the existence of external objects, which the vulgar believe upon the bare authority of their senses; but those philosophers were not aware, that this theory made it equally necessary for them to find arguments to prove the existence of things past, which we remember, and to support the authority of memory.

All the arguments they advanced to support the authority of our senses, were easily refuted by bishop Berkeley and Mr. Hume, being indeed very weak and inconclusive. And it would have been as easy to answer every argument they could have brought, consistent with their theory, to support the authority of memory.

For, according to that theory, the immediate object of memory, as well as of every other operation of the understanding, is an idea present in the mind. And, from the present existence of this idea of memory I am left to infer, by reasoning, that six months, or six years ago, there did exist an object similar to this idea.

But what is there in the idea that can lead me to this conclusion? What mark does it bear of the date of its archetype? Or what evidence have I that it had an archetype, and that it is not the first of its kind?

Perhaps it will be said, that this idea or image in the mind must have had a cause.

I admit, that if there is such an image in the mind it must have had a cause, and a cause able to produce the effect; but what can we infer from its having a cause? Does it follow that the effect is a type, an image, a copy of its cause? Then it will follow, that a picture is an image of the painter, and a coach of the coachmaker.

A past event may be known by reasoning, but that is not remembering it. When I remember a thing distinctly, I disdain equally to hear reasons for it or against it. And so I think does every man in his senses.

4thly, Another first principle is our own personal identity and continued existence, as far back as we remember any thing distinctly.

This we know immediately, and not by reasoning. It seems, indeed, to be a part of the testimony of memory. Every thing we remember has such a relation to ourselves, as to imply necessarily our existence at the time remembered. And there cannot be a more palpable absurdity than that a man should remember what happened before he existed. He must therefore have existed as far back as he remembers any thing distinctly, if his memory be not fallacious. This principle, therefore, is so connected with the last mentioned, that it may be doubtful whether both ought not to be included in one. Let every one judge of this as he sees reason. The proper notion of identity, and the sentiments of Mr. Locke on this subject, have been considered before under the head of memory.

5thly, Another first principle is, That those things do really exist which we distinctly perceive by our senses, and are what we perceive them to be.

It is too evident to need proof, that all men are by nature led to give implicit faith to the distinct testimony of their senses, long before they are capable of any bias from prejudices of education or of philosophy.

How came we at first to know that there are certain beings about us whom we call father, and mother, and

sisters, and brothers, and nurse? Was it not by the testimony of our senses? How did these persons convey
to us any information or instruction? Was it not by
means of our senses?

It is evident we can have no communication, no correspondence or society with any created being, but by
means of our senses, And until we rely upon their
testimony, we must consider ourselves as being alone
in the universe, without any fellow creature, living
or inanimate, and be left to converse with our own
thoughts.

Bishop Berkeley surely did not duly consider, that
it is by means of the material world that we have
any correspondence with thinking beings, or any knowledge of their existence, and that by depriving us of
the material world, he deprived us at the same time
of family, friends, country, and every human creature;
of every object of affection, esteem or concern, except
ourselves.

The good bishop surely never intended this. He
was too warm a friend, too zealous a patriot, and too
good a Christian, to be capable of such a thought.
He was not aware of the consequences of his system,
and therefore they ought not to be imputed to him;
but we must impute them to the system itself. It
stifles every generous and social principle.

When I consider myself as speaking to men who
hear me, and can judge of what I say, I feel that respect which is due to such an audience. I feel an enjoyment in a reciprocal communication of sentiments
with candid and ingenious friends, and my soul blesses
the Author of my being, who has made me capable of
this manly and rational entertainment.

But the bishop shows me, that this is all a dream;
that I see not a human face; that all the objects I
see, and hear, and handle, are only the ideas of my

own mind ; ideas are my only companions. Cold company, indeed ! Every social affection freezes at the thought.

But, my lord bishop, are there no minds left in the universe but my own ?

Yes, indeed ; it is only the material world that is annihilated ; every thing else remains as it was.

This seems to promise some comfort in my forlorn solitude. But do I see those minds ? No. Do I see their ideas ? No. Nor do they see me or my ideas. They are then no more to me than the inhabitants of Solomon's isles, or of the moon ; and my melancholy solitude returns. Every social tie is broken, and every social affection is stifled.

This dismal system, which, if it could be believed, would deprive men of every social comfort, a very good bishop, by strict and accurate reasoning, deduced from the principles commonly received by philosophers concerning ideas. The fault is not in the reasoning, but in the principles, from which it is drawn.

All the arguments urged by Berkeley and Hume against the existence of a material world are grounded upon this principle, that we do not perceive external objects themselves, but certain images or ideas in our own minds. But this is no dictate of common sense, but directly contrary to the sense of all who have not been taught it by philosophy.

We have before examined the reasons given by philosophers, to prove that ideas, and not external objects, are the immediate objects of perception, and the instances given to prove the senses fallacious. Without repeating what has before been said upon those points, we shall only here observe, that if external objects be perceived immediately, we have the same reason to believe their existence as philosophers have to believe the existence of ideas, while they hold them to be the immediate objects of perception.

6thly, Another first principle, I think, is, That we have some degree of power over our actions, and the determinations of our will.

All power must be derived from the fountain of power, and of every good gift. Upon his good pleasure its continuance depends, and it is always subject to his control.

Beings to whom God has given any degree of power, and understanding to direct them to the proper use of it, must be accountable to their Maker. But those who are intrusted with no power, can have no account to make ; for all good conduct consists in the right use of power ; all bad conduct in the abuse of it.

To call to account a being who never was intrusted with any degree of power, is an absurdity no less than it would be to call to an account an inanimate being. We are sure, therefore, if we have any account to make to the Author of our being, that we must have some degree of power, which, as far as it is properly used, entitles us to his approbation ; and, when abused, renders us obnoxious to his displeasure.

It is not easy to say in what way we first get the notion or idea of power. It is neither an object of sense nor of consciousness. We see events, one succeeding another ; but we see not the power by which they are produced. We are conscious of the operations of our minds ; but power is not an operation of mind. If we had no notions but such as are furnished by the external senses, and by consciousness, it seems to be impossible that we should ever have any conception of power. Accordingly Mr. Hume, who has reasoned the most accurately upon this hypothesis, denies that we have any idea of power, and clearly refutes the account given by Mr. Locke of the origin of this idea.

But it is in vain to reason from a hypothesis against a fact, the truth of which every man may see by attending to his own thoughts. It is evident, that all men, very early in life, not only have an idea of power, but a conviction that they have some degree of it in themselves: for this conviction is necessarily implied in many operations of mind, which are familiar to every man, and without which no man can act the part of a reasonable being.

1st, It is implied in every act of volition. "Volition, it is plain," says, Mr. Locke, "is an act of the mind, knowingly exerting that dominion which it takes itself to have over any part of the man, by employing it in, or withholding it from any particular action." Every volition, therefore, implies a conviction of power to do the action willed. A man may desire to make a visit to the moon, or to the planet Jupiter; but nothing but insanity could make him will to do so. And if even insanity produced this effect, it must be by making him think it to be in his power.

2dly, This conviction is implied in all deliberation; for no man in his wits deliberates whether he shall do what he believes not to be in his power.

3dly, The same conviction is implied in every resolution or purpose formed in consequence of deliberation. A man may as well form a resolution to pull the moon out of her sphere, as to do the most insignificant action which he believes not to be in his power. The same thing may be said of every promise or contract wherein a man plights his faith; for he is not an honest man who promises what he does not believe he has power to perform.

As these operations imply a belief of some degree of power in ourselves; so there are others equally common and familiar, which imply a like belief with regard to others.

When we impute to a man any action or omission as a ground of approbation or of blame, we must believe he had power to do otherwise. The same is implied in all advice, exhortation, command, and rebuke, and in every case, in which we rely upon his fidelity in performing any engagement, or executing any trust.

It is not more evident that mankind have a conviction of the existence of a material world, than that they have the conviction of some degree of power in themselves, and in others; every one over his own actions, and the determinations of his will: a conviction so early, so general, and so interwoven with the whole of human conduct, that it must be the natural effect of our constitution, and intended by the Author of our being to guide our actions.

It resembles our conviction of the existence of a material world in this respect also, that even those who reject it in speculation, find themselves under a necessity of being governed by it in their practice; and thus it will always happen when philosophy contradicts first principles.

7thly, Another first principle is, that the natural faculties, by which we distinguish truth from error, are not fallacious. If any man should demand a proof of this, it is impossible to satisfy him. For suppose it should be mathematically demonstrated, this would signify nothing in this case; because, to judge of a demonstration, a man must trust his faculties, and take for granted the very thing in question.

If a man's honesty were called in question, it would be ridiculous to refer it to the man's own word, whether he be honest or not. The same absurdity there is in attempting to prove, by any kind of reasoning, probable or demonstrative, that our reason is not fallacious, since the very point in question is, whether reasoning may be trusted.

If a skeptic should build his skepticism upon this foundation, that all our reasoning, and judging powers

are fallacious in their nature, or should resolve at least
to withhold assent until it be proved that they are not;
it would be impossible by argument to beat him out of
this strong hold, and he must even be left to enjoy his
skepticism.

Des Cartes certainly made a false step in this matter; for having suggested this doubt among others,
that whatever evidence he might have from his consciousness, his senses, his memory, or his reason; yet
possibly some malignant being had given him those faculties on purpose to impose upon him; and therefore,
that they are not to be trusted without a proper voucher: to remove this doubt, he endeavours to prove
the being of a Deity who is no deceiver; whence he
concludes, that the faculties he had given him are true
and worthy to be trusted.

It is strange that so acute a reasoner did not perceive,
that in this reasoning there is evidently a begging of the
question.

For if our faculties be fallacious, why may they not
deceive us in this reasoning as well as in others? And if
they are to be trusted in this instance without a voucher, why not in others?

Every kind of reasoning for the veracity of our faculties, amounts to no more than taking their own
testimony for their veracity; and this we must do
implicitly, until God give us new faculties to sit in
judgment upon the old; and the reason why Des Cartes satisfied himself with so weak an argument for the
truth of his faculties, most probably was, that he never
seriously doubted of it.

If any truth can be said to be prior to all others in
the order of nature, this seems to have the best claim;
because in every instance of assent, whether upon intuitive, demonstrative, or probable evidence, the truth
of our faculties is taken for granted, and is, as it

were, one of the premises on which our assent is grounded.

How then come we to be assured of this fundamental truth on which all others rest? Perhaps evidence, as in many other respects it resembles light, so in this also, that as light, which is the discoverer of all visible objects, discovers itself at the same time : so evidence, which is the voucher for all truth, vouches for itself at the same time.

This, however, is certain, that such is the constitution of the human mind, that evidence discerned by us, forces a corresponding degree of assent. And a man who perfectly understood a just syllogism, without believing that the conclusion follows from the premises, would be a greater monster than a man born without hands or feet.

We are born under a necessity of trusting to our reasoning and judging powers; and a real belief of their being fallacious cannot be maintained for any considerable time by the greatest skeptic, because it is doing violence to our constitution. It is like a man's walking upon his hands, a feat which some men upon occasion can exhibit; but no man ever made a long journey in this manner. Cease to admire his dexterity, and he will, like other men, betake himself to his legs.

We may here take notice of a property of the principle under consideration, that seems to be common to it with many other first principles, and which can hardly be found in any principle that is built solely upon reasoning; and that is, that in most men it produces its effect without ever being attended to, or made an object of thought. No man ever thinks of this principle, unless when he considers the grounds of skepticism; yet it invariably governs his opinions. When a man in the common course of life gives credit to the testimony of his senses, his memory, or his reason, he does not put the question to himself, whether these faculties may deceive him; yet the trust he reposes in them supposes an inward conviction, that, in that instance at least, they do not deceive him.

It is another property of this and of many first principles, that they force assent in particular instances, more powerfully than when they are turned into a general proposition. Many skeptics have denied every general principle of science, excepting perhaps the existence of our present thoughts; yet these men reason, and refute, and prove, they assent and dissent in particular cases. They use reasoning to overturn all reasoning, and judge that they ought to have no judgment, and see clearly that they are blind. Many have, in general, maintained that the senses are fallacious, yet there never was found a man so skeptical as not to trust his senses in particular instances when his safety required it; and it may be observed of those who have professed skepticism, that their skepticism lies in generals, while in particulars they are no less dogmatical than others.

8thly, Another first principle relating to existence, is, that there is life and intelligence in our fellow men with whom we converse.

As soon as children are capable of asking a question, or of answering a question, as soon as they show the signs of love, of resentment, or of any other affection, they must be convinced that those with whom they have this intercourse are intelligent beings.

It is evident they are capable of such intercourse long before they can reason. Every one knows, that there is a social intercourse between the nurse and the child before it is a year old. It can, at that age, understand many things that are said to it.

It can, by signs, ask and refuse, threaten and supplicate. It clings to its nurse in danger, enters into her grief and joy, is happy in her soothing and caresses, and unhappy in her displeasure : that these things cannot be without a conviction in the child that the nurse is an intelligent being, I think must be granted.

Now, I would ask how a child of a year old comes by this conviction? Not by reasoning surely, for children do not reason at that age. Nor is it by external senses, for life and intelligence are not objects of the external senses.

By what means, or upon what occasions, nature first gives this information to the infant mind, is not easy to determine. We are not capable of reflecting upon our own thoughts at that period of life, and before we attain this capacity, we have quite forgot how or on what occasion we first had this belief; we perceive it in those who are born blind, and in others who are· born deaf; and therefore nature has not connected it solely either with any object of sight, or with any object of hearing. When we grow up to the years of reason and reflection, this belief remains. No man thinks of asking himself what reason he has to believe that his neighbour is a living creature. He would be not a little surprised if another person should ask him so absurd a question ; and perhaps could not give any reason which would not equally prove a watch or a puppet to be a living creature.

But, though you should satisfy him of the weakness of the reasons he gives for his belief, you cannot make him in the least doubtful. This belief stands upon another foundation than that of reasoning; and therefore, whether a man can give good reasons for it or not, it is not in his power to shake it off.

Setting aside this natural conviction, I believe the best reason we can give, to prove that other men are living and intelligent, is, that their words and actions indicate like powers of understanding as we are conscious of in ourselves. The very same argument applied to the works of nature leads us to conclude, that there is an intelligent Author of nature, and appears equally strong and obvious in the last case as in the first; so that it may be doubted whether men, by the mere exercise of reasoning, might not as soon discover the existence of a Deity, as that other men have life and intelligence.

The knowledge of the last is absolutely necessary to our receiving any improvement by means of instruction and example; and, without these means of improvement, there is no ground to think that we should ever be able to acquire the use of our reasoning powers. This knowledge, therefore, must be antecedent to reasoning, and therefore must be a first principle.

It cannot be said, that the judgments we form concerning life and intelligence in other beings are at first free from error: but the errors of children in this matter lie on the safe side; they are prone to attribute intelligence to things inanimate. These errors are of small consequence, and are gradually corrected by experience and ripe judgment. But the belief of life and intelligence in other men, is absolutely necessary for us before we are capable of reasoning; and therefore the Author of our being has given us this belief antecedently to all reasoning.

9thly, Another first principle I take to be, That certain features of the countenance, sounds of the voice, and gestures of the body, indicate certain thoughts and dispositions of mind.

That many operations of the mind have their natural signs in the countenance, voice, and gesture, I suppose every man will admit. *Omnis enim motus animi*, says Cicero, *suum quemdam habet a natura vultum, et vocem et gestum.* The only question is, whether we understand the signification of those signs, by the constitution of our nature, by a kind of natural perception similar to the perceptions of sense; or whether we gradually learn the signification of such signs from experience, as we learn that smoke is a sign of fire, or that the freezing of water is a sign of cold? I take the first to be the truth.

It seems to me incredible, that the notions men have of the expression of features, voice, and gesture, are entirely the fruit of experience. Children, almost as soon as born, may be frighted, and thrown into fits by a threatening or angry tone of voice. I knew a man who could make an infant cry, by whistling a melancholy tune in the same or in the next room; and again, by altering his key, and the strain of his music, could make the child leap and dance for joy.

It is not by experience surely that we learn the expression of music; for its operation is commonly strongest the first time we hear it. One air expresses mirth and festivity; so that, when we hear it, it is with difficulty we can forbear to dance. Another is sorrowful and solemn. One inspires with tenderness and love; another with rage and fury.

> Hear how Timotheus's vary'd lays surprise,
> And bid alternate passions fall and rise;
> While at each change, the son of Lybian Jove
> Now burns with glory, and then melts with love.
> Now his fierce eyes with sparkling fury glow,
> Now sighs steal out, and tears begin to flow.
> Persians and Greeks, like turns of nature, found,
> And the world's victor stood subdu'd by sound.

It is not necessary that a man have studied either music or the passions, in order to his feeling these effects. The most ignorant and unimproved, to whom nature has given a good ear, feel them as strongly as the most knowing.

The countenance and gesture have an expression no less strong and natural than the voice. The first time one sees a stern and fierce look, a contracted brow, and a menacing posture, he concludes that the person is inflamed with anger. Shall we say, that previous to experience, the most hostile countenance has as agreeable an appearance as the most gentle and benign? This surely would contradict all experience; for we know that an angry countenance will fright a child in the cradle. Who has not observed, that children, very early, are able to distinguish what is said to them in jest from what is said in earnest, by the tone of the voice, and the features of the face? They judge by these natural signs, even when they seem to contradict the artificial.

If it were by experience that we learn the meaning of features, and sound, and gesture, it might be expected that we should recollect the time when we first learned those lessons, or, at least, some of such a multitude.

Those who give attention to the operations of children, can easily discover the time when they have their earliest notices from experience, such as that flame will burn, or that knives will cut. But no man is able to recollect in himself, or to observe in others, the time when the expression of the face, voice, and gesture, were learned.

Nay, I apprehend that it is impossible that this should be learned from experience.

When we see the sign, and see the thing signified always conjoined with it, experience may be the instructor, and teach us how that sign is to be interpreted. But how shall experience instruct us when we see the sign only, when the thing signified is invisible? Now is this the case here; the thoughts and passions of the mind, as well as the mind itself, are invisible, and therefore their connection with any sensible sign cannot be first discovered by experience; there must be some earlier source of this knowledge.

Nature seems to have given to men a faculty or sense, by which this connection is perceived. And the operation of this sense is very analogous to that of the external senses.

When I grasp an ivory ball in my hand, I feel a certain sensation of touch. In the sensation, there is nothing external, nothing corporeal. The sensation is neither round nor hard; it is an act of feeling of the mind, from which I cannot, by reasoning, infer the existence of any body. But, by the constitution of my nature, the sensation carries along with it the conception and belief of a round hard body really existing in my hand.

In like manner, when I see the features of an expressive face, I see only figure and colour variously modified. But, by the constitution of my nature, the visible object brings along with it the conception and belief of a certain passion or sentiment in the mind of the person.

In the former case, a sensation of touch is the sign, and the hardness and roundness of the body I grasp, is signified by that sensation. In the latter case, the features of the person is the sign, and the passion or sentiment is signified by it.

The power of natural signs, to signify the sentiments and passions of the mind, is seen in the signs of dumb persons, who can make themselves to be understood in a considerable degree, even by those who are wholly unexperienced in that language.

It is seen in the traffic which has been frequently carried on between people that have no common acquired language. They can buy and sell, and ask and refuse, and show a friendly or hostile disposition by natural signs.

It was seen still more in the actors among the ancients who performed the gesticulation upon the stage,
while others recited the words. To such a pitch was
this art carried, that we are told, Cicero and Roscius
used to contend whether the orator could express any
thing by words, which the actor could not express in
dumb show by gesticulation ; and whether the same
sentence or thought could not be acted in all the
variety of ways in which the orator could express it in
words.

But the most surprising exhibition of this kind,
was that of the pantomimes among the Romans, who
acted plays, or scenes of plays, without any recitation,
and yet could be perfectly understood.

And here it deserves our notice, that although it required much study and practice in the pantomimes to
excel in their art ; yet it required neither study nor
practice in the spectators to understand them. It was
a natural language, and therefore understood by all
men, whether Romans, Greeks, or Barbarians, by the
learned and the unlearned.

Lucian relates, that a king, whose dominions border-
ed upon the Euxine sea, happening to be at Rome in the
reign of Nero, and having seen a pantomime act, begged
him of Nero that he might use him in his intercourse
with all the nations in his neighbourhood : for, said he,
I am obliged to employ I don't know how many inter-
preters, in order to keep a correspondence with neigh-
bours who speak many languages, and do not understand mine ; but this fellow will make them all understand him.

For these reasons, I conceive, it must be granted,
not only that there is a connection established by nature
between certain signs in the countenance, voice, and
gesture, and the thoughts and passions of the mind ;
but also, that by our constitution, we understand the

meaning of those signs, and from the sign conclude the existence of the thing signified.

10thly, Another first principle appears to me to be, That there is a certain regard due to human testimony in matters of fact, and even to human authority in matters of opinion.

Before we are capable of reasoning about testimony or authority, there are many things which it concerns us to know, for which we can have no other evidence. The wise Author of nature has planted in the human mind a propensity to rely upon this evidence before we can give a reason for doing so. This, indeed, puts our judgment almost entirely in the power of those who are about us, in the first period of life; but this is necessary both to our preservation and to our improvement. If children were so framed, as to pay no regard to testimony or to authority, they must, in the literal sense, perish for lack of knowledge. It is not more necessary that they should be fed before they can feed themselves, than that they should be instructed in many things, before they can discover them by their own judgment.

But when our faculties ripen, we find reason to check that propensity, to yield to testimony and to authority, which was so necessary and so natural in the first period of life. We learn to reason about the regard due to them, and see it to be a childish weakness to lay more stress upon them than reason justifies. Yet, I believe, to the end of life, most men are more apt to go into this extreme than into the contrary; and the natural propensity still retains some force.

The natural principles, by which our judgments and opinions are regulated before we come to the use of reason, seem to be no less necessary to such a being as man, than those natural instincts which the Author of nature has given us to regulate our actions during that period.

11thly, There are many events depending upon the will of man, in which there is a self-evident probability, greater or less, according to circumstances.

There may be in some individuals such a degree of phrenzy and madness, that no man can say what they may or may not do. Such persons we find it necessary to put under restraint, that, as far as possible, they may be kept from doing harm to themselves or to others. They are not considered as reasonable creatures, or members of society. But, as to men who have a sound mind, we depend upon a certain degree of regularity in their conduct; and could put a thousand different cases, wherein we could venture, ten to one, that they will act in such a way, and not in the contrary.

If we had no confidence in our fellow men that they will act such a part in such circumstances, it would be impossible to live in society with them: for that which makes men capable of living in society, and uniting in a political body under government, is, that their actions will always be regulated in a great measure by the common principles of human nature.

It may always be expected, that they will regard their own interest and reputation, and that of their families and friends; that they will repel injuries, and have some sense of good offices; and that they will have some regard to truth and justice, so far at least as not to swerve from them without temptation.

It is upon such principles as these, that all political reasoning is grounded. Such reasoning is never demonstrative; but it may have a very great degree of probability, especially when applied to great bodies of men.

12thly, The last principle of contingent truths I mention, is, That, in the phenomena of nature, what is to be, will probably be like to what has been in similar circumstances.

We must have this conviction as soon as we are capable of learning any thing from experience ; for all experience is grounded upon a belief that the future will be like the past. Take away this principle, and the experience of an hundred years makes us no wiser with regard to what is to come.

This is one of those principles, which, when we grow up and observe the course of nature, we can confirm by reasoning. We perceive that nature is governed by fixed laws, and that if it were not so, there could be no such thing as prudence in human conduct ; there would be no fitness in any means to promote an end ; and what. on one occasion, promoted it, might as probably, on another occasion, obstruct it.

But the principle is necessary for us before we are able to discover it by reasoning, and therefore is made a part of our constitution, and produces its effects before the use of reason.

This principle remains in all its force when we come to the use of reason : but we learn to be more cautious in the application of it. We observe more carefully the circumstances on which the past event depended, and learn to distinguish them from those which were accidentally conjoined with it.

In order to this, a number of experiments, varied in their circumstances, is often necessary. Sometimes a single experiment is thought sufficient to establish a general conclusion. Thus, when it was once found, that in a certain degree of cold, quicksilver became a hard and malleable metal, there was good reason to think, that the same degree of cold will always produce this effect to the end of the world.

I need hardly mention, that the whole fabric of natural philosophy is built upon this principle, and, if it be taken away, must tumble down to the foundation.

Therefore the great Newton lays it down as an axiom, or as one of his laws of philosophizing, in these words, *Effectuum naturalium ejusdem generis easdem esse causas*. This is what every man assents to as soon as he understands it, and no man asks a reason for it. It has therefore the most genuine marks of a first principle.

It is very remarkable, that although all our expectation of what is to happen in the course of nature is derived from the belief of this principle, yet no man thinks of asking what is the ground of this belief.

Mr. Hume, I think, was the first who put this question; and he has shown clearly and invincibly, that it is neither grounded upon reasoning, nor has that kind of intuitive evidence which mathematical axioms have. It is not a necessary truth.

He has endeavoured to account for it upon his own principles. It is not my business at present to examine the account he has given of this universal belief of mankind; because, whether his account of it be just or not, and I think it is not, yet, as this belief is universal among mankind, and is not grounded upon any antecedent reasoning, but upon the constitution of the mind itself, it must be acknowledged to be a first principle, in the sense in which I use that word.

I do not at all affirm, that those I have mentioned are all the first principles from which we may reason concerning contingent truths. Such enumerations, even when made after much reflection, are seldom perfect.

CHAP. VI.

FIRST PRINCIPLES OF NECESSARY TRUTHS.

ABOUT most of the first principles of necessary truths there has been no dispute, and therefore it is the less necessary to dwell upon them. It will be sufficient to divide them into different classes; to mention some, by way of specimen, in each class; and to make some remarks on those of which the truth has been called in question.

They may, I think, most properly be divided according to the science to which they belong.

1st, There are some first principles that may be called grammatical; such as, that every adjective in a sentence must belong to some substantive expressed or understood; that every complete sentence must have a verb.

Those who have attended to the structure of language, and formed distinct notions of the nature and use of the various parts of speech, perceive, without reasoning, that these, and many other such principles, are necessarily true.

2dly, There are logical axioms; such as, that any contexture of words which does not make a proposition, is neither true nor false; that every proposition is either true or false; that no proposition can be both true and false at the same time; that reasoning in a circle proves nothing; that whatever may be truly affirmed of a genus, may be truly affirmed of all the species, and all the individuals belonging to that genus.

3dly, Every one knows there are mathematical axioms. Mathematicians have, from the days of Euclid, very wisely laid down the axioms or first principles on which they reason. And the effect which this appears to have had upon the stability and happy progress of this science, gives no small encouragement to attempt to lay the foundation of other sciences in a similar manner, as far as we are able.

Mr. Hume has discovered, as he apprehends, a weak side, even in mathematical axioms; and thinks, that it is not strictly true, for instance, that two right lines can cut one another in one point only.

The principle he reasons from is, that every simple idea is a copy of a preceding impression; and therefore, in its precision and accuracy, can never go beyond its original. From which he reasons in this manner: no man ever saw or felt a line so straight, that it might not cut another, equally straight, in two or more points. Therefore there can be no idea of such a line.

The ideas that are most essential to geometry, such as, those of equality, of a straight line, and of a square surface, are far, he says, from being distinct and determinate; and the definitions destroy the pretended demonstrations. Thus, mathematical demonstration is found to be a rope of sand.

I agree with this acute author, that, if we could form no notion of points, lines, and surfaces, more accurate than those we see and handle, there could be no mathematical demonstration.

But every man that has understanding, by analyzing, by abstracting, and compounding the rude materials exhibited by his senses, can fabricate, in his own mind, those elegant and accurate forms of mathematical lines, surfaces, and solids.

If a man finds himself incapable of forming a precise and determinate notion of the figure which mathematicians call a cube, he not only is no mathematician, but is incapable of being one. But, if he has a precise and determinate notion of that figure, he must perceive, that it is terminated by six mathematical surfaces, perfectly square, and perfectly equal. He must perceive, that these surfaces are terminated by twelve mathematical lines, perfectly straight, and perfectly equal, and that those lines are terminated by eight mathematical points.

When a man is conscious of having these conceptions distinct and determinate, as every mathematician is, it is in vain to bring metaphysical arguments to convince him that they are not distinct. You may as well bring arguments to convince a man racked with pain, that he feels no pain.

Every theory that is inconsistent with our having accurate notions of mathematical lines, surfaces, and solids, must be false. Therefore it follows, that they are not copies of our impressions.

The Medicean Venus is not a copy of the block of marble from which it was made. It is true, that the elegant statue was formed out of the rude block, and that too by a manual operation, which, in a literal sense, we may call abstraction. Mathematical notions are formed in the understanding by an abstraction of another kind, out of the rude perceptions of our senses.

As the truths of natural philosophy are not necessary truths, but contingent, depending upon the will of the Maker of the world, the principles from which they are deduced must be of the same nature, and therefore belong not to this class.

4thly, I think there are axioms, even in matters of taste. Notwithstanding the variety found among men, in taste, there are, I apprehend, some common principles, even in matters of this kind. I never heard of any man who thought it a beauty in a human face to want a nose, or an eye, or to have the mouth on one side. How many ages have passed since the days of Homer! Yet, in this long tract of ages, there never was found a man who took Thersites for a beauty.

The *fine arts* are very properly called the *arts of taste,* because the principles of both are the same ;

and in the fine arts, we find no less agreement among those who practise them than among other artists.

No work of taste can be either relished or understood by those who do not agree with the author in the principles of taste.

Homer, and Virgil, and Shakespeare, and Milton, had the same taste ; and all men who have been acquainted with their writings, and agree in the admiration of them, must have the same taste.

The fundamental rules of poetry, and music, and painting, and dramatic action and eloquence, have been always the same, and will be so to the end of the world.

The variety we find among men in matters of taste is easily accounted for, consistently with what we have advanced.

There is a taste that is acquired, and a taste that is natural. This holds, with respect both to the external sense of taste, and the internal. Habit and fashion have a powerful influence upon both.

Of tastes that are natural, there are some that may be called rational, others that are merely animal.

Children are delighted with brilliant and gaudy colours, with romping and noisy mirth, with feats of agility, strength, or cunning; and savages have much the same taste as children.

But there are tastes that are more intellectual. It is the dictate of our rational nature, that love and admiration are misplaced when there is no intrinsic worth in the object.

In those operations of taste which are rational, we judge of the real worth and excellence of the object, and our love or admiration is guided by that judgment. In such operations, there is judgment as well as feeling, and the feeling depends upon the judgment we form of the object.

I do not maintain that taste, so far as it is acquired, or so far as it is merely animal, can be reduced to principles. But as far as it is founded on judgment, it certainly may.

The virtues, the graces, the muses, have a beauty that is intrinsic. It lies not in the feelings of the spectator, but in the real excellence of the object. If we do not perceive their beauty, it is owing to the defect, or to the perversion of our faculties.

And as there is an original beauty in certain moral and intellectual qualities, so there is a borrowed and derived beauty in the natural signs and expressions of such qualities.

The features of the human face, the modulations of the voice, and the proportions, attitudes, and gesture of the body, are all natural expressions of good or bad qualities of the person, and derive a beauty or a deformity from the qualities which they express.

Works of art, express some quality of the artist, and often derive an additional beauty from their utility or fitness for their end.

Of such things, there are some that ought to please, and others that ought to displease. If they do not, it is owing to some defect in the spectator. But what has real excellence will always please those who have a correct judgment, and a sound heart.

The sum of what has been said upon this subject is, that, setting aside the tastes which men acquire by habit and fashion, there is a natural taste, which is partly animal, and partly rational. With regard to the first, all we can say is, that the Author of nature, for wise reasons, has formed us so as to receive pleasure from the contemplation of certain objects, and disgust from others, before we are capable of perceiving any real excellence in the one, or defect in the other. But that taste which we may call rational, is that part of our constitution by which we are made to receive pleasure from the contemplation of what we conceive to be excellent in its kind; the pleasure being annexed to this judgment, and regulated by it. This taste may be true or false, according as it is founded on a true or false judgment. And if it may be true or false, it must have first principles.

5thly, There are also first principles in morals.

That an unjust action has more demerit than an ungenerous one: that a generous action has more merit than merely a just one: that no man ought to be blamed for what it was not in his power to hinder: that we ought not to do to others what we would think unjust or unfair to be done to us in like circumstances: these are moral axioms, and many others might be named which appear to me to have no less evidence than those of mathematics.

Some, perhaps, may think, that our determinations, either in matters of taste or in morals, ought not to be accounted necessary truths: that they are grounded upon the constitution of that faculty which we call taste, and of that which we call the moral sense or conscience; which faculties might have been so constituted as to have given determinations different, or even contrary to those they now give: that as there is nothing sweet or bitter in itself, but according as it agrees or disagrees with the external sense called taste; so there is nothing beautiful or ugly in itself, but according as it agrees or disagrees with the internal sense, which we also call taste; and nothing morally good or ill in itself, but according as it agrees or disagrees with our moral sense.

This, indeed, is a system, with regard to morals and taste, which has been supported in modern times by great authorities. And if this system be true, the consequence must be, that there can be no principles, either of taste or of morals, that are necessary truths, For, according to this system, all our determinations, both with regard to matters of taste, and with regard to morals, are reduced to matters of fact. 1 mean to such as these, that by our constitution   have on such occasions, certain agreeable feelings, and on other occasions, certain disagreeable feelings.

But I cannot help being of a contrary opinion, being persuaded, that a man who determined that polite behaviour has great deformity, and that there is great beauty in rudeness and ill breeding, would judge wrong whatever his feelings were.

In like manner, I cannot help thinking, that a man who determined that there is more moral worth in cruelty, perfidy, and injustice, than in generosity, justice, prudence, and temperance, would judge wrong whatever his constitution was.

And if it be true that there is judgment in our determinations of taste and of morals, it must be granted, that what is true or false in morals, or in matters of taste, is necessarily so. For this reason, I have ranked the first principles of morals and of taste under the class of necessary truths.

6thly, The last class of first principles I shall mention, we may call metaphysical.

I shall particularly consider three of these, because they have been called in question by Mr. Hume.

The *first* is, That the qualities which we perceive by our senses must have a subject, which we call body, and that the thoughts we are conscious of must have a subject, which we call mind.

It is not more evident that two and two make four, than it is that figure cannot exist, unless there be something that is figured, nor motion without something that is moved. I not only perceive figure and motion, but I perceive them to be qualities: they have a necessary

relation to something in which they exist as their subject. The difficulty which some philosophers have
found in admitting this, is entirely owing to the theory
of ideas. A subject of the sensible qualities which we
perceive by our senses, is not an idea either of sensation or of consciousness; therefore, say they, we have
no such idea. Or, in the style of Mr. Hume, from what
impression is the idea of substance derived? It is
not a copy of any impression; therefore there is no
such idea.

The distinction between sensible qualities, and the
substance to which they belong, and between thought,
and the mind that thinks, is not the invention of philosophers; it is found in the structure of all languages,
and therefore must be common to all men who speak
with understanding. And, I believe, no man, however
skeptical he may be in speculation, can talk on the
common affairs of life for half an hour, without saying
things that imply his belief of the reality of these distinctions.

Mr. Locke acknowledges, "That we cannot conceive how simple ideas of sensible qualities should subsist alone; and therefore we suppose them to exist in,
and to be supported by, some common subject." In his
Essay, indeed, some of his expressions seem to leave it
dubious, whether this belief, that sensible qualities
must have a subject, be a true judgment, or a vulgar
prejudice. But in his first letter to the bishop of
Worcester, he removes this doubt, and quotes many
passages of his Essay, to show that he neither denied,
nor doubted of the existence of substances, both thinking and material; and that he believed their existence
on the same ground the bishop did, to wit, "on the repugnancy to our conceptions, that modes and accidents
should subsist by themselves." He offers no proof of
this repugnancy; nor, I think, can any proof of it be
given, because it is a first principle.

It were to be wished that Mr. Locke, who inquired so accurately, and so laudably into the origin, certainty, and extent of human knowledge, had turned his attention more particularly to the origin of these two opinions which he firmly believed; to wit, that sensible qualities must have a subject, which we call body, and that thought must have a subject, which we call mind. A due attention to these two opinions which govern the belief of all men, even of skeptics in the practice of life, would probably have led him to perceive, that sensation and consciousness are not the only sources of human knowledge; and that there are principles of belief in human nature, of which we can give no other account, but that they necessarily result from the constitution of our faculties; and that if it were in our power to throw off their influence upon our practice and conduct, we could neither speak nor act like reasonable men.

We cannot give a reason why we believe even our sensations to be real, and not fallacious; why we believe what we are conscious of; why we trust any of our natural faculties. We say, it must be so, it cannot be otherwise. This expresses only a strong belief, which is indeed the voice of nature, and which therefore in vain we attempt to resist. But if, in spite of nature, we resolve to go deeper, and not to trust our faculties, without a reason to show that they cannot be fallacious; I am afraid, that seeking to become wise, and to be as gods, we shall become foolish, and being unsatisfied with the lot of humanity, we shall throw off common sense.

The *second* metaphysical principle, I mention, is that whatever begins to exist, must have a cause which produced it.

Philosophy is indebted to Mr. Hume in this respect among others, that, by calling in question many of the first principles of human knowledge, he has put speculative men upon inquiring more carefully than was done before, into the nature of the evidence upon which they rest. Truth can never suffer by a fair inquiry; it can bear to be seen naked and in the fullest light; and the strictest examination will always turn out in the issue to its advantage. I believe Mr. Hume was the first who ever called in question, whether things that begin to exist must have a cause.

With regard to this point, we must hold one of these three things, either that it is an opinion, for which we have no evidence, and which men have foolishly taken up without ground; or, *secondly*, that it is capable of direct proof by argument; or, *thirdly*, that it is self-evident, and needs no proof, but ought to be received as an axiom, which cannot, by reasonable men, be called in question.

The fisrt of these suppositions would put an end to all philosophy, to all religion, to all reasoning that would carry us beyond the objects of sense, and to all prudence in the conduct of life.

As to the second supposition, that this principle may be proved by direct reasoning, I am afraid we shall find the proof extremely difficult, if not altogether impossible.

I know only of three or four arguments that have been urged by philosophers, in the way of abstract reasoning, to prove, that things which begin to exist must have a cause.

One is offered by Mr. Hobbes, another by Dr. Samuel Clarke, another by Mr. Locke. Mr. Hume, in his Treatise of Human Nature, has examined them all; and, in my opinion, has shown, that they take for granted the thing to be proved; a kind of false reasoning, which men are very apt to fall into when they attempt to prove what is self-evident.

It has been thought, that, although this principle does not admit of proof from abstract reasoning, it may be proved from experience, and may be justly drawn by induction from instances that fall within our observation.

I conceive this method of proof will leave us in great uncertainty, for these three reasons:

1st, Because the proposition to be proved, is not a contingent, but a necessary proposition. It is not, that things which begin to exist commonly have a cause, or even that they always in fact have a cause; but that they must have a cause, and cannot begin to exist without a cause.

Propositions of this kind, from their nature, are incapable of proof by induction. Experience informs us only of what is, or has been, not of what must be; and the conclusion must be of the same nature with the premises.

For this reason, no mathematical proposition can be proved by induction. Though it should be found by experience in a thousand cases, that the area of a plane triangle is equal to the rectangle under the altitude and half the base, this would not prove that it must be so in all cases, and cannot be otherwise; which is what the mathematician affirms.

In like manner, though we had the most ample experimental proof, that things which have begun to exist had a cause, this would not prove that they must have a cause. Experience may show us what is the established course of nature, but can never show what connections of things are in their nature necessary.

2dly, General maxims, grounded on experience, have only a degree of probability proportioned to the extent of our experience, and ought always to be understood so as to leave room for exceptions, if future experience shall discover any such.

The law of gravitation has as full a proof from experience and induction as any principle can be supposed to have. Yet if any philosopher should by clear experiment, show that there is a kind of matter in some bodies which does not gravitate, the law of gravitation ought to be limited by that exception.

Now it is evident, that men have never considered the principle of the necessity of causes, as a truth of this kind which may admit of limitation or exception; and therefore it has not been received upon this kind of evidence.

3dly, I do not see that experience could satisfy us that every change in nature actually has a cause.

In the far greatest part of the changes in nature that fall within our observation, the causes are unknown; and therefore, from experience, we cannot know whether they have causes or not.

Causation is not an object of sense. The only experience we can have of it, is in the consciousness we have of exerting some power in ordering our thoughts and actions. But this experience is surely too narrow a foundation for a general conclusion, that all things that have had, or shall have a beginning, must have a cause.

For these reasons, this principle cannot be drawn from experience, any more than from abstract reasoning.

The *third* supposition is, That it is to be admitted as a first or self evident principle. Two reasons may be urged for this.

1st, The universal consent of mankind, not of philosophers only, but of the rude and unlearned vulgar.

Mr. Hume, as far as I know, was the first that ever expressed any doubt of this principle. And when we consider that he has rejected every principle of human knowledge, excepting that of consciousness, and has not even spared the axioms of mathematics, his authority is of small weight.

Indeed, with regard to first principles, there is no reason why the opinion of a philosopher should have more authority than that of another man of common sense, who has been accustomed to judge in such cases. The illiterate vulgar are competent judges; and the philosopher has no prerogative in matters of this kind; but he is more liable than they to be misled by a favourite system, especially if it is his own.

Setting aside the authority of Mr. Hume, what has philosophy been employed in, since men first began to philosophize, but in the investigation of the causes of things? This it has always professed, when we trace it to its cradle. It never entered into any man's thought, before the philosopher we have mentioned, to put the previous question, whether things have a cause or not? Had it been thought possible that they might not, it may be presumed, that, in the variety of absurd and contradictory causes assigned, some one would have had recourse to this hypothesis.

They could conceive the world to arise from an egg, from a struggle between love and strife, between moisture and drought, between heat and cold; but they never supposed that it had no cause. We know not any Atheistic sect that ever had recourse to this topic, though by it they might have evaded every argument that could be brought against them, and answered all objections to their system.

But rather than adopt such an absurdity, they contrived some imaginary cause; such as chance, a concourse of atoms, or necessity, as the cause of the universe.

The accounts which philosophers have given of particular phenomena, as well as of the universe in general, proceed upon the same principle. That every phenomenon must have a cause, was always taken for granted. *Nil turpius physico*, says Cicero, *quam fieri sine causa quicquam dicere.* Though an academic, he was dogmatical in this. And Plato, the father of the academy, was no less so. "Πάντι γὰρ ἀδύναῑον χωρις αἰτίας γένεσιν σχεῖν." Timeus. It is impossible that any thing should have its origin without a cause.

I believe Mr. Hume was the first who ever held the contrary. This, indeed, he avows, and assumes the honour of the discovery. " It is," says he, " a maxim in philosophy, that whatever begins to exist, must have a cause of existence. This is commonly taken for granted in all reasonings, without any proof given or demanded. It is supposed to be founded on intuition, and to be one of those maxims, which, though they may be denied with the lips, it is impossible for men in their hearts really to doubt of. But, if we examine this maxim by the idea of knowledge, above explained, we shall discover in it no mark of such intuitive certainty." The meaning of this seems to be, that it did not suit with his theory of intuitive certainty, and therefore he excludes it from that privilege.

The vulgar adhere to this maxim as firmly and universally as the philosophers. Their superstitions have the same origin as the systems of philosophers, to wit, a desire to know the causes of things. *Felix qui potuit rerum cognoscere causas*, is the universal sense of men ; but to say that any thing can happen without a cause, shocks the common sense of a savage.

This universal belief of mankind is easily accounted for, if we allow that the necessity of a cause of every event is obvious to the rational powers of a man. But it is impossible to account for it otherwise. It cannot be ascribed to education, to systems of philosophy, or to priestcraft. One would think, that a philosopher who takes it to be a general delusion or prejudice, would endeavour to show from what causes in human nature such a general error may take its rise. But I forget that Mr. Hume might answer upon his own principles, that since things may happen without a cause, this error and delusion of men may be universal without any cause.

A second reason why I conceive this to be a first principle, is, That mankind not only assent to it in speculation, but that the practice of life is grounded upon it in the most important matters, even in cases· where experience leave us doubtful; and it is impossible to act with common prudence if we set it aside.

In great families there are so many bad things done by a certain personage called *nobody*, that it is proverbial, that there is a nobody about every house who does a great deal of mischief; and even where there is the exactest inspection and government, many events will happen of which no other author can be found: So that, if we trust merely to experience in this matter, nobody will be found to be a very active person, and to have no inconsiderable share in the management of affairs. But whatever countenance this system may have from experience, it is too shocking to common sense to impose upon the most ignorant. A child knows that when his top, or any of his playthings are taken away, it must be done by somebody. Perhaps it would not be difficult to persuade him that it was done by some invisible being, but that it should be done by nobody he cannot believe.

Suppose a man's house to be broke open, his money and jewels taken away: such things have happened times innumerable without any apparent cause; and were he only to reason from experience in such a case, how must he behave? He must put in one scale the instances wherein a cause was found of such an event, and in the other scale, the instances wherein no cause was found, and the preponderant scale must determine, whether it be most probable that there was a cause of this event, or that there was none. Would any man of common understanding have recourse to such an expedient to direct his judgment?

Suppose a man to be found dead on the highway, his skull fractured, his body pierced with deadly wounds, his watch and money carried off. The coroner's jury sits upon the body, and the question is put, What was the cause of this man's death, was it accident, or *felo de se*, or murder by persons unknown? Let us suppose an adept in Mr. Hume's philosophy to make one of the jury, and that he insists upon the previous question, whether there was any cause of the event; or whether it happened without a cause?

Surely, upon Mr. Hume's principles, a great deal might be said upon this point; and, if the matter is to be determined by past experience, it is dubious on which side the weight of argument might stand. But we may venture to say, that, if Mr. Hume had been of such a jury, he would have laid aside his philosophical principles, and acted according to the dictates of common prudence.

Many passages might be produced, even in Mr. Hume's philosophical writings, in which he, unawares, betrays the same inward conviction of the necessity of causes, which is common to other men. I shall mention only one, in the Treatise of Human Nature, and in that part of it where he combats this very principle. "As to those impressions," says he, "which arise from the senses, their ultimate cause is, in my opinion, perfectly inexplicable by human reason; and it will always be impossible to decide with certainty, whether they arise immediately from the object, or are produced by the creative power of the mind, or are derived from the Author of our being."

Among these alternatives, he never thought of their not arising from any cause.

The arguments which Mr. Hume offers, to prove that this is not a self-evident principle, are three. *First,* That all certainty arises from a comparison of ideas, and a discovery of their unalterable relations, none of which relations imply this proposition, That whatever has a beginning must have a cause of existence. This theory of certainty has been examined before, in chap. 3. of this Essay.

The *second* argument is, that whatever we can conceive is possible. This has likewise been examined.

The *third* argument is, that what we call a cause, is only something antecedent to, and always conjoined with the effect. This is also one of Mr. Hume's peculiar doctrines, which we may have occasion to consider afterward. It is sufficient here to observe, that we may learn from it that night is the cause of day, and day the cause of night: for no two things have more constantly followed each other since the beginning of the world.

The *last* metaphysical principle I mention, which is opposed by the same author, is, That design, and intelligence in the cause, may be inferred with certainty, from marks or signs of it in the effect.

Intelligence, design, and skill, are not objects of the external senses, nor can we be conscious of them in any person but ourselves. Even in ourselves, we cannot, with propriety, be said to be conscious of the natural or acquired talents we possess. We are conscious only of the operations of mind in which they are exerted. Indeed, a man comes to know his own mental abilities, just as he knows another man's, by the effects they produce, when there is occasion to put them to exercise.

A man's wisdom is known to us only by the signs of it in his conduct; his eloquence by the signs of it in his speech. In the same manner we judge of his virtue, of his fortitude, and of all his talents and qualities of mind.

Yet it is to be observed, that we judge of men's talents with as little doubt or hesitation as we judge of the immediate objects of sense.

One person, we are sure, is a perfect idiot; another who feigns idiocy to screen himself from punishment, is found upon trial to have the understanding of a man, and to be accountable for his conduct. We perceive one man to be open, another cunning; one to be ignorant, another very knowing; one to be slow of understanding, another quick. Every man forms such judgments of those he converses with; and the common affairs of life depend upon such judgments. We can as little avoid them as we can avoid seeing what is before our eyes.

From this it appears, that it is no less a part of the human constitution, to judge of men's characters, and of their intellectual powers, from the signs of them in their actions and discourse, than to judge of corporeal objects by our senses : that such judgments are common to the whole human race that are endowed with understanding; and that they are absolutely necessary in the conduct of life.

Now, every judgment of this kind we form, is only a particular application of the general principle, that intelligence, wisdom, and other mental qualities in the cause, may be inferred from their marks or signs in the effect.

The actions and discourses of men are effects, of which the actors and speakers are the causes. The effects are perceived by our senses ; but the causes are behind the scene. We only conclude their existence and their degrees from our observation of the effects.

From wise conduct we infer wisdom in the cause; from brave actions we infer courage; and so in other cases.

This inference is made with perfect security by all men. We cannot avoid it; it is necessary in the ordinary conduct of life; it has therefore the strongest marks of being a first principle.

Perhaps some may think that this principle may be learned either by reasoning or by experience, and therefore that there is no ground to think it a first principle.

If it can be shown to be got by reasoning, by all, or the greater part of those who are governed by it, I shall very readily acknowledge that it ought not to be esteemed a first principle. But I apprehend the contrary appears from very convincing arguments.

1st, The principle is too universal to be the effect of reasoning. It is common to philosophers and to the vulgar; to the learned and the most illiterate; to the civilized and to the savage : and of those who are governed by it, not one in ten thousand can give a reason for it.

2dly, We find philosophers, ancient and modern, who can reason excellently in subjects that admit of reasoning, when they have occasion to defend this principle, not offering reasons for it, or any *medium* of proof, but appealing to the common sense of mankind ; mentioning particular instances, to make the absurdity of the contrary opinion more apparent, and sometimes using the weapons of wit and ridicule, which are very proper weapons for refuting absurdities, but altogether improper in points that are to be determined by reasoning.

To confirm this observation, I shall quote two authors, an ancient and a modern, who have more expressly undertaken the defence of this principle than any others I remember to have met with, and whose good sense and ability to reason, where reasoning is proper, will not be doubted.

The first is Cicero, whose words, lib. 1. cap. 13. *De divinatione*, may be thus translated. " Can any thing done by chance have all the marks of design ? Four dice may by chance turn up four aces ; but do you think that four hundred dice, thrown by chance, will turn up four hundred aces ? Colours thrown upon canvas without design may have some similitude to a human face ; but do you think they might make as beautiful a picture as that of the Coan Venus ? A hog turning up the ground with his nose may make something of the form of the letter A ; but do you think that a hog might describe on the ground the Andromache of Ennius ? Carneades imagined, that in the stone quarries at Chios he found, in a stone that was split, a representation of the head of a little pan, or sylvan deity. I believe he might find a figure not unlike ; but surely not such a one as you would say had been formed by an excellent sculptor like Scopas. For so, verily, the case is, that chance never perfectly imitates design." Thus Cicero.

Now, in all this discourse I see very good sense, and what is apt to convince every unprejudiced mind ; but I see not in the whole a single step of reasoning. It is barely an appeal to every man's common sense.

Let us next see how the same point is handled by the excellent archbishop Tillotson, 1st Sermon, vol. 1.

" For I appeal to any man of reason, whether any thing can be more unreasonable, than obstinately to impute an effect to chance which carries in the face of it all the arguments and characters of design ? Was ever any considerable work, in which there was required a great variety of parts, and an orderly and regular adjustment of these parts done by chance ? Will chance fit means to ends, and that in ten thousand instances, and not fail in any one ? How often might a man, after

he had jumbled a set of letters in a bag, fling them out
upon the ground before they would fall into an exact
poem, yea or so much as make a good discourse in prose?
And may not a little book be as easily made as this
great volume of the world? How long might a man
sprinkle colours upon canvas with a careless hand before they would make the exact picture of a man? And
is a man easier made by chance than his picture? How
long might twenty thousand blind men, which should be
sent out from the remote parts of England, wander up
and down before they would all meet upon Salisbury
plains, and fall into rank and file in the exact order of
an army? And yet this is much more easy to be imagined than how the innumerable blind parts of matter
should rendezvous themselves into a world. A man
that sees Henry the Seventh's chapel at Westminster,
might, with as good reason maintain, yea, and much better, considering the vast difference between that little
structure and the huge fabric of the world, that it was
never contrived or built by any man, but that the stones
did by chance grow into those curious figures into
which we see them to have been cut and graven; and
that upon a time, as tales usually begin, the materials
of that building, the stone, mortar, timber, iron, lead,
and glass, happily met together and very fortunately
ranged themselves into that delicate order in which we
see them now so close compacted, that it must be a very
great chance that parts them again. What would the
world think of a man that should advance such an opinion as this, and write a book for it? If they would do
him right, they ought to look upon him as mad. But
yet he might maintain this opinion with a little more
reason than any man can have to say that the world
was made by chance. or that the first men grew out of
the earth, as plants do now. For can any thing be more
ridiculous and against all reason, than to ascribe the

production of men to the first fruitfulness of the
earth, without so much as one instance or experiment
in any age or history to countenance so monstrous a
supposition? The thing is at first sight so gross and
palpable, that no discourse about it can make it more
apparent. And yet these shameful beggars of principles, who give this precarious account of the original
of things, assume to themselves to be the men of reason, the great wits of the world, the only cautious and
wary persons, who hate to be imposed upon, that
must have convincing evidence for every thing, and
can admit nothing without a clear demonstration for it."

In this passage, the excellent author takes what I
conceive to be the proper method of refuting an absurdity, by exposing it in different lights, in which every
man of common understanding perceives it to be ridiculous. And although there is much good sense, as well
as wit, in the passage I have quoted, I cannot find one
medium of proof in the whole.

I have met with one or two respectable authors who
draw an argument from the doct rne o chances, to
show how improbable it is that a regular arrangement
of parts should be the effect of chance, or that it should
not be the effect of design.

I do not object to this reasoning ; but I would observe, that the doctrine of chances is a branch of mathematics little more than an hundred years old. But the
conclusion drawn from it has been held by all men from
the beginning of the world. It cannot, therefore, be
thought, that men have been led to this conclusion by
that reasoning. Indeed, it may be doubted whether
the first principle upon which all the mathematical
reasoning about chances is grounded, is more self-
evident than this conclusion drawn from it, or whether
it is not a particular instance of that general conclusion.

We are next to consider whether we may not learn
this truth from experience, that effects which have all

the marks and tokens of design must proceed from a designing cause.

I apprehend that we cannot learn this truth from experience, for two reasons.

1st, Because it is a necessary truth, not a contingent one. It agrees with the experience of mankind since the beginning of the world, that the area of a triangle is equal to half the rectangle under its base and perpendicular. It agrees no less with experience that the sun rises in the east and sets in the west. So far as experience goes, these truths are upon an equal footing. But every man perceives this distinction between them, that the first is a necessary truth, and that it is impossible it should not be true ; but the last is not necessary, but contingent, depending upon the will of him who made the world. As we cannot learn from experience that twice three must necessarily make six, so neither can we learn from experience that certain effects must proceed from a designing and intelligent cause. Experience informs us only of what has been, but never of what must be.

2dly, It may be observed, that experience can show a connection between a sign, and the thing signified by it, in those cases only, where both the sign and thing signified are perceived, and have always been perceived in conjunction. But if there be any case where the sign only is perceived, experience can never show its connection with the thing signified. Thus, for example, thought is a sign of a thinking principle or mind. But how do we know that thought cannot be without a mind ? If any man should say that he knows this by experience, he deceives himself. It is impossible he can have any experience of this; because, though we have an immediate knowledge of the existence of thought in ourselves by consciousness, yet we have no immediate knowledge of a mind. The mind is not an immediate object either of sense or of consciousness. We may therefore justly conclude, that the necessary connection between thought and a mind, or thinking being, is not learned from experience.

The same reasoning may be applied to the connection between a work excellently fitted for some purpose, and design in the author or cause of that work. One of these, to wit, the work, may be an immediate object of perception. But the design and purpose of the author cannot be an immediate object of perception; and therefore experience can never inform us of any connection between the one and the other, far less of a necessary connection.

Thus I think it appears, that the principle we have been considering, to wit, that from certain signs or indications in the effect, we may infer, that there must have been intelligence, wisdom, or other intellectual or moral qualities in the cause, is a principle which we get, neither by reasoning nor by experience; and therefore, if it be a true principle, it must be a first principle. There is in the human understanding a light, by which we see immediately the evidence of it, when there is occasion to apply it.

Of how great importance this principle is in common life, we have already observed. And I need hardly mention its importance in natural theology.

The clear marks and signatures of wisdom, power, and goodness, in the constitution and government of the world, is, of all arguments that have been advanced for the being and providence of the Deity, that which in all ages has made the strongest impression upon candid and thinking minds; an argument, which has this peculiar advantage, that it gathers strength as human knowledge advances, and is more convincing at present than it was some centuries ago.

King Alphonsus might say, that he could contrive a better planetary system than that which astronomers

held in his day. That system was not the work of
God, but the fiction of men.

But since the true system of the sun, moon, and
planets, has been discovered, no man, however atheisti-
cally disposed, has pretended to show how a better
could be contrived.

When we attend to the marks of good contrivance
which appear in the works of God, every discovery
we make in the constitution of the material or intellectual system becomes a hymn of praise to the great
Creator and Governor of the world. And a man who
is possessed of the genuine spirit of philosophy, will
think it impiety to contaminate the divine workmanship, by mixing it with those fictions of human fancy,
called theories and hypotheses, which will always bear
the signatures of human folly, no less than the other
does of divine wisdom.

I know of no person who ever called in question the
principle now under our consideration, when it is applied to the actions and discourses of men : for this
would be to deny that we have any means of discerning
a wise man from an idiot, or a man that is illiterate in
the highest degree from a man of knowledge and learning, which no man has the effrontery to deny.

But, in all ages, those who have been unfriendly to
the principles of religion, have made attempts to weak-
en the force of the argument for the existence and perfections of the Deity, which is founded on this principle. That argument has got the name of the argument from final causes; and as the meaning of this
name is well understood, we shall use it.

The argument from final causes, when reduced to a
syllogism, has these two premises : *First*, That design
and intelligence in the cause, may with certainty be inferred from marks or signs of it in the effect. This
is the principle we have been considering, and we may

call it the *major* proposition of the argument. The *second*, which we call the *minor* proposition, is, that there are, in fact, the clearest marks of design and wisdom in the works of nature ; and the conclusion is, that the works of nature are the effects of a wise and intelligent cause. One must either assent to the conclusion, or deny one or other of the premises.

Those among the ancients who denied a God or a providence, seem to me to have yiel'ed the major proposition, and to have denied the minor ; conceiving that there are not in the constitution of things such marks of wise contrivance as are sufficient to put the conclusion beyond doubt. This, I think, we may learn from the reasoning of Cotta the academic, in the third book of Cicero, of the nature of the gods.

The gradual advancement made in the knowledge of nature has put this opinion quite out of countenance.

When the structure of the human body was much less known than it is now, the famous Galen saw such evident marks of wise contrivance in it, that though he had been educated an Epicurean, he renounced that system, and wrote his book of the use of the parts of the human body, on purpose to convince others of what appeared so clear to himself, that it was impossible that such admirable contrivance should be the effect of chance.

Those, therefore, of later times, who are dissatisfied with this argument from final causes, have quitted the strong hold of the ancient Atheists, which had become untenable, and have chosen rather to make a defence against the major proposition.

Des Cartes seems to have led the way in this, though he was no Atheist. But, having invented some new arguments for the being of God, he was perhaps led to disparage those that had been used before, that he

might bring more credit to his own. Or, perhaps, he
was offended with the Peripatetics, because they often
mixed final causes with physical, in order to account for
the phenomena of nature.

He maintained therefore that physical causes only
should be assigned for phenomena; that the philosopher has nothing to do with final causes; and that it
is presumption in us to pretend to determine for what
end any work of nature is framed. Some of those
who were great admirers of Des Cartes, and followed
him in many points, differed from him in this; particularly, Dr. Henry More, and the pious archbishop Fenelon: but others, after the example of Des Cartes,
have shown a contempt of all reasoning from final
causes. Among these, I think, we may reckon Mau-
pertuis and Buffon. But the most direct attack has
been made upon this principle by Mr. Hume, who puts
an argument in the mouth of an Epicurean, on which
he seems to lay great stress.

The argument is, That the universe is a singular
effect, and therefore we can draw no conclusion from it,
whether it may have been made by wisdom or not.

If I understand the force of this argument, it amounts
to this, that if we had been accustomed to see worlds
produced, some by wisdom and others without it, and had
observed, that such a world as this which we inhabit was
always the effect of wisdom, we might then, from past
experience, conclude, that this world was made by wisdom; but having no such experience, we have no means
of forming any conclusion about it.

That this is the strength of the argument, appears,
because if the marks of wisdom seen in one world be no
evidence of wisdom, the like marks seen in ten thousand
will give as little evidence, unless, in time past, we perceived wisdom itself conjoined with the tokens of it;
and, from their perceived conjunction in time past,

conclude, that although, in the present world, we see only one of the two, the other must accompany it.

Whence it appears, that this reasoning of Mr. Hume is built on the supposition, that our inferring design from the strongest marks of it, is entirely owing to our past experience of having always found these two things conjoined. But I hope I have made it evident that this is not the case. And indeed it is evident, that, according to this reasoning, we can have no evidence of mind or design in any of our fellow men.

How do I know that any man of my acquaintance has understanding? I never saw his understanding. I see only certain effects, which my judgment leads me to conclude to be marks and tokens of it.

But, says the skeptical philosopher, you can conclude nothing from these tokens, unless past experience has informed you that such tokens are always joined with understanding. Alas! sir, it is impossible I can ever have this experience. The understanding of another man is no immediate object of sight, or of any other faculty which God has given me; and unless I can conclude its existence from tokens that are visible, I have no evidence that there is understanding in any man.

It seems then, that the man who maintains, that there is no force in the argument from final causes, must, if he will be consistent, see no evidence of the existence of any intelligent being but himself.

CHAP. VII.

I KNOW no writer who has treated expressly of first principles before Aristotle; but it is probable, that, in the ancient Pythagorean school, from which both Plato and Aristotle borrowed much, this subject had not been left untouched.

Before the time of Aristotle, considerable progress had been made in the mathematical sciences, particularly in geometry.

The discovery of the forty-seventh proposition of the first book of Euclid, and of the five regular solids, is, by antiquity, ascribed to Pythagoras himself; and it is impossible he could have made those discoveries without knowing many other propositions in mathematics. Aristotle mentions the incommensurability of the diagonal of a square to its side, and gives a hint of the manner in which it was demonstrated. We find likewise some of the axioms of geometry mentioned by Aristotle as axioms, and as indemonstrable principles of mathematical reasoning.

It is probable, therefore, that, before the time of Aristotle, there were elementary treatises of geometry, which are now lost; and that in them the axioms were distinguished from the propositions which require proof.

To suppose, that so perfect a system as that of Euclid's Elements was produced by one man, without any preceding model or materials, would be to suppose Euclid more than a man. We ascribe to him as much as the weakness of human understanding will permit, if we suppose that the inventions in geometry, which had been made in a tract of preceding ages, were by him not only carried much further, but digested into so admirable a system, that his work obscured all that went before it, and made them be forgot and lost.

Perhaps, in like manner, the writings of Aristotle with regard to first principles, and with regard to many other abstract subjects, may have occasioned the loss of what had been written upon those subjects by more ancient philosophers.

Whatever may be in this, in his second book upon demonstration he has treated very fully of first principles; and though he has not attempted any enumeration of them, he shows very clearly, that all demonstration must be built upon truths which are evident of themselves, but cannot be demonstrated. His whole doctrine of syllogisms is grounded upon a few axioms, from which he endeavours to demonstrate the rules of syllogism in a mathematical way; and in his topics he points out many of the first principles of probable reasoning.

As long as the philosophy of Aristotle prevailed, it was held as a fixed point, that all proof must be drawn from principles already known and granted.

We must observe, however, that, in that philosophy, many things were assumed as first principles, which have no just claim to that character; such as, that the earth is at rest; that nature abhors a vacuum; that there is no change in the heavens above the sphere of the moon; that the heavenly bodies move in circles, that being the most perfect figure; that bodies do not gravitate in their proper place; and many others.

The Peripatetic philosophy, therefore, instead of being deficient in first principles, was redundant; instead of rejecting those that are truly such, it adopted, as first principles, many vulgar prejudices and rash judgments: and this seems, in general, to have been the spirit of ancient philosophy.

It is true, there were, among the ancients, skeptical philosophers, who professed to have no principles, and held it to be the greatest virtue in a philosopher to withhold assent, and keep his judgment in a perfect equilibrium between contradictory opinions. But though this sect was defended by some persons of great erudition and acuteness, it died of itself, and the dogmatic philosophy of Aristotle, obtained a complete triumph over it.

What Mr. Hume says of those who are skeptical with regard to moral distinctions, seems to have had its accomplishment in the ancient sect of skeptics. " The only way," says he, " of converting antagonists of this kind, is to leave them to themselves; for finding that nobody keeps up the controversy with them, it is probable they will at last of themselves, from mere weariness, come over to the side of common sense and reason."

Setting aside this small sect of the skeptics, which was extinct many ages before the authority of Aristotle declined, I know of no opposition made to first principles among the ancients. The disposition was, as has been observed, not to oppose, but to multiply them beyond measure.

Men have always been prone, when they leave one extreme to run into the opposite ; and this spirit in the ancient philosophy, to multiply first principles beyond reason, was a strong presage, that, when the authority of the Peripatetic system was at an end, the next reigning system would diminish their number beyond reason.

This accordingly happened in that great revolution of the philosophical republic brought about by Des Cartes. That truly great reformer in philosophy, cautious to avoid the snare in which Aristotle was taken, of admitting things as first principles too rashly, resolved to doubt of every thing, and to withhold his assent, until it was forced by the clearest evidence.

Thus Des Cartes brought himself into that very state of suspense, which the ancient skeptics recommended as the highest perfection of a wise man, and the only road to tranquillity of mind. But he did not remain long in this state; his doubt did not arise from despair of finding the truth, but from caution, that he might not be imposed upon, and embrace a cloud instead of a goddess.

His very doubting convinced him of his own existence; for that which does not exist, can neither doubt, nor believe, nor reason.

Thus he emerged from universal skepticism by this short enthymeme, *cogito ergo sum.*

This enthymeme consists of an antecedent proposition, *I think,* and a conclusion drawn from it, *therefore I exist.*

If it should be asked, how Des Cartes came to be certain of the antecedent proposition, it is evident, that for this he trusted to the testimony of consciousness. He was conscious that he thought, and needed no other argument.

So that the first principle which he adopts in this famous enthymeme is this, that those doubts, and thoughts, and reasonings, of which he was conscious, did certainly exist, and that his consciousness put their existence beyond all doubt.

It might have been objected to this first principle of Des Cartes, how do you know that your consciousness cannot deceive you? You have supposed, that all you see, and hear, and handle, may be an illusion. Why, therefore, should the power of consciousness have this prerogative, to be believed implicitly, when all our other powers are supposed fallacious?

To this objection, I know no other answer that can be made, but that we find it impossible to doubt of things of which we are conscious. The constitution of our nature forces this belief upon us irresistibly.

This is true, and is sufficient to justify Des Cartes, in assuming, as a first principle, the existence of thought, of which he was conscious.

He ought, however, to have gone further in this track, and to have considered whether there may not be other first principles, which ought to be adopted for the same reason. But he did not see this to be necessary, conceiving that, upon this one first principle, he could support the whole fabric of human knowledge.

To proceed to the conclusion of Des Cartes's enthymeme. From the existence of his thought he infers his own existence. Here he assumes another first principle, not a contingent, but a necessary one; to wit, that where there is thought, there must be a thinking being or mind.

Having thus established his own existence, he proceeds to prove the existence of a supreme and infinitely perfect Being; and from the perfection of the Deity, he infers that his senses, his memory, and the other faculties which God had given him, are not fallacious.

Whereas other men, from the beginning of the world, had taken for granted, as a first principle, the truth and reality of what they perceive by their senses, and from thence inferred the existence of a Supreme Author and Maker of the world. Des Cartes took a contrary course, conceiving that the testimony of our senses, and of all our faculties, excepting that of consciousness, ought not to be taken for granted, but to be proved by argument.

Perhaps some may think that Des Cartes meant only to admit no other first principle of contingent truths besides that of consciousness; but that he allowed the axioms of mathematics, and of other necessary truths, to be received without proof.

But I apprehend this was not his intention : for the truth of mathematical axioms must depend upon the truth of the faculty by which we judge of them. If the faculty be fallacious, we may be deceived by trusting to it. Therefore, as he supposes, that all our faculties, excepting consciousness, may be fallacious, and attempts to prove by argument that they are not, it follows, that according to his principles, even mathematical axioms require proof. Neither did he allow that there are any necessary truths ; but maintained, that the truths which are commonly so called, depend upon the will of God. And we find his followers, who may be supposed to understand his principles, agree in maintaining, that the knowledge of our own existence is the first and fundamental principle from which all knowledge must be deduced by one who proceeds regularly in philosophy.

There is, no doubt, a beauty in raising a large fabric of knowledge upon a few first principles. The stately fabric of mathematical knowledge, raised upon the foundation of a few axioms and definitions, charms every beholder. Des Cartes, who was well acquainted with this beauty in the mathematical sciences, seems to have been ambitious to give the same beautiful simplicity to his system of philosophy ; and therefore sought only one first principle as the foundation of all our knowledge, at least of contingent truths.

And so far has his authority prevailed, that those who came after him have almost universally followed him in this track. This, therefore, may be considered as the spirit of modern philosophy, to allow of no first principles of contingent truths but this one, that the thoughts and operations of our own minds, of which we are conscious, are self-evidently real and true ; but that every thing else that is contingent is to be proved by argument.

The existence of a material world, and of what we perceive by our senses, is not self-evident, according to this philosophy.   Des Cartes founded it upon this argument, that God, who has given us our senses, and all our faculties, is no deceiver, and therefore they are not fallacious.

I endeavoured to show, that if it be not admitted as a first principle, that our faculties are not fallacious, nothing else can be admitted; and that it is impossible to prove this by argument, unless God should give us new faculties to sit in judgment upon the old.

Father Malebranche agreed with Des Cartes, that the existence of a material world requires proof; but being dissatisfied with Des Cartes's argument from the perfection of the Deity, thought that the only solid proof is from divine revelation.

Arnauld, who was engaged in controversy with Malebranche, approves of his antagonist in offering an argument to prove the existence of the material world, but objects to the solidity of his argument, and offers other arguments of his own.

Mr. Norris, a great admirer of Des Cartes and of Malebranche, seems to have thought all the arguments offered by them and by Arnauld to be weak; and confesses, that we have at best only probable evidence of the existence of the material world.

Mr. Locke acknowledges, that the evidence we have of this point is neither intuitive nor demonstrative; yet he thinks it may be called knowledge, and distinguishes it by the name of sensitive knowledge; and, as the ground of this sensitive knowledge he offers some weak arguments, which would rather tempt one to doubt than to believe.

At last bishop Berkeley and Arthur Collier, without any knowledge of each other, as far as appears by their writings, undertook to prove, that there neither is nor can be a material world. The excellent style and elegant composition of the former have made his writings to be known and read, and this system to be attributed to him only, as if Collier had never existed.

Both, indeed, owe so much to Malebranche, that if we take out of his system the peculiarities of our seeing all things in God, and our learning the existence of an external world from divine revelation, what remains is just the system of bishop Berkeley. I make this observation by the way, in justice to a foreign author, to whom British authors seem not to have allowed all that is due.

Mr. Hume has adopted bishop Berkeley's arguments against the existence of matter, and thinks them unanswerable.

We may observe, that this great metaphysician, though in general he declares in favour of universal skepticism, and therefore may seem to have no first principles at all, yet, with Des Cartes, he always acknowledges the reality of those thoughts and operations of mind, of which we are conscious. So that he yields the antecedent of Des Cartes's enthymeme *cogito*, but denies the conclusion *ergo sum;* the mind, being, according to him, nothing but that train of impressions and ideas of which we are conscious.

Thus we see, that the modern philosophy, of which Des Cartes may justly be accounted the founder, being built upon the ruins of the Peripatetic, has a spirit quite opposite, and runs into a contrary extreme. The Peripatetic not only adopted, as first principles, those which mankind have always rested upon in their most important transactions, but, along with them, many vulgar prejudices; so that this system was founded upon a wide bottom, but in many parts unsound. The modern system has narrowed the foundation so much, that every superstructure raised upon it appears top heavy.

From the single principle of the existence of our own thoughts, very little, if any thing, can be deduced by just reasoning, especially if we suppose that all our other faculties may be fallacious.

Accordingly, we find that Mr. Hume was not the first that was led into skepticism by the want of first principles. For soon after Des Cartes, there arose a sect in France called *Egoists*, who maintained, that we have no evidence of the existence of any thing but ourselves.

Whether these Egoists, like Mr. Hume, believed themselves to be nothing but a train of ideas and impressions, or to have a more permanent existence, I have not learned, having never seen any of their writings; nor do I know whether any of this sect did write in support of their principles. One would think, they who did not believe that there was any person to read, could have little inducement to write, unless they were prompted by that inward monitor, which Persius makes to be the source of genius and the teacher of arts. There can be no doubt, however, of the existence of such a sect, as they are mentioned by many authors, and refuted by some, particularly by Buffier, in his Treatise of First Principles.

Those Egoists and Mr. Hume seem to me to have reasoned more consequentially from Des Cartes's principle than he did himself; and indeed I cannot help thinking, that all who have followed Des Cartes's method, of requiring proof by argument of every thing except the existence of their own thoughts, have escaped the abyss of skepticism by the help of weak reasoning and strong faith, more than by any other means. And they seem to me to act more consistently, who, having rejected the first principles on which belief must be grounded, have no belief, than they, who like the others, rejecting first principles, must yet have a system of belief, without any solid foundation on which it may stand.

The philosophers I have hitherto mentioned, after the time of Des Cartes, have all followed his method, in resting upon the truth of their own thoughts as a first principle, but requiring arguments for the proof of every other truth of a contingent nature; but none of them, excepting Mr. Locke, has expressly treated of first principles, or given any opinion of their utility or inutility. We only collect their opinion from their following Des Cartes in requiring proof, or pretending to offer proof of the existence of a material world, which surely ought to be received as a first principle, if any thing be, beyond what we are conscious of.

I proceed, therefore, to consider what Mr. Locke has said on the subject of first principles or maxims.

I have not the least doubt of this author's candour in what he somewhere says, that his essay was mostly spun out of his own thoughts. Yet it is certain, that, in many of the notions which we are wont to ascribe to him, others were before him, particularly, Des Cartes, Gassendi, and Hobbes. Nor is it at all to be thought strange, that ingenious men, when they are got into the same track, should hit upon the same things.

But, in the definition which he gives of knowledge in general, and in his notions concerning axioms or first principles, I know none that went before him, though he has been very generally followed in both.

His definition of knowledge, that it consists solely in the perception of the agreement or disagreement of our ideas, has been already considered. But supposing it to be just, still it would be true, that some agreements and disagreements of ideas must be immediately perceived; and such agreements or disagreements, when they are expressed by affirmative or negative proposi-

tions, are first principles, because their truth is immediately discerned as soon as they are understood.

This I think is granted by Mr. Locke, book 4. chap. 2.
"There is a part of our knowledge," says he, "which
we may call intuitive. In this the mind is at no pains
of proving or examining, but perceives the truth as the
eye does light, only by being directed toward it. And
this kind of knowledge is the clearest and most certain
that human frailty is capable of. This part of knowledge is irresistible, and, like bright sunshine, forces
itself immediately to be perceived, as soon as ever the
mind turns its view that way."

He further observes, "That this intuitive knowledge is necessary to connect all the steps of a demonstration."

From this, I think, it necessarily follows, that, in
every branch of knowledge, we must make use of
truths that are intuitively known, in order to deduce
from them such as require proof.

But I cannot reconcile this with what he says, sect.
8. of the same chapter. "The necessity of this intuitive knowledge in every step of scientifical or demonstrative reasoning gave occasion, I imagine, to
that mistaken axiom, that all reasoning was *ex præ-
cognitis et præconcessis*, which, how far it is mistaken, I shall have occasion to show more at large,
when I come to consider propositions, and particularly
those propositions which are called maxims, and to
show, that it is by a mistake. that they are supposed
to be the foundation of all our knowledge and reasonings."

I have carefully considered the chapter on maxims,
which Mr. Locke here refers to ; and though one
would expect, from the quotation last made, that it
should run contrary to what I have before delivered
concerning first principles, I find only two or three

sentences in it, and those chiefly incidental, to which
I do not assent; and I am always happy in agreeing
with a philosopher whom I so highly respect.

He endeavours to show, that axioms, or intuitive
truths, are not innate.

To this I agree. I maintain only, that when the
understanding is ripe, and when we distinctly apprehend such truths, we immediately assent to them.

He observes, that self-evidence is not peculiar to
those propositions, which pass under the name of axioms, and have the dignity of axioms ascribed to them.

I grant that there are innumerable self-evident
propositions, which have neither dignity nor utility,
and therefore deserve not the name of axioms, as that
name is commonly understood to imply, not only self-
evidence, but some degree of dignity or utility. That
a man is a man, and that a man is not a horse, are
self-evident propositions; but they are, as Mr. Locke
very justly calls them, trifling propositions. Tillotson very wittily says of such propositions, that they
are so surfeited with truth, that they are good for
nothing; and as they deserve not the name of axioms, so neither do they deserve the name of knowledge.

He observes, that such trifling self-evident propositions as we have named are not derived from axioms,
and therefore that all our knowledge is not derived
from axioms.

I grant that they are not derived from axioms, because they are themselves self-evident. But it is an
abuse of words to call them knowledge, as it is to call
them axioms; for no man can be said to be the wiser
or more knowing for having millions of them in store.

He observes, that the particular propositions contained under a general axiom are no less self-evident
than the general axiom, and that they are sooner

known and understood. Thus, it is as evident, that my hand is less than my body, as that a part is less than the whole ; and I know the truth of the particular proposition sooner, than that of the general.

This is true. A man cannot perceive the truth of a general axiom, such as, that a part is less than the whole, until he has the general notions of a part and a whole formed in his mind ; and before he has these general notions, he may perceive that his hand is less than his body.

A great part of this chapter on maxims is levelled against a notion, which, it seems, some have entertained, that all our knowledge is derived from these two maxims ; to wit, whatever is, is ; and it is impossible for the same thing to be and not to be.

This I take to be a ridiculous notion, justly deserving the treatment which Mr. Locke has given it, if it at all merited his notice. These are identical propositions ; they are trifling and surfeited with truth. No knowledge can be derived from them.

Having mentioned how far I agree with Mr. Locke concerning maxims or first principles, I shall next take notice of two or three things wherein I cannot agree with him.

In the seventh section of this chapter, he says, That concerning the real existence of all other beings, besides ourselves, and a first cause, there are no maxims.

I have endeavoured to show, that there are maxims, or first principles, with regard to other existences. Mr. Locke acknowledges, that we have a knowledge of such existences, which, he says, is neither intuitive nor demonstrative, and which, therefore, he calls sensitive knowledge. It is demonstrable, and was long ago demonstrated by Aristotle, that every proposition to which we give a rational assent, must either have its evidence in itself, or derive it from some antecedent proposition. And the same thing may be said of the antecedent proposition. As, therefore, we cannot go back to antecedent propositions without end, the evidence must at last rest upon propositions, one or more, which have their evidence in themselves, that is, upon first principles.

As to the evidence of our own existence, and of the existence of a first cause, Mr. Locke does not say whether it rests upon first principles or not. But it is manifest, from what he has said upon both, that it does.

With regard to our own existence, says he, we perceive it so plainly, and so certainly, that it neither needs, nor is capable of any proof. This is as much as to say, that our own existence is a first principle; for it is applying to this truth the very definition of a first principle.

He adds, that if I doubt, that very doubt makes me perceive my own existence, and will not suffer me to doubt of that. If I feel pain, I have as certain perception of my existence as of the pain I feel.

Here we have two first principles plainly implied : 1st, That my feeling pain, or being conscious of pain, is a certain evidence of the real existence of that pain. And, 2dly, that pain cannot exist without a mind, or being that is pained. That these are first principles, and incapable of proof, Mr. Locke acknowledges. And it is certain, that if they are not true, we can have no evidence of our own existence. For if we may feel pain when no pain really exists, or if pain may exist without any being that is pained, then it is certain that our feeling pain can give us no evidence of our existence.

Thus it appears, that the evidence of our own existence, according to the view that Mr. Locke gives of it, is grounded upon two of those first principles which we had occasion to mention.

If we consider the argument he has given for the existence of a first intelligent cause, it is no less evident that it is grounded upon other two of them. The first, that what begins to exist must have a cause of its existence; and the second, that an unintelligent and unthinking being, cannot be the cause of beings that are thinking and intelligent. Upon these two principles, he argues very convincingly for the existence of a first intelligent cause of things. And if these principles are not true, we can have no proof of the existence of a first cause, either from our own existence, or from the existence of other things that fall within our view.

Another thing advanced by Mr. Locke upon this subject is, that no science is, or has been built upon maxims.

Surely Mr. Locke was not ignorant of geometry, which has been built upon maxims prefixed to the elements, as far back as we are able to trace it. But though they had not been prefixed, which was a matter of utility rather than necessity, yet it must be granted, that every demonstration in geometry is grounded, either upon propositions formerly demonstrated, or upon self-evident principles.

Mr. Locke further says, that maxims are not of use to help men forward in the advancement of the sciences, or new discoveries of yet unknown truths: that Newton, in the discoveries he has made in his never enough to be admired book, has not been assisted by the general maxims, whatever is, is; or the whole is greater than a part, or the like.

I answer, the first of these is, as was before observed, an identical trifling proposition, of no use in mathematics, or in any other science. The second is often used by Newton, and by all mathematicians, and many demonstrations rest upon it. In general Newton, as well as all other mathematicians, grounds his demonstrations of mathematical propositions upon the axioms laid down by Euclid, or upon propositions which have been before demonstrated by help of those axioms.

But it deserves to be particularly observed, that Newton, intending in the third book of his *Principia*, to give a more scientific form to the physical part of astronomy, which he had at first composed in a popular form, thought proper to follow the example of Euclid, and to lay down first, in what he calls, *Regulæ Philosophandi*, and in his *Phenomena*, the first principles which he assumes in his reasoning.

Nothing, therefore, could have been more unluckily adduced by Mr. Locke to support his aversion to first principles, than the example of sir Isaac Newton, who, by laying down the first principles upon which he reasons in those parts of natural philosophy which he cultivated, has given a stability to that science which it never had before, and which it will retain to the end of the world.

I am now to give some account of a philosopher, who wrote expressly on the subject of first principles, after Mr. Locke.

Pere Buffier, a French jesuit, first published his *Traité des premiers Veritez, et de la source de nos jugements*, in 8vo. if I mistake not, in the year 1724. It was afterward published in folio, as a part of his *Cours des sciences*. Paris, 1732.

He defines first principles to be propositions so clear, that they can neither be proved, nor combated by those that are more clear.

The first source of first principles he mentions, is that intimate conviction which every man has of his own existence, and of what passes in his own mind. Some philosophers, he observes, admitted these as first principles, who were unwilling to admit any others:

and he shows the strange consequences that follow
from this system.

A second source of first principles he makes to be
common sense ; which, he observes. philosophers have
not been wont to consider. He defines it to be the disposition which nature has planted in all men, or the
far greater part, which leads them, when they come to
the use of reason, to form a common and uniform
judgment upon objects which are not objects of consciousness, nor are founded on any antecedent judgment.

He mentions not as a full enumeration, but as a specimen, the following principles of common sense.

1st, That there are other beings, and other men in the
universe, besides myself.

2dly, That there is in them something that is called
truth, wisdom, prudence ; and that these things are
not purely arbitrary.

3dly, That there is something in me which I call intelligence, and something which is not that intelligence,
which I call my body, and that these things have different properties.

4thly, That all men are not in a conspiracy to deceive
me and impose upon my credulity.

5thly, That what has not intelligence cannot produce
the effects of intelligence, nor can pieces of matter
thrown together by chance form any regular work,
such as a clock or watch.

He explains very particularly the several parts of
his definition of common sense, and shows how the dictates of common sense may be distinguished from common prejudices ; and then enters into a particular consideration of the primary truths that concern being in
general ; the truths that concern thinking beings ;
those that concern body ; and those on which the various branches of human knowledge are grounded.

I shall not enter into a detail of his sentiments on
these subjects. I think there is more which I take to

be original in this treatise, than in most books of the metaphysical kind I have met with; that many of his notions are solid; and that others, which I cannot altogether approve, are ingenious.

The other writers I have mentioned, after Des Cartes, may, I think, without impropriety, be called Cartesians: for though they differ from Des Cartes in some things, and contradict him in others, yet they set out from the same principles, and follow the same method, admitting no other first principle with regard to the existence of things but their own existence, and the existence of those operations of mind of which they are conscious; and requiring that the existence of a material world, and the existence of other men and things, should be proved by argument.

This method of philosophizing is common to Des Cartes, Malebranche, Arnauld, Locke, Norris, Collier, Berkeley, and Hume; and, as it was introduced by Des Cartes, I call it the Cartesian system, and those who follow it, Cartesians, not intending any disrespect by this term, but to signify a particular method of philosophizing common to them all, and begun by Des Cartes.

Some of these have gone the utmost length in skepticism, leaving no existence in nature but that of ideas and impressions. Some have endeavoured to throw off the belief of a material world only, and to leave us ideas and spirits. All of them have fallen into very gross paradoxes, which can never sit easy upon the human understanding, and which, though adopted in the closet, men find themselves under a necessity of throwing off and disclaiming when they enter into society.

Indeed, in my judgment, those who have reasoned most acutely and consequentially upon this system, are they that have gone deepest into skepticism.

Father Buffier, however, is no Cartesian in this sense. He seems to have perceived the defects of the Cartesian system while it was in the meridian of its glory, and to have been aware that a ridiculous skepticism is the natural issue of it, and therefore nobly attempted to lay a broader foundation for human knowledge, and has the honour of being the first, as far as I know, after Aristotle, who has given the world a just treatise upon first principles.

Some late writers, particularly Dr. Oswald, Dr. Beattie, and Dr. Campbell, have been led into a way of thinking somewhat similar to that of Buffier; the two former, as I have reason to believe, without any intercourse with one another, or any knowledge of what Buffier had wrote on the subject. Indeed, a man, who thinks, and who is acquainted with the philosophy of Mr. Hume, will very naturally be led to apprehend, that, to support the fabric of human knowledge, some other principles are necessary than those of Des Cartes and Mr. Locke. Buffier must be acknowledged to have the merit of having discovered this, before the consequences of the Cartesian system were so fully displayed as they have been by Mr. Hume. But I am apt to think, that the man who does not see this now, must have but a superficial knowledge of these subjects.

The three writers above mentioned have my high esteem and affection as men; but I intend to say nothing of them as writers upon this subject, that I may not incur the censure of partiality. Two of them have been joined so closely with me in the animadversions of a celebrated writer, that we may be thought too near of kin to give our testimony of one another.

CHAP. VIII.

OF PREJUDICES, THE CAUSES OF ERROR.

OUR intellectual powers are wisely fitted by the Author of our nature for the discovery of truth, as far as suits our present state. Error is not their natural issue, any more than disease is of the natural structure of the body. Yet, as we are liable to various diseases of body from accidental causes, external and internal; so we are, from like causes, liable to wrong judgments.

Medical writers have endeavoured to enumerate the diseases of the body, and to reduce them to a system, under the name of *nosology ;* and it were to be wished that we had also a nosology of the human understanding.

When we know a disorder of the body, we are often at a loss to find the proper remedy; but in most cases the disorders of the understanding point out their remedies so plainly, that he who knows the one must know the other.

Many authors have furnished useful materials for this purpose, and some have endeavoured to reduce them to a system. I like best the general division given of them by lord Bacon, in his fifth book *De augmentis scientiarum,* and more fully treated in his *Novum Organum.* He divides them into four classes; *idola tribus, idola specus, idola fori,* and *idola the atri.* The names are perhaps fanciful; but I think the division judicious, like most of the productions of that wonderful genius. And as this division was first made by him, he may be indulged the privilege of giving names to its several members.

I propose in this chapter to explain the several members of this division, according to the meaning of the author, and to give instances of each, without confining myself to those which lord Bacon has given, and without pretending to a complete enumeration.

To every bias of the understanding, by which a man may be misled in judging, or drawn into error, lord Bacon gives the name of an idol. The understanding, in its natural and best state, pays its homage to truth only. The causes of error are considered by him as so many false deities, who receive the homage which is due only to truth.

The first class are the *idola tribus.* These are such as beset the whole human species; so that every man is in danger from them. They arise from principles of the human constitution, which are highly useful and necessary in our present state; but, by their excess or defect, or wrong direction, may lead us into error.

As the active principles of the human frame are wisely contrived by the Author of our being, for the direction of our actions, and yet, without proper regulation and restraint, are apt to lead us wrong; so it is also with regard to those parts of our constitution that have influence upon our opinions. Of this we may take the following instances.

1st, *First,* Men are prone to be led too much by authority in their opinions.

In the first part of life we have no other guide; and without a disposition to receive implicitly what we are taught, we should be incapable of instruction, and incapable of improvement.

When judgment is ripe, there are many things in which we are incompetent judges. In such matters, it is most reasonable to rely upon the judgment of those whom we believe to be competent and disinterested. The highest court of judicature in the nation relies upon the authority of lawyers and physicians in matters belonging to their respective professions.

Even in matters which we have access to know, authority always will have, and ought to have, more or less weight, in proportion to the evidence on which our own judgment rests, and the opinion we have of the judgment and candour of those who differ from us, or agree with us. The modest man, conscious of his own fallability in judging, is in danger of giving too much to authority; the arrogant of giving too little.

In all matters belonging to our cognizance, every man must be determined by his own final judgment, otherwise he does not act the part of a rational being. Authority may add weight to one scale; but the man holds the balance, and judges what weight he ought to allow to authority.

If a man should even claim infallibility, we must judge of his title to that prerogative. If a man pretend to be an ambassador from heaven, we must judge of his credentials. No claim can deprive us of this right, or excuse us for neglecting to exercise it.

As therefore our regard to authority may be either too great or too small, the bias of human nature seems to lean to the first of these extremes; and, I believe, it is good for men in general that it should do so.

When this bias concurs with an indifference about truth, its operation will be the more powerful.

The love of truth is natural to man, and strong in every well disposed mind. But it may be overborne by party zeal, by vanity, by the desire of victory, or even by laziness. When it is superior to these, it is a manly virtue, and requires the exercise of industry, fortitude, self-denial, candour, and openness to conviction.

As there are persons in the world of so mean and abject a spirit, that they rather choose to owe their subsistence to the charity of others, than by industry to acquire some property of their own; so there are many more who may be called mere beggars with regard to their opinions. Through laziness and indifference about truth, they leave to others the drudgery of digging for this commodity; they can have enough at second hand to serve their occasions. Their concern is not to know what is true, but what is said and thought on such subjects; and their understanding, like their clothes, is cut according to the fashion.

This distemper of the understanding has taken so deep root in a great part of mankind, that it can hardly be said that they use their own judgment in things that do not concern their temporal interest; nor is it peculiar to the ignorant; it infects all ranks. We may guess their opinions when we know where they were born, of what parents, how educated, and what company they have kept. These circumstances determine their opinions in religion, in politics, and in philosophy.

2dly, A *second* general prejudice arises from a disposition to measure things less known, and less familiar, by those that are better known and more familiar.

This is the foundation of analogical reasoning, to which we have a great proneness by nature, and to it, indeed, we owe a great part of our knowledge. It would be absurd to lay aside this kind of reasoning altogether, and it is difficult to judge how far we may venture upon it. The bias of human nature is to judge from too slight analogies.

The objects of sense engross our thoughts in the first part of life, and are most familiar through the whole of it. Hence in all ages men have been prone to attribute the human figure and human passions and frailties to superior intelligences, and even to the Supreme Being.

There is a disposition in men to materialize every thing, if I may be allowed the expression; that is, to apply the notions we have of material objects to things of another nature. Thought is considered as analogous to motion in a body; and as bodies are put in motion by impulses, and by impressions made upon them by contiguous objects, we are apt to conclude that the mind is made to think by impressions made upon it, and that there must be some kind of contiguity between it and the objects of thought. Hence the theories of ideas and impressions have so generally prevailed.

Because the most perfect works of human artists are made after a model, and of materials that before existed, the ancient philosophers universally believed that the world was made of a pre-existent, uncreated matter; and many of them, that there were eternal and uncreated models of every species of things which God made.

The mistakes in common life, which are owing to this prejudice, are innumerable, and cannot escape the slightest observation. Men judge of other men by themselves, or by the small circle of their acquaintance. The selfish man thinks all pretences to benevolence and public spirit to be mere hypocrisy or self-deceit. The generous and open hearted believe fair pretences too easily, and are apt to think men better than they really are. The abandoned and profligate can hardly be persuaded that there is any such thing as real virtue in the world. The rustic forms his notions of the manners and characters of men from those of his country village, and is easily duped when he comes into a great city.

It is commonly taken for granted, that this narrow way of judging of men is to be cured only by an extensive intercourse with men of different ranks, professions, and nations; and that the man whose acquaintance has been confined within a narrow circle, must have many prejudices and narrow notions, which a more extensive intercourse would have cured.

3dly, Men are often led into error by the love of simplicity, which disposes us to reduce things to few principles, and to conceive a greater simplicity in nature than there really is.

To love simplicity, and to be pleased with it wherever we find it, is no imperfection, but the contrary. It is the result of good taste. We cannot but be pleased to observe, that all the changes of motion produced by the collision of bodies, hard, soft, or elastic, are reducible to three simple laws of motion, which the industry of philosophers has discovered.

When we consider what a prodigious variety of effects depend upon the law of gravitation ; how many phenomena in the earth, sea, and air, which, in all preceding ages, had tortured the wits of philosophers, and occasioned a thousand vain theories, are shown to be the necessary consequences of this one law ; how the whole system of sun, moon, planets, primary and secondary, and comets, are kept in order by it, and their seeming irregularities accounted for and reduced to accurate measure ; the simplicity of the cause, and the beauty and variety of the effects, must give pleasure to every contemplative mind. By this noble discovery, we are taken, as it were, behind the scene in this great drama of nature, and made to behold some part of the art of the divine Author of this system, which, before this discovery, eye had not seen, nor ear heard, nor had it entered into the heart of man to conceive.

There is, without doubt, in every work of nature, all the beautiful simplicity that is consistent with the end for which it was made. But if we hope to discover how nature brings about its ends, merely from this principle, that it operates in the simplest and best way, we deceive ourselves, and forget that the wisdom of

Nature is more above the wisdom of man, than man's wisdom is above that of a child.

If a child should sit down to contrive how a city is to be fortified. or an army arranged in the day of battle, he would, no doubt, conjecture what, to his understanding, appeared the simplest and best way. But could he ever hit upon the true way? No surely. When he learns from fact how these effects are produced, he will then see how foolish his childish conjectures were.

We may learn something of the way in which nature operates, from fact and observation; but if we conclude that it operates in such a manner, only because to our understanding, that appears to be the best and simplest manner, we shall always go wrong.

It was believed, for many ages, that all the variety of concrete bodies we find on this globe is reducible to four elements, of which they are compounded, and into which they may be resolved. It was the simplicity of this theory, and not any evidence from fact, that made it to be so generally received; for the more it is examined, we find the less ground to believe it.

The Pythagoreans and Platonists were carried further by the same love of simplicity. Pythagoras, by his skill in mathematics, discovered, that there can be no more than five regular solid figures, terminated by plain surfaces which are all similar and equal; to wit, the tetrahedron, the cube, the octahedron, the dodecahedron, and the eicosihedron. As nature works in the most simple and regular way, he thought that all the elementary bodies must have one or other of those regular figures; and that the discovery of the properties and relations of the regular solids would be a key to open the mysteries of nature.

This notion of the Pythagoreans and Platonists has undoubtedly great beauty and simplicity. Accordingly it prevailed, at least, to the time of Euclid. He was a Platonic philosopher, and is said to have wrote all the books of his Elements, in order to discover the properties and relations of the five regular solids. This ancient tradition of the intention of Euclid in writing his Elements, is countenanced by the work itself. For the last books of the Elements treat of the regular solids, and all the preceding are subservient to the last,

So that this most ancient mathematical work, which, for its admirable composition, has served as a model to all succeeding writers in mathematics, seems, like the two first books of Newton's Principia, to have been intended by its author to exhibit the mathematical principles of natural philosophy.

It was long believed, that all the qualities of bodies, and all their medical virtues, were reducible to four, moisture and dryness, heat and cold : and that there are only four temperaments of the human body ; the sanguine, the melancholy, the bilious, and the phlegmatic. The chymical system, of reducing all bodies to salt, sulphur, and mercury, was of the same kind. For how many ages did men believe, that the division of all the objects of thought into ten categories, and of all that can be affirmed or denied of any thing, into five universals or predicables, were perfect enumerations?

The evidence from reason that could be produced for those systems was next to nothing, and bore no proportion to the ground they gained in the belief of men ; but they were simple and regular, and reduced things to a few principles ; and this supplied their want of evidence.

Of all the systems we know, that of Des Cartes was most remarkable for its simplicity. Upon one proposition, *I think*, he builds the whole fabric of human knowledge. And from mere matter, with a certain

quantity of motion given it at first, he accounts for all
the phenomena of the material world.

The physical part of this system was mere hypothesis. It had nothing to recommend it but its simplicity;
yet it had force enough to overturn the system of Aristotle, after that system had prevailed for more than a
thousand years.

The principle of gravitation, and other attracting
and repelling forces, after sir Isaac Newton had given
the strongest evidence of their real existence in nature,
were rejected by the greatest part of Europe for half
a century, because they could not be accounted for by
matter and motion. So much were men enamoured
with the simplicity of the Cartesian system.

Nay, I apprehend, it was this love of simplicity, more
than real evidence, that led Newton himself to say, in
the preface to his Principia, speaking of the phenomena of the material world.   "Nam multa me movent ut
nonnihil suspicer, ea omnia ex viribus quibusdam pen-
dere posse, quibus corporum particulæ, per causas non-
dum cognitas, vel in se mutuo impelluntur, et secundum
figuras regulares cohærent, vel ab invicem fugantur et
recedunt." For certainly we have no evidence from
fact, that all the phenomena of the material world are
produced by attracting or repelling forces.

With his usual modesty, he proposes it only as a
slight suspicion; and the ground of this suspicion could
only be, that he saw that many of the phenomena of nature depended upon causes of this kind; and therefore
was disposed, from the simplicity of nature, to think
that all do.

When a real cause is discovered, the same love of
simplicity leads men to attribute effects to it which are
beyond its province.

A medicine that is found to be of great use in one
distemper, commonly has its virtues multiplied, till it

becomes a *panacea.* Those who have lived long, can
recollect many instances of this. In other branches of
knowledge, the same thing often happens. When the
attention of men is turned to any particular cause, by
discovering it to have remarkable effects, they are in
great danger of extending its influence, upon slight evidence, to things with which it has no connection. Such
prejudices arise from the natural desire of simplyfying
natural causes, and of accounting for many phenomena
from the same principle.

4thly, One of the most copious sources of error in
philosophy, is the misapplication of our noblest intellectual power to purposes for which it is incompetent.

Of all the intellectual powers of man, that of invention bears the highest price. It resembles most the
power of creation, and is honoured with that name.

We admire the man who shows a superiority in the
talent of finding the means of accomplishing an end;
who can, by a happy combination, produce an effect, or
make a discovery beyond the reach of other men ; who
can draw important conclusions from circumstances
that commonly pass unobserved ; who judges with the
greatest sagacity of the designs of other men, and the
consequences of his own actions. To this superiority
of understanding we give the name of genius, and look
up with admiration to every thing that bears the marks
of it.

Yet this power so highly valuable in itself, and so
useful in the conduct of life, may be misapplied ; and
men of genius, in all ages, have been prone to apply it
to purposes for which it is altogether incompetent.

The works of men and the works of nature are not
of the same order. The force of genius may enable a
man perfectly to comprehend the former, and to see
them to the bottom. What is contrived and executed
by one man may be perfectly understood by another

man. With great probability, he may from a part, conjecture the whole, or from the effects may conjecture
the causes; because they are effects of a wisdom not
superior to his own.

But the works of nature are contrived and executed
by a wisdom and power infinitely superior to that of
man; and when men attempt, by the force of genius,
to discover the causes of the phenomena of nature,
they have only the chance of going wrong more ingeniously. Their conjectures may appear very probable
to beings no wiser than themselves, but they have no
chance to hit the truth. They are like the conjectures
of a child how a ship of war is built, and how it is managed at sea.

Let the man of genius try to make an animal, even
the meanest; to make a plant, or even a single leaf
of a plant, or feather of a bird; he will find that all
his wisdom and sagacity can bear no comparison with
the wisdom of nature, nor his power with the power
of nature.

The experience of all ages shows how prone ingenious men have been to invent hypotheses to explain
the phenomena of nature; how fond, by a kind of an-
ticipation, to discover her secrets. Instead of a slow
and gradual ascent in the scale of natural causes, by
a just and copious induction, they would shorten the
work, and, by a flight of genius get to the top at once.
This gratifies the pride of human understanding; but
it is an attempt beyond our force, like that of Phæton
to guide the chariot of the sun.

When a man has laid out all his ingenuity in fabricating a system, he views it with the eye of a parent;
he strains phenomena to make them tally with it, and
make it look like the work of nature.

The slow and patient method of induction, the only
way to attain any knowledge of nature's work, was
little understood until it was delineated by lord Bacon,

and has been little followed since. It humbles the
pride of man, and puts him constantly in mind that his
most ingenious conjectures with regard to the works
of God are pitiful and childish.

There is no room here for the favourite talent of
invention. In the humble method of information, from
the great volume of nature we must receive all our
knowledge of nature. Whatever is beyond a just interpretation of that volume, is the work of man ; and
the work of God ought not to be contaminated by any
mixture with it.

To a man of genius, self-denial is a difficult lesson
in philosophy as well as in religion. To bring his fine
imaginations and most ingenious conjectures to the fiery
trial of experiment and induction, by which the greater part, if not the whole, will be found to be dross, is
a humiliating task. This is to condemn him to dig
in a mine, when he would fly with the wings of an
eagle.

In all the fine arts, whose end is to please, genius is
deservedly supreme. In the conduct of human affairs
it often does wonders ; but in all inquiries into the constitution of nature it must act a subordinate part, ill
suited to the superiority it boasts. It may combine,
but it must not fabricate: it may collect evidence, but
must not supply the want of it by conjecture: it may
display its powers by putting nature to the question
in well contrived experiments, but it must add nothing
to her answers.

5thly, In avoiding one extreme, men are very apt to
rush into the opposite.

Thus, in the rude ages, men, unaccustomed to search
for natural causes, ascribe every uncommon appearance to the immediate interposition of invisible beings ;
but when philosophy has discovered natural causes of
many events, which in the days of ignorance, were

ascribed to the immediate operation of gods or demons, they are apt to think, that all the phenomena of nature may be accounted for in the same way, and that there is no need of an invisible Maker and Governor of the world.

Rude men are at first disposed to ascribe intelligence and active power to every thing they see move or undergo any change. " Savages," says the Abbe Raynal, " wherever they see motion which they cannot account for, there they suppose a soul." When they come to be convinced of the folly of this extreme, they are apt to run into the opposite, and to think that every thing moves only as it is moved, and acts as it is acted upon.

Thus, from the extreme of superstition, the transition is easy to that of atheism ; and from the extreme of ascribing activity to every part of nature, to that of excluding it altogether, and making even the determinations of intelligent beings, the links of one fatal chain, or the wheels of one great machine.

The abuse of occult qualities in the Peripatetic philosophy, led Des Cartes and his followers to reject all occult qualities ; to pretend to explain all the phenomena of nature by mere matter and motion, and even to fix disgrace upon the name of occult quality.

6thly, Men's judgments are often perverted by their affections and passions.   This is so commonly observed, and so universally acknowledged, that it needs no proof nor illustration.

The second class of idols in lord Bacon's division, are the *idola specus.*

These are prejudices which have their origin, not from the constitution of human nature, but from something peculiar to the individual.

As in a cave objects vary in their appearance according to the form of the cave and the manner in which it receives the light, lord Bacon conceives the mind of every man to resemble a cave, which has its particular form and its particular manner of being enlightened; and, from these circumstances, often gives false colours and a delusive appearance to objects seen in it.

For this reason, he gives the name of *idola specus* to those prejudices which arise from the particular way in which a man has been trained, from his being addicted to some particular profession, or from something particular in the turn of his mind.

A man whose thoughts have been confined to a certain track by his profession or manner of life, is very apt to judge wrong when he ventures out of that track. He is apt to draw every thing within the sphere of his profession, and to judge by its maxims of things that have no relation to it.

The mere mathematician is apt to apply measure and calculation to things which do not admit of it. Direct and inverse ratios have been applied by an ingenious author to measure human affections, and the moral worth of actions. An eminent mathematician attempted to ascertain by calculation, the ratio in which the evidence of facts must decrease in the course of time, and fixed the period when the evidence of the facts on which Christianity is founded shall become evanescent, and when, in consequence, no faith shall be found on the earth. I have seen a philosophical dissertation published by a very good mathematician, wherein, in opposition to the ancient division of things into ten categories, he maintains that there are no more, and can be no more than two categories, to wit *data* and *quæsita*.

The ancient chymists were wont to explain all the mysteries of nature, and even of religion, by salt, sulphur, and mercury.

Mr. Locke, I think, mentions an eminent musician who believed that God created the world in six days and rested the seventh, because there are but seven notes in music. I knew one of that profession, who thought that there could be only three parts in harmony, to wit, bass, tenor, and treble, because there are but three persons in the trinity.

The learned and ingenious Dr. Henry More having very elaborately and methodically compiled his Enchiridium Metaphysicum, and Enchiridium Ethicum, found all the divisions and subdivisions of both to be allegorically taught in the first chapter of Genesis. Thus even very ingenious men are apt to make a ridiculous figure, by drawing into the track, in which their thoughts have long run, things altogether foreign to it.

Different persons, either from temper or from education, have different tendencies of understanding, which, by their excess, are unfavourable to sound judgment.

Some have an undue admiration of antiquity, and contempt of whatever is modern; others go as far into the contrary extreme. It may be judged, that the former are persons who value themselves upon their acquaintance with ancient authors, and the latter such as have little knowledge of this kind.

Some are afraid to venture a step out of the beaten track, and think it safest to go with the multitude; others are fond of singularities, and of every thing that has the air of paradox.

Some are desultory and changeable in their opinions; others unduly tenacious. Most men have a predilection for the tenets of their sect or party, and still more for their own inventions.

The *idola fori* are the fallacies arising from the imperfections and the abuse of language, which is an instrument of thought, as well as of the communication of our thoughts.

Whether it be the effect of constitution or of habit, I will not take upon me to determine; but, from one or both of these causes, it happens, that no man can pursue a train of thought or reasoning without the use of language. Words are the signs of our thoughts; and the sign is so associated with the thing signified, that the last can hardly present itself to the imagination, without drawing the other along with it.

A man who would compose in any language, must think in that language. If he thinks in one language what he would express in another, he thereby doubles his labour, and, after all, his expressions will have more the air of a translation than of an original.

This shows, that our thoughts take their colour in some degree from the language we use; and that, although language ought always to be subservient to thought, yet thought must be at some times, and in some degree, subservient to language.

As a servant that is extremely useful and necessary to his master, by degrees acquires an authority over him, so that the master must often yield to the servant; such is the case with regard to language. Its intention is to be a servant to the understanding; but it is so useful and so necessary, that we cannot avoid being sometimes led by it when it ought to follow. We cannot shake off this impediment, we must drag it along with us; and therefore must direct our course, and regulate our pace, as it permits.

Language must have many imperfections when applied to philosophy, because it was not made for that use, in the early periods of society, rude and ignorant men use certain forms of speech, to express their wants, their desires, and their transactions with one another. Their language can reach no further than their speculations and notions; and if their notions be vague and ill defined, the words by which they express them must be so likewise.

It was a grand and noble project of bishop Wilkins, to invent a philosophical language, which should be free from the imperfections of vulgar languages. Whether this attempt will ever succeed, so far as to be generally useful, I shall not pretend to determine. The great pains taken by that excellent man in this design have hitherto produced no effect. Very few have ever entered minutely into his views; far less have his philosophical language and his real character been brought into use.

He founds his philosophical language and real character upon a systematical division and subdivision of all the things which may be expressed by language, and, instead of the ancient division into ten categories, has made forty categories, or *summa genera*. But whether this division, though made by a very comprehensive mind, will always suit the various systems that may be introduced, and all the real improvements that may be made in human knowledge, may be doubted. The difficulty is still greater in the subdivisions; so that it is to be feared, that this noble attempt of a great genius will prove abortive, until philosophers have the same opinions and the same systems in the various branches of human knowledge.

There is more reason to hope, that the language used by philosophers may be gradually improved in copiousness and in distinctness; and that improvements in knowledge and in language may go hand in hand, and facilitate each other. But I fear the imperfections of language can never be perfectly remedied while our knowledge is imperfect.

However this may be, it is evident that the imperfections of language, and much more the abuse of it, are the occasion of many errors; and that in many disputes which have engaged learned men, the difference has been partly, and in some wholly, about the meaning of words.

Mr. Locke found it necessary to employ a fourth part of his Essay on Human Understanding about words ; their various kinds ; their imperfection and abuse, and the remedies of both ; and has made many observations upon these subjects, well worthy of attentive perusal.

The fourth class of prejudices are the *idola theatri,* by which are meant prejudices arising from the systems or sects, in which we have been trained, or which we have adopted.

A false system once fixed in the mind, becomes, as it were, the medium through which we see objects : they receive a tincture from it, and appear of another colour than when seen by a pure light.

Upon the same subject, a Platonist, a Peripatetic, and an Epicurean, will think differently, not only in matters connected with his peculiar tenets, but even in things remote from them.

A judicious history of the different sects of philosophers, and the different methods of philosophizing, which have obtained among mankind, would be of no small use to direct men in the search of truth. In such a history, what would be of the greatest moment is not so much a minute detail of the *dogmata* of each sect, as a just delineation of the spirit of the sect, and of that point of view in which things appeared to its founder. This was perfectly understood, and, as far as concerns the theories of morals, is executed with great judgment and candour by Dr. Smith in his theory of moral sentiments.

As there are certain temperaments of the body that dispose a man more to one class of diseases than to another ; and, on the other hand, diseases of that kind when they happen by accident, are apt to induce the temperament that is suited to them ; there is something analogous to this in the diseases of the understanding.

A certain complexion of understanding may dispose a man to one system of opinions more than to another; and, on the other hand, a system of opinions, fixed in the mind by education or otherwise, gives that complexion to the understanding which is suited to them.

It were to be wished, that the different systems that have prevailed could be classed according to their spirit, as well as named from their founders.   Lord Bacon has distinguished false philosophy into the sophistical, the empirical, and the superstitious, and has made judicious observations upon each of these kinds.   But I apprehend this subject deserves to be treated more fully by such a hand, if such a hand can be found.

ESSAY VII.

OF REASONING.

CHAP. I.

OF REASONING IN GENERAL, AND OF DEMONSTRATION.

THE power of reasoning is very nearly allied to that of judging; and it is of little consequence in the common affairs of life to distinguish them nicely. On this account, the same name is often given to both. We include both under the name of reason. The assent we give to a proposition is called judgment, whether the proposition be self-evident, or derive its evidence by reasoning from other propositions.

Yet there is a distinction between reasoning and judging. Reasoning is the process by which we pass from one judgment to another which is the consequence of it. Accordingly, our judgments are distinguished into intuitive, which are not grounded upon any preceding judgment, and discursive, which are deduced from some preceding judgment by reasoning.

In all reasoning, therefore, there must be a proposition inferred, and one or more from which it is inferred. And this power of inferring, or drawing a conclusion, is only another name for reasoning; the proposition inferred, being called the *conclusion*, and the proposition, or propositions from which it is inferred, the *premises*.

710

Reasoning may consist of many steps ; the first conclusion being a premise to a second, that to a third, and so on, till we come to the last conclusion. A process consisting of many steps of this kind, is so easily distinguished from judgment, that it is never called by that name. But when there is only a single step to the conclusion, the distinction is less obvious, and the process is sometimes called judgment, sometimes reasoning.

It is not strange, that, in common discourse, judgment and reasoning should not be very nicely distinguished, since they are in some cases confounded even by logicians. We are taught in logic, that judgment is expressed by one proposition, but that reasoning requires two or three. But so various are the modes of speech, that what in one mode is expressed by two or three propositions, may in another mode be expressed by one. Thus I may say, *God is good ; therefore good men shall be happy.* This is reasoning, of that kind which logicians call an enthymeme, consisting of an antecedent proposition, and a conclusion drawn from it. But this reasoning may be expressed by one proposition, thus : *Because God is good, good men shall be happy.* This is what they call a casual proposition, and therefore expresses judgment ; yet the enthymeme, which is reasoning, expresses no more.

Reasoning, as well as judgment, must be true or false ; both are grounded upon evidence which may be probable or demonstrative, and both are accompanied with assent or belief.

The power of reasoning is justly accounted one of the prerogatives of human nature ; because by it many important truths have been, and may be discovered, which without it would be beyond our reach ; yet it seems to be only a kind of crutch to a limited understanding. We can conceive an understanding, superior to human, to which that truth appears intuitively, which we can only discover by reasoning. For this cause, though we must ascribe judgment to the Almighty, we do not ascribe reasoning to him, because it implies some defect or limitation of understanding. Even among men, to use reasoning in things that are self-evident, is trifling; like a man going upon crutches when he can walk upon his legs.

What reasoning is, can be understood only by a man who has reasoned, and who is capable of reflecting upon this operation of his own mind. We can define it only by synonymous words or phrases, such as inferring, drawing a conclusion, and the like. The very notion of reasoning, therefore, can enter into the mind by no other channel than that of reflecting upon the operation of reasoning in our own minds ; and the notions of premises and conclusion, of a syllogism, and all its constituent parts, of an enthymeme, sorites, demonstration, paralogism, and many others, have the same origin.

It is nature undoubtedly that gives us the capacity of reasoning. When this is wanting, no art nor education can supply it. But this capacity may be dormant through life, like the seed of a plant, which, for want of heat and moisture, never vegetates. This is probably the case of some savages.

Although the capacity be purely the gift of Nature, and probably given in very different degrees to different persons; yet the power of reasoning seems to be got by habit, as much as the power of walking or running. Its first exertions we are not able to recollect in ourselves, or clearly to discern in others. They are very feeble, and need to be led by example, and supported by authority. By degrees it acquires strength, chiefly by means of imitation and exercise.

The exercise of reasoning on various subjects not only strengthens the faculty, but furnishes the mind with a store of materials. Every train of reasoning, which is familiar, becomes a beaten track in the way to many others. It removes many obstacles which lay in our way, and smooths many roads which we may have occasion to travel in future disquisitions.

When men of equal natural parts apply their reasoning powers to any subject, the man who has reasoned much on the same, or on similar subjects, has a like advantage over him who has not; as the mechanic who has store of tools for his work, has of him who has his tools to make, or even to invent.

In a train of reasoning, the evidence of every step, where nothing is left to be supplied by the reader or hearer, must be immediately discernible to every man of ripe understanding who has a distinct comprehension of the premises and conclusion, and who compares them together. To be able to comprehend, in one view, a combination of steps of this kind, is more difficult, and seems to require a superior natural ability. In all, it may be much improved by habit.

But the highest talent in reasoning is the invention of proofs; by which, truths remote from the premises are brought to light. In all works of understanding, invention has the highest praise; it requires an extensive view of what relates to the subject, and a quickness in discerning those affinities and relations which may be subservient to the purpose.

In all invention, there must be some end in view: and sagacity in finding out the road that leads to this end, is, I think, what we call invention. In this chiefly, as I apprehend, and in clear and distinct conceptions, consist that superiority of understanding which we call *genius*.

In every chain of reasoning, the evidence of the last conclusion can be no greater than that of the weakest link of the chain, whatever may be the strength of the rest.

The most remarkable distinction of reasonings is, that some are probable, others demonstrative.

In every step of demonstrative reasoning, the inference is necessary, and we perceive it to be impossible that the conclusion should not follow from the premises. In probable reasoning, the connection between the premises and the conclusion is not necessary, nor do we perceive it to be impossible that the first should be true while the last is false.

Hence demonstrative reasoning has no degrees, nor can one demonstration be stronger than another, though, in relation to our faculties, one may be more easily comprehended than another. Every demonstration gives equal strength to the conclusion, and leaves no possibility of its being false.

It was, I think, the opinion of all the ancients, that demonstrative reasoning can be applied only to truths that are necessary, and not to those that are contingent. In this, I believe, they judged right. Of all created things, the existence, the attributes, and consequently the relations resulting from those attributes, are contingent. They depend upon the will and power of him who made them. These are matters of fact, and admit not of demonstration.

The field of demonstrative reasoning, therefore, is the various relations of things abstract, that is, of things which we conceive, without regard to their existence. Of these, as they are conceived by the mind, and are nothing but what they are conceived to be, we may have a clear and adequate comprehension. Their relations and attributes are necessary and immutable. They are the things to which the Pythagoreans and Platonists gave the name of ideas. I would beg leave to borrow this meaning of the word *idea* from those ancient philosophers, and then I must agree with them, that ideas are the only objects about which we can reason demonstratively.

There are many even of our ideas about which we can carry on no considerable train of reasoning. Though they be ever so well defined and perfectly comprehended, yet their agreements and disagreements are few, and these are discerned at once. We may go a step or two in forming a conclusion with regard to such objects, but can go no further. There are others, about which we may, by a long train of demonstrative reasoning, arrive at conclusions very remote and unexpected.

The reasonings I have met with that can be called strictly demonstrative, may, I think, be reduced to two classes. They are either metaphysical, or they are mathematical.

In metaphysical reasoning, the process is always short. The conclusion is but a step or two, seldom more, from the first principle or axiom on which it is grounded, and the different conclusions depend not one upon another.

It is otherwise in mathematical reasoning. Here the field has no limits. One proposition leads on to another, that to a third, and so on without end.

If it should be asked, why demonstrative reasoning has so wide a field in mathematics, while, in other abstract subjects, it is confined within very narrow limits? I conceive this is chiefly owing to the nature of quantity, the object of mathematics.

Every quantity, as it has magnitude, and is divisible into parts without end, so in respect of its magnitude, it has a certain ratio to every quantity of the kind. The ratios of quantities are innumerable, such as, a half, a third, a tenth, double, triple. All the powers of number are insufficient to express the variety of ratios. For there are innumerable ratios which cannot be perfectly expressed by numbers, such as, the ratio of the side to the diagonal of a square, of the circumference of a circle to the diameter. Of this infinite variety of ratios, every one may be clearly conceived, and distinctly expressed, so as to be in no danger of being mistaken for any other.

Extended quantities, such as lines, surfaces, solids, besides the variety of relations they have in respect of magnitude, have no less variety in respect of figure; and every mathematical figure may be accurately defined, so as to distinguish it from all others.

There is nothing of this kind in other objects of abstract reasoning. Some of them have various degrees; but these are not capable of measure, nor can be said to have an assignable ratio to others of the kind. They are either simple, or compounded of a few indivisible parts; and therefore, if we may be allowed the expression, can touch only in a few points. But mathematical quantities being made up of parts without number, can touch in innumerable points, and be compared in innumerable different ways.

There have been attempts made to measure the merit of actions by the ratios of the affections and principles of action from which they proceed. This may perhaps, in the way of analogy, serve to illustrate what was before known; but I do not think any truth can be discovered in this way. There are, no doubt, degrees of benevolence, self love, and other affections; but, when we apply ratios to them, I apprehend we have no distinct meaning.

Some demonstrations are called direct, others indirect. The first kind leads directly to the conclusion to be proved. Of the indirect some are called demonstrations *ad absurdum*. In these the proposition contradictory to that which is to be proved is demonstrated to be false, or to lead to an absurdity; whence it follows, that its contradictory, that is, the proposition to be proved, is true. This inference is grounded upon an axiom in logic, that of two contradictory propositions, if one be false, the other must be true.

Another kind of indirect demonstration proceeds by enumerating all the suppositions that can possibly be made concerning the proposition to be proved, and then demonstrating, that all of them, excepting that which is to be proved, are false; whence it follows, that the excepted supposition is true. Thus one line is proved to be equal to another, by proving first that it cannot be greater, and then that it cannot be less: for it must be either greater, or less, or equal; and two of these suppositions being demonstrated to be false, the third must be true.

All these kinds of demonstration are used in mathematics, and perhaps some others. They have all equal strength. The direct demonstration is preferred where it can be had, for this reason only, as I apprehend, because it is the shortest road to the conclusion. The nature of the evidence and its strength is the same in all; only we are conducted to it by different roads.

CHAP. II.

WHETHER MORALITY BE CAPABLE OF DEMONSTRATION.

WHAT has been said of demonstrative reasoning may help us to judge of an opinion of Mr. Locke, advanced in several places of his Essay; to wit, "That morality is capable of demonstration, as well as mathematics."

In book 3. chap. 11. having observed, that mixed modes, especially those belonging to morality, being such combinations of ideas as the mind puts together of its own choice, the signification of their names may be perfectly and exactly defined, he adds,

Sect. 16. "Upon this ground it is that I am bold to think, that morality is capable of demonstration as well as mathematics: since the precise real essence of the things moral words stand for may be perfectly known, and so the congruity or incongruity of the things themselves be certainly discovered, in which consists perfect knowledge. Nor let any one object. that the names of substances are often to be made use of in morality, as well as those of modes, from which will arise obscurity: for as to substances, when concerned in moral discourses, their divers natures are not so much inquired into as supposed: *v. g.* When we say that man is subject to law, we mean nothing by man but a corporeal rational creature. What the real essence or other qualities of that creature are, in this case, is no way considered.

Again, in book 4. chap. 3. §18. "The idea of a Supreme Being, whose workmanship we are, and the idea of ourselves, being such as are clear in us, would. I suppose, if duly considered and pursued, afford such foundation of our duty and rules of action, as might place morality among the sciences capable of demonstration. The relation of other modes may certainly be perceived, as well as those of number and extension; and I cannot see why they should not be capable of demonstration, if due methods were thought on to examine or pursue their agreement or disagreement."

He afterwards gives as instances, two propositions as moral propositions, of which we may be as certain as of any in mathematics; and considers at large what may have given the advantage to the ideas of quantity, and made them be thought more capable of certainty and demonstration.

Again, in the 12th chapter of the same book, § 7, 8. "This I think I may say, that if other ideas that are the real, as well as nominal essences of their several species, were pursued in the way familiar to mathematicians, they would carry our thoughts further, and with greater evidence and clearness, than possibly we are apt to imagine. This gave me the confidence to advance that conjecture which I suggest, chap. 3. viz. That morality is capable of demonstration as well as mathematics."

From these passages it appears, that this opinion was not a transient thought, but what he had revolved in his mind on different occasions. He offers his reasons for it, illustrates it by examples, and considers at length the causes that have led men to think mathematics more capable of demonstration than the principles of morals.

Some of his learned correspondents, particularly his friend Mr. Molyneux, urged and importuned him to compose a system of morals according to the idea he had advanced in his Essay; and, in his answer to these solicitations, he only pleads other occupations, without suggesting any change of his opinion, or any great difficulty in the execution of what was desired.

The reason he gives for this opinion is ingenious and his regard for virtue, the highest prerogative of the human species, made him fond of an opinion which seemed to be favourable to virtue, and to have a just foundation in reason.

We need not, however, be afraid, that the interest of virtue may suffer by a free and candid examination of this question, or indeed of any question whatever. For the interests of truth and of virtue can never be found in opposition. Darkness and error may befriend vice, but can never be favourable to virtue.

Those philosophers who think that our determinations in morals are not real judgments, that right and wrong in human conduct are only certain feelings or sensations in the person who contemplates the action, must reject Mr. Locke's opinion without examination. For if the principles of morals be not a matter of judgment, but of feeling only, there can be no demonstration of them; nor can any other reason be given for them, but that men are so constituted by the Author of their being, as to contemplate with pleasure the actions we call virtuous, and with disgust those we call vicious.

It is not therefore to be expected, that the philosophers of this class should think this opinion of Mr. Locke worthy of examination, since it is founded upon what they think a false hypothesis. But if our determinations in morality be real judgments, and, like all other judgments, be either true or false, it is not unimportant to understand upon what kind of evidence those judgments rest.

The argument offered by Mr. Locke, to show that morality is capable of demonstration, is, "That the precise real essence of the things moral words stand for may be perfectly known, and so the congruity or incongruity of the things themselves be perfectly discovered, in which consists perfect knowledge."

It is true, that the field of demonstration is the various relations of things conceived abstractly, of which we may have perfect and adequate conceptions. And Mr. Locke, taking all the things which moral words stand for to be of this kind, concluded that morality is as capable of demonstration as mathematics.

I acknowledge, that the names of the virtues and vices, of right and obligation, of liberty and property, stands for things abstract, which may be accurately defined, or, at least, conceived as distinctly and adequately as mathematical quantities. And thence indeed it follows, that their mutual relations may be perceived as clearly and certainly as mathematical truths.

Of this Mr. Locke gives two pertinent examples. The first, " where there is no property, there is no injustice, is," says he, " a proposition as certain as any demonstration in Euclid."

When injustice is defined to be a violation of property, it is as necessary a truth, that there can be no injustice where there is no property, as that you cannot take from a man that which he has not.

The second example is, " that no government allows absolute liberty." This is a truth no less certain and necessary.

Such abstract truths I would call metaphysical, rather than moral. We give the name of mathematical, to truths that express the relations of quantities considered abstractly ; all other abstract truths may be called metaphysical. But if those mentioned by Mr. Locke are to be called moral truths, I agree with him, that there are many such that are necessarily true, and that have all the evidence that mathematical truths can have.

It ought however to be remembered, that, as was before observed, the relations of things abstract, perceivable by us, excepting those of mathematical quan-

tities, are few, and for the most part immediately discerned, so as not to require that train of reasoning
which we call demonstration. Their evidence resembles more that of mathematical axioms, than mathematical propositions.

This appears in the two propositions given as examples by Mr. Locke. The first follows immediately
from the definition of injustice; the second from the
definition of government. Their evidence may more
properly be called intuitive than demonstrative: and
this I apprehend to be the case, or nearly the case, of
all abstract truths that are not mathematical, for the
reason given in the last chapter.

The propositions which I think are properly called
moral, are those that affirm some moral obligation to
be, or not to be incumbent on one or more individual
persons. To such propositions, Mr. Locke's reasoning
does not apply, because the subjects of the proposition
are not things whose real essence may be perfectly
known. They are the creatures of God; their obligation results from the constitution which God has given
them, and the circumstances in which he has placed
them. That an individual has such a constitution,
and is placed in such circumstances, is not an abstract
and necessary, but a contingent truth. It is a matter
of fact, and therefore not capable of demonstrative evidence, which belongs only to necessary truths.

The evidence which every man has of his own existence, though it be irresistible, is not demonstrative.
And the same thing may be said of the evidence which
every man has, that he is a moral agent, and under
certain moral obligations. In like manner, the evidence we have of the existence of other men is not demonstrative; nor is the evidence we have of their being endowed with those faculties which make them
moral and accountable agents.

If a man had not the faculty given him by God of perceiving certain things in conduct to be right, and others to be wrong, and of perceiving his obligation to do what is right, and not to do what is wrong, he would not be a moral and accountable being.

If a man be endowed with such a faculty, there must be some things, which, by this faculty, are immediately discerned to be right, and others to be wrong ; and therefore there must be in morals, as in other sciences, first principles, which do not derive their evidence from any antecedent principles, but may be said to be intuitively discerned.

Moral truths, therefore, may be divided into two classes ; to wit, such as are self-evident to every man whose understanding and moral faculty are ripe, and such as are deduced by reasoning from those that are self-evident. If the first be not discerned without reasoning, the last never can be, by any reasoning.

If any man could say with sincerity, that he is conscious of no obligation to consult his own present and future happiness ; to be faithful to his engagements ; to obey his Maker ; to injure no man ; I know not what reasoning, either probable or demonstrative, I could use to convince him of any moral duty. As you cannot reason in mathematics with a man who denies the axioms, as little can you reason with a man in morals who denies the first principles of morals. The man who does not, by the light of his own mind, perceive some things in conduct to be right, and others to be wrong, is as incapable of reasoning about morals, as a blind man is about colours. Such a man, if any such man ever was, would be no moral agent, nor capable of any moral obligation.

Some first principles of morals must be immediately discerned, otherwise we have no foundation on which others can rest, or from which we can reason.

Every man knows certainly, that, what he approves in other men he ought to do in like circumstances, and that he ought not to do what he condemns in other men. Every man knows that he ought, with candour, to use the best means of knowing his duty. To every man who has a conscience, these things are self-evident. They are immediate dictates of our moral faculty, which is a part of the human constitution; and every man condemns himself, whether he will or not, when he knowingly acts contrary to them. The evidence of these fundamental principles of morals, and of others that might be named, appears therefore to me to be intuitive rather than demonstrative.

The man who acts according to the dictates of his conscience, and takes due pains to be rightly informed of his duty, is a perfect man with regard to morals, and merits no blame, whatever may be the imperfections or errors of his understanding. He who knowingly acts contrary to them is conscious of guilt, and self-condemned. Every particular action that falls evidently within the fundamental rules of morals is evidently his duty; and it requires no reasoning to convince him that it is so.

Thus I think it appears, that every man of common understanding knows certainly, and without reasoning, the ultimate ends he ought to pursue, and that reasoning is necessary only to discover the most proper means of attaining them; and in this, indeed, a good man may often be in doubt.

Thus, a magistrate knows that it is his duty to promote the good of the community which has intrusted him with authority; and to offer to prove this to him by reasoning would be to affront him. But whether such a scheme of conduct in his office, or another, may best serve that end, he may in many cases be doubtful. I believe, in such cases, he can very rarely have demonstrative evidence. His conscience determines the end he ought to pursue, and he has intuitive evidence that his end is good; but prudence must determine the means of attaining that end; and prudence can very rarely use demonstrative reasoning, but must rest in what appears most probable.

I apprehend, that in every kind of duty we owe to God or man, the case is similar: that is, that the obligation of the most general rules of duty is self-evident; that the application of those rules to particular actions is often no less evident; and that, when it is not evident, but requires reasoning, that reasoning can very rarely be of the demonstrative, but must be of the probable kind. Sometimes it depends upon the temper, and talents, and circumstances of the man himself; sometimes upon the character and circumstances of others; sometimes upon both; and these are things which admit not of demonstration.

Every man is bound to employ the talents which God has given him to the best purpose; but if, through accidents which he could not foresee, or ignorance which was invincible, they be less usefully employed than they might have been, this will not be imputed to him by his righteous Judge.

It is a common and a just observation, that the man of virtue plays a surer game in order to obtain his end than the man of the world. It is not, however, because he reasons better concerning the means of attaining his end; for the children of this world are often wiser in their generation than the children of light. But the reason of the observation is, that involuntary errors, unforeseen accidents, and invincible ignorance, which affect deeply all the concerns of the present world, have no effect upon virtue or its reward.

In the common occurrences of life, a man of integrity, who has exercised his moral faculty in judging what

is right and what is wrong, sees his duty without reasoning, as he sees the highway. The cases that require reasoning are few, compared with those that require none ; and a man may be very honest and virtuous who cannot reason, and who knows not what demonstration means.

The power of reasoning, in those that have it, may
be abused in morals, as in other matters. To a man
who uses it with an upright heart, and a single eye to
find what is his duty, it will be of great use ; but when
it is used to justify what a man has a strong inclination
to do, it will only serve to deceive himself and others.
When a man can reason, his passions will reason, and
they are the most cunning sophists we meet with.

If the rules of virtue were left to be discovered by
demonstrative reasoning, or by reasoning of any kind,
sad would be the condition of the far greater part of
men, who have not the means of cultivating the power
of reasoning. As virtue is the business of all men, the
first principles of it are written in their hearts, in characters so legible, that no man can pretend ignorance of
them, or of his obligation to practise them.

Some knowledge of duty and of moral obligation is
necessary to all men. Without it they could not be
moral and accountable creatures, nor capable of being
members of civil society. It may therefore be presumed, that nature has put this knowledge within the
reach of all men. Reasoning and demonstration are
weapons which the greatest part of mankind never was
able to wield. The knowledge that is necessary to all,
must be attainable by all. We see it is so in what pertains to the natural life of man.

Some knowledge of things that are useful, and things
that are hurtful, is so necessary to all men, that without it the species would soon perish. But it is not by
reasoning that this knowledge is got, far less by

demonstrative reasoning. It is by our senses, by memory, by experience, by information; means of knowledge that are open to all men, and put the learned and the unlearned, those who can reason and those who cannot, upon a level.

It may therefore be expected, from the analogy of nature, that such a knowledge of morals as is necessary to all men, should be had by means more suited to the abilities of all men than demonstrative reasoning is.

This, I apprehend, is in fact the case. When men's faculties are ripe, the first principles of morals, into which all moral reasoning may be resolved, are perceived intuitively, and in a manner more analogous to the perceptions of sense than to the conclusions of demonstrative reasoning.

Upon the whole, I agree with Mr. Locke, that propositions expressing the congruities and incongruities of things abstract, which moral words stand for, may have all the evidence of mathematical truths. But this is not peculiar to things which moral words stand for. It is common to abstract propositions of every kind. For instance, you cannot take from a man what he has not. A man cannot be bound and perfectly free at the same time. I think no man will call these moral truths, but they are necessary truths, and as evident as any in mathematics. Indeed, they are very nearly allied to the two which Mr. Locke gives as instances of moral propositions capable of demonstration. Of such abstract propositions, I think it may more properly be said, that they have the evidence of mathematical axioms, than that they are capable of demonstration.

There are propositions of another kind, which alone deserve the name of moral propositions. They are such as affirm something to be the duty of persons that really exist. These are not abstract propositions; and therefore Mr. Locke's reasoning does not apply to

them. The truth of all such propositions depends upon
the constitution and circumstances of the persons to
whom they are applied.

Of such propositions, there are some that are self-
evident to every man that has a conscience ; and these
are the principles from which all moral reasoning must
be drawn. They may be called the axioms of morals.
But our reasoning from these axioms to any duty that
is not self-evident, can very rarely be demonstrative.
Nor is this any detriment to the cause of virtue, because to act against what appears most probable in a
matter of duty, is as real a trespass against the first
principles of morality, as to act against demonstration ;
and because he who has but one talent in reasoning, and
makes the proper use of it, shall be accepted, as well as
he to whom God has given ten.

CHAP. III.

OF PROBABLE REASONING.

THE field of demonstration, as has been observed, is necessary truth ; the field of probable reasoning is contingent truth, not what necessarily must be at all times, but what is, or was, or shall be.

No contingent truth, is capable of strict demonstration ; but necessary truths may sometimes have probable evidence.

Dr. Wallis discovered many important mathematical truths, by that kind of induction which draws a general conclusion from particular premises. This is not strict demonstration, but, in some cases, gives as full conviction as demonstration itself ; and a man may be certain, that a truth is demonstrable before it ever has been demonstrated. In other cases, a mathematical proposition may have such probable evidence from induction or analogy, as encourages the mathematician to investigate its demonstration. But still the reasoning proper to mathematical and other necessary truths, is demonstration ; and that which is proper to contingent truths, is probable reasoning.

These two kinds of reasoning differ in other respects. In demonstrative reasoning, one argument is as good as a thousand. One demonstration may be more elegant than another ; it may be more easily comprehended, or it may be more subservient to some purpose beyond the present. On any of these accounts it may deserve a preference : but then it is sufficient by itself ; it needs no aid from another ; it can receive none. To add more demonstrations of the same conclusion, would be a kind of tautology in reasoning ; because one demonstration, clearly comprehended, gives all the evidence we are capable of receiving.

The strength of probable reasoning, for the most part, depends not upon any one argument, but upon many, which unite their force, and lead to the same conclusion. Any one of them by itself would be insufficient to convince; but the whole taken together may have a force that is irresistible, so that to desire more evidence would be absurd. Would any man seek new arguments to prove that there were such persons as king Charles the first, or Oliver Cromwell?

Such evidence may be compared to a rope made up of many slender filaments twisted together. The rope has strength more than sufficient to bear the stress laid upon it, though no one of the filaments of which it is composed would be sufficient for that purpose.

It is a common observation, that it is unreasonable to require demonstration for things which do not admit of it. It is no less unreasonable to require reasoning of any kind for things which are known without reasoning. All reasoning must be grounded upon truths which are known without reasoning. In every branch of real knowledge there must be first principles whose truth is known intuitively, without reasoning, either probable or demonstrative. They are not grounded on reasoning, but all reasoning is grounded on them. It has been shown, that there are first principles of necessary truths, and first principles of contingent truths. Demonstrative reasoning is grounded upon the former, and probable reasoning upon the latter.

That we may not be embarrassed by the ambiguity of words, it is proper to observe, that there is a popular meaning of *probable evidence,* which ought not to be confounded with the philosophical meaning above explained.

In common language, probable evidence is considered as an inferior degree of evidence, and is opposed to certainty: so that what is certain is more than probable, and what is only probable is not certain. Philosophers consider probable evidence, not as a degree, but as a species of evidence which is opposed, not to certainty, but to another species of evidence called demonstration.

Demonstrative evidence has no degrees; but probable evidence, taken in the philosophical sense, has all degrees, from the very least, to the greatest, which we call certainty.

That there is such a city as Rome, I am as certain as of any proposition in Euclid; but the evidence is not demonstrative, but of that kind which philosophers call probable. Yet, in common language, it would sound oddly to say, it is probable there is such a city as Rome; because it would imply some degree of doubt or uncertainty.

Taking probable evidence, therefore, in the philosophical sense, as it is opposed to demonstrative, it may have any degree of evidence, from the least to the greatest.

I think, in most cases, we measure the degrees of evidence by the effect they have upon a sound understanding, when comprehended clearly and without prejudice. Every degree of evidence perceived by the mind, produces a proportioned degree of assent or belief. The judgment may be in perfect suspense between two contradictory opinions, when there is no evidence for either, or equal evidence for both. The least preponderancy on one side inclines the judgment in proportion. Belief is mixed with doubt, more or less, until we come to the highest degree of evidence, when all doubt vanishes, and the belief is firm and immoveable. This degree of evidence, the highest the human faculties can attain, we call certainty.

Probable evidence not only differs in kind from demonstrative, but is itself of different kinds. The chief of these I shall mention, without pretending to make a complete enumeration.

The first kind is that of human testimony, upon which the greatest part of human knowledge is built.

The faith of history depends upon it, as well as the judgment of solemn tribunals, with regard to men's acquired rights, and with regard to their guilt or innocence when they are charged with crimes. A great part of the business of the judge, of counsel at the bar, of the historian, the critic, and the antiquarian, is to canvass and weigh this kind of evidence; and no man can act with common prudence in the ordinary occurrences of life, who has not some competent judgment of it.

The belief we give to testimony in many cases is not solely grounded upon the veracity of the testifier. In a single testimony, we consider the motives a man might have to falsify. If there be no appearance of any such motive, much more if there be motives on the other side, his testimony has weight independent of his moral character. If the testimony be circumstantial, we consider how far the circumstances agree together, and with things that are known. It is so very difficult to fabricate a story, which cannot be detected by a judicious examination of the circumstances, that it acquires evidence, by being able to bear such a trial. There is an art in detecting false evidence in judicial proceedings, well known to able judges and barristers; so that I believe few false witnesses leave the bar without suspicion of their guilt.

When there is an agreement of many witnesses in a great variety of circumstances, without the possibility of a previous concert, the evidence may be equal to that of demonstration.

A second kind of probable evidence, is the authority of those who are good judges of the point in question. The supreme court of judicature of the British nation is often determined by the opinion of lawyers in a point of law, of physicians in a point of medicine, and of other artists, in what relates to their several professions. And, in the common affairs of life, we frequently rely upon the judgment of others, in points of which we are not proper judges ourselves.

A third kind of probable evidence, is that by which we recognize the identity of things, and persons of our acquaintance. That two swords, two horses, or two persons, may be so perfectly alike, as not to be distinguishable by those to whom they are best known, cannot be shown to be impossible. But we learn either from nature, or from experience, that it never happens; or so very rarely, that a person or thing, well known to us, is immediately recognized without any doubt, when we perceive the marks or signs by which we were in use to distinguish it from all other individuals of the kind.

This evidence we rely upon in the most important affairs of life; and, by this evidence, the identity, both of things and of persons, is determined in courts of judicature.

A fourth kind of probable evidence, is that which we have of men's future actions and conduct, from the general principles of action in man, or from our knowledge of the individuals.

Notwithstanding the folly and vice that is to be found among men, there is a certain degree of prudence and probity which we rely upon in every man that is not insane. If it were not so, no man would be safe in the company of another, and there could be no society among mankind. If men were as much disposed to hurt, as to do good, to lie as to speak truth, they could not live together; they would keep at as great distance from one another as possible, and the race would soon perish.

We expect that men will take some care of themselves, of their family, friends, and reputation: that they will not injure others without some temptation: that they will have some gratitude for good offices, and some resentment of injuries.

Such maxims with regard to human conduct are the foundation of all political reasoning, and of common prudence in the conduct of life. Hardly can a man form any project in public or in private life, which does not depend upon the conduct of other men, as well as his own, and which does not go upon the supposition that men will act such a part in such circumstances. This evidence may be probable in a very high degree, but can never be demonstrative. The best concerted project may fail, and wise counsels may be frustrated, because some individual acted a part which it would have been against all reason to expect.

Another kind of probable evidence, the counterpart of the last, is that by which we collect men's characters and designs from their actions, speech, and other external signs.

We see not men's hearts, nor the principles by which they are actuated; but there are external signs of their principles and dispositions, which, though not certain, may sometimes be more trusted than their professions; and it is from external signs that we must draw all the knowledge we can attain of men's characters.

The next kind of probable evidence I mention, is that which mathematicians call the probability of chances.

We attribute some events to chance, because we know only the remote cause which must produce some one event of a number; but know not the more immediate cause which determines a particular event of that number, in preference to the others.

I think all the chances about which we reason in mathematics are of this kind. Thus, in throwing a just die upon a table, we say it is an equal chance which of the six sides shall be turned up; because neither the person who throws, nor the bystanders know the precise measure of force and direction necessary to turn up any one side rather than another. There are here, therefore, six events, one of which must happen; and as all are supposed to have an equal probability, the probability of any one side being turned up, the ace, for instance, is as one to the remaining number five.

The probability of turning up two aces with two dice is as one to thirty-five; because here there are thirty-six events, each of which has equal probability.

Upon such principles as these, the doctrine of chances has furnished a field of demonstrative reasoning of great extent, although the events about which this reasoning is employed be not necessary, but contingent, and be not certain, but probable.

This may seem to contradict a principle before advanced, that contingent truths are not capable of demonstration; but it does not : for, in the mathematical reasonings about chance, the conclusion demonstrated, is not, that such an event shall happen, but that the probability of its happening bears such a ratio to the probability of its failing; and this conclusion is necessary upon the suppositions on which it is grounded.

The last kind of probable evidence I shall mention, is that by which the known laws of nature have been discovered, and the effects which have been produced by them in former ages, or which may be expected in time to come.

The laws of nature are the rules by which the Supreme Being governs the world. We deduce them only from facts that fall within our own observation, or are properly attested by those who have observed them.

The knowledge of some of the laws of nature is necessary to all men in the conduct of life. These are soon discovered, even by savages. They know that fire burns, that water drowns, that bodies gravitate toward the earth. They know that day and night, summer and winter, regularly succeed each other. As far back as their experience and information reach, they know that these have happened regularly ; and, upon this ground, they are led, by the constitution of human nature, to expect that they will happen in time to come, in like circumstances.

The knowledge which the philosopher attains of the laws of nature differs from that of the vulgar, not in the first principles on which it is grounded, but in its extent and accuracy. He collects with care the phenomena that lead to the same conclusion, and compares them with those that seem to contradict or to limit it. He observes the circumstances on which every phenomenon depends, and distinguishes them carefully from those that are accidentally conjoined with it. He puts natural bodies in their various situations, and applies them to one another in various ways, on purpose to observe the effect ; and thus acquires from his senses a more extensive knowledge of the course of nature in a short time, than could be collected by casual observation in many ages.

But what is the result of his laborious researches? It is, that, as far as he has been able to observe, such things have always happened in such circumstances, and such bodies have always been found to have such properties. These are matters of fact, attested by sense, memory and testimony, just as the few facts which the vulgar know are attested to them.

And what conclusions does the philosopher draw from the facts he has collected? They are, that like events have happened in former times in like circumstances, and will happen in time to come; and these conclusions are built on the very same ground on which the simple rustic concludes that the sun will rise to-morrow.

Facts reduced to general rules, and the consequences of those general rules, are all that we really know of the material world. And the evidence that such general rules have no exceptions, as well as the evidence that they will be the same in time to come as they have been in time past, can never be demonstrative. It is only that species of evidence which philosophers call probable. General rules may have exceptions or limitations which no man ever had occasion to observe. The laws of nature may be changed by him who established them. But we are led by our constitution to rely upon their continuance with as little doubt as if it was demonstrable.

I pretend not to have made a complete enumeration of all the kinds of probable evidence; but those I have mentioned are sufficient to show, that the far greatest part, and the most interesting part of our knowledge, must rest upon evidence of this kind; and that many things are certain for which we have only that kind of evidence which philosophers call probable.

CHAP. IV.

OF MR. HUME'S SKEPTICISM WITH REGARD TO REASON.

In the Treatise of Human Nature, book 1. part 4. sect. 1. the author undertakes to prove two points: 1st, that all that is called human knowledge, meaning demonstrative knowledge, is only probability; and 2dly, that this probability, when duly examined, vanishes by degrees, and leaves at last no evidence at all: so that in the issue, there is no ground to believe any one proposition rather than its contrary, and " all those are certainly fools who reason or believe any thing."

According to this account, reason, that boasted prerogative of man, and the light of his mind, is an *ignis fatuus,* which misleads the wandering traveller, and leaves him at last in absolute darkness.

How unhappy is the condition of man, born under a necessity of believing contradictions, and of trusting to a guide who confesses herself to be a false one!

It is some comfort, that this doctrine can never be seriously adopted by any man in his senses. And after this author had shown that " all the rules of logic require a total extinction of all belief and evidence," he himself, and all men that are not insane, must have believed many things, and yielded assent to the evidence which he had extinguished.

This indeed he is so candid as to acknowledge. " He finds himself absolutely and necessarily determined to live and talk and act like other people in the common affairs of life. And since reason is incapable of dispelling these clouds, most fortunately it happens, that nature herself suffices to that purpose, and cures him of this philosophical melancholy and delirium." See sect. 7.

This was surely a very kind and friendly interposition of nature; for the effects of this philosophical delirium, if carried into life, must have been very melancholy.

But what pity is it, that nature, whatever is meant by that personage, so kind in curing this delirium, should be so cruel as to cause it. Doth the same fountain send forth sweet waters and bitter? Is it not more probable, that if the cure was the work of nature, the disease came from another hand, and was the work of the philosopher?

To pretend to prove by reasoning that there is no force in reason, does indeed look like a philosophical delirium. It is like a man's pretending to see clearly, that he himself and all other men are blind.

A common symptom of delirium is, to think that all other men are fools or mad. This appears to have been the case of our author, who concluded, "That all those are certainly fools who reason or believe any thing."

Whatever was the cause of this delirium, it must be granted, that if it was real and not feigned, it was not to be cured by reasoning: for what can be more absurd than to attempt to convince a man by reasoning who disowns the authority of reason. It was therefore very fortunate that nature found other means of curing it.

It may, however, not be improper to inquire, whether, as the author thinks, it was produced by a just application of the rules of logic, or, as others may be apt to think, by the misapplication and abuse of them.

First, Because we are fallible, the author infers that all knowledge degenerates into probability.

That man, and probably every created being, is fallible; and that a fallible being cannot have that

perfect comprehension and assurance of truth which
an infallible being has, I think ought to be granted.
It becomes a fallible being to be modest, open to new
light, and sensible, that by some false bias, or by rash
judging, he may be misled. If this be called a degree of skepticism, I cannot help approving of it, being persuaded, that the man who makes the best use
he can of the faculties which God has given him, without thinking them more perfect than they really are,
may have all the belief that is necessary in the conduct
of life, and all that is necessary to his acceptance with
his Maker.

It is granted then, that human judgments ought always to be formed with an humble sense of our fallibility in judging.

This is all that can be inferred by the rules of logic from our being fallible. And if this be all that is
meant by our knowledge degenerating into probability,
I know no person of a different opinion.

But it may be observed, that the author here uses
the word *probability* in a sense for which I know no
authority but his own. Philosophers understand probability as opposed to demonstration; the vulgar as opposed to certainty; but this author understands it as
opposed to infallibility, which no man claims.

One who believes himself to be fallible, may still
hold it to be certain that two and two make four, and
that two contradictory propositions cannot both be
true. He may believe some things to be probable only,
and other things to be demonstrable, without making
any pretence to infallibility.

If we use words in their proper meaning, it is impossible that demonstration should degenerate into
probability from the imperfection of our faculties.
Our judgment cannot change the nature of the things
about which we judge. What is really demonstration,

will still be so, whatever judgment we form concerning it. It may likewise be observed, that when we mistake that for demonstration, which really is not, the consequence of this mistake is, not that demonstration degenerates into probability, but that what we took to be demonstration is no proof at all; for one false step in a demonstration destroys the whole, but cannot turn it into another kind of proof.

Upon the whole, then, this first conclusion of our author, that the fallibility of human judgment turns all knowledge into probability, if understood literally, is absurd; but if it be only a figure of speech, and means no more, but that, in all our judgments, we ought to be sensible of our fallibility, and ought to hold our opinions with that modesty that becomes fallible creatures, which I take to be what the author meant, this, I think, nobody denies, nor was it necessary to enter into a laborious proof of it.

One is never in greater danger of transgressing against the rules of logic, than in attempting to prove what needs no proof. Of this we have an instance in this very case : for the author begins his proof, that all human judgments are fallible, with affirming that some are infallible.

" In all demonstrative sciences," says he, " the rules are certain and infallible ; but when we apply them, our fallible and uncertain faculties are very apt to depart from them, and fall into error."

He had forgot, surely, that the rules of demonstrative sciences are discovered by our fallible and uncertain faculties, and have no authority but that of human judgment. If they be infallible, some human judgments are infallible ; and there are many in various branches of human knowledge which have as good a claim to infallibility as the rules of the demonstrative sciences.

We have reason here to find fault with our author for not being skeptical enough, as well as for a mistake in reasoning, when he claims infallibility to certain decisions of the human faculties, in order to prove that all their decisions are fallible.

The *second* point which he attempts to prove, is, that this probability, when duly examined, suffers a continual diminution, and at last a total extinction.

The obvious consequence of this is, that no fallible being can have good reason to believe any thing at all ; but let us hear the proof.

" In every judgment, we ought to correct the first judgment derived from the nature of the object, by another judgment derived from the nature of the understanding. Besides the original uncertainty inherent in the subject, there arises another, derived from the weakness of the faculty which judges. Having adjusted these two uncertainties together, we are obliged, by our reason, to add a new uncertainty, derived from the possibility of error in the estimation we make of the truth and fidelity of our faculties. This is a doubt, of which, if we would closely pursue our reasoning, we cannot avoid giving a decision. But this decision, though it should be favourable to our preceding judgment, being founded only on probability, must weaken still further our first evidence. The third uncertainty must in like manner be criticised by a fourth, and so on without end.

" Now, as every one of these uncertainties takes away a part of the original evidence, it must at last be reduced to nothing. Let our first belief be ever so strong, it must infallibly perish, by passing through so many examinations, each of which carries off somewhat of its force and vigour. No finite object can subsist under a decrease repeated *in infinitum*.

" When I reflect on the natural fallibility of my judgment, I have less confidence in my opinions, than when I only consider the objects concerning which I reason. And when I proceed still further, to turn the scrutiny against every successive estimation I make of my faculties, all the rules of logic require a continual diminution, and at last a total extinction of belief and evidence."

This is the author's Achillean argument against the evidence of reason, from which he concludes, that a man who would govern his belief by reason, must believe nothing at all, and that belief is an act not of the cogitative, but of the sensitive part of our nature.

If there be any such thing as motion, said an ancient skeptic, the swift-footed Achilles could never overtake an old man in a journey. For, suppose the old man to set out a thousand paces before Achilles, and that while Achilles has travelled the thousand paces, the old man has gone five hundred; when Achilles has gone the five hundred, the old man has gone two hundred and fifty; and when Achilles has gone the two hundred and fifty, the old man is still one hundred and twenty-five before him. Repeat these estimations *in infinitum*, and you will still find the old man foremost; therefore Achilles can never overtake him; therefore there can be no such thing as motion.

The reasoning of the modern skeptic against reason is equally ingenious, and equally convincing. Indeed, they have a great similarity.

If we trace the journey of Achilles two thousand paces, we shall find the very point where the old man is overtaken: but this short journey, by dividing it into an infinite number of stages, with corresponding estimations, is made to appear infinite. In like manner, our author, subjecting every judgment to an infinite number of successive probable estimations, reduces the evidence to nothing.

To return then to the argument of the modern skeptic. I examine the proof of a theorem of Euclid. It appears to me to be strict demonstration. But I may have overlooked some fallacy ; therefore I examine it again and again, but can find no flaw in it. I find all that have examined it agree with me. I have now that evidence of the truth of the proposition, which I and all men call demonstration, and that belief of it, which we call certainty.

Here my skeptical friend interposes, and assures me, that the rules of logic reduce this demonstration to no evidence at all. I am willing to hear what step in it he thinks fallacious, and why. He makes no objection to any part of the demonstration, but pleads my fallibility in judging. I have made the proper allowance for this already, by being open to conviction. But, says he, there are two uncertainties, the first inherent in the subject, which I have already shown to have only probable evidence ; the second arising from the weakness of the faculty that judges. I answer, It is the weakness of the faculty only that reduces this demonstration to what you call probability. You must not therefore make it a second uncertainty ; for it is the same with the first. To take credit twice in an account for the same article is not agreeable to the rules of logic. Hitherto therefore there is but one uncertainty ; to wit, my fallibility in judging.

But, says my friend, you are obliged by reason to add a new uncertainty, derived from the possibility of error in the estimation you make of the truth and fidelity of your faculties. I answer,

This estimation is ambiguously expressed ; it may either mean an estimation of my liableness to err by the misapplication and abuse of my faculties ; or it may mean an estimation of my liableness to err, by conceiving my faculties to be true and faithful while they may be false and fallacious in themselves, even when applied

in the best manner.   I shall consider this estimation in
each of these senses.

If the first be the estimation meant, it is true that
reason directs us, as fallible creatures, to carry along
with us, in all our judgments, a sense of our fallibility.
It is true also, that we are in greater danger of erring
in some cases, and less in others ; and that this danger
of erring may, according to the circumstances of the
case, admit of an estimation, which we ought likewise
to carry along with us in every judgment we form.

When a demonstration is short and plain ; when the
point to be proved does not touch our interest or our
passions ; when the faculty of judging in such cases, has
acquired strength by much exercise, there is less danger of erring ; when the contrary circumstances take
place, there is more.

In the present case, every circumstance is favourable to the judgment I have formed.   There cannot be
less danger of erring in any case, excepting perhaps
when I judge of a self-evident axiom.

The skeptic further urges, that this decision, though
favourable to my first judgment, being founded only on
probability, must still weaken the evidence of that
judgment.

Here I cannot help being of a quite contrary opinion,
nor can I imagine how an ingenious author could impose upon himself so grossly, for surely he did not intend to impose upon his reader.

After repeated examination of a proposition of Euclid, I judge it to be strictly demonstrated ; this is my
first judgment.   But as I am liable to err from various
causes, I consider how far I may have been misled by
any of these causes in this judgment.   My decision
upon this second point is favourable to my first judgment, and therefore, as I apprehend, must strengthen
it.   To say, that this decision, because it is only proba-

ble, must weaken the first evidence, seems to me contrary to all rules of logic, and to common sense.

The first judgment may be compared to the testimony of a credible witness; the second, after a scrutiny into the character of the witness, wipes off every objection that can be made to it, and therefore surely must confirm and not weaken his testimony.

But let us suppose, that, in another case, I examine my first judgment upon some point, and find, that it was attended with unfavourable circumstances. What, in reason, and according to the rules of logic, ought to be the effect of this discovery?

The effect surely will be, and ought to be, to make me less confident in my first judgment, until I examine the point anew in more favourable circumstances. If it be a matter of importance, I return to weigh the evidence of my first judgment. If it was precipitate before, it must now be deliberate in every point. If at first I was in passion, I must now be cool. If I had an interest in the decision, I must place the interest on the other side.

It is evident, that this review of the subject may confirm my first judgment, notwithstanding the suspicious circumstances that attended it. Though the judge was biassed or corrupted, it does not follow, that the sentence was unjust. The rectitude of the decision does not depend upon the character of the judge, but upon the nature of the case. From that only, it must be determined whether the decision be just. The circumstances that rendered it suspicious are mere presumptions, which have no force against direct evidence.

Thus, I have considered the effect of this estimation of our liableness to err in our first judgment, and have allowed to it all the effect that reason and the rules of logic permit. In the case I first supposed, and in every case where we can discover no cause of error, it affords a presumption in favour of the first judgment. In other cases, it may afford a presumption against it. But the rules of logic require, that we should not judge by presumptions, where we have direct evidence. The effect of an unfavourable presumption should only be, to make us examine the evidence with the greater care.

The skeptic urges, in the last place, that this estimation must be subjected to another estimation, that to another, and so on *in infinitum;* and as every new estimation takes away from the evidence of the first judgment, it must at last be totally annihilated.

I answer, *first,* It has been shown above, that the first estimation, supposing it unfavourable, can only afford a presumption against the first judgment; the second, upon the same supposition, will be only the presumption of a presumption; and the third, the presumption that there is a presumption of a presumption. This infinite series of presumption resembles an infinite series of quantities decreasing in geometrical proportion, which amounts only to a finite sum. The infinite series of stages of Achilles's journey after the old man, amounts only to two thousand paces; nor can this infinite series of presumptions outweigh one solid argument in favour of the first judgment, supposing them all to be unfavourable to it.

2dly, I have shown, that the estimation of our first judgment may strengthen it; and the same thing may be said of all the subsequent estimations. It would, therefore, be as reasonable to conclude, that the first judgment will be brought to infallible certainty when this series of estimations is wholly in its favour, as that its evidence will be brought to nothing by such a series supposed to be wholly unfavourable to it. But, in reality, one serious and cool re-examination of the evidence by which our first judgment is supported, has, and in reason ought to have, more force to strengthen or weaken it, than an infinite series of such estimations as our author requires.

3dly, I know no reason nor rule in logic, that requires that such a series of estimations should follow every particular judgment.

A wise man who has practised reasoning knows that he is fallible, and carries this conviction along with him in every judgment he forms. He knows likewise, that he is more liable to err in some cases than in others. He has a scale in his mind, by which he estimates his liableness to err, and by this he regulates the degree of his assent in his first judgment upon any point.

The author's reasoning supposes, that a man, when he forms his first judgment, conceives himself to be infallible; that by a second and subsequent judgment, he discovers that he is not infallible; and that by a third judgment, subsequent to the second, he estimates his liableness to err in such a case as the present.

If the man proceed in this order, I grant, that his second judgment will, with good reason, bring down the first from supposed infallibility to fallibility; and that his third judgment will, in some degree, either strengthen or weaken the first, as it is corrected by the second.

But every man of understanding proceeds in a contrary order. When about to judge in any particular point, he knows already that he is not infallible. He knows what are the cases in which he is most or least liable to err. The conviction of these things is always present to his mind, and influences the degree of his assent in his first judgment, as far as to him appears reasonable.

If he should afterward find reason to suspect his first judgment, and desires to have all the satisfaction his faculties can give, reason will direct him not to form such a series of estimations upon estimations, as this author requires, but to examine the evidence of his first judgment carefully and cooly; and this review may very reasonably, according to its result, either strengthen or weaken, or totally overturn his first judgment.

This infinite series of estimations, therefore, is not the method that reason directs in order to form our judgment in any case. It is introduced without necessity, without any use but to puzzle the understanding, and to make us think, that to judge, even in the simplest and plainest cases, is a matter of insurmountable difficulty and endless labour; just as the ancient skeptic, to make a journey of two thousand paces appear endless, divided it into an infinite number of stages.

But we observed, that the estimation which our author requires may admit of another meaning, which indeed is more agreeable to the expression, but inconsistent with what he advanced before.

By the possibility of error in the estimation of the truth and fidelity of our faculties, may be meant, that we may err by esteeming our faculties true and faithful, while they may be false and fallacious, even when used according to the rules of reason and logic.

If this be meant, I answer, 1st, that the truth and fidelity of our faculty of judging is, and must be taken for granted in every judgment and in every estimation.

If the skeptic can seriously doubt of the truth and fidelity of his faculty of judging when properly used, and suspend his judgment upon that point till he finds proof, his skepticism admits of no cure by reasoning, and he must even continue in it until he have new faculties given him, which shall have authority to sit in judgment upon the old. Nor is there any need of an endless succession of doubts upon this subject, for the first puts an end to all judgment and reasoning, and to the possibility of conviction by that means. The skeptic has here got possession of a strong hold which is impregnable to reasoning, and we must leave him in possession of it, till nature, by other means, makes him give it up.

2dly, I observe, that this ground of skepticism, from the supposed infidelity of our faculties, contradicts what the author before advanced in this very argument; to wit, that "the rules of the demonstrative sciences are certain and infallible, and that truth is the natural effect of reason, and that error arises from the irruption of other causes."

But perhaps he made these concessions unwarily. He is therefore at liberty to retract them, and to rest his skepticism upon this sole foundation, that no reasoning can prove the truth and fidelity of our faculties. Here he stands upon firm ground: for it is evident, that every argument offered to prove the truth and fidelity of our faculties, takes for granted the thing in question, and is therefore that kind of sophism which logicians call *petitio principi.*

All we would ask of this kind of skeptic is, that he would be uniform and consistent, and that his practice in life do not belie his profession of skepticism with regard to the fidelity of his faculties: for the want of faith, as well as faith itself, is best shown by works. If a skeptic avoid the fire as much as those who believe it dangerous to go into it, we can hardly avoid thinking his skepticism to be feigned, and not real.

Our author indeed was aware, that neither his skepticism, nor that of any other person, was able to endure this trial, and therefore enters a caveat against it.

"Neither I," says he, "nor any other person, was ever sincerely and constantly of that opinion. Nature, by an absolute and uncontrollable necessity, has determined us to judge, as well as to breathe and feel. My intention, therefore," says he, "in displaying so carefully the arguments of that fantastic sect, is only to make the reader sensible of the truth of my hypothesis, that all our reasonings concerning causes and effects, are derived from nothing but custom, and that belief is more properly an act of the sensitive than of the cogitative part of our nature."

We have before considered the first part of this hypothesis, Whether our reasoning about causes be derived only from custom?

The other part of the author's hypothesis here mentioned is darkly expressed, though the expression seems to be studied, as it is put in italics. It cannot surely mean that belief is not an act of thinking. It is not, therefore, the power of thinking that he calls the cogitative part of our nature. Neither can it be the power of judging, for all belief implies judgment; and to believe a proposition means the same thing as to judge it to be true. It seems, therefore, to be the power of reasoning that he calls the cogitative part of our nature.

If this be the meaning, I agree to it in part. The belief of first principles is not an act of the reasoning power: for all reasoning must be grounded upon them. We judge them to be true, and believe them without reasoning. But why this power of judging of first principles should be called the sensitive part of our nature, I do not understand.

As our belief of first principles is an act of pure judgment without reasoning; so our belief of the conclusions drawn by reasoning from first principles, may, I think, be called an act of the reasoning faculty.

Upon the whole, I see only two conclusions that can be fairly drawn from this profound and intricate reasoning against reason. The first is, that we are fallible in all our judgments and in all our reasonings. The second, that the truth and fidelity of our faculties can never be proved by reasoning; and therefore our belief of it cannot be founded on reasoning. If the last be what the author calls his hypothesis, I subscribe to it, and think it not an hypothesis, but a manifest truth; though I conceive it to be very improperly expressed, by saying, that belief is more properly an act of the sensitive than of the cogitative part of our nature.

ESSAY VIII.

OF TASTE.

CHAP. I.

OF TASTE IN GENERAL.

THAT power of the mind by which we are capable of discerning and relishing the beauties of nature,
and whatever is excellent in the fine arts, is called
taste.

The external sense of taste, by which we distinguish
and relish the various kinds of food, has given occasion
to a metaphorical application of its name to this internal power of the mind, by which we perceive what is
beautiful, and what is deformed or defective in the various objects that we contemplate.

Like the taste of the palate, it relishes some things,
is disgusted with others; with regard to many, is indifferent or dubious, and is considerably influenced by
habit, by associations, and by opinion. These obvious
analogies between external and internal taste, have led
men, in all ages, and in all, or most polished languages, to give the name of the external sense to this
power of discerning what is beautiful with pleasure,
and what is ugly and faulty in its kind with disgust.

In treating of this as an intellectual power of the
mind, I intend only to make some observations, first on
its nature, and then on its objects.

1st, In the external sense of taste, we are led by reason and reflection to distinguish between the agreeable sensation we feel, and the quality in the object which occasions it. Both have the same name, and on that account are apt to be confounded by the vulgar, and even by philosophers. The sensation I feel when I taste any sapid body is in my mind; but there is a real quality in the body which is the cause of this sensation. These two things have the same name in language, not from any similitude in their nature, but because the one is the sign of the other, and because there is little occasion in common life to distinguish them.

This was fully explained in treating of the secondary qualities of bodies. The reason of taking notice of it now is, that the internal power of taste bears a great analogy in this respect to the external.

When a beautiful object is before us, we may distinguish the agreeable emotion it produces in us, from the quality of the object which causes that emotion. When I hear an air in music that pleases me, I say, it is fine, it is excellent. This excellence is not in me; it is in the music. But the pleasure it gives is not in the music; it is in me. Perhaps I cannot say what it is in the tune that pleases my ear, as I cannot say what it is in a sapid body that pleases my palate; but there is a quality in the sapid body which pleases my palate, and I call it a delicious taste; and there is a quality in the tune that pleases my taste, and I call it a fine, or an excellent air.

This ought the rather to be observed, because it is become a fashion among modern philosophers, to resolve all our perceptions into mere feelings or sensations in the person that perceives, without any thing corresponding to those feelings in the external object. According to those philosophers, there is no heat in the fire, no taste in a sapid body; the taste and the heat being only in the person that feels them. In like manner, there is no beauty in any object whatsoever; it is only a sensation or feeling in the person that perceives it.

The language and the common sense of mankind contradict this theory. Even those who hold it, find themselves obliged to use a language that contradicts it. I had occasion to show, that there is no solid foundation for it when applied to the secondary qualities of body; and the same arguments show equally, that it has no solid foundation when applied to the beauty of objects, or to any of those qualities that are perceived by a good taste.

But though some of the qualities that please a good taste resemble the secondary qualities of body, and therefore may be called occult qualities, as we only feel their effect, and have no more knowledge of the cause, but that it is something which is adapted by nature to produce that effect; this is not always the case.

Our judgment of beauty is in many cases more enlightened. A work of art may appear beautiful to the most ignorant, even to a child. It pleases, but he knows not why. To one who understands it perfectly, and perceives how every part is fitted with exact judgment to its end, the beauty is not mysterious; it is perfectly comprehended; and he knows wherein it consists, as well as how it affects him.

2dly, We may observe, that, though all the tastes we perceive by the palate are either agreeable or disagreeable, or indifferent; yet, among those that are agreeable, there is great diversity, not in degree only, but in kind. And as we have not generical names for all the different kinds of taste, we distinguish them by the bodies in which they are found.

In like manner, all the objects of our internal taste are either beautiful, or disagreeable, or indifferent; yet of beauty there is a great diversity, not only of degree, but of kind: the beauty of a demonstration, the beauty of a poem, the beauty of a palace, the beauty of a piece of music, the beauty of a fine woman, and many more that might be named, are different kinds of beauty; and we have no names to distinguish them but the names of the different objects to which they belong.

As there is such diversity in the kinds of beauty as well as in the degrees, we need not think it strange that philosophers have gone into different systems in analyzing it, and enumerating its simple ingredients. They have made many just observations on the subject; but, from the love of simplicity, have reduced it to fewer principles than the nature of the thing will permit, having had in their eye some particular kinds of beauty, while they overlooked others.

There are moral beauties as well as natural; beauties in the objects of sense, and in intellectual objects; in the works of men, and in the works of God; in things inanimate, in brute animals, and in rational beings; in the constitution of the body of man, and in the constitution of his mind. There is no real excellence which has not its beauty to a discerning eye, when placed in a proper point of view; and it as difficult to enumerate the ingredients of beauty as the ingredients of real excellence.

3dly, The taste of the palate may be accounted most just and perfect, when we relish the things that are fit for the nourishment of the body, and are disgusted with things of a contrary nature. The manifest intention of nature in giving us this sense, is, that we may discern what it is fit for us to eat and to drink, and what it is not. Brute animals are directed in the choice of their food merely by their taste. Led by this guide, they choose the food that nature intended for them, and seldom make mistakes, unless they be pinched by hunger, or deceived by artificial compositions. In infants, likewise, the taste is commonly sound and uncorrupted, and of the simple productions of nature they relish the things that are most wholesome.

In like manner, our internal taste ought to be accounted most just and perfect, when we are pleased with things that are most excellent in their kind, and displeased with the contrary. The intention of nature is no less evident in this internal taste than in the external. Every excellence has a real beauty and charm that makes it an agreeable object to those who have the faculty of discerning its beauty ; and this faculty is what we call a good taste.

A man, who, by any disorder in his mental powers, or by bad habits, has contracted a relish for what has no real excellence, or what is deformed and defective, has a depraved taste, like one who finds a more agreeable relish in ashes or cinders, than in the most wholesome food. As we must acknowledge the taste of the palate to be depraved in this case, there is the same reason to think the taste of the mind depraved in the other.

There is therefore a just and rational taste, and there is a depraved and corrupted taste. For it is too evident, that, by bad education, bad habits, and wrong associations, men may acquire a relish for nastiness, for rudeness, and ill breeding, and for many other deformities. To say that such a taste is not vitiated, is no less absurd than to say, that the sickly girl who delights in eating charcoal and tobacco pipes, has as just and natural a taste as when she is in perfect health.

4thly, The force of custom, of fancy, and of casual associations, is very great both upon the external and internal taste. An Esquimaux can regale himself with a draught of whale oil, and a Canadian can feast upon a dog. A Kamtschadale lives upon putrid fish, and is sometimes reduced to eat the bark of trees. The taste of rum, or of green tea, is at first as nauseous as that of ipecacuanha, to some persons, who may be brought by use to relish what they once found so disagreeable.

When we see such varieties in the taste of the palate produced by custom and associations, and some perhaps by constitution, we may be the less surprised that the same causes should produce like varieties in the taste of beauty ; that the African should esteem thick lips and a flat nose; that other nations should draw out their ears, till they hang over their shoulders ; that in one nation ladies should paint their faces, and in another should make them shine with grease.

5thly, Those who conceive that there is no standard in nature by which taste may be regulated, and that the common proverb, *That there ought to be no dispute about taste,* is to be taken in the utmost latitude, go upon slender and insufficient ground. The same arguments might be used with equal force against any standard of truth.

Whole nations by the force of prejudice are brought to believe the grossest absurdities ; and why should it be thought that the taste is less capable of being perverted than the judgment ? It must indeed be acknowledged, that men differ more in the faculty of taste than in what we commonly call judgment ; and therefore it may be expected that they should be more liable to have their taste corrupted in matters of beauty and deformity, than their judgment in matters of truth and error.

If we make due allowance for this, we shall see that it is as easy to account for the variety of tastes, though there be in nature a standard of true beauty, and consequently of good taste; as it is to account for the variety and contrariety of opinions, though there be in nature a standard of truth, and consequently of right judgment.

6thly, Nay, if we speak accurately and strictly, we shall find, that in every operation of taste, there is judgment implied.

When a man pronounces a poem or a palace to be beautiful, he affirms something of that poem or that palace; and every affirmation or denial expresses judgment. For we cannot better define judgment, than by saying that it is an affirmation or denial of one thing concerning another. I had occasion to show, when treating of judgment, that it is implied in every perception of our external senses. There is an immediate conviction and belief of the existence of the quality perceived, whether it be colour, or sound, or figure; and the same thing holds in the perception of beauty or deformity.

If it be said that the perception of beauty is merely a feeling in the mind that perceives, without any belief of excellence in the object, the necessary consequence of this opinion is, that when I say Virgil's Georgics is a beautiful poem, I mean not to say any thing of the poem, but only something concerning myself and my feelings. Why should I use a language that expresses the contrary of what I mean?

My language, according to the necessary rules of construction can bear no other meaning but this, that there is something in the poem, and not in me, which I call beauty. Even those who hold beauty to be merely a feeling in the person that perceives it, find themselves under a necessity of expressing themselves, as if beauty were solely a quality of the object, and not of the percipient.

No reason can be given why all mankind should express themselves thus, but that they believe what they say. . It is therefore contrary to the universal sense of mankind, expressed by their language, that beauty is not really in the object, but is merely a feeling in the person who is said to perceive it. Philosophers should be very cautious in opposing the common sense of mankind; for, when they do, they rarely miss going wrong.

Our judgment of beauty is not indeed a dry and unaffecting judgment, like that of a mathematical or metaphysical truth. By the constitution of our nature, it is accompanied with an agreeable feeling or emotion, for which we have no other name but the sense of beauty. This sense of beauty, like the perceptions of our other senses, implies not only a feeling, but an opinion of some quality in the object which occasions that feeling.

In objects that please the taste, we always judge that there is some real excellence, some superiority to those that do not please. In some cases, that superior excellence is distinctly perceived, and can be pointed out; in other cases, we have only a general notion of some excellence which we cannot describe. Beauties of the former kind may be compared to the primary qualities perceived by the external senses; those of the latter kind, to the secondary.

7thly, Beauty or deformity in an object, results from its nature or structure. To perceive the beauty therefore, we must perceive the nature or structure from which it results. In this the internal sense differs from the external. Our external senses may discover qualities which do not depend upon any antecedent perception. Thus I can hear the sound of a bell, though I never perceived any thing else belonging to it. But it is impossible to perceive the beauty of an object, without perceiving the object, or at least conceiving it. On this account, Dr. Hutcheson called the senses of beauty and harmony reflex or secondary senses; because the beauty cannot be perceived unless the object be perceived by some other power of the mind. Thus the sense of harmony and melody in sounds supposes the external sense of hearing, and is a kind of secondary to it. A man born deaf may be a good judge of beauties of another kind, but can have no notion of melody or harmony. The like may be said of beauties in colouring and in figure, which can never be perceived without the senses, by which colour and figure are perceived.

CHAP. II.

OF THE OBJECTS OF TASTE; AND FIRST, OF NOVELTY.

A PHILOSOPHICAL analysis of the objects of taste is like applying the anatomical knife to a fine face. The design of the philosopher, as well as of the anatomist, is not to gratify taste, but to improve knowledge. The reader ought to be aware of this, that he may not entertain an expectation in which he will be disappointed.

By the objects of taste, I mean those qualities or attributes of things, which are by nature adapted to please a good taste. Mr. Addison, and Dr. Akenside after him, have reduced them to three; to wit, novelty, grandeur, and beauty. This division is sufficient for all I intend to say upon the subject, and therefore I shall adopt it; observing only, that beauty is often taken in so extensive a sense as to comprehend all the objects of taste; yet all the authors I have met with, who have given a division of the objects of taste, make beauty one species.

I take the reason of this to be, that we have specific names for some of the qualities that please the taste, but not for all; and therefore all those fall under the general name of beauty, for which there is no specific name in the division.

There are, indeed, so many species of beauty, that it would be as difficult to enumerate them perfectly, as to enumerate all the tastes we perceive by the palate. Nor does there appear to me sufficient reason for making, as some very ingenious authors have done, as many different internal senses as there are different species of beauty or deformity.

The division of our external senses is taken from the organs of perception, and not from the qualities perceived. We have not the same means of dividing the internal; because, though some kinds of beauty belong only to objects of the eye, and others to objects of the ear, there are many which we cannot refer to any bodily organ; and therefore I conceive every division that has been made of our internal senses to be in some degree arbitrary. They may be made more or fewer, according as we have distinct names for the various kinds of beauty and deformity; and I suspect the most copious languages have not names for them all.

Novelty is not properly a quality of the thing to which we attribute it, far less is it a sensation in the mind to which it is new; it is a relation which the thing has to the knowledge of the person. What is new to one man, may not be so to another; what is new this moment, may be familiar to the same person some time hence. When an object is first brought to our knowledge, it is new, whether it be agreeable or not.

It is evident, therefore, with regard to novelty, whatever may be said of other objects of taste, that it is not merely a sensation in the mind of him to whom the thing is new; it is a real relation which the thing has to his knowledge at that time.

But we are so constituted, that what is new to us, commonly gives pleasure upon that account, if it be not in itself disagreeable. It rouses our attention, and occasions an agreeable exertion of our faculties.

The pleasure we receive from novelty in objects has so great influence in human life, that it well deserves the attention of philosophers; and several ingenious authors, particularly, Dr. Gerard in his Essay on taste, have, I think, successfully accounted for it, from the principles of the human constitution.

We can perhaps conceive a being so made, that his happiness consists in a continuance of the same unvaried sensations or feelings, without any active exertion on his part. Whether this be possible or not, it is evident that man is not such a being; his good consists in the vigorous exertion of his active and intellective powers upon their proper objects; he is made for action and progress, and cannot be happy without it; his enjoyments seem to be given by Nature, not so much for their own sake, as to encourage the exercise of his various powers. That tranquillity of soul in which some place human happiness, is not a dead rest, but a regular progressive motion.

Such is the constitution of man by the appointment of Nature. This constitution is perhaps a part of the imperfection of our nature; but it is wisely adapted to our state, which is not intended to be stationary, but progressive. The eye is not satiated with seeing, nor the ear with hearing; something is always wanted. Desire and hope never cease, but remain to spur us on to something yet to be acquired; and, if they could cease, human happiness must end with them. That our desire and hope be properly directed, is our part; that they can never be extinguished, is the work of Nature.

It is this that makes human life so busy a scene. Man must be doing something, good or bad, trifling or important; and he must vary the employment of his faculties, or their exercise will become languid, and the pleasure that attends it sicken of course.

The notions of enjoyment, and of activity, considered abstractly, are no doubt very different, and we cannot perceive a necessary connection between them. But, in our constitution, they are so connected by the wisdom of Nature, that they must go hand in hand; and the first must be led and supported by the last.

An object at first, perhaps, gave much pleasure, while attention was directed to it with vigour. But attention cannot be long confined to one unvaried object, nor can it be carried round in the same narrow circle. Curiosity is a capital principle in the human constitution, and its food must be what is in some respect new. What is said of the Athenians, may in some degree be applied to all mankind, That their time is spent in hearing, or telling, or doing some new thing.

Into this part of the human constitution, I think, we may resolve the pleasure we have from novelty in objects.

Curiosity is commonly strongest in children and in young persons, and accordingly novelty pleases them most. In all ages, in proportion as novelty gratifies curiosity, and occasions a vigorous exertion of any of our mental powers in attending to the new object, in the same proportion it gives pleasure. In advanced life, the indolent and inactive have the strongest passion for news, as a relief from a painful vacuity of thought.

But the pleasure derived from new objects, in many cases, it is not owing solely, or chiefly to their being new, but to some other circumstance that gives them value. The new fashion in dress, furniture, equipage, and other accommodations of life, gives pleasure, not so much, as I apprehend, because it is new, as because it is a sign of rank, and distinguishes a man from the vulgar.

In some things, novelty is due, and the want of it a real imperfection. Thus, if an author adds to the num- of books, with which the public is already overloaded, we expect from him something new; and if he says nothing but what has been said before in as agreeable a manner, we are justly disgusted.

When novelty is altogether separated from the conception of worth and utility, it makes but a slight impression upon a truly correct taste. Every discovery in nature, in the arts, and in the sciences, has a real value, and gives a rational pleasure to a good taste. But things that have nothing to recommend them but novelty, are fit only to entertain children, or those who are distressed from a vacuity of thought. This quality of objects may therefore be compared to the cypher in arithmetic, which adds greatly to the value of significant figures; but, when put by itself, signifies nothing at all.

CHAP. III.

OF GRANDEUR.

THE qualities which please the taste are not more various in themselves than are the emotions and feelings with which they affect our minds.

Things new and uncommon, affect us with a pleasing surprise, which rouses and invigorates our attention to the object. But this emotion soon flags, if there is nothing but novelty to give it continuance, and leaves no effect upon the mind.

The emotion raised by grand objects is awful, solemn, and serious.

Of all objects of contemplation, the Supreme Being is the most grand. His eternity, his immensity, his irresistible power, his infinite knowledge and unerring wisdom, his inflexible justice and rectitude, his supreme government, conducting all the movements of this vast universe to the noblest ends, and in the wisest manner, are objects which fill the utmost capacity of the soul, and reach far beyond its comprehension.

The emotion which this grandest of all objects raises in the human mind, is what we call devotion; a serious recollected temper, which inspires magnanimity, and disposes to the most heroic acts of virtue.

The emotion produced by other objects which may be called grand, though in an inferior degree, is, in its nature and in its effects, similar to that of devotion. It disposes to seriousness, elevates the mind above its usual state to a kind of enthusiasm, and inspires magnanimity, and a contempt of what is mean.

Such, I conceive, is the emotion which the contemplation of grand objects raises in us. We are next to consider what this grandeur in objects is.

To me it seems to be nothing else but such a degree of excellence, in one kind or another, as merits our admiration.

There are some attributes of mind which have a real and intrinsic excellence, compared with their contraries, and which, in every degree, are the natural objects of esteem, but, in an uncommon degree are objects of admiration. We put a value upon them because they are intrinsically valuable and excellent.

The spirit of modern philosophy would indeed lead us to think, that the worth and value we put upon things is only a sensation in our minds, and not any thing inherent in the object; and that we might have been so constituted as to put the highest value upon the things which we now despise, and to despise the qualities which we now highly esteem.

It gives me pleasure to observe, that Dr. Price, in his Review of the Questions concerning morals, strenuously opposes this opinion, as well as that which resolves moral right and wrong into a sensation in the mind of the spectator. That judicious author saw the consequences which these opinions draw after them, and has traced them to their source; to wit, the account given by Mr. Locke, and adopted by the generality of modern philosophers, of the origin of all our ideas; which account he shows to be very defective.

This proneness to resolve every thing into feelings and sensations, is an extreme into which we have been led by the desire of avoiding an opposite extreme, as common in the ancient philosophy.

At first, men are prone by nature and by habit to give all their attention to things external. Their notions of the mind, and its operations, are formed from some analogy they bear to objects of sense; and an external existence is ascribed to things which are only conceptions or feelings of the mind.

This spirit prevailed much in the philosophy both of Plato and of Aristotle, and produced the mysterious notions of eternal and self-existent ideas, of *materia prima*, of substantial forms, and others of the like nature.

From the time of Des Cartes, philosophy took a contrary turn. That great man discovered, that many things supposed to have an external existence, were only conceptions or feelings of the mind. This track has been pursued by his successors to such an extreme, as to resolve every thing into sensations, feelings, and ideas in the mind, and to leave nothing external at all.

The Peripatetics thought, that heat and cold which we feel to be qualities of external objects. The moderns make heat and cold to be sensations only, and allow no real quality of body to be called by that name : and the same judgment they have formed with regard to all secondary qualities.

So far Des Cartes and Mr. Locke went. Their successors being put into this track of converting into feelings things that were believed to have an external existence, found that extension, solidity, figure, and all the primary qualities of body, are sensations or feelings of the mind; and that the material world is a phenomenon only, and has no existence but in our mind.

It was then a very natural progress to conceive, that beauty, harmony, and grandeur, the objects of taste, as well as right and wrong, the objects of the moral faculty, are nothing but feelings of the mind.

Those who are acquainted with the writings of modern philosophers, can easily trace this doctrine of feelings from Des Cartes down to Mr. Hume, who put the finishing stroke to it, by making truth and error to be feelings of the mind, and belief to be an operation of the sensitive part of our nature.

To return to our subject: If we hearken to the dictates of common sense, we must be convinced that there is real excellence in some things, whatever our feelings or our constitution be.

It depends no doubt upon our constitution, whether we do, or do not perceive excellence where it really is: but the object has its excellence from its own constitution, and not from ours.

The common judgment of mankind in this matter sufficiently appears in the language of all nations, which uniformly ascribes excellence, grandeur, and beauty to the object, and not to the mind that perceives it. And I believe in this, as in most other things, we shall find the common judgment of mankind and true philosophy not to be at variance.

Is not power in its nature more excellent than weakness; knowledge than ignorance; wisdom than folly; fortitude than pusillanimity?

Is there no intrinsic excellence in self-command, in generosity, in public spirit? Is not friendship a better affection of mind than hatred; a noble emulation, than envy?

Let us suppose, if possible, a being so constituted, as to have a high respect for ignorance, weakness, and folly; to venerate cowardice, malice, and envy, and to hold the contrary qualities in contempt; to have an esteem for lying and falsehood, and to love most those who imposed upon him, and used him worst. Could we believe such a constitution to be any thing else than madness and delirium? It is impossible. We can as easily conceive a constitution, by which one should perceive two and three to make fifteen, or a part to be greater than the whole.

Every one who attends to the operations of his own mind will find it to be certainly true, as it is the common belief of mankind, that esteem is led by opinion, and that every person draws our esteem, as far only as he appears either to reason or fancy to be amiable and worthy.

There is therefore a real intrinsic excellence in some qualities of mind, as in power, knowledge, wisdom, virtue, magnanimity. These, in every degree, merit esteem; but in an uncommon degree, they merit admiration; and that which merits admiration, we call grand.

In the contemplation of uncommon excellence, the mind feels a noble enthusiasm, which disposes it to the imitation of what it admires.

When we contemplate the character of Cato, his greatness of soul, his superiority to pleasure, to toil, and to danger, his ardent zeal for the liberty of his country; when we see him standing unmoved in misfortunes, the last pillar of the liberty of Rome, and falling nobly in his country's ruin, who would not wish to be Cato rather than Cæsar in all his triumph?

Such a spectacle of a great soul struggling with misfortune, Seneca thought not unworthy of the attention of Jupiter himself, " Ecce spectaculum Deo dignum, ad quod respiciat Jupiter suo operi intentus vir fortis cum mala fortuna compositus."

As the Deity is of all objects of thought the most grand, the descriptions given in holy writ of his attributes and works, even when clothed in simple expression, are acknowledged to be sublime. The expression of Moses, "And God said, let there be light, and there was light," has not escaped the notice of Longinus, a heathen critic, as an example of the sublime.

What we call sublime in description, or in speech of any kind, is a proper expression of the admiration and enthusiasm which the subject produces in the mind of the speaker. If this admiration and enthusiasm appears to be just, it carries the hearer along with it involuntarily, and by a kind of violence rather than by cool conviction: for no passions are so infectious as those which hold of enthusiasm.

But, on the other hand, if the passion of the speaker appears to be in no degree justified by the subject or the occasion, it produces in the judicious hearer no other emotion but ridicule and contempt.

The true sublime cannot be produced solely by art in the composition; it must take its rise from grandeur in the subject, and a corresponding emotion raised in the mind of the speaker. A proper exhibition of these, though it should be artless, is irresistible, like fire thrown into the midst of combustible matter.

When we contemplate the earth, the sea, the planetary system, the universe, these are vast objects; it requires a stretch of imagination to grasp them in our minds. But they appear truly grand, and merit the highest admiration, when we consider them as the work of God, who, in the simple style of Scripture, stretched out the heavens, and laid the foundation of the earth; or, in the poetical language of Milton,

> In his hand
> He took the golden compasses, prepar'd,
> In God's eternal store, to circumscribe
> This universe, and all created things.
> One foot he center'd, and the other turn'd
> Round thro' the vast profundity obscure;
> And said, thus far extend, thus far thy bounds;
> This be thy just circumference, O world.

When we contemplate the world of Epicurus, and conceive the universe to be a fortuitous jumble of atoms, there is nothing grand in this idea. The clashing of atoms by blind chance has nothing in it fit to raise our conceptions, or to elevate the mind. But the regular structure of a vast system of beings produced by creating power, and governed by the best laws which perfect wisdom and goodness could contrive, is a spectacle which elevates the understanding, and fills the soul with devout admiration.

A great work is a work of great power, great wisdom, and great goodness, well contrived for some important end. But power, wisdom, and goodness, are properly the attributes of mind only: they are ascribed to the work figuratively, but are really inherent in the author : and, by the same figure, the grandeur is ascribed to the work, but is properly inherent in the mind that made it.

Some figures of speech are so natural and so common in all languages, that we are led to think them literal and proper expressions. Thus an action is called brave, virtuous, generous; but it is evident, that valour, virtue, generosity, are the attributes of persons only, and not of actions. In the action considered abstractly, there is neither valour, nor virtue, nor generosity. The same action done from a different motive may deserve none of those epithets. The change in this case is not in the action, but in the agent; yet, in all languages, generosity and other moral qualities are ascribed to actions. By a figure, we assign to the effect a quality which is inherent only in the cause.

By the same figure, we ascribe to a work that grandeur which properly is inherent in the mind of the author.

When we consider the Iliad as the work of the poet, its sublimity was really in the mind of Homer. He conceived great characters, great actions, and great events in a manner suitable to their nature, and with those emotions which they are naturally fitted to produce ; and he conveys his conceptions and his emotions by the most proper signs. The grandeur of his thoughts is reflected to our eye by his work, and therefore it is justly called a grand work.

When we consider the things presented to our mind in the Iliad, without regard to the poet, the grandeur is properly in Hector and Achilles, and the other great personages, human and divine, brought upon the stage.

Next to the Deity and his works, we admire great talents and heroic virtue in men, whether represented in history or in fiction. The virtues of Cato, Aristides, Socrates, Marcus Aurelius, are truly grand. Extraordinary talents and genius, whether in poets, orators, philosophers, or lawgivers, are objects of admiration, and therefore grand. We find writers of taste seized with a kind of enthusiasm in the description of such personages.

What a grand idea does Virgil give of the power of eloquence, when he compares the tempest of the sea, suddenly calmed by the command of Neptune, to a furious sedition in a great city, quelled at once by a man of authority and eloquence.

> Sic ait, ac dicto citius tumida æquora placat :
> Ac veluti magno in populo, si forte coorta est
> Seditio, sævitque animis ignobile vulgus ;
> Jamque faces et saxa volant, furor arma ministrat ;
> Tum pietate gravem, et meritis, si forte virum quem
> Conspexere, silent, arrectisque auribus adstant.
> Ille regit dictis animos, et pectora mulcet.
> Sic cunctus pelagi cecidit fragor.

The wonderful genius of sir Isaac Newton, and his sagacity in discovering the laws of nature, is admirably expressed in that short but sublime epitaph by Pope :

> Nature and nature's laws lay hid in night ;
> God said, Let Newton be, and all was light.

Hitherto we have found grandeur only in qualities of mind; but it may be asked, Is there no real grandeur in material objects?

It will perhaps appear extravagant to deny that there is; yet it deserves to be considered, whether all the grandeur we ascribe to objects of sense be not derived from something intellectual, of which they are the effects or signs, or to which they bear some relation or analogy.

Besides the relations of effect and cause, of sign and thing signified, there are innumerable similitudes and analogies between things of very different nature, which lead us to connect them in our imagination, and to ascribe to the one what properly belongs to the other.

Every metaphor in language is an instance of this; and it must be remembered, that a very great part of language, which we now account proper, was originally metaphorical; for the metaphorical meaning becomes the proper as soon as it becomes the most usual; much more when that which was at first the proper meaning falls into disuse.

The poverty of language, no doubt, contributes in part to the use of metaphor; and therefore we find the most barren and uncultivated languages the most metaphorical. But the most copious language may be called barren, compared with the fertility of human conceptions, and can never, without the use of figures, keep pace with the variety of their delicate modifications.

But another cause of the use of metaphor is, that we find pleasure in discovering relations, similitudes, analogies, and even contrasts that are not obvious to every eye. All figurative speech presents something of this kind; and the beauty of poetical language seems to be derived in a great measure from this source.

Of all figurative language, that is the most common, the most natural, and the most agreeable, which either gives a body, if we may so speak, to things intellectual, and clothes them with visible qualities; or which, on the other hand, gives intellectual qualities to the objects of sense.

To beings of more exalted faculties, intellectual objects may perhaps appear to most advantage in their naked simplicity. But we can hardly conceive them but by means of some analogy they bear to the objects of sense. The names we give them are almost all metaphorical or analogical.

Thus the names of grand and sublime, as well as their opposites, mean and low, are evidently borrowed from the dimensions of body; yet it must be acknowledged, that many things are truly grand and sublime, to which we cannot ascribe the dimensions of height and extension.

Some analogy there is, without doubt, between greatness of dimension, which is an object of external sense, and that grandeur, which is an object of taste. On account of this analogy, the last borrows its name from the first; and the name being common, leads us to conceive that there is something common in the nature of the things.

But we shall find many qualities of mind, denoted by names taken from some quality of body to which they have some analogy, without any thing common in their nature.

Sweetness and austerity, simplicity and duplicity, rectitude and crookedness, are names common to certain qualities of mind, and to qualities of body to which they have some analogy; yet he would err greatly who ascribed to a body that sweetness or that simplicity which are the qualities of mind. In like manner, greatness and meanness are names common to qualities perceived by the external sense, and to qualities perceived by taste; yet he may be in an error, who ascribes to the objects of sense that greatness or that meanness, which is only an object of taste.

As intellectual objects are made more level to our apprehension by giving them a visible form; so the objects of sense are dignified and made more august, by ascribing to them intellectual qualities which have some analogy to those they really possess. The sea rages, the sky lowers, the meadows smile, the rivulets murmur, the breezes whisper, the soil is grateful or ungrateful; such expressions are so familiar in common language, that they are scarcely accounted poetical or figurative; but they give a kind of dignity to inanimate objects, and make our conception of them more agreeable.

When we consider matter as an inert, extended, divisible, and moveable substance, there seems to be nothing in these qualities which we can call grand; and when we ascribe grandeur to any portion of matter, however modified, may it not borrow this quality from something intellectual, of which it is the effect, or sign, or instrument, or to which it bears some analogy; or, perhaps, because it produces in the mind an emotion that has some resemblance to that admiration which truly grand objects raise?

A very elegant writer on the sublime and beautiful, makes every thing grand or sublime that is terrible. Might he not be led to this by the similarity between dread and admiration? Both are grave and solemn passions; both make a strong impression upon the mind: and both are very infectious. But they differ specifically, in this respect, that admiration supposes some uncommon excellence in its object, which dread does not. We may admire what we see no reason to dread; and we may dread what we do not admire. In dread, there is nothing of that enthusiasm which naturally accompanies admiration, and is a chief ingredient of the emotion raised by what is truly grand or sublime.

Upon the whole, I humbly apprehend, that true grandeur is such a degree of excellence as is fit to raise an enthusiastical admiration; that this grandeur is found originally and properly in qualities of mind; that it is discerned in objects of sense only by reflection, as the light we perceive in the moon and planets is truly the light of the sun; and that those who look for grandeur in mere matter, seek the living among the dead.

If this be a mistake, it ought at least to be granted, that the grandeur which we perceive in qualities of mind, ought to have a different name from that which belongs properly to the objects of sense, as they are very different in their nature, and produce very different emotions in the mind of the spectator.

CHAPTER IV.

OF BEAUTY.

BEAUTY is found in things, so various, and so very different in nature, that it is difficult to say wherein it consists, or what there can be common to all the objects in which it is found.

Of the objects of sense, we find beauty, in colour, in sound, in form, in motion. There are beauties of speech, and beauties of thought; beauties in the arts, and in the sciences; beauties in actions, in affections, and in characters.

In things so different, and so unlike, is there any quality, the same in all, which we may call by the name of beauty? What can it be that is common to the thought of a mind, and the form of a piece of matter, to an abstract theorem, and a stroke of wit?

I am indeed unable to conceive any quality in all the different things that are called beautiful, that is the same in them all. There seems to be no identity, nor even similarity, between the beauty of a theorem and the beauty of a piece of music, though both may be beautiful. The kinds of beauty seem to be as various as the objects to which it is ascribed.

But why should things so different be called by the same name? This cannot be without a reason. If there be nothing common in the things themselves, they must have some common relation to us, or to something else, which leads us to give them the same name.

All the objects we call beautiful agree in two things, which seem to concur in our sense of beauty. 1st, When they are perceived, or even imagined, they produce a certain agreeable emotion or feeling in the mind; and 2dly, this agreeable emotion is accompanied with an opinion or belief of their having some perfection or excellence belonging to them.

Whether the pleasure we feel in contemplating beautiful objects may have any necessary connection with the belief of their excellence, or whether that pleasure be conjoined with this belief, by the good pleasure only of our Maker, I will not determine. The reader may see Dr. Price's sentiments upon this subject, which merit consideration, in the second chapter of his Reveiw of the Questions concerning morals.

Though we may be able to conceive these two ingredients of our sense of beauty disjoined, this affords no evidence that they have no necessary connection. It has indeed been maintained, that whatever we can conceive, is possible : but I endeavoured, in treating of conception, to show, that this opinion, though very common, is a mistake. There may be, and probably are, many necessary connections of things in nature, which we are too dim sighted to discover.

The emotion produced by beautiful objects is gay and pleasant. It sweetens and humanizes the temper, is friendly to every benevolent affection, and tends to allay sullen and angry passions. It enlivens the mind, and disposes it to other agreeable emotions, such as those of love, hope, and joy. It gives a value to the object, abstracted from its utility.

In things that may be possessed as property, beauty greatly enhances the price. A beautiful dog or horse, a beautiful coach or house, a beautiful picture or prospect, is valued by its owner and by others, not only for its utility, but for its beauty.

If the beautiful object be a person, his company and conversation are, on that account, the more agreeable, and we are disposed to love and esteem him. Even in a perfect stranger, it is a powerful recommendation, and disposes us to favour and think well of him, if of our own sex, and still more if of the other.

"There is nothing," says Mr. Addison, "that makes its way more directly to the soul than beauty, which, immediately diffuses a secret satisfaction and complacence through the imagination, and gives a finishing to any thing that is great and uncommon. The very first discovery of it strikes the mind with an inward joy, and spreads a cheerfulness and delight through all its faculties."

As we ascribe beauty, not only to persons, but to inanimate things, we give the name of love or liking to the emotion, which beauty, in both these kinds of objects, produces. It is evident, however, that liking to a person is a very different affection of mind from liking to an inanimate thing. The first always implies benevolence; but what is inanimate cannot be the object of benevolence. The two affections, however different, have a resemblance in some respects; and, on account of that resemblance, have the same name: and perhaps beauty, in these two different kinds of objects, though it has one name, may be as different in its nature as the emotions which it produces in us.

Besides the agreeable emotion which beautiful objects produce in the mind of the spectator, they produce also an opinion or judgment of some perfection or excellence in the object. This I take to be a second ingredient in our sense of beauty, though it seems not to be admitted by modern philosophers.

The ingenious Dr. Hutcheson, who perceived some of the defects of Mr. Locke's system, and made very important improvements upon it, seems to have been carried away by it, in his notion of beauty. In his inquiry concerning beauty, sect. 1. "Let it be observed," says he, "that, in the following papers, the word *beauty* is taken for the idea raised in us, and the sense of beauty, for our power of receiving that idea." And

again ; " Only let it be observed, that, by absolute or
original beauty, is not understood any quality supposed
to be in the object which should, of itself, be beautiful,
without relation to any mind which perceives it : for
beauty, like other names of sensible ideas, properly denotes the perception of some mind ; so cold, hot, sweet,
bitter, denote the sensations in our minds, to which
perhaps there is no resemblance in the objects which
excite these ideas in us ; however, we generally imagine otherwise.　Were there no mind, with a sense of
beauty, to contemplate objects, I see not how they could
be called beautiful."

There is no doubt an analogy between the external
senses of touch and taste, and the internal sense of
beauty.　This analogy led Dr. Hutcheson, and other
modern philosophers, to apply to beauty, what Des
Cartes and Locke had taught concerning the secondary
qualities, perceived by the external senses.

Mr. Locke's doctrine concerning the secondary qualities of body, is not so much an error in judgment, as an
abuse of words.　He distinguished very properly between the sensations we have of heat and cold, and that
quality or structure in the body which is adapted by
nature to produce those sensations in us.　He observed very justly, that there can be no similitude between
one of these and the other.　They have the relation of
an effect to its cause, but no similitude.　This was a
very just and proper correction of the doctrine of the
Peripatetics, who taught, that all our sensations are the
very form and image of the quality in the object by
which they are produced.

What remained to be determined was, whether the
words, heat and cold, in common language, signify the
sensations we feel, or the qualities of the object which
are the cause of these sensations.　Mr. Locke made
heat and cold to signify only the sensations we feel, and

not the qualities which are the cause of them. And in this, I apprehend, lay his mistake. For it is evident, from the use of language, that hot and cold, sweet and bitter, are attributes of external objects, and not of the person who perceives them. Hence it appears a monstrous paradox to say, there is no heat in the fire, no sweetness in sugar: but when explained according to Mr. Locke's meaning, it is only, like most other paradoxes, an abuse of words.

The sense of beauty may be analyzed in a manner very similar to the sense of sweetness. It is an agreeable feeling or emotion, accompanied with an opinion or judgment of some excellence in the object, which is fitted by nature to produce that feeling.

The feeling is, no doubt, in the mind, and so also is the judgment we form of the object: but this judgment, like all others, must be true or false. If it be a true judgment, there is some real excellence in the object. And the use of all languages shows, that the name of beauty belongs to this excellence of the object, and not to the feelings of the spectator.

To say that there is in reality no beauty in those objects in which all men perceive beauty, is to attribute to man fallacious senses. But we have no ground to think so disrespectfully of the Author of our being; the faculties he has given us are not fallacious; nor is that beauty, which he has so liberally diffused over all the works of his hands, a mere fancy in us, but a real excellence in his works, which express the perfection of their Divine Author.

We have reason to believe, not only that the beauties we see in nature are real, and not fanciful, but that there are thousands which our faculties are too dull to perceive. We see many beauties, both of human and divine art, which the brute animals are incapable of perceiving; and superior beings may excel us

as far in their discernment of true beauty as we excel
the brutes.

The man who is skilled in painting or statuary, sees
more of the beauty of a fine picture or statue, than a
common spectator. The same thing holds in all the
fine arts. The most perfect works of art have a beauty that strikes even the rude and ignorant; but they
see only a small part of that beauty which is seen in
such works by those who understand them perfectly
and can produce them.

This may be applied with no less justice to the works
of nature. They have a beauty that strikes even the
ignorant and inattentive. But the more we discover
of their structure, of their mutual relations, and of
the laws by which they are governed, the greater
beauty, and the more delightful marks of art, wisdom,
and goodness we discern.

Thus the expert anatomist sees numberless beautiful contrivances in the structure of the human body,
which are unknown to the ignorant.

Although the vulgar eye sees much beauty in the
face of the heavens, and in the various motions and
changes of the heavenly bodies, the expert astronomer,
who knows their order and distances, their periods,
the orbits they describe in the vast regions of space,
and the simple and beautiful laws by which their motions are governed, and all the appearances of their stations, progressions, and retrogradations, their eclipses,
occultations, and transits are produced, sees a beauty,
order, and harmony reign through the whole planetary
system, which delights the mind. The eclipses of the
sun and moon, and the blazing tails of comets, which
strike terror into barbarous nations, furnish the most
pleasing entertainment to his eye, and a feast to his understanding.

In every part of nature's works, there are numberless beauties, which, on account of our ignorance, we
are unable to perceive. Superior beings may see more
than we; but he only who made them, and, upon a
review, pronounced them all to be very good, can see
all their beauty.

Our determinations with regard to the beauty of
objects, may, I think, be distinguished into two kinds;
the first we may call instinctive, the other rational.

Some objects strike us at once, and appear beautiful
at first sight, without any reflection, without our being
able to say why we call them beautiful, or being able
to specify any perfection which justifies our judgment.
Something of this kind there seems to be in brute
animals; and in children before the use of reason;
nor does it end with infancy, but continues through
life.

In the plumage of birds, and of butterflies, in the
colours and form of flowers, of shells, and of many
other objects, we perceive a beauty that delights; but
cannot say what it is in the object that should produce
that emotion.

The beauty of the object may in such cases be called
an occult quality. We know well how it affects our
senses; but what it is in itself we know not. But this,
as well as other occult qualities, is a proper subject of
philosophical disquisition; and, by a careful examination of the objects to which nature has given this
amiable quality, we may perhaps discover some real
excellence in the object, or at least, some valuable purpose that is served by the effect which it produces
upon us.

This instinctive sense of beauty, in different species
of animals, may differ as much as the external sense
of taste, and in each species be adapted to its manner
of life. By this perhaps the various tribes are led to

associate with their kind, to dwell among certain objects rather than others, and to construct their habitation in a particular manner.

There seem likewise to be varieties in the sense of beauty in the individuals of the same species, by which they are directed in the choice of a mate, and in the love and care of their offspring.

"We see," says Mr. Addison, "that every different species of sensible creatures has its different notions of beauty, and that each of them is most affected with the beauties of its own kind. This is no where more remarkable than in birds of the same shape and proportion, where we often see the mate determined in his courtship by the single grain or tincture of a feather, and never discovering any charms but in the colour of its own species."

> "Scit thalamo servare fidem, sanctasque veretur
> Connubii leges ; non illum in pectore candor
> Sollicitat niveus ; neque pravum accendit amorem
> Splendida lanugo, vel honesta in vertice crista ;
> Purpureusve nitor pennarum ; ast agmina latè
> Fœminea explorat cautus, maculasque requirit
> Cognatus, paribusque interlita corpora guttis :
> Ni faceret, pictis sylvam circum undique monstris
> Confusam aspiceres vulgo, partusque biformes,
> Et genus ambiguum, et veneris monumenta nefandæ,
>
> "Hinc merula in nigro se oblectat nigra marito ;
> Hinc socium lasciva petit philomela canorum,
> Agnoscitque pares sonitus ; hinc noctua tetram
> Canitiem alarum, et glaucos miratur ocellos.
> Nempe sibi semper constat, crescitque quotannis
> Lucida progenies, castos confessa parentes :
> Vere novo exultat, plumasque decora juventus
> Explicat ad solem, patriisque coloribus ardet."

In the human kind, there are varieties in the taste of beauty, of which we can no more assign a reason than of the variety of their features, though it is easy to perceive that very important ends are answered by both. These varieties are most observable in the judgments we form of the features of the other sex; and in this the intention of nature is most apparent.

As far as our determinations of the comparative beauty of objects are instinctive, they are no subject of reasoning or of criticism; they are purely the gift of nature, and we have no standard by which they may be measured.

But there are judgments of beauty that may be called rational, being grounded on some agreeable quality of the object which is distinctly conceived, and may be specified.

This distinction between a rational judgment of beauty and that which is instinctive, may be illustrated by an instance.

In a heap of pebbles, one that is remarkable for brilliancy of colour, and regularity of figure will be picked out of the heap by a child. He perceives a beauty in it, puts a value upon it, and is fond of the property of it. For this preference, no reason can be given, but that children are, by their constitution, fond of brilliant colours, and of regular figures.

Suppose again that an expert mechanic views a well constructed machine. He sees all its parts to be made of the fittest materials, and of the most proper form; nothing superfluous, nothing deficient; every part adapted to its use, and the whole fitted in the most perfect manner to the end for which it is intended. He pronounces it to be a beautiful machine. He views it with the same agreeable emotion as the child viewed the pebble; but he can give a reason for his judgment, and point out the particular perfections of the object on which it is grounded.

Although the instinctive and the rational sense of beauty may be perfectly distinguished in speculation, yet, in passing judgment upon particular objects, they

are often so mixed and confounded, that it is difficult
to assign to each its own province. Nay, it may often
happen, that a judgment of the beauty of an object,
which was at first merely instinctive, shall afterward
become rational, when we discover some latent perfection of which that beauty in the object is a sign.

As the sense of beauty may be distinguished into
instinctive and rational; so I think beauty itself may
be distinguished into original and derived.

As some objects shine by their own light, and many
more by light that is borrowed and reflected; so I conceive the lustre of beauty in some objects is inherent
and original, and in many others, is borrowed and reflected.

There is nothing more common in the sentiments of
all mankind, and in the language of all nations, than
what may be called a communication of attributes; that
is, transferring an attribute, from the subject to which
it properly belongs, to some related or resembling subject.

The various objects which nature presents to our
view, even those that are most different in kind, have
innumerable similitudes, relations, and analogies, which
we contemplate with pleasure, and which lead us naturally to borrow words and attributes from one object
to express what belongs to another. The greatest
part of every language under heaven is made up of
words borrowed from one thing, and applied to something supposed to have some relation or analogy to
their first signification.

The attributes of body we ascribe to mind, and the
attributes of mind to material objects. To inanimate
things we ascribe life, and even intellectual and moral
qualities. And although the qualities that are thus
made common belong to one of the subjects in the
proper sense, and to the other metaphorically, these

different senses are often so mixed in our imagination, as to produce the same sentiment with regard to both.

It is therefore natural, and agreeable to the strain of human sentiments and of human language, that in many cases the beauty which originally and properly is in the thing signified, should be transferred to the sign; that which is in the cause, to the effect; that which is in the end, to the means; and that which is in the agent, to the instrument.

If what was said in the last chapter of the distinction between the grandeur which we ascribe to qualities of mind, and that which we ascribe to material objects be well founded, this distinction of the beauty of objects will easily be admitted as perfectly analogous to it. I shall therefore only illustrate it by an example.

There is nothing in the exterior of a man more lovely and more attractive than perfect good breeding. But what is this good breeding? It consists of all the external signs of due respect to our superiors, condescension to our inferiors, politeness to all with whom we converse or have to do, joined in the fair sex with that delicacy of outward behaviour which becomes them. And how comes it to have such charms in the eyes of all mankind? For this reason only, as I apprehend, that it is a natural sign of that temper, and those affections and sentiments with regard to others, and with regard to ourselves, which are in themselves truly amiable and beautiful.

This is the original, of which good breeding is the picture; and it is the beauty of the original that is reflected to our sense by the picture. The beauty of good breeding, therefore, is not originally in the external behaviour in which it consists, but is derived from the qualities of mind which it expresses. And though there may be good breeding without the amiable qualities of mind, its beauty is still derived from what it naturally expresses.

Having explained these distinctions of our sense of beauty into instinctive and rational, and of beauty itself into original and derived, I would now proceed to give a general view of those qualities in objects, to which we may justly and rationally ascribe beauty, whether original or derived.

But here some embarrassment arises from the vague meaning of the word *beauty*, which I had occasion before to observe.

Sometimes it is extended, so as to include every thing that pleases a good taste, and so comprehends grandeur and novelty, as well as what in a more restricted sense is called beauty. At other times, it is even by good writers confined to the objects of sight, when they are either seen, or remembered, or imagined. Yet it is admitted by all men, that there are beauties in music; that there is beauty as well as sublimity in composition, both in verse and in prose; that there is beauty in characters, in affections, and in actions. These are not objects of sight; and a man may be a good judge of beauty of various kinds, who has not the faculty of sight.

To give a determinate meaning to a word so variously extended and restricted, I know no better way than what is suggested by the common division of the objects of taste into novelty, grandeur, and beauty. Novelty, it is plain, is no quality of the new object, but merely a relation which it has to the knowledge of the person to whom it is new. Therefore, if this general division be just, every quality in an object that pleases a good taste, must, in one degree or another, have either grandeur or beauty. It may still be difficult to fix the precise limit between grandeur and beauty; but they

must together comprehend every thing fitted by its
nature to please a good taste, that is, every real perfection and excellence in the objects we contemplate.

In a poem, in a picture, in a piece of music, it is
real excellence that pleases a good taste. In a person,
every perfection of the mind, moral or intellectual,
and every perfection of the body, gives pleasure to
the spectator as well as to the owner, when there is
no envy nor malignity to destroy that pleasure.

It is therefore in the scale of perfection and real excellence that we must look for what is either grand or
beautiful in objects. What is the proper object of admiration is grand, and what is the proper object of love
and esteem is beautiful.

This, I think, is the only notion of beauty that corresponds with the division of the objects of taste
which has been generally received by philosophers.
And this connection of beauty, with real perfection,
was a capital doctrine of the Socratic school. It is
often ascribed to Socrates in the dialogues of Plato and
of Zenophon.

We may therefore take a view, first, of those qualities of mind to which we may justly and rationally ascribe beauty, and then of the beauty we perceive in
the objects of sense. We shall find, if I mistake not,
that, in the first, original beauty is to be found, and
that the beauties of the second class are derived from
some relation they bear to mind, as the signs or expressions of some amiable mental quality, or as the
effects of design, art, and wise contrivance.

As grandeur naturally produces admiration, beauty
naturally produces love. We may therefore justly
ascribe beauty to those qualities which are the natural
objects of love and kind affection.

Of this kind chiefly are some of the moral virtues,
which in a peculiar manner constitute a lovely char-

acter. Innocence, gentleness, condescension, humanity, natural affection, public spirit, and the whole train of the soft and gentle virtues. These qualities are amiable from their very nature, and on account of their intrinsic worth.

There are other virtues that raise admiration, and are therefore grand; such as magnanimity, fortitude, self-command, superiority to pain and labour, superiority to pleasure, and to the smiles of fortune, as well as to her frowns.

These awful virtues constitute what is most grand in the human character; the gentle virtues, what is most beautiful and lovely. As they are virtues, they draw the approbation of our moral faculty; as they are becoming and amiable, they affect our sense of beauty.

Next to the amiable moral virtues, there are many intellectual talents which have an intrinsic value, and draw our love and esteem to those who possess them. Such are, knowledge, good sense, wit, humour, cheerfulness, good taste, excellence in any of the fine arts, in eloquence, in dramatic action; and we may add, excellence in every art of peace or war that is useful in society.

There are likewise talents which we refer to the body, which have an original beauty and comeliness; such as health, strength, and agility, the usual attendants of youth; skill in bodily exercises, and skill in the mechanic arts. These are real perfections of the man, as they increase his power, and render the body a fit instrument for the mind.

I apprehend, therefore, that it is in the moral and intellectual perfections of mind, and in its active powers, that beauty originally dwells; and that from this as the fountain, all the beauty which we perceive in the visible world is derived.

This, I think, was the opinion of the ancient philosophers before named; and it has been adopted by lord Shaftesbury and Dr. Akenside among the moderns.

> "Mind, mind alone! bear witness earth and heav'n,
> The living fountains in itself contains
> Of beauteous and sublime. Here hand in hand
> Sit paramount the graces. Here enthron'd,
> Celestial Venus, with divinest airs,
> Invites the soul to never fading joy."   AKENSIDE.

But neither mind, nor any of its qualities or powers, is an immediate object of perception to man. We are, indeed, immediately conscious of the operations of our own mind; and every degree of perfection in them gives the purest pleasure, with a proportional degree of self esteem, so flattering to self-love, that the great difficulty is to keep it within just bounds, so that we may not think of ourselves above what we ought to think.

Other minds we perceive only through the medium of material objects, on which their signatures are impressed. It is through this medium that we perceive life, activity, wisdom, and every moral and intellectual quality in other beings. The signs of those qualities are immediately perceived by the senses; by them the qualities themselves are reflected to our understanding; and we are very apt to attribute to the sign, the beauty or the grandeur, which is properly and originally in the things signified.

The invisible Creator, the fountain of all perfection, has stamped upon all his works signatures of his divine wisdom, power and benignity, which are visible to all men. The works of men in science, in the arts of taste, and in the mechanical arts, bear the signatures of those qualities of mind which were employed in their production. Their external behaviour and conduct in life expresses the good or bad qualities of their mind.

In every species of animals, we perceive by visible signs their instincts, their appetites, their affections, their sagacity. Even in the inanimate world there are many things analogous to the qualities of mind; so that there is hardly any thing belonging to mind which may not be represented by images taken from the objects of sense; and on the other hand, every object of sense is beautified, by borrowing attire from the attributes of mind.

Thus the beauties of mind, though invisible in themselves, are perceived in the objects of sense, on which their image is impressed.

If we consider, on the other hand, the qualities in sensible objects to which we ascribe beauty, I apprehend we shall find in all of them some relation to mind, and the greatest in those that are most beautiful.

When we consider inanimate matter abstractly, as a substance endowed with the qualities of extension, solidity, divisibility, and mobility, there seems to be nothing in these qualities that affects our sense of beauty. But when we contemplate the globe which we inhabit, as fitted by its form, by its motions, and by its furniture, for the habitation and support of an infinity of various orders of living creatures, from the lowest reptile up to man, we have a glorious spectacle indeed! with which the grandest and the most beautiful structures of human art can bear no comparison.

The only perfection of dead matter is its being, by its various forms and qualities, so admirably fitted for the purposes of animal life, and chiefly that of man. It furnishes the materials of every art that tends to the support or the embellishment of human life. By the Supreme Artist, it is organized in the various tribes of the vegetable kingdom, and endowed with a kind of life; a work which human art cannot imitate, nor human understanding comprehend.

In the bodies and various organs of the animal tribes, there is a composition of matter still more wonderful and more mysterious, though we see it to be admirably adapted to the purposes and manner of life of every species. But in every form, unorganized, vegetable, or animal, it derives its beauty from the purposes to which it is subservient, or from the signs of wisdom, or of other mental qualities which it exhibits.

The qualities of inanimate matter, in which we perceive beauty, are, sound, colour, form, and motion; the first an object of hearing, the other three of sight; which we may consider in order.

In a single note, sounded by a very fine voice, there is a beauty which we do not perceive in the same note, sounded by a bad voice, or an imperfect instrument. I need not attempt to enumerate the perfections in a single note, which give beauty to it. Some of them have names in the science of music, and there perhaps are others which have no names. But I think it will be allowed, that every quality which gives beauty to a single note, is a sign of some perfection, either in the organ, whether it be the human voice or an instrument, or in the execution. The beauty of the sound is both the sign and the effect of this perfection; and the perfection of the cause is the only reason we can assign for the beauty of the effect.

In a composition of sounds, or a piece of music, the beauty is either in the harmony, the melody, or the expression. The beauty of expression must be derived, either from the beauty of the thing expressed, or from the art and skill employed in expressing it properly.

In harmony, the very names of concord and discord are metaphorical, and suppose some analogy between the relations of sound, to which they are figuratively applied, and the relations of minds and affections, which they originally and properly signify.

As far as I can judge by my ear, when two or more persons of a good voice and ear, converse together in amity and friendship, the tones of their different voices are concordant, but become discordant when they give vent to angry passions ; so that, without hearing what is said, one may know by the tones of the different voices, whether they quarrel or converse amicably. This, indeed, is not so easily perceived in those who have been taught, by good breeding, to suppress angry tones of voice, even when they are angry, as in the lowest rank, who express their angry passions without any restraint.

When discord arises occasionally in conversation, but soon terminates in perfect amity, we receive more pleasure than from perfect unanimity. In like manner, in the harmony of music, discordant sounds are occasionally introduced, but it is always in order to give a relish to the most perfect concord that follows.

Whether these analogies, between the harmony of a piece of music, and harmony in the intercourse of minds, be merely fanciful, or have any real foundation in fact, I submit to those who have a nicer ear, and have applied it to observations of this kind. If they have any just foundation, as they seem to me to have, they serve to account for the metaphorical application of the names of concord and discord to the relations of sounds ; to account for the pleasure we have from harmony in music ; and to show, that the beauty of harmony is derived from the relation it has to agreeable affections of mind.

With regard to melody, I leave it to the adepts in the science of music, to determine whether music, composed according to the established rules of harmony and melody, can be altogether void of expression ; and

whether music that has no expression can have any
beauty. To me it seems, that every strain in melody
that is agreeable, is an imitation of the tones of the human voice in the expression of some sentiment or passion, or an imitation of some other object in nature ;
and that music, as well as poetry is an imitative art.

The sense of beauty in the colours, and in the motions of inanimate objects, is, I believe, in some cases
instinctive. We see, that children and savages are
pleased with brilliant colours and sprightly motions.
In persons of an improved and rational taste, there
are many sources from which colours and motions may
derive their beauty. They, as well as the forms of objects, admit of regularity and variety. The motions
produced by machinery, indicate the perfection or imperfection of the mechanism, and may be better or
worse adapted to their end, and from that derive their
beauty or deformity.

The colours of natural objects, are commonly signs
of some good or bad quality in the object ; or they may
suggest to the imagination something agreeable or disagreeable.

In dress and furniture, fashion has a considerable influence on the preference we give to one colour above
another.

A number of clouds of different and ever changing
hue, seen on the ground of a serene azure sky at the
going down of the sun, present to the eye of every man
a glorious spectacle. It is hard to say, whether we
should call it grand or beautiful. It is both in a high
degree. Clouds towering above clouds, variously tinged,
according as they approach nearer to the direct rays
of the sun, enlarge our conceptions of the regions above
us. They give us a view of the furniture of those regions, which, in an unclouded air, seem to be a perfect
void; but are now seen to contain the stores of wind

and rain, bound up for the present, but to be poured down upon the earth in due season. Even the simple rustic does not look upon this beautiful sky, merely as a show to please the eye, but as a happy omen of fine weather to come.

The proper arrangement of colour, and of light and shade, is one of the chief beauties of painting; but this beauty is greatest, when that arrangement gives the most distinct, the most natural, and the most agreeable image of that which the painter intended to represent.

If we consider, in the last place, the beauty of form or figure in inanimate objects, this, according to Dr. Hutcheson, results from regularity, mixed with variety. Here it ought to be observed, that regularity in all cases, expresses design and art : for nothing regular was ever the work of chance ; and where regularity is joined with variety, it expresses design more strongly. Besides, it has been justly observed, that regular figures are more easily and more perfectly comprehended by the mind, than the irregular, of which we can never form an adequate conception.

Although straight lines and plain surfaces have a beauty from their regularity, they admit of no variety, and therefore are beauties of the lowest order. Curve lines and surfaces admit of infinite variety, joined with every degree of regularity ; and therefore, in many cases, excel in beauty those that are straight.

But the beauty arising from regularity and variety, must always yield to that which arises from the fitness of the form for the end intended. In every thing made for an end, the form must be adapted to that end ; and every thing in the form that suits the end, is a beauty ; every thing that unfits it for its end, is a deformity.

The forms of a pillar, of a sword, and of a balance, are very different. Each may have great beauty ; but that beauty is derived from the fitness of the form, and of the matter for the purpose intended.

Were we to consider the form of the earth itself, and the various furniture it contains, of the inanimate kind; its distribution into land and sea, mountains and vallies, rivers and springs of water, the variety of soils that cover its surface, and of mineral and metallic substances laid up within it, the air that surrounds it, the vicissitudes of day and night, and of the seasons; the beauty of all these, which indeed is superlative, consists in this, that they bear the most lively and striking impression of the wisdom and goodness of their Author, in contriving them so admirably for the use of man, and of their other inhabitants.

The beauties of the vegetable kingdom are far superior to those of inanimate matter, in any form which human art can give it. Hence, in all ages, men have been fond to adorn their persons and their habitations with the vegetable productions of nature.

The beauties of the field, of the forest, and of the flower garden, strike a child long before he can reason. He is delighted with what he sees; but he knows not why. This is instinct, but it is not confined to childhood; it continues through all the stages of life. It leads the florist, the botanist, the philosopher, to examine and compare the objects which nature, by this powerful instinct, recommends to his attention. By degrees, he becomes a critic in beauties of this kind, and can give a reason why he prefers one to another. In every species, he sees the greatest beauty in the plants or flowers that are most perfect in their kind, which have neither suffered from unkindly soil, nor inclement weather; which have not been robbed of their nourishment by other plants, nor hurt by any accident. When he examines the internal structure of those productions of nature, and traces them from their

embryo state in the seed to their maturity, he sees a
thousand beautiful contrivances of nature, which feast
his understanding more than their external form delighted his eye.

Thus, every beauty in the vegetable creation, of
which he has formed any rational judgment, expresses
some perfection in the object, or some wise contrivance
in its Author.

In the animal kingdom, we perceive still greater
beauties than in the vegetable. Here we observe life,
and sense, and activity, various instincts and affections,
and, in many cases, great sagacity. These are attributes of mind, and have an original beauty.

As we allow to brute animals a thinking principle or
mind, though far inferior to that which is in man ; and
as, in many of their intellectual and active powers, they
very much resemble the human species, their actions,
their motions, and even their looks, derive a beauty from
the powers of thought which they express.

There is a wonderful variety in their manner of life ;
and we find the powers they possess, their outward
form, and their inward structure, exactly adapted to
it. In every species, the more perfectly any individual
is fitted for its end and manner of life, the greater is its
beauty.

In a racehorse, every thing that expresses agility,
ardour, and emulation, gives beauty to the animal. In
a pointer, acuteness of scent, eagerness on the game,
and tractableness, are the beauties of the species. A
sheep derives its beauty from the fineness and quantity
of its fleece ; and in the wild animals, every beauty is a
sign of their perfection in their kind.

It is an observation of the celebrated Linnæus, that,
in the vegetable kingdom, the poisonous plants have
commonly a lurid and disagreeable appearance to the
eye, of which he gives many instances. I apprehend

the observation may be extended to the animal kingdom, in which we commonly see something shocking to
the eye in the noxious and poisonous animals.

The beauties which anatomists and physiologists
describe in the internal structure of the various tribes
of animals; in the organs of sense, of nutrition, and of
motion, are expressive of wise design and contrivance,
in fitting them for the various kinds of life, for which
they are intended.

Thus, I think, it appears, that the beauty which
we perceive in the inferior animals, is expressive, either of such perfections as their several natures may receive, or expressive of wise design in him who made
them, and that their beauty is derived from the perfections which it expresses.

But of all the objects of sense, the most striking
and attractive beauty is perceived in the human species, and particularly in the fair sex.

Milton represents Satan himself, in surveying the
furniture of this globe, as struck with the beauty of
the first happy pair.

> Two of far nobler shape, erect and tall,
> Godlike erect! with native honour clad
> In naked majesty, seem'd lords of all.
> And worthy seem'd; for in their looks divine,
> The image of their glorious Maker, shone
> Truth, wisdom, sanctitude severe, and pure;
> Severe, but in true filial freedom plac'd,
> Whence true authority in man, though both
> Not equal, as their sex not equal seem'd,
> For contemplation he, and valour form'd,
> For softness she, and sweet attractive grace.

In this well known passage of Milton, we see that
this great poet derives the beauty of the first pair in
Paradise from those expressions of moral and intellectual qualities which appeared in their outward form
and demeanour.

The most minute and systematical account of beauty in the human species, and particularly in the fair sex, I have met with, is in *Crito; or a Dialogue on Beauty*, said to be written by the author of Polymetis, and republished by Dodsley in his collection of fugitive pieces.

I shall borrow from that author some observations, which, I think, tend to show that the beauty of the human body is derived from the signs it exhibits of some perfection of the mind or person.

All that can be called beauty in the human species may be reduced to these four heads; colour, form, expression, and grace. The two former may be called the body, the two latter the soul of beauty.

The beauty of colour is not owing solely to the natural liveliness of flesh colour and red, nor to the much greater charms they receive from being properly blended together; but is also owing, in some degree, to the idea they carry with them of good health, without which all beauty grows languid and less engaging, and with which it always recovers an additional strength and lustre. This is supported by the authority of Cicero. *Venustas et pulchritudo corporis secerni non potest a valetudine.*

Here I observe, that as the colour of the body is very different in different climates, every nation preferring the colour of its climate; and as among us one man prefers a fair beauty, another a brunette, without being able to give any reason for his preference; this diversity of taste has no standard in the common principles of human nature, but must arise from something that is different in different nations, and in different individuals of the same nation.

I observed before, that fashion, habit, associations, and perhaps some peculiarity of constitution, may have great influence upon this internal sense, as well as upon the external. Setting aside the judgments arising from such causes, there seems to remain nothing that, according to the common judgment of mankind, can be called beauty in the colour of the species, but what expresses perfect health and liveliness, and in the fair sex, softness and delicacy; and nothing that can be called deformity but what indicates disease and decline. And if this be so, it follows, that the beauty of colour is derived from the perfections which it expresses. This, however, of all the ingredients of beauty is the least.

The next in order is form, or proportion of parts. The most beautiful form, as the author thinks, is that which indicates delicacy and softness in the fair sex, and in the male either strength or agility. The beauty of form, therefore, lies all in expression.

The third ingredient, which has more power than either colour or form, he calls expression, and observes, that it is only the expression of the tender and kind passions that gives beauty; that all the cruel and unkind ones add to deformity; and that, on this account, good nature may very justly be said to be the best feature, even in the finest face. Modesty, sensibility, and sweetness, blended together, so as either to enliven or to correct each other, give almost as much attraction as the passions are capable of adding to a very pretty face.

It is owing, says the author, to the great force of pleasingness which attends all the kinder passions, that lovers not only seem, but really are, more beautiful to each other than they are to the rest of the world; because, when they are together, the most pleasing passions are more frequently exerted in each of their faces than they are in either before the rest of the world. "There is then," as a French author very well expresses it, "a soul upon their countenances, which does not appear when they are absent from one another, or even in company that lays a restraint upon their features.

There is a great difference in the same face, according as the person is in a better or a worse humour, or more or less lively. The best complexion, the finest features, and the exactest shape, without any thing of the mind expressed in the face, is insipid and unmoving. The finest eyes in the world, with an excess of malice or rage in them, will grow shocking. The passions can give beauty without the assistance of colour or form, and take it away where these have united most strongly to give it; and therefore this part of beauty is greatly superior to the other two.

The last and noblest part of beauty is grace, which the author thinks undefinable.

Nothing causes love so generally and irresistibly as grace. Therefore, in the mythology of the Greeks and Romans, the graces were the constant attendants of Venus the goddess of love. Grace is like the cestus of the same goddess, which was supposed to comprehend every thing that was winning and engaging, and to create love by a secret and inexplicable force, like that of some magical charm.

There are two kinds of grace, the majestic and the familiar; the first more commanding, the last more delightful and engaging. The Grecian painters and sculptors used to express the former most strongly in the looks and attitudes of their Minervas, and the latter in those of Venus. This distinction is marked in the description of the personages of virtue and pleasure in the ancient fable of the choice of Hercules.

> Graceful, but each with different grace they move,
> This striking sacred awe, that softer winning love.

In the persons of Adam and Eve in Paradise, Milton has made the same distinction.

For contemplation he, and valour form'd,
For softness she, and sweet attractive grace.

Though grace be so difficult to be defined, there are
two things that hold universally with relation to it.
1st, There is no grace without motion ; some genteel
or pleasing motion, either of the whole body or of some
limb, or at least some feature. Hence, in the face,
grace appears only on those features that are moveable, and change with the various emotions and sentiments of the mind, such as the eyes and eyebrows, the
mouth and parts adjacent. When Venus appeared to
her son Eneas in disguise, and, after some conversation
with him, retired, it was by the grace of her motion in
retiring that he discovered her to be truly a goddess.

Dixit, et avertens roseâ cervice refulsit,
Ambrosiæque comæ divinum vertice odorem
Spiravere ; pedes vestis defluxit ad imos ;
Et vera incessu patuit dea. Ille ubi matrem
Agnovit, &c.

A *second* observation is, that there can be no grace
with impropriety, or that nothing can be graceful that
is not adapted to the character and situation of the person.

From these observations, which appear to me to be
just, we may, I think, conclude, that grace, as far as it
is visible, consists of those motions, either of the whole
body, or of a part or feature, which express the most
perfect propriety of conduct and sentiment in an amiable character.

Those motions must be different in different characters; they must vary with every variation of emotion and
sentiment; they may express either dignity or respect,
confidence or reserve, love or just resentment, esteem or
indignation, zeal or indifference. Every passion, sentiment, or emotion, that in its nature and degree is just
and proper, and corresponds perfectly with the charac

ter of the person, and with the occasion, is what we may call the soul of grace. The body or visible part consists of those motions and features which give the true and unaffected expression of the soul.

Thus, I think, all the ingredients of human beauty, as they are enumerated and described by this ingenious author, terminate in expression: They either express some perfection of the body, as a part of the man, and an instrument of the mind, or some amiable quality or attribute of the mind itself.

It cannot indeed be denied, that the expression of a fine countenance may be unnaturally disjoined from the amiable qualities which it naturally expresses : but we presume the contrary, till we have a clear evidence ; and even then, we pay homage to the expression, as we do to the throne when it happens to be unworthily filled.

Whether what I have offered, to show that all the beauty of the objects of sense is borrowed, and derived from the beauties of mind which it expresses or suggests to the imagination, be well founded or not ; I hope this terrestrial Venus will not be deemed less worthy of the homage which has always been paid to her, by being conceived more nearly allied to the celestial, than she has commonly been represented.

To make an end of this subject, taste seems to be progressive as man is. Children, when refreshed by sleep, and at ease from pain and hunger, are disposed to attend to the objects about them ; they are pleased with brilliant colours, gaudy ornaments, regular forms, cheerful countenances, noisy mirth, and glee. Such is the taste of childhood, which we must conclude to be given for wise purposes. A great part of the happiness of that period of life is derived from it ; and therefore it ought to be indulged. It leads them to attend to objects which they may afterward find worthy of their attention. It puts them upon exerting their in-

fant faculties of body and mind, which, by such exertions, are daily strengthened and improved.

As they advance in years and in understanding, other
beauties attract their attention, which, by their novelty
or superiority, throw a shade upon those they formerly
admired. They delight in feats of agility, strength,
and art ; they love those that excel in them, and strive
to equal them. In the tales and fables they hear, they
begin to discern beauties of mind. Some characters
and actions appear lovely, others give disgust. The
intellectual and moral powers begin to open, and, if
cherished by favourable circumstances, advance gradually in strength, till they arrive at that degree of perfection, to which human nature, in its present state,
is limited.

In our progress from infancy to maturity, our faculties open in a regular order appointed by nature ; the
meanest first ; those of more dignity in succession, until the moral and rational powers finish the man. Every
faculty furnishes new notions, brings new beauties into
view, and enlarges the province of taste ; so that we
may say, there is a taste of childhood, a taste of youth,
and a manly taste. Each is beautiful in its season ;
but not so much so, when carried beyond its season.
Not that the man ought to dislike the things that please
the child, or the youth, but to put less value upon them,
compared with other beauties, with which he ought to
be acquainted.

Our moral and rational powers justly claim dominion over the whole man. Even taste is not exempted
from their authority ; it must be subject to that authority in every case wherein we pretend to reason or
dispute about matters of taste ; it is the voice of reason
that our love or our admiration ought to be proportioned to the merit of the object. When it is not grounded on real worth, it must be the effect of constitution,

or of some habit or casual association.   A fond mother may see a beauty in her darling child, or a fond author in his work, to which the rest of the world are blind. In such cases, the affection is pre-engaged, and, as it were, bribes the judgment, to make the object worthy of that affection.   For the mind cannot be easy in putting a value upon an object beyond what it conceives to be due.   When affection is not carried away by some natural or acquired bias, it naturally is, and ought to be led by the judgment.

As, in the division which I have followed of our intellectual powers, I mentioned moral perception and consciousness, the reader may expect that some reason should be given, why they are not treated of in this place.

As to consciousness; what I think necessary to be said upon it has been already said, Essay 6. chap. 5. As to the faculty of moral perception, it is indeed a most important part of human understanding, and well worthy of the most attentive consideration, since without it we could have no conception of right and wrong, of duty and moral obligation, and since the first principles of morals, upon which all moral reasoning must be grounded, are its immediate dictates; but as it is an active as well as an intellectual power, and has an immediate relation to the other active powers of the mind, I apprehend that it is proper to defer the consideration of it till these be explained.